Dictionary of

FIRST
NAMES

An indispensable guide to
more than 10,000 names

Julia Cresswell

CHAMBERS
An imprint of Chambers Harrap Publishers Ltd
7 Hopetoun Crescent, Edinburgh, EH7 4AY

Chambers Harrap is an Hachette UK company

© Julia Cresswell 2009

Chambers® is a registered trademark of Chambers Harrap Publishers Ltd

First published by Chambers Harrap Publishers Ltd 2009

A CIP catalogue record for this book is available from the British Library.

ISBN 978 0550 10429 8

10 9 8 7 6 5 4 3 2 1

Publishing Manager: Hazel Norris
Copy Editor: Kate Sleight
Chambers Editors: Hazel Norris *and* Liam Rodger
Prepress: Andrew Butterworth *and* Becky Pickard
Editorial Director: Vivian Marr

www.chambers.co.uk

Designed by Chambers Harrap Publishers Ltd, Edinburgh
Typeset in Optima by Chambers Harrap Publishers Ltd, Edinburgh
Printed and bound in UK by CPI Cox & Wyman

Contents

About the author

Julia Cresswell is the author of over a dozen books, all of which are connected with the history and development of words, names and language.

She was educated at St Hugh's College, Oxford, where she studied English with a special emphasis on medieval literature and the history of the language. There she first became fascinated with the way the English language has developed and the influences that have directed its course. She subsequently gained a PhD at the University of Reading.

Her working life has been split between writing and teaching, and she has taught for both the Oxford universities and at some of the many US university programmes in Oxford. She now concentrates on the US colleges and summer schools for the Department of External Studies at the University of Oxford.

Julia is a recognized expert on first names and has published widely on the subject with great success. She is frequently called upon to comment upon trends in naming and news stories relating to first names in the print, broadcast and on-line media.

Introduction

The names in this book are those of the Western European tradition, and those names introduced into the culture by immigration. More precisely, the book focuses on names found in the United Kingdom, Ireland and the USA. Names from cultures such as Japan and China have not been included, partially for reasons of space and partially because of the author's ignorance. The entries aim to give information on the origin of each name, the history of how and why it is used, its current status and, in many cases, the names of prominent real and fictional bearers. Unfortunately, reliable sources of such information for Far Eastern names are not available in English, and only limited information is available for Islamic and Indian names; hence the briefer entries for such names and the focus on the Western canon.

Indo-European and Semitic names

Names in the West fall into two main groups, the Indo-European (comprising most European and a number of Asian cultures) and the Semitic (Hebrew and Arabic). The main differences lie in the ways in which the names are formed. The majority of Indo-European names are formed by combining two elements, each of which has an independent meaning, although the combined form may not in fact have a clear sense. Semitic names are often simple vocabulary words.

Indo-European is a term which covers a whole family of languages, all descended from a language which developed in prehistoric times, probably somewhere in the Black Sea area, although both time and place are argued over by academics. Over centuries these people, or at least their language and customs, spread. With each generation the language changed slightly, each group making its own subtle changes and developing its own terms as it met new things. Over time these changes amounted to new languages. In the modern world we can see how this process works, both over time through listening to old recordings of voices and noting how different they sound from the way people speak today, and over distance, noting the differences that have arisen in just a few generations between the English spoken in the UK, in America and Australia. Eventually, Indo-European languages spread to parts of India and China in the East, and West as far as Britain. In the 19th century they were taken to every continent by European colonists. In most of these languages the two-part, compound names predominated. From ancient Greece we find names such as Philip formed from the Greek *philos* 'friend, lover' and *hippos* 'horse', and thus interpretable as 'lover of horses'. From the other side of Europe we find names such as the Irish Fergal, formed from the Gaelic elements *fear* 'man' and *gal* 'valour' and thus interpretable as 'man of valour'.

Roman names

An exception to the compound type among European names is found in the Roman tradition. This, among the wealthy at least – and most of our records for early uses of first names are confined to the wealthy – used three or more names for men, which are often of obscure origin, and when we do know the origin are usually based on simple vocabulary words. This obscurity comes from the fact that many of the names were of Etruscan origin, and the Etruscans spoke a non-Indo-European language, now long extinct and of which we only understand a few words. The Roman three-name system consisted of a very limited number of first names, such as Marcus and Titus, and names which numbered one's place in the family, such as Quintus ('fifth'); these first names (the *praenomen*) would only be used by family or really close friends. Then came the tribal name (*nomen*), which showed which of the large family groupings one belonged to and which was important when one came to vote. Examples of these are Claudius and Julius. The third name (*cognomen*) indicated which family within the clan you belonged to. Examples of these are Crispus and Rufus. These final names were much more flexible than the others. They often started out as nicknames which were then passed down to descendants. They could be used to form a middle name by adding the ending *-i(a)nus*, to indicate adoption or a special relationship with a given family. This explains why we have pairs of names such as Augustus and Augustine (*Augustinus*). Further nicknames could be added to the three names. For Roman women the situation was very different. In early times they simply bore the feminine form, ending in *-a*, of their father's middle name, giving forms such as Claudia or Valeria, sometimes followed by a number name to indicate where they came in the family. Later on this sometimes expanded to two or more names.

These Roman names passed into the stock of Western first names by three routes. The earliest and most prolific source of Latin names is the vast pool of early Christian saints and martyrs. These names were adopted early on the Continent, but were rare in Britain before the 11th century. The other two sources of Roman names were the New Testament, particularly the Acts of the Apostles, where the people are very much a part of the extended Roman world, and names drawn directly from classical culture.

Celtic names

The earliest records we have of British first names are those of the Celtic Britons, a few of whose names have been preserved in Roman writings, albeit in Latinized forms. It is difficult to know how many ancient names have come down to us through the languages descended from Old Celtic or British (Welsh and less directly Irish and Scottish Gaelic), particularly given the way names are regularly revived by fashion. However, many Celtic names are undoubtedly ancient, and it is worth noting that Buddug, the Welsh equivalent of Victoria, is, allowing for sound changes over time, to all intents and purposes the same name as Boudicca, the name of the British woman who led a revolt against the Romans in 60 AD.

Germanic names

However, the main stock of names used by English speakers comes not from Celtic, but from another branch of Indo-European, the German languages. The modern Germanic languages, such as English, German, Dutch and those spoken in Scandinavia, are all descended from a dead language referred to as Old Germanic. These languages all shared a large pool of name elements that could be combined in pairs, creating a vast number of potential names. Sometimes these pairings made some kind of sense, as in a name such as Robert formed by combining elements meaning 'bright' and 'fame'; sometimes the pairings were just random. However, certain name elements tended to be used within certain families. This is why we have so many names beginning with Ed- (Edward, Edmund, Edgar, Edwyn) for Ed (Old English *ead* 'fortunate, prosperous') was one of the elements used by an English ruling house. As great houses intermarried there would be some carrying over of name elements between families and these would gradually spread throughout the general populace. These types of names were the norm not only in the Old English of the Anglo-Saxon population, but throughout much of Europe. This was because of the Dark Age tribal movements which saw the Franks conquer Gaul, which would later become France; took the Vandals down into Spain and on to North Africa; the Goths to Italy, and others throughout western Europe. As these invaders became the ruling classes their names were spread through conquered populations and survived even when, as with the Franks, the conquerors' original Germanic languages were given up for those used by the native population. One result of this is that Germanic names often appear in different forms derived from different branches of Old Germanic, so that Reginald, Ronald and Reynold are all variants of the same name which arrived in English by different routes. Ronald, for example was originally introduced into Scotland by the Old-Norse-speaking invaders from Scandinavia who plagued Britain and Ireland with their raids from the eighth to eleventh centuries. Reynold was the French form of the same name and Reginald was originally the form of the name as written down in Latin. By the 11th century this name creation slowed down, and names became more fixed in form. Again these fixed names were often connected to certain families and then spread through marriage alliances.

French names

The Norman Conquest of England after 1066 brought about a radical change in naming habits. Within a couple of generations the bulk of the Old English names had died out, at least among the upper classes, although they lingered on among the rural poor. The Old English names were replaced by French names, both the French versions of Germanic names, and the names of saints. Initially these came from Norman French, the dialect spoken by the invaders, but they were later added to by names from the more standard Parisian form of Medieval French. At the same time, the form of English spoken gradually changed from Old English to Middle English, with early Middle English dating from about 1100. Many of what we think of as standard English names, such as Richard, Thomas, Margaret and Catherine, came into use in this period.

Reformation and Renaissance

This situation continued, with variations in the popularity of names, and with a steady increase in saint's names, up until the Reformation in the 16th century. There was some continuity thereafter, but there was in general a sharp drop in the number of saint's names used as first names. This was because of the Protestant rejection of the doctrine of the power of saints to intercede for those who prayed to them. This meant that in Protestant countries children were no longer named after the saint on whose day they were born, or one particularly favoured by their parents. These traditions did continue in Roman Catholic countries, but elsewhere, instead of saint's names, parents now often used names taken from the New Testament, either the Roman ones discussed above, or Semitic ones. They also plundered the Old Testament for names such as Elijah and David. While many of these are still standard names, some of the more obscure biblical names are strongly associated with the more extreme forms of Protestantism, particularly Puritanism. The term Puritan has been used quite loosely in the text to indicate these naming trends. Another Puritan naming trend was to use abstract names. Some of these were simple virtues such as Hope and Prudence, but there was also a fashion for long, religious abstract names, such as Fear-no-evil or Labour-in-the-love-of-the-Lord. These were not in fact very common, but because they are so striking they have attracted a good deal of attention. The time of the Reformation was also the time of the Renaissance. Names taken from the Greek and Latin classics had appeared occasionally in England from the 12th century, but among the more learned classes their use now became more frequent, although often first in literary texts, and only later, once the names had become familiar there, were they adopted in real life.

The 18th century

The 18th century saw these trends continue, but with the arrival of the German Hanoverians on the throne of the United Kingdom there was a new German influence, introducing names such a Frederick, one of the names favoured by German royalty. The feminine names used by the Germans were often Latin, which suited the growing fashion for all things Classical, and names such as Augusta were introduced and Latinate forms such as Clara rather than Claire were often chosen.

The 19th century

The 19th century introduced some radical changes in name patterns, increasing the fund of names. As tastes swung away from the Classical in architecture and elsewhere to the Gothic, so a fashion arose for reviving medieval names. Names such as Alfred, which had died out after the Norman Conquest, were revived and often became very fashionable. New names were invented by authors and passed into real-life use. Other new names, particularly those based on flowers and jewels, were introduced. The trend for using surnames as first names increased enormously. Surnames had long been used as first names by the upper classes to indicate relationship to important families, particularly wives' maiden names. Aristocratic surnames such as Howard or Sidney now became popular with the general public who had no blood relationship to these families. The surnames of admired people were also adopted, giving us names such as Stanley. A minor but significant trend, which is once again influencing names today, was to name people after the place they were born, or one their families were associated with. Thus soldiers might name their children after barracks or battles, sometimes with what now seem extraordinary results, but also giving names, such as Florence and Kimberley, now accepted without question.

The 20th century

These trends continued into the 20th century with ever more names being added, and with the rate at which names go in and out of fashion speeding up. The range of countries that names were taken from also expanded, with names like Gemma from Italian and Zoe from Greek becoming popular. A particular source of new names in the 20th century, expanding a trend begun in the 19th, was the adoption of Celtic names into mainstream English usage.

While English names were developing as described above, Celtic names had followed their own history, just as Welsh and Gaelic changed over time, partly under pressure from English. The Celtic-speaking peoples of Wales, Ireland and Scotland had already included many new names of religious origin, sometimes in the same form as in English, but sometimes modified to conform to the patterns of their native language. However, once English speakers gained power in Wales and Ireland, the Celtic languages themselves came under attack. Irish, Welsh and later Scots Gaelic were banned from official use, and children were punished for speaking these languages in schools well into the 20th century. With no educated standard form of the language to impose uniformity, variants proliferated, which explains why Irish names, for example, may have different spellings or pronunciations in different regions of the country. This official disapproval also explains why many of these names have both an anglicized form or forms, as well as an original spelling. It also explains the peculiarities of non-Celtic names being used to 'translate' native names. These non-native forms would be for public or official use, while the frowned-on Celtic names would be used at home. A similar situation can be found today in the Chinese community and among some Native American groups, where people may have a name from the Western tradition for use in public, and an indigenous name which is used at home.

America

First names in the USA have followed the same main trends as those in Britain, but with their own regional twists and emphases. While everyone knows that the Pilgrim Fathers and other Puritan groups settled New England, it is often forgotten that Royalists and other dissident groups settled further south, giving a number of very different naming traditions. In addition, America has been subject to extensive settlement by speakers of other languages. As well as the obvious Spanish influence from the south, Louisiana was originally a French colony, and its French nature was reinforced by the arrival of the Cajuns, French-speakers exiled from the Canadian area called Arcadia in the 18th century, who brought with them their own dialect of French. In the 19th century there was extensive immigration from Scandinavia, Germany and Russia, and more recently from Eastern Asia. Each wave of immigrants has brought with it its own naming traditions, adding to the pool of potential names. This is one reason why the variety of names used in the USA is so great.

The Puritan settlers in America brought with them the then current fashions in England, using the names of abstract virtues and biblical names. These remained in popular use for rather longer than in England, many surviving in use into living memory, and it is from the USA that the current trend for reviving names such as Elijah and Zebulon seems to have come. There was also a determination among early settlers to break with the conventions of the past, and entirely new names started to appear early on. Another early tradition was a great emphasis on using surnames as first names. Those descended from the founding families became the new elite, and liked to mark their descent in their children's first names, much as aristocratic families in England had done. As a result, first names formed from surnames were regarded as having high status, which may explain the wide use of such names in the USA today. Further South the formation of first names from the surnames of famous people is more marked. This is particularly noticeable from the Civil War period, when the use of the surnames of generals and politicians was widespread. The most successful of these has been Lee. Linked to this was a trend for using the names of the famous from the past, giving such typically American first names as Homer, Virgil and Myron.

African-American names

More recently in the USA there has been a growth of distinctly African-American names. This has been most noticeable since the 1960s, when it became identified with the Black Pride and Civil Rights movements. In fact, many of these names have origins that go back to the 19th century. In particular, by the later 19th century we can see surnames such as the French Laverne, Lamar and Lafayette being used as first names, and Laverne developed forms such as Laverna by the early years of the 20th century. This encouraged a feeling that La- was a combining form for names, helped, of course, by the fact that the La in many of the names was indeed a separate element coming from the equivalent of 'the' in French or Spanish. These names remained in general use well into the 20th century, and some developed further. By World War I Laverne had given rise to Lavonne, as if based on Yvonne, and by the end of the 1920s forms such as Ladonna were beginning to appear. Thus although the use of La- as a name element is thought of as a typically African-American trend from the 1970s, it is both much older and not African-American in origin. A similar development can be traced for the other well-known supposedly African-American element De-. Another distinctive feature of modern American naming is the effects of the large number of Spanish speakers now living in the country. This has led to a growth in the incidence of both Spanish and Latin-American names, so that, for example, the Spanish Jorge is now more frequently given there than George, and Francisco is more common than Francis.

Names today

Thanks to Hollywood and modern communications the influence of the USA on the names of the rest of the world has been considerable, but there are still distinct national differences in name use. Indeed, even within the UK differences in naming patterns can be found not just in the different countries, but even within cities. This reflects the enormous fund of names now available. This is in part because we are such a cosmopolitan country, and have become open not only to Sanskrit names introduced by Hindu immigrants and Arabic names introduced by Muslims, but also to a wide variety of variant forms of names from Continental languages. (Note that Islamic names have mainly been listed under the regional variants most used in the UK, rather than the classical Arabic form.) A look at the variants in use for a name like Mary will amply illustrate this point. But it is not this alone that has led to the enormous increase in the number of different names used. In the past first names were comparatively rarely used. They were restricted to use among close family members, if at all. Victorian novels show the most formal of married couples even addressing each other as Mr or Mrs Whatever in bed. Under such circumstances society could make do with only a limited choice of first names. Nowadays, when complete strangers will address you by your first name, we need a large stock of names to distinguish one another.

About this book

The entries in this book are laid out alphabetically with the headword either giving a single name or, often, both the masculine and feminine form. The source and any significant history of the name is given and this is followed by a listing of any pet names or variants. However, this format is not rigid. If the masculine and feminine forms have significantly different histories they are listed separately, and important variants are given their own entries. If the feminine form is rare, it is listed among the variants. The main variants are followed by variants from other languages. Again this is not a rigid rule. Names in other languages that are the same as in English are not listed, even if there are other forms from these languages. Thus the name Agnes is found in German, Dutch and Scandinavian (a catch-all term to cover Danish, Norwegian, Swedish and Icelandic), and is not listed, although the Scandinavian Agnetta is listed among foreign variants. Nor is it practically possible to include all variants from all languages – the book would simply become too unwieldy. Portuguese (including Brazilian) variants are only listed if they are significantly different from the Spanish, and variants are only included from other languages if they are likely to be encountered by the general reader, or are of particular interest. Language labels have been used loosely, so that Hebrew covers both biblical and modern forms and may have some overlap with Yiddish forms. The term 'Irish' covers both the Gaelic spellings of the name, the anglicized form of these names, and any particularly Irish variants of non-Irish names. 'Scots Gaelic' labels both original and anglicized forms, while 'Scots' covers Lowland uses and distinctively Scottish naming habits. Similarly, the listing of famous real and fictional bearers has been flexible. If there are no famous bearers, I have not usually searched round for lesser-known examples, except in a few cases where they provide evidence about usage or proof of the existence of the name.

Conversely, when a name is so common that there are multiple candidates, it seemed best not to choose between rivals.

Further information

The information in this book has come from a wide variety of sources. Anyone writing on first names is heavily dependent on those who have gone before, and I have made full use of the most authoritative sources. Academic research on first names is scattered through numerous journals, but there are two main sources, in the journals *Nomina* published by the Society for Names Studies in Britain and Ireland and *Names*, published by the American Names Society. In recent years the internet has revolutionized the study of names. Unfortunately, many of the baby names sites are most inaccurate, but there are some that are reliable, in particularly *Behind the Name* (*http://www.behindthename.com/*). Other useful sites include the more specialised pages on Irish names at *http://www.namenerds.com/irish/* and Scottish Gaelic Given Names at *http://www.medievalscotland.org/scotnames/gaelicgiven/*. This is a site tracing the history of these names for role-players, but like many such sites it has some genuinely useful research. More information on Scottish names can be found at the Clan Macmillan site *http://www.clanmacmillan.org/MAOL.htm* which lists Gaelic names and their anglicized equivalents. More important are the various government statistics sites, which include the Office for National Statistics for England and Wales, the Central Statistics Office for Ireland and the General Register Office for Scotland. These publish various amounts of information. The English site lists just the top hundred names for each sex for the year and a few previous years; the Irish site gives a more detailed breakdown, while the Scottish site includes every name chosen in the year in question. The Rolls Royce of such sites is that of the American Government, which lists the top 1000 names for every year back to the 1880s, and is searchable in multiple formats. That is why it is so much easier to speak confidently about names in the USA. The on-line edition of the British Dictionary of National Biography, accessible from home via your local library site, provides a useful database of the names over the centuries of the rich and successful.

Acknowledgements

Finally, I have a number of people to thank. Professor Laurence Eldridge provided information about the history of his surname in North America; and Torin Douglas of the BBC generously supplied information about his name. Professor Emilie Savage-Smith gave generously of her time to help me with the more difficult of the Arabic names (remaining errors, are, of course, entirely my fault). My editor at Chambers, Hazel Norris, is to be thanked for all the support she provided. And as ever, my family, Philip and Alexander, provided cups of tea at my desk and other invaluable forms of support.

Julia Cresswell
Oxford, 2009

A

Aali, Aaliyah *see* **Ali**

Aamin, Aamina *see* **Amin**

Aamir, Aamira *see* **Amir**

Aarif, Aarifa *see* **Arif**

Aaron *m*
This is a biblical name. In the Old Testament Aaron is the brother of Moses and Miriam, and becomes the first high priest of the Israelites (Exodus 4.14 onwards). There have been various attempts to link the name with the Hebrew *har*, 'mountain', or with *ron*, 'sing', but it is most likely that Aaron's name, like those of his siblings, was Egyptian in origin and that its meaning has been lost. The name only came into regular use in England after the Reformation, and it wasn't until the 1990s that it became widely popular among English speakers. As a result, it has developed a wide number of different spellings, some of which overlap with ARRAN and ARUN. These variations are due in part to the unusual spelling of the standard form, and in part to a shift in pronunciation. Thirty years ago the standard pronunciation was with the first syllable pronounced as in 'air', but nowadays a short 'a' sound is frequently heard.
PET FORMS **Ron, Ronnie** • VARIANTS **Arron, Aron, Arren, Aran, Ehrin, Aaryn** *Arabic* **Harun** *Hebrew* **Ahron**
★ Aaron Burr (1756–1836), US vice-president and duellist
★ Aaron Copland (1900–90), US composer

Abbas *m*
This is the Arabic for someone who is stern or frowns a lot. It was the name of the Prophet Muhammad's uncle.

Abbey, Abbie, Abbi, Abby *see* **Abigail, Gabriel**

Abdul, Abdullah, Abd~ *m*
The Arabic word *abd* means 'male servant' and is used as an element combined with many of the titles of Allah to form compound names. Abdullah, shortened to Abdul, meaning 'servant of Allah' is one of the most common. It was the name of both the father and a son of the Prophet Muhammad. Others include *Abdulaziz*, 'servant of the Mighty'; *Abdulkarim*, 'servant of the Generous'; *Abdullatif*, 'servant of the Kind'; *Abdulmalik*, 'servant of the King'; *Abdulrahman*, 'servant of the Merciful' and many, many more. The feminine equivalent is *Ama(t)*, producing names such as *Amatulkarim* and *Amatullah*.
VARIANTS **Abd-al-Aziz, Abd-al-Karim, Abd-Allah, Abd-al-Latif, Abd-al-Malik, Abd-al-Rahim, Abder-Rahman**

Abe *see* **Abraham**

Abeera *see* **Abira**

Abel *m*
In the biblical book of Genesis, Abel is the younger son of Adam and Eve who is murdered by his brother CAIN. Since Cain was 'a tiller of the soil' while his brother was a shepherd, the story may reflect a clash between these two ways of life, a theme which has been repeated many times since. The name

appears to be from the Hebrew word for breath, *hevel*, but may in fact be from the Assyrian *ablu* meaning 'son'. The name was adopted by the Puritans who took it to the USA, where it has always been used quietly but regularly. As with many other of the less common biblical names, use currently seems to be on the increase.

PET FORMS **Abe, Nab** (archaic) • VARIANT *Hebrew* **Hevel**

★ Abel Tasman (1603–c.1659), Dutch explorer after whom Tasmania is named

☆ Abel Magwitch, transported criminal and benefactor in Charles Dickens's *Great Expectations* (1861)

Abelone *see* Apollo

Abi *see* Abigail

Abid *m* Abida *f*
These come from the Arabic for a worshipper, someone who is devout.

Abie *see* Abraham

Abigail *f*
This biblical name is formed from the elements *av(i)*, 'father', and *gayil*, 'joy'. This has variously been interpreted as meaning 'father rejoiced', 'father of joy', 'my father is joy' and other similar terms. In the Old Testament Abigail is the beautiful wife of a man called Nabal, who refuses to supply David and his troops with food when they need it. Abigail goes behind her husband's back to provide the needed food and, after Nabal's death, David marries her. Abigail describes herself to David as 'your servant', and it may be because of this that in the 17th century the name became a term for a lady's-maid, which naturally led to a decline in use. It has, however, been very popular in recent years, both in its full form and in shortened forms.

PET FORMS **Ab(b)i(e), Abb(e)y, Gail,**

Ga(y)le • VARIANTS *French* **Abigaïl, Abigaël(le)** *Hebrew* **Avigayil, Aviga'yil, Avigal**

Abir *m* Abira *f*
Abir is a Hebrew name meaning 'hero, strong', while Abira is explained as 'my strength'.

VARIANTS **Abeera, Abiri** (m) 'my hero', (f) 'my powerful one'

Abla *f*
This is the Arabic for 'well-rounded, perfectly formed' and was the name of the woman to whom the 7th-century poet Antara wrote his poetry.

Abner *m*
This is a biblical name interpreted as meaning 'father of light', but which could also be interpreted as 'my father is Ner', as was indeed true of the biblical character. He was a cousin and general of King Saul. Abner was used occasionally by British Puritans in the 17th century, but has always been more common in the USA.

VARIANT *Hebrew* **Avner**

★ Abner Doubleday (1819–93), US army officer, popularly credited with having invented baseball

☆ Li'l Abner Yokum in Al Capp's strip cartoon which ran 1934–77

Abraham *m*
Abraham means, according to Genesis 17.5, 'father of a multitude'. His name was originally *Abram* ('High Father'), but when God made a covenant with him that his descendants should possess the land of Caanan, he changed it to one that suited his role as the patriarch of his nation.

PET FORMS **Abe, Abie, Aby, Bram, Ham** • VARIANTS *Arabic* **Ibrahim** *Hebrew* **Avram, Avraham, Avi** *Russian* **Abram** *Spanish* **Abramo** *Yiddish* **Avrom**

★ Abraham Lincoln (1809–65), 16th president of the USA

★ Abraham 'Bram' Stoker (1847–1912),
Irish author of *Dracula* (1897)

Absalom *m*

Absalom, which means 'father of
peace', is a name used in the Bible
for one of the favourite sons of David,
but who nevertheless rebels against
him. In a battle against his father he
rides under an oak tree and is caught
by his hair. While he is trapped in this
way his father's general Joab kills him,
despite David's orders that Absalom
should not be hurt (2 Samuel 15–18).
The name was a popular one in the
Middle Ages, but has not been used
much since, except in Scandinavia.
VARIANTS **Absolon, Absolom** *Scandinavian*
Axel (from this the French have
developed a feminine form **Axelle**), **Acke**

Abu *m*

Although Abu is occasionally found
as a stand-alone name, it is really
an Arabic combining-form meaning
'father', used to form what is called
a *kunya* (roughly translatable as
'nickname'). Nicknames can then be
used as first names if they have been
borne by someone famous. The most
frequent of these is *Abubakar*, meaning
'father of the young camel', who was
one of the ten to whom the Prophet
Muhammad gave the good news about
entering paradise. Others include
the names of two of the uncles of the
Prophet, *Abu Fazl* and *Abu Talib*. The
female equivalent is *Umm*.
VARIANT **Abu Bakr**

Aby *see* **Abraham**

Acacia *f*

This is the name of a flowering tree
which is the source of the florist's
mimosa (itself a rare first name).
The species is particularly found in
Australia where it is a national symbol
and popularly known as the wattle. As
a result Acacia is particularly found
in Australia, although it has spread
elsewhere.

Achilles *m*

The meaning of the name Achilles is
much disputed. It is spelt *Akhilleus*
in Greek (Achilles is the Latin form),
and it has been linked to the Greek
word *achos*, 'pain', and to the name
of the river *Akheloös*, among other
theories. The name may be, like that of
many of Homer's heroes, pre-Greek.
There is no doubt about Achilles'
military fame; in Homer's *Iliad* he is
the greatest warrior among the Greeks,
his success helped by the fact that he
is invulnerable to weapons, except on
one heel. This is where his mother, the
sea nymph Thetis, held him when she
dipped him in the River Styx to give
him this protection. The name gained
respectability by being given to several
minor saints – although as is so often
the case with saints taking names from
Greek mythology, their authenticity is
suspect – and so entered the general
stock of Western names. Unlike the
name of Achilles' great rival HECTOR, it
has never been much used by English
speakers, but is established in the
Romance languages, and was regularly
used in France in the 17th and 18th
centuries.
VARIANTS *French* **Achille** (pronounced
'a-SHEEL', while all other forms are
pronounced with a hard 'k' sound) *Italian*
Achille, Achilleo *Spanish* **Aquiles**
☆ Achille Poirot, twin brother of Agatha
Christie's detective Hercule Poirot
(though possibly Hercule himself in
disguise)

Achim *see* **Joachim**

Acke *see* **Absalom**

Ada *f*

Ada can have several origins. It is
usually derived from the Germanic
element *adal*, 'noble' (see also ADELE).

As such, it was in use by the 7th century, when it is recorded as the name of a French abbess, but did not become widespread until the 18th century. The poet Byron was an early user in 1815 when he chose the name for his only legitimate child, whom he describes as 'Ada! sole daughter of my house and heart' (*Childe Harold*, Canto 3 1.3). She later achieved fame in her own right as Ada, Countess of Lovelace, writing on scientific subjects and working with William Babbage on what was to be the prototype of the computer. She also wrote what is considered the first computer program and, as a result, in 1979 the programming language that was developed as the official language of the US Department of Defense was named Ada after her. Ada is also recorded as an ancient Greek name, having been the name of the sister of Mausolus of Halicarnassus (now Bodrum in Turkey), who finished the building of his magnificent tomb, the original Mausoleum. It is also sometimes used as a spelling of ADAH, and as a pet form of ALEXANDRA and *Adriana* (see ADRIANNA).

PET FORMS **Ad**, **Addie**, **Adie**

☆ Ada Clare, character in Charles Dickens's novel *Bleak House* (1853)

Adah *f*

This is a biblical name, borne by the wives of *Lamech* (Genesis 4.19) and ESAU (Genesis 36.2). It is the Hebrew for 'adornment'.

PET FORM **Ada**

Adalbert, Adalbrecht *see* **Albert**

Adaliah *see* **Adlai**

Adam *m*

In the biblical book of Genesis Adam is the first human, created from earth, which is the probable meaning of the name. However, in Genesis 'Adam' is used as a term to mean 'human' rather than as a personal name. Adam was popular with English speakers from the Norman Conquest until the 14th century, and was often given to women. It appears in Latin texts with a feminine ending, in the form *Adama*, and this is found as a rare feminine given name, along with *Adamina*, which is thought of as a particularly Scottish name. Adam was taken up again in the Reformation, but thereafter declined in social status, until by the 19th century it was considered a rustic name. It came back into fashion in the 1970s.

PET FORM **Adie** (mainly Scottish) • VARIANTS **Edom** (old Northern English and Scottish form) *Irish* **Ádhamh**, **Adamnan** *Scots Gaelic* **Àdhamh**, **Adaidh** *Welsh* **Adda** *Italian* **Adamo** *Portuguese* **Adão** *Spanish* **Adán**

☆ Adam Bede, eponymous hero of George Eliot's 1859 novel

Adamnan *m*

This is an Irish name meaning 'little Adam' (although some Irish scholars see it as coming from the Irish word meaning 'timorous one'). It came into wider use through the fame of St Adamnan of Iona, in his day a famous author, a campaigner for religious reform and whose *Life* contains the first recorded mention of the Loch Ness Monster.

VARIANTS **Adhamhnan**, **Eunan**, **Onan**, **Awnan**

Adán, Adão, Adda *see* **Adam**

Addie, Adie *see* **Addison, Adelaide, Adele, Adeline, Adrian**

Addison *mf*

This was originally a surname derived from the first name ADAM. It came into fashion as a first name for boys in the USA in the 1980s, appearing as a girl's name some ten years later. It has since spread to other English-speaking areas. In 2006 the name for girls, which had been climbing steadily in use, shot up to 27th place in the USA, probably due to the popularity of a character by this name in the television series *Grey's Anatomy*.

PET FORMS **Addie, Addy**

Addolorata *see* **Dolores**

Addy *see* **Adelaide**

Ade *see* **Adrian**

Adeel, Adeela *see* **Adil**

Adela *see* **Adele**

Adelaide *f*
The German name *Adalheid*, formed from the Germanic elements *adal*, 'noble', and *heid*, 'kind, sort', became *Adélaïde* in French and Adelaide in English. The name was used on the Continent from at least the 9th century, where it gave rise to a number of pet forms, most notably ALICE, which only became an independent name in the 12th century. Adelaide became popular in the 19th century in England, when it was the name of the German-born wife of King William IV, after whom the Australian city of Adelaide is named.

PET FORMS **Ada, Ad(d)ie, Addy** • VARIANTS **Adelia** *Dutch* **Aleid, Aleida** *German* **Adelheid, Aleit, Alina, Alke, Heida, Heidi** *Hungarian* **Aleeda, Alida**

Adelbrecht *see* **Albert**

Adele, Adeline *f*
This is one of a group of names based on the Germanic element *adal*, 'noble', such as ADELAIDE, for which this serves as a short form. These names were popular with the Frankish aristocracy, as they emphasized the marriageable nobility of their daughters. Their popularity was enhanced by the

sanctity of St Adele (c.675–734), and the name rapidly spread through the French population. Adele developed a pet form Adeline, which in turn was shortened to forms such as *Aline*. The name came to England with William the Conqueror for it was the name of one of his daughters, who was mother to King Stephen. It died out in the later Middle Ages, but was revived in the 19th century. The variant *Adella* has given rise to the independent name DELLA.

PET FORMS **Ad(dy), Ad(d)ie** • VARIANTS **Adel(l)a, Adelle, Adelina** *French* **Adèle, Adélie, Adélia, Aline, Alina, Alette**
☆ *Sweet Adeline*, a 1903 song by Richard H Gerard and Harry Armstrong

Adelmar *see* **Elmira**

Aden *see* **Aidan**

Ádhamh, Àdhamh *see* **Adam**

Adhamhnan *see* **Adamnan**

Adie *see* **Ada, Adam, Adelaide, Adele, Aidan**

Adil *m* **Adila** *f*
This is a popular name from the Arabic for 'just, righteous, fair'.
VARIANTS **Adeel, Adeela**

Adina *mf*
This is from the Hebrew word *adin*, meaning 'slender, delicate', and in the Bible (1 Chronicles 11.42) it is mentioned in passing as the name of a captain of soldiers. However, its *-a* ending makes it look feminine, and it is now generally used as a female name. It is particularly popular in Romania.
★ Adina Howard (1974–), US singer
☆ Adina is the name of a wealthy landowner in Donizetti's 1832 opera *L'elisir d'amore*
☆ 'Adina' is the title of an 1874 story by Henry James, set in Italy

Aditya *m*

This is an Indian name, from a term for the children of *Aditi*, the Hindu mother goddess of the sky and fertility, whose name means 'boundless, entire' and also 'freedom, security'. Tradition varies as to whether there are seven or eight Aditya. The name is popular among Hindus.

Adlai *m*

Adlai is the Aramaic form of a Hebrew name which probably means 'God is just', although it is often interpreted as meaning 'my ornament'. It is the name of a minor character in the Bible (1 Chronicles 27.29), who was chief shepherd to King David. It was not unusual as a Puritan name in the USA, and is kept alive there today by the Stevenson political dynasty, who have produced a string of politicians bearing the name.

VARIANT *Hebrew* **Adaliah**

★ Adlai Stevenson (1900–65), US Democratic politician and lawyer

Adnan *m*

This is an Arabic name, which probably means 'settler'. In tradition Adnan is the son of Ismail, (see ISHMAEL), who was famous for his eloquence, and whose descendants settled in the northern parts of Arabia. It is a popular name throughout the Islamic world.

★ Adnan Khashoggi (1935–   ), Saudi businessman

Adolph *m*

After the Norman Conquest the Old English name *Æthelwulf*, made up of elements meaning 'noble' and 'wolf', was replaced by the form *Adolf*, now usually spelt Adolph in English, which the Normans had inherited from the Old Germanic form *Adalwolf*. However, the name was comparatively rare in the Middle Ages. The Latin form of the name, Adolphus, was brought over to the UK in the 18th century with the Hanoverians, and was given to George III's seventh son Adolphus, Duke of Cambridge (1774–1850). The popularity of Adolphus and Adolf among the German and Scandinavian upper classes at this time was in part out of respect for the Swedish King Gustavus Adolphus. The name was also particularly popular in France in the 19th century. The rise and fall of Adolf Hitler has severely affected use of the name in northern Europe, although shortened forms are sometimes found.

PET FORMS **Dolph, Dolphus, Dolly** (archaic) • VARIANTS *French* **Adolphe, Adolphie** (f), **Adolphine** (f) *Italian, Spanish* **Adolfo**

★ Gustavus Adolphus (1594–1632), King of Sweden

Adonis *m*

Adonis comes from *Adonai*, a Semitic term for 'Lord' and used in the Levant in the past as a term for a number of different gods. The rites of one of these, a fertility god, were imported into Greece, where the myth was told that Adonis was a beautiful youth with whom the goddess of love, APHRODITE, fell in love. He was wounded in the thigh while hunting wild boar, and died from loss of blood. The scarlet anemone flower, a symbol of spring and rebirth, sprang from the blood. The gods comforted Aphrodite by allowing Adonis to return to life for part of the year. Adonis is thus something of a male counterpart to PERSEPHONE. The name has been largely literary in use, but has been used quietly in the USA since the 1990s.

FEMININE **Adonia**

Adrian *m*

The Roman town of Hadria or Adria, in the Veneto region of Italy, gave its name both to the Adriatic Sea and to a Roman family, the best-known member of which was Publius Aelius Hadrianus, who ruled as Roman emperor from AD 117 to 138 and who was responsible for the building of Hadrian's Wall. The meaning of the name is not known, although it has been suggested that it may come from the Latin *ater*, 'black', or that it may be of Etruscan origin. The name was quite common in the Roman Empire, and was borne by a 4th-century soldier who was martyred in Turkey. Since he had his limbs broken with a large hammer before being martyred, he became the patron saint of blacksmiths. In the 12th century the only Englishman to have become pope, Nicolas Breakspear, took the papal name of Adrian IV or Hadrian. Adrian was particularly popular in the middle of the 20th century, and has returned to popularity again in a number of countries. It is occasionally used now for women.

PET FORMS **Addie, Ade, Adie** • VARIANTS *Dutch* **Adriaan, Adrianus, Arie, Arjan** *French* **Adrien** *Italian* **Adriano** *Spanish* **Adrián**

Adrianna *f*
This is one of a number of different feminine forms of the name ADRIAN, others of which are listed below.
PET FORMS **Drina, Drene, Riana, Rianna** • VARIANTS **Adriane, Adrianne, Adria** *French* **Adrienne** *Italian, Spanish* **Adriana**

Aed, Aedan, Áedán *see* **Aidan**

Aegle *see* **Aglaia**

Aelwen *f* **Aelwyn** *m*
This is a Welsh name formed from *ael*, 'fair', and *wen*, 'brow'.
VARIANT **Aylwyn** (m)

Aeneas *m*
Aeneas was regarded by the Romans as the founding father of their nation.

Said to be the son of APHRODITE, he was supposed to have fled from Troy after the Greeks sacked it at the end of the Trojan War and, after many adventures, to have obeyed the demands of the gods to travel to Italy and to found a great nation there. The story was told in the great national epic *The Aeneid* written by VIRGIL in the 1st century BC. The Romans derived the name from the Greek word *ainein* meaning 'to praise'. The name has not been used much by English speakers outside literary contexts, but was used in Scots Gaelic areas to anglicize the name *Aonghas* (see ANGUS).
VARIANTS *Italian* **Enea** *Portuguese* **Enéas**
★ Aeneas Silvius Piccolomini (1405–64), Italian scholar and writer who became Pope Pius II

Aengus *see* **Angus**

Aeron *mf* **Aeronwy** *f*
Aeron is the name of a river in Ceredigion, best-known from the place name Aberaeron. The river may have been named after the Celtic goddess of battle (*aer* means 'battle' in Welsh) who is known as *Agrona* in Roman inscriptions. However, since in Modern Welsh *aeron* means 'fruit, berries', the name is associated with this. Aeronwy, which is formed from Aeron plus the ancient suffix *-wy*, of obscure meaning, received a boost in 1943 when the poet Dylan Thomas chose it for his daughter.
VARIANTS **Aeronwen** (f) formed from Aeron + *wen*, 'white, fair, blessed', **Aerona** (f)

Afanasi, Afanasiy, Afanasy *see* **Athanasius**

Affery, Afra *see* **Aphra**

Afrodite *see* **Aphrodite**

Agatha *f*
The Greek word *agathos* meaning

'good, brave' gave rise to the names *Agathe* and the masculine *Agathon*. In Latin Agathe became Agatha. The name was in use in England even before the Norman Conquest. In the Middle Ages the spoken form of the name would normally have been *Agate* but, as it is written in Latin documents as *Agat(h)a*, when the name was revived in the 19th century Agatha was the form used. In 19th-century literature, the name tends to be used for heroines whose virtue is in peril. This is because of the legend of St Agatha, who was a 3rd-century Sicilian martyr. She was said to be a Christian virgin who was offered the chance to escape prosecution for her faith if she gave in to the evil intentions of her prosecutor. When she refused, she was put in a brothel, but kept her virtue by resolutely refusing to co-operate, whatever was done to her. Among the various tortures that were part of her martyrdom, she had her breasts cut off. In pictures she is painted carrying her breasts on a dish. This iconography has made her the patron saint of wet nurses, bread makers and bell-founders; the latter two because the objects she carries have been misinterpreted.

PET FORM **Aggie** • VARIANTS *French, German, Greek* **Agathe** *Scandinavian* **Agathe, Agata, Agda, Agot** *Spanish* **Águeda**

★ Agatha Christie (1890–1976), English crime novelist

Aggie *see* Agatha, Agnes

Aghaistin *see* Augustine

Aglaia *f*
Aglaia, which means 'brightness, splendour', was the name of the youngest of the Three Graces in Greek mythology; the other two being *Euphrosyne* and THALIA. It is also the name of at least four other minor characters in Greek mythology. The name is most likely to be found in Russia and Romania.

VARIANTS **Aglaea, Aegle** *French* **Aglaé** *Russian* **Aglaya**

Agnes *f*
The Greek adjective *hagnos*, meaning 'pure, chaste, holy', gave the name *Hagnē*. When the name crossed over into Latin the 'h' was dropped and the name became associated with the Latin *agnus*, 'lamb', which fitted well with the original sense, since in Judaeo-Christian iconography the lamb is a symbol of innocence and purity. St Agnes is thus shown in art accompanied by a lamb. While her very existence is in doubt, she was a very popular saint. By the end of the Middle Ages Agnes was one of the three most popular names in England, often in the form ANNIS. In many languages the 'g' is not pronounced or serves to do no more than modify the 'n' to a 'ny' sound. There are two traditions as to St Agnes's story. While both versions place her in the 4th century, the Western tradition has her die while still a child, but in the East her story is very similar to St AGATHA's, except that the man who tries to violate her in a brothel is struck dead, only to be restored to life by Agnes.

PET FORMS **Aggie, Nessie** • VARIANTS **Annis** *Irish* **Aignéis** *Welsh* **Nest, Nesta** *Czech* **Anežka** *French* **Agnès** *German* **Agnethe** *Italian* **Agnese** *Polish* **Agnieszka, Jagienka, Jagna, Jagusia** *Russian* **Agnessa** *Scandinavian* **Agnet(h)a, Agnet(h)e** *Slovene* **Neža** *Spanish* **Inés, Inez**

★ Agnès Sorel (c.1422–50), mistress of Charles VII of France and model for Jean Fouquet's famous painting of the Virgin and Child

★ Nest ferch Rhys (died after 1136), Welsh princess famous for her beauty

☆ Agnes Grey, eponymous heroine of Anne Brontë's 1847 novel

☆ Agnes Nitt, witch and singer, in Terry Pratchett's *Discworld* novels

Agostina, Agostinho, Agostino *see* **Augustine**

Agot *see* **Agatha**

Águeda *see* **Agatha**

Agustijn, Agustín *see* **Augustine**

Ahmed *m*
This is an Arabic name based on *hamida*, 'to praise', and means 'very praiseworthy, highly praised'. It is one of the most popular names in the Islamic world and is one of the epithets of the Prophet Muhammad.
VARIANTS **Ahmad** *Turkish* **Ahmet**
★ Ahmed Jamal (1930–), US jazz pianist
★ Ahmed Zewail (1946–), Egyptian Nobel Prize winner for Chemistry

Ahron *see* **Aaron**

Aibhistin *see* **Augustine**

Aibhlin *see* **Eileen, Evelyn**

Aïcha, Aïchoucha *see* **Aisha**

Aidan *m*
The ancient Irish name *Aodh* (pronounced 'ee'), which also has a modern form *Aed*, means 'fire' and was the name of an ancient Celtic sun god. Aidan was initially a pet form of Aodh. The name dates from an early period, for example Aidan the False was placed on the throne of the Dalriada Scots by St Columba in about 575. But the man who made the name famous was St Aidan, who played a major role in converting the Scots and people of northern England to Christianity in the 7th century. This meant that, until comparatively recently, the name was mainly restricted to the northern parts of the British Isles. However, in the later 20th century the name spread widely through the English-speaking world, and has been particularly popular in the USA, where it has taken on a multiplicity of spellings and is beginning to be given to girls. The standard forms for girls can be seen under ENAT.
PET FORM **Adie** • VARIANTS **Aiden, Aden, Aedan, Ayden, Edan** *Irish* **Áedán, Aod(h)an** *Scottish* **Iagan**

Aifric *see* **Effie**

Aignéis *see* **Agnes**

Ailbe *mf*
This is an old Irish name, which probably comes from the Irish word for 'white'. It was frequently used in early times, being the name of a legendary female warrior and a miracle-working female saint, among others. The name is more commonly feminine. It is pronounced 'al-by'. See also ELVIS.
VARIANTS **Ailbhe, Alby, Elli, Elva, Elvy, Oilbhe**

Ailbeart *see* **Albert**

Aileas *see* **Alice**

Aileen *see* **Eileen**

Ailie *see* **Ailsa, Alice, Eilidh**

Ailig *see* **Alexander**

Ailin, Ailean *see* **Alan**

Ailish, Eilish *f*
Strictly speaking Ailish and Eilish are, respectively, Irish pet forms of ALICE and ELIZABETH, but as they are both pronounced 'ay-lish' (the 'ay' as in hay or EYE-leesh), there is no practical distinction between the two.
VARIANTS **Elish, Eillish**
★ Eilís Dillon (1920–94), Irish author

Ailpean *see* **Alpin**

Ailsa f

This name, popular in Scotland and to a lesser extent in Australia, has a complex history. On the surface it appears to come from a place name, the island of Ailsa Craig in the Firth of Clyde, Scotland. Ailsa in this case is a reduced form of the Old Norse name *Alfsigr*, 'elf victory', which is still occasionally used, particularly in fantasy contexts. This looks quite straightforward, until one discovers that the Gaelic name for the island is either Allasa or Cread Ealasaid, *Ealasaid* being a Gaelic form of ELIZABETH. Since ELSA is also a form of Elizabeth, it has been suggested that the name may represent a Scottish form of this; alternatively the name may come from *Ailsie*, a Scottish pet form of ALICE. To add further complications, although the name is normally pronounced as it is spelt, 'ale-sa', there is a variant pronunciation 'eye-la', the same as the Scottish name ISLA. In most probability, the island is the main source with the other names helping to reinforce its popularity. Its spread was no doubt boosted by the fact that the name Ailsa Craig was given to varieties of onion and tomato popular with gardeners, and that this name was easily misinterpreted as a first name and surname by those not familiar with Scottish geography.

PET FORM **Ailie**

Aimée, Aimie *see* Amy

Aindrea, Aindréas, Aindrias, Aindriú *see* Andrew

Aine f

Aine, pronounced 'on-ya' or 'awn-ya', is the Irish Gaelic word for 'splendour, radiance', and was the name of the queen of the fairies who lived under Knockainey ('Aine's Hill') in County Limerick. The kings of Munster claimed her as an ancestor and so, through them, did the prominent Fitzgerald family (see under GERALDINE) for whom the name has been traditional. It has been steadily popular in Ireland for a number of years. In the past, when Irish names were rarely used officially, the name was written Anna or Anne.

VARIANT **Anya**

Aingeal *see* Angel

Ainsley *mf*

This is a surname used as a first name. The surname comes in turn from various place names formed from Old English *an*, 'one, only', and *leah*, 'clearing', and is usually interpreted as meaning 'solitary clearing'.

★ Ainsley Harriot (1957–), English chef

Aisha f

This Arabic name comes from the word for 'alive, thriving, prosperous'. As the name of the Prophet Muhammad's influential third wife, it is popular throughout the Islamic world. The name is pronounced 'eye-EE-sha', but in the West is sometimes reduced to two syllables, overlapping with the name ASIA. It has been well used by African Americans, with use peaking in the 1970s and 80s.

VARIANTS **Aishah, Aye(i)sha, Ie(a)sha**
French **Aïcha, Aïchoucha, Aoucha**

★ Aisha bint-Abu-Bakr (c.613–73), third wife of the Prophet Muhammad
☆ Ayesha, 'She Who Must Be Obeyed' in H Rider Haggard's 1887 novel *She*

Aisling f

This is a modern Irish name, from *aisling* the Irish for 'dream'. It has nationalist associations, for in the 17th and 18th centuries it was a poetic term used to describe a vision of Ireland in the form of a woman in peril. It is pronounced 'ash-ling'.

VARIANTS **Ashlin, Ashling, Aisli, Aislin, Isleen**

Ajay, Ajit *m*
These are Indian names, from the Sanskrit for 'unconquered, invincible'. Ajay is also sometimes formed from the English initials A J.
VARIANT **Ajaya** (used for both sexes)

Akeem *see* **Hakim**

Akim *see* **Joachim**

Akiva *see* **Jacob**

Aksinya *see* **Xenia**

Al *mf*
A short form of almost any name beginning *Al-*, most commonly ALEXANDER.

Alan *m*
This is a Celtic name of uncertain origin, although a number of suggestions have been made. In England in 2006, an Iron Age coin was discovered bearing the name *Ale*, and it may be that this is our earliest evidence of the name. It is thought that it may be from the same root as the Gaelic word *ailin*, 'little rock'. The name was reintroduced to England with the Norman Conquest, by Breton followers of William the Conqueror who included Alan, Duke of Brittany. The Bretons had a particular affection for the name because it was that of a local 6th-century saint.
PET FORM **Al** • VARIANTS **Allan, Allen** *Irish* **Ailin** *Scots Gaelic* **Ailean** *Welsh* **Alun** *French* **Alain**
★ Alan Bennett (1934–), English dramatist, actor and director
★ Allan Breck Stewart (fl.1745–63), Scottish Jacobite who appears in fiction in Sir Walter Scott's *Rob Roy* (1817) and Robert Louis Stevenson's *Kidnapped* (1886)

Alana *f*
This is a feminine form of ALAN which has been in regular use since the 1940s. LANA is usually regarded as its short form, although it can also be a shortening of SVETLANA. However, the dating evidence presents a problem, for Lana was being used in the USA by the 1880s, which suggests that in some cases it may have another, unknown, source. In Ireland the name, particularly in the spelling *Alannah*, can have another interpretation, as coming from the Gaelic *leanbh*, 'child', with the affectionate *a*, the equivalent of 'Oh' placed in front.
PET FORM **Lana** • VARIANTS **Alanna, Allana(h), Alanis**
★ Alanis Morissette (1974–), Canadian-American singer, with whom general use of this form seems to have started

Alaois *see* **Aloysius**

Alastair *m*
This is a Scottish form of ALEXANDER. Alexander was an important name in Scotland in the Middle Ages, when it developed this Gaelic form. It was then reintroduced as an independent name to English speakers, and this anglicization explains the wide variety of forms the name takes.
FEMININE **Alastriona** • PET FORMS **Al, Ali, Allie, Aly** • VARIANTS **Alistair, Allastar, Alister** *Scots Gaelic* **Alasdair** *Irish* **Alastar**
★ Alistair MacLean (1922–87), Scottish author
★ Alistair Cooke (1908–2004), English-born US journalist and broadcaster

Alatheia, Alathia *see* **Alethea**

Alba *see* **Alban, Aurora**

Alban *m* Albina, Albinia *f*
This probably derives from the Latin word *albus*, meaning white, either directly or via a place name, Alba, from the same source. An alternative

is that the name comes from the Celtic *alp*, 'rock, crag'. Whichever the source may be, Alban is an important name in British history, being the name of St Alban, the first Christian martyr in Britain, who was executed around AD 209 near the city named after him. The name was revived in the 19th century, but is little used now. The feminine forms can be either from Alban's name, or directly from the Latin adjective (compare BLANCHE).

PET FORMS **Albie** • VARIANTS **Alba, Albin**

☆ Albus Dumbledore, headmaster of Hogwarts school in J K Rowling's *Harry Potter* books

Alberic *see* **Aubrey**

Albert *m*

Albert is a Germanic first name formed from the elements *adal*, 'noble', and *berht*, 'bright, famous'. It was brought to England with the Norman Conquest, and replaced, usually in the form *Aubert*, the Anglo-Saxon form of the name ETHELBERT. However, although popular on the Continent, it was not much used in Britain until the 19th century, when Albert of Saxe-Coburg-Gotha became Prince Consort to Queen Victoria. It is, however, recorded in the USA from the 17th century, which may be because of German and Dutch immigrants. Prince Albert's influence made the name popular, but use had largely died out by the 1920s. The various feminine forms of the name were again established on the Continent, but introduced to the UK in honour of Prince Albert, and were used for both a daughter and goddaughter of Queen Victoria.

FEMININES **Alberta, Albertina, Berta** • PET FORMS **Al** (mainly USA), **Bert(ie), Alby** • VARIANTS *Scots Gaelic* **Ailbeart** *French* **Alberte, Albertine** (fs) *German* **Albrecht,**

Adalbert, Adalbrecht, Adelbrecht *Italian, Portuguese, Spanish* **Alberto**

★ Albert Einstein (1879–1955), German-Swiss-US physicist

★ Albert Camus (1913–60), French existentialist writer

★ Princess Louise Caroline Alberta (1848–1939), daughter of Queen Victoria after whom the Canadian province of Alberta is named

☆ Albertine Simonet is the main love interest in Marcel Proust's *À la recherche du temps perdu* (1913–27)

Alby *see* **Ailbe, Albert, Elvis**

Aldous *m*

The Germanic element *ald*, 'old', appears in a number of obsolete names, and Aldous seems to be derived from pet forms of these. It was widespread in East Anglia in the Middle Ages, but was never much used elsewhere in the UK. The element is found in other countries, particularly Italy, where *Aldo* is not an uncommon name. However, the story in Italy is somewhat muddied, for the most famous bearer of the name there is *Aldus* Manutius, also called Aldo Manuzio (c.1449–1515), humanist scholar and widely regarded as printer of the finest books ever produced. Although he appears to be one of the bearers of the name, he was in fact christened Teobaldo (see THEOBALD) and it is impossible at this stage to say whether he used Aldus merely as a pet form of his given name, or if he deliberately chose to try to change it.

VARIANTS **Aldis** *French* **Alde** (m), **Aude** (f) *Italian, Spanish* **Aldo**

★ Aldous Huxley (1894–1963), English novelist

★ Aldo Moro (1916–78), Italian politician assassinated by the Red Brigades

☆ In medieval French stories of the hero Roland, the Fair Aude is the sister of

Oliver and betrothed of Roland, who dies of grief at the news of his death

Aldred m
The Old English name Aldred, 'old council', was the name of the last Anglo-Saxon archbishop of York, who died in 1069. It was revived in the 19th century along with other Anglo-Saxon religious names, but was never particularly popular, and is now rare.
VARIANTS **Eldred, Ealdred**

Alease see **Alice**

Alec, Aleck see **Alexander**

Alecia see **Alice**

Aled m
The name of the River Aled in Clwyd entered the Welsh stock of names after it was adopted by the poet Tudor Aled (fl.1480–1526) as his bardic name.
FEMININE **Aledwen**
★ Aled Jones (1970–), Welsh singer

Aleece see **Alice**

Aleeda see **Adelaide**

Aleesha see **Alice**

Aleeza see **Aliza**

Aleid, Aleida, Aleit see **Adelaide**

Alena, Alyona see **Helen**

Alessa, Alessia see **Alexandra**

Alèssio see **Alexis**

Alethea f
This name dates from the 16th century, and was used regularly through to at least the 18th century, although it is rare now. It comes from the Greek alēthea, 'truth'. It may have become popular as part of the contemporary fashion for virtue names, or it may have been taken from the name of the Spanish princess Maria Aletea, who was at one time intended as a bride

for the future Charles II. There are two possible pronunciations of the name, 'Al-a-THEE-a', and 'Al-EE-thia', the latter being more common in the USA. There is some confusion between this name and ALTHEA.
VARIANTS **Alathia, Alatheia, Alithea**
☆ Alethea Pontifex is a character in Samuel Butler's novel *The Way of all Flesh* (1903)

Alette see **Adele**

Alexander m
The Greek *Alexandros* is formed from the verb *alexein*, 'to help, defend', and *andros*, 'of man'. In mythology it was given by some shepherds to the Trojan PARIS after he drove off brigands who were attacking them. The name was traditional in the Macedonian ruling family, and was most notably borne by Alexander the Great (356–323 BC). Alexander was an expert at manipulating his public image, and fictionalized versions of his life began to circulate soon after his death. These built up into a vast cycle of stories that spread his fame throughout Europe and Asia, which explains why the name is so widely distributed. The name has been particularly important in Scotland, where it was introduced by St Margaret of Scotland (c.1038–93), wife of King Malcolm III. She was the daughter of an exiled Anglo-Saxon prince and a Hungarian princess, and had been brought up in Hungary where Alexander was already a well-established name. One of her sons came to the throne as Alexander I, and in the 13th century Alexander II and his successor Alexander III were on the throne for a combined reign of over 70 years, which meant that many of the inhabitants had never known a king of any other name. It is not surprising, therefore, that the name was well used thereafter. Many of the

short forms of the name are used as independent names. Some of the short forms are indistinguishable from those used for ALEXIS.

PET FORMS **Al, Alec, Aleck, Alex, Alick, Allie, Ally, Lex, Sandy** (particularly in Scotland), **Xander, Zander** • VARIANTS *Scots Gaelic* **Alasdair, Ailig, Sandaidh** *Arabic* **Iskander** *French* **Alexandre, Sasha** *Greek* **Alexandros** *Hungarian* **Sandor** *Italian* **Alessandro** *Polish* **Aleksandar, Olek** *Russian* **Aleksandr, Alyosha, Lyosha, Sacha, Sasha, Shura** *Scandinavian* **Sander** *Spanish* **Alejandro, Alondro** *Yiddish* **Sender**

★ Sir Alexander Fleming (1881–1955), Scottish bacteriologist involved in the discovery of penicillin

Alexandra *f*

Alexandra is the base form of the many feminine forms of ALEXANDER. The name was rare in the UK until the Danish Princess Alexandra, later to be Queen Alexandra, married the Prince of Wales in 1863. As with Alexander, many of the short forms are used as independent names. Some of the short forms are indistinguishable from those used for ALEXIS or ALICE.

PET FORMS **Alex, Alix, Alexa, Alyx, Lexa, Lexi, Lexie, Sandi, Sandy, Sandie** • VARIANTS **Alexandrea, Alexandria, Alexandrina, Drina, Alexia, Alexaina, Alexis** *Scottish* **Alickina, Kina, Alexina, Zena** *French* **Alexandrine, Sandra, Sandrine, Sasha** *Italian* **Alessandra, Aless(i)a, Sandra** *Polish* **Ola** *Spanish* **Alejandra, Alondra** (this also means 'lark' in Spanish) *Russian* **Sasha, Shura**

★ Alexandrina Victoria (1819–1901), better known as Queen Victoria

Alexis *mf* Alexia *f*

The Greek name *Alexios*, frequently used in the Byzantine royal families and which comes from the same root meaning 'to help' as ALEXANDER, became *Alexius* in Latin and was then shortened again to Alexis. It is particularly well used in Russia and other areas that come under the Orthodox Church, thanks to the popularity of St Alexis of Edessa. His is a highly romantic story of a nobleman from Constantinople who abandons his family on the day of his marriage to go and live among the poor. Alexis was originally exclusively masculine, with Alexia used for females, but Alexis is now predominantly feminine. The name shares many short forms with Alexander and ALEXANDRA, and it is not always possible to distinguish between the two groups.

VARIANTS **Alexa, Lexus** *French* **Alexie, Alexiane** (fs) *German* **Alexius** *Italian* **Alèssio, Alessa** *Russian* **Aleksei**

☆ Alexis Carrington, much-married ruthless schemer in the television series *Dynasty* and its spin-offs, played by Joan Collins from 1981 onwards. Although this was not the first use of Alexis as a feminine name, it contributed heavily to its spread

Alfonso *see* Alphonse

Alfred *m*

Made famous by Alfred the Great (849–99), this name is formed from the Old English elements *ælf*, 'elf', and *ræd*, 'counsel'. The name has had a somewhat chequered history, for although it survived the Norman Conquest, which was unusual for an Anglo-Saxon name, it was radically altered by Norman French speakers. Norman French had difficulty pronouncing groups of consonants, so the *lfr* in the name presented a problem. The pronunciation of the name was changed by them to *Avery*, now better known as a surname, but still found as a first name, particularly in the USA where it is used for both sexes and is a popular girl's name. At the same time scribes writing Latin felt that a 'v' was a more appropriate spelling of Alfred than an 'f'. However, in the writing of the time the form of the letter v used in the middle of a word had an identical form to a 'u', so that the name appeared to be spelt *Alured*. In the Middle Ages the name would always have been pronounced Alfred, but when Alfred was revived with other Anglo-Saxon names at the end of the 18th century, Alured, pronounced as spelt, was revived alongside it. Alfred is not currently much used as a given name, but the pet form *Alfie* is one of the most popular choices for boys. The feminine form *Alfreda* is strictly speaking a form of ELFRIDA, but is used as a feminine of Alfred.

PET FORMS **Alf, Alfie, Avery, Fred** • VARIANTS **Averie** *French* **Alfréda, Alfréde, Alfrédie, Alfrédine** (fs) *Italian, Spanish* **Alfredo, Alfreda** *Scandinavian* **Alf**

★ Alfred Nobel (1833–96), Swedish inventor and founder of the Nobel Prize
★ Alfred Hitchcock (1899–1980), English film-maker
☆ Alfie Moon in the television soap opera *EastEnders*, appearing 2002–5, and credited with being behind the current popularity of Alfie

Algernon *m*

This name started out as a nickname, for the medieval French *als gernons* means 'with whiskers'. In 1066 one of the soldiers who came over to England with William the Conqueror was William de Percy. He had moustaches, when the majority of Normans were clean shaven, so was nicknamed *als gernons*. In the 15th century, the Percy family, by now earls of Northumberland, revived the name within the family, and from them it was taken into other families by marriage. By the 19th century it was being widely used by the general public, although it is now out of favour.

PET FORMS **Algie, Algy**

★ Algernon Charles Swinburne (1837–1909), English poet and critic
☆ Algernon Moncrieff in Oscar Wilde's 1895 play *The Importance of Being Earnest*

Ali[1] *m* Alia *f*

This comes from the Arabic for 'lofty, sublime', its popularity in Islam being due to the fact that Ali was the name of the Prophet Muhammad's cousin and son-in-law, who became the first caliph. The names are well used by black Muslims in the USA.

VARIANTS **Aali, Aliyya(h), Aliya(h), Aaliyah**

★ Muhammad Ali (1942–), US boxer
★ Aaliyah Haughton (1979–2001), US singer, known as Aaliyah. It was her popularity, coupled with her early death, that established her name as the most popular feminine form in the West
☆ Ali Baba and the Forty Thieves in the *Arabian Nights*

Ali[2] *see* **Alastair, Alexander, Alice, Alison**

Alice, Alicia *f*

Alice started out as a pet form of the name that gives us ADELAIDE. The Old German *Adalheidis* was shortened first to *Adaliz* then to *Aliz* which was then respelt Alice. Adelaide and Alice had separated into distinct names by the 13th century, appearing in forms that look like modern developments such as *Alys* and *Alix*. The form Alicia also appears in Latin written texts from this date, but did not come into general use as a given name until reintroduced in 19th-century literature. Alice was enormously popular in the Middle Ages but died out around the 17th century, although it too was revived in the 19th. Forms of the name are currently experiencing worldwide popularity, with derivatives of Alicia such as *Alisha* or *Alyssa*, being particularly popular in English-speaking countries.

PET FORMS **Ali, Aly, Alison** • VARIANTS **Alease, Alecia, Aleece, Aleesha, Alishia, Alisia, Alys(h)a, Alyse, Alysha, Lecia, Lesia, Lisha, Lyssa** *Irish* **Ailís** *Scots Gaelic* **Aileas, Ailie** *Welsh* **Alis** *German* **Elke** *Polish* **Alicja** *Russian* **Alisa**

★ Alice Liddle (1852–1934), child for whom Lewis Carroll wrote *Alice's Adventures in Wonderland* (1865)

Alick *see* **Alexander**

Alickina *see* **Alexandra**

Alida, Alina *see* **Adelaide**

Alienor *see* **Eleanor**

Alina, Aline *see* **Adele**

Alisha *see* **Alice**

Alison *f*
Alison was originally a pet form of ALICE, and was equally popular in the Middle Ages. It is, like Alice, widely popular at the moment, but it is one of the names that shows distinct spelling differences between the UK and the USA. In the UK, Alison is the standard spelling, while in the USA, Allison is currently much more popular.

PET FORMS **Al, Ali, Ally** • VARIANTS **Allison, Alyson, Alysson**

★ Alyson Hannigan (1974–), US actress

☆ Alisoun, the Wife of Bath in Chaucer's *Canterbury Tales*

Alistair, Alister *see* **Alastair**

Alita *f*
This name comes from the Hebrew for 'high, excellent'.

Alithea *see* **Alethea**

Alivia *see* **Olivia**

Alix *see* **Alexandra, Alice**

Aliya, Aliyah *see* **Ali**

Aliz *see* **Alice**

Aliza *f*
This is a Jewish name, meaning 'joy, happiness', which is growing in use.

MASCULINE **Ali(t)z** • VARIANTS **Aleeza, Alitza(h), Alizah**

Alke *see* **Adelaide**

Allan *see* **Alan**

Allana, Allanah *see* **Alana**

Allastar *see* **Alastair**

Allegra *f*
This is the Italian word for 'lively, happy' introduced as a name when it was chosen for the short-lived child that the poet Byron had by Claire Clairmont, stepsister of Mary Shelley. Born in 1817, and raised in a nunnery, she died in 1822.

Allen *see* **Alan**

Allie *see* **Alastair, Alexander, Alice**

Allison *see* **Alison**

Allon *see* **Alon**

Ally *see* **Alexander, Alice, Alison**

Alma *f*
There was a rare name Alma, derived either from the Latin for 'soul' or for 'nourishing' (as in the expression *alma mater*), already in use when this name became more popular in the UK after the Crimean Battle of Alma in 1854. It has been used more in the USA than in the UK, particularly between the 1880s and 1920s, possibly because it is also the Spanish for 'soul'. In Persia and a number of other languages, Alma can be a name meaning 'apple'.

★ Alma Mahler (1878–1964), Austrian composer and noted beauty, wife of the composer Gustav Mahler, the architect Walter Gropius and the novelist Franz Werfel

☆ Alma Halliwell (previously Baldwin and Sedgewick), character in the television soap opera *Coronation Street*

☆ Alma Del Mar, character in Annie Proulx's short story *Brokeback Mountain*, published 1997, filmed 2005

Almeric *see* America

Almira *see* Elmira

Almitra *f*
Almitra is the name given to a seeress in Kahlil Gibran's book *The Prophet* (1923), and seems to have been made up by him, as it does not correspond to anything in Persian or Arabic. Since this book was something of a hippy bible in the 1960s, the name has passed into more general circulation.

Alon *m* Alona *f*
These are Jewish names, from the Hebrew for 'oak tree'.
VARIANT **Allon**

Alondra *see* Alexandra

Alondro *see* Alexander

Alonso, Alonzo *see* Alphonse

Aloysius *m*
It is possible that this name may come, at least in part, directly from a lost Germanic name containing the elements *al*, 'all', and *wis*, 'wise', but since the Middle Ages it has been considered a Latinized form of the Provençal name *Aloys*, itself one of the many variant forms of LEWIS. Use spread from the 17th century onwards in honour of St Aloysius Gonzaga (1568–91), an Italian nobleman who gave up his inheritance to join the Jesuits. In English the name is pronounced 'al-oo-(w)ish-us'.
FEMININE **Aloysia** • VARIANTS *Irish* **Alaois**

French **Aloïs, Aloïse, Aloyse, Eloise** (feminines) *German* **Alois** *Italian* **Aloisio**

Alphonse *m*
When the Visigoths invaded Spain in the Dark Ages, they took with them a Germanic name which appears variously as *Alfonso, Alonso* or *Alonzo*. Its original Germanic form seems to have been something like *Adalfons* from *adal*, 'noble', and *funs*, 'prompt, ready', although elements such as *ala*, 'all', *hadu*, 'struggle', or *hild*, 'battle', have been suggested for the first syllable. It seems likely that this confusion stems from the fact that Germanic elements were very flexible in the way they combined, and Alfonso may represent the local version of more than one name. The name was adopted from the Spanish by the French, making its mark in the 18th century, and given a Latinate twist by turning the 'f' into 'ph'. The name has been more used in the USA and West Indies than in the UK, but is currently out of favour.
FEMININE **Alphonsina** • PET FORMS **Fons(ie), Fonz(ie), Fonzo, Lonnie** • VARIANTS **Alphonsus** *French* **Alphonsine** (f) *Italian* **Alonzo**

Alpin *m*
This Highland Scottish name is more likely to be found in family trees rather than used today. Its earlier popularity is attested by the surname McAlpin. Since it has not been possible to find a Gaelic origin for this name, it is thought to be a survival of the extinct Pictish language.
VARIANT *Scots Gaelic* **Ailpean**

Alta *f*
Alta can be interpreted as either from the Spanish and Latin for 'high, elevated', or else as a form of the Yiddish name *Alte*, 'old'. In Yiddish-speaking communities girls could

be called *Alte*, boys *Alter* or *Altman* ('old man'), both to confer long life by association, and as a way of frustrating the Angel of Death if it should be looking for a baby. *Alta* was well used in the USA in the later 19th century, but had more or less died out by the 1950s.

★ Claudia Alta Taylor, better known as 'Lady Bird' Johnson (1912–2007), First Lady of the USA

Althea *f*

This name occurs in Greek mythology in the form *Althaia* or *Althæa*, as the mother of the hero Meleager. The name appears to be from the Greek *althein*, 'to heal', although given her story this does not seem appropriate. Sitting by the fire after her son's birth she was told his life would last only as long as a certain log lasted. She snatched the log from the fire and preserved it, but when, as a young hero, her son got into a fight and killed her two brothers, she threw the branch into the fire in fury and so killed him. Althea is also the Latin name for the mallow plant, given because of its healing properties. The name was revived in the modern form, probably with reference to its meaning rather than the story, by the Cavalier poet Richard Lovelace for his famous poem 'To Althea, from Prison' (1642) with its opening lines 'Stone walls do not a prison make, Nor iron bars a cage'. Althea, which is sometimes confused with ALETHEA, is generally pronounced with the stress on the first syllable by the British, but on the second in the USA.

★ Althea Braithwaite (1940–   ), children's writer and illustrator

★ Althea Gibson (1927–2003), US tennis player

☆ 'Althea' is the title of a 1980 Grateful Dead song

Alton *m*

This is a common place name which became a surname and then a first name. The place name can have various origins, the most common of which means 'settlement by a spring'. The name was well used in the USA in the first two decades of the 20th century, but is rarely chosen now. It is usually pronounced with the first syllable as in 'all', but is sometimes pronounced 'al'.

Alun *m*

While Alun is often a variant of ALAN, it can also be a separate Welsh name. The Riven Alun (Alyn in English) rises in Clwyd and is a tributary of the Dee. This name has been used as a first name since the 9th century, and was the name of a hero of the kingdom of Dyfed. In the 19th century it was adopted as a bardic name by the popular poet John Blackwell, and this helped its spread.

Alured *see* Alfred

Alva *mf*

It is impossible to sort out the various sources of this name from each other. As a boy's name it comes from the Hebrew name *Alvah*, 'height', found as a minor biblical name and well used in the USA from the 19th century into the first part of the 20th. This form appears feminine, so may be one source of the female name. However, the feminine has also been derived from the Irish *Ailbhe* (see ELVIS), as a feminine of the Scandinavian name *Alf* from the word for 'elf', or as a feminine form of ALVAR or ALVIN.

★ Thomas Alva Edison (1847–1931), US inventor and physicist

Alvar *m*

Two similar names have fallen together in modern use of this name. The Old English *Ælfhere*, 'elf army or warrior', is one source. A Spanish name once also found in the form Alvar, but now usually *Alvaro*, is the other. This is formed from Germanic elements meaning 'all' and 'army, warrior' and was taken by the conquering Visigoths to Spain.

★ Alvar Aalto (1898–1976), Finnish architect and designer

☆ Álvar Fáñez de Minaya, the Cid's nephew and closest adviser in the 12th-century Spanish epic poem *El Cantar de Mio Cid*

Alvin *m*

This is Old English in origin, from the elements *ælf*, 'elf', and *wine*, 'friend'. It has always been more popular in the USA than in the UK, being used steadily since records began, and peaking in the 1920s and 30s. See also ELVINA.

FEMININE **Alvina** • PET FORMS **Al, Elvina** • VARIANTS **Alwyne, Alwyn, Aylvin, Alvy, Elvin, Elwin**

☆ *Elfwine*, the old form of Alvin, was used by J R R Tolkien for the son of Éomer of the Rohirrim in *The Lord of the Rings*

Alvis *see* **Elvis**

Alwyn *m* Alwen *f*

Superficially, this is a Welsh name derived from the River Alwen in Clwyd. However, it is complicated by the fact that Alwyn can also be a variant of ALVIN, and that *Aylwyn*, which looks like a further variant can also be a form of Welsh *Aelwyn* from *ael*, 'brow', and *wen*, 'fair, white', which has a feminine AELWEN.

VARIANT **Alwena**

☆ *Alwen Hoff* ('Alwen Mine') is a popular Welsh song by J M Lloyd

Aly *see* **Alastair, Alice**

Alyosha *see* **Alexander**

Alys, Alysa, Alyse, Alysha, Alyssa

see **Alice**

Alyson, Alysson *see* **Alison**

Alyth *f*

Although still rare, this name is increasingly being noticed. In some cases it may be a variant of names in the ALICE group, but in others it is a transferred use of a place name. Alyth is a small town in Perth and Kinross, Scotland. The meaning of the place name is obscure, although 'place overlooking soft ground' has been suggested. Although the name is of Scottish origin, Alyth is also found in other places, particularly New Zealand which has historical connections with the town of Alyth.

★ Alyth McCormack (1970–), Scottish singer

Alyx *see* **Alexandra, Alice**

Ama *see* **Abdul**

Amabel *f*

This comes from the Latin *amabilis*, 'deserving love, loveable', and was a popular name in the Middle Ages, although rare today. It is, however, the source of both ANNABEL and MABEL, and was sometimes used in the 19th and first half of the 20th centuries under the influence of literary models.

VARIANT **Amabilla**

☆ Amabel Bloundel, beautiful heroine of William Harrison Ainsworth's once influential 1841 novel *Old St Paul's*

Amadeus *m*

Amadeus is the Latin translation of the Greek name THEOPHILUS, 'love God'. Use by English speakers is mostly with direct reference to the musician Wolfgang Amadeus Mozart (1757–91). This is actually a Latin translation of the German name GOTTLIEB, which has the same meaning.

FEMININE **Amadea** • VARIANTS *French*

Amadé, Amedée *Italian* **Amadeo, Amedeo**

Amadou *m*

Amadou is an old French name which is a reduced form of *Amadour*, derived in turn from the Latin *Amator*, 'lover [of God]'. The name is rare even in France, but is used in Africa, particularly in Francophone areas.

★ Amadou Bagayoko (1954–), Malian musician

Amal *f*

This is an Arabic name meaning 'hope, expectation'.

VARIANTS **Amaal, Amahl**

☆ *Amahl and the Night Visitors* is a 1951 children's opera by Gian Carlo Menotti

Amalie *f*

This is a name of Germanic origin, probably originally a shortened form of a name containing the element *amal*, 'work', recorded among the Goths as early as the 1st century AD. Amalie influenced the development of the name AMELIA, and is sometimes regarded as a variant.

VARIANTS **Amalia, Amaline**

Amalric *see* America

Aman *mf*

This is the Arabic for 'trust, safety'. There is some overlap with AMANI.

Amanda *f*

Although there were plenty of medieval masculine names derived from the Latin verb *amare*, 'to love', such as *Ama(n)ce, Amant* and *Amand(in)*, some of which are still in use in other languages, there is little evidence for feminine forms until the 17th century. Amanda, from the Latin for 'worthy to be loved', appears in 1696 in Colly Cibber's *Love's Last Shift*, and then is much used for literary heroines for the next century or so. It was well used in the USA in the later

19th century, but really became widely popular in the 1960s, and was in the top ten US names from 1976 to 1995.

PET FORMS **Manda, Mandi(e), Mandy**

• VARIANTS **Amata** *French* **Amandine** *Italian* **Amato** (m) *Spanish* **Amado, Amador, Amancio** (ms)

☆ 'Mandy' was a hit song for Barry Manilow in 1974

Amani *mf*

This is the Arabic for 'wishes, aspirations'. It is mainly a feminine name and in the USA, where it is almost exclusively female, it is also interpreted as coming from the Swahili for 'peace'. It is also the Persian form of AMAN.

Amaryllis *f*

Use of this name goes back to the Greek poet Theocritus in the 3rd century BC. Its etymology is uncertain, but the Greek *amaryssein*, 'to sparkle', has been suggested. The name was taken up by the Latin poets Ovid and Virgil, and the latter uses the name in his *Eclogues* for a typical country girl or pastoral shepherdess. This use was adopted in England by poets in the 16th and 17th centuries, most famously by Milton, who writes in *Lycidas* (1637) about the desire to 'Sport with Amaryllis in the shade'. The name has always been predominantly literary, and was most often used as a given name in the 19th century. It may at times have been used as a flower name, Amaryllis having been given as a name to the South African bulb also known as the Jersey or belladonna lily.

PET FORM **Rilla** • VARIANT **Marilla**

Amat *see* Abdul

Amata *see* Amity

Amber *f*

The Arabic word *anbar*, which was used for the perfume ingredient we now call ambergris, passed into Western languages in the Middle Ages and soon became the name for the fossilized resin used for jewellery. It was not adopted as a first name until the late 19th century when it joined other jewel names. However, it only really came to public attention in 1944 with the publication of Kathleen Winsor's scandalous bestseller *Forever Amber*. Amber St Clair, heroine of *Forever Amber* is anachronistically named Amber after the colour of her eyes. The novel is set in the 17th century, and tells how the orphaned Amber sleeps her way to power and riches. Occasionally Amber is a shortened form of *Amberl(e)y*, which is an English place name, and may play on the compound name *Amber-Leigh*. The name was well used in the 1960s, and has been popular with English speakers internationally since the mid-1990s.

PET FORM **Ambie** • VARIANTS **Ambretta, Ambreen** *Arabic* **Amb(a)rin, Ambara** *French* **Ambre, Ambrine** *Italian* **Ambra**
★ Amber Valletta (1974–   ), US model and actress

Ambrose *m*

Ambrose comes from the Greek meaning 'immortal' and shares a root with the food of the gods, ambrosia. The Latin form of the name is found attached to the supposed Romano-British leader in the 5th century AD, *Ambrosius Aurelianus*. It was the name of a number of saints, most notably St Ambrose who became bishop of Milan in AD 374. He was a prolific theologian and famously barred the emperor himself from entering church over a doctrinal dispute. The name was used regularly in the past but is little used now.

FEMININES **Ambrosine, Ambrosina**
• VARIANTS *Irish* **Ambrós** *Welsh* **Emrys**

French **Ambroise** *Hungarian* **Ambrus** *Italian* **Ambrogio, Ambrogino** *Polish* **Ambrozy** *Portuguese, Spanish* **Ambrosio**
★ Ambrose Philips (c.1674–1749), English poet. The term 'namby-pamby', based on his name, was coined by his critics to describe his writing

Amedeo, Amedée *see* Amadeus

Ameer, Ameera *see* Amir

Amelia *f*

This name developed from a falling together of the Germanic name AMALIE with the Latin name *Æmelia*, source of EMILY. The name came into use in the 16th century, but was most popular in the 18th, helped by Henry Fielding's novel *Amelia* (1751), and the choice of the name for Princess Amelia (often known as Emily), third daughter of George III, in 1783. Use of the French form has increased radically since the international success of the 2001 French film *Amélie*.

PET FORMS **Melia, Millie, Milly** • VARIANTS **Emilia** *French* **Amélie** *German* **Amalie**
★ Amelia Earhart (1897–1937), US pioneer aviator

Amer, Amera *see* Amir

America *f* Amerigo *m*

It is well known that the explorer Amerigo Vespucci (1451–1512) gave his name to the continent of America. His name was either the Italian form of the Germanic name *Amalric*, formed from the elements *amal*, 'work', and *ric*, 'rule', or a local form of HENRY. Amalric goes back to at least the 6th century, when it was the name of a Visigothic king. In France the name developed into *Amaury*, which in turn became the English surnames *Emery* or *Emory* and *Emerson*, now starting to be used as first names for both sexes. America was used in the USA as a girl's name in the 19th century, but then fell out of use, until there was a sudden revival after the events of 9/11. However, the name has a different history in Mexico, where girls are not infrequently called América, the name being chosen by fathers who are supporters of the Club América football team.

★ America Ferrara (1984–), US actress

Amethyst *f*

This is one of the rarer jewel names. The name of the gem comes from the Greek *amethustos*, 'not drunk', for it was believed in the past that wearing the stone, or drinking from a cup containing it, would protect against drunkenness.

Amey *see* **Amy**

Amhladh, Amhlaidh *see* **Aulay**

Amhlaoibh *see* **Aulay, Olaf**

Ami *see* **Amy**

Amias *see* **Amyas**

Amice, Amicia *see* **Amity**

Amie *see* **Amy**

Amilcar, Amilcare *see* **Hamilcar**

Amin *m* Amina *f*

This name comes from the Arabic meaning 'trustworthy, loyal' which in turn comes from the verb *amana*, 'to trust or believe [in God]', which is also the source of the name IMAN.

PET FORM **Aminata (f)** • VARIANTS **Aamin, Amine, Aamina, Aminah**

★ Amina bint Wahab (d.576), mother of the Prophet Muhammad

☆ Amina is the name of the heroine of Bellini's 1831 opera *La Sonnambula*

Aminta, Amynta *see* Araminta

Amir *m* Amira *f*

This is the Arabic for 'leader, commander' which has entered

English vocabulary as the word Emir. Amir is often used in combination with another name, such as *Amir Ali* or *Amir Hassan*. The name should not be confused with *Amr* which means 'life'.

PET FORM **Mir** • VARIANTS **Aamir, Aamira, Amer, Ameer, Amera, Ameera** *Turkish* **Emir**

★ Amir Khan (1986–), English boxer

Amit, Amitabh *m*

In Sanskrit Amit means 'unlimited' and Amitabh 'of unlimited splendour', which is one of the titles of the Buddha.

FEMININE **Amita** • VARIANT **Amitav**

Amity *f*

This is one of a number of rare names, more common in the past, which derive ultimately from the Latin *amo*, 'to love, like'. Amity, *Amice, Amita* and *Amicia* come from *amicitia*, the Latin for 'friendship'. *Amata* means 'beloved'. The names have largely been replaced by AMANDA and AMY.

VARIANT *French* **Ami**

Amos *m*

Amos is one of the prophets of the Old Testament, who warned his people of their forthcoming doom. The name probably comes from the Hebrew word for 'to carry' and is interpreted as meaning either 'borne by God' or 'bearer of a burden'. It was adopted by the Puritans, and was well used until the end of the 19th century, by which time it had rather rustic connotations. The name shows some signs of returning to use.

★ Amos Oz (1939–), Israeli author

Amr *see* Amir

Amrit *m* Amrita *f*

This comes from the Sanskrit meaning 'without death', although it is often translated 'nectar, elixir', for it refers to the ambrosial substance drunk by the Hindu gods that keeps them immortal.

Amy *f*

Amy is a development of the names listed under AMITY, which in Old French developed the pet form *Amée*, which then became *Aimée*, 'loved, beloved'. It is on record by the 13th century, began to fade in the 17th, but was revived in the early 19th century with the publication of Sir Walter Scott's *Kenilworth* in 1821. This told the story of Amy Robsart who died in 1560, murdered, it was rumoured, by her husband, Elizabeth I's favourite the Earl of Leicester. The name is widely popular at the moment both in the form Amy and *Aimee*, and is a popular first element in compound names.

VARIANTS **Aimie, Ami(e), Amey**

Amyas *m*

This probably comes from the French name *Amis*, the hero of a medieval romance and the masculine equivalent of *Amice* (see AMITY). It had entered the stock of English names by the 12th century. It has strong literary associations, having been used by Spenser in his *Faerie Queene* (1596) and by Charles Kingsley in *Westward Ho!* (1855). The latter started something of a fashion for the name, but it is now rare.

VARIANT **Amias**

Amynta *see* **Araminta**

Ana *see* **Anne**

Anabel, Anabella *see* **Annabel**

Anacletus *m*

This is a Greek name, meaning 'invoked', which was the name of the third pope who died c.88 AD.

PET FORM **Cletus** • VARIANTS *Italian, Spanish* **Anacleto, Cleto**

Anaëlle *see* **Anne**

Anaïs *f*

This name, pronounced 'a-na-EES', is a Catalan form of the name ANNA. It had a certain currency in the 19th century in France, but only became popular there in the 1980s after it was used in the name of a perfume. This also led to wider use in the rest of the world.

PET FORM **Naïs** • VARIANT **Anais**

★ Anaïs Nin (1903–77), French-born US writer

☆ Anaïs is a character in the 1900 novel *Claudine at School (Claudine à l'école)* by Colette

Anand *m* Ananda *f*

These come from the Sanskrit word for 'happiness, bliss' which can have strong religious connotations.

VARIANT **Anandi (f)**

Anastasia *f*

The Greek word *anastasis* means 'resurrection' (literally 'a rising up'). Although it is recorded centuries before the advent of Christianity, it rapidly took on Christian overtones thereafter, and became a name particularly frequently used for those born around Easter. *Anastasius*, the masculine form of the name, has never been much used by English speakers, but Anastasia has a long record. It was the name of a popular 4th-century martyr, whose feast day is celebrated on 25 December, which may be why it is also the traditional name for the Virgin Mary's midwife. It was in use in England by the 13th century, where it usually took such forms as *Anstace* or *Anstice*, which are still occasionally used.

MASCULINE **Anastasius** • PET FORMS **Nastasia, Stasia, Stacey, Tansy, Tacy** • VARIANTS **Anastacia** *French* **Anastasie, Anastase (m)** *German* **Nastassja** *Greek* **Tasia, Tasoula, Anastasios (m)** *Italian* **Anastasio (m)** *Polish* **Anastazja, Anastazy (m)** *Russian* **Anastasiya, Asya, Nastasia, Nastasya,**

Nastya, Atasya, Anastas (m) *Spanish* **Anastasio** (m)

★ Anastasia (1901–?18), Grand Duchess of Russia and daughter of the last Tsar of Russia

★ Nastassja Kinski (1961?–   ), German actress

Anatole *m*

This comes from the Greek word for 'sunrise, east'. In ancient Greece the name was used for both sexes (and today is occasionally construed as feminine from the shared sounds with ANNA) and was the name of one of the Hours. The name is thought of as typically French but it is not, in fact, particularly common there.

★ Anatole France (1844–1924), French author

☆ Anatole is the name of the superb French chef employed by Bertie's Aunt Dahlia in the *Jeeves and Wooster* stories of P G Wodehouse

Anchoret *see* **Angharad**

Andela *see* **Angela**

Andrea *f*

This is the commonest feminine form of ANDREW, although in Italy it is also a masculine name. It has been recorded from the 17th century, but only became popular in the middle of the 20th century.

PET FORMS **Andi(e), Andy** • VARIANTS **Andree, Andria, Andriana, Andrena, Andrene, Andrine**

Andrew *m*

This comes from the Greek word *aner*, 'man', which becomes *andros* when it means 'of a man', and probably started out as a short form of compound names such as *Alexandros* (ALEXANDER). It was the name of the first of the Apostles, who was a very popular saint in the Middle Ages, and became the patron saint of Greece, Russia and Scotland. The x-shaped cross of St Andrew, found on the Scottish flag, comes from the story that St Andrew was crucified on an x-shaped cross.

PET FORMS **Andy, Drew** • VARIANTS *Irish* **Aindrias, Aindréas, Aindriú** *Scots Gaelic* **Aindrea, Anndra** *Scottish* D**and(y)** *Welsh* **Andras** *Czech* **Andrej, Ondrej** *Dutch* **Andries** *Finnish* **Antero, Antii, Tero** *French* **André** *German* **Andreas, Andies** *Greek* **Andreas** *Hungarian* **András, Andor, Endre** *Italian* **Andrea** *Polish* **Andrzej, Jedrzej, Jed** *Russian* **Andrei** *Scandinavian* **Anders** *Spanish* **Andrés**

Ane *see* **Anne**

Anéislis *see* **Stanislas**

Aneke *see* **Anneke**

Aneurin *m*

This has come to be the dominant form of an ancient Welsh name *Aneirin*. Its oldest form seems to have been *Neirin*, with the initial 'A' only added in the 13th century. There has been much debate as to the meaning of the name. Some think it may come from a Celtic root meaning 'noble', in which case the added *A* would have been emphatic in Welsh. Others, more doubtfully, have suggested that the name is derived from *an*, 'very', and *eur*, 'gold'. It is traditionally described as the Welsh form of *Honorius* (see HONORIA), which also means 'noble'. It is pronounced 'an-EYE-rin' in the south of Wales and 'an-AY-rin' in the north.

PET FORMS **Ni, Nye, Neirin**

★ Aneurin 'Nye' Bevan (1897–1960), Welsh Labour politician, who introduced the National Health Service

★ Aneurin or Aneirin, (fl.6th–7th century), ancient British poet

Anežka *see* **Agnes**

Angel *mf*

The Greek word *angelos* originally simply meant 'messenger', but in the

Bible acquired a special meaning of 'messenger from God', hence our word angel. In Spain and the USA, Angel is well-established as a masculine name, and has been so used occasionally in England. The masculine form is currently popular in the USA, and is moderately well used for girls, although *Angelina* and ANGELA occur more frequently. In the UK Angel is predominantly a feminine name, and is currently more popular than Angela.

PET FORM **Ang(i)e** • VARIANTS **Angelle** *Irish* **Aingeal** (f) *French* **Ange, Angèle** *Italian* **Angelo, Gelo, Lito** *Spanish* **Ángel, Angeles** (f) from Nuestra Señora de los Ángeles, 'Our Lady of the Angels'

☆ Angel Clare (m) is a character in Thomas Hardy's 1891 novel *Tess of the D'Urbervilles*

☆ Angel is the name of the (masculine) vampire with a soul in the television series *Buffy the Vampire Slayer* and *Angel*

Angela, Angelica *f*

There are two basic forms for feminine names from the word 'angel', the first formed from adding a feminine ending to the vocabulary word, as in the case of Angela; the second formed from an adjective, as in the French *Angelique*, 'angelic'. Some names combine the two. They are listed together here as they share the same function. Forms of the names have been in use since the Middle Ages, but English speakers did not use the name very frequently until the 19th century. Angela is currently less commonly given in the UK than the USA where it has been popular for a number of years, peaking in the 1970s. See also under ANGEL, with which there is considerable overlap, and EVANGELINE.

PET FORMS **Ange, Angie** • VARIANTS **Angelia, Anjelica** *Czech* **Andĕla** *Dutch* **Angelien** *French* **Angeline, Angelique** *German*

Angelika *Greek* **Angeliki** *Italian* **Angelina** *Polish* **Aniela, Anielka** *Russian* **Anzhela, Anzhelina** *Spanish* **Ángela, Angelita, Lita, Angélica**

★ Angelika Kauffmann (1741–1807), Swiss painter

★ Angelina Jolie (1975–), US actress

☆ Angelica was the name of the heroine in Boiardo's 15th-century Italian epic *Orlando Innamorato* (*Orlando in Love*) and Ariosto's 16th-century sequel *Orlando Furioso* (*Orlando Mad*), both of which were influential in later literature

Angharad *f*

This is a Welsh name formed from *car*, 'love', found in a number of Welsh names such as CARYS, with the intensifying *an* placed in front, giving a meaning 'much loved'. The name was in use by the 9th century, and was one of the three most frequent female names in Wales from the 13th century right through to the 17th, and enjoyed a revival in the 20th century. The name is also thought to be behind the medieval English name *Anchoret* or *Ankaret*. Angharad is pronounced 'ang-HAR-ad'.

VARIANT **Angharead**

★ Angharad Rees (1949–), Welsh actress

☆ Angharad Golden Hand is the heroine of the medieval Welsh romance *Peredur*

Angus *m*

Angus is the English spelling of the Gaelic name formed from *aon*, 'one, single', and *ghus*, 'choice', and was the name of a Celtic god of youth and love. In the past it was confined to Ireland and the Scottish Highlands, where AENEAS could be used as a substitute, but in modern times it is widely used, while still keeping its Scottish flavour. In Gaelic it is pronounced 'EEN-yis'.

FEMININE **Angusina** (mainly confined to
the Scottish Highlands) • PET FORMS **Angie**
(with a hard 'g'), **Gus** • VARIANTS *Scots
Gaelic* **Aonghas, Angaidh, Aonghus**
Scottish **Innes** *Irish* **Aengus, Oengus**

★ Aonghas Og ('the Young') (d.1490),
last independent Lord of the Isles, who
declared war on his father, and was
assassinated by his own harper

Anibal, Anibale *see* **Hannibal**

Anice *see* **Annis**

Anicetos, Aniketos *see* **Nikita**

Aniela, Anielka *see* **Angela**

Anika *see* **Anneke**

Anil *m* **Anila** *f*
The Hindu god of the wind, whose
job is to drive the sun's chariot, is
called Anil, the name simply being the
Sanskrit for 'wind'.

Anis[1] *see* **Annis**

Anis[2] *m* **Anisa** *f*
The Arabic *anis* means 'courteous,
kind, good friend'.
VARIANTS **Anisse, Anissa**

Anish *m*
This comes from Sanskrit and means
'supreme, born without an equal'. It is
one of the thousand names of the god
Vishnu.

★ Anish Kapoor (1954–), British
sculptor

Anisha *f*
Anisha, 'unending, uninterrupted'
in Sanskrit, is one of the titles of the
goddess LAKSHMI. The word can also be
interpreted as meaning 'light', from a
combination of the name NISHA, 'night',
with a negative prefix. In the West the
name is occasionally an elaboration
of ANNE.

Anita *f*
Anita was originally a Spanish pet form

of *Ana*, the Spanish form of ANNA, but
is now used as an independent name.
PET FORM **Nita**

★ Anita Brookner (1928–), English
novelist and art historian

★ Dame Anita Roddick (1942–2007),
English retail entrepreneur

Anja *see* **Anne**

Anjali
This name uses the Sanskrit word for a
religious offering. See also GITANJALI.

Anjelica *see* **Angela**

Ankaret *see* **Angharad**

Ann, Anna *see* **Anne**

Annabel *f*
Although it appears to be a compound
name formed from ANNA and BEL (see
BELLE), and is often analysed as such,
this is probably a form of the name
AMABEL. It is an old name, already in
use in Scotland by the 12th century.
In England it was used regularly until
the end of the 16th century, and had a
strong revival in the middle of the 20th
century.
PET FORMS **Bel, Belle, Bella** • VARIANTS
Anabel, Annabell, Annabelle, Anabella
Irish **Nápla**

☆ 'Annabel Lee' is an influential poem
Edgar Allan Poe published in 1849. It
may commemorate the death of his
cousin and wife

Annaëlle *see* **Anne**

Annalise, Anneli *f*
These are variants of a compound
name made from forms of ANNA and
LISA. The base form seems to have been
the German form *Anneliese*, while the
Scandinavian form Anneli has also been
influential. The name takes many forms,
but parents need to be careful, as there
is at least one child going round with
the unfortunate spelling *Analyse*.

VARIANTS **Annalisa, Annaliesa, Annelise, Annelies, Annaliesse, Annalie**
☆ Annalise Kratz, née Hartman, was a character in the Australian soap opera *Neighbours*

Anndra *see* **Andrew**

Anne, Anna *f*
These are the English and English-Latin forms of the Hebrew name HANNAH. In Christian legend Anne, or Anna, was the name of the Virgin Mary's mother, possibly because it was also the name of the mother of Samuel, and both are said to have become pregnant through divine intervention. As the cult of the Virgin spread, so did reverence for her mother and the spread of the name. Anna was particularly popular among the Byzantine ruling classes, which further helped spread the name. In 19th-century England the form *Ann* was the most popular, but in the 20th century Anne became the more common spelling, although Ann is still standard in the USA. However, both forms are currently heavily overshadowed by Anna. These names have been so popular for so long that they have developed a multitude of different forms and pet forms in different languages. The more common ones which have drifted furthest from their roots are listed separately, and to make the list more manageable have only been listed below if they do not begin *An-*. Anne is also a popular element in compound names, giving innumerable forms such as *Annemarie* or *Anne-Margaret*.
PET FORMS **Annie, Nan, Nancy, Ninon, Ninette** • VARIANTS *Breton* **Anaëlle, Annaëlle** *Danish* **Ane** *Dutch* **Ans, Antje** *Scandinavian* **Anja** *Spanish* **Ana**
★ Princess Anne (1950–), British princess and only daughter of Queen Elizabeth II

Anneke *f*
There is a long tradition in a number of Western languages of adding a 'k' sound to form a pet form of nouns. In English it used to be *kin* giving obsolete forms such as *Peterkin*. It is this -*kin* that lies behind JACK as a pet form of JOHN. Thus Anneke would have started life with a form such as *Anniken*. Variants of Anneke appear in a number of languages as a pet form of ANNE, either through direct formation or borrowing. In France the pet form *Annick* has developed a further pet form *Anouk*, and in Russian it has become *Anuska*, more often found as *Anouska, Anoushka* or *Anouchka* in other languages.
VARIANTS **Aneke, Anika, Anneka, Annika**
★ Anneka Rice (1958–), Welsh television presenter
★ Anouk Aimée (1932–), French actress

Annette *f*
This was originally a French pet form of ANNE, now used as an independent name.
PET FORMS **Netta, Nettie** • VARIANTS **Annetta, Annett**

Annika *see* **Anneke**

Annis *f*
This is a medieval form of AGNES, which is still occasionally revived. Some variant spellings may be influenced by the French vocabulary word *anice*, 'aniseed'.
VARIANTS **Anice, Annice, Annys, Anis**

Annora *see* **Honoria**

Annunziata *f*
This is an Italian name referring to the feast day of the Annunciation, when Gabriel told the Virgin Mary she would have a child. It is most likely to be used for children born about the time of the feast, on 25 March.

PET FORMS **Nunzia, Nunziatina** • VARIANTS
Spanish **Anunciación, Anunciata**

Annwen see **Anwen**

Annwyl *m*
The Welsh word *annwyl* means 'dear,
beloved'. This is found as both a first
name and a surname in Wales.
VARIANT **Anwyl**

Anora see **Honoria**

**Anouchka, Anouk, Anoushka,
Anouska, Anuska** see **Anneke**

Anraí see **Henry**

Ans see **Anne**

Anselm *m*
This is a Germanic name formed from
the element *ans*, 'god' (found in other
names such as OSBERT in the form
os-) combined with *helm*, 'helmet,
protection'. The name was taken to
northern Italy by invading Lombards
and it became quite common there –
used frequently enough, for example,
for four bishops of Milan to bear the
name between 896 and 1136. One
such Italian, Anselm, born in 1033,
was a distinguished Italian theologian
who was first of all prior of the Abbey
of Bec in Normandy, taking the name
to France, and then in 1093 became
archbishop of Canterbury, thus
bringing the name to England. He was
later canonized. The name Anselm was
revived in the 19th century, along with
those of other British saints, although it
has never been very common.
FEMININE **Anselma** • VARIANTS **Ansel(l)**
French **Anselme** *Italian* **Anselmo**
★ Ansel Adams (1902–84), US landscape
photographer

Anshel see **Asher**

Anstace, Anstice see **Anastasia**

Antero see **Andrew**

Anthea *f*
This comes from the Greek meaning
'flowery', and was one of the titles
of the goddess Hera. It was in use
as a literary name in Latin by the
4th century AD. Its introduction to
the English-speaking world was also
literary, as it was used by 17th-century
poets such as Robert Herrick in their
pastoral writings. However, it did not
enter the general stock of names until
the middle of the 20th century.
★ Anthea Turner (1960–   ), English
television presenter

Anthony *m* **Antonia** *f*
These are forms of the Roman family
name *Antonius*. The origin of the
name is uncertain, and may have been
Etruscan, but the Roman family liked
to interpret it as deriving from a word
meaning 'inestimable', or else to claim
that they were descended from *Antius*,
the son of the Greek hero Hercules.
The silent 'h' (sometimes pronounced
in the USA) in Anthony comes from a
later attempt to link the name, falsely,
with the Greek word *anthos*, 'flower',
found in ANTHEA. A related family name
Antoninus is the source of *Antonin*,
hardly used in English, but found in
other languages. Anthony passed into
the general stock of European names
in the Middle Ages, in honour of two
major saints, St Anthony the Great
from the 3rd century, who lived as
a hermit in the Egyptian desert and
whose temptations are the subject of
many paintings, and St Anthony of
Padua from the 13th century, still one
of the most popular Catholic saints.
PET FORMS **Tony, Toni, Tonia, Tonya**
• VARIANTS **Antony, Antwan** (USA),
Antonietta, Antonina *Irish* **Antain(e)**
Dutch **Antonius, Teun(is), Ton** *French*
Antoine, Antoinette, Toinette *German,
Russian, Scandinavian* **Anton** *Hungarian*

Antal *Italian, Spanish* **Antonio** *Italian*
Antonello, Tonio, Antonella

★ Mark Antony (c.83–30 BC), Roman
politician and soldier, follower of Julius
Caesar and lover of Cleopatra

Antigone *f*

In Greek mythology Antigone is one
of the daughters of the unwittingly
incestuous marriage between Oedipus
and Jocasta. Hence her name, from
anti, 'against', and *gen*, *gon*, 'born'.
After her brothers, as traitors to the
state, are refused burial by her uncle,
she defies him and releases their souls
by giving them the proper rites, feeling
that this is a stronger moral duty than
obedience. As a punishment she is
buried alive. Her story and moral
strength were celebrated not only
in the play by Sophocles in the 5th
century BC, but also in the 1944 play
by the French writer Jean Anouilh.
This latter was very influential, for it
used the moral themes of the story as
an allegory for the Nazi occupation of
France and, moreover, was for many
years a standard school text. Despite
her sad history Antigone's name has
been given regularly, if rarely, since
at least the 13th century. Her sister's
name *Ismene* ('knowledge') has been
even rarer. Antigone is pronounced
with four syllables, 'an-TIG-e-nee',
although the French pronounce it 'on-
ti-GONE'.

Antii *see* **Andrew**

Antje *see* **Anne**

Antwan *see* **Anthony**

Anunciación, Anunciata *see*
Annunziata

Anwar *m*
This is the Arabic for 'brighter'.
FEMININE **Anwaar** ('rays of light') • VARIANT
Anwer

★ Anwar el-Sadat (1918–81), president
of Egypt

Anwen *f*
This is from the Welsh word *(g)wen*
meaning 'fair, blessed'.
VARIANT **Annwen**

Anwyl *see* **Annwyl**

Anya *f*
The Spanish form of ANNE is *Ana*,
pronounced with a 'ny' sound in the
middle, which has been anglicized as
Anya. See also AINE.

★ Anya Seton (1904–90), US historical
novelist, who did much to spread the
name

Anzhela, Anzhelina *see* **Angela**

Aodan, Aodh, Aodhan *see* **Aidan**

Aodhnait *see* **Enat**

Aoibheann, Aoibhinn *see* **Eavan**

Aoife *f*
Aoife is a Gaelic name which is
currently very popular in Ireland
and well used in Scotland. It means
'radiant, brilliant' and was one of
the many words associated with
brightness and light that were used
for Celtic gods and goddesses. There
are a number of divine or semi-divine
figures in Irish legend that bear the
name, and it has been frequently
used for historical figures as well.
Because the pronunciation of the
name is very close to that of EVA (see
EVE), the difference being at most the
pronunciation of 'f' for 'v', Eva has
long been used as an equivalent,
and many historical Evas were in fact
called Aoife.

Aonghas, Aonghus *see* **Angus**

Aoucha *see* **Aisha**

Aphra *f*
This is a name of obscure origin, which

seems to have flourished mainly from the 17th to 19th centuries, although it is still found occasionally today. It resembles the late Roman name *Afra* which means 'woman from Africa', and was the name of a number of minor saints, but the main or most probable source is the biblical quote 'in the house of Aphrah roll thyself in the dust' (Micah 1.10). This is actually a place name meaning 'dust' but was taken to be a personal name.

PET FORM **Affery** • VARIANTS **Afra, Ayfara**

★ Aphra Behn (1640–89), known as 'the incomparable Astrea', was a playwright (and probably the first Englishwoman to earn her living as a writer), an adventuress and spy. Most modern uses of Aphra are in reference to her

☆ Affery Flintwinch in Charles Dickens's *Little Dorrit* (1857)

Aphrodite *f*

This is the name of the ancient Greek goddess of love and generation, which may mean 'risen from the foam', a reference to her birth from foam (Greek *aphros*) in the sea. The name is not very common outside Greece, where it is in regular use. The Roman equivalent VENUS is slightly more frequently used elsewhere.

VARIANT **Afrodite**

Apollo *m* Apollinaria *f*

The origin of the Greek god Apollo's name is obscure, and may be pre-Greek. Although it is used in Greece, it is rare elsewhere, except as a nickname with reference to someone's good looks, but there are records of it having been used to commemorate the 1969 Apollo moon landings. More common are names based on the Latin *Apollinaris*, 'of Apollo, devotee of Apollo'. These include *Apollinaire* and *Appolonia*, both 3rd-century martyrs.

PET FORMS **Pollonie, Pollonia** • VARIANTS

Apollonia *French* **Apollinie, Apolline** (fs) *Italian* **Apollinare** (m) *Scandinavian* **Abelone** (f)

☆ Captain Lee 'Apollo' Adama, from the television series *Battlestar Galactica*

April *f*

This is the month of the year used as a first name. The month, in Latin *mensis aprillis*, probably comes from the Latin *aperire*, 'to open', referring to flowers and leaves. The form *Avril*, although ostensibly the French word for the month, is not used as a first name in France, and may be a form of AVERIL. April is a 20th-century name.

VARIANTS **Apryl** *Welsh* **Ebrilla, Ebrilwen**

Aquiles *see* Achilles

Arabella *f*

This is another name with a difficult history. It is first recorded in Scotland used by a 12th-century noblewoman, appearing in a Latin document in the form *Orabilis*. This seems to be from the Latin *orare*, 'to pray', and could mean something like 'moved by prayer, open to supplication' which could either be interpreted on a religious level, or indicate someone with a compassionate nature. However, the name appears in a wide variety of forms, and it may be that it is simply a variant of ANNABEL which appears in Scotland at the same time.

PET FORMS **Bel(le), Bella** • VARIANTS **Arabel(l)(e), Arbel, Arbella**

★ Arabella Weir (1957–), British comedian and writer

Araceli *f*

This is a fairly recently introduced Spanish name, used more in the Americas than in Spain itself, formed from the Latin *ara*, 'altar', and *celi*, 'of heaven'.

VARIANTS **Aracely, Aracelia**

Araminta *f*
This is a name with strong literary
associations. There was a Macedonian
Greek name *Amyntas*, 'protector',
which was used by the Elizabethan
poet Edmund Spenser in his 1596
poem *Colin Clout*. The feminine
form of this, *Aminta*, had already
been used a few years earlier for
the eponymous heroine of a play by
the Italian, Torquato Tasso, and was
picked up again by the Restoration
poet Sir Charles Sedley. Araminta also
seems to date from the Restoration,
and can be seen as an elaboration of
Aminta, perhaps under the influence
of ARABELLA. It seems to have been used
first by Congreve in his 1693 play *The
Old Bachelor* and then by Vanbrugh in
his 1705 play *The Confederacy*.
PET FORMS **Minta, Minty** • VARIANTS
Amynta, Aramynta
☆ Minta Doyle is a character in Virginia
  Woolf's *To the Lighthouse* (1927)

Aran *see* **Aaron, Arran**

Aranka *see* **Aurelia**

Aranrhod *see* **Arianrhod**

Arantxa *f*
This is the pet form of the Basque
name *Aranzazu*, which has spread
to the rest of Spain. The name means
'thornbush' and refers to a miracle
when an image of the Virgin Mary was
found in a thornbush.
★ Arantxa Sánchez Vicario (1971–),
  Spanish tennis player

Aranwen *see* **Arianwen**

Arbel, Arbella *see* **Arabella**

Archibald *m*
This is a Germanic name, brought over
at the Norman Conquest, formed from
the elements *erchen*, 'true, genuine',
and *bald*, 'bold'. It is particularly
associated with Scotland, where it

survived long after it had died out in
England. The rather puzzling reason
for this was that it was used to translate
the totally unrelated Highland name
Gillespie. The usual explanation for
this is that the final element was
misinterpreted as literally meaning
'bald', and that since Gillespie
means 'servant of the bishop' and the
servant would have been a tonsured
priest or monk, the two names were
thought to be linked. However, this
seems unnecessarily elaborate, and
presupposes a consistency in the
spelling of Archibald, while the name
was actually very variable in the
Middle Ages. Currently the full form of
the name is comparatively rare, but the
short form *Archie* is popular in both
England and Scotland.
PET FORMS **Archie, Archy** • VARIANTS
Archibold *Scots Gaelic* **Eairdsidh,
Eairrsidh**

Ardal *m*
This Irish name is probably from *ard*,
'high', and *gal*, 'valour', although as
so many Celtic names incorporate
the element *art*, meaning 'bear', it
may signify 'brave as a bear'. It is an
old name, which probably made its
way into English literature in the form
Arthgallo in Geoffrey of Monmouth's
1135 *History of the Kings of Britain*.
VARIANTS *Irish* **Ardg(h)al**
★ Ardal O'Hanlon (1965–), Irish
  comedian and actor

Areef, Areefa *see* **Arif**

Arel *see* **Ariel**

Arethusa *f*
This name probably comes from the
Greek *arete*, 'excellence, virtue'. In
Greek mythology she was a water
nymph, who wished to remain chaste
so that she could be a follower of
the virgin goddess Artemis. She
transformed herself into a spring in

order to avoid the unwanted advances of the river god Alpheus. The name is not common, but has been used on occasion. The same Greek root probably lies behind the rare name *Aretha*, and the Greek name *Areti*.

★ Aretha Franklin (1942–), US soul singer

☆ Arethusa Skimpole in Charles Dickens's *Bleak House* (1853)

☆ Arethusa, heroine of Beaumont and Fletcher's play *Philaster, or Love Lies Bleeding* (1609)

Arfon *m*

Arfon is a district name from Wales. The area in Gwynedd that lies opposite the island of Anglesey is called Arfon, from Welsh *ar*, 'opposite', and *Fon*, the Welsh name for Anglesey, *Môn*, with the first sound changed to reflect the grammatical relationship, as is normal in Welsh.

FEMININES **Arfona, Arfonia**

Aria *f*

This is a recent addition to the list of girls' names derived from musical terms, such as HARMONY and MELODY. In some cases uses may be a short form of *Ariane* (see ARIADNE) and the variant *Arya* may at times be taken from a character in Christopher Paolini's *Inheritance* trilogy of fantasy novels.

Ariadne *f*

Ariadne, whose name means 'very holy', appears in Greek mythology as the Cretan king's daughter who helps Theseus escape from the labyrinth after killing the Minotaur. After they escape from Crete he abandons her on the island of Naxos, where the god Dionysus makes her his consort. A Cretan goddess probably lies behind this story. The name has been particularly used in recent years in the USA, usually in variants that do not include the 'd' in the name.

VARIANTS **Ariana, Aryan(n)a** *French* **Arianne** *Italian* **Arianna**

★ Arianna Huffington (1950–), Greek-born US columnist and political activist

☆ Ariane is the name for the European-developed space rocket

Arianrhod *f*

This is the name of an ancient Celtic moon goddess, with the appropriate meaning of 'silver circle or wheel'. In Welsh the name for the Milky Way is *Caer Arianrhod* ('Arianrhod's Castle').

VARIANT **Aranrhod**

Arianwen *f*

Arianwen comes from the Welsh for 'silver' combined with a common ending meaning 'white, fair, blessed'. Traditionally, St Arianwen was one of many children of King Brychan, who evangelized the surrounding areas, stories of whom, it has been suggested, reflect a dim memory of ancient settlement patterns.

MASCULINE **Arianwyn** • VARIANT **Aranwen**

Arica *see* **Erica**

Arie *see* **Adrian**

Ariel[1] *f*

Ariel started to be used as a girl's name in the USA in the 1970s. Its exact origin is unclear. While it could be a transferred use of Ariel[2], it is more likely to be a direct borrowing from Shakespeare's character in *The Tempest*, particularly as so many other names have been taken from his works. Given that Shakespeare's Ariel is an air spirit, as the name implies, it seems rather contrary that Disney should choose the name for the lead role in their 1989 film *The Little Mermaid*. Use of the name increased enormously after the film was shown, and the name is now strongly associated with the mermaid. In the

UK the name tends to be pronounced with the first syllable as in 'air' but in the USA it is more often an 'ah' sound, and the stress is sometimes on the final syllable.

VARIANT **Arielle**

Ariel² *m*
This is a Hebrew name, translated as 'lion of God'. It is used in the Bible as a name for Jerusalem, and is a personal name in the book of Ezra. It is popular in Israel, and well used in Spanish-speaking America.

PET FORMS **Arik, Ari** • VARIANT **Arel**

Arif *m* Arifa *f*
This is an Arabic name meaning 'learned, expert'.

VARIANTS **Aarif** (m), **Areef** (mf), **Areefa, Aarifa**

Arjan *see* Adrian

Arjit *m*
This is the Sanskrit for 'invincible'.

Arjun *m*
This is the Sanskrit for 'bright, shining', used of things as varied as silver, the dawn and milk. Arjun is the main hero of the great Indian epic *The Mahabharata* to whom the god Krishna gave the text of the holy book the *Bhagavad Gita*.

VARIANT **Arjuna**

Arlene *f*
The name in the form *Arline* seems to have been invented by Michael William Balfe for the heroine of his successful 1843 opera *The Bohemian Girl*. In the 20th century the US filmstar, and later newspaper columnist, Arlene Dahl helped establish this spelling as the dominant form.

PET FORM **Arli** • VARIANT **Arleen**

Arlette *f*
This is a French name, probably a shortening of the Old French *Charlette*, an old form of CHARLOTTE. It is an old name, for the mother of William the Conquerer, born about 1027, was called Arlette de Falaise. However, it did not make much of a mark, even in France, until the 20th century.

★ Arletty (1898–1992), French actress

Arline *see* Arlene

Arlo *m*
This name was used regularly in the USA in the first part of the 20th century, and may represent a form of the surname Harlow, 'rocky hill'. Its revival is directly connected with the fame of Arlo Guthrie.

★ Arlo Guthrie (1947–), US folk singer and activist

Armand *m*
This is a French form of HERMAN.

FEMININES **Armande, Armandine** • VARIANTS German **Armin** *Italian, Spanish* **Armando**

★ Armand Jean Duplessis, Cardinal Richelieu (1585–1642), French cardinal, duke and politician

★ Armin Shimerman (1949–), US actor

☆ Armand is a vampire in Anne Rice's series of novels *The Vampire Chronicles* (1976–), played by Antonio Banderas in the 1994 film of the first novel *Interview with the Vampire*

☆ Armand St Just is the brother-in-law of Sir Percy Blakeney in Baroness Orczy's *Scarlet Pimpernel* books

Armani *mf*
This is a name used in recent years, mainly in the USA, and more for boys than girls. It appears to be the most successful of the names from a recorded minor trend to use high status brand names, such as Bacardi and Timberland, as first names. In this case it is the name of the Italian fashion designer Giorgio Armani (b.1935). His surname comes from an Italian form of

the name HERMAN. There may, however, be some confusion in the minds of some users between Armani and AMANI.

Armin see **Armand**

Arnold m
This is a Germanic name formed from the elements *arn*, 'eagle', and *wald*, 'ruler'. It was popular in France, and brought over to the UK by the Norman conquerors. It died out after the Middle Ages, although it survived as a surname, and was revived along with many other medieval names in the 19th century.
PET FORMS **Arn**, **Arnie** • VARIANTS *French* **Arnauld** *German* **Arno** *Italian, Spanish* **Arnaldo**
★ Arnold Bennett (1867–1931), English novelist
★ Arnold Schwarzenegger (1947–), Austrian-born US actor and politician

Aroldo see **Harold**

Aron see **Aaron**

Arran m
It is difficult to tell to what extent this form is a variant spelling of AARON, and to what extent it is the Scottish island used as a first name. However, given the frequency with which Arran occurs in Scotland, it seems likely that at least some are uses of the place name. This reflects a trend in Scotland, where local place names are popular. Some of these are well-established in the common fund of names (IONA, ISLA, KYLE), but others such as *Argyle* are uniquely Scottish. *Aran*, as in the Irish islands, has also been recorded.
VARIANT **Aran**

Arren, **Arron** see **Aaron**

Arrigo see **Henry**

Arsène m
This the French form of the Greek name *Arsnios* meaning 'manly, virile'.
VARIANTS *Italian, Spanish* **Arsenio** *Russian* **Arseni(y)**
★ Arsène Wenger (1949–), French football manager
☆ Arsène Lupin, gentleman thief in the works of Maurice Leblanc (1864–1941)

Art m
As well as being a short form of Arthur, this is an Irish name meaning 'bear'.
PET FORM **Artan**

Artemis f
In ancient Greek religion Artemis was the name of the goddess of childbirth and all young things, of the moon and, above all, of wild animals. She is usually described as a virgin huntress, and demanded chastity from her followers. The Romans identified her with their god DIANA. The name cannot be explained as Greek, and she is probably pre-Greek, going back to goddesses such as Astarte and the Cretan goddess called by archaeologists the 'Mistress of the Animals' after depictions of her that have survived, but whose real name is not known. There are various forms of names for those who were particular followers of Artemis, including *Artemisia* for women and *Artemus* and *Artemas* for men. The use of the latter in the New Testament meant that it has been used occasionally since the 17th century. Artemis remains rare, never having had the success of the related CYNTHIA and Diana.
★ Artemisia Gentileschi (c.1597–c.1652), Italian painter
☆ Artemis Fowl, hero of the series of children's books by Eoin Colfer. In this case the name is masculine, which may be a cause of confusion in the future

Arthur *m*

This name is famous as the legendary king of the Britons, with his associations with knighthood and chivalry. Its origin, as with so many such figures, is debated. The most popular interpretations either link it to the Roman family name *Artorius*, or with the Celtic *Art* meaning 'bear'. The name was used regularly from the Middle Ages onwards, although never particularly frequently, until its popularity was greatly boosted in the 19th century by the success and popularity of Arthur Wellesley, Duke of Wellington (1769–1852).

PET FORMS **Art(ie)**, **Arty** (mainly USA)
• VARIANTS *Scots Gaelic* **Artair** *German, Russian* **Artur** *Italian, Spanish* **Arturo**
★ Sir Arthur Conan Doyle (1859–1930), Scottish writer of detective stories and creator of Sherlock Holmes
★ Arthur C Clarke (1917–2008), English science fiction writer

Arun *m*

This is the Sanskrit colour word, often translated as 'reddish-brown', but actually used as the word to describe the colour of rubies or dawn. It is also the name of the person who drives the chariot of the sun in Hindu mythology.
VARIANT **Aruna** (mf)

Arwel *m*

This is a Welsh name. It has been variously interpreted as meaning 'prominent' or 'wept over'.
★ Arwel Hughes (1909–88), Welsh conductor and composer

Arwen *f* Arwyn *m*

These names are from the Welsh for 'fair, good looking'. The feminine form has taken on new connotations in recent years as the name of J R R Tolkien's elf-princess in *The Lord of the Rings*. In Tolkien's story the name is said to mean 'noble lady' in the elvish Sindarin language.

Aryana, Aryanna *see* Ariadne

Aryn *see* Erin

Asa *m*

This is a Hebrew name meaning 'healer, physician'. It is the name of a king in the Old Testament who ruled for 40 years. It was introduced to the UK by the Puritans, and came to be associated with Yorkshire. It is not now much used in the UK, but has shown signs of a revival in the USA.
★ Asa Briggs (1921–   ), English historian

Asad *m*

An Arabic name, from the word for 'happy'.

Asante *see* Ashanti

Asastasiya *see* Anastasia

Asdrubale *see* Hannibal

Asha *f*

This is an Indian name, from the Sanskrit for 'hope, aspiration'.

Ashanti *mf*

The Ashanti are the dominant tribe in southern Ghana. The name is usually chosen by those who want to emphasize their West African lineage. The tribe is known for both its power and its matrilineal society, and consequently the name is more often used for females than males.
PET FORMS **Shanti, Sante** • VARIANT **Asante**
★ Ashanti Douglas (1980–   ), US singer

Asher *m*

According to the Old Testament, the name Asher was given to one of the sons of Jacob, because Leah said 'Happy am I, for the daughters will call me blessed; and she called his name Asher', the name being derived from the Hebrew for 'happy, fortunate'. The name is traditionally masculine, but in recent years has been more often used as a feminine name. Asher is also used as a pet name for ASHLEY.

PET FORM **Ash** • VARIANTS **Ashur, Osher** *Yiddish* **Anshel**

Ashik *m*
This is from the Arabic for 'devotee, lover'.

VARIANT **Ashiq**

Ashish *m*
This is an Indian name from the Sanskrit for 'prayer, benediction'.

VARIANT **Ashis**

Ashley *mf*
This was originally a surname, which is in turn a common English place name, usually from elements meaning 'clearing in an ash-wood'. It has been recorded as a first name since the 16th century, but its popularity in the 20th century probably comes from its use in Margaret Mitchell's 1936 novel *Gone with the Wind* and the subsequent film. The name was initially masculine, but was in use for females by the 1940s. Recently, it has been a particularly popular girl's name in the USA and Australia, and has spawned many variants, which are mainly used for girls. *Ashlyn(n)* may be considered a variant of this, or else either a blend of *Ashly* and LYN or a US version of AISLING.

PET FORMS **Ash, Asher** • VARIANTS **Ashlea, Ashlee, Ashleigh, Ashlie, Ashly**

★ Anthony Ashley Cooper, 7th Earl of Shaftesbury (1801–85), social reformer who was instrumental in limiting working hours

☆ Ashley Wilkes, the young man desired by Scarlett O'Hara in Margaret Mitchell's *Gone with the Wind* (1936)

Ashlin, Ashling *see* Aisling

Ashok *m*
This is an Indian name, from the Sanskrit for 'without sorrow'. It is also the name of a variety of tree found in India, which is not only admired for its fine flowers, but also widely revered, both for being the tree under which the Buddha was born and as the tree sacred to Kama Deva, the god of love.

VARIANT **Ashoka**

★ Emperor Asóka (ruled c.269–232 BC), ruled an empire which stretched from Afghanistan to Sri Lanka, and was a mighty warrior before converting to Buddhism

Ashton *mf*
This is a surname, like ASHLEY, derived from a place name, and which has followed a similar path, starting out as a masculine name, but now also being used for girls. The place name means 'settlement where ash trees grow'.

PET FORM **Ash** • VARIANT **Ashtyn**

★ Ashton Kutcher (1978–), US actor

Asia *f*
This name can be derived from several different sources. Most frequently nowadays, it is simply the name of the continent, which probably comes from a word found in several Middle Eastern languages, meaning 'east'. It can be a variant of AISHA, it can be a Polish pet form of JOANNA or it can be a form of the Arabic name *Asiya* meaning 'firm, powerful'.

VARIANTS **Asya, Aysia**

★ Asia Argento (1975–), Italian actress, writer, director

Asif *m*
This is the Arabic for 'forgiveness'.

Asil *m* Asila *f*
This is an Arabic name meaning 'noble, pure, highborn'.

Asim *m* Asima *f*
Arabic names, from the word meaning 'protector, guardian'.

Asma *f*
This is an Arabic name meaning 'higher, more exalted, more eminent'. There are other Arabic names that may come out in European script with the same or similar spelling, the situation being complicated by the fact that the ' , which represents a sound in Arabic, is not generally taken over into the English spelling. These names include *Asmaa'*, meaning 'names' which is taken from the Koranic line which reads 'All beautiful names belong to Him [Allah]' (surat al-Hashr 59.24) and '*Asmaa*, 'chaste, precious'.

Aspen *f*
This tree name is a fashionable name for girls in the USA, probably with reference to the resort of Aspen, Colorado.

Assa *see* Astrid

Assisi *f*
The name of the northern Italian town, particularly associated with St Francis and with early Italian art, is occasionally used as a first name, much as SIENNA is.

Assumpta *f*
This is a name most likely to be found in Ireland. It is the Latin for Assumption, used with reference to the Assumption of the Virgin Mary.
VARIANTS *Italian* Assunta *Portuguese* Assunção *Spanish* Asunción

Astrid *f*
This is a Scandinavian name, which has been well used by the royal families there. It comes from the Old Norse elements *ass*, 'god', and *frithr*, 'beautiful', and so is often interpreted as meaning 'divine beauty'.

PET FORMS Assa, Sassa • VARIANTS Astrud, Estrid
★ Astrid, Queen of the Belgians (1905–35), Swedish-born princess, married to King Leopold III of the Belgians
★ Astrid Lindgren (1907–2002), Swedish children's writer, best-known for the Pippi Longstocking books

Asunción *see* Assumpta

Asya *see* Anastasia, Asia

Atalanta *f*
In Greek mythology Atalanta, a follower of ARTEMIS, was a keen huntress and very fast runner. She was determined not to marry, so said that she would only marry a man who could outrun her. This proved impossible, until Hippomenes raced against her equipped with three golden apples. These he rolled in front of her every time she was getting too far ahead. She paused to pick up each one, thus slowing her down, and he was able to win her hand. The name is uncommon, but used regularly. See also ATLANTA.
PET FORMS Lanta, Lanty

Atara *f*
This is the modern form of the Hebrew name *Atarah*, 'crown', a minor character in the Old Testament (1 Chronicles 2.26). It is well used in Israel.

Atanasio *see* Athanasius

Atasya *see* Anastasia

Athairne *see* Hercules

Athanasius *m* Athanasia *f*
This name is formed from the Greek negative element *a-* combined with *thanatos*, 'death', and thus means 'immortal'. Athanasius was the name of a 4th-century saint who used his skills as a theologian to combat the Arian heresy. The Athanasian creed

is named after him. Although it is an uncommon name among English speakers, it is popular in other countries, particularly Greece. The feminine form, Athanasia, was given as a Latin name to the plant known as tansy, which is used both as a short form of the name and as a flower name.

PET FORMS **Athan, Nathan, Nass** (m), **Tansi** • VARIANTS *French* **Athanase** (m), **Athanasie** (f) *Greek* **Athanasio, Thanasis, Thanos** *Italian, Spanish* **Atanasio** *Russian* **Afanasi, Afanas(i)y**

Athelstan *m*

Athelstan is an Old English name formed from the elements *æthal*, 'noble', and *stan*, 'stone'. It was a royal name in Wessex, but died out along with so many other Saxon names after the Norman Conquest. It was one of the old names revived in the 19th century, and continues to be used occasionally.

☆ Athelstane, last of the Saxon royal line in Sir Walter Scott's novel *Ivanhoe* (1820)

Athene *f*

The name of the Greek goddess of wisdom and crafts, who is also a warrior and patroness of Athens, is found as far back as the Linear B tablets from ancient Crete, so it is no surprise that the meaning of her name has been lost. The name is used regularly, especially in Greece, but is uncommon elsewhere. Athene is the form most likely to be found in England, the Latinate *Athena* is more usual in the USA. See also MINERVA.

PET FORM **Nana** • VARIANTS **Athena** *French* **Athénaïs, Athanaïs**

★ Athene Seyler (1889–1990), English actress

Atholl *mf*

This is a predominantly masculine name, but in Scotland has been recorded as a feminine. Atholl is a Highland place name, from Gaelic *ath fodla* meaning 'New Ireland' (*fodla* being a poetic term for Ireland). It is a duchy in Perthshire, and shows the Scottish liking for place names as first names. An early earl of Atholl was a staunch supporter of Robert the Bruce against the English.

VARIANTS **Athol, Athold**

★ Athol Fugard (1932–), South African playwright and actor

Atif *m* Atifa *f*

This is an Arabic name meaning 'loving, compassionate'.

Atlanta *f*

This is a name that is still unusual, but growing in popularity. In the past it has been recorded used for children born in ships crossing the Atlantic, but nowadays the US city is an influence. The Atlantic ocean got its name from the mythical Greek giant Atlas, who reportedly stood near its shores, holding up the sky on his shoulders. There is some blurring between this name and ATALANTA.

PET FORMS **Lanta, Lanty**

Atticus *m*

This Roman nickname, meaning 'of Attica' (ie the area around Athens) is growing in use in the USA. This is undoubtedly owing to the influence of the quietly heroic figure of Atticus Finch, the Southern lawyer who defends an innocent man accused as a result of racial prejudice in Harper Lee's 1960 novel *To Kill a Mockingbird*. The original Atticus was a 1st-century BC Roman, given his nickname because of his love of all things Greek. His letters to Cicero are still preserved.

Aubert *see* Albert

Aubrey *mf*

The Germanic name *Alberic*, 'elf ruler', presented the Norman French, who found pronouncing groups of consonants a challenge, with a problem, which they solved by shortening it to Aubrey. *Auberon* is probably a pet form of this. Since in Germanic mythology Alberic is the name of the ruler of the elves, it is no surprise to find a form of the name, *Oberon*, used for the King of the Fairies in Shakespeare's *A Midsummer Night's Dream*. Shakespeare borrowed the name from the 13th-century romance *Huon of Bordeaux*, a version of which was still popular in Shakespeare's day. This group of names has traditionally been masculine, but in recent years Aubrey has been used for girls, particularly in the USA. The variants below are feminine.

PET FORM **Bron** • VARIANTS **Aubree, Aubrie**
★ Aubrey Beardsley (1872–98), English illustrator
★ Auberon Waugh (1932–2001), English journalist and novelist

Aude *see* Aldous

Audrey *f*

This is a name that has been radically altered from its original form. It is the name of a 7th-century Anglo-Saxon saint who was called *Æthelthryth*, 'noble strength'. This became *Atheldreda* or *Etheldreda* in Latin documents. She was an East Anglian princess who founded the religious community at Ely that eventually developed into the magnificent cathedral there. The name evolved further into Audrey during the Middle Ages, when a big fair was held on her feast day. The word 'tawdry' developed from running together 'St Audrey' and was originally used to describe the cheap and cheerful stuff sold at the fair. It has developed a number of modern elaborations. The old form Etheldreda, sometimes shortened to DREDA, is very occasionally found.

PET FORM **Audie** • VARIANTS **Audrie, Audry, Audra, Audreen, Audrianna, Audrina**
★ Audrey Hepburn (1929–93), Belgian-born actress

Augustine *m* Augusta *f*

The Latin name *Augustus* (feminine *Augusta*) means 'great, majestic', and was originally a title awarded to Octavian, nephew and heir of Julius Caesar, who is known to history as the Emperor Augustus. The title became a standard one for Roman emperors, with the feminine form being used for members of their families. The Roman name Augustine, 'appertaining to Augustus', developed as a Roman name thereafter and was given to one of the most influential early fathers of the Church, St Augustine of Hippo (AD 354–430). The rules of conduct he formulated for religious communities took his name all over Europe. Use in England was further encouraged by the fact that the principal missionary to Dark Age England was St Augustine of Canterbury, who converted the English in the 6th century. In medieval English use the name was shortened to *Austin*, which became a common surname, and is undergoing a marked revival in the USA, as well as beginning to make an impression in the UK. Augusta was given a boost in the UK in the 18th century when Princess Augusta of Saxe-Coburg-Gotha (1719–72) married Frederick, Prince of Wales, and later became mother of George III.

PET FORMS **Augie, Gus(sie)** • VARIANTS **Augustina, Austen, Austyn** *Irish* **Aghaistin, Aibhistin** *Welsh* **Awstin** *Dutch* **Agustijn, Gusta, (S)tijn** *French* **Auguste** *German* **August, Augustin** *Italian* **Agostina, Agostino, Augusto** *Polish* **August, Augustyn(a)** *Portuguese*

Agostinho *Russian* **Avgustin** *Spanish*
Agustín, Augusto
★ Augustus John (1878–1961), Welsh
painter
☆ Austin Powers, spoof spy in the
eponymous series of films

Aulay *m*
This is a Scottish form of OLAF.
VARIANTS **Awl(a)y, Auliffe** *Irish Gaelic*
Amhlaoibh *Scots Gaelic* **Amhladh,
Amhlaidh**

Auliffe *see* **Olaf**

Aurelia *f* **Aurelian** *m*
The Roman family name *Aurelius*
or Aurelia comes from the word for
'golden' and was the name of an
important family in ancient Rome.
Aurelian is derived from Aurelius.
Aurelia came into European use in
honour of a French saint who perhaps
lived in the 9th century, but the name
did not appear in English much before
the 17th century. Aurelius or Aurelian
is not much used by English speakers,
but is part of the basic fund of names
in other countries. See also ORIANA.
VARIANTS **Aurelie, Oralie, Oralee,
Oriel, Oriole** *French* **Aurélie, Aurélien,
Aurélienne** *German* **Aurel, Oral, Orel**
Hungarian **Aranka** *Italian, Spanish* **Aurelio**
Polish **Aureliusz**
★ Marcus Aurelius (AD 121–180), Roman
emperor and philosopher

Auriane *see* **Oriana**

Auriol *f*
It is unclear whether Auriol and its
variants should be taken as forms of
AURELIA, or represent a new coinage
from the Latin *aureus*, meaning
'golden'. The name only seems to have
been in use since the 19th century.
PET FORMS **Aurie, Aury** • VARIANTS **Auriel,
Auriole, Oriel**

Aurnia *see* **Orla**

Auron *see* **Euron**

Aurora *f*
This is the Latin word for DAWN. It does
not seem to have been used before
the Renaissance, and only really took
off as a name in the 18th century. The
Spanish equivalent, *Alba*, is currently
popular in Spain, and is also used in Italy.
VARIANT *French* **Aurore**
★ Aurore Dupin (1804–76), was the
real name of the French author who
published as George Sand
☆ Aurora or Aurore is the traditional
name of the princess in the fairytale
Sleeping Beauty
☆ 'Aurora Leigh' (1857) is a poem by
Elizabeth Barrett Browning

Austen, Austin, Austyn *see*
Augustine

Autumn *f*
This is a season name that has been
particularly popular in the USA in
recent years.

Ava *f*
Despite the fact that this name has
recently become very popular in
a number of countries, its origin is
unclear. There is a 9th-century saint
called Ava or *Avia*, whose name is
thought to be the Latinate form of
some lost Germanic name, but she is
a one-off. The name does not seem to
reappear until the 19th century, when
it is probably a variant of EVA, although
some would link it to *avis*, the Latin
for 'bird'. The name came to public
attention through Ava Lowle Willing
(1868–1958) a beautiful Philadelphian
heiress. She was a prominent star of
society first in the USA as the wife of
John Jacob Astor IV, and then in the
UK as the wife of Lord Ribbesdale. Her
daughter was also called Ava. This put
a high gloss on the name, which was
further enhanced by the glamour of
the film star Ava Gardner. By the time

Gardner died in 1990 the name had fallen into obscurity, only to be revived shortly afterwards.

Avdotya *see* **Eudocia**

Aveline *f*
Aveline is the old form of the name more usually found today as EVELYN. It was a common name in the Middle Ages, particularly among the Normans, whose bearers included the great-grandmother of William the Conqueror.

Averie *see* **Alfred**

Averil *f*
Although sometimes used as a variant of APRIL, this is also a form of an Old English name formed from the elements *eofer*, 'boar' (once a pagan religious symbol), and *hild*, 'battle'. St *Eberhilda*, as her name appears in Latin, was a minor English saint. The surname from the name, *Averill*, has occasionally been used as a masculine name.
VARIANTS **Avril, Averilla, Everilda**

Avery *see* **Alfred**

Avgustin *see* **Augustine**

Avi *see* **Abraham**

Avice *see* **Avis**

Avigal, Avigayil, Aviga'yil *see* **Abigail**

Avis *f*
This is a form of the old Germanic name, recorded in Latin texts as *Aveza*. It would appear to be a shortening of a longer name, and its meaning is not known, although some have related it to HEDWIG. Historically it has no connection to the Latin *avis*, 'bird', although some like to link it to this meaning. It was revived in the 18th century, but although regularly

encountered, it has never been popular.
VARIANT **Avice**

Avital *see* **Abigail**

Avner *see* **Abner**

Avraham, Avram, Avrom *see* **Abraham**

Avril *see* **April, Averil**

Awen *mf* **Awena** *f*
The word *awen* in Welsh means 'poetic inspiration', and is sometimes glossed as 'muse'.

Awlay, Awley, Awly *see* **Aulay**

Awnan *see* **Adamnan**

Awstin *see* **Augustine**

Axel, Axelle *see* **Absalom**

Ayden *see* **Aidan**

Ayesha, Ayeisha *see* **Aisha**

Ayfara *see* **Aphra**

Aylvin *see* **Alvin**

Ayesha *see* **Aisha**

Aylmer *see* **Elmer**

Aylwyn *see* **Aelwen, Alwyn**

Aymé *see* **Esme**

Aysia *see* **Asia**

Ayub *see* **Job**

Azalia *f*
This is one of the less common flower names, recorded from the 19th century. The plant was given its name by Linnaeus from the Greek *azaleos*, 'dry, arid', because of the conditions in which it flourishes.
VARIANT **Azelia**

Azaria *mf*
In the Bible the name appears as

Azariah, and is the name of several minor characters. In the book of Daniel it is the Hebrew name of one of the three who are thrown into, and miraculously rescued from, the fiery furnace, called *Abednigo* by the Babylonians. The name, appropriately, means 'helped by God'. Because of its ending in -*a*, Azaria is now usually found as a feminine name, although it is still used as a masculine name in Israel.

PET FORM **Azzy** • VARIANTS **Azarias, Azarya**

★ Azaria Chamberlain (1980), Australian baby stolen by a dingo whose mother was wrongly accused of murdering her

Aziz *m* **Aziza** *f*
This name comes from the Arabic for 'honoured, powerful, beloved'. *Al-Aziz*, the 'All Powerful', is one of the titles of the Prophet Muhammad in the Koran. Aziz is often combined with ABDUL to form *Abdulaziz*, 'servant of the All Powerful'.

Azzy *see* **Azaria**

B

Baariq *see* **Burak**

Babar *m*
This name, mainly used in Pakistan and by Muslims in India, comes from the Turkish for 'tiger' and was a nickname given both to Zahir ud-Din Muhammad (1483–1530), founder of the Mughal Empire, and to his son.
VARIANTS **Babur, Bobur, Baber**
☆ Babar the Elephant in the series of children's books by Jean de Brunhoff

Babette *f*
This is used as a pet form of both ELIZABETH and BARBARA in France, but English speakers usually regard it as a form of Barbara, with which it shares pet forms.
☆ *Babette's Feast* is a 1987 film adapted from a short story by Karen Blixen

Babs *see* **Barbara**

Babur *see* **Babar**

Badr *mf*
This is from the Arabic for 'full moon', used to indicate beauty in a person. *Budur* is the plural form, mainly used for women. The description *Badr-al Budur*, 'full moon of full moons', is a great compliment, and is a name traditionally used for the princess in the story of Aladdin.

Bahar *see* **Banu**

Baibin *see* **Barbara**

Bailey *mf*
This is a surname, most often given to someone who worked as a bailiff or estate official. It became a popular first name in the USA in the 1990s, where

it is used more for girls than for boys. In recent years it has become popular in other English-speaking areas, where it is predominantly masculine, although feminine use is catching up. It is one of the names, like the similar-sounding HAYLEY, which attract too many spelling variations to list more than the most common.
VARIANTS **Bailee, Baily, Baileigh, Bayley**

Báirbhe *see* **Barbara**

Bairre *see* **Finbar**

Bairtliméad *see* **Bartholomew**

Bala *mf*
This is an Indian name from the Sanskrit for 'young'.
PET FORM **Balu**

Baldric *m*
A Germanic name formed from *bald*, 'bold, brave' and *ric*, 'power, rule'. It was found throughout the West in the early Middle Ages, but was rare thereafter. The name is widely known today through the character of that name in the television series *Blackadder*, shown from 1983 onwards.

Baldwin *m*
This is formed from the Germanic elements *bald*, 'bold, brave', and *wine*, 'friend'. It was particularly popular among the nobility in the north-west region of France in the early Middle Ages, and was brought over to England by the Normans. The name is still used in the Belgian royal family.
VARIANTS *Welsh* **Maldwyn** *Dutch*

Boudewijn *French* **Baudoin** *Italian*
Baldovino *Spanish* **Balduino**

★ Baldwin of Boulogne (c.1058–1118), crowned king of Jerusalem in 1100, after the first Crusade

Balthasar *m*

This is the name of one of the Three Kings of the Nativity (see also CASPER and MELCHIOR) in Western tradition. Since they represent the idea that Jesus's ministry was for everyone, it is not surprising that the name is pagan. In origin it is a Babylonian name, meaning 'Ba'al protect the king' and is the same name as the biblical *Belshazzar*. It has never been much used by English speakers, but is found elsewhere, particularly in the Italian Renaissance.

VARIANTS *German* **Balzar**, **Balthazar** *Italian* **Baldassare** *Spanish* **Baltasar**

★ Count Baldassare Castiglione (1478–1529), Italian diplomat, scholar and author, most famously of *The Book of the Courtier*

★ Baldassaro Galuppi (1706–85), Italian composer, celebrated in Robert Browning's poem 'A Toccata of Galuppi's'

Balu *see* Bala

Banu *f*

This name comes from the Persian word for 'lady, princess, bride'. It is mainly used on the Indian sub-continent, Iran and Turkey. It can be found combined with *Bahar*, 'spring, blossom', to form the name *Bahar Banu*, 'blooming princess'.

VARIANT **Bano**

Baptist *m*

This name, taken from the name of John the Baptist, is unusual among English speakers, but has been recorded among US evangelicals. Otherwise, it is mainly used in Catholic countries, and has been particularly popular in France in recent years.

VARIANTS *French* **Baptiste**, **Jean-Baptiste** *Italian* **Battista**, **Giambattista** *Portuguese* **Batista** *Spanish* **Bautista**

☆ Baptista Minola, father of Katharina in Shakespeare's *The Taming of the Shrew*

Barack, Barak *see* Baruch

Barbara *f*

Barbara was the Latin word, borrowed from Greek, for 'foreigner, stranger', and may initially have been a slave's name. The original Greek word appears to have imitated the supposed 'gabble' that foreign languages sounded like to civilized Greek ears. The word is also the source of 'barbarian'. Barbara came to be used throughout the Christian world from the 9th century in honour of St Barbara, who was a very popular saint, although there is now some doubt that she ever existed. She is said to have been locked in a tower by her father and later murdered by him. He in turn was struck down by a thunderbolt. This meant that Barbara became the patron saint of all those who deal with gunpowder and explosions, as well as those who have jobs that would have been involved in the building of her tower. The name was little used between the Reformation and the 20th century, when it became very popular and developed a number of pet forms and variants. It is currently little used by English speakers, but is widespread in Poland.

PET FORMS **Babs**, **Barb(ie)** (mainly USA), **Babette**, **Bobbie** • VARIANTS **Barbra** *Irish* **Báirbhe**, **Baibin** *French* **Barbe**, **Barberine**, **Babette** *Greek* **Varvara** *Russian* **Varvara**, **Varya** *Scandinavian* **Barbro**

★ Barbra Streisand (1942–   ), US singer and actress

☆ The Barbie doll®

Barack *m*
President Barack Obama gets his name from the Arabic name more usually spelt *Barak*, meaning 'blessing'. As a Hebrew name Barak means 'lightning'.

Barclay *m*
The Barclay family was one of the most powerful in Scotland, which led to the name being adopted as a first name. The surname actually comes from an English place name, Berkeley in Gloucestershire, meaning 'birch clearing or wood', but was taken to Scotland in the 12th century. The Irish name, *Parthalan*, supposedly the name of a mythical founder of Ireland but probably a form of BARTHOLOMEW, was sometimes anglicized as Barclay or its variants.
VARIANTS **Barkley, Berk(e)ley**

Bareeq *see* Burak

Barnabas, Barnaby *m*
The name Barnabas appears in the New Testament as a nickname for Joseph, who was surnamed by the apostles Barnabas because it meant 'Son of Exhortation' (Acts 4.36), although modern commentators gloss it as 'son of prophecy or encouragement'. This Barnabas was a companion of St Paul in his missionary work. The name became Barnaby in medieval English use, and in turn was shortened to *Barny* (shared with BERNARD).
PET FORM **Barn(e)y** • VARIANTS *French* **Barnabé** *Polish* **Barnaba** *Spanish* **Bernabé**

Barney, Barny *see* Barnabas, Bernard

Barr, Barra *see* Finbar

Barry *m*
This is a name that can have a number of origins. The most frequent source is from the Irish *Barra* (Old Irish *Bairre*), a pet form of FINBAR. It can also be a form of *Bearach*, an Irish name meaning 'sharp, spear'. In this case, there is a St Barry, who was a missionary to Scotland. Finally, there is a Welsh surname, which comes from the Welsh *ap Harry*, 'son of Harry'. In the 1970s the name Barry was so common in Australia that it was thought of as typically Australian. The name is currently only quietly used, even in Ireland.
PET FORM **Baz(za)** (Australian) • VARIANT **Barrie**
★ Barry Goldwater (1909–98), US politician and author
☆ *Barry Lyndon*, an 1844 novel by W M Thackeray, which helped bring the name to public attention

Bartholomew *m*
The Hebrew name *Talmai* is said to mean 'furrowed' (Bible, Numbers 13.22). The element *bar*, 'son of', placed in front of the name gives a meaning 'son of Talmai', the origin of Bartholomew. This custom of calling people after their fathers is still in use in the Middle East, but can be confusing for those not in the know. Bartholomew is mentioned as an Apostle in three of the gospels, and there has been debate over which of the Apostles has this alternative name. The majority identify him as the one also known as NATHANIEL. In Ireland there is a name *Parthalan*, which was probably a local form of Bartholomew, although Parthalan was said to have been the leader of those who settled Ireland after Noah's Flood and to have introduced agriculture to Ireland. The histories of this name and that of Bartholomew are inextricably linked, and Ireland has developed its own pet forms of both names. Bartholomew was popular and widespread in the Middle Ages, but is not much used today.

PET FORMS **Bart, Barty, Bat, Tolly,
Tolom(e)y** • VARIANTS *Irish* **Bairtliméad,
Bartley, Bert(ie), Part(h)lan, Partnan**
Scots Gaelic **Pàlan** *Welsh* **Barti** *Czech*
Bartoloměj *Dutch* **Bartholomeus,
Bartel, Mees, Mies** *French* **Barthélemy,
Bartholomé** *German* **Bartholomäus**
Hungarian **Bartal, Bartos, Bartó**
Italian **Bartolo(m)mèo, Bàrtolo**
Polish **Bartlomeu, Bartosz** *Portuguese*
Bartolomeu *Russian* **Varfolomei,
Varfolomey**

★ Bartolomeu Diaz (c.1450–1500),
  Portuguese explorer, first European to
  sail round the western coast of Africa
★ Patrick Bartholomew 'Bertie' Ahern
  (1951–   ), Irish politician
☆ Bart Simpson, a principal character
  in the cartoon television series *The
  Simpsons*

Bartold *see* Berthold

Bàrtolo *see* Bartholomew

Baruch *m*
This is a Hebrew name, meaning
'blessed'. Baruch appears in the
Bible as a companion of the
prophet Jeremiah, and there are four
apocryphal books bearing his name,
one of which is a major source of
information on contemporary belief
in angels. It is little used by English
speakers, although it was occasionally
used by Puritans, but is common in
Israel.

★ Baruch Spinoza (1632–77), Dutch
  philosopher
☆ Baruch is the name of one of the
  angels in Philip Pullman's *His Dark
  Materials* trilogy

Bashir *m* Bashira *f*
This name comes from the Arabic for
'bringer of good news', and is one of
the epithets of Muhammad.

Basil *m*
The Greek name *Basileios*, 'royal',

appears in English as Basil. There
are more than a dozen saints of this
name, the most important of whom is
St Basil the Great (c.330–75) who was
bishop of Caesarea (in what is now
Turkey), and an immensely influential
theologian who is particularly revered
in the Eastern Orthodox Church. Thus
the name is most often used in the area
of influence of the Orthodox Church,
although there was a certain vogue
for it in the UK in the late 19th and
early 20th century. The herb basil was
so named because its many uses in
cookery and herbal medicine made it
the king of herbs.

FEMININES (RARE) **Basilia, Basilla, Basilie** • PET
FORMS **Bas, Baz(za)** • VARIANTS *Dutch* **Basiel**
French **Basile** *Greek* **Vasili(o)s** (m), **Vasiliki**
(f) *Italian, Spanish* **Basilio** *Polish* **Bazyli**
Russian **Vasili(y), Vaska** (ms), **Vasilisa** (f)

★ Cardinal Basil Hume (1923–99),
  English Benedictine monk and head of
  the Roman Catholic Church in the UK
☆ Basil Fawlty, manic hotelier in the
  television series *Fawlty Towers*, first
  shown in 1975
☆ Basil Brush, television fox puppet

Basim *m* Basima *f*
This is from the Arabic for 'smiling,
smile'.

VARIANT **Basma**

Bastian, Bastiaan, Bastien *see* Sebastian

Bat *see* Bartholomew

Bathaney *see* Bethany

Bathsheba
This is a biblical name. In the Old
Testament King David sees Bathsheba
taking what she thinks is a private bath
and falls for her. He engineers the
death of her husband, marries her, and
she becomes the mother of Solomon.
The name can be interpreted as
meaning 'daughter of an oath'.

PET FORM **Sheba** • VARIANTS *French*
Bethsabée *Hebrew* **Bat-Sheva, Bat-Shua**
☆ Bathsheba Everdene, femme fatale in
Thomas Hardy's *Far From the Madding
Crowd* (1874)

Batista, Battista *see* **Baptist**

Baudoin *see* **Baldwin**

Bautista *see* **Baptist**

Bayley *see* **Bailey**

Baz, Bazza *see* **Barry, Basil**

Bazyli *see* **Basil**

Bearnard *see* **Bernard**

Bearnas *see* **Berenice**

Beata *f*
This is the Latin for 'blessed' and was
the name of an early Christian martyr
who was popular throughout Europe,
although the name has never been
much used in the UK. When it is, it is
often as a short form of BEATRICE.
VARIANTS *German Swiss* **Beat** (m), **Beate** (f)

Beathag *f* **Beathan** *m*
These are names from the Gaelic
beatha, 'life'. Beathan is mainly found
in Scotland, although Ireland has at
least one St *Bean*, an alternative form
of the masculine name. Scotland also
has a St Bean, and the two are often
confused. In old records Beathan is
often turned into BENJAMIN. The Scottish
king known today as Macbeth bore this
name. In Ireland the feminine Beathag
appears as *Beatha*, *Betha* or *Bethoc*,
and can appear as *Bethia*, otherwise an
occasional pet form of ELIZABETH.

Beatrice *f*
The Latin name *Viator* meant 'voyager'
and was used by Christians with a
specific sense of one travelling through
this life to the life after death. The
feminine form of this was *Viatrix*.
However, in Late Latin the sounds of

'b' and 'v' fell together, and similar
words beginning with these two
sounds were often confused. In this
case the word *beatus*, source of BEATA,
got mixed up with Viatrix to produce
the name *Beatrix*. This was the name
of a 4th-century Roman martyr whose
cult spread the name to other parts of
the world. The name had arrived in
the UK by the 11th century, where it
developed the English form Beatrice.
PET FORMS **Bea, Bee, Beattie, Tris(s), Trix,
Trixi, Trixie** • VARIANTS **Beatrix** *Scots Gaelic*
Beitris *Welsh* **Betrys** *French* **Béatrice**
Polish **Beatrycze** *Spanish* **Beatriz**
★ Beatrice Portinari (1266–90), was the
Beatrice of Dante's *Divine Comedy*
☆ Beatrice, a principal character in
Shakespeare's *Much Ado About
Nothing*

Beau *mf*
The French surname *Beauregard*,
'handsome view, appearance', derives
either from a French place, named for
its fine aspect, or else from someone
who was considered 'easy on the eye'.
It was taken to the USA where it was
the surname of the French-descended
Confederate General Pierre Gustave
Toutant Beauregard (1818–93).
Southerners adopted his surname as
a first name, particularly in his native
New Orleans, and it was usually
shortened to Beau. *Beau*, French for
'fine, good-looking', was also used as
a nickname for someone handsome
and, particularly in Britain during the
Regency period of the early 1800s,
for someone well turned out. From
these sources Beau has entered the
stock of first names, and in recent
years has come to be given, rather
confusingly, to girls. It is sometimes
spelt phonetically as *Bo*, in which case
it can also be from the Scandinavian
name meaning 'householder'.
VARIANT *Scandinavian, from Bo* **Bosse**

★ George 'Beau' Brummell (1778–1840), English dandy

★ Beau Bridges (1941–   ), US actor, nicknamed Beau by his parents after Beau Wilkes (see below)

☆ Beau Wilkes is a character in Margaret Mitchell's 1936 novel *Gone with the Wind*

Bebhinn, Bébhinn, Bébhionn, Bébinn *see* **Beibhinn**

Beca, Becca, Beck, Beckie, Becky *see* **Rebecca**

Bede *m*
Baeda, the original form of Bede, probably comes from the Old English for 'prayer' which, since prayers were usually said using the beads of a rosary, is also the source of the word 'bead'. St Bede or 'the Venerable Bede', as he is now known, was an 8th-century monk at the monastery of Jarrow. He was an intellectual giant in his day, writing on science, theology and, the work he is best-known for, the seminal *Ecclesiastical History of the English People*. His was one of the names revived in the 19th century, and it is still occasionally encountered, particularly in the region where he once lived.

Bedelia *see* **Bidelia**

Bedwyr *m*
This is the modern Welsh form of the name that became *Bedevere* in Arthurian romance. The name is an ancient one, found in the earliest Arthurian stories, and the meaning of it has been lost.

★ Professor Bedwyr Lewis Jones (1933–92), was an expert on the Welsh language and a popular broadcaster

Bee *see* **Beatrice**

Beibhinn *f*
This name is formed from the Irish words *bean*, 'woman, lady', and *finn*, 'white, fair', and it has been suggested that it was coined to describe a blonde Viking woman. In Irish mythology Beibhinn was a beautiful giantess who fled to Finn Macool to avoid a forced marriage. However, her betrothed followed her and killed her, and she was buried at a place which was named the Ridge of the Dead Woman after her. There was also a goddess of the same name who appears to have presided over childbirth. The name is pronounced 'bee-veen' or 'bay-vin' depending on which part of Ireland it is used in. In the past it was anglicized as VIVIAN, which may explain the form *Vevina* chosen by James Macpherson as the Scottish equivalent for his Ossianic poems.

VARIANTS **Béb(h)inn, Bébhionn, Bevin, Bevan**

★ In the 10th and 11th centuries, Beibhinn was the name of both the mother and the daughter of the great Irish king Brian Boru

Beileag *see* **Elizabeth, Isabel**

Beitidh *see* **Betty**

Beitris *see* **Beatrice**

Bel *see* **Annabel, Arabella**

Belén *f*
This is the Spanish form of Bethlehem used as a first name. It is popular in Latin America and has spread from there to the USA.

Belinda *f*
Belinda is a name of uncertain origin, but it was probably formed from the Italian *bella*, 'beautiful', and is certainly usually analysed that way today. It first appeared in English in Sir John Vanbrugh's 1697 comedy *The Provok'd Wife*, and was then made famous by its use for the society beauty

in Pope's satiric poem 'The Rape of the Lock' in 1712.

PET FORM **Bindy**

Bella, Belle f

These can be either short forms of names such as *Isabella*, *Isabelle* (see *Isabel*), ARABELLA or ANNABEL, or uses of the Italian and Spanish adjective *bella*, or French equivalent *belle*, 'beautiful'.

VARIANT **Bel**

☆ The fairy story of *Beauty and the Beast* is *La Belle et la Bête* in its French original, and the heroine is often still called Belle in English versions

Beltrán *see* Bertram

Ben m

Ben is usually a short form of BENJAMIN, but can be a shortening of any name beginning *Ben-* such as BENEDICT. It is often given as an independent name.

PET FORMS **Bennie**, **Benny**

Benazir f

This is an Arabic name meaning 'incomparable, matchless, unique'.

★ Benazir Bhutto (1953–2007), Pakistani politician

Benedict m

The Latin *Benedictus* means 'blessed'. This was the name of the 6th-century Italian saint who wrote a rule for communal religious living that became the foundation of Western monasticism. He also founded the famous monastery at Monte Cassino which is still the centre of the Benedictine order named after him. His name became very popular in Europe and, because it is rather long, the middle part was often swallowed. Thus in English Benedict became *Bennett* which is still a common surname, and is sometimes used as a first name, either as an old first name or taken from the surname. There are feminines *Benedicta* and *Benedetta*

(most likely to be encountered in Ireland), but these names are rare in English. Feminine forms are more common in other languages.

PET FORM **Ben** • VARIANTS **Benedick**, **Ben(n)et(t)** *Scots Gaelic* **Benneit** *Danish* **Benedikte**, **Ben(d)t** (ms), **Bente** (f) *French* **Benoît**, **Bénédict** (ms), **Benoîte**, **Bénédicte** (fs) *German* **Benedikt** *Italian* **Benedetto**, **Benito**, **Bettino** (ms), **Benedetta**, **Bettina** (fs) *Norwegian* **Bendik** *Polish* **Benedykt** (m), **Benedykta** (f) *Portuguese* **Benedito**, **Bento** (ms), **Benedita** *Russian* **Venedikt** *Swedish* **Bengt** *Yiddish* **Benesh**

★ Benedict XVI (1927–), present pope

★ Benedict Arnold (1741–1801), American general who changed sides during the American Revolution

☆ Benedick is the soldier and wit in Shakespeare's *Much Ado About Nothing*

Benjamin m

The Hebrew name *Binyamin*, the source of Benjamin, can be interpreted as coming from *ben*, 'son', and *yamin*, meaning 'right hand'. Thus it is often defined as 'son of my right hand', the right having positive connotations. In the Bible, Benjamin is the youngest son of Jacob. Since the second element of the name can mean not only 'right' but also 'south', it is sometimes interpreted as 'son of the South' on the grounds that, while his other eleven brothers were born in Mesopotamia, Benjamin was born in the southern land of Canaan. Yet another explanation takes the second element as being from *yamim*, 'days, years', and interprets the name as meaning 'son of my old age', which again fits the biblical story. This latter is the meaning that was most influential, as Benjamin was often used for a late-born child. Since Benjamin's mother Rachel died at his birth, the name was also a traditional one in the past for children born in similar circumstances. The name was well used by Puritans and taken by them to the USA, where it became a typical US name. The name is widely popular at the moment, although in Scotland Ben is noticeably more popular than the full form. The name is unusual among stock names for not having developed a feminine in most languages, although the form *Benjamine* has been recorded in France.

PET FORMS **Ben, Bennie, Benny, Benjy, Benji(e)** • VARIANTS *Italian* **Beniamino** *Portuguese* **Benjamim** *Russian* **Veniamin, Venyamnin**

★ Benjamin Franklin (1706–90), US statesman and scientist

★ Benjamin Disraeli (1804–81), English statesman and novelist

Bennett *see* **Benedict**

Benno *see* **Bernard**

Beppe *see* **Joseph**

Berenice, Bernice *f*

The Greek name *Pherenike*, 'bringer of victory', became *Berenike* in the Macedonian dialect. It was in use among the Macedonian aristocracy, who took it with them when they conquered much of the known world east of Greece, under the leadership of Alexander the Great in the 4th century BC. It was the name of the wife of one of Alexander's generals, who went on to marry Ptolemy the Great, ruler of Egypt. In this way it was introduced into the Egyptian royal family, and spread to other ruling families in the area. In the 3rd century BC one Egyptian Berenice became the stuff of legend. It is said that she sacrificed her particularly beautiful hair as an offering to the gods for the safe return of her husband. The gods took the offering and placed her hair in the heavens in the form of the

constellation still called Berenice's Hair. The name was also used by the rulers of Judaea, which led to the name appearing in the New Testament as Bernice, which is the more usual form of the name in the USA. The two forms have led to some confusion over pronunciation. In the past the longer form was usually pronounced 'Ber-e-NI-see', but nowadays both forms are more usually pronounced 'Ber-NEES'. This name is also probably the origin of VERONICA.

PET FORMS **Bernie, Binnie** (sometimes also used for other names beginning *B-*), **Bunnie, Berry, Bib** • VARIANTS *Scots Gaelic* **Bearnas** (also used as a feminine form of, **Bernard**) *French* **Bérénice, Bernicé**

Berinthia *see* **Berry**

Berit *see* **Bridget**

Berkeley, Berkley *see* **Barclay**

Bernabé *see* **Barnabas**

Bernadette *f*

This was originally a French feminine form of BERNARD. Use increased in the 19th century in response to the fame of St Bernadette of Lourdes (Marie-Bernarde Soubirous, 1844–79), whose Marian visions turned LOURDES into the great centre of pilgrimage and healing it is today. The name is most likely to be found used in Ireland.

PET FORMS **Bernie, Detta** (shared with *Benedetta*, see, **Benedict**) • VARIANTS **Bernardet(te)** *French* **Bernardine, Nadine, Bernarde** *Italian* **Bernardetta** *Spanish* **Bernardita**

★ Bernadette McAliskey (née Devlin) (1947–), Irish political activist

★ Baroness Detta O'Cathain (1938–), Irish businesswoman

Bernard *m*

The Germanic name *Bernhard* was made up of the elements *bern*, 'bear', and *hard*, 'brave, strong'. There

have been a number of saints with the name, with perhaps the most famous being St Bernard of Menthon (923–1008), who founded shelters on the two St Bernard passes in the Alps and after whom the dogs are named. The Normans brought the name to England, where it replaced the Old English counterpart *Beornheard*. In the UK the stress is on the first syllable, but in the USA it is often on the second.
PET FORMS **Bernie, Barney** • VARIANTS *Irish* **Bearnard** *Dutch* **Bernhard** *German* **Bernhard(t), Bernd(t), Benno** (also used for, **Benedict**) *Italian, Spanish* **Bernardo** *Scandinavian* **Bernt**

Bernice *see* Berenice

Berry *mf*
This name can have a number of sources. From about the 1880s it was a given name referring to the berries of a plant. For women it can be a pet form of names such as BERENICE or BERYL. In the case of one of the best-known bearers, the US model, actress and photographer Berry Berenson, it was a pet form of the unusual name *Berinthia*. This was a literary coinage of the 17th century, having been used by Colly Cibber in 1696 in his play *Love's Last Shift* and picked up by Sir John Vanbrugh in the same year for *The Relapse*. It later appeared in Sheridan's 1777 reworking of *The Relapse*, called *A Trip to Scarborough*. As a masculine name it can also be a pet form of names beginning with *Ber-*. In the case of the Dornford Yates character Berry Pleydell, it is a pet form of BERTRAM. The Welsh name AERON can mean berry.

Bert *m*
A short form of a number of names containing the Germanic element *berht*, meaning 'bright, famous', such as ALBERT, BERTRAM, ETHELBERT or HERBERT.

In Ireland it can be found as a pet form of BARTHOLOMEW.
See also BURT.
PET FORM **Bertie**

Berta *see* Albert, Roberta

Bertha *f*
This is a Germanic name from the element *berht*, 'bright, famous'. The name is old, and is probably a shortening of a lost name that had the usual Germanic two-element form. The name was well used by the Frankish conquerors of France, being borne by two 7th-century saints, and an influential royal in the form of Bertha Bigfoot (d.783), mother of the Emperor Charlemagne. There was something of a revival of the name in the later 19th century, but it is little used now.
VARIANTS *French* **Berthe** *German, Polish, Spanish* **Birta** *Scandinavian* **Birta, Birthe**
★ Bertha Krupp (1886–1957), heiress to the Krupp armaments firm, after whom the 'Big Bertha' guns used in World War I were named

Berthold *m*
A German name formed from elements meaning 'bright' and 'splendid'.
VARIANTS **Bartold, Bertoldt** *Scandinavian* **Bertil, Bertel**
★ Bertolt Brecht (1898–1956), German playwright and poet

Bertie *see* Bartholomew, Bert

Bertram *m*
The respect that Germanic culture had for ravens as symbols of wisdom and power lies behind this name, made up of elements *berht*, 'bright, famous', and *hramm*, 'raven'. Although the raven element is rare in names used by English speakers, it was common in medieval France and Germany, where it is represented in names such as *Wolfram, Enguerrand* and *Gontran*. Bertram was particularly popular

in France, but was also regularly used in England, where it had been introduced by the Normans. It was among the medieval names revived in the 19th century, but is now felt to be rather old-fashioned and is rarely used, although its short forms are occasionally found.

PET FORMS **Bert, Bertie, Berry** • VARIANTS **Bertrand, Bertran** Hungarian **Bertók** Italian **Bertrando** Spanish **Beltrán, Bettan**

★ Bertrand Russell (1872–1970), English philosopher, mathematician, writer and Nobel Prize winner

☆ Bertie (Bertram Wilberforce) Wooster, man about town and well-meaning ass in P G Wodehouse's Jeeves and Wooster books

Berwyn m

Berwyn is the name of a range of Welsh mountains and a popular personal name in Wales. The name is made up of the elements barr, 'head', and (g)wyn, 'white'. Although it is primarily thought of today as deriving from the place name, use for people is age-old, with Berwyn being the name of one of King Arthur's knights in Welsh tradition.

Beryl f

This is one of the jewel names introduced in the late 19th century. It was popular in the early 20th century but then largely went out of use. The name flourished in the US Bible Belt, perhaps because of its use as one of the foundations of the Heavenly City in the biblical book of Revelation. It has been recorded regularly as a masculine name in that region, but is strictly feminine elsewhere.

PET FORM **Berry**

★ Dame Beryl Bainbridge (1934–   ), English novelist

★ Beryl Reid (1916–96), English comedian and actress

Bess f

A short form of ELIZABETH that has come to be used as an independent name.

VARIANT **Bessie**

Beth f

Another short form of ELIZABETH that has come to be used as an independent name.

PET FORM **Bet**

Bethan f

This started life as a Welsh name, a pet form of ELIZABETH formed by adding the affectionate ending -an on to BETH. It has now spread throughout the English-speaking world, where it is used as an independent name, without associations with Elizabeth.

☆ Bethan is the name of the lost sister in Jenny Nimmo's acclaimed children's book, set in Wales, The Snow Spider (1986)

Bethany f

On the surface this is a biblical place name, meaning 'house of figs', which was the home of Mary of Bethany, her sister MARTHA, and LAZARUS. However, many users do so without any sense of religious association, and it is often considered an elaboration of BETHAN or other form of ELIZABETH.

PET FORMS **Beth, Bethan** • VARIANTS **Bathaney, Bethanie**

Bethia see **Beathag**

Bethsabée see **Bathsheba**

Betrys see **Beatrice**

Betsan see **Betty**

Bettan see **Bertram**

Bettina see **Benedict, Betty**

Bettino see **Benedict**

Betty

This is another short form of ELIZABETH used as an independent name. The elaboration *Bettina* is well used in Germany as a form of Elizabeth, but in Italy it is a pet form of *Bernadetta* (see BERNADETTE) and *Benedetta* (see BENEDICT).

VARIANTS **Bet, Bette, Bettie, Betsy** *Scots Gaelic* **Beitidh** *Welsh* **Beti, Betsan** *German* **Bettina, Bettine**

★ Betty Grable (1916–73), US film star

Beulah *f*

In the Old Testament book of Isaiah, Beulah, meaning 'married woman', is used as a metaphor for the land of Israel, and came to be seen also as an image of heaven. It was introduced as a personal name during the Reformation and taken by the Puritans to the USA, where it has been most used. It was common there in the late 19th century, reaching its peak in 1900, and continued in use until the 1940s. However, it came to be regarded as a typically African-American name as well as being associated with servants, after it was immortalized first in Mae West's line to her maid: 'Beulah, peel me a grape' in the film *I'm No Angel* (1933), and then in the television series of the 1950s, *Beulah*, about an African-American cook to a white Southern family.

★ Beulah Bondi (1888–1981), US film star

Bevan, Bevin *see* Beibhinn

Beverly, Beverley *mf*

Some would like to distinguish between Beverley, masculine, and Beverly, feminine, but the name is so rarely used today as a masculine that the distinction, if it was ever there, has ceased to exist. Beverly is a reused surname, originally from a place, which got its name from the Old English meaning 'beaver-stream'. The name is primarily American, although it was widespread in the UK in the

1960s. Interest in the name seems to have been sparked by an enormously popular, highly romantic novel *Beverly of Graustark* by G B McCutcheon published in 1904. Certainly, Beverly first enters the list of most-used 1000 names in the USA in 1905. Use peaked there in the 1930s, and did not go into decline until the 1990s. Beverly was still being used regularly for men in the USA until the end of the 1940s.

★ Beverley Nichols (1898–1983), English writer, playwright and composer

Bevin *see* Beibhinn

Bevis *m*

In the Middle Ages there was a popular and interminable romance called *Sir Bevis of Hamptoun* (Southampton). The story was an international hit, appearing in translations in languages from Russian to Yiddish to Italian. The name disappeared after the end of the Middle Ages, but was revived by the delightful pastoral novel by Richard Jefferies, *Bevis, the Story of a Boy* (1882). It enjoyed a mild popularity thereafter, but is unlikely to be much used until all memory of the related name *Beavis*, used in the 1990s television cartoon *Beavis and Butthead*, is forgotten.

★ Bevis Hillier (1940–   ), English art historian and writer

Beyoncé *f*

This is a name created by the parents of the US singer and actress, Beyoncé Knowles, for their daughter. Since she became famous there have been slight signs of others adopting it.

Bhaltair *see* Walter

Bhaskar *m*

This is an Indian name, formed from the Sanskrit *bhasa*, 'light', and *kara*, 'shining'. It is one of the titles of the god Shiva.

VARIANT **Bhaskara**

★ Bhaskara Acharya ('the teacher') (1114–85), Indian mathematician and astronomer

Bhàtair see Walter

Bhavini f

This is an Indian name meaning 'beautiful, illustrious' and is one of the titles of the goddess PARVATI.

VARIANT **Bhavani**

Bhictoria see Victoria

Biaggio, Biagino, Biagio see Blaise

Bianca f

This is the Italian for 'white'. It came to public attention in the early 1970s when the Nicaraguan Bianca Pérez-Mora Macías married Mick Jagger, and achieved international fame as Bianca Jagger. Thereafter, it entered the mainstream of English names, and is currently well used in the USA and Australia. Compare BLANCHE and CANDIDA.

PET FORM **Bibi** • VARIANTS Polish **Blanka** Portuguese **Branka** Spanish **Blanca**

☆ Bianca is the 'good' daughter in Shakespeare's The Taming of the Shrew

Bib see Berenice

Bibi¹ f

Meaning 'lady', this is used on the Indian subcontinent and by those who have inherited its culture, both as a title of respect and as part of a first name.

Bibi² f

This is used as a pet name for BIANCA and BRITTANY, and sometimes for other female names beginning with 'B', or for those with the initials B B.

Biddy see Bridget

Bidelia f

This is an elaboration of the name BRIDGET (compare the form Biddy). Its history is obscure, but it was in use by the 18th century. It is one of the sources of DELIA.

VARIANT **Bedelia**

Bijay, Bijoy see Vijay

Bilal m

This comes from the Arabic for 'moistening, refreshment', a name with very positive associations in a desert culture. It was the name of the first ever muezzin (caller to prayer) in Islam.

VARIANT **Bilel**

Bill m Billie f

Bill is a pet form of WILLIAM, now used as an independent name. The history of the name is obscure. There is no record of Will becoming Bill in the Middle Ages, but it seems well established by the time William of Orange (King William III from 1689 to 1702) came to be known in parts of Ireland as King Billy. It has been suggested that a Celtic sound shift may have influenced the change. Billie for girls (now sometimes Billy) also presents some problems. It has been in regular use in the USA since the 19th century and, since feminine forms of William, such as Wilhelmina, were more common in the USA, having been introduced by German immigrants, it may well have started as a pet form of these names. Billie peaked as a girl's name in the USA in the 1920s and 30s, although it was still well used into the 1970s, but has only recently become more prominent in the UK. It is often used in combinations such as Billie-Jo.

PET FORM **Billy**

★ Billie Piper (1982–), English singer and actress

★ Billie Jean King (1943–), US tennis player

Bilqis see **Sheba**

Bina¹ f
This is a Jewish name that can be interpreted as coming either from the Hebrew for 'understanding, intelligence, wisdom', or from the Yiddish bin(e), 'bee', making it a translation of the name DEBORAH.
PET FORM **Binke** • VARIANTS **Binah, Bine**

Bina² f
A short form of names ending in these syllables, such as SABINA.

Bindy see **Belinda**

Binnie see **Berenice**

Birgit, Birgitta see **Bridget**

Birta, Birthe see **Bertha**

Bishen m
This is a north Indian variant of VISHNU.

Björk f
This is a Scandinavian name, meaning 'birch tree', that has become internationally famous through the Icelandic singer Björk Gudmundsdottir.

Bjorn m
This is a Scandinavian name, meaning 'bear'. The Swedish spelling is Björn, the Danish and Norwegian Bjørn.
★ Björn Ulvaeus (1945–), Swedish member of the pop group Abba
★ Björn Borg (1956–), Swedish tennis player

Blaine
The Scots Gaelic name Bláán comes from blá, 'yellow', and would mean something like 'little yellow one'. It would originally have been a nickname given to someone who was blond. It developed into both the surname and first name Blaine. Its spread was helped by there being a 6th-century saint called Blane who was a bishop and missionary. Dunblane ('Blaine's Fort') Cathedral is said by some to be built over the site of a monastery he founded. The name is used regularly in both Scotland and the USA.
VARIANT **Blane**

Blair mf
The Gaelic blar, 'field, plane', gives us the Scottish surname Blair, also found as a first name mainly in Scotland and North America, and more frequently male than female. The coincidence that it was a UK prime minister's surname does not seem to have affected its use in Scotland, where its familiarity as a place name probably means that it shares in the popularity of other national place names.
VARIANTS **Blaire, Blayre**

Blaise mf
The Roman name Blasius probably came from the word blaesus, 'stuttering, lisping'. It was the name of a 4th-century saint from what is now Turkey, about whom little is known for certain, but about whom a rich and fictitious set of legends evolved. The Crusaders brought these stories back with them, and the name was widely popular in the Middle Ages, particularly as he was the patron saint not only of wool-workers – an important trade then – but also, more significantly, of those with sore throats. Canterbury Cathedral claimed to have a relic of him. Use of the name shows signs of a slight revival, and it is occasionally used for girls. It sometimes appears as Blaze, which may also be a use of the vocabulary word.
VARIANTS Greek **Vlas(s)is** Italian **Biag(g)io, Biagino** Polish **Błażes** Portuguese **Bras** Russian **Vlas(i)** Spanish **Blas**
★ Blaise Pascal (1623–62), French

mathematician, physicist, theologian
and man-of-letters

Bláithín *see* **Bláthnait**

Blake *m*
This is an English surname, now used
as quite a popular first name. There
are two Old English sources for the
name. The first is the word *blac*, the
source of modern 'black', which would
have been originally given to someone
swarthy. The second is *blaek*, source
of the modern word 'bleak', but which
originally meant 'white, shining'. It too
would have started life as a nickname.
The name is now occasionally found
as a girl's name.
★ Blake Edwards (1922–   ), US
  screenwriter, director and film
  producer

Blanaid *see* **Bláthnait**

Blanca *see* **Bianca**

Blanche *f*
This is the French for 'white, pure', and
has been in use in the UK since the
Middle Ages. Other related names can
be found under BIANCA, In the Middle
Ages the name *Blanchefleur*, 'white
flower', was used and was the name
of the heroine of a popular romance,
but this seems to have died out now,
except as a surname.
VARIANT **Blanch**
★ Blanche, Duchess of Lancaster
  (1345–69), wife of John of Gaunt and
  one of the greatest heiresses of her
  day. Chaucer wrote *The Book of the
  Duchess* in her memory
☆ Blanche DuBois, mentally unstable
  Southern belle in Tennessee Williams's
  play *A Streeetcar Named Desire* (1947)

Blane *see* **Blaine**

Blanid *see* **Bláthnait**

Blanka *see* **Bianca**

Bláthnait *f*
This is formed from the Irish word
blath, 'flower', with an added
affectionate ending. The related name
Bláithín is formed in the same way. It
is an old name, and in Irish mythology
Bláthnait was a married woman who
fell in love with the hero Cuchulainn
and arranged to betray her husband
to him. Cuchulainn carried her off,
but she was swiftly killed by one of
her husband's followers in revenge for
her perfidy. The name is pronounced
'blaw-nit'. Many FLORAS or FLORENCES in
Irish records were really Bláthnaits, as,
having the same meanings, these were
used to translate the name.
PET FORM **Blath** • VARIANTS **Bláthnaid,
Blanaid, Blanid**

Blaze, Błażes *see* **Blaise**

Bleddyn *m*
This is a Welsh name, formed from
blaidd, meaning 'wolf', a word often
used to indicate a heroic fighter in the
Middle Ages, when it was a popular
name. It gave rise to surnames such
as Blethyn. The 'dd' is pronounced as
a 'th'.
★ Bleddyn Williams (1923–   ), Welsh
  rugby captain

Blodeuwedd *f*
In the Welsh *Mabinogion* story of
'Math son of Mathonwy' we are told
that Blodeuwedd, whose name means
'flower face', was created by Math out
of the flowers of meadowsweet, broom
and oak, to be a wife for Lleu. But she
was heartless and unfaithful, and her
story ends in tragedy.
PET FORM **Blod** • VARIANT **Blodwedd**
☆ The story of Blodeuwedd is retold in
  Alan Garner's 1967 novel for young
  adults *The Owl Service*

Blodwen *f*
This name is formed from the Welsh
blodau, 'flowers' (also the source

of *Blodyn* and *Blodeyn*), and *gwyn*, 'white', and is the most popular of the Welsh names formed from *blodau*. It is a direct translation of *Blanchefleur* (see BLANCHE). It was a popular medieval name, and was revived in the 19th century.

PET FORM **Blod**

Blossom *f*
A fairly unusual flower name, based on the vocabulary word. It has been recorded since the 19th century.
★ Blossom Dearie (1926–), US jazz singer and pianist

Blue *mf*
There has been something of a fashion for this name among celebrities since the 1970s, and it is now spreading to the general public. *Bleu*, the French form, is also used by English speakers. See also under BONNIE.
★ Dakota Blue Richards (1994–), English actress

Bluebell *f*
One of the more unusual flower names, which has been in occasional use since the late 19th century.

Blythe *fm*
Only occasionally used for boys, but regularly found for girls, this may sometimes be a transferred use of the surname, but is more often a form of the vocabulary word *blithe* meaning 'happy, cheerful'. It seems to be particularly popular in Scotland.

VARIANT **Blyth**
★ Blythe Danner (1943–), US actress, mother of Gwyneth Paltrow

Bo *see* Beau

Boaz *m*
This is a Hebrew name of uncertain meaning, although both 'strength' and 'swiftness' have been suggested. In the Bible, Ruth was gleaning in a cornfield and Boaz, taking a liking

to her, told his men to deliberately drop grain where she could collect it. They later married and became the ancestors of King David. The name was used by Puritans in the 16th and 17th centuries, but is now mainly confined to the Jewish community.

Boba *see* Boris

Bobby, Bobbie *mf*
Bobby is usually masculine and is a short form of ROBERT, *Rob* becoming *Bob* and then Bobby. Bobbie is more usually feminine, although all forms are sometimes used for both sexes. As a feminine name it can come from either ROBERTA or BARBARA. Bobby and Bobbie are increasingly being used as independent names, and there is a trend to combine them with other names, producing forms such as *Bobby-Lee*.

PET FORMS **Bob, Bobbi**

Bobur *see* Babar, Babur

Boniface *m*
This name started out as the Latin *Bonifatius*, 'well fated', but in Late Latin there was much confusion between spellings -*ti*- and -*ci*- and so the name was reinterpreted as deriving from *bonum*, 'good', and *facere*, 'to do', thus meaning 'doer of good deeds'. It was the name of a number of saints and nine popes and was quite popular in the Middle Ages, but is rare among English speakers today, although it is still found in other languages.

VARIANTS *Dutch* **Bonifaas, Faas** *German* **Bonifaz** *Italian, Spanish, Portuguese* **Bonifacio** *Polish* **Bonifacy**
★ St Boniface (c.680–c.754), poet, Latin grammarian, church reformer and missionary

Bonita *f*
This is the Spanish for 'pretty [girl]'

used as a first name. It was in use in the USA at the beginning of the 20th century (earlier than is usually stated), and has always been more popular there than in other English-speaking areas. Other names derived ultimately from the Latin *bonus*, 'good', are listed below although, strictly speaking, they are related names rather than variants.

PET FORM **Bonnie** • VARIANTS *French* **Bon**, **Bonne** *Italian* **Bona**, **Bonito**

★ Bonnie Langford (1964–), English actress, singer and dancer has Bonita as her full name

Bonnie

This is the Scottish vocabulary word meaning 'fine, pretty', ultimately derived from Latin *bonus*, 'good' (as are many other names beginning *Bon-*), used as a first name. It was in use in the USA in the 19th century, but only reached Scotland itself comparatively recently. The rise of the name may have been political: Margaret Mitchell, in her novel *Gone with the Wind* which is set in the American Civil War, described how the daughter of Scarlett and Rhett Butler was christened Eugenie Victoria, but known as Bonnie or Bonnie BLUE because her eyes were as blue as the Bonnie Blue Flag. This flag, which was bright blue with a single white star, was one of the unofficial flags used by the Confederates during the war and was celebrated in a popular marching song. Although the popularity of the name has often been attributed to Mitchell's novel it was, in fact, already widespread by the time the book was published.

★ Bonnie Parker (1911–34), US thief and murderess
★ Bonnie Bedelia (1948–), US actress

Boris *m*

There are a number of Eastern European names, such as *Bojan* (pronounced 'boy-an') and *Borislav*, 'battle glory', which derive from the Old Slavic element *boi*, 'fight, struggle', and Boris has been linked to this. However, it is thought more likely that it comes from a Turkic, perhaps Tartar, nickname meaning 'little, short'. The name is a popular one in many Slavic and central European countries, particularly Russia (where the stress is on the second syllable), as it was the name of a number of well-known saints and rulers.

PET FORMS **Borya**, **Boba**

★ Boris Pasternak (1890–1960), Russian author
★ Boris Johnson (1964–), English journalist and politician

Bosse *see* Beau

Botros, Boutros *see* Peter

Boudewijn *see* Baldwin

Boyd *m*

A Scottish and Irish surname, now increasingly used as a first name. Its origin is uncertain, but the Gaelic *buidhe*, 'yellow', or the Gaelic name for the Isle of Bute are the most popular explanations.

Bracken *mf*

A new plant name which is just beginning to make itself felt. The name bracken for the common fern goes back to Old English.

Brad *m*

A short form of names such as BRADLEY, also used as an independent name.

VARIANT **Bradd**

★ Brad Pitt (1963–), US actor

Braden, Bradan *m*

This is an Irish surname meaning 'salmon', which has become common as a first name in the USA and is increasing in use in the UK. Its popularity reflects the fashion in the

USA both for names that rhyme with
AIDAN, which form a high percentage
of popular boys' names, and for names
beginning with *Br-*.

VARIANTS **Bradon, Braydon, Brayden,
Braeden, Bralen, Braylon**

Bradley *m*
A surname, originally given to
someone who lived in a *brad*, 'broad',
leah, 'wood, clearing'. It has been used
since the 19th century. In the USA it
was among the top 100 names there
from 1960 to 1997 and is still among
the top 200. It became popular in the
UK in the 1990s.

PET FORM **Brad** • VARIANTS **Bradly, Bradlie**
☆ Bradley Headstone, spurned lover in
 Charles Dickens's *Our Mutual Friend*
 (1865)

Brady *m*
This is an Irish surname, of uncertain
origin, perhaps originally a nickname
given to someone with a broad chest.
It has a long history of quiet use as
a first name, but has become much
more popular in the USA since the
mid-1990s and is beginning to make
its mark elsewhere.

VARIANTS **Bradie, Braidy**

Braith *mf*
A Welsh name, from the vocabulary
word for 'speckled'.

Bram *see* **Abraham**

Bramble *see* **Briar**

Bran *m* **Branwen** *f*
Bran is an ancient Welsh name
meaning 'raven', and the name
of a Celtic god. He appears in the
important medieval Welsh story
collection, known as *The Mabinogion*,
as *Bendiedfran*, 'Bran the Blessed'. In
these stories Branwen, formed from
Bran plus *(g)wen*, 'holy, white, fair',
is his beautiful sister. Branwen may
sometimes be used as a variant of the

more popular BRONWEN. Bran is also a
short form of names beginning with
that syllable.

Brand *see* **Brenda**

Brandon *m*
An Old English place name formed
from *brom*, 'broom, gorse', and *dun*,
'hill', is the most usual source of
the surname Brandon, which later
became a first name. The name is often
confused with BRENDAN, and when
Charles Kingsley writes of 'St Brandon's
fairy isle' in *The Water Babies* (1862)
he appears to be referring to legends
of St Brendan. Although the name has
been recorded from the 19th century,
Brandon became popular in the USA
in the 1950s, and has been in the top
30 names there since 1975.

VARIANTS **Branden, Brandin, Brandyn,
Branton**
★ Brandon de Wilde (1942–72), US actor
 who made his name as a child actor
 in films such as *Shane* (1953), and
 who probably did much to spread the
 popularity of the name

Brandy *f*
It may seem strange that someone
would choose to name their daughter
after an alcoholic drink, but Brandy
serves to fill the gap as a female
equivalent of the many fashionable
boys' names beginning *Bra-*,
particularly the very popular BRANDON.
Although recorded earlier, at least as
a nickname, Brandy came into more
general use in the USA in the 1960s,
its popularity peaking in the late 1970s
to early 80s. It has had less success
in other countries. It is occasionally
found as a masculine name.

VARIANTS **Brandi(e), Brandee**
★ Brandy Norwood (1979–   ), US
 singer-songwriter and actress
☆ 'Brandy (You're a Fine Girl)' 1972

song, written by Elliot Lurie and recorded by Looking Glass

Branka see **Bianca**

Branwen see **Bran**

Bras see **Blaise**

Brea f
This is a Gaelic name meaning 'fine, splendid, beautiful'. The Irish Gaelic word from which it is taken is breá, the Scots Gaelic word is brèagha, and spellings reflecting both forms and intermediate forms are found. It has yet to spread much outside Gaelic-speaking areas. It is pronounced 'bria'. There may be some overlap with BREE.
VARIANTS **Breagh**, **Breagha**

Bréanainn see **Brendan**

Breanna f
This is often analysed as a feminine form of BRIAN, but may be regarded by some users as a blend of BREE and ANNA or similar names.
VARIANTS **Breann**, **Breeanna**, **Breeanne**, **Brieanna**

Breda see **Bridget**

Bree f
This is the anglicized form, reflecting the pronunciation, of the Irish name Brighe which is a pet form of BRIDGET.
VARIANTS **Brie**, **Breda**

Brenda f
Brenda came to public attention in 1821 when it was used by Sir Walter Scott in his 1821 novel *The Pirate*. In the novel it is the name of a Shetlander, the daughter of a man who claims noble Viking descent. Scott is generally regarded as historically accurate, in that the name is thought to be a Shetland name, and to be of Old Norse origin, being the feminine of the name *Brand*, 'sword'. In Ireland, however, it is used as the feminine

form of BRENDAN. It was mainly confined to Scotland until the mid-20th century when it became popular throughout the UK, although it is not much used now.

Brendan m
This is an Irish name which belonged to a number of saints, the most famous of whom is the 6th-century St Brendan the Navigator who, despite having a career worthy of celebration, is better known from the romance written of his travels to the mythical Land of Promise, and who is generally credited with having reached America. The origin of the name has been the subject of much speculation, but is now generally thought to be from a Celtic word meaning 'prince'. The name became widely popular in the 20th century but BRANDON, often regarded as a variant in Ireland, has largely replaced it, even in the Republic of Ireland.
VARIANTS **Brenden**, **Brendon** *Irish Gaelic* **Breandán**, **Bréanainn**

Brenna f **Brennan** m
The Irish surname Brennan comes from the old name *Braonán*, meaning 'drop, moisture, tear'. Brenna seems to have been formed as a feminine form of Brennan. However, there is much confusion and variation between the currently fashionable names for both sexes beginning *Br-*.
VARIANTS **Brennah**, **Brenan**, **Brennen**, **Brennon**

Brent m
This is a surname, originally a place name, which can come either from an Old English word meaning 'burnt' or else from a West Country term for a hill. It is now used, particularly in the USA, as a first name. *Brenton* is probably best seen as an elaboration, although it is also a separate surname.

★ Brent Spiner (1949–), US actor best-known as Data in the television series *Star Trek: The Next Generation*

Brett *mf*
This is a surname, originally meaning 'Breton', which has been used as a first name, particularly since the second half of the 20th century. It is more usually male than female. The variant Bret is also found as a pet form for BRITTANY.
VARIANT **Bret**
★ Bret Harte (1836–1902), US poet and story writer

Bri *see* Bryony

Briallen *f*
This is the Welsh for 'primrose'.

Brian *m*
This is an Irish name, the meaning of which is unclear. It may be from a word meaning 'high', perhaps by extension meaning 'noble', although others prefer 'hill', or it may be from *brigh* meaning 'strength, power'. The name was also used by the Celtic-speaking Bretons, and it was probably they who brought the name to England in the Middle Ages. *Bryant*, a surname derived from Brian, functions as a variant.
VARIANT **Bryan**
★ Brian Boru (c.926–1014), King of Ireland, who defeated the Dublin Vikings
★ Bryan Ferry (1945–), English singer

Brianna *f*
This is the commonest of the feminine forms of the name BRIAN. It has been particularly popular in the USA since the 1990s. Some forms such as *Breanne* blend into variants of BREE or BREANNA.
VARIANTS **Brianne, Briana, Briann, Bryanne**

Briar *f*
This is an occasional first name, used with reference to the rose plant. *Briar Rose* is a traditional name for the princess in the *Sleeping Beauty* story. Briar can also be used for the bramble or blackberry, and *Bramble* is also found as an even rarer name.

Brice *see* Bryce

Bridget *f*
This Irish first name, meaning 'The High One' was originally the name of a pagan goddess, but its popularity stems from Ireland's most famous female saint, St Bridget, who lived c.450–c.523. However, we can be sure of very little in her life, as her legend seems to have incorporated material from stories of the earlier pagan goddess. The Irish Gaelic form of the name is *Brighid*, pronounced 'breed', which explains the multiple forms the name takes. For many years it was the archetypical Irish name, but it no longer gets into the top 100 names even in the Republic of Ireland.
PET FORM **Biddy** • VARIANTS **Brigit, Bridgette** *Irish* **Bidelia, Breda, Bree, Bríd, Bride, Bridie, Brighe** *Welsh* **Ffraid** *French* **Brigitte** *German* **Brigitta, Gitta** *Italian, Spanish* **Brigida** *Polish* **Brygida** *Portuguese* **Brígida** *Scandinavian* **Birgit(ta), Berit, Brit(t)(a), Gittan**
★ Brigitte Bardot (1934–), French actress
★ St Birgitta (c.1303–73), Swedish visionary and author

Brie *see* Bree

Brieanna *see* Breanna

Brielle *f*
This is a short form of *Gabrielle* (see GABRIEL) which has been used as a independent name since the 1990s.

Brígida *see* Bridget

Brin *see* Bryn

Brion, Briony *see* **Bryony**

Brittany *f*
This is the French place name used as
a first name. No one has really come
up with a convincing explanation
for why it should have become so
popular in the USA in the 1980s and
90s, although it is worth noting that in
recent decades place names have been
growing in popularity, and that names
such as CHELSEA were particularly
fashionable at the same time. Brittany
has enjoyed much less popularity in
other English-speaking areas. In the
USA it has developed innumerable
variants; one source has counted 83.
PET FORMS **Bibi, Bret, Brittie, Britty**
• VARIANTS **Britny, Britani, Britni, Brittiny**
★ Britney Spears (1981–), US singer

Brizio *see* **Bryce**

Brock *m*
This is a surname now used as a first
name, particularly in the USA and
to a lesser extent in Australia. Brock
is another word for badger, and the
name would probably have started
out as a nickname for someone with
a distinguishing mark reminiscent of a
badger, such as a white streak in their
hair.
VARIANT **Broc**

Broderick *m*
This is a Welsh surname occasionally
used as a first name. The name is an
anglicized form of *ap Roderick*, 'son of
Roderick'.

Brodie, Brody *mf*
This is a surname, derived from a place
name, and now used as a first name.
Brodie Castle in Moray probably gets
its name from the Gaelic *brothhach*,
'muddy place', although an alternative
word meaning 'ditch' has been
suggested. Brodie is the usual form
of the name in Scotland, where –

although still most often a masculine
name – it is also more likely to be used
for girls than elsewhere. In the USA
and Australia it is more often Brody,
and mainly masculine.
VARIANT **Brodi**

Brogan *mf*
This is an old Irish name, perhaps
from the Gaelic *bróg*, 'shoe'. It was
originally masculine, but is now used
for both sexes.
VARIANT **Broghan**

Bron *see* **Aubrey, Bronwen**

Bronagh *f*
This is an Irish name from *bronach*,
'sad, sorrowful'. St Bronach was a 6th-
century abbess whose monastery was
in Kilbroney Valley, which is named
after her, in Northern Ireland.
VARIANTS **Brona, Bronya** *Irish* **Brónach**
★ Bronagh Gallagher (1972–),
    Northern Irish singer and actress

Brontë *f*
This is the surname of the three
19th-century sisters (Charlotte,
Emily and Anne), whose novels have
been enduringly popular. It is a rare
surname, because it was changed
by their father from the much more
common name Prunty. This was an
Irish surname meaning 'descendant of
an open-handed person'. It is thought
that the Rev Patrick Brontë changed
his name when Admiral Nelson was
awarded the title 'Duke of Bronte'
(named after a place in Sicily), by the
king of Sicily in 1799.
☆ Bronte Parrish is a character in the
    1990 film *Green Card*. This character
    is thought to have increased use of
    the name, although it was already in
    circulation

Bronwen *f*
Bronwen is a Welsh name formed from
bron, 'breast', and *(g)wen*, 'white,

fair, blessed'. *Branwen* (see BRAN) is sometimes used as a variant.

PET FORM **Bron** • VARIANT **Bronwyn**

Brooke *f*

Brooke comes from a surname which would originally have been given to someone who lived near a brook. A prominent person with an early use of the name was the long-lived socialite and philanthropist Brooke Astor (1902–2007). Born Roberta Brooke Russell, her middle name, by which the public knew her, was a family surname. Brooke is occasionally used for males, but has been a popular choice for women in a number of countries for some years.

VARIANT **Brook**

★ Brooke Shields (1965–   ), US actress and model, whose fame has been influential in spreading the name

Brooklyn *mf*

This is the borough of New York City used as a first name. It gets its name not from a brook, but from the Dutch *Breukelen* meaning 'broken land'. In the USA, where it first became popular, it is predominantly a female name, and often takes forms that make it look like a blend of BROOKE and LYN. However, in the UK it is predominantly male, having been introduced to the British largely by David and Victoria Beckham. They chose it for their first son in 1999, as they were in Brooklyn when they discovered they were expecting him.

VARIANTS **Brookelyn, Brooklin, Brooklynn**

Bruce *m*

This is a surname turned first name. The famous Scottish Bruce family was of Norman descent, and took its surname from a place in Normandy, although which of several possible candidates is unclear. It was first used in Scotland in honour of King Robert the Bruce (1274–1329), famous for the story of his learning persistence in adversity from watching a spider. The name was taken round the world by Scottish emigrants. It was very popular in Australia in the middle of the 20th century, and by the 1970s had come to epitomize the butch Australian. Curiously around the same time in the USA, where it had been equally popular, it came to be associated with homosexuality which led to a considerable decline in use, although the association is now dying out.

PET FORM **Brucie**

★ Bruce Springsteen (1949–   ), US rock singer
★ Bruce Willis (1955–   ), US actor
☆ Bruce Wayne, real name of Batman

Brunhilde *f*

The name of the most famous of the Valkyries in Germanic mythology, this name is formed from *brun*, here meaning 'armour, protection', and *hild* meaning 'battle'. Most modern English-language uses are with reference to Wagner's operas.

VARIANTS **Brunhild(a), Brynhild** *German* **Brünhild(e)** *Italian, Spanish, Portuguese* **Brunilda, Nilda**

Bruno *m*

This simply means brown, and would originally have been a nickname for someone with brown hair. The name is better used by speakers of Spanish, Italian and German than by English speakers. It entered the common stock of European names in honour of the German-born St Bruno who, in the 11th century, founded a religious house which was to evolve into the Carthusian Order.

FEMININES **Brunella, Brunette**

★ Bruno Walter (1876–1972), German-born US conductor
★ Bruno Bettelheim (1903–90), Austrian-

born US psychologist, known for his writing on fairy tales

Bryan *see* **Brian**

Bryanne *see* **Brianna**

Bryce, Bryson *m*
The French first name *Brice* developed into a surname more usually spelt Bryce, which in turn developed into a self-explanatory surname Bryson. The French name seems to be of Gaulish origin, and probably meant 'speckled, freckled'. It was the name of a saint who was a follower of St Martin, and who became bishop of Tours in AD 444. Use of Bryce increased steadily in the USA in the 1990s, and it is also making its mark in the UK.
VARIANTS **Brycen** *French* **Brice** *Italian* **Brizio** (also used as a short form of *Fabrizio*)

Brygida *see* **Bridget**

Bryn, Brynmor *mf*
Bryn Mawr, the source of Brynmor, is a Welsh place name meaning 'big hill'. Bryn, 'hill', is either a short form of this or an independent name. In the USA Bryn, particularly in the form *Brynn*, is now usually a feminine name, growing in popularity since the 1980s, which is beginning to appear as such in the UK.
VARIANTS **Brin, Brynne**
★ Bryn Terfel (1965–), Welsh baritone

Brynhild *see* **Brunhilde**

Bryony *f*
This is the name of a hedgerow climber with pretty berries, used as a first name. The plant name comes ultimately from a Greek word meaning 'to grow luxuriantly'. It seems to be a 20th-century name and, while it has been popular in the UK, does not seem to have been much used elsewhere. At times it probably serves as a feminine of BRIAN.
PET FORMS **Bry(on), Bri(on)** • VARIANT **Briony**

Buck *m*
This term for a vigorous young man, derived from the term for a deer, is more often a nickname than a given name.
★ Buck Duke (1858–1925), US tobacco magnate, after whom Duke University is named
☆ Anthony 'Buck' Rogers, spaceman, who was created by Philip Francis Nowlan in 1928 for short stories, and subsequently appeared in strip cartoons, films and television series

Buddy
This word for 'friend' is more often a nickname, but has been recorded as a given name. Its origin is either from a child's pronunciation of 'brother' or from the Scots Gaelic *a bhodaich*, 'old man'.
PET FORM **Bud**
★ Buddy Holly (1936–59), US musician, whose fame helped spread the name

Budur *see* **Badr**

Buffy *f*
A pet form of ELIZABETH, based on a child's attempt to say the name.
★ Buffy Sainte-Marie (1941/42–), Native American musician and social activist
☆ Buffy Summers, heroine of the television series *Buffy the Vampire Slayer*, which ran 1997–2003

Bunnie *see* **Berenice**

Bunty *f*
This name seems to have come from a dialect word for a hand-reared lamb, and started out as a term of endearment. It came to public attention in 1911 with a successful play called *Bunty Pulls the Strings* and later through a girls' comic called *Bunty*, which was published between 1958 and 2001.

Burak *m*

This is an Arabic, particularly Turkish, name. It was the name of a legendary, heavenly steed that carried the Prophet Muhammad on his night journey to heaven. It is described as being white, smaller than a donkey, but larger than a mule. In art it is often shown as a sort of winged horse, sometimes with a human head. The name comes from the Arabic root for 'lightning', also the source of *Baariq*, 'bright', and *Bareeq*, 'lightning, lustre, brilliance'.

VARIANT *Arabic* **Buraq**

Burt *m*

This is now an independent name which started out either as a respelling of BERT, as a short form of any of the many names containing that syllable, or else as a shortening of *Burton*, a first name derived from a surname in turn derived from a place name, meaning 'fortified settlement'.

★ Burt Lancaster (1913–94), US actor
★ Burt Bacharach (1928–) US songwriter and pianist
★ Burt Reynolds (1936–), US actor

Buster *m*

This is usually a nickname, and mainly used in the USA. It was brought to public attention by the silent movie comedy star Buster Keaton (1895–1966).

Butros *see* **Peter**

Byron *m*

This is used in memory of the poet Lord Byron (more properly George Gordon, 6th Baron Byron, 1784–1824). Byron's daughter ADA, Countess of Lovelace, gave the name Byron to her eldest son, born in 1836. It has been used more often in the USA than the UK and is rather out of fashion, but still chosen occasionally.

C

Cabhan *see* **Cavan**

Cäcilia *see* **Cecilia**

Caddy *see* **Candace, Caroline**

Cade *m*
The Old English word *cada* meant 'lump' and was probably used as a nickname for someone fat. This became a surname and then a first name. It appears as a first name in Margaret Mitchell's influential novel *Gone with the Wind* (1936) but has only been used with any regularity in the last 30 years or so.

VARIANT **Kade**

Cadell *m*
This is a Welsh name, based on *cad* 'battle'. As the ending is one used to create pet forms, it probably started out as a pet form of one of the many medieval Welsh male names beginning *Cad-*.

VARIANT **Cadel**

Caden *m*
This is a fashionable name in the USA, having first appeared in the 1000 most common boys' names in 1993, and having climbed rapidly to 92nd place by 2007, currently the most recent figures available. It can be construed as coming from the Scottish surname McCadden, but this usually has a short 'a' sound, while Caden has the same 'a' sound as 'may'. It is more likely that it is based on CADE, with the *-en* added to give the very fashionable '-aden' sound, which currently dominates US boys' names. The enormous variety of forms the name takes, only a few of

which are listed below, suggests it is a modern coinage.

VARIANTS **Kaden, Cadan, Cadon, Cadyn, Caedan, Kadin, Kadyn, Kaeden**

Cadence *f*
This is part of the recent trend to use musical terms for first names, only making its mark since 2000, but already developing a number of variants. It supplies a feminine name linked with fashionable masculines such as CADEN.

PET FORM **Cady** • VARIANTS **Cadance, Kadence, Kaydence**

☆ Cadence Roth is the main character in Armistead Maupin's 1992 novel *Maybe the Moon*

☆ Cadence Flaherty is a character in the 2003 film *American Wedding*

Cadfael *m*
This ancient Welsh name is formed from *cad*, 'battle', and *mael*, 'metal, iron'. St Cadfael, better known by the pet form of his name as St *Cadog*, was a 6th-century saint whose popularity means that there are 15 churches dedicated to him in his native South Wales. A single 'f' is pronounced as a 'v 'in Welsh.

VARIANT **Cadoc**

Cadfan *m*
This is the name of a Breton who in the 5th century founded a monastery on Bardsey Island where, according to a Welsh poem, 20,000 saints lie buried. The name is formed from the elements *cad*, 'battle', and *ban*, 'peak'.

Cadhla *see* **Keeley**

Cadi *see* **Caroline, Catherine**

Cadog *see* **Cadfael**

Cadogan *m*
This is the anglicized form of a Welsh name produced from *cad*, 'battle', and *gwogawn*, 'honour, glory'. It was a popular name in early medieval Wales, and was revived in the 19th century.
VARIANT *Welsh* **Cadwgan**

Cadwalader *m*
This Welsh name is formed from *cad*, 'battle', and *gwaladr*, 'leader'. It was the name of a number of early Welsh leaders including St Cadwalader in the 7th century, who died defending his stronghold against the invading Saxons.
VARIANTS **Cadwallader** *Welsh* **Cadwaladr**

Caecilia *see* **Cecilia**

Caedan *see* **Caden**

Caedmon *m*
Caedmon was the name of the 7th-century cowherd who had a vision which inspired him to write the first English vernacular religious poetry. The origin of the name is not known, but may in fact have been British, and share the same *cad* element as the names above. The name was revived in the 19th century, and is still occasionally used, often by those with associations with Caedmon's native Northumberland.

Cael *see* **Cale**

Caelainn *see* **Caoilainn**

Caelan *see* **Caoilainn, Caolan**

Caelen *see* **Caolan**

Caelyn *see* **Caoilainn**

Caeo *m*
This is the name of a village and parish in Carmarthenshire used as a first name in Wales.
VARIANTS **Caio, Cayo**

Caera *see* **Cara**

Caerwyn *m*
Although this Welsh name looks as if it is formed from *caer*, 'fort', and *(g)wyn*, 'white, fair', both common elements in Welsh place names, it is generally accepted that in origin it is a respelling of CARWYN.
★ Professor J E Caerwyn Williams (1912–99), scholar of Welsh and Irish

Caesar *m*
The most famous bearer of this name was Julius Caesar (c.104–44 BC). His fame and power were such that Caesar became a title for the succeeding Roman emperors and passed into other languages as a term for 'ruler', becoming Tsar in Russian and Kaiser in German. Romans derived the name from *caesaries*, 'head of hair', but later scholars have doubted their interpretation and prefer to regard it as an ancient name of unknown origin. The Spanish form of the name is well used in the USA.
VARIANTS *Italian* **Cesare** *French, Spanish* **César**
★ Cesare Borgia (c.1476–1507), violent scion of the notorious Borgia family during the Italian Renaissance
★ César Chávez (1927–93), US labour activist

Caetano *see* **Gaetano**

Cahal *see* **Cathal**

Cahir *see* **Cathair**

Cai *m*
While some uses of this may represent a respelling of KAI, in Wales this is the name of King Arthur's seneschal, known in English Arthurian stories as Sir Kay. The origin of this name is

debated. Some link it to the Roman name CAIUS while others see Cai, who in Welsh tradition has supernormal powers, as the remnants of a Celtic god.

VARIANTS **Kai, Caio, Caw**

Cailean see Colin

Cain m

From the Hebrew for 'acquired', this name is best-known through the biblical character who was both the first son, born to Adam and Eve, and the first murderer, after he killed his younger brother ABEL in a jealous rage. As it seems unlikely that parents would deliberately choose such a role model with the frequency with which this name appears, it should be regarded as an unfortunate respelling of similar-sounding names such as KANE or CIAN. The fashionable sound is probably the key to its use. For Cain as a feminine name see CEINWEN.

Cainneach see Kenneth

Caio see Caeo

Cairbre m

An Irish first name meaning 'charioteer'. It is well-attested in early Irish stories that lie half way between fact and myth. One bearer was said to have been a noted satirist, reputed to be the son of the god of eloquence; another to have been a 3rd-century warrior High King of Ireland; while a third was a son of Niall of the Nine Hostages. Carbury in County Kildare is said to be named after him.

VARIANT **Carbr(e)y**

Cairistìona, Cairstìne see Christina

Cáit see Caitlin, Kate

Caitìona, Caitriona see Catriona

Cáitir see Catriona

Caitlin f

This is an Irish form of CATHERINE which also lies behind KATHLEEN. In Ireland it is pronounced in various ways depending on what part of Ireland the speaker comes from: 'koit-leen' and 'kath-leen' are the most usual. Elsewhere, the name tends to be pronounced as if a blend of Kate and Lyn. As a result in the USA, where the name has been enormously popular for many years, the spelling *Kaitlyn* is currently the most common. Its popularity throughout the English-speaking world has meant that a vast number of variants have evolved, only the most common of which are listed below.

PET FORMS **Cait, Cáit** • VARIANTS **Caitlinn, Caitlyn(n), Kaitlin, Kaitlyn, Katelyn(n)**

Caius m

This ancient Roman first name, which the Romans spelt both as Caius and *Gaius*, is occasionally still used as a first name. As the Romans had only a handful of first names it was very common among them, although it had no discernible meaning.

Caje, Cajé, Cajetan see Gaetano

Cal m

This is usually a pet form of names such as CALVIN or CALLUM, but in Northern Ireland is a variant of CATHAL.

Cale m

A recent name of uncertain or mixed origin. It could be a short form of CALEB, or it could be from the surname. What is important is the fashionable sound.

VARIANTS **Cael, Kale**

Caleb m

Of all those who left Egypt with Moses, only Caleb and JOSHUA survived to see the Promised Land (Numbers 26.65). Caleb appears in the Bible as a difficult man, one who is not afraid to make himself unpopular with the people, but who is regarded as a champion of the Lord. The name appears to mean 'dog', and is interpreted as reflecting his faithfulness. It was a popular name among the Puritans who took it with them to the USA. It has been popular there again in recent years, and has spread from there to other English-speaking areas.

PET FORM **Cale** • VARIANTS **Kaleb** *Hebrew* **Kalev**

Calie *see* **Callie**, **Kayleigh**

Calixta, Calixtus *see* **Callista**

Callan *m*

This is a surname used as a first name. It can have two sources: either an Irish surname derived from CATHAN, or a Scottish surname from *ail*, 'rock'. This also gives the surname Allen, the 'c' in this form being carried over from a form such as 'MacAllen'. The name is particularly found in Scotland. Once again the fashionable 'Cal-' sound has probably played a part in its growth.

VARIANTS **Calan**, **Kallan**

Callie *f*

This is now an independent name, well used in the USA for many years and growing elsewhere. It is a short form of a number of names, particularly those beginning with the element *kalos*, 'fair', but including other names beginning *Cal-* and the name CAROLINE. See also KAYLEIGH.

VARIANTS **Cally**, **Calli**, **Kalli(e)**

Callista *f*

Two names seem to have fallen together inextricably here. There is a Greek name *Callisto*, from *kalos* 'beautiful', which means 'most beautiful'. This was the name of one of the many Greek nymphs who had the misfortune to attract the sexual attention of Zeus, king of the gods.

His jealous wife, Hera, turned Callisto into a bear as punishment. The name became Callista in Latin, and in Late Latin could have developed the form *Callixta*, because of sound changes that had taken place. However, there was another Latin word *calix*, meaning 'cup', origin of the botanical term and, ultimately, of the word 'chalice'. This took on the specifically Christian sense of the chalice for communion wine, making *Calixtus* or *Callistus* a suitable name for Christians and, indeed, it was taken as a papal name by three popes. Users may choose which sense they wish to give these names. The masculine forms have never been much used by English speakers, but are used in other languages as listed below.

PET FORM **Callie** • VARIANTS **Calista**, **Kalysta** *French* **Cal(l)ixte** (used for both sexes until the 19th century, now m) *Italian* **Callisto** *Spanish* **Calisto**, **Calixto**, **Calixta** ★ Calista Flockhart (1964–), US actress

Callum, Calum *m*

The Late Latin name COLUMBA, 'dove', became Callum or Calum in Scots Gaelic. There is no significance in the two spellings which are merely a matter of fashion. While Calum is sometimes described as the traditional Scottish spelling of the name, the version with -*ll*- is currently used more than twice as often as the -*l*- form there. The latest available figures, however, put Callum at number 5 in Scotland and Calum at 33, so the confusion over spelling has not diminished the popularity of the name. A similar situation exists in Ireland, and the -*ll*- spelling is also currently the more popular in England and Australia. Curiously, despite its popularity among other English-speakers, the name is hardly used at all in the USA in either form. The name entered Scottish culture early on thanks to St Columba. He was an Irish noble who became a monk and took the religious name of Columba; in 563, he settled on IONA and began to preach Christianity to the Scots and Picts. Columba was also responsible for the introduction of MALCOLM.

FEMININE **Calumina** (rare) • PET FORM **Cal** • VARIANT *Irish* **Colm**

Calvin *m*

The Latin word *calvus* meant 'bald' and became *Chauve* in French. With a pet-form ending this became a surname, Chauvin or Cauvin, with a sense something like 'baldy'. When Jean Cauvin became a prominent theologian in the 16th century, a time when most serious writing was done in Latin, the name was given a learned, Latinate form, and he became the man known in English as John Calvin (1509–64). His reforming, Protestant theology was so influential that a whole branch of Protestant thought was named Calvinism after him. The name has always been regularly used in the USA, where it is only in the last few years that it has dropped out of the top 200 names for the first time since records began in 1880. Use is increasing elsewhere.

PET FORM **Cal** • VARIANTS *Irish* **Calbhach**, **Calvagh** (independent name of same meaning and origin) *Italian* **Calvino**

Calypso *f*

In Homer's *Odyssey* Calypso, whose name means 'hider, concealer', was a demi-goddess and enchantress who lived on the hidden island of Ogygia, and kept Odysseus as her prisoner and lover for seven years. It is difficult to tell if people are using the name directly after the nymph, or after the West Indian style of music. In France, where the name has had a certain currency since the late 20th century,

it has been suggested that the fact the research boat of the French underwater researcher Jacques Cousteau was called *Calypso* may have been influential.

☆ The mythical Calypso features as a character in the *Pirates of the Caribbean* films

Camellia *f*

This flower name is occasionally used as a first name, most frequently in France and in the French form. Use was inspired by Alexandre Dumas the Younger's 1848 story *La Dame aux Camélias* ('The Lady with the Camellias'), which was turned by Verdi into the opera *La Traviata* (1853). The plant family, which includes not only the beautiful flowering shrub but also the tea plant, gets its name from Georg Joseph Kamel (1661–1706) a Moravian Jesuit missionary to the Far East. See also CAMILLA.

VARIANT *French* **Camélia**

Cameron *mf*

The origin of this name lies in a Gaelic nickname *cam sròn* meaning 'crooked nose'. The name developed into the Scottish clan name and surname Cameron. It has been used as a first name since at least the 19th century. It was originally solely masculine, but has been used increasingly as a feminine since the 1980s.

VARIANTS **Camron, Camryn, Kam(e)ron, Kamryn**

★ Cameron Mackintosh (1946–), British theatrical producer

★ Cameron Diaz (1972–), US actress

Camilla *f*

The Roman family name *Camillus* was an ancient one, probably taken from the Etruscans. In Virgil's *Aeneid*, the feminine form Camilla appears as the name of a warrior queen who battles AENEAS, and who was said to be so fast a runner that she could cross a wheatfield without a stalk bending. Curiously, use of the French form of the name, *Camille* (used for both sexes in France), increased by 50 per cent in the USA in the year immediately after Hurricane Camille struck the Gulf Coast in 1969. The masculine forms of the name have never made their mark among English speakers, but are used in other languages.

PET FORMS **Cam(mie)**, **Millie**, **Milly**, **Milla**
• VARIANTS *French* **Camille** (m&f) *German* **Kamil** (m), **Kamilla** (m) *Italian* **Camillo** (m) *Spanish* **Camila**, **Camilo** (m)
★ Camilla, Duchess of Cornwall (1946–), British duchess and wife of Charles, Prince of Wales
★ Camille Paglia (1947–), US author and academic

Campbell *mf*

This is a Scottish surname formed from the Gaelic *cam béul*, 'crooked mouth', a nickname which later became a clan name. It is used as a masculine name in Scotland, but is used for both sexes in the USA.

Candace *f*

Candace is the traditional name of the queens of Ethiopia. The name appears in the New Testament, which made it available for the Puritans to use. They would have pronounced the name 'can-DAY-see', but modern users usually say 'can-diss'. The meaning is not known, although a Nubian word meaning 'queen mother' has been suggested.

PET FORMS **Caddy**, **Candy**, **Candi**, **Kandy**
• VARIANTS **Candice**, **Candis**, **Kandace**, **Kandice**
★ Candice Bergen (1946–), US actress
★ Candace Bushnell (1958–), author of *Sex and the City*

Candia *f*

This is the name of the town of Candia, now Heraklion in Crete, used as a first name. The usually reliable Withycombe in the *Oxford Dictionary of English Christian Names* tells us that it is 'a name used in the Barrow family and other Quaker families. The first bearer of the name, Candia Palmer, was born while her father was on a voyage to Candia' but fails to give any kind of date. However, the name was established in the West Country by the late 18th century, so it was presumably some time in that century. A prominent bearer was Candia Barrow, the wife of John Cadbury, founder of the chocolate company. She lived 1805–55.
★ Candia McWilliam (1955–), Scottish author

Candida *f*

The Latin word *candidus* meant 'bright white', but also acquired the senses 'pure, sincere, loyal'. A Roman politician wore a specially whitened toga to show he possessed these qualities, which gave us the word 'candidate' as well as 'candid'. Although Candida was the name of several saints, it was hardly used by English speakers until the 20th century. This use seems to have been inspired by George Bernard Shaw's play *Candida* (1897). Shaw in turn had based the name on that of the hero of Voltaire's 1759 novel *Candide*, this being the French equivalent used for both sexes. Names with the same meaning are BIANCA and BLANCHE.

PET FORMS **Candi(e)**, **Candy** • VARIANT *Spanish* **Candido**

Candra *see* Chandra

Candy *see* Candace, Candida

Canna *f*

A recent flower name, taken from the exotic bloom of the canna lily. The botanical name comes from the Greek for 'reed'. The name has been in use since at least the 1940s and is found particularly in Australia.

Cannelle see **Cinnamon**

Caoilainn f
An Irish name formed from *caol*, 'slender', and *fionn*, 'white, fair, pure', and the name of a number of saints. It is anglicized as *Kalin* (pronounced 'kay-lin') or KEELIN ('key-lin') depending on which regional pronunciation is chosen.
VARIANTS **Caoilfhionn, Caoilfinn, Caoilinn, Caelainn, Caelan, Caelyn, Keelan**

Caoimhe f
This is an Irish name, pronounced 'key-va' or 'kwey-va'. Despite its difficult spelling it usually keeps its Irish form, in Ireland at least. It has been among the most popular names there for a number of years. The name means 'gentle, precious'.
VARIANTS **Ke(e)va, Keavy**

Caoimhín see **Kevin**

Caolan m
This is a Gaelic name formed from *caol*, 'slender', and is thus the masculine of CAOILAINN. The pronunciation is reflected in the anglicized form KEELAN. The name is particularly popular in Northern Ireland.
VARIANTS **Caolain, Caelan, Caelen, Kealan, Kealon, Keelin**

Capri f
This is the name of the Italian island, famed for its beauty, used as a first name. It is a 20th-century introduction.
VARIANT **Capree**

Caprice f
This is the vocabulary word used as a first name. It is a 20th-century innovation.
★ Caprice Bourret (1971–), US model

Cara[1] f
Cara is the feminine form of the Latin word for 'dear', which was passed down to Italian. The name came into use in the 19th century, and is more usual in the USA than the UK. In practice, it is not possible to tell if users of this and its variants are using Cara[1] or Cara[2].
VARIANT **Kara**

Cara[2] f
In Irish *cara* means 'friend'. The name can either be pronounced 'car-a' or 'keer-a'. It is a popular choice in Ireland.
VARIANTS **Caragh, Caera, Carah**

Caradoc m
This Welsh name is based on the word *câr*, 'love'. It is one of the earliest recorded British names, for in the form *Caractacus* or *Caratacus* it is known from Roman sources as the name of a British leader who fought against them in the 1st century AD. In the Middle Ages it was known as the name of a knight at King Arthur's court.
VARIANT **Caradog**

Carenza see **Karenza**

Carbrey, Carbry see **Cairbre**

Caress f
This is the vocabulary word used as a first name. However, it has numerous variant spellings which blend imperceptibly into forms of other Car- or Char- feminines.

Cari f
As well as being a respelling of Carrie, a pet form of CAROLINE, in Wales this can be a name based on *câr*, 'love, dear', or a pet form of CERIDWEN. See also CARY.

Caridad, Caridade see **Charity**

Carina *f*
This looks like a pet form of CARA[1], a view reinforced by the existence of *Carita*, another such pet form, but some users consider it a Latinate form of KAREN. It is mainly found in English, German and in the Scandinavian countries. Carita can also be interpreted as coming from *caritas*, 'charity, love'.

VARIANTS *French* **Carine** *Scandinavian* **Karita**

Carinthia *f*
The name of this province of Austria came into limited circulation as a first name after George Meredith used it as the name of the heroine in his 1895 novel *The Amazing Marriage*.

★ Carinthia 'Kinta' Beevor (1911–95), English author

Carissa, Caris *f*
This name has been interpreted variously as an emphatic pet form of CARA, or as a variant of either CARYS, CHARIS or related names.

VARIANT **Karis(s)a**

Carl *m*
One of the many forms of the name CHARLES. This is a German form, closer to the original Germanic term *karl*, 'free man', than many others.

VARIANTS **Karl** *Italian* **Carlo** *Spanish, Portuguese* **Carlos**, **Carlito(s)**

★ Carl Jung (1875–1961), Swiss psychiatrist

Carla *f*
This is a feminine form of CARL, used in many countries.

PET FORMS **Carly**, **Karly** • VARIANT **Karla**

Carlene, Carline *f*
These are further plays on feminine forms of the CARL–CHARLES group of names. They are usually described as modern variants, but the Latinate form *Carlina* has been recorded from at least 1803, and Carlene first entered the records of the US top 1000 names in 1919.

VARIANTS **Carlyn**, **Carline**

Carlotta *f*
This is the Italian form of CHARLOTTE, sometimes used by English speakers as an independent name.

Carlton *m*
Carlton was originally a surname, now used as a first name. The surname in turn came from a place name formed from the Old English *ceorl*, 'free man, peasant' and *tun*, 'settlement'.

VARIANTS **Charlton**, **Karlton**

Carly *f*
This is yet another variant of the many feminines of the CARL–CHARLES group of names. It is sometimes used as a pet form of CARLA or CAROL, but is most often found as an independent name.

VARIANTS **Carley**, **Carlee**, **Carli**, **Carleigh**, **Karli(e)**, **Karly**

★ Carly Simon (1945–   ), US singer-songwriter

Carmel *f*
Carmel is the Hebrew for 'orchard, garden' and is the name of an area near the city of Haifa. In the 12th century a monastery was founded there, from which the Carmelite monastic order developed. The monastery was dedicated to the Virgin Mary and Carmel became one of the many names taken from Marian titles (for example DOLORES, MERCEDES), in this case 'Our Lady of Carmel'.

PET FORMS **Carmelina**, **Carmelita** • VARIANTS **Carmella** *Italian, Spanish* **Carmela** *Spanish* **Carmelo** (m)

Carmen *f*
This was originally a Spanish respelling of CARMEL, apparently influenced by the Latin word *carmen* meaning 'song'. Nowadays, its strongest association is with the tempestuous Spanish

gypsy heroine of Bizet's 1875 opera *Carmen*, based on a short story by fellow Frenchman, Prosper Mérimée. The name is currently popular in Spain, and increasing in use in the UK. Carmen is also used frequently as a masculine name in the USA, where it probably represents a respelling of the regular Italian masculine *Carmine*, which is also found in the USA.

VARIANTS **Carmine, Carmina, Karmen**

Carol[1] *m*

As a masculine name, Carol can have several sources. It can share two sources with the feminine, either as a form of the Latin for CHARLES, *Carolus*, or as a use of the vocabulary word for children born around Christmas. Very occasionally it can be a form of the Irish name CEARBHALL, although this is usually anglicized as *Carroll*. Finally, it can be an Eastern European form of Charles, respelling either the Polish *Karol*, Czech *Karel* or Romanian Carol, all of which are also derived from *Carolus*. Carol first appears as a man's name in English in the 18th century, and was in regular use as a masculine name in the USA, sometimes in the form *Carroll* as if from the surname, throughout the first half of the 20th century.

VARIANT **Karol**

★ Sir Carol Reed (1906–76), English film director, born 30 December

Carol[2] *f*

The Latin form of the name Charles is *Carolus*, which can become *Carola* or Carol (used for both sexes, see above), in the feminine. Part of the name's history is as a short form of the earlier CAROLINE, as Carol does not seem to have come into general use until the later 19th century. It had its peak popularity in the mid-20th century. Since the name is also an unrelated vocabulary word associated

with Christmas, the name has also taken on a role of being given to those born around late December. As the name's use has waned, this role has become more important. Carol is one of the names which has been popular as a compound, particularly in forms combined with Anne perhaps because the resulting names have a similar sound to CAROLINE.

VARIANTS **Caryl, Karol** *French* **Carole**

Carolina *f*

This is a form of CAROLINE used in Italy, Spain and Portugal. Some uses in the USA may be from the two states called Carolina, which got their name from Charles II in whose reign they were settled.

Caroline *f*

The Latin masculine form of CHARLES, *Carolus*, appeared as a feminine form in French, Caroline, by the 8th century. It was found in England by the 17th century, but only came into general use with the arrival of King George II's wife, Caroline of Ansbach (1683–1737). The name was very prevalent in the mid-20th century and, although not currently one of the most popular names in the UK, it is well used in the USA and in a number of European countries.

PET FORMS **Caddy, Callie, Cari, Carol, Carrie, Carry** • VARIANTS **Carolyn, Karaline** *Dutch* **Carolein** *German* **Carolin, Karolina, Karoline** *Scandinavian* **Karolina, Karoline**

★ Lady Caroline Lamb (1785–1828), wife of Lord Melbourne and lover of Lord Byron
★ Caroline (1957–), princess of Monaco
☆ Carrie Bradshaw, principal character in the television series *Sex and the City*

Carolyn *f*

A 19th-century name, which can

be interpreted as either a variant of CAROLINE or a blend of CAROL and LYN.

VARIANTS **Carolynn, Karolyn(n)**

Caron[1] *f*

This is a Welsh name from *caru*, 'to love'. It is also used as a variant of KAREN.

VARIANT **Caronwen** (Caron + *(g)wen*, 'fair, white')

Caron[2] *m*

A Welsh saint's name and place name used as a first name.

Carreen *f*

This is one of the less common names introduced by Margaret Mitchell in her novel *Gone with the Wind*. In this case Carreen O'Hara, younger sister of SCARLETT, 'had been born Caroline Irene' but was generally known as Carreen. Some users may regard it as a variant of KAREN.

VARIANTS **Careen, Karine**

Carrick *m*

Mainly used in Ireland and Scotland, Carrick is a Celtic word for 'rock, crag' which has the same root and meaning as CRAIG.

VARIANT **Carrig**

Carrie *see* **Caroline**

Carroll *see* **Cearbhall**

Carson *mf*

This is a Scottish surname, of uncertain origin, used as a first name. It is mainly used as a masculine name, although its most famous bearer is female.

VARIANTS **Cason, Ka(r)son**

★ Carson McCullers (1917–67), US author

Carsten *see* **Christian**

Carter *m*

This is the surname, taken from the occupation, used as a first name. It has been popular in the USA for some years and is spreading to the UK, in particular to Northern Ireland where the role played in the peace process by former US president, Jimmy Carter, may have had an influence.

Carwen *f* **Carwyn** *m*

These are Welsh names formed from *câr*, 'love', and the word for 'fair, blessed'.

VARIANT **Caerwyn**

★ Carwyn James (1929–83), influential Welsh Rugby player and coach
★ Carwyn Jones (1967–), Leader of the House in the Welsh National Assembly

Cary *m*

This is a surname, based on a number of place names – most commonly derived from an Old Celtic river name – which is used as a first name. It has been recorded since the 19th century, but only became popular as a first name after it was given prominence by the film star Cary Grant. It is difficult to tell if feminine uses, found most often as *Carey* or even *Cari*, should be classed as forms of this name or as variants of *Carrie*, a pet form of CAROLINE.

VARIANT **Carey**

★ Cary Grant (1904–86), English-born Hollywood film star

Caryl *f*

This is usually a variant of CAROL, but among Welsh speakers can be a name formed from *câr*, 'love'.

Carys *f*

This is a Welsh name formed from *câr*, 'love', which has spread from Wales and now become popular elsewhere. There is some overlap between variants of this name and CHARIS, as both are pronounced in the same way.

VARIANTS **Cerys, Caris, Karys**

Casey *mf*

This name has a number of sources.

There is an Irish surname Casey, from an old name meaning 'descendant of *Chathasach*' (probably meaning 'the vigilant one'). It can be a pet form of names such as CASIMIR and CASSANDRA, or a nickname for someone with the initials KC. In the case of its most famous bearer, Luther 'Casey' Jones (1863–1900), it was a nickname derived from his home town, correctly spelt Cayce. He was a US engine driver who gave his life saving the lives of his passengers, and whose heroism was turned into a popular song. The name has been steadily popular in the USA for both sexes for a number of years, and has become increasingly widespread in the UK, particularly in Scotland. It has developed innumerable variant spellings, only a sample of which are listed here. In Kingston-upon-Hull the name has taken on special significance for Hull City football fans, following the inauguration of the KC Stadium, where the team plays, named after the Kingston Communications company who sponsored it. There are records of forms such as Kaycee being chosen with specific reference to the stadium by parents who support the team.

VARIANTS (MOSTLY FEMININE) **Casi(e)**, **Casee**, **Casy**, **Kas(e)y**, **Kaci(e)**, **Ka(y)cee**

Cashel *m*
The name of the town, which means 'castle, fort' in Irish, used as a first name.

☆ Cashel Byron, character in George Bernard Shaw's *The Admirable Bashville* (1901)

Casilda *f*
The meaning of this Spanish saint's name is not known, and may have been Arabic in origin. The 11th-century St Casilda is the patron saint of Toledo.

Casimir *m*
There have been various attempts to analyse this Polish name. The traditional meaning for it is 'proclamation of peace', but many modern commentators analyse it as being from *kazic*, 'to destroy', and *mir*, 'peace', although the elements *kazac*, 'to command, order', and *meri*, 'famous', have also been put forward. It was a traditional name in the Polish royal family.

PET FORMS **Casey**, **Kaz** • VARIANTS *German* **Kasimir** *Italian, Spanish, Portuguese* **Casimiro** *Polish* **Kazimierz**, **Kazimiera**, **Kazia** (fs) *Russian* **Kazimir**

★ St Casimir (1458–84), Polish prince and patron saint of Poland

Cason *see* **Carson**

Casper *m*
This is a form of the name JASPER and is traditionally the name of one of the Three Wise Men, or Magi, from the Christmas story. It means 'treasurer'. The name is currently popular in Scandinavia, and use seems to be increasing in the UK.

PET FORM **Cas** • VARIANTS *Dutch* **Caspar** *French* **Gaspard** *Italian* **Gaspare**, **Gasparo** *Polish* **Kacper**, **Kasper** *Scandinavian, Spanish* **Kaspar**

★ Caspar Weinberger (1917–2006), US politician

☆ *Casper the Friendly Ghost*, originally a 1930s cartoon, but best-known from the 1995 film adaptation

Caspian *m*
The introduction of this name comes from its use in C S Lewis's *Narnia* stories, where a character called Caspian first features in the book *Prince Caspian* (1951). The name appears to be the same as that of the Caspian Sea, which gets its name from the prehistoric Caspi people who once lived there.

☆ Caspian, villain in the television series *Highlander: the Series*, which ran 1992–98

Cass *m*

This can be a short form of any name beginning *Cas-*, but became established as an independent name in the USA. In some cases it can be a use of the surname originally given to a box- or case-maker. For feminine uses see under CASSANDRA.

★ 'Mama' Cass Elliot (1941–74), US singer with The Mamas and the Papas

Cassandra *f*

In the stories told about the Trojan War, Cassandra was a beautiful Trojan princess offered the gift of true prophecy by the god Apollo, in return for her love. However, when she refused to sleep with him he cursed her with the fate of never being believed. She was captured at the fall of Troy and later killed. In the medieval period these stories were transmitted via Roman versions, rather than the Greek versions more familiar today, and as the Romans considered themselves descendants of Trojans, their stories were always pro-Trojan. This may explain why, despite her unpleasant fate, the name had appeared in England by the beginning of the 13th century, when classical names were not common. It was sufficiently well used in the Middle Ages to be a source of surnames such as Cass and Cash. Use declined thereafter, but it continued to appear, if rarely, often in its short forms Cass or *Cassie* rather than its full form. Cassie is currently more popular in the UK than the full form, although Cassandra is the more popular in the USA.
PET FORMS **Cass(ie)**, **Casey**, **Sandra**, **Sandy** • VARIANT **Kas(s)andra**

★ Cassandra Austen (1773–1845), elder sister of the novelist Jane Austen

Cassia *see* Keziah

Cassidy *mf*

This is the Irish surname used as a first name. The surname comes from the Irish for 'curly-haired'. The name has been popular in the USA for a number of years, particularly as a female name.
PET FORM **Cass** • VARIANT **Kassidy**

Cassius *m*

This Roman family name is best-known as one of the main assassins of Julius Caesar. For Revolutionary Americans in the 18th century this made him something of a hero, and the name was sometimes given, developing the independent short form CASS. At the same time, there was a fashion in the Southern States of giving slaves names taken from the classics, which led to the name entering the stock of African-American names.

★ Cassius Clay (1942–), birth name of the US boxer who later changed his name to Muhammad Ali

Casy *see* Casey

Cathair, Cahir *m*

This is an Irish name, formed from *cath*, 'battle', and *vir*, 'man', thus indicating 'warrior'. Cahir is a respelling to reflect the pronunciation.
VARIANT **Cathaoir**

Cathal, Cahal

This Irish name is formed from *cath*, 'battle', and *val*, 'rule, strength', usually interpreted as meaning 'battle-mighty, strong in battle'. Cathal has been a quite popular name in Ireland in the 21st century, and was one of the most popular in the Middle Ages, being a name borne by many kings.

★ Cardinal Cahal Daly (1917–), former Primate of All Ireland

Cathan *m*

An Irish name formed from *cath*, 'battle', plus a pet ending. It may have started life as a pet form of a longer name. See also KANE.

Catherine f

This is the name of a virgin saint martyred, in Alexandria in AD 307, on the wheel to which she gave her name. The original Greek name, *Aikaterine*, became *Katerina* in Latin and *Catharina* in Late Latin. We do not know the meaning of the name, and attempts to find an origin lie behind the number of different forms the name takes. Some have linked the name to Greek *aikia*, 'wound, torture', with reference to her martyrdom; others have linked it to Greek *kathara*, 'pure', with reference to her virtue and virginity. The first of these explain forms such as *Katharine* and *Catharine*, while *kathara* accounts for the introduction of 'th' into the original form. The cult of St Catherine seems to have been brought back to Europe from the Middle East by the Crusaders, and subsequently became popular throughout Europe. Her name first appears in England in 1100. The 'C' and 'K' forms of the name have been in use in England since the Middle Ages. Currently in the UK the forms Catherine and Katherine are more or less equally popular; spellings with a medial 'a' are less common. Many regional varieties of the name are also popular.

PET FORMS **Cath(ie)**, **Cat(e)**, **Kate**, **Katie**, **Katy**, **Kay**, **Kat**, **Kathy**, **Kit**, **Kitty**, **Trina** • VARIANTS **Katheryn**, **Kathryn**, **Cathryn**, *Irish* **Caitlin**, **Kathleen**, **Riona** *Scots Gaelic* **Catriona** *Welsh* **Catrin**, **Cadi** *Dutch* **Katrien**, **Cato**, **Katelijn(e)** *German* **Kat(h)arine**, **Kat(h)arina**, **Katrine**, **Katinka** *Greek* **Ekaterini**, **Katina** *Italian* **Caterina** *Polish* **Katarzyna**, **Kasia** *Russian* **Yekaterina**, **Katerina**, **Ekaterina**, **Katia** *Scandinavian* **Katarina**, **Karen**

Cathleen see Kathleen

Cato m

This is a Roman family name, probably meaning 'wise'. There were two famous Catos in Roman history, both politicians, and known for their stern, unbending philosophies. Cato was occasionally chosen as a name in the 19th century, but as the world-view of the famous Romans has become less popular, the name has pretty well died out as a parental choice, except as a family tradition. As a feminine name Cato can be a pet form of CATHERINE.

Catriona f

This is a Gaelic form of CATHERINE, particularly associated with Scotland, but also traditional in Ireland. Its spread beyond Celtic areas was greatly helped by the success of Robert Louis Stevenson's 1893 novel *Catriona*. In Gaelic the accent is on *-tri-*, but English speakers usually accent it on the first and third syllables.

PET FORM **Tri(o)na** • VARIANTS **Catrina**, **Catrine**, **Katrina** *Scots Gaelic* **Catrìona**, **Caitìona**, **Cáitir** *Irish* **Caitriona**, **Riona**

Cavan m

This is the name of the Ulster county used as a first name. The place name means 'hollow'.

VARIANTS **Ke(e)van** *Irish* **Cabhan**

Caw see Cai

Cayetano see Gaetano

Cayo see Caeo

Ceallach see Kelly

Cearbhall m

This is a traditional Irish name, perhaps from *cearbh*, 'hacking', traditionally interpreted as 'fierce in battle'. It was a popular medieval name with royal associations. It is sometimes anglicized as *Carroll*, which reflects the pronunciation.

VARIANT **Cearul**

★ Cearbhall O Dalaigh (1911–78), president of Ireland

Cebrián see Cyprian

Cecil m

This is one of the aristocratic family names that became well used as a first name in the 19th century. The Cecil family first flourished under the Tudors, and have remained prominent in public life ever since. Their surname was Welsh, and came from *Seissylt*, a Welsh form of SEXTUS. Since the name appears to come from the earliest levels of Welsh, it may actually be a remnant of the Roman occupation. At the same time Cecil could also be used as an English form of the Latin name *Caecilius*, and thus function as a masculine form of CECILIA, which was popular at the same time as Cecil.

★ Cecil Rhodes (1853–1902), English-born South African statesman and founder of the Rhodes Scholarship

★ Cecil B De Mille (1881–1959), US film producer and director

Cecile, Cecily see Cicily

Cecilia f

Cecilia is the feminine form of an ancient Roman family name. The Roman bearers derived it from *caecus*, 'blind', and claimed it was a name given to a distinguished ancestor. However, the chances are that the name is Etruscan in origin, and since we known so little about that language, the true meaning of the name is lost. The name was popular in the Middle Ages in honour of St Cecilia, virgin martyr and patron saint of music. The name was introduced to England with the Norman Conquest, although Cecilia is the learned form of the name, which would usually have been CICILY (where other shortened forms are dealt with) or *Cecile*.

PET FORM **Celia** • VARIANTS *Irish* **Sheila**

French **Cécile** *German* **Cäcilia, Caecilia** *Polish* **Cecylia** *Russian* **Tsetsiliya**

Cedric m

This name was coined by Sir Walter Scott for the Anglo-Saxon thegn in his 1820 historical novel *Ivanhoe*. He seems to have misread the genuine Old English name *Cerdic* in his creation of the name. Cerdic is the traditional founder of the kingdom of Wessex. However there is another old name that could be the origin of Cedric, the Welsh *Cedrych*, formed from elements meaning 'pattern of bounty'. This would mean that, despite his learning, Scott could not (or chose not to) distinguish between Welsh and Saxon culture. *Ivanhoe* was a great success, and coincided with the beginning of the 19th-century revival of old names, so Cedric rapidly entered the stock of 19th-century names. It gained further prominence with the publication of Frances Hodgson Burnett's 1886 novel *Little Lord Fauntleroy*, where the eponymous hero was called Cedric Errol Fauntleroy. In the novel the boy is rather admirable, but the portrayal of him in film by Mary Pickford, complete with ringlets and velvet suit, weakened the reputation of the name and use went into steep decline. There was a mild revival of use in the USA between the 1970s and 1990s.

PET FORMS **Ced, Ric(k)** • VARIANT **Sedric(k)**
☆ Cedric Diggory is a character in the *Harry Potter* books

Cees see Cornelius

Ceferino see Zephyr

Ceilidh f

This vocabulary word for a social event involving music and dancing in Scotland and Ireland has recently been taken up as a girl's name in Scotland, perhaps originally as a variant of KEELEY.

It has the useful property of combining the same sounds as the name KAYLEIGH, with cultural nationalism. The word *ceilidh* comes from a Gaelic word for 'visit, visiting'.

VARIANT **Keilidh**

Ceinlys *f*
A Welsh name formed from the element *cain*, 'beautiful', and either *melys*, 'sweet', or *glwys*, 'fair'.

Ceinwen *f*
This Welsh name is formed from *cain*, 'beautiful' combined with *(g)wen*, 'fair, blessed'. However, since the plural *ceinion* can mean 'beauties' or 'gems' the name is sometimes interpreted as 'beautiful gems'. St Ceinwen, an 5th-century Welsh saint, gave her name to Keynsham near Bristol. The area is known for its fossil ammonites, which legend says are snakes miraculously turned to stone by the saint. Pronunciation of the name varies regionally, being broadly 'CAIN-wen' in North Wales and 'KINE-wen' in South Wales.

VARIANTS **Cain, Keyne**

Ceirios *f*
The Welsh for 'cherry' used as a first name.

Ceit *see* **Kate**

Celeste *f*
The Latin word *caelestis*, 'heavenly', was taken up by Christians as a first name. The masculine form, *Celestin*, has been chosen as a name by five popes, the first one in AD 422. *Caelestis* gives a feminine of Celeste, with a pet form *Celestina*.

VARIANTS **Celesta, Celine** *French* **Céleste, Célestine** *Italian, Spanish* **Celestina** *Polish* **Celestyna**

☆ Celeste is the wife of Babar in the *Babar the Elephant* children's books

Celia *f*
Celia is often treated as pet form of CECILIA, but it is also an independent name which probably comes from *caelum*, Latin for 'heaven'. It has been recorded in England from the 16th century, but did not become widely used until the 19th century.

MASCULINE *Italian, Spanish, Portuguese* **Celio**
• VARIANTS *French* **Célie** *German* **Silke**
★ Dame Celia Johnson (1908–82), English actress
★ Celia Imrie (1952–), English actress
☆ Celia is a character in Shakespeare's *As You Like It*

Celida *f*
This is a Spanish name, from the Spanish vocabulary word for a swallow.

Celina *see* **Selina**

Celine *f*
There is some debate as to the origin of this French name. It probably comes from the same root as CELIA, but can also be a short form of *Marceline* (see MARCEL), and a variant of CELESTE. In addition, the variant *Celina* means that there is some overlap with SELINA.

VARIANT **Ciline**

Celyn *m*
This is a Welsh name from the vocabulary word for 'holly'. The 'C' is hard.

Cephas *m*
This is the Aramaic word for 'rock', and was the original form of the nickname which became the name of the Apostle better known as PETER.

Ceredig *m*
This is the name of a Welsh prince who would have lived in the 5th century. He was one of the sons of Cunedda, ruler of the Gododdin in Scotland, who is said to have moved to Wales to protect the country against

Irish invaders. The Welsh district of Ceredigion is named after him.

Ceri *mf*

There have been several explanations of this Welsh name, but the majority of users regard it as coming from the word *caru*, meaning 'to love'. Despite not being recorded before the 1940s, it is popular in Wales. It is pronounced in the same way as KERRY. See also CERIDWEN.

PET FORM **Cerian** • VARIANT **Keri**

Ceridwen *f*

In Welsh tradition this is the name of the goddess of poetic inspiration, formed from the words *cerdd*, 'poetry', and *(g)wen*, 'white, fair, holy'. She was also the mother of the great poet TALIESIN. Although she appears in early stories, the name was not much used in the Middle Ages, but was revived in the 19th century.

PET FORMS **Ceri, Cari** • VARIANT **Cerridwyn**

Cerys *f*

This is a variant form of CARYS, 'love'. While Carys is mainly restricted to Wales, Cerys has now spread further and is well used in the rest of the UK.

★ Cery Matthews (1969–   ), Welsh singer-songwriter

Cesar, César, Cesare *see* Caesar

Chad *m*

This is the modern form of the name of an Old English saint, *Ceadda*. St Chad was a 7th-century bishop, famous for his humility and preaching. The cathedral at Lichfield, where he was bishop, is dedicated to him. The name was not uncommon in Saxon times but died out after the Norman Conquest except locally around his cathedral. Like so many other Old English names it was revived in the 19th century. During World War II the cartoonist Chat (George Chatterton) created a little cartoon figure known as Chad, showing the bald head, eyes, nose and fingers of a man peering over a wall, accompanied by the slogan 'Wot no ...?', which became a popular graffito for complaining about shortages. This figure was ubiquitous for many years after the end of the war, although as shortages ceased it came to be associated with the legend 'Kilroy was here'. It may be no coincidence that it was in 1945 that Chad first appeared in US names statistics, having been virtually unknown in the USA before. Thereafter, it became steadily more popular there, peaking in use in the 1970s. It is unclear where the name *Ceadda* came from. It may be that it was British in origin, and is based on the same element *cad*, 'battle', that is the source of so many early Welsh names.

★ Chad Varah (1911–2007), Anglican priest, founder of the Samaritans

Chaim *m* Chaya *f*

This is a variant of the name *Hyam*, from the Hebrew *hayyim*, 'life'. Use is restricted to Jewish communities. The 'Ch' is pronounced as a heavy 'h' sound. See also HYMAN.

VARIANT **Haim**

★ Chaim Herzog (1918–97), Israeli president

Chance *mf*

This name, mainly American and mainly masculine, would appear on the surface to be the vocabulary word, or the surname derived from it, used as a first name. However, the influence of *Chaunce*, the short form of the much older name CHAUNCEY should not be discounted.

VARIANT **Chanse**

Chandan *m* Chandana *f*

This Indian name comes from the Sanskrit *chandana*, 'sandalwood',

which plays an important role in
Hindu ceremonies.

PET FORM **Chandanika** (f) • VARIANT
Chandanpreet

Chandler *m*

This surname comes from the French
chandelier, 'candlemaker'. It began
to be used as a first name in the USA
in the 1980s, and peaked in 1999 in
the middle of the run of the television
series *Friends* (1994–2004) which had
brought the name to prominence. It is
occasionally used for girls.

Chandra *mf*

Chandra is the Sanskrit *candra*,
'moon', and is usually interpreted as
'shining'. It is the name of the Hindu
god of the moon.

VARIANTS **Chader, Candra**

★ Chandra Shekhar (1927–2007), prime
   minister of India
★ Chandra Wilson (1969–   ), US actress

Chandrakant *m* Chandrakanta *f*

Formed from the Sanskrit *candra*,
'moon', and *kanta*, 'beloved'. It not
only means 'beloved of the moon'
but is also the vocabulary word for
both moonstone and a type of night-
flowering water-lily. The feminine
form is a title for the wife of the moon,
CHANDRA.

Chanel, Chanelle *f*

This is the name of the famous French
perfume and fashion house used as a
first name. It first came into use in the
1970s among African Americans, and
has spread to the UK more recently.
The spelling Chanelle is currently
more common in the UK than the
original, although this has not been
the case in the USA. The change has
the advantage of making clear that
the name is not pronounced in the
same way as channel, and looks more
feminine, making the name conform
with others such as MICHELLE, which

has a similar final stress. It is worth
noting that the spelling Chanelle
is even found in France, where the
pronunciation is not in doubt.

VARIANT **Shanel(le)**

Chanoch *see* Enoch

Chantal, Chantelle *f*

This is the surname of St Jeanne de
Chantal (1572–1641) used as a first
name. In France, where children
were only meant to be given
names from an official list of those
permitted, the pressure of this name's
popularity forced it to be added to
the list. Unfortunately after a surge of
popularity in the 1950s Chantal came
to play much the same role in France
that SHARON and TRACY came to play
in the UK. The name was exported to
other countries and remains popular,
particularly in Scotland. The spelling
Chantelle is much more frequently
used than the original by English
speakers, probably for much the same
reasons as CHANEL became Chanelle.

VARIANTS **Chantale, Chantel, Shantal,
Shantel(le), Shontelle**

Chardonnay *f*

This is the name of the very popular
variety of wine, and the grape from
which it is made, used as a first
name. It has been in occasional use
for at least 20 years, but received a
brief boost in 2001–3 in the UK as a
result of the name being used in the
television series *Footballers' Wives*.

VARIANT **Chardonay**

Charis *f*

This name comes from the Greek
kharis, 'grace', and so is pronounced
in English with a 'k' sound, although
the French form is pronounced with a
'sh'. The form *Charissa* first appeared
in a literary context, having been used
by Spenser for a character in his poem
The Faerie Queene (1590–96), with

direct reference to the meaning of the name. Charis was introduced in the 17th century as one of the names based on Christian virtues that were used by the Puritans, who took the name to the USA. It is difficult to sort out the variant spellings of this name from the variants of CARISSA (see CARA) and CARYS.

VARIANTS **Caris(sa)**, **Karis(sa)** *French* **Charisse**

Charisma *f*
A rarely-used name, taken from the vocabulary word which shares a source with CHARIS.

★ Charisma Carpenter (1970–), US actress who won fame playing Cordelia in the television series *Buffy the Vampire Slayer*

Charity *f*
This is one of the Christian virtues which has been used as a first name since the 16th century. The word comes from the Latin *caritas* which can be translated as both 'love' and 'charity'. CHERRY was originally a pet form of Charity.

PET FORM **Chattie** • VARIANTS **Charita** *Portuguese* **Caridade** *Scandinavian* **Karita** *Spanish* **Caridad**

☆ Charity Pecksniff, character in Charles Dickens's novel *Martin Chuzzlewit* (1844)

Charlene *f*
A feminine form of the name CHARLES which came into use in the 1950s, mainly in the USA and Australia. As it is pronounced in the French manner with a 'sh' sound, it may be a reworking of the old French feminine form of Charles, *Charline*.

PET FORM **Charlie** • VARIANTS **Charleen**, **Sharlene**

☆ Charlene was the name of the character played by Kylie Minogue in the long-running Australian soap opera *Neighbours*

Charles *m*
This is the commonest form of a group of names, which includes CARL, that come from the old Germanic root *karl* meaning 'free man'. This was turned into a Latin form *Carolus*, which was then softened to Charles in French. The name became an important one in France, having been established early on as a royal name. It belonged to Charles Martel ('the Hammer'), founder of the Carolingian empire and, most famously, to his grandson Charles the Great or, in French, *Charlemagne*. The name was not that common among English speakers in the Middle Ages, but became much more widespread after the French-reared Mary, Queen of Scots named her son Charles James in 1566. He ascended the throne of Scotland as James VI, and then later became James I of England. His son and grandson became Charles I and II respectively, which firmly established the name among the common stock of names. Other languages have mostly kept the hard 'k' sound of the original form of the name, and these forms are listed under CARL. At the time of writing, the pet form CHARLIE is more popular as a given name than the more formal Charles in the UK, although the reverse is true in the USA.

PET FORMS **Charlie**, **Chaz**, **Chilla**, **Chuck** • VARIANTS **Carl** *Irish* **Séarlas** *Scots Gaelic* **Teàrlach** *Welsh* **Siarl**

Charlie *mf*
This is a pet form of CHARLES or CHARLOTTE, now used as an independent name. The more exotic spellings are mainly, but not entirely, restricted to women.

VARIANTS **Charl(e)y**, **Charlee**, **Charleigh**, **Charli**

Charlize

This variant on the name of CHARLES has been popularized by the South African actress Charlize Theron, who was named after her father Charles.

Charlotte *f*

In the Middle Ages in France it was very common to make a pet form of a name by adding *-ot* on the end. Thus CHARLES could become *Charlot*, and it was then only a small step to turn it feminine and create Charlotte. The name is used in a number of languages. Although it was in use in Britain from the 17th century, its popularity since the 18th century is due to German influence. In 1761 George III married Duchess Sophia Charlotte of Mecklenburg-Strelitz, and she remained as Queen Charlotte until 1818.

PET FORMS **Charlie, Lottie, Chattie, Tottie**
• VARIANTS **Sharlotte** *Irish* **Searlait**
★ Charlotte Brontë (1816–55), English novelist

Charlton *m*

This, like CARLTON, is a first name taken from a surname, taken in turn from a place name. Both names come from Old English *Ceorlatun*, 'settlement of the free peasants'. Charlton entered the general stock of names as a result of the fame of US actor Charlton Heston (b.1923 as John Charles Carten) who took his stage first name from his mother's maiden name, and his surname from his step-father.

Charmaine *f*

This name would appear to be a US coinage, created for a 1924 play *What Price Glory?* by Maxwell Anderson and Laurence Stallings. The play was made into a very successful silent film in 1926 and was remade in 1952. The name was used for the love interest in the film, a French innkeeper's daughter. This would explain the 'sh' pronunciation of the 'Ch'. The release of the film was accompanied by a song called 'Charmaine', written by Emo Rapee and Lew Pollack. This has since been recorded by many artists, helping to keep the name before the public.

VARIANT **Sharmaine**

Charmian *f*

Shakespeare took this name from his source, Lord North's translation of Plutarch, and used it for Cleopatra's witty maid in *Antony and Cleopatra*. It comes from the Greek *kharma*, and means 'little joy'. As it comes from Greek the initial 'Ch' would normally be pronounced with a hard 'k' sound, and this pronunciation is usually retained in performances of the play. However, elsewhere the 'Ch' is often softened.

Charulata *f*

Charulata is a Hindi name meaning 'beautiful vine'.

PET FORM **Charu**
☆ *Charulata* is the title of a famous 1964 Indian film, directed by Satyajit Ray, sometimes retitled *The Lonely Wife* in English-speaking countries

Chase *mf*

This name is mainly masculine and predominantly found in the USA, although it is beginning to be used in the UK. On the surface it appears to be simply the surname, originally given to a hunter, used as a first name. However, it may represent part of the trend for using high-status brand names, as the Chase Bank (called the Chase Manhattan until 2000, some 30 years after the name started to become popular) has associations with old money and power, with roots going back to the 18th century.

Chasity, Chastity *f*

In 1969 the singing duo Sonny

and Cher revived the Puritan name Chastity for their daughter, and by 1972 both Chastity and Chasity began to appear in US names statistics. Chastity disappeared 20 years later, but Chasity is still in use. Given these circumstances, the best explanation for the name Chasity that has been put forward is that it is a mishearing or misinterpretation of Chastity.

Chattie *see* **Charity, Charlotte**

Chauncey *m*

This is a Norman surname, from a village near Amiens, used as a first name mainly in the USA. The Chauncey family was prominent in the early days of New England and, as so often happened with the major families, prominent surnames which might otherwise disappear from the family branch through marriage came to be used as first names. The first Chauncey to make a major impact on the country was Charles Chauncey (1592–1672), 2nd president of Harvard.

PET FORMS **Chaunce, Chance** • VARIANT **Chancy**

Chaz *m*

Chas was originally a scribe's abbreviation of the name CHARLES, which has now been converted to a pet form and occasional independent name.

Che *m*

Che is a distinctively Argentine way of calling out 'Hey' to a person, and when the Argentine revolutionary Ernesto Guevara (1928–67) moved to Cuba this was given to him as a nickname. It was used as a given name for a few years in the 1970s and, with the recent publicity surrounding the anniversary of his death and a film about him, has made a minor comeback.

Chelle *see* **Michelle**

Chelo *see* **Consuelo**

Chelsea *f*

This place name, from the Old English meaning 'chalk landing-place', was in use by the 1950s, initially in Australia and the USA, but did not become really popular until the 1980s. It is assumed to be used with reference to a glamorous part of London, although there are numerous other places named Chelsea throughout the world.

VARIANTS **Chelsie, Chelsey, Chelci(e)**

★ Chelsea Clinton (1980–   ), daughter of Bill and Hillary Clinton. Her parents have said that she was named after the Joni Mitchell song 'Chelsea Morning'

Cher *f*

This is a name which has moved from being a short form of names such as CHERYL to an independent name, thanks to the success of the singer and actress Cher (b.1946, as Cherilyn Sarkisian LaPierre).

VARIANT **Chere**

Cherida *f*

This is a 20th-century name, introduced at a time when other *Cher-* names were popular. It may be an adaptation of the Spanish *querida*, 'darling', changed to fit with names such as CHERIE, or may be a blend of attractive elements such as those in CHERYL and PHYLLIDA (see PHYLLIS).

Cherie *f*

This is the French vocabulary word *chérie*, 'dear', used as a first name in the USA since the 1920s, but only making its mark in Britain 20 to 30 years later. Variants overlap with other names starting with a 'sh' sound plus 'r'.

PET FORM **Chere** • VARIANTS **Cheri, Cheree, Sherry**

★ Cherie Lunghi (1952–), English actress

★ Cherie Booth (1954–), English barrister, wife of former prime minister Tony Blair

☆ *Chéri* was the title of a 1920 novel by Colette, which may have had an influence on the growth of the name

Cherilyn *f*
A blend of CHERYL with the fashionable ending -*lyn*.

VARIANTS **Cheralyn, Sherilyn**

Cherise *f*
This is the Old French word for CHERRY, although this may be mere coincidence. The name may be a variant of *Cerise*, the modern French for Cherry; a blend of Cerise and any of the associated *Ch*- names, such as Cherie; or simply an invention using fashionable sounds.

Cherish *f*
This is a relatively recent introduction, a use of the vocabulary word which also expresses the parents' feelings about the child.

Cherith *f*
In the Bible Cherith, meaning 'stream bed', is the name of the brook where Elijah hid himself from King Ahab (1 Kings 17). As a name it is usually pronounced with a 'ch' sound, but historically should be pronounced with a 'k' sound; consequently it is sometimes spelt *Ker(r)ith* and found as a masculine name. Some, however, prefer to see the name as a modern blend of fashionable sounds.

VARIANTS **Cheryth, Kerith**

★ Cherith Baldry (1947–), English writer

★ Kerrith Brown (1962–), English judo expert

Cherokee *mf*
The Native American people known as the Cherokee probably got their name from the word in the Creek language *tciloki*, 'people of a different speech' (compare CHEYENNE, below). It is one of the less common names chosen as part of the current trend in the USA to use Native American groupings as first names.

Cherry *f*
Cherry can have three sources as a name. It can simply be the fruit used as a first name; it can be an adaptation of CHERIE; or it can be a pet form of the name CHARITY.

Cheryl *f*
Names beginning with the sound *Cher-* have been very popular for the last hundred or so years, as can be seen from the previous entries. There are too many coinages, many of them one-offs, to put in a book of this sort. Cheryl seems to have been one such coinage that first appeared around the 1920s, and was at its most popular between the 1940s and 80s. It is pronounced both with a 'ch' and a French 'sh' sound, and has numerous variants.

VARIANTS **Cheryll, Cher(r)el(le), Sherill, Sheryl, Shar(r)el(le)**

★ Cheryl Ladd (1951–), US actress

★ Sheryl Crow (1962–), US singer

Chesney *m*
This is a surname, originally from Le Quesney in France, used as a first name.

PET FORMS **Ches, Chet**

★ Chesney Allen (1893–1982), English comedian

★ Chesney 'Chet' Baker (1929–88), US jazz musician

Chester *m*
This is the place name, from the Latin *castra* meaning 'army camp, fort', used as a first name, possibly via the surname. It was well used in the USA

in the 19th and early 20th centuries, but not now particularly common.
PET FORM **Chet**
★ Chester Arthur (1830–86), 21st president of the USA
★ Chester 'Chet' Atkins (1924–2001), US country music guitarist

Chevonne *see* **Siobhan**

Cheyenne *mf*
The name Cheyenne comes from the Dakota language *shahiyena*, 'people whose language we cannot understand'. It is, along with DAKOTA, the most successful of the names based on Native American peoples, which began to be used in the 1980s. Because of its irregular pronunciation, spellings which reflect the pronunciation 'shy-anne' are common. The name is more usually feminine than masculine.
VARIANTS **Cheyanne, Cheyanna, Shiane, Shyann(e)**

Chiara *f*
This is the Italian form of the name CLARE, and was the given name of the follower of St Francis usually known in English as St Clare. There is, however, an overlap between the use of this name and of CIARA and KIARA. The 'Ch' is pronounced as 'k'.
PET FORM **Chiarina**

Chica *see* **Frances**

Chico *see* **Francis**

Chilla *m*
Australian pet form of CHARLES.

Chimène *see* **Ximena**

China *mf*
This is the name of the country used as a first name. The country got its name from the Qin or Ch'in dynasty that ruled it in the 3rd century BC.
VARIANTS **Chyna, Chynna** (fs)

★ China Miéville (1972–), English writer
★ Chynna Phillips (1968–), US actress and singer

Chip *see* **Christopher**

Chirsty *see* **Kirsten**

Chístìona *see* **Christina**

Chita *see* **Concepta**

Chloe *f*
Chloe has been one of the most popular names in the UK in recent years, as well as being widespread in Australia, the USA, Ireland and France. It comes from the Greek for 'green shoot' and was one of the epithets of the fertility goddess Demeter. It was frequently used as a girl's name in classical literature, a use that was taken up by English writers, but was also given Christian respectability by being the name of someone mentioned by St Paul. Chloe is increasingly hyphenated with other names, to form compounds such as *Chloe-Anne* or *Chloe-Louise*.
VARIANTS **Chloë, Cloe, Khloe** *French* **Chloé, Cloé**

Chloris *f*
This comes from *Khloris*, meaning 'green, greenish-yellow', which was the name of a nymph in Greek mythology who functioned as the goddess of spring. The name is thus the Greek equivalent of FLORA.
VARIANT **Cloris**
★ Cloris Leachman (1926–), US actress

Choire *f*
One of the rarer of the new names derived from vocabulary words associated with music, such as HARMONY and MELODY.

Chris *mf*
A short form of any name beginning

with *Chris-*, now used as an independent name.

VARIANT **Kris(s)**

★ Kriss Akabusi (1958–), English athlete and television presenter

Chrissie *f*

A pet form of CHRISTINE and other *Chris-*names, now used independently.

VARIANTS **Chrissy, Krissie, Krissy**

Christabel

A medieval name, formed by combining Christ with Latin *bel(la)*, 'fair, beautiful', to give a name meaning 'beautiful Christian'. In the Middle Ages it was mainly a literary name, but was in general use by the 17th century. Modern use is often with conscious reference to the suffragette Christabel Pankhurst (1880–1958).

VARIANTS **Christabella, Christabelle**

☆ 'Christabel' was the title of a 1797 poem by Coleridge, which led to a revival of the name

Christal *see* Crystal

Christelle *f*

A French name formed by replacing the ending of CHRISTINE with the common feminine ending *-elle*. The separate name CRYSTAL was no doubt influential.

VARIANT **Christel**

Christian *mf*

This is the vocabulary word, which has been used as a first name since the Middle Ages. Currently, it is mainly masculine in the UK, but in the past it has been well used for women.

PET FORMS **Chris, Christie, Christy**

• VARIANTS **Christiana, Christianna, Christianne, Cristian** *Scots Gaelic* **Crìsdean** *Dutch* **Christiaan, Carsten** *French* **Chrétien** (ms), **Christiane, Chrétienne** (fs) *German* **Karsten** (ms), **Christiane, Christa** (fs) *Italian, Spanish, Portuguese* **Cristiano, Cristiana** *Polish*

Krysztian *Scandinavian* **Christer, Kristen, Stian**

Christina *f*

This is the English form of the Latin *Christiana*, a form of the name CHRISTIAN. It came into use in the 17th century, and was well used in the 20th.

PET FORM **Tina** • VARIANTS **Krystina, Kryssa** *Irish* **Chístìona** *Scots Gaelic* **Cairistìona, Cairstìne** *Dutch, German* **Kristin, Kristina** *Italian, Spanish, Portuguese* **Cristina** *Polish* **Kr(z)ystyna** *Russian* **Kristina** *Scandinavian* **Kristina, Kerstin, Kirsten**

★ Christina Aguilera (1980–), US singer

★ Christina Ricci (1980–), US actress

Christine *f*

This was originally a French form of CHRISTINA which has been part of the general stock of English names since the 19th century.

PET FORMS **Chris, Chrissie, Christy, Kirsty, Christa** • VARIANTS **Christen, Kristen, Kristin, Kristine** *Welsh* **Crystin**

Christopher *m*

This name is formed from Greek elements *Khristos*, 'Christ', and *pherein*, 'carry'. The legend of St Christopher tells of a gigantic man who, having converted to Christianity, used to carry people across a river. One night he carried a child on his back, but felt as if it was the whole weight of the world on his shoulders. He was later told that it was the Christ child who had weighed him down so, and he became the patron saint of travellers. St Christopher's popularity made the name one of the core names in the European tradition.

PET FORMS **Chris, Crystal, Kester, Kit, Chip, Kip, Topher** • VARIANTS **Kristopher** *Irish* **Criostóir** *Dutch* **Christofoor** *French* **Christophe** *German* **Christoph** *Italian* **Cristoforo** *Polish* **Krzysztof, Krzyś**

Portuguese **Cristóvão** *Scandinavian* **Christoffer, Kristoffer** *Spanish* **Cristóbal**

Christy *mf*
This is a short form of any name created from the name *Christ*. In particular, it is a pet form of CHRISTOPHER in Ireland and Scotland, where it can also be given as an independent name for both sexes.
VARIANT **Christie**

Chrystal *see* Crystal

Chucho *see* Jesus

Chuck *m*
A pet form of the name CHARLES, particularly in the USA. It is now used as an independent name.
★ Chuck Jones (1912–2002), US animator and director of many of the Warner Brothers classic cartoons
★ Chuck Yeager (1923–), US test pilot, first man to break the sound barrier

Chulda *see* Hulda

Chus, Chuy *see* Jesus

Chyna, Chynna *see* China

Cian *m* Ciannait *f*
This is an Irish name meaning 'ancient, enduring'. In the past the masculine could be anglicized as CAIN, reflecting one pronunciation (others being 'KEE-an' and 'keen', with the feminine form adding 'it' on the end). The name is currently among the most popular Irish names in Ireland. It is the source of KEAN.
VARIANTS **Kian, Kean, Keane**
★ Cian Mac Muad (d.1014), son-in-law of Brian Boru, who died leading the troops from Desmond in the Battle of Clontarf against the Dublin Vikings

Ciara *f*
This is a modern feminine form of CIARAN. All 'c's are pronounced hard in Irish, and the name is often respelt with a 'K' to make this clear, either as *Kiera* or, more recently, the form KEIRA which has become dominant and now almost counts as an independent name. Ciara is still the norm in Ireland, as one would expect, and is well represented there, but otherwise the 'K' forms are most common. The water is further muddied by the existence of KYRA and KIARA, and the fact that use of CHIARA sometimes overlaps. Furthermore, in the USA Ciara is sometimes pronounced with a soft 'c', in which case it represents either a respelling of SIERRA or a use of the name of a brand of perfume (compare CHANEL) pronounced in the same way.
VARIANTS **Kiera, Keira**

Ciaran *m*
This is an old Irish name formed from *ciar* meaning 'black'. It was the name of at least 26 early saints, including the one who founded the beautiful monastery at Clonmacnoise. As with CIARA, the 'c' is hard and this has led to forms with a 'K' spelling being more popular outside Ireland. The name has been widespread in recent decades. *Ciar* can also be found as an Irish masculine name.
VARIANTS **Ciarán, Cieran, Kieran, Kieren, Kieron, Keiran**

Cicily *f*
From the Middle Ages onwards, this was the normal form of the name CECILIA, with *Cecily* being a later, hypercorrect form.
PET FORMS **Cis(sie), Cissy, Sis(sie), Sissy**
• VARIANTS **Sisley, Cecile, Cecily**
★ Dame Cicely Courtneidge (1893–1980), English actress
★ Cicely Mary Barker (1895–1973), English illustrator, best-known for the children's *Flower Fairy* books
☆ Cecily Cardew in Oscar Wilde's 1895 play *The Importance of Being Earnest*

Cieran *see* **Ciaran**

Ciline *see* **Celine**

Cilla *f*
A short form of PRISCILLA, now used as
an independent name.
★ Cilla Black (1943–), English singer
and television presenter

Cillian *m*
This is the name of a number of
Irish saints, two of whom made
considerable contributions to the
conversion of the Franks to Christianity.
Like all Irish names beginning *Ci-* the *c*
is hard. The name is popular in Ireland,
as well as in France where it also
appears as *Kyl(l)ian*.
VARIANTS **Kil(l)ian**, **Kyl(l)ian**
★ Cillian Murphy (1976–), Irish actor

Cimmie *see* **Cynthia**

Cindy *f*
Originally a short form of names such
as CYNTHIA and LUCINDA, this is now used
as an independent name.
VARIANTS **Cindi**, **Sindy**
★ Cindy Crawford (1966–), US model
★ Cindi Lauper (1953–), US singer
☆ Sindy, British doll launched in 1963

Cinead *see* **Kenneth**

Cinnamon *f*
A rare use of the spice as a first name.
Although really a 20th-century name,
it has been recorded as a masculine
slave name in the 18th century. The
French also use their equivalent,
Cannelle, as a first name.

Cinneidigh *see* **Kennedy**

Cintia, **Cinzia** *see* **Cynthia**

Ciorstag, **Ciorstaidh** *see* **Kirsten**

Cipriano *see* **Cyprian**

Circe *f*
This is the name of the nymph-

witch who transforms Odysseus's
companions into pigs and then
keeps him on her beautiful island,
as her lover, for ten years. The name
may come from the Greek for 'bird'.
Despite the fact that the name has hard
'k' sounds in Greek, they are always
pronounced with 's' sounds in English.
The name is rare, but is probably used
as a first name because it has come to
have associations with a 'bewitching'
woman.

Cirillo *see* **Cyril**

Cis, **Cissie**, **Cissy** *see* **Cicily**

Citlali *mf*
This is the word for 'star' in the
Nahuatl (Aztec) language and is
growing in popularity as a first name
in Mexico and among Mexican-
Americans. It is currently more usually
given to girls.
VARIANT **Xitlalli**

Claire *see* **Clare**

Clancy *mf*
This is an Irish surname used as a first
name, although sometimes it is a pet
form of CLARENCE. The surname appears
in Irish as *Mac Fhlannchaidh* and
means 'son of the red warrior'.
VARIANT **Clancey**
☆ Chief Clancy Wiggum from the
television cartoon *The Simpsons*

Clara, **Clare**, **Claire** *f*
The Latin adjective *Clara* means
'bright, famous'. It came to England
with the Normans, in the French form
Claire, although it usually appeared
in the English form, Clare. The French
form was reintroduced in the 19th
century. The name became widespread
in honour of St Clare (CHIARA), an Italian
associate of St Francis of Assisi in the
13th century, who founded the order
of the Poor Clares.
VARIANTS **Clair**, **Klara**

Clarence *m*

In the 14th century, the third son of King Edward III, Lionel, was created Duke of Clarence in honour of his lucrative marriage to an heiress to large estates in Clare, Suffolk. The form of the name was reached via his Latin title, *dux Clarensis*, the ending added to Clare indicated that he was 'Duke *of* Clare'. The Suffolk place name has no connection with the personal name CLARE, but comes from a Celtic river name. This title became a traditional one for younger sons of the royal family. It has been claimed that the name was adopted in the 19th century because of the popularity of the elder son of Edward VII, who was made Duke of Clarence in 1890 only to die two years later, but the name was already among the most popular masculine names in the USA well before this date.

PET FORMS **Clarrie, Clancy**

★ Clarence Birdseye (1886–1956), US businessman and pioneer of frozen food

☆ Clarence Harvey is the hero of Maria Edgeworth's 1801 novel *Belinda*. This may have introduced the name

Claribel *f*

A name formed from the same Latin adjective *clara*, 'bright, famous', that gives CLARE, combined with the ending *bel*, 'beautiful'. In English it has strong literary associations, having been used first by Spenser in *The Faerie Queen*, then in passing by Shakespeare in *The Tempest*, and in a rather overblown poem by Tennyson published in 1830. It may be the latter that gave the name a certain currency on both sides of the Atlantic in the late 19th and early 20th centuries.

☆ Claribel Cow was an early Walt Disney character

Clarice *f*

This is the English form of the French *Clarisse*, in turn a form of CLARISSA. It is a name found in several medieval romances, was in use in the 12th century in England and was revived in the 19th century. While never particularly common, it was in regular use in the USA until the mid-20th century.

VARIANT **Claris**

★ Clarice Cliff (1899–1972), English ceramic designer

☆ Clarice Starling, a principal character in Thomas Harris's novel *The Silence of the Lambs* (1988)

Clarinda *f*

This is another elaboration of CLARE, this time with the intensifying suffix *-inda* found in a number of other literary names. It appears, like CLARIBEL, to have first been used by Spenser in *The Faerie Queen* (1596). It was taken up as a literary name, and enjoyed some use in real life in the 18th and 19th centuries.

☆ Clarinda was used by Robert Burns (1759–96) for poems he addressed to Agnes MacLehose

Clarissa *f*

In Latin Clarissa means 'most bright, most famous'. The name is occasionally found in the Middle Ages, but really made its mark when Samuel Richardson published one of the first major novels, with the title *Clarissa, or the History of a Young Lady*, in 1747.

PET FORMS **Clarrie, Clarry, Claris** • VARIANTS **Clarice** *French* **Clarisse** (see CLARICE) *Spanish* **Clarisa, Clariz(z)a**

Clark *m*

This is a surname meaning 'clerk', originally referring to someone in holy orders, used as a first name. It is found primarily in the USA.

VARIANT **Clarke**

★ Clark Gable (1901–60), US actor
☆ Clark Kent is the alter ego of Superman

Clarrie, Clarry see Clarissa

Claude m
This is the French form of the Roman name *Claudius* (see CLAUDIA). Claudius was a Roman family name, interpreted as coming from the Latin word *claudus*, 'lame'. In France it was used for both sexes, although the feminine is now rare, but it is usually restricted to males by English speakers. The French pronunciation has a vowel sound as in the English 'owed', but in English the pronunciation sounds like 'or'.
VARIANTS **Claud** *Italian, Spanish* **Claudio**
★ Claude Rains (1889–1967), English actor
★ Claude Monet (1840–1926), French Impressionist painter

Claudette f
A French feminine form of *Claudius*, introduced to the English-speaking world through the success of the French-born Hollywood actress Claudette Colbert (1903–96).

Claudia f
This is the most used of the feminine forms of CLAUDE. Because it is mentioned in the New Testament it was available to those looking for religious names, which were not those of saints, after the Reformation. It has been recorded from the 16th century.
PET FORM **Claudie** • VARIANTS *French* **Claudie** *Polish* **Klaudia** *Russian* **Klavdiya, Klava**
★ Claudia Schiffer (1970–   ), German model
★ Claudia Cardinale (1938–   ), Italian actress

Claudine f
This is an old French pet form of CLAUDE. Use by English speakers is usually with conscious reference to the *Claudine* novels of the French author Collette (1875–1954).

Claus m
Originally a Germanic shortening of various forms of the name NICHOLAS, this is now used as an independent name. Users generally pronounce it 'klows', rather than the 'claws' sound used by English speakers in the name Santa Claus (originally St Nicholas).
VARIANTS *Dutch* **Klaas** *German* **Klaus, Klaas** *Russian* **Kolya** *Scandinavian* **Claes**

Clay m
The surname, originally from a clayey place, used as a first name. It is also a short form of CLAYTON. The name appears in the 19th century, and some uses are thought to be in honour of the popular US statesman Henry Clay (1777–1852).
★ Clay Allison (1840–87), US gunfighter
★ Clay Jones (1923–96), Welsh horticulturist and regular broadcaster on radio programme *Gardeners' Question Time*

Clayton m
This is a surname from a common place name, indicating a settlement built of clay. Although mainly found in the USA, it is beginning to make its presence felt elsewhere.
PET FORM **Clay**
★ Clayton Moore (1914–99), US actor who played the Lone Ranger in the US television series
☆ Clayton Farlow, oil baron in the 1978–91 television series *Dallas*

Clea f
A name introduced to English speakers by Lawrence Durrell in his novels *The Alexandria Quartet*, for the character of Clea Montis, most particularly in the volume written from her point of view, *Clea* (1958). It is a contraction of CLEOPATRA, although it can also be identified with an ancient name based

on the same Greek element *klea*, 'glory', as is found in Cleopatra.
VARIANTS *French* **Cléa** *Italian* **Clèa**
★ Clea DuVall (1977–   ), US actress

Clearie *m*
An Irish surname, meaning 'scholar, minstrel', which has now come into use as a first name in Ireland.
VARIANT **Clearay**

Cledwyn
This is the name of a river in Conwy, Wales, used as a first name. It is made up of the elements *caled*, 'hard, rough', and *(g)wyn*, 'white, blessed'.
PET FORM **Cled**
★ Cledwyn Hughes, Baron Cledwyn of Penrhos (1916–2001), Welsh Labour politician

Clelia *f*
This is the modern Italian form of the Latin name *Cloelia*. While most of the heroines of Roman history are rather uninspiring by modern standards, being chiefly praised for domestic or sexual virtues, Cloelia was rather more feisty than average, according to her legend. Having been given by the Romans to the Etruscans as a hostage, she escaped by swimming the River Tiber back to Rome. She was returned, but out of admiration the Etruscans released her, along with other hostages.
VARIANT **Cloelia**
★ St Clelia Barbieri (1847–70), Italian, patron saint of those mocked for their faith

Clem, Clemmie *mf*
These are used as short forms for any of the following names beginning *Clem-*.
VARIANT **Clemmy**

Clematis *f*
This is one of the more unusual modern flower names. The British

stress the plant name on the first syllable, the Americans on the second. The name for this pretty climbing plant comes ultimately from the Greek for 'vine shoot'.

Clemence, Clemency *f*
Clemence was the medieval form of the name derived from the Latin *Clementia*, both from the root that gives us the vocabulary word clemency. Clemence has been quite popular in France in recent years, while there was something of a vogue for Clemency in the 1980s and 90s.
VARIANTS **Clementia**, **Cleamence** *French* **Clémence**
★ Clémence was the pseudonym used by Louise Michel (1830–1905), a French anarchist active in the Paris Commune, who had two battalions of the International Brigades fighting in the Spanish Civil War named after her
★ Clemence Dane (1888–1965), English novelist and playwright
★ Clemency Burton-Hill (1981–   ), English actress and journalist

Clement *m*
From the Latin *clemens*, 'merciful', this was an early Christian name, being adopted by the third pope and by 13 of his successors, as well as being the name of several early saints. The name was popular in the Middle Ages and was revived in the 19th century.
VARIANTS *Scots Gaelic* **Cliamain** *French* **Clément** *German* **Clemens**, **Klemens** *Italian* **Clemente** *Russian* **Kliment** *Scandinavian* **Klemens**
★ Clement 'Clem' Atlee (1883–1967), English Labour statesman and prime minister
★ Sir Clement Freud (1924–   ), British chef, politician and broadcaster, born in Berlin
☆ Sir Clement Willoughby in Fanny Burney's novel, *Evelina* (1778), was a

use that may have helped the name's revival

Clementine *f*

Clementine or *Clementina* was the name of the 11,000 virgins supposedly martyred with St URSULA in the 4th century AD. However, the name did not really make its mark until the 19th century. The relationship between the fruit and the name is peripheral, the fruit getting its name from Father Clement Rodier, who bred it in 1902.

VARIANTS **Clementina** *Polish* **Klementyna**

★ Clementine 'Clemmie' Churchill (1885–1977), wife of Sir Winston Churchill

☆ 'Oh My Darling Clementine', song of disputed authorship, which dates from the 1880s

Cleo *f*

Pet form of CLEOPATRA, now used as an independent name. See also CLIO, CLEA.

★ Dame Cleo Laine (1927–), English jazz singer and actress

Cleona *see* **Cliona**

Cleone *f*

This would appear to be a feminine form of the Greek masculine name *Cleon*, from *kleos* meaning 'glory'. Racine used the name for Hermione's confidante in his 1667 play *Andromache*. It was used in English by the now obscure playwright, Robert Dodsley, for his enormously successful tragedy, *Cleone*, in 1758. Being Greek, it is pronounced with three syllables, the final 'e' being sounded.

Cleopatra *f*

The Greek name *Kleopatra*, formed from *kleos*, 'glory', and *patros*, 'of the father', was a traditional one in the Ptolemaic royal family, just as BERENICE was. This family was Greek in origin, the first Ptolemy having been one of the generals in the army of Alexander the Great (who himself had a sister called Cleopatra). Ptolemy managed to take over as King of Egypt when Alexander's empire was broken up after his death. The most famous bearer of the name Cleopatra was the last Queen of Egypt, who ruled before the country was absorbed by the expanding Roman Empire. Her fame for beauty, seduction and political skill made the name difficult to use, but it is now becoming more common, particularly with those wishing to mark their African roots. It is still, however, more likely to be found in fiction, and when used for real people it is usually shortened to CLEO.

PET FORMS **Cleo, Clea**

★ Cleopatra Stratan (2002–), Moldovan child singer

☆ *Cleopatra Jones*, a 1973 film

Cleto *see* **Anacletus**

Cletus *m*

Kleitos, probably from *kleos* meaning 'glory', was the name of one of Alexander the Great's generals. The name is now rare, although it was quietly but steadily used in the USA from the 19th century until the middle of the 20th. Cletus can also be used as a shortening of ANACLETUS.

☆ Cletus is the name of the 'slack-jawed yokel' in the cartoon television series *The Simpsons*

Cliamain *see* **Clement**

Clifford *m*

This is a surname, derived from a place name indicating a ford by a cliff, used as a first name. It has been recorded sporadically from the 17th century, but really made its mark in the 19th. The Clifford family have been prominent in English history since the 13th century, and theirs was the name of the former earls of Cumberland. Thus the rise in popularity of the name belongs with the group of 19th-century names based on aristocratic surnames.

PET FORM **Cliff** • VARIANT **Clifton** 'cliff settlement'

★ Sir Cliff Richard (1940–), English pop singer
★ Cliff Michelmore (1919–), English broadcaster

Clint, Clinton *m*

This is another place name turned surname turned first name, but this time by a rather devious route. The River Glyme in Oxfordshire gave its name to the village of Glympton. The French-speaking Norman lords, who came to hold the land, had difficulty pronouncing the uncouth English consonant clusters of the place they took their surname from, and so it changed to Clinton. The Clinton family grew in power and came to be dukes of Newcastle. However, this is not one of the many aristocratic surnames turned first name. In fact the name, which is primarily American, is used with reference to the Clinton family in the USA. The US Clintons produced many prominent people, including George Clinton (1739–1812) who was instrumental in the fight for American independence, and became vice-president of the new country.

★ Clint Eastwood (1930–), US film actor and director

Clio *f*

This is the name of the Greek Muse of History, spelt *Kleio* in Greek. Her name is probably from *kleos*, 'glory, praise', for it is her function to record the deeds of outstanding people. It thus shares a root with CLEO and is sometimes used as a respelling of that name. However, when used of the Muse the name is said with the 'i' pronounced as in the word 'my'. Clio is also found as a shortening of CLIONA.

Cliona *f*

An Irish first name from mythology, where Cliona is a goddess of beauty who falls in love with a mortal. They run away together, but the god of the sea sends a great wave that pulls Cliona back to the realm of the gods. In later tradition Cliona becomes a fairy queen, honoured at Carriag Cliodhna ('Cliona's Rock'), Cork. The name is pronounced with the stress on the first syllable, 'KLEE-o-na'.

PET FORM **Clio** • VARIANTS **Clíodhna, Cleona**

Clive *m*

This is a surname which comes from the Old English word for 'cliff'. It seems to have become a first name in honour of Robert Clive (1725–74), 'Clive of India', perhaps inspired by the name's use for the character of Clive Newcome in Thackeray's novel *The Newcomes* (1853–55).

VARIANT **Clyve**

★ Clive James (1939–), Australian writer and broadcaster
★ Clive Anderson (1952–), English broadcaster

Clodagh *f*

This is the name of the Tipperary river, also called the Clody, which was the name of the pagan goddess of the river. It seems to have been first used in 1879 by the Marquis of Waterford, who named one of his daughters after the local river, and has since entered the stock of Irish names. The 'gh' at the end of the name is silent.

★ Clodagh Rogers (1947–), Northern Irish singer
☆ Sister Clodagh was the Mother Superior in the 1946 film *Black Narcissus*

Cloe, Cloé *see* Chloe

Cloelia *see* Clelia

Cloris *see* Chloris

Clornélie *see* **Cornelia**

Clothilde *f*
This is the Old French form of the
Germanic name *Hlothilda* formed
from *hlod*, 'fame', and *hilde*, 'battle'.
It entered the stock of French names
thanks to St Clothilde (c.470–545),
who married Clovis, King of the
Franks, and converted him to
Christianity. There has been a slight
revival of use of the name in France,
where the middle 'th' is pronounced
as a 't'.
VARIANT **Clotilde**

Cloudy *f*
An unusual name, based on the
vocabulary word (compare STORM,
STORMY).

Clove *f*
An uncommon name, from the spice
(compare CINNAMON). The spice gets
its name from the French word *clou*,
'nail', because of the shape of the
bud and stem that are used, which
resembles an old-fashioned handmade
nail. Clove may also function as a
short form of CLOVER.

Clover *f*
The name of the flower used as a
first name. It has been used since the
19th century, and there was a certain
vogue for the name in the late 1960s
and early 70s. It is impossible to tell if
Clova should be regarded as a variant
of this or a feminine of CLOVIS.
☆ Clover Carr was the younger sister
in Susan Coolidge's *Katie* books,
published 1870–90

Clovis *m*
This is the Germanic name *Chlodowic*,
made up of *hlod*, 'glory', and *wic*,
'battle'. It became LOUIS in most cases,
but the Merovingian king of the Franks
who converted to Christianity under
the influence of his queen, CLOTHILDE,

whose name has the same meaning,
is always referred to as Clovis. Clovis
never had the popularity of Louis, but
has recently been revived in France as
part of a fashion for medieval names.
☆ Clovis is one of the regular narrators in
the short stories of 'Saki' (H H Munro,
1870–1916)

Cluny *f*
The place name, found in both France
and Scotland, used as a first name. It
is rare.

Clyde *m*
The name of the Scottish river, used
as a first name. It has been in use
since the 19th century, and although
found in Scotland, has been most
common in the USA. The river name
is very ancient, predating the Romans,
and is thought to mean 'the washer',
representing the name of a local
goddess.
★ Clyde Barrow (1909–34), US thief and
murderer of Bonnie and Clyde fame

Clyve *see* **Clive**

Cnochúr *see* **Connor**

Coan *see* **Comgan**

Cobain *m*
This is the surname, internationally
known as that of the US singer Kurt
Cobain who committed suicide in
1994, which has now come to be used
as a first name.
VARIANT **Coben**

Cobi *mf*
This is a Dutch pet form of JACOB.
However, it may be that its recent
appearance among English speakers
represents a respelling of the
fashionable name KOBE.
VARIANT **Coby**

Coco *f*
Although it is possible to find it used

as a pet form of names beginning *Co-*, this fashionable name is used with reference to Gabrielle 'Coco' CHANEL (1883–1971), who got her nickname from a song she sang when she worked in cabaret.

★ Coco Rocha (1988–   ), Canadian supermodel

Cody *mf*
This is an Irish surname, from various sources, used as a first name. It has been popular in the USA for some time, is well used in Australia and is becoming popular in the UK. The variants are mainly, but not exclusively, feminine.

VARIANTS **Codi(e)**, **Codee**, **Kody**, **Kodi(e)**, **Kodee**

Colby *mf*
This is a surname, originally from an English place name meaning 'Koli's settlement', *Koli* being a nickname for someone dark, from the Norse word for charcoal. Despite being the name of a type of cheese in the USA, it has been used since the late 1960s, mainly as a boy's name, and peaked at the turn of the millennium. It grew in popularity in the 1980s when there was a television soap opera called *The Colbys*.

VARIANTS **Kolby**, **Colbie**

Cole *m*
This is a surname used as a first name. The surname is recorded from the Middle Ages and is either from a pet form of NICHOLAS, or else from a nickname for someone dark, from the Old English word *col*, 'charcoal'. The name has been popular in the USA for some years, and is well used in Scotland. Perhaps this is because the Cole of the nursery rhyme 'Old King Cole' has been identified with a man called *Coel Hen* ('Old Coel') who was

a king in Scotland in the 4th century AD. See also COMGALL.

VARIANT **Kole**

★ Cole Porter (1891–1964), US composer and lyricist, who did much to establish the name. He was given his mother's maiden name

Colette *f*
In the Middle Ages the name NICHOLAS could be shortened to *Nichol*. This was given a feminine ending to give *Nicholette*, which in turn was shortened to Colette. It was a common name in England in the Middle Ages, but died out some time in the 17th century. However, it survived in France where it also became a surname, and was taken as an ambiguous pen name by the writer Colette (Sidonie-Gabrielle Colette, 1873–1954). Modern use among English speakers is largely due to her fame.

VARIANT **Collette**

Colin *m*
This is a name with several sources. The commonest is as a double diminutive of NICHOLAS. *Col* was used as a pet form of NICHOLAS in the Middle Ages, and it in turn acquired the pet ending *-in*, giving Colin. This was a common name in the Middle Ages, but then died out. It was reintroduced in the 19th century, probably from Scotland. There Colin had become the anglicized form of the name *Cailean*. This is a medieval name which also has two interpretations. One is from a word meaning 'pup, whelp', the other is from the name of St COLUMBA combined with an ending which indicates devotion to the saint. There is a further Irish name *Coilin*, interpreted as deriving from *coll*, 'chief', which is also anglicized as Colin.

FEMININES **Colinette**, **Colina** • PET FORM **Coll**

Coll *m*

As well as being a pet form of COLIN, this can be a Scots Gaelic name meaning 'high, exalted'.

Colleen *f*

From the Irish word *cailin*, meaning 'girl, wench', this was originally used as a first name in the 19th century by people of Irish extraction in the USA and Australia, where the name became popular in the 1940s. It took several more decades before the name appeared in Ireland itself.

VARIANTS **Coleen, Coline**

★ Colleen Moore (1900–88), US silent film star whose role in the shocking 1923 film *Flaming Youth* brought the name to public attention

★ Colleen McCullough (1937–), Australian novelist

Collen *m*

A Welsh name from the Welsh word for 'hazel'. It is also the name of a saint, after whom the town of Llangollen is named.

Colm *m*

This is the Irish form of CALLUM, from the name of the great Irish saint COLUMBA.

VARIANTS **Colum, Colom**

Colton *m*

A surname meaning 'Koli's settlement' (see COLBY) which has been well used in the USA.

PET FORM **Colt** • VARIANTS **Coleton, Kolton**

Columba *m* Columbine *f*

Columba comes from the Latin for 'dove', that symbol not only of peace but also, to Christians, of the Holy Spirit. Consequently, it was widely used as a first name by early Christians, the most famous of whom was the Irish saint, Columba, source of the names CALLUM and MALCOLM. The saint was a 6th-century missionary to Scotland who founded the Abbey on Iona, and who was widely revered in Ireland and Scotland. The Italians developed a pet form of this name into the feminine *Columbina*, which became *Columbine* in English. This 'little dove' became the standard name for the girl loved by Harlequin in the *Commedia dell'Arte*. Modern use for English speakers, though, probably comes directly from the flower name. The plant got its name because the flowers, before modern breeders developed double forms or ones with the flowers facing upwards, when seen from above looked like a cluster of little doves, with the spurs forming the head and neck and the bell of the petal the body.

VARIANTS *Irish* **Colmán, Coleman** *French* **Colombe** (f), **Colombain** (m) *German* **Kol(o)man** (m) *Italian* **Colombano, Colombo** (ms), **Colombina** (f)

Colwyn *m*

The river and place name in North Wales used as a first name. The river name probably means 'whelp, puppy'.

Côme *see* **Cosmo**

Comfort *f*

One of the virtue names introduced at the Reformation, when it was most common. It is still occasionally used.

Comgall *m*

An old Irish name formed from elements *comh*, 'together', and *gall*, 'hostage, pledge'. St Comgall (c.515–602) was a prominent churchman, who followed COLUMBA to Iona. The name is pronounced 'KO-gal'.

VARIANTS **Comhgall, Comgal, Comghall, Conghaile, Cowall, Cole**

Comgan *m*

An Irish name formed from *comh*, 'together', and *gan*, 'born', which may originally have been used for a twin.

It is pronounced 'KO-gan'. St Comgan was an Irish prince who founded a monastery in Scotland after he was driven from power.

VARIANTS **Comhghán, Congan, Cowan, Coan**

Comhnall *see* **Conal**

Comyn *see* **Cuimin**

Conal *m*
A Celtic name formed from elements meaning 'strong as a wolf'. It is a name that is prominent in the royal families in early Irish history.

PET FORM **Con** • VARIANTS **Con(n)all, Comhnall, Connel(l)**

Conan *m*
An Irish name which comes from *cú* meaning 'hound' or 'wolf'. In some Irish names *cú* can have implications of 'watch-dog, protector'. It is not an uncommon name in early Irish history. One legendary Conan was famous for his violent and uncouth behaviour, making it a suitable name for Robert E Howard's invention Conan the Cimmerian, better known as Conan the Barbarian. The name was also in use in Brittany, and medieval use of the name in England comes from Bretons who came over with the Norman conquerors. The Irish pronounce the name with a short 'o'; elsewhere it is usually long.

VARIANTS **Connan, Conant**
★ Sir Arthur Conan Doyle (1859–1930), Scottish writer of detective stories and creator of Sherlock Holmes

Concepta *f*
A name mainly used by devout Irish Catholics with reference to the immaculate conception by the Virgin Mary.

VARIANTS *Italian* **Concetta, Concettina** *Spanish* **Concepción, Conchita, Concha, Chita**

☆ Concepta Regan, barmaid at the Rovers Return in the television soap *Coronation Street* in the 1960s and 70s

Congan *see* **Comgan**

Conghaile *see* **Comgall**

Conley *m*
An Irish name which comes either from *connla*, 'pure', or *conn*, 'high, chief'. It was the name of an early Irish saint who was the first bishop of Kildare.

VARIANTS **Conloadh, Conla, Conleth, Con(n)(o)l(l)y**

Conn *m*
As well as being a pet form of names beginning *Con-*, this is an Irish name from the word for 'chief'.

VARIANT **Con**
★ Conn Céad Cathach ('Conn of the Hundred Battles'), semi-legendary hero after whom the province of Connacht was named

Connie *f*
A short form of CONSTANCE and other names beginning with similar sounds, sometimes given as an independent name.

PET FORM **Con** • VARIANT **Konnie**
★ Connie Francis (1938–   ), US singer and film actress
★ Konnie Huq (1975–   ), English broadcaster

Connor, Conor *m*
Con(n)or is the modern form of the ancient Irish name *Conchobhar* which probably means 'lover of hounds'. It was the name of one of the most famous of the kings of Ulster, whose doings are celebrated in the great Irish epic, *The Tain*, set some two thousand years ago. In recent years the name has been immensely popular among all English speakers. There seems to be no general agreement as to whether the name should be spelt with one or

two 'n's. In Ireland, the single *n* form is vastly more popular that the double, although both forms get into the top 100 names. In England, Scotland, the USA, Canada and Australia the double *nn* spelling is the preferred one.

PET FORM **Con(n)** • VARIANTS **Con(n)ar, Con(n)er, Ko(n)ner, Ko(n)nor** *Irish* **Cnochúr**

★ Conor Cruise O'Brien (1917–2008), Irish politician and writer

Conrad *m*

A Germanic name formed from *kuon*, 'bold', and *rad*, 'counsel'. It was a prominent name in Germanic ruling families, and was used in a number of countries in the Middle Ages in honour of the 10th-century St Conrad of Constance, who is said to have swallowed a spider in the course of saying mass, only to have the creature emerge unscathed at the end of the service. The name died out among English speakers thereafter, but was reintroduced in the 19th century.

PET FORMS **Kurt, Curt, Con, Conradin** (archaic) • VARIANTS *Dutch* **Koenraad** *German* **Konrad, Cort, Kort** *Italian,* *Spanish* **Corrado** *Polish* **Konrad, Kondrat**

★ Conrad Hilton (1887–1979), founder of the hotel chain
★ Konrad Lorenz (1903–89), groundbreaking Austrian zoologist
☆ Conrade, a minor character in Shakespeare's *Much Ado About Nothing* at a time when the name was unusual in England

Constance *f*

The Latin *constantia* was the Christian virtue of constancy or perseverance. The spread of the name was helped by the fact that Constance the daughter of Constantine the Great came to be regarded as one of the virgin saints, despite the fact that she had been married twice and had never shown any particular sign of piety. It was a popular name with the Normans, who brought the name to England, an early bearer being a daughter of William the Conqueror. The name was also well used by the Puritans, with their liking for abstract names, and was the name of one of the passengers on the *Mayflower*. It became very popular again in the later 19th and early 20th centuries. It fell out of fashion again thereafter, but has come back into use in recent years.

PET FORM **Connie** • VARIANTS **Constantia** *German* **Konstanze, Constanze** *Polish* **Konstancja** *Portuguese* **Constança** *Spanish* **Constanza**

☆ Lady Constance Chatterley in D H Lawrence's 1928 novel *Lady Chatterley's Lover*

Constant *m*

A medieval equivalent of CONSTANCE. The name was used by the Puritans and revived in the 19th century. While it was then very popular in France, it never made much headway in the UK.

VARIANTS **Constancy** *Italian* **Costanso** *Polish* **Konstanty**

★ Constant Lambert (1905–51), English composer and conductor

Constantine *m*

A Roman name meaning 'constant, steadfast' from the same root as CONSTANCE. The name spread because its most famous bearer was the Roman Emperor Constantine the Great (c.288–337), who adopted Christianity as the official religion of the Roman Empire. The name also belonged to two kings of Scotland. In their case it would have been the standard, official, written form of the Gaelic name CONN. The name is well used in Greece and Romania, reflecting their proximity to Constantinople (modern Istanbul), the city Constantine the Great established as his base and named after himself.

PET FORM **Con(n)** • VARIANTS *Welsh*

Cystenian, Cystennin *Dutch* **Constantijn** *French* **Constantin** *German* **Konstantin**, **Constantin** *Greek* **Kostantyn**, **Costa(s)** *Italian* **Costantino** *Polish* **Konstantyn** *Romanian* **Constantin**, **Costel**, **Costica**, **Costin** *Russian* **Konstantin**, **Kostya**

Consuelo *f*

This is a Spanish name adopted in the USA, particularly in the 1920s. It comes from *Neustra Señora del Consuelo*, 'Our Lady of Consolation'. Because the *-o* ending seems counter-intuitive for a feminine name, it is sometimes found as *Consuela*.

PET FORMS **Chelo, Suelo, Connie** • VARIANT *Italian* **Consolata**

★ Consuelo Vanderbilt, Duchess of Marlborough (1877–1964), US heiress and beauty, whose marriage to one of the premier dukes in England was representative of the transatlantic trade in money and rank during the Edwardian period

Cooper *m*

The surname, from the trade of barrel-maker, which has been well used as a first name in the USA and Australia for some years, and is starting to make its mark in the UK. It is occasionally used for girls.

PET FORM **Coop** • VARIANT **Coupar**

Cora *f*

Cora is a bit of a mystery. It looks as though it is formed from the Greek *kore*, 'maiden', but does not appear to be old. It seems to have been invented by James Fenimore Cooper for the character of Cora Munro, fictional daughter of a real British army commander in the province of New York, when it was still ruled by the British. Cora is of mixed race, being one-quarter black, and her dark hair and good sense contrasts with the blonde softness of her younger half-sister. In the end Cora dies, but

she enables her sister to survive the ordeals they endure in order to marry and give birth to the next generation. It may be that Cooper coined the name from *Kore*, an epithet of Persephone, the goddess of the dark underworld who lives there in winter, before her return in spring causes the cycle of life to continue.

VARIANTS **Coretta**, **Corah**

★ Coretta Scott King (1927–2006), US civil rights activist, widow of Martin Luther King

Coral *f*

This is one of the semi-precious jewel names introduced in the later 19th century. It has been out of favour for some years, but is showing signs of coming back.

★ Coral Browne (1913–91), Australian actress

Coralie *f*

Coralie is usually taken as a variant of CORAL, or perhaps CORA, but may in fact be a development of the Italian *Coralina*. This is the traditional name of the cunning young woman in the *Commedia dell'Arte*. This makes the name much older than CORAL or CORA, and fits with the fact that Coralie is used for the French girl, Coralie Brack, in Thackeray's 1850 novel *Pendennis*, well before Coral came into general use.

PET FORMS **Cory** • VARIANTS **Cora-Lee** *French* **Coraline**

Corazon *f*

This is a Spanish name meaning 'heart' originally used with reference to the Sacred Heart. It is particularly found in the Philippines.

★ Corazon 'Cory' Aquino (1933–), Philippine politician and former president

Corbin *m*
A surname, from the French for 'raven', which is used as a first name.

VARIANTS **Corbyn**, **Corben**

★ Corbin Bernsen (1954–), US actor, whose success in the television series *LA Law* probably boosted interest in the name in the 1990s

Cordelia *f*
A name introduced by Shakespeare in his 1605 play, *King Lear*. It may be a form of the name *Cordula*, which belonged to one of the virgins martyred with St Ursula, and which is thought to be derived from the Latin for 'heart'. Shakespeare seems to have adopted the name from *Cordeilla*, the form used in his source, Holinshed's *Chronicles* (1577). However, it has recently been pointed out that Shakespeare may have known of a contemporary Londoner called *Cordell* Annesley who tried to stop her father being declared insane by her two older married sisters, a situation with strong echoes of the play, and that this may have influenced the form of the name.

PET FORMS **Cordy**, **Delia** • VARIANT *Welsh* **Creiddylad**

☆ Cordelia Chase, character in the television series *Buffy the Vampire Slayer* and *Angel*

☆ Cordelia Naismith, a character in Lois McMaster Bujold's *Barrayar* novels

Corey *mf*
A surname of unknown origin which has been very popular as a given name in the USA, particularly between the 1970s and 90s, arriving in the 1990s in the UK. It was initially used for boys, but is now used for both sexes, although the variants are more likely to be feminine.

VARIANTS **Cory**, **Cori(e)**, **Corrie**

Corin *mf*
This was originally a French masculine name derived from the Latin *Quirinus*, the name of a god associated with the foundation of Rome, but about whom remarkably little is actually known. It entered the stock of names used by Christians because it was borne by several early martyrs. However, nowadays it is usually regarded as a variant of the CORINNA names, and is used for both sexes.

★ Corin Redgrave (1939–), English actor

Corinna *f*
This name goes back to ancient Greece, where *Korinna* was the name of a poetess whose work only survives in fragments. It was then used by the Roman poet Ovid, in the 1st century BC, for the name of the woman to whom he addressed some of his love poems, and entered the stock of literary names in this way. It was taken up by English poets in the 16th and 17th centuries, most famously by Robert Herricks in his poem 'Corinna's going a-Maying' (1648). The French form gained literary fame in Madame de Staël's novel *Corinne* (1807). From these sources the name passed into general use.

VARIANTS **Coreen**, **Corrin(n)(a)** *French* **Corinne** *Spanish* **Corina**

Corisande *f*
This is an old French name, used for a character in the romance *Amadis of Gaul*. 'La Belle Corisande' was a title given to Diane de Poitiers (1499–1566), beautiful mistress of the French king, Henry II. It was not an uncommon name in the 19th century, when it was also given to a character in Disraeli's *Lothair* (1870).

Cormac *m*
This is an ancient Irish name of unknown meaning, although interpretations have included

'charioteer' and 'son of the raven'. It is steadily popular in Ireland.

VARIANTS **Corma(c)k** *Scottish* **Cormag**

★ Cormac Murphy-O'Connor (1932–), Cardinal Archbishop of Westminster
★ Cormac McCarthy (1933–), US writer

Cornelia *f*

Cornelia is the feminine form of the Roman name CORNELIUS. The most famous of the women of this name in Rome was the mother of the Gracchi, two brothers who tried to reform the state and were both killed. She is said to have devoted herself to their upbringing and, when a visitor was showing off her jewels and asked to see her hostess's, Cornelia sent for her boys and presented them with the words 'these are my jewels'.

PET FORMS **Cornie, Corrie, Nellie** • VARIANTS *French* **Cornélia, Clornélie** *German* **Nele** *Polish* **Kornelia**

★ Cornelia Funke (1958–), German children's author

Cornelius *m*

This name, from the Roman Cornelii family, probably comes from the Latin word *cornu* meaning 'horn'. Legend has it that one Cornelius was a Roman legionary converted by St Peter, and another was pope in the 3rd century AD. The name was particularly popular in the Low Countries in the Middle Ages.

PET FORMS **Cornie, Corn(e)y, Cornel** • VARIANTS *Dutch* **Cornelis, Cor, Cees, Kerneels, Kees** *French* **Corneille** *Italian, Spanish* **Cornelio** *Polish* **Kornel**

★ Cornelius Vanderbilt (1794–1877), US financier
☆ Dr Cornelius, chimpanzee archaeologist and historian in the *Planet of the Apes* books and films

Corrado, Cort *see* **Conrad**

Cory *see* **Corey, Coralie**

Cosette *f*

French *cose* is the old form of *chose*, 'thing', so Cosette means 'little thing'. It is the name of a character in Victor Hugo's novel *Les Misérables*, and is rarely used except by fans of the book.

Cosima *f*

A feminine form of COSMO, this name got into the stock of English names from Cosima Wagner (1837–1930), daughter of Franz Liszt and mistress, then wife, of Richard Wagner.

VARIANT **Cosma**

Cosmo *m*

The Byzantine Greek name *Kosmas*, 'order, harmony', was turned into *Cosmas* or *Cosmus* in Latin and became Cosmo or *Cosimo* in Italian. St Cosmas and his brother, St DAMIAN, were early Christian martyrs; they were doctors who had practised for free among the poor, and who became the patron saints of Milan. This explains why the name is found prominently in northern Italy during the Renaissance. In the 18th century the name was transferred to Scotland when the Gordon family, who had links with the dukes of Tuscany, adopted the name, and it became traditional in their family.

VARIANT *French* **Côme**

★ Cosimo de Medici (1389–1464), Florentine financier, statesman and philanthropist
★ Cosmo Gordon Lang (1864–1945), Scottish Archbishop of Canterbury

Costa, Costas *see* **Constantine**

Costanso *see* **Constant**

Costantino, Costel, Costica, Costin *see* **Constantine**

Coty *m*

Although it can be analysed as the use of a surname from the French for 'river bank', it is more likely that this name, which was in use in the USA in the 1980s and 90s, is simply a variant of CODY, the sounds of 't' and 'd' being indistinct in some US accents. As a boy's name it is highly unlikely that it represents the name of the perfume house.

VARIANT **Koty**

Coupar see Cooper

Courtney mf

Courtney started out as a French surname, based on any of several place names originally meaning 'property of Curtius'. However, it sounds as if it comes from the French *court nez*, 'short nose', which was the nickname of a famous hero from a medieval story who had lost the tip of his nose in battle, and it came to be interpreted as having this meaning. It has been in occasional use for both sexes since the 19th century, but its modern popularity started in the 1960s as a masculine name in the USA. However, it quickly became a feminine name, and use rapidly overtook the masculine. Courtney was among the most popular names for girls in the 1980s and 90s in the USA, and it has been among the top 100 girls' names in most English-speaking areas. It has developed many variant spellings, of which a sample are listed below, and is increasingly used in combinations such as *Courtneylee*.

VARIANTS **Courteney, Courtenay, Courtny**
★ Courtney Pine (1964–), English jazz saxophonist
★ Courtney Love (1964–), US singer

Cowall see Comgall

Cowan see Comgan

Craig m

Craig is the Scottish vocabulary word meaning 'rock, cliff', used as

a surname and then as a first name. It was popular in the USA from the 1940s to 70s, in Australia and the UK in the 1970s and 80s, and is currently well used in its native Scotland and in Ireland.
★ Craig David (1981–), English singer-songwriter

Cree mf

The name of a Native American grouping, used as part of the fashionable trend to use tribal names as first names. Compare DAKOTA.
★ Cree Summer (1969–), US actress and musician

Creiddylad see Cordelia

Cressida f

The story of *Troilus and Cressida* came to England from Italy, in a translation of Boccaccio's *Il Filostrato* by Geoffrey Chaucer, and was taken up by Shakespeare, among others. In the story Cressida is a beautiful Trojan woman at the time of the Trojan War. She and Troilus fall in love, but Cressida is unfaithful. Despite this, the name has been used regularly in the 20th century, mostly in the UK. It comes ultimately from the Greek word *khrysos* meaning 'gold'.

PET FORM **Cressy**
★ Cressida Dick (1960–), Police Commissioner and one of the most senior women in the British police force

Crete see Lucretia

Criostóir see Christopher

Crìsdean see Christian

Crispin m

Crispin and his brother *Crispinian* got their names from the old Roman family name *Crispus*, 'curly-haired'. They were martyred for their faith in the later 3rd century AD and became the patron saints of shoemakers. The name is famous from the speech in Shakespeare's *Henry V*, which Henry delivers on the eve of the Battle of Agincourt: 'And gentlemen in England now a-bed / Shall think themselves accurs'd they were not here, / And hold their manhoods cheap while any speaks / That fought with us upon Saint Crispin's day.'

VARIANTS **Crispian**, **Krispin**

Cristian, Cristiana, Cristiano *see* Christian

Cristina *see* Christina

Cristoforo, Cristóbal, Cristóvão *see* Christopher

Cronan *m*

A traditional Irish name, originally a pet form of *crón*, 'dark, swarthy'.

VARIANTS **Crónán**, **Cronin**

Cruz *mf*

A Spanish name meaning 'cross'. In Spain it is usually feminine, but in the Americas it is usually masculine. The Beckhams' choice of the name for their third son led to a great increase in its use in the UK.

Crystal *f*

This name, from the vocabulary word, was introduced to English in the later part of the 19th century, at around the same time as other similar names such as CORAL, although the Welsh form has been in use since the 12th century. The word ultimately goes back to the Greek for 'ice'. In Scotland Crystal is also a masculine name, an old form of CHRISTOPHER.

VARIANTS **Christal**, **Christelle**, **Krystal** *Welsh* **Crisiant**

★ Crystal Gayle (1951–), US country singer

Crystin *see* Christine

Cuddy *see* Cuthbert

Cuimin *m*

A traditional Irish name from *cam*, 'crooked'.

VARIANT **Comyn**

Cuithbeart *see* Cuthbert

Curro *see* Francis

Curt *see* Conrad, Kurt

Curtis *m*

A surname, now a well-used first name, originally from the Old French *curteis* 'courteous'.

PET FORM **Curt**

★ Curtis James Jackson III (1975–), US rapper better known as 50 Cent

Cushla *f*

This is an uncommon name based on the Irish endearment *cushla macree* (*cuisle mo croidhe* in Gaelic), meaning 'beat of my heart'.

Cuthbert *m*

An Old English name from the Old English words *cuth*, 'famous, known', and *beorht*, 'bright, famous'. It was one of the few Old English names that continued in use after the Norman Conquest, thanks to the popularity of St Cuthbert, a 7th-century archbishop, whose tomb in Durham was an important place of pilgrimage. It continued in use in the north of England, and had a more general revival in the 19th century. However, it came to be used in World War I as a slang term for a conscientious objector, or someone who evaded military service, which led to a steep decline in use.

PET FORM **Cuddy** • VARIANT *Scots Gaelic* **Cuithbeart**

Cybill *see* Sybil

Cynan *m*

This is a Welsh name based on *cyn*

meaning 'chief, pre-eminent'. It was popular among the medieval Welsh ruling families.

VARIANTS **Cynin, Cynon**

Cynth *see* **Hyacinth**

Cynthia *f*

The Greek goddess ARTEMIS (DIANA to the Romans) was reportedly born on Mount Kynthos, on the island of Delos, and so Cynthia ('of Kynthos') became one of her titles. The name was in use in ancient Rome, where the 1st-century BC poet Procopius used it in his love poetry. This was picked up in the 16th century by the Elizabethan poets who used Cynthia as a title for Queen Elizabeth I, as Artemis was a virgin goddess and Elizabeth liked her role as Virgin Queen to be stressed. By the 17th century, when classical names started to come into fashion, it had started to be used as a given name, but only really became popular in the later 19th century.

PET FORMS **Cindy, Cimmie, Cyn(th)** • VARIANTS *Italian* **Cinzia** *Portuguese* **Cintia**

Cynyr *m*

A Welsh name formed from *cyn*, 'chief', and *(g)wr*, 'hero'. It was the name of St David's grandfather.

Cyprian *m*

St Cyprian, whose name means 'man of Cyprus', was a 3rd-century bishop of Carthage who was martyred for his faith. The name was used in England in the Middle Ages, but is now rare, although it is found in other languages. One reason for the name's lack of popularity in English may be that it was an old term for a prostitute,

because the goddess APHRODITE had strong associations with Cyprus.

VARIANTS *French* **Cyprien** (m), **Cyprienne** (f) *Italian* **Cipriano** *Spanish* **Cebrián**

Cyril *m*

This name comes from the Greek *Kyrillos*, 'lord'. There were numerous early saints called Cyril, including one who introduced Christianity to Russia. He designed an alphabet, based on his native Greek, in order to write down the language, which is why the Russian alphabet is known as Cyrillic script. It is also why the name is popular in Russian Orthodox areas.

FEMININE **Cyrilla** • PET FORM **Cy** • VARIANTS **Syril** *French* **Cyrille** (m & f) *Italian* **Cirillo** *Polish* **Cyryl** *Russian* **Kirill**

Cyrus *m* Cyra *f*

This is the biblical form of a name used by the kings of Persia. Its meaning is debated – some associate it with the Persian word for 'throne', others with the same root as CYRIL. It came into the stock of Western names, not only from the Bible, but also from a number of early saints. It is more often found in the USA than the UK, and use of the rare feminine has been growing since the 20th century.

PET FORM **Cy**

★ Cyrus Vance (1917–2002), US lawyer and politician

★ Cyrus West Field (1819–92), US businessman, whose company laid the first transatlantic telegraph cable in 1858

★ Cyra McFadden (c.1939–   ), US writer

Cystenian, Cystennin *see* **Constantine**

D

Daan *see* **Daniel**

Daffodil *f*
One of the more uncommon of the flower names introduced in the late 19th century. Daffodil is a medieval corruption of the Greek flower name asphodel. Compare JONQUIL.
PET FORMS **Daf(fy)** (also used for DAPHNE), **Dil(ly)**

Dafydd *see* **David**

Dag *m*
A Scandinavian name, from the Old Norse *dagr*, 'day'.
★ Dag Hammarskjöld (1905–61), Swedish statesman and second secretary general of the United Nations

Dagmar *f*
In the 13th century a Czech princess named *Dragomir* (from *dorog*, 'dear', and *meri*, 'peace') became queen of Denmark, through marriage, under the name *Margarethe*. Her true name was changed to Dagmar, and reinterpreted as coming from the Old Danish *dag*, 'day', and *mar*, 'maid'. From Denmark the name spread to the rest of Scandinavia and surrounding Germanic countries; from there it was taken to the USA, where it is much more common than in the UK.
★ Dagmar Nordstrom (1903–76), US pianist, composer and singer, who performed as one-half of the Nordstrom Sisters
★ Dagmar (1921–2001), US actress specializing in 'dumb blonde' roles

Dahey *see* **Daithi**

Dahlia *f*
This garden flower, originating in Mexico, was named after the Swiss botanist Anders Dahl (1751–89). It seems to have been introduced to the general public as a first name by George Meredith in his 1865 novel *Rhoda Fleming*. It has never been particularly popular, although it is currently enjoying a mild vogue in the USA. In English the name is usually pronounced as in 'dale', but in some other countries it is pronounced with a long 'ah' sound. See also DALIA.
VARIANTS **Dalya** *Italian, Arabic* **Dalia**
☆ Bertie Wooster's favourite aunt in P G Wodehouse's *Jeeves and Wooster* stories was called Aunt Dahlia

Dahy *see* **Daithi**

Dai, Dàibhidh *see* **David**

Daire *m*
This Irish name comes from the word meaning 'fertile, fruitful', and was probably originally that of a god. The name is well used in early legend, and is currently popular in Ireland. There is, however, considerable overlap with the similar DARA and DARRAGH. See also DARINA.
VARIANTS **Dáire, Dary**

Daisy *f*
The daisy flower gets its name from the Old English *daegeseage* (pronounced pretty much the same way) which is made up of words meaning 'day's eye'. This describes the way in which the flower opens up the rays of its petals round the sunny yellow centre when the sun comes

up, and closes them in the evening. Because the French form of MARGARET, *Marguerite*, is also a general French term for the daisy family, Daisy was originally a punning nickname for someone called Margaret. However, in the 19th century when flower names were fashionable, Daisy was well established as an independent name. It was popular in the later 19th century, particularly in the USA where it remained in regular use, but went out of fashion in the UK. In the 21st century it has once again become very popular in the UK.

☆ Daisy Buchanan, character in F Scott Fitzgerald's novel *The Great Gatsby* (1925)
☆ Daisy Miller, eponymous heroine of Henry James's novel (1878)

Daithi *m*
Pronounced 'da-hee', this Old Irish name, usually interpreted to mean 'swift', was the name of the last pagan king of Ireland in the 5th century. So many legends exist about him that it is impossible to distinguish fact from fiction.
VARIANTS **Dahey**, **Dahy**

Daividh *see* **David**

Dakota *mf*
The name of a Native American nation, meaning 'friend' in their language. Part of the fashion for such names, it has been making its mark as a first name since the 1980s. It has been more popular for boys in the USA, but is more common for girls in the UK.
VARIANT **Dakotah**
★ Dakota Stanton (1930–2007), US jazz singer
★ Dakota Fanning (1994–), US actress
★ Dakota Blue Richards (1994–), English actress

Dale *mf*
A surname from the self-explanatory

place name, turned into a first name. It has been in use for both sexes since the 19th century and was among the top 100 names for boys in the USA from the start of the 1920s to the end of the 60s.
★ Dale Carnegie (1888–1955), US self-help writer
☆ Dale Arden, girlfriend of the comic-book hero Flash Gordon

Daley *m*
An Irish surname used as a first name. The surname means descendant of *Dalach*, which in turn means 'a frequenter of gatherings'. The name of the Irish parliament, the Dáil (pronounced 'doyle'), comes from the same root.
VARIANTS **Daly** *Irish* **Dalaigh**

Dalia *f*
A Jewish name, from the Hebrew for 'bough, branch'. Since it is also a form of DAHLIA, it is often impossible to distinguish between the two names.
PET FORM **Dalika** • VARIANTS **Dalya**, **Daliah**
★ Daliah Lavi (1940–), Israeli film actress

Dalil *m* **Dalila** *f*
An Arabic name meaning 'guide, leader, model'. Dalila can also be a French form of DELILAH.

Dallas *mf*
This was originally a Scottish surname based on the Gaelic *dalfhas*, a term for a meadow used as an overnight stop by cattle drovers. The city in Texas was named after George Mifflin Dallas, lawyer and vice-president of the USA. Dallas has been steadily used as a first name since the middle of the 19th century. It was originally used in honour of George Dallas, but modern use may be due to the glamour of the city, and the television series of the same name that ran from the 1970s to 1990s.

★ Dallas Stoudenmire (1845–82), Texas ranger and gunman, born the year George Mifflin Dallas became vice-president

Dallin *m*
This name, mainly used in the USA, can be analysed as a reused surname, taken from a place name referring either to a dale, or to a settlement belonging to someone with the Old English name *Dalla*. However, it is more likely that it is used because it combines fashionable sounds.

Dalton *m*
This surname has been regularly used as a first name in the USA since the 19th century, but became popular in the late 1990s. It comes from a number of English places meaning 'settlement in the dale'. It is spreading to other countries.

Dalya *see* **Dahlia**

Damaris *f*
This is the name of a woman mentioned in passing in the biblical Act of the Apostles (17.34), as an early convert to Christianity. Since she encountered St Paul in Athens, she was probably Greek, and it is thought that the name is a late variant of the Greek name *Damalis*, meaning 'calf'. The name has been in quiet use since the 16th century, but has been increasingly common, particularly in the USA, since the early 1990s. It may be no coincidence that this increase coincided with the 1991 publication of a novel called *A Woman Named Damaris* by the successful evangelical novelist Janette Oke.

Damayanti *f*
This is a Hindu name meaning 'subduing [men]'. In one of the great love stories of the *Mahabharata*, Damayanti is a princess who is admired not just for her beauty, but also for her intelligence.

Damhnait *see* **Davnat**

Damian, Damien *m*
St Damian shared martyrdom with his brother, St Cosmas (see COSMO). The name is *Damianos* in Greek, and comes from the root *daman*, 'to rule, subdue'. The name was used quietly from the 13th century, but only became prominent in the 20th century. The French Damien is now the more commonly used form in the UK, the change being influenced by the character of Damien, born to be the Antichrist, in the 1976 film *The Omen*.
FEMININE **Damiana** • VARIANTS **Damion** *Italian* **Damiano** *Russian* **Demyan**
★ Damien Hirst (1965–), English artist
★ St Peter Damian (Pietro Damiani) (1007–72), Italian church reformer

Damodar *m* Damodari *f*
The Hindu stories of KRISHNA include an episode in his childhood when he was creating chaos in his foster-mother's home. To keep Krishna under control, his foster-mother tied a rope round his middle and tethered him to a large pot. Being the Sanskrit for 'having a rope tied round his belly', these names originated from this story.

Damon *m*
Damon comes from the same root as DAMIAN, the Greek for 'to tame'. The name Damon became a byword for friendship and loyalty because of a story, told in varying forms, from the 4th century BC. According to the tale, Pythias had been sentenced to death by Dionysius, tyrant of Syracuse. He was allowed to go home to settle his affairs first, after his friend Damon offered to stand surety for him and be killed in his place if he did not return. Pythias was delayed returning, and Damon was about to be executed, but

Pythias arrived just in time. Dionysius was so impressed by their loyalty that he pardoned them both. Some versions of the story swap the roles. The name was very rare before the 20th century.

★ Damon Runyon (1884–1946), US writer of comic stories
★ Damon Hill (1962–   ), English racing driver

Dan *m*

As well as being a pet form of DANIEL, Dan can be an independent name from the Hebrew for 'he judged'. In the Bible (Genesis 30.6), Dan was the name of one of the twelve sons of Jacob, founders of the Jewish tribes.

Dana¹ *m*

This is the surname of Richard Henry Dana (1815–82), a member of a prominent New England family, a noted reforming lawyer and politician, and writer. The origin of the surname is unclear, but may mean 'a Dane'.

★ Dana Andrews (1909–92), US film actor
★ Dana Carvey (1955–   ), US actor and comedian

Dana² *m*

An Arabic name meaning 'wise, learned'.

Dana³ *f*

As a feminine name Dana can have a number of origins. It can be a feminine form of DANIEL; it can be a shortening of other feminines of Daniel; and it can be a variant or pet form of names such as DIANA, DONNA or a number of Slavic names ending in -*dana*. Alternatively, it can be a transference of the masculine name which, with its -*a* ending, can easily be taken to be feminine. There is also an ancient Irish mother goddess called Dana. The situation is further complicated by the fact that it is found with both a short and long first 'a' sound.

VARIANT **Danna**

★ Dana (1951–   ), Northern Irish singer and politician
☆ Dana Scully, the sceptical one in the television series *The X Files*

Danaë *f*

This is a name from Greek mythology. Danaë was a princess whose father had received a prophecy that his future grandson would kill him. To avoid this, he locked Danaë in a tower, where she was visited by Zeus in the form of a shower of gold, and by him had a son, the hero Perseus. The meaning of the name is not clear, but Danaë was great-granddaughter of *Danaus*, the originator of the Greek tribal grouping, the Danai, and the name probably comes from this. The name is mildly fashionable at the moment. The lines from Tennyson's song in *The Princess* written in 1850 may have influenced use: 'Now lies the Earth all Danaë to the stars, / And all thy heart lies open unto me.'

Dand, Dandy *see* Andrew

d'Andre *see* DeAndre

Dane *m*

The surname Dane, the origin of the first name, is usually from a regional variant of DEAN, although it is often interpreted as coming from the nationality.

Danesh *see* Danish

Danette *f*

One of the more uncommon feminines of DANIEL.

D'Angelo *see* DeAngelo

Dani *see* Danielle

Danica *f*

This is a Slavic name, meaning 'morning star', which is being increasingly used by English speakers.

They usually pronounce it 'DAN-i-ka', but in Slavic languages it is pronounced something like 'dan-i-tsa'.
VARIANT **Danika**

Daniel *m*
This is a Hebrew name, meaning 'God is my judge', from the Old Testament. The story of how Daniel stood up to the King of Babylon and miraculously escaped from the lion's den is one of the most exciting in the Bible, and it is not surprising that it created interest in the name early on in the Middle Ages. It has been used steadily ever since, and is currently one of the most popular names among both English speakers and speakers of other languages.
PET FORMS **Dan, Danny, Danni** • VARIANTS **Danial, Danyal** *Scots Gaelic* **Dàniel** *Welsh* **Deiniol** *Dutch* **Daniël, Daan** *Italian* **Daniele, Danilo** *Russian* **Daniil**

Danielle, Daniella *f*
These are the most common feminine forms of DANIEL used by English speakers. The former was originally French, the latter is the English form of *Daniela*, used by many languages including Italian, German, Polish and Spanish.
PET FORM **Da(n)ni** • VARIANTS *French* **Danièle** *Italian* **Daniele** *Slavic* **Danijela** *Spanish* **Dania**

Danish *m*
This is a Persian name, also used in other Muslim areas, meaning 'sagacity, wisdom'.
VARIANTS **Danesh, Danush**

Danni *see* **Danielle**

Dante *m*
This is a name derived from *Durante* meaning 'enduring, steadfast'. Dante is used in honour of the early Italian poet Dante Alighieri (1265–1321), author of the *Divine Comedy*.

VARIANT **Donte**
★ Dante Gabriel Rossetti (1828–82), English poet and Pre-Raphaelite artist

Danush *see* **Danish**

Danuta *f*
This Polish name, which has now spread to the English-speaking world, is probably a feminine form of DANIEL.

Danya *f*
An uncommon modern feminine form of DAN or DANIEL.

Daood *see* **David**

Daphne *f*
The Greek word for a laurel tree, in mythology Daphne was a nymph desired by the god Apollo. He chased Daphne and nearly caught her, but she prayed to her father, the local river god, and as Apollo was about to lay hands on her, she was changed into a laurel tree. Apollo swore to wear a wreath made from her leaves, which is the supposed origin of laurel wreaths as signs of success. The subject was a popular one in Renaissance art. Daphne came into use in the 18th century, and in the UK was at its most popular from the late 19th through to the first third of the 20th century, although in the USA it was at its peak in the 1960s and early 2000s.
PET FORMS **Daph, Daff(y)**
★ Dame Daphne du Maurier (1907–89), English novelist
☆ Daphne Moon is a character in the television sitcom *Frasier*
☆ Daphne was the name adopted by the character played by Jack Lemmon in the 1959 film *Some Like It Hot*

Dara *mf*
Dara is a shortened form of the Irish name, originally local to Connemara, *Mac Dara*, meaning 'son of the oak'. This was the name of the local patron saint of fishermen. However, there is

considerable overlap in use between Dara, DAIRE and DARRAGH. The name, which has been well used for a number of years in Ireland, has spread beyond the country and, because of its feminine-sounding -a ending, is now used for girls. See also DARIUS.

Darby, **Derby** m
This is a surname based on the place name Derby, which could refer to either the English city or one of the smaller places bearing that name. The name comes from the Old Norse *diur*, 'deer', and *byr*, 'settlement'. In Ireland it was used to anglicize DERMOT.
VARIANT **D'arby**
☆ The term 'Darby and Joan', used for a happily married couple, dates back to at least the 18th century

Darcy mf
This was originally a Norman surname given to someone who came from (indicated by *d'*) the village of Arcy in northern France. The d'Arcy family settled in Ireland in the 14th century, where the name was adopted as a first name. Despite the associations of the name with Mr Darcy in Jane Austen's *Pride and Prejudice* (1813), the name is now predominantly feminine, particularly in its variant forms.
VARIANTS **Darci(e)**, **Darcey**, **D'arcy**
★ Darcey Bussell (1969–   ), English ballerina

Daria f
This is a feminine form of DARIUS which has spread to many countries thanks to St Daria, a Greek converted by her husband St Crysanthus, and martyred alongside him.
VARIANTS **Dariea** *French* **Darie** *Greek* **Dareia** *Slavic* **Darja**, **Darinka** *Russian* **Darya**

Darian mf
A modern name, used more for boys than girls, which probably represents

a variant of DARIUS perhaps influenced by DARREN or DAMIAN, or modelled on DORIAN. It appeared in the USA in the 1960s and peaked in the 1990s.
VARIANTS **Darien**, **Darion**, **Darrien**, **Darrion**

Darija *see* **Dorothy**

Darina f
This is the anglicized version of the Irish name *Dáirine*, the feminine form of DAIRE.

Darion *see* **Darian**

Darius m
This is the Latin form, transferred via the Greek *Dareios*, of a Persian royal name. The exact form and meaning of the original is not clear, although *Darayavahush* is one suggestion, and it is generally accepted that it is based on a form of the word *daraya*, 'to hold, possess'. The most famous Persian rulers bearing this name were Darius the Great, whose troops were defeated at the Battle of Marathon in 490 BC, and Darius III, who was deposed by Alexander the Great in 330 BC. Use of the name in the West is thanks to St Darius, an early Christian martyr. The name has two pronunciations. That with the stress on the second syllable and a long 'i' sound is the one usually used by scholars speaking of the ancient kings; that with the stress on the first syllable is used for vernacular forms of the name. The name was moderately popular in the USA in the 1990s, where it developed forms *LaDarius* and less commonly *LeDarius* (both masculine).
VARIANTS **Der(r)ius** *Arabic* **Dara** *Iranian* **Dariush**, **Daryush** *Italian* **Dario** *Polish* **Dariusz**
★ Darius Milhaud (1892–1974), French composer
★ Dario Fo (1926–   ), Nobel Prize-winning Italian dramatist

Darla *f*

One of a group of 20th-century first names based on the word 'darling'. Use has mainly been confined to the USA. It was the birth name of Darla Hood (1931–79), who must have been one of the first to be given it. She was a child actress, who first appeared on screen in 1935 in the popular *Our Gang* series of films, playing a character also known as Darla. The name must have been an instant hit with the public, for it first appears in the US names charts that year, as the 673rd most popular name, and climbed steadily thereafter, until peaking in the 1960s, when the related DARLENE was also popular.
☆ Darla, vampire in the cult television series *Buffy the Vampire Slayer* and *Angel*

Darlene *f*

A name based on the vocabulary word 'darling', mainly found in Australia and the USA, where it first appeared right at the beginning of the 20th century.
VARIANTS **Darleen, Darylyne**

Darnell

There is a surname Darnell which can either be from the Old French *darnel*, a term for a type of grass, or else from the Old English *derne halh*, 'hidden nook'. However, as the name first came into use, mainly in the USA, in the 1940s and peaked in the 1980s, at the same time as names such as DARRYL were also popular, the sounds may have been the main attraction.
☆ Darnell, character in the television series *My Name is Earl*

Darragh *m*

An Irish name derived from *dair* meaning 'oak'. It has been very popular in Ireland for some years and has spread elsewhere. It also serves as an anglicized form of the unrelated DAIRE, and as an alternative spelling of the related DARA.
VARIANTS **Darrach, Darroch**

Darren *m*

A name of uncertain origin first brought to public attention by the US actor Darren McGavin (1922–2006), born William Richardson. He began to make his name as an actor in the late 1940s. It has long been well used in the USA, and has been popular in recent years in Scotland and Ireland, but not in England.
FEMININES **Darrene, Dareen, Der(r)yn(e)**
• VARIANTS **Dar(r)an, Dar(r)in, Dar(r)on, Derrin, Derryn**
★ Darren Shan (1972–), pen name of children's author Darren O'Shanghnessy, as well as the name of the vampire protagonist of a series of his books
☆ Darrin was the name of the husband in the 1960s television series *Bewitched*. This is often credited with spreading the name, although it was already well-established in the USA by that time

Darrien, Darrion *see* Darian

Darryl *mf*

This was originally a surname, from the Norman family who were the knights *d'Airelle* in the Calvados region of France. Despite some prominent female bearers, the name is still mostly masculine.
VARIANTS **Dar(r)el(l), Daryl(l)**
★ Daryl Hannah (1960–), US actress
★ Darryl F Zanuck (1902–79), US film producer
☆ Darrell Rivers is the heroine of Enid Blyton's *Malory Towers* (1946–51) series of stories set in a girls' boarding school. In this case, Darrell seems to have been taken from the middle name of Blyton's second husband

Dary *see* Daire

Dashawn *see* **DeShawn**

Dashiell *m*
This is a surname used as a first name. The French surname De Chiel, of unknown meaning, was brought by settlers to the USA, where it was turned into Dashiell. It was the maiden name of the mother of Samuel Dashiell Hammett (1894–1961), who wrote detective novels such as *The Maltese Falcon* under the name Dashiell Hammett. It is now a quietly fashionable name.
PET FORM **Dash**

Dassa, **Dassah** *see* **Hadassah**

David *m*
This is a Hebrew name meaning 'beloved'. It has become so much part of the Western tradition of names that its biblical associations have been largely obscured, but King David is one of the greatest kings in the Old Testament. As well as being famous for killing Goliath as a boy, he was a poet, musician and efficient administrator and politician. The name has strong associations with both Wales and Scotland: St David is the patron saint of the former, and there were two kings of the name in the Middle Ages in the latter. David I in particular was important in the development of the Scottish nation. The name is currently popular in many countries.
PET FORMS **Dave**, **Davie**, **Davey** • VARIANTS *Irish* **Dáibhíd** *Scots Gaelic* **Dàibhidh**, **Daividh** *Welsh* **Dafydd**, **Dai**, **Dewi**, **Taffy** *Cornish* **Daveth** *Arabic* **Daud**, **Dawud**, **Daood**, **Dawood** *Italian* **Davide** *Polish* **Dawid** *Yiddish* **Dovid**, **Dudel**, **Dov**

Davina *f*
Originally a Scottish feminine of DAVID, this is now used in other English-speaking communities. Other Scottish feminine forms less commonly found include *Davida* and *Davita*.

PET FORMS **Vina**, **Vida** • VARIANTS **Davinia**, **Davena**
★ Davina McCall (1967–), English television presenter

Davion *m*
A name in use in the USA since the 1990s. It is probably a shortening of *Octavian* (*Tavion* is a less common variant), with the first sound slightly altered.
VARIANT **Davius**

Davis *m*
A surname, based on the first name DAVID, now used as a first name. It was originally used to commemorate Jefferson Davis (1808–89), sole president of the Confederate States during the American Civil War.
VARIANT **Davies**

Davnat *f*
This is the anglicized form of the Irish name *Damhnait*, a name formed from the Irish *damh* meaning 'fawn'. It was the name of a 6th-century Irish saint who founded a monastery at Tedavnet, County Monaghan, and whose crosier is preserved in the National Museum of Ireland. See also DYMPHNA.
VARIANT **Devnet**

DaVon *see* **Devon**

Dawid *see* **David**

Dawn *f*
The vocabulary word used as a first name, possibly as a translation of AURORA. It came into use at the beginning of the 20th century and in the UK was most prominent in the 1920s and 30s, while in the USA it was popular from the 1950s to 80s.
PET FORM **Dawnie**
★ Dawn French (1957–), Welsh comedienne and actress

Dawood *see* **David**

Dawson *m*
Daw was an old pet form of DAVID which became the surname Dawson, now back in use as a first name. It is recorded in occasional use in the USA in the 19th century and early 20th, but suddenly came back into use in the 1990s, its growing popularity influenced by the character of Dawson Leery in the television series *Dawson's Creek*.

Dawud *see* **David**

Dayton *m*
The Dayton family was prominent in the early history of the USA, which may explain why the first name is primarily found there. The surname comes from a common place name which can mean either 'dairy settlement' or 'ditch settlement'. The name was used occasionally in the first half of the 20th century, and was revived in the 1990s.

Deacon *m*
A surname from the occupation which is showing signs of becoming fashionable as a first name.

Dean *m*
A surname used as a first name. Although it looks as if it comes from the occupation, in many cases the surname comes from an old world meaning 'valley' (compare DALE). It can also be an adaptation of the Italian name *Dino*, formed from the ending of names such as *Bernardino*.
VARIANTS **Deane, Dene**
★ Dean Martin (1917–95), US singer and actor
★ Dean Acheson (1893–1971), US politician

DeAndre *m*
One of the most popular of the many names formed in the USA by putting the prefix *De-* in front of an already

established name or variant thereof. It came into use in the 1970s and peaked in the 90s.
VARIANTS **d'Andre, Diondre**

DeAngelo *m*
One of the many *De-* names fashionable in the USA in the 1990s.
VARIANTS **DiAngelo, D'Angelo**

Deanna
Depending on how this is pronounced, this is either a variant of DIANA, or a feminine of DEAN.
VARIANTS **Deena, Deana**
★ Deanna Durbin (1921–   ), Canadian actress and singer

Deanne *see* **Diane**

Dearbhla *see* **Dervla**

Deasún *see* **Desmond**

Deb *see* **Dev**

Debdan *see* **Devdan**

Deborah *f*
A biblical name from the Hebrew for 'bee'. It was the name of a woman who was a judge and prophet, and who even led the army of Israel. It came into use among English speakers in the 16th century, not so much because the Puritans relished the idea of such a strong-minded woman, but because the bee was then an important symbol of industriousness. It enjoyed great popularity in the 1960s. In the USA, in the 1950s, it was occasionally used for boys. See also BINA.
PET FORMS **Deb(s), Debbi(e), Debby**
• VARIANTS **Debora, Deb(b)ra, Debrah**
French **Débora(h)** *Hebrew* **Devorah, Dvorah** *Italian* **Debora** *Spanish* **Débora**
★ Deborah Kerr (1921–2007), Scottish actress
★ Debbie Harry (1945–   ), US singer

Decima *f* **Decimus** *m*
This, now rare, name is based on

the Latin for 'tenth'. Decimus was a common Roman first name, and was used occasionally in the English-speaking world, particularly in the 19th century when large families were in fashion and it could be used for a tenth child.

★ Decimus Burton (1800–81), English architect

Declan m

This is the more usual spelling of the Irish name *Deaglán*. although even in Ireland this latter form is comparatively rare. St Declan was a missionary to south-east Ireland even before the arrival of St Patrick, but the meaning of his name has been lost. The name has spread well beyond Ireland, and is currently a more popular choice for parents in England and Scotland than in its native land.

PET FORM **Dec** • VARIANTS **Deklan, Declyn**

★ Declan Donnelly (1975–   ), one-half of the British 'Ant and Dec' television presenting team

Dedrick see Derek

Dee mf

This started out as a pet form of any name beginning with 'D', but is now found as an independent name.

VARIANTS **Dee-Dee, Didi**

Deena see Deanna, Dena, Dinah

Deepak see Dipak

DeForest m

An American name, thought to have come into use with reference to the US writer John DeForest (1826–1906), whose American Civil War novels were very popular in their day. The surname simply means 'of the forest'.

VARIANT **Deforrest**

★ DeForest Kelly (1920–99), US actor who played Dr McCoy in the original *Star Trek* television series

★ Humphrey DeForest Bogart (1899–1957), US actor

Deiniol m

This is the name of an early Welsh saint, reputedly the first bishop of Bangor, who is also revered in Brittany. Its meaning is not known. It also functions as the Welsh equivalent of DANIEL.

VARIANT *Breton* **Denoual**

Deirdre f

Deirdre of the Sorrows is the heroine of one of the great tragic love stories of early Irish mythology. The beautiful Deirdre was betrothed to King Conchobhar (see CONNOR) but fell in love with Naoise. They eloped, but Naoise was murdered in revenge and Deirdre killed herself. The story was taken up by Irish nationalists as a parallel to the fate of their country, particularly as retold in 1907 by W B Yeats, and in 1910 by J M Synge. This led to widespread use both in Ireland and elsewhere. The name takes many forms and has varied pronunciations. In England it is usually pronounced 'deer-dree', but in Ireland 'deer-dra' or 'dare-dreh' is more common, and these pronunciations are also used in the USA.

VARIANTS **Deidre, Deidra, Diedra, Derdre**

Deklan see Declan

Del m

This is a pet form of names beginning with Del, such as DELBERT, and of DEREK, which came to be used as a first name after it was given exposure by the US singer Del Shannon (1934–90), who was born Charles Westover.

☆ Del Boy Trotter (Derek Edward Trotter) in the television series *Only Fools and Horses*

Delaney mf

This surname has become a

fashionable girl's name in the USA in the 21st century. It can come from a Norman French name *de l'aunaie*, 'from the alder grove', but is more prominently from an Irish surname. This comes from an old name *Dubhshlaine*, 'black defiance', which was re-formed under the influence of the Norman name.

Delbert *m*
A name which has been in use in the USA, from where it travelled to the West Indies, from at least the 1870s. It may be a blend of two common elements, or it may be a shortening of *Adelbert*, a German variant of ALBERT. The name was quite popular in the USA in the first two decades of the 20th century, but acquired a reputation for rusticity and had all but died out by the end of the 1980s.
★ Delbert Mann (1920–2007), US film director
☆ Delbert Wilkins was a comic West Indian character created by the comedian Lenny Henry in the 1980s

Delia *f*
Delia means 'of Delos' and, like CYNTHIA, was one of the titles of the goddess ARTEMIS, referring to the Greek island on which she was said to have been born. In Ireland it could also be a shortening of BIDELIA. It entered the stock of names via poetic use from the 16th century onwards, but has never been common.
★ Delia Smith (1941–), English cookery writer and broadcaster whose reliable recipes have given a whole new resonance to the name

Delilah *f*
In the Bible this is the name of Samson's mistress, who betrayed him to the Philistines. The name probably means 'delicate, nimble'. Surprisingly, it was well used among the Puritans on both sides of the Atlantic between the 16th and 18th centuries, and seems to be staging a comeback in the USA. Since the Puritans were sometimes prepared to give their children very negative-sounding names as reminders of human weakness, they may have chosen the name as a warning of women's perfidy.
VARIANTS **Delila** *French* **Dalila**

Della *f*
This is now established as an independent name, but was originally a short form of ADELA or sometimes of names such as DELIA.

Delma *see* **Fidelma**

Delmar *m*
This is the Spanish for 'of the sea'. It is the name of a number of places in the USA, where the name is mainly used, and Maria Reina del Mar, 'Mary, Queen of the Sea', is one of the Spanish titles of the Virgin Mary. It was in use from the 19th century in the USA, but came to be regarded as rather old-fashioned and unsophisticated, and had more or less died out by the end of the 1970s.
☆ Delmar is the name of the least intelligent of the trio of adventurers in the cult Coen brothers film *O Brother, Where Art Thou?* (2000)

Delphine *f*
This name, meaning 'of Delphi', comes from one of the titles of the Greek god Apollo, whose main oracle was at Delphi. The name entered the stock of late Roman names, and there was a masculine form, as borne by 4th-century St Delphinus of Bordeaux. The Blessed Delphine (1283–1358), a Provençal nun, probably took her name in his honour. However, the name only really came to the attention of the French when Madame de Staël published a successful novel called

Delphine in 1802. The name became fashionable in France thereafter, but died out in the earlier 20th century, only to come back temporarily in the 1970s. It also came into quiet English use in the 19th century.

VARIANTS **Dephin(i)a** *Italian, Spanish* **Delfina**

Delroy *m*

This is generally thought to have been an alteration of LEROY, perhaps influenced by DELMAR, although as Leroy means 'the king', and was originally given to servants of the king (*'de le roy'*), it could be a hangover from this. It has been most often used by the West Indian community.

Delta *f*

Although this is the name of the fourth letter in the Greek alphabet, as a first name it is more likely to have been used with reference to the type of river mouth named after the letter's triangular shape. Certainly, modern uses seem to be associated with the Mississippi Delta. The name has been in use in the USA since the 19th century.

★ Delta Goodrem (1984–), Australian singer and actress, said to have been named after the song 'Delta Lady'

Delun *f*

This is a Welsh name meaning 'pretty one'. See DELWEN.

Delwen *f* Delwyn *m*

These names are formed from the Welsh element *del*, 'neat, pretty', and the masculine and feminine of a common Welsh name element meaning 'fair, white, blessed'. Delwyn is sometimes used for females.

★ Delwyn Young (1982–), US baseball player

Delyth *f*

This name is formed from the Welsh element *del*, 'neat, pretty', combined with the ending -*yth* found in Welsh feminine names.

★ Delyth Morgan, Baroness Morgan of Drefelin (1961–), Welsh Labour peer

DeMarcus *m*

A name combining the fashionable prefix *De-* with MARCUS. It was introduced with other such names in the 1970s, and was particularly used by African Americans.

Demelza *f*

This is a Cornish place name used as a first name. The place name is in turn based on a first name, for it means 'hill-fort of Maeldaf'. Use of the name is recent, and it may have been created by Winston Graham for his *Poldark* series of novels of which the first, *Demelza*, was published in 1946. The name received a boost in the 1970s when the novels were very successfully adapted for television.

Demetrius *m*

In the ancient Greek religion, Demeter was the goddess of fertility and the patroness of a mystery religion. The name probably means 'earth mother'. Demetrius meant 'follower of Demeter'. This did not stop the name becoming that of several Christian saints, including one 4th-century martyr who became very popular with followers of the Eastern Orthodox Church. The name has been mildly popular in the USA since the 1960s.

VARIANTS **Demitris, Dimitrius** *Greek* **Demitrios, Dimitris, Dimos** *Italian, Spanish* **Demitrio** *Russian* **Dimitri, Dmitri, Dmitry, Mitya** *Slavic* **Demitar, Dimitar**

☆ Demetrius and LYSANDER are the two male leads in Shakespeare's *A Midsummer Night's Dream*

Demi *f*

Demi was originally a pet form of *Demitria*, feminine form of DEMETRIUS.

It came to public attention through the actress Demi Moore (born Demetria Gene Guynes). It subsequently spread to the general public, and has become popular in the UK. It is a name that is quite often combined with others to form compounds such as *Demi-Lee*. Demi Moore stresses her name on the second syllable, but others often stress it on the first.

VARIANTS **Demmi, Demie, Demitra, Dimitra**

Demyan *see* **Damian**

Dena *f*
This name can represent feminine coinages from names such as DEAN or DENIS, a respelling of DINAH, or a short form of names ending in *-dina*.

VARIANT **Deena**

Dene *see* **Dean**

Denham *m*
A surname used as a first name. The surname comes from a common place name meaning 'settlement in a valley'.

Denholm *m*
Originally a surname from a place name which means 'water-meadow in a valley'.

★ Denholm Elliott (1922–92), English actor

Denis, Dennis *m*
Denis, one the French spellings of the name, is now the most usual spelling of the name in the UK, although Dennis is still preferred in the USA. It has travelled a long way from its origins, which go back to the Greek god Dionysos. He was god of wine and inspiration, and was the object of a mystery religion so secret that we know almost nothing about it. His name possibly means 'son of Zeus', the king of the gods. The Greek name *Dionysios*, 'follower of Dionysos', became *Dionisius* in Latin, and spread across the Roman Empire. Among its bearers was a 3rd-century Christian who became the evangelist of the Gauls, and gave his name to the Parisian suburb of St Denis, the place of his burial. The shortening from Dionisius to Denis occurred in the popular speech of the Gauls. See also DION.

PET FORMS **Den, Denny** • VARIANT **Denys** (originally an Old French form)

★ Denis Healey (1917–   ), English Labour politician
★ Dennis Hopper (1936–   ), US actor
☆ Dennis the Menace, cartoon character

Denise *f*
The feminine form of DENIS, Denise was originally adopted from the French, where it represents a form of *Dionysia*, by the same process that turned *Dionisius* into Denis.

PET FORM **Deni** • VARIANTS **Denice, Deniese, Denyse, Denisa**

Denisha *f*
A modern coinage, used in the 1980s and 90s mainly by African Americans, presumably formed from DENISE combined with the fashionable *-isha* ending.

Denoual *see* **Deiniol**

Denver *mf*
This is a place name meaning 'Dane ford', which became a surname. The best-known place of that name, Denver, Colorado, was in turn named after James W Denver, governor of Kansas. Denver has been used as a first name in the USA since the 19th century.

☆ Denver is the name of a character in Toni Morrison's 1987 novel *Beloved*

Denzel *m*
This was originally a Cornish place name, perhaps derived from a word meaning 'fort', which became a

surname for the Denzell family. When they married into the Hollis family, the surname was preserved as a first name, and then spread to the wider public. The name has had a higher profile in the USA than in the UK in recent years.

VARIANT **Denzil**

★ Denzel Washington (1954–), US actor

★ Denzil Douglas (1953–), Prime Minister of St Kitts and Nevis

Deo see **Dev**

Deodan see **Devdan**

Deònaid see **Shona**

Deòrsa see **George**

Dephina, Dephinia see **Delphine**

Derby see **Darby**

Derdre see **Deirdre**

Derek m
The Germanic name *Theodoric*, 'ruler of the people', became prominent in early European history as the name of a number of famous people, including two kings of the Visigoths and, above all, Theodoric the Great, leader of the Ostrogoths in the 5th century. He was so famous that his name, and a very distorted version of his life, entered the mainstream of European legend. As a result the name spread through Europe, taking many forms. Romance languages tended to keep the 'T' form of his name, as in the French *Thierry*, which became TERRY. Germanic forms often have an initial 'D', as in *Dietrich*, the current form of the older *Diederich*. Derek derives from a Dutch form of this name, also found as *Dirk*. It was a popular name in the UK in the mid-20th century, but is not notably common now. In the USA it became popular rather later, peaking in the

1990s, and is still well used. Theodoric is also one of the sources of Terry.

PET FORMS **Ric(k), Del •** VARIANTS **Der(r)ic(k), Deryc(k), Der(r)ec(k), Dedrick, Dirk**

★ Sir Derek Jacobi (1938–), English actor

★ Sir Dirk Bogarde (1921–99), English actor

Derius see **Darius**

Dermot m
This is an Irish name that has spread well beyond its country of origin. The meaning of the name is not firmly established, but it may be 'free from envy'. It is a common name among the Irish saints (there are at least eleven of them) and in Irish mythology. The most famous bearer is Dermot of the Love Spot, who eloped with GRAINNE, the betrothed of FINN, with tragic results. In the past it was anglicized as Darby or DERBY.

VARIANTS **Dermod** *Irish* **Diarmaid, Diarmait, Dermuid** *Scots Gaelic* **Dermid, Diarmad**

Derrin see **Darren**

Derrius see **Darius**

Derry m
This is usually from a pet form of names such as DEREK and DERMOT, but in some cases may refer to the Northern Irish town, in which case it comes from the Irish word for an 'oak wood', and is thus related to DARRAGH.

★ Derry Irvine, Baron Irvine of Lairg (1940–), former Lord Chancellor

Dervla f
Two early Irish names have fallen together here. One is *Dearbháil*, the other *Deirbhile*. Both have a first element formed from *der* meaning 'daughter'. Dearbháil's second element is *Fál*, an old poetic term for Ireland. Deirbhile's second element is *file*

meaning 'poet'. St Deirbhile was a 6th-century Irish saint, whose well in County Mayo is said to cure eye problems.

VARIANTS **Dervila, Dervilla, Dearbhla, Derval**

★ Dervla Murphy (1931–), Irish travel writer

★ Dervla Kirwan (1971–), Irish actress

Deryn, Derryne f

This is the Welsh for 'blackbird', and the name is beginning to travel outside Wales. However, since forms such as *Derryn* are also found used for boys, some forms may represent reworkings of names such as DARREN.

Desdemona f

The name of the heroine of Shakespeare's *Othello* is still occasionally used, despite her tragic end. The name is thought to be derived from the Greek *dysdaimon* meaning 'ill-starred'. Shakespeare appears to have stressed the name on the second syllable, but modern use stresses it on the first and third.

DeShawn m

One of the more regularly used of the fashionable *De-* compound names, mainly used among African Americans. It is compounded from various spellings of SEAN, and also appears as *Keshawn* or *Keyshawn*. It has been in use since the early 1970s.

VARIANTS **Deshaun, Dashawn**

Desirée f

Latin had the names *Desideratus* and *Desiderata* meaning 'desired, wished for', and interpreted as having been chosen for a much-wanted child. These developed into various forms in various languages, Desirée being the French feminine form. It was in early use in France, as Desirée, or Desiderata, was the name of Charlemagne's wife in the 8th century,

named after her father DIDIER, King of the Lombards. There do not seem to be old forms in English, although *Desire* is recorded as a 17th-century man's name. What seems to have introduced the name into English was a film first shown in 1954; this is certainly the year in which the name first appears in the top 1000 feminine names in the USA, where it has remained in steady use ever since. The film, called *Desirée*, which starred Jean Simmons in the title role and Marlon Brando as Napoleon, was based on the bestselling novel of the same name by Annemarie Selinko. This in turn was based on the real-life character of Bernardine Eugénie Désirée Clary, known as Désirée Clary, one-time fiancee of Napoleon, and later Queen of Sweden and Norway, under the name of *Desideria*.

VARIANTS **Desiree, Desirae** *French* **Desiré** (m) *Italian, Spanish, Portuguese* **Desiderio** (m)

★ Desiderius Erasmus (c.1466–1536), Dutch humanist and scholar

★ Des'ree (Desirée Weeks) (1968–), English singer

Desmond m

This was originally a surname, which in Gaelic is *Deas-Mhumhan* meaning 'someone from south Munster'. It was also the title of the earls of Desmond, and this may be why it came into use as a first name in the 19th century, when aristocratic names were popular.

PET FORMS **Des, Desi, Desy, Dez(z)I**

• VARIANT *Irish* **Deasún**

★ Desmond Lynam (1942–), Irish-born British sports presenter

★ Des O'Connor (1932–), English singer

Destiny f

This is the vocabulary word used as a first name. It has been in use in the USA since the mid-1970s, and has been in the top 50 girls' names there for the last decade. It is beginning to make its mark in the UK. Parents need to be careful with their spelling, as there is at least one child on record who has ended up with the name *Density*. There is a much rarer masculine equivalent, *Destin*.

VARIANTS **Destinee, Destiney, Destini**

☆ Destiny is the eldest of 'The Endless' in Neil Gaiman's cult graphic novel series *The Sandman* (1989–96)

Desya *see* **Modestine**

Detta *see* **Bernadette**

Dev *m* **Devi** *f*
This is a Sanskrit term for 'god'. The masculine form is also a title of the god INDRA, as well as being used to address royalty. Devi is a title of the Hindu mother goddess.

VARIANTS **Deo, Deb**

Devaki *f*
This name, meaning 'black', belonged to the god KRISHNA's mother in Hindu mythology.

Devdan *m*
This is a Sanskrit name formed from *deva*, 'god', and *dana*, 'gift', and thus means 'gift of the gods'.

VARIANTS **Deodan, Debdan**

Devdas *m*
This is a Sanskrit name formed from *deva*, 'god', and *dasa*, 'servant', so means 'servant of the gods'.

VARIANT **Devadas**

Devika *f*
This is a Sanskrit name formed from DEVI with the ending *ka* meaning 'little, like'. It is usually glossed as 'little goddess'.

Devin *mf*
This has been analysed as a reuse of the Irish surname Devin, in Gaelic

O Damháin which is 'descendant of *Damháin*', with *Damháin* meaning 'fawn'. However, given the wide variety of forms the name DEVON takes, it seems more likely that it functions as much as variant of this name. Devin is currently popular in the USA.

VARIANT **Devyn**

Devlin *m*
The Irish and Scottish surname, of uncertain meaning but sometimes glossed as either 'fiercely brave' or 'unlucky', used as a first name.

VARIANT **Devlyn**

Devnet *see* **Davnat**

Devon *mf*
This is the English county name, also found as a surname, used as a first name. Devon got its name from the ancient British tribe of the Dumnonii who lived there. Their name is thought to mean 'worshippers of the god Dumnonos'. There is much variation in the form of the name, and considerable overlap with DEVIN.

VARIANTS **Devan, DaVon, Devyn**

★ Devon Malcolm (1963–), Jamaican-born England cricketer

★ Devon Aoki (1982–), US supermodel and actress

Devorah *see* **Deborah**

Devorgilla
This is the anglicized form of the Scots Gaelic name *Diobhail*, 'true testimony'. It was a common name among the Highlanders and Islanders of Scotland, from the Middle Ages onwards, although its frequency is masked by the fact that it was often turned into DOROTHY or *Doll* in written documents. When it does appear in its own form it is in a bewildering number of different spellings and transitional forms between Latin and Gaelic. There is some overlap between forms of this

name and the ones that lie behind DERVLA.

VARIANT **Diorbhall**

★ Dervorg(u)illa, Princess of Galloway (c.1210–90), was co-founder of Balliol College, Oxford, with her son John I of Scotland

DeWayne *see* Duane

Dewey *m*

There is disagreement about the origin of this name. Some see it as an English spelling of *Dewi*, which is one Welsh form of DAVID. Others link it to the surname, which is of unknown meaning. As the name has been in use in the USA since the 19th century, and the Dewey family was prominent in early US history, the latter interpretation seems the more likely, particularly as Dewi was mainly restricted to sacred use as the name of the national saint, until the 20th century. Dewey can also be a pet form of DUANE.

VARIANT **Dewy**

☆ Dewey, along with Huey and Louie, is one of the nephews of the cartoon character Donald Duck

☆ Dewey Denouement is a character in the children's books *A Series of Unfortunate Events* by Lemony Snicket

Dexter *m*

As a surname, Dexter means 'a (female) dyer'. However, in Latin the word means 'right handed, fortunate', and the name may be taken from this.

FEMININE **Dextra** • PET FORM **Dex**

Dez, Dezi, Dezz, Dezzi *see* Desmond

Dhani *m*

This name, pronounced much the same as *Danny*, was chosen by the musician George Harrison for his son, and a number of others have followed suit. It is formed from the

names of two notes of a musical scale in Indian music. It may be that the current trend to respell other names normally beginning *Da-*, with *Dha-*, was inspired by this.

Diamond *f*

One of the less common jewel names. Diamonds get their name from a corruption of the word 'adamant', meaning 'very hard'. This is turn comes from the Greek *a*, 'not', and *daman*, 'to tame' (see DAMON), used because, as the hardest of materials, diamonds cannot be marked by anything else.

Diana *f*

Diana was the name of the Roman goddess of the moon and the hunt, the equivalent of the Greek ARTEMIS. Her name appears to be from the same root as *deus*, the Latin for 'god'. In the Elizabethan period the name was well used in a literary context, particularly with reference to Elizabeth, the Virgin Queen, for Diana was also symbolic of chastity (compare CYNTHIA). However, it was comparatively rare as a given name until the 19th century, when it experienced a popularity which lasted into the first part of the 20th century. Surprisingly, the enormous popularity of Diana, Princess of Wales, has only had a mild influence on the frequency of a name that had become a deeply unpopular choice for parents.

PET FORM **Di** • VARIANTS **Dianna, Dean(n)a** *Hawaiian* **Kiana** *Slavic* **Dijana**

★ Diana Dors (1931–84), English actress

★ Diana Ross (1944–), US singer

Diane *f*

The French form of DIANA. The famously beautiful mistress of King Henri II of France, Diane de Poitiers (1499–1566), was an early bearer of the name, and gave it long-lasting glamour.

PET FORM **Di** • VARIANTS **Diann(e), Dyan, Deanne**

DiAngelo *see* **DeAngelo**

Diarmad, Diarmaid, Diarmait *see* **Dermot**

Dick, Dickie *m*
This is a pet form of RICHARD that has taken on a life of its own. People love to play with the sounds of pet names and the change of a first or last sound is not uncommon. Thus ROBERT gets shortened to *Rob* and then changed to *Bob*. It has been suggested that the change from *Rick*, as a shortening of Richard, to Dick occurred because the English could not manage the rolled 'r' of a Norman French name, but this does not seem necessary – 'r' is a notoriously unstable sound. The surname from Dick, Dickson, is occasionally also used as a first name.
VARIANT **Dicky**
★ Dick Turpin (1705–39), English highwayman
★ Dickie Davies (1933–), English television presenter

Dickon *m*
This is the old equivalent of DICKIE, with the French pet-form ending *-on* instead of the English *-ie*. It was popular in the Middle Ages and is still occasionally used.

Dicky *see* **Richard**

Didi *see* **Dee**

Didier *m*
Didier is the French masculine equivalent of DÉSIRÉE, being a form of *Desideratus*. This was an early Christian name meaning 'longed for, desired'. It was a popular name among Christians and was the name of many early saints.
PET FORM **Didi**
★ Didier Drogba (1978–), Ivory Coast-born Chelsea FC player

Dido *f*
The name of the tragic Queen of Carthage who killed herself for love after Aeneas, founder of the Roman people, left her, despite the fact that she had been a successful and enterprising ruler up to this point. This ancient story, often retold in literature, drama and opera, has kept the name alive, although it has not been used very much in real life.
★ Dido (1971–), English singer
★ Dido Elizabeth Belle (1761–1804), illegitimate great-niece of the Earl of Mansfield, whose mother was a black slave. Mansfield raised her in his household, and she is thought to have influenced rulings he made as Lord Chief Justice which led to the abolition of slavery
☆ Dido Twite, heroine of Joan Aiken's *Wolves* series of books for children

Diedra *see* **Deirdre**

Diego *m*
There is some doubt about the origin of this name. It is generally thought to be a form of SANTIAGO with the first three letters dropped, and then a slight modification of the sound. Others see it as a form of the name of a saint, *Didacus*, a name of obscure origin found in medieval Spain and sometimes linked to the Greek *didache* meaning 'teaching'.
VARIANT *Portuguese* **Tiego**
★ Diego Rivera (1886–1957), Mexican painter
★ Diego Maradona (1960–), Argentine footballer

Dieter *m*
This is a German name, formed ultimately from the elements *theud*, 'people', and *heri*, 'army', and usually interpreted as 'warrior of the people'.
★ Dieter Schnebel (1930–), German composer

★ Dieter Brummer (1976–), Australian actor who played Shane Parrish in the television soap opera *Home and Away*

Dietrich *see* **Derek**

Dieudonne *see* **Donata**

Digby *m*
This is a place name in Lancashire, from the Old Norse *diki*, 'ditch', and *byr*, 'settlement', used first as a surname and then as a first name.
★ Digby Jones, Baron Jones of Birmingham (1955–), English businessman and politician
☆ Digby was Dan Dare's loyal batman in the strip cartoon adventure series in the *Eagle* comic

Diggory *m*
This now rare name appears to be an early example of a name adopted from English literature. The history of the name is not entirely clear, but the best bet seems to be that it comes from a hero of medieval romance, Sir Degaré. His name, in turn, comes from the French *égaré*, 'lost', for the story tells of his being separated from his family as a baby, and how he is eventually reunited with them. The name was well used in the 16th century, but by the 18th had come to seem rustic. As a result, most notable uses of the name are reserved for literary rustics. The most prominent 20th-century use was in the respelt form of Digory Kirk, in C S Lewis's *Narnia* stories, and modern uses are likely to be connected to this. Otherwise, the name is now better known as a surname.
☆ Diggory Venn in Thomas Hardy's *The Return of the Native* (1878)
☆ Diggory Compton was a character in the television soap opera *Coronation Street* (2005–6).

Dijana *see* **Diana**

Dil *see* **Daffodil**

Dilek *f*
This is a Muslim name, from the Turkish for 'wish, desire'.

Dilip *m*
An Indian name, borne by several legendary kings, which probably means 'defender of Delhi'.
VARIANTS **Duleep, Dilipa, Dileep**

Dillan, Dillon *see* **Dylan**

Dilly *f*
This is a pet form of names such as DAFFODIL, DILYS and DILWEN sometimes found as an independent name.

Dilwen *f* **Dilwyn** *m*
This is usually said to be a modern Welsh name, a blend of the *Dil-* from names such as DILYS and the common Welsh name ending *wen* (f) or *wyn* (m), which can be translated as 'fair', 'white', 'blessed' or 'holy', depending on the context. However, the name may have been inspired by the surname Dillwyn which, although well-established in Wales, actually comes from a Herefordshire place name, Dilwyn, from an English term meaning 'a secret or hidden place'.

Dilys *f*
This is the Welsh for 'genuine, sincere, true'. According to Trefor Davies in *A Book of Welsh Names* the name was first used 'by William and Jane Davis for their daughter who was born on the 11th June, 1857, at St Pancras, Middlesex. It is said to have been taken from the xxiii Psalm in the metrical version written by Edmund Prys (1544–1623)'.
PET FORM **Dilly** • VARIANTS **Dylis, Dyllis**
★ Dilys Powell (1901–95), English film critic

Dima *f*
This is an Arabic name, a term for the sort of steady rain that soaks into the ground and makes the desert bloom.

Dimitar *see* **Demetrius**

Dimitra *see* **Demi**

Dimitri, **Dimitris**, **Dimitrius**, **Dimos** *see* **Demetrius**

Dina *f* **Dino** *m*
An Italian first name, created from the pet forms of names that end with corresponding sounds, such as *Bernardina* or *Bernardino*.
★ Dino De Laurentiis (1919–   ), Italian film producer

Dinah *f*
Although many use this name as a variant of DIANA, it was originally a completely separate name, coming from the Hebrew *din*, 'judgement', the same root as DANIEL. The name came into use in the 16th century, after the Reformation.
VARIANTS *French* **Dina** *Hebrew* **Deena**
★ Dinah Washington (1924–63), US jazz and rhythm-and-blues singer

Dinesh *m*
This is the Sanskrit for 'lord of the day', which is a title of the sun.

Dino *see* **Dina**

Dinsdale
A place name meaning 'settlement by a moat' used first as a surname and then as an occasional first name.
★ Dinsdale Landen (1932–2003), English actor
☆ Dinsdale is one of the Piranha brothers in a 1970 Monty Python sketch, based on the East End gangsters of the time

Dion *m* **Dionne** *f*
Dion was originally a short form of *Dionysius* and similar names, and thus related to DENIS. It has been recorded among English speakers since the 16th century, and is nowadays particularly associated with African Americans. Dionne is one of several feminine

versions, although the full form, *Dionysia*, was in regular use in England between the 14th and 17th centuries.
VARIANTS **Dione**, **Dion(n)a**
★ Dion Boucicault (1820–90), Irish actor and playwright
★ Dionne Warwick (1940–   ), US soul and pop singer

Diondre *see* **DeAndre**

Dior *f*
The name of the fashion and perfume house, which came from its founder Christian Dior, used as a first name. Compare the more common CHANEL.

Diorbhall *see* **Devorgilla**

Dipak *m*
An Indian name meaning 'little light', one of the titles of Karma, the god of love.
VARIANT **Deepak**

Dipesh *m*
An Indian name meaning 'lord of light'.

Dirk *see* **Derek**

Divine *mf*
This seems to be used as part of the modern trend for Evangelical names, echoing the Puritan use of the 16th and 17th centuries. It has been recorded in punning, but overtly Christian, compounds such as *Divine-Will* and *Divine-Grace*.

Dixie *f*
This is an American name, particularly associated with the Southern States, from the term for the American South used in Daniel Emmett's 1959 song 'Dixie'. The name is thought to come from *dix*, the French for 'ten' which was printed on the $10 bills issued in New Orleans where French was a second language. It was in use in

the 19th century, and peaked during World War II.

Djamil, Djamila see **Jamil**

Dmitri, Dmitry see **Demetrius**

Dod see **Robert**

Dodie f
A pet form of DOROTHY, sometimes given as a name in its own right.
VARIANT **Dodo**
★ Dodie Smith (1896–1990), English writer

Doirind see **Doreen**

Dolag see **Donald**

Dolf see **Randolf**

Dolina see **Donald**

Dolly f
Dolly, or *Doll*, was originally a pet form of DOROTHY. In the 17th century the name was so common that it came to be given to the little model babies played with by children. Dolly has been used as an independent name since the 18th century. It is now sometimes also used as a pet form of DOLORES. See also ADOLPH.
VARIANT **Dolley**
★ Dolly Parton (1946–   ), US country singer
★ Dolly the Sheep (1996–2003), was the first cloned sheep

Dolores f
This was originally a Spanish name, taken from the title *Maria de los Dolores*, 'Mary of the Sorrows'. The name was well used in the USA in the first half of the 20th century.
PET FORMS **Lola, Lolita, Dolly** • VARIANT *Italian* **Addolorata**
★ Dolores del Rio (1905–83), Mexican actress

Dolph, Dolphus see **Adolph, Randolf**

Dominic m
The Latin vocabulary word *dominus*, 'lord, master', developed into a name *Dominicus*, which became Dominic in popular speech. It became a widely used name in honour of St Dominic (1170–1221), a Spaniard who founded the order of Dominican Friars, and who is also the patron saint of astronomers. Since the name has the same root as the word for Sunday in Romance languages (eg *domingo* in Spanish, *domenica* in Italian) it has been particularly used for children born on Sunday. In Ireland the name was sometimes used as the equivalent of *Domhnall*, DONALD.
PET FORMS **Dom, Nic** • VARIANTS **Domenic, Domini(c)k** *Dutch* **Dominicus** *French* **Dominique** *German, Polish, Slavic* **Dominik** *Italian* **Domenico** *Portuguese* **Domigos** *Spanish* **Domingo**

Dominica f
A feminine form of DOMINIC. There were at least two St Dominicas, one was a supporter of St Lawrence, another was an early martyr whose legend says that she was so pure, the wild animals set to devour her refused to touch her.
VARIANTS *Italian* **Domenica** *Polish, Russian, Slavic* **Dominika** *Spanish* **Dominga**

Dominique f
This is the French feminine form of DOMINIC, used for both sexes in France, and regularly used as a masculine in the USA since the 1970s.
PET FORM **Minique**

Domitilla f
There was a Roman family name *Domitianus* which was that of the emperor we call Domitian (AD 51–96). Domatilla is a feminine pet form of the name. There is a saint called Flavia Domitilla who was martyred during Domitian's persecution of Christians, and is said to have been a relative of

the emperor. The name is mainly used in Italy.

VARIANT *French* **Domitille**

Donald *m*

This is the standard English form of the Scots Gaelic name *Domhnall*, formed from Old Celtic elements *dubno*, 'world', and *val*, 'rule'. The name was at one time thought of as typically Scottish, but from the mid-19th century it was taken to North America and Australasia by Scottish emigrants, and by the 1920s was being widely used throughout the English-speaking world. Shakespeare's *Donalbain*, in *Macbeth*, was properly *Domhnall Ban*, 'Donald the Fair', who ruled as king of Scotland (1093–97). As with many Highland names, there are a number of feminine forms, some of which are not uncommon in 19th-century Highland school registers, but which are much rarer now.

FEMININES **Dolina, Donalda, Donaldina, Donella** *Scots Gaelic* **Dolag** • PET FORMS **Don, Donnie, Donny** • VARIANTS *Irish* **Dónal, Donal(l)**

★ Donald Campbell (1921–67), English land and water speed record breaker
★ Donald Sutherland (1935–), Canadian actor
☆ The Walt Disney character Donald Duck

Donata *f* Donatus *m*

This is a name from the Latin for 'given', adopted with a spiritual sense by early Christians. French uses the even more explicit *Dieudonné(e)* compounded from the French for 'God' and 'given'. Compare DOROTHY and THEODORE. These names have never been much used by English speakers, but are in regular use on the Continent. See also DONNACHADH.

PET FORM **Donna** • VARIANTS *French* **Donat, Donatien** *Italian* **Donatello, Donatella**

★ Donatello (Donato di Niccolo) (c.1386–1466), Italian sculptor
★ Donatella Versace (1955–), Italian designer

Donla *f*

This is the modern Irish form of the old name *Dúnflaith* meaning either 'brown lady' or 'lady of the *dún* ('fort')'. The name was well used in the Middle Ages, occurring both in saga and real life, and was revived in the 19th century.

VARIANT **Dunla**

Donna *f*

This is the Italian word for 'lady', often given as a title of respect, used as a first name. Although it is often described as a 20th-century name, it was in fact well established in the USA in the latter part of the 19th century, and was extremely popular there from the 1920s to the 1970s. It was not until the second half of the 20th century that it really began to make its mark in the UK. It is sometimes used as a feminine for DONALD. Compare MADONNA.

★ Donna Summer (1948–), US singer
★ Donna Tartt (1963–), US writer

Donnachadh *m*

This Irish name is pronounced 'don-a-HA', and is a compound of *donn*, 'brown', and *chadh*, 'chief'. In Scotland it became DUNCAN. In the past it was sometimes anglicized as *Donat* (see DONATA). This was the name of a High King of Ireland, the son of Brian Boru, who died in 1064.

VARIANTS **Donnach, Donagh, Donough**

Donny *see* Donald

Donovan *m*

This is an Irish surname, derived from a name meaning 'dark brown', used as a first name since at least the end of the 19th century. It was first brought to public attention in

1882 when Edna Lyall published a novel called *Donovan*, but only really came to prominence in the 1960s with the success of the Scottish singer-songwriter Donovan (Donovan Leitch, b.1946). The name has been moderately popular in the USA in recent years.

PET FORM **Don(ny)** • VARIANT **Donavan**

Donte *see* Dante

Dora *f*
This was originally a short form of names ending in *-dora* which usually share a derivation from the Greek *doron* meaning 'gift'. It was particularly a pet form of DOROTHY or *Dorothea*. It is now usually regarded as an independent name.

PET FORM **Dor(r)y** • VARIANTS **Doria, Doretta, Dorette, Dorita**
- ★ Dora Bryan (1924–   ), English actress
- ★ Dora Carrington (1893–1932), English painter
- ☆ Dora the Explorer, children's animated character

Doran *m*
An Irish first name which is a transferred used of the surname. This, in Irish, is *O Deoradháin* 'descendant of *Deoradhin*', a name which meant 'stranger, exile, pilgrim'.

Dorcas *f*
This is from the Greek word for a doe or gazelle. It was not used as a first name in ancient Greece, but in the Acts of the Apostles (9.3) we are told 'there was at Joppa a certain disciple named Tabitha, which by interpretation is called Dorcas', who was 'full of good works and almsdeeds' who was miraculously restored to life by St Peter. The name was enthusiastically adopted by the Puritans as a suitable role model for their daughters. In 1834 the first Dorcas Society was founded to emulate her charitable deeds by providing clothing and necessities to the poor. In Scotland, in the past, the name Dorcas might represent an anglicization of the Scots Gaelic name *Deòiridh*, from the Scots Gaelic for 'pilgrim', which is pronounced something like 'JOR-ee'.

Doreen *f*
There is some debate over the origin of this name. There is one view that it is a blend of names such as DORA with the *-een* ending of names such as KATHLEEN. This would make it a separate name from the Irish name *Dorean*, an anglicized form of *Dáireann*, an old name which may mean 'daughter of Finn'. The book that brought Doreen to public attention, Edna Lyall's *Doreen, The Story of a Singer* (1894), treats the name as Irish, which would support the Dorean theory. The name was popular in the UK in the first part of the 20th century, but is little used now; it peaked in the USA in the 1950s and 60s.

VARIANT *Irish* **Doirind**

Dorian *mf*
This name seems to have been invented by Oscar Wilde for his novella *The Portrait of Dorian Gray* (1891). The name was probably modelled on DORIS, with which it shares a root, and which was popular at the time. The name was taken up, despite the disreputable nature of the character for whom it was coined, and soon came to be used for both sexes. The name has been out of fashion for a long time in the UK, although there are hints that it may be coming back, but is used regularly in the USA.

VARIANTS **Dor(r)ien, Dorion, Dorianne** (f)
- ★ Dorian Williams (1914–85), English sports commentator
- ★ Dorian Leigh (1917–2008), US photographic model, sometimes

described as the world's first supermodel

Dorinda *f*

This is a literary coinage of the 17th century, probably modelled on such literary names as BELINDA and CLARINDA, which is now used as a first name, possibly influenced by DORINE.

★ Dorinda Clark Cole (1957–   ), US singer

☆ Dorinda is the daughter of Lady Bountiful in George Farquhar's comedy *The Beaux' Stratagem* (1707)

Dorine *f*

A French name, either based on DOROTHY or from the same root as DORIS. Like *Dorinda*, it started out in the 17th century as a literary name, most notably in Molière's *Tartuffe* (1664).

VARIANTS **Dorina, Doraine**

Doris *f*

This is a Greek name meaning 'Dorian woman' referring to one of the main tribal groupings of ancient Greece. Doris was also the name of a sea goddess, the wife of Nereus and mother of the Nereids (see NERISSA).

PET FORM **Dorrie**

★ Doris Day (1924–   ), US singer and actress

★ Doris Lessing (1919–   ), Rhodesian Nobel Prize-winning novelist

Doron *m*

Doron comes from the Greek for 'gift', but has been adopted into the stock of Jewish names. It is occasionally given to girls.

Dorothy *f*

Dorothy means 'gift of God', being formed from the Greek *doron*, 'gift', and *theos*, 'god', elements also found in THEODORA. The romantic legend of St Dorothy tells that while she was going to her martyrdom a pagan offered to convert if she would send him roses

and apples picked in Paradise after her death, a miracle which she performed.

PET FORMS **Dot, Dotty, Dottie, Dodie, Dorrit, Dolly, Dora, Dory, Thea**

• VARIANTS **Dorothea** *French* **Dorothée** *German* **Dörthe, Tea** *Greek* **Dorotheos** *Polish* **Dorota** *Russian* **Dorofei, Darija** *Scandinavian* **Dorote, Dorthe, Tea** *Spanish* **Dorita, Dorotea**

★ Dorothy Parker (1893–1967), US writer and wit

★ Dorothy L Sayers (1893–1957), English detective-story writer

☆ Dorothy is the heroine of Frank L Baum's novel *The Wonderful Wizard of Oz* (1900) and the later film

Douce, Douceline, Doucette *see* Dulcie

Dougal *m*

The Scots Gaelic name *Dubhgall* is formed from *dubh*, 'black, dark', and *gall*, 'stranger', said originally to have been applied to the dark-haired Danish Viking invaders, as opposed to the FINGAL, given to the blond Swedes. It is thought of as a typically Scottish name, and not widely used outside the country.

PET FORMS **Dug(gie), Doug(ie), Duggy**

• VARIANTS **Dugal, Dugald** *Scots Gaelic* **Dughall**

☆ Dougal, puppet dog from the children's television series *The Magic Roundabout*

Douglas *m*

This is the surname of one of the most powerful and influential families in Scottish history. Sir James Douglas, known as 'the Black Douglas', was a follower of Robert the Bruce. He founded the family fortune and captured the castle of Douglas, named after the 'black stream' nearby, from the English. The name was used for both sexes in the 17th and 18th

centuries, but is now exclusively
masculine.

FEMININE **Douglasina** • PET FORMS **Dug(gie),
Doug(ie), Duggy**

Dougray *m*
This name was adopted by the Scottish
actor, Dougray Scott, who took his
grandmother's surname in place of
his birth name of Stephen. The name
has started to be used by the general
public.

Dov *m*
This is a Jewish name, meaning 'bear'.
It can also be a form of DAVID.

Dovid *see* David

Doyle *m*
The Irish surname *O Dubhghaill*,
'descendant of *Dugal*', was anglicized
as Doyle, which has subsequently
been used as a first name, mainly in
the USA.

Drake *m*
A surname used as a first name, which
has been increasingly popular in the
USA since the early 1990s.

Dre *m*
Originally a pet form of *André*, the
French form of ANDREW, which has been
well used in the USA since the 1960s.
It was popularized by the rap singer
known as Dr Dre (André Romelle
Young) and is now being used as an
independent name.

Dreda *f*
A 19th-century name, originally a
short form of ETHELDREDA, or a pet form
of *Eldreda* (see ELDRED).

Dreena *f*
A Scottish first name, originally from
Andrene, a feminine form of ANDREW.

Drena *see* Drina

Drene *see* Adrianna

Drew *mf*
This was originally a Scottish pet
form of ANDREW, which became an
independent name, still well used
in Scotland. Drew also became a
surname. In the case of the actress
Drew Barrymore, who has brought the
name to public attention as a feminine
name, it was a family surname reused
as a first name.

Drina *f*
A short form of ADRIANNA and similar
feminine forms of ADRIAN. It is also used
as a short form of *Alexandrina* (see
ALEXANDRA).

VARIANT **Drena**

Drogo *m*
This was a name prominent among
the European aristocracy in the early
Middle Ages, and introduced to
England with the Norman Conquest,
but which is now all but obsolete.
Its meaning is not known, but it may
come from a Slavic element meaning
'dear'.

☆ Drogo Baggins, father of Frodo Baggins
in J R R Tolkien's *The Lord of the Rings*
trilogy (1954–5)

Drusilla *f*
This is a Roman family name used
as a first name. According to Roman
legend, it was adopted by an ancestor
who had killed a Gaulish chieftain
named *Drausus* in battle, and
thereafter called himself *Drusus*. There
is a brief mention of a woman called
Drusilla in the Acts of the Apostles
(24.24) which made it available to
users in the 17th century when New
Testament names were popular.

PET FORMS **Dru, Drue**

Duaa *f*
An Arabic name meaning 'prayer'.
VARIANT **Dua**

Duald *m*
An Irish name, from *dubh fholtach*
which means 'black-haired'.
VARIANTS **Dualta** *Irish* **Dubhaltach**

Duane *m*
An anglicized form of the Gaelic
Dubhan, from *dubh* meaning 'dark'
with a pet ending. The name was
fashionable from the 1940s to 1970s.
VARIANTS **Dwane, Dwayne, Dwain,**
DeWayne (US variant)
★ Duane Eddy (1938–), US guitarist

Duarte *see* **Edward**

Dubhaltach *see* **Duald**

Dubhdara *m*
The Irish name DARA, 'oak', with the
element *dubh*, 'black', in front.

Dudel *see* **David**

Dudley *m*
The name of the English town of
Dudley, also an aristocratic surname,
from the Old English meaning
'Dudda's clearing' became a first name
in England in the 19th century. In the
USA the name was introduced earlier
as a first name by the descendants of
Thomas Dudley who emigrated from
England to Massachusetts in 1630.
In Ireland it was used, in the past, to
anglicize DARA or DUBHDARA.
PET FORM **Dud**
★ Dudley Moore (1935–2002), English
   actor and musician

Duff *m*
A Scottish surname turned first name,
originally from the Gaelic *dubh*,
'black', which would have been a
nickname for somone dark-haired.
★ Duff Cooper, 1st Viscount Norwich
   (1890–1954), English diplomat,
   politician and writer

Dug *see* **Dougal, Douglas**

Dugal, Dugald *see* **Dougal**

Duggie, Duggy *see* **Dougal,**
Douglas

Dughall *see* **Dougal**

Duha *f*
This is an Arabic name which, as well
as meaning 'morning', is also the title
of the 93rd sura of the Koran.

Duke *m*
Usually a nickname, but sometimes a
given name, from the aristocratic title.
This can also be a short form of the
name MARMADUKE.
★ Duke Ellington (1899–1974), US jazz
   pianist and composer

Dulcie *f*
A name based on the Latin *dulcis*,
'sweet'. Although it became popular in
the 19th century, there was an earlier
English name, *Dowse*, based on the
Latin name *Dulcia* which came from
the same source, and other languages
had similar names based on the
same root. The best-known of these is
Dulcinea, the object of Don Quixote's
affections.
VARIANTS **Dulcibella** *French* **Douce,**
Douceline, Doucette *Spanish* **Dulce**
★ Dulcie Gray (1919–), British actress,
   born in Malaya

Duleep, Dulip *see* **Dilip**

Duncan *m*
This is the anglicized form of the
Scots Gaelic *Donnchadh* (compare
DONNACHADH) meaning 'brown chief'.
The Duncan murdered by Macbeth in
Shakespeare's play was the first king
of all the Scots who died in 1040,
apparently while still a young man.

Dunla *see* **Donla**

Dunstan *m*
St Dunstan was a popular Anglo-Saxon
saint, with a lively legend which
depicts him in conflict with the Devil,

including one occasion when he is said to have grabbed the Devil by the nose with a pair of blacksmith's tongs. In real life he was a reforming archbishop of Canterbury. The name comes from Old English elements meaning 'brown stone'.

Durante see **Dante**

Dustin m
This name entered the stock of English names through the US actor Dustin Hoffman. He in turn is said to have been named after an earlier actor, Dustin Farnam. The name is thought to be from a French surname which comes from THURSTAN.
VARIANTS **Dustan, Dusten**

Dvorah see **Deborah**

Dwayne, Dwain, Dwane see **Duane**

Dwight m
This is a transferred use of a French surname which comes from *Diot*, a pet form of *Dionysia*. The Dwight family was prominent in the early years of US history. Modern use comes from President Dwight D Eisenhower (1890–1969), supreme commander of the Allied forces in western Europe during World War II. He in turn was named after the philosopher Timothy Dwight (1752–1817).
★ Dwight Yoakam (1956–   ), US country singer and actor

Dwyer m
An Irish surname, from an Irish nickname *Duibhuidhir* combining words for 'dark' and 'tawney', now sometimes found as a first name.

Dyan see **Diane**

Dyddgu f
A Welsh name which was popular in the Middle Ages and early modern period. It has been revived because it was the name of the dark-haired beauty to which Dafydd ap Gwilym, one of Wales's most famous medieval poets, addresses his despairing love poetry. The name is pronounced something like 'dith-gee'.
★ Dyddgu Owen (1906–92), author of Welsh children's books

Dylan m
This is an ancient Welsh name, probably coming from the word for 'sea', found in the *Mabinogion*, one of the most important collections of early Welsh literature. The fame of the singer Bob Dylan has done much to popularize the name outside Wales.
VARIANTS **Dillon, Dillan, Dylin, Dyllan**
★ Dylan Thomas (1914–53), Welsh poet

Dylis, Dyllis see **Dilys**

Dymphna f
This is a form of the name of St *Dympna* of Gheel in Belgium, patron saint of the insane. Her legend says that she was a medieval Irish princess who fled her home in horror at her father's incestuous advances. Because of this story the name is sometimes used in Ireland. It has been suggested that the original form of the name may have been *Damhnait* (DAVNAT).

E

Eachann *m*
Eachann is a Scots Gaelic name, made up of the elements *each*, 'horse', and *donn*, 'brown'. In the past it was anglicized as HECTOR, which is how that came to be a typically Scottish name. The correspondence is easier to understand when you realize that Hector can become *Eachtar* in Gaelic. Eachann is pronounced 'ACH-an', with the 'ch' as in the Scottish word 'loch'.
VARIANT **Eachan**

Éadaoin, Eadan *see* **Etain**

Eadbhárd *see* **Edward**

Eairdsidh, Eairrsidh *see* **Archibald**

Ealasaid *see* **Ailsa, Elizabeth**

Ealdred *see* **Aldred**

Ealga *f*
An Irish name meaning 'noble, brave'. *Innis Ealga*, 'the noble island', is a poetic term for Ireland. The name is pronounced 'ale-ga'.

Eamonn *m*
This is the Irish form of EDMUND.
VARIANTS **Eamon, Eaman(n)** *Irish* **Éamon(n), Éaman(n)**
★ Eamonn Holmes (1959–), Northern Irish television presenter
★ Éamon de Valera (1882–1975), Irish statesman

Ean *see* **John**

Eanna, Éanna *see* **Enda**

Eanraig *see* **Henry**

Earl *m*
The aristocratic title, or the surname given originally to a person who worked for an earl, used as a first name, mainly in the USA.
FEMININES **Earla, Earleen, Earlene, Earline**
• VARIANT **Earle**
☆ Earl J Hickey, principal character in the television series *My Name is Earl*

Earnán *see* **Ernan**

Earnest *see* **Ernest**

Eartha *f*
A rare name, most likely to be found among African Americans. In the past there was a tradition in the southern states of the USA, that if you had lost two children in infancy you could try to prevent further loss by giving a subsequent child a name linked with death or burial, such as ASHLEY (as in 'dust to dust, ashes to ashes') or Eartha (based on 'earth').
VARIANTS **Ertha, Erthel**
★ Eartha Kitt (1927–2008), US singer

Easton *m*
This is a surname, from a place name meaning 'settlement in the east', now used as a first name.

Eavan *f*
This is the anglicized form of the Irish name *Aoibheann*, an old name meaning 'beautiful' that was given to a number of medieval princesses.
VARIANT **Aoibhinn**
★ Eavan Boland (1944–), Irish poet

Ebbe *see* **Eberhard, Everard**

Ebenezer *m*
This is a biblical name meaning 'stone of help' in Hebrew. Its use as

a first name is peculiar as it is not a personal name, and suggests that the Puritans who adopted it may have misunderstood a slightly odd passage in the Bible. The story told in 1 Samuel is of an Israelite defeat of the Philistines, after God has manipulated the weather to help them. Samuel sets up a memorial stone 'and called the name of it Ebenezer, saying, Hitherto has the Lord helped us' (1 Samuel 7.12). The name was in use into the 19th century, but fell out of favour because of the unpleasant character of Ebenezer Scrooge in Charles Dickens's *A Christmas Carol* (1843), although its short form is occasionally found.

PET FORM **Eben**

☆ The 1992 song *Ebeneezer Goode* by The Shamen has heavy drug references

Eber *see* **Eibhear**

Eberardo *see* **Everard**

Eberhard *m*
A German name formed from the elements *eber*, 'boar', and *hard*, 'brave'. The Old English form is EVERARD. Compare AVERIL.

PET FORM **Ebbe** • VARIANT **Evert**

Ebeth *see* **Elizabeth**

Ebony *f*
This is the vocabulary word for the black wood, used as a first name. Because of its associations with blackness it is often chosen by African Americans. It is also well used in Australia.

PET FORM **Ebo** • VARIANT **Eboni(e)**

Ebrahim *see* **Ibrahim**

Ebrilla, Ebrilwen *see* **April**

Ecbert, Eckbert *see* **Egbert**

Edan *m* **Edana** *f*
These are variant forms of AIDAN,

particularly found in Scotland. There are saints of both names.

Edda *see* **Hedwig**

Eddie, Eddy *see* **Edgar, Edmund, Edward, Edwin**

Eden *mf*
This is the name of the biblical garden of Eden (Hebrew for 'place of pleasure') used as a first name. It started to occur in significant numbers in the early 1990s and is increasing in popularity, mainly for girls. Some uses of the name, particularly early ones, may be from the surname, or may be a variant of AIDAN. Use of the name seems to have started in Israel, where it is primarily masculine.

VARIANTS **Edyn, Edin**

☆ Eden McCain, character in the television series *Heroes*

Edgar *m*
An Anglo-Saxon name formed from the common element which gives so many *Ed-* names, *ead*, meaning 'fortunate, prosperous', combined with *gar*, 'spear'. It survived the Norman Conquest better than most Anglo-Saxon names, perhaps because it was the name of St Edgar the Peaceful, a king who died in 975, and who was the father of two other saints, EDWARD and EDITH. However, the name had died out by the end of the Middle Ages, only to be revived again in the 19th century, particularly in the USA where it is still much more widely used than in the UK. Important in the revival of the name in the USA was the publication of the novel *Edgar Huntly* (1799), by Charles Brockden Brown who is widely regarded as the first purely American novelist. In the UK, Sir Walter Scott brought the name to public attention via the character of Edgar Ravenswood in *The Bride of Lammermoor*.

PET FORMS **Ed, Eddie, Eddy** • VARIANTS *French*
Ogier, Edgard *Italian, Spanish* **Edgardo**
★ Edgar Allen Poe (1809–49), US writer
★ Edgar Degas (1834–1917), French artist
★ J Edgar Hoover (1895–1972), US law
  enforcement official

Edin *see* Eden

Edina *see* Edna, Edwina

Edison *m*
From the surname, meaning 'son of
EDWARD'. The name was used in the
USA in the 19th century and first half
of the 20th, in honour of the inventor
Thomas Alva Edison. It then dropped
out of the statistics for many years, but
has just started to reappear.
★ Edison James (1943–   ), prime
  minister of Dominica

Edith *f*
The Anglo-Saxon name *Eadgyth*, made
up of the elements *ead*, 'fortunate,
prosperous', and *gyth*, 'battle', was
borne by two Anglo-Saxon princesses,
both better known as 'St Edith'. One
was the daughter of St EDGAR who
refused to leave her nunnery when
offered the chance to become queen.
The other, who lived a century later, is
far more obscure and little is known
about her. The name remained in
use after the Norman Conquest, and
continued to be quietly used until the
19th century when it came back into
fashion. In the later part of the 20th
century it was out of fashion again, but
it is showing signs of coming back into
favour.
PET FORM **Edie** • VARIANTS **Editha, Edyth**
★ Edith Wharton (c.1861–1937), US
  novelist
★ Edith Cavell (1865–1915), English
  nurse executed in World War I

Edme *see* Esme

Edmund *m*
An Anglo-Saxon name formed from
ead, 'fortunate, prosperous', and
mund, 'protector'. The name has
survived because of the martyred
East Anglian King Edmund, who took
the Christian message of pacifism to
unusual lengths for the time and, as a
result, was captured and killed by the
pagan Vikings. The town of Bury St
Edmunds is named after him and many
miracles were said to have happened
at his tomb, which is in the abbey
there.
PET FORMS **Ed, Eddie, Eddy, Ned(die),
Ted(dy), Teddie** • VARIANTS *Irish* **Eamonn**
Scots Gaelic **Eumann** *Welsh* **Edmwnd**
French **Edmond, Edme** (ms), **Edmonde,
Edmondine, Edmée** (fs) *Italian* **Edmonda**
(f), **Edmondo** (m) *Spanish, Portuguese*
Edmundo
★ Edmund Spenser (c.1552–99), English
  poet
★ Sir Edmund Hillary (1919–2008), New
  Zealand mountaineer.
☆ Edmund Blackadder, principal
  character in the television series
  Blackadder
☆ Edmund Pevensie in the *Narnia* books
  by C S Lewis

Edna *f*
In the book of Tobit, one of the
apocryphal books of the Bible, Edna
is the name of the mother-in-law of
Tobias (TOBY), and is also found as
the name of Enoch's wife. The name
Edna comes from the Hebrew for
'pleasure'. It was used in Ireland as
an anglicization of the name EITHNE,
but it is not clear if this was a direct
borrowing from the Hebrew form. It
was found occasionally in England
from the 15th century onwards, but
only became popular in the later
19th century. An important influence
on this was the novelist Edna Lyall
(1857–1903) who, although now little
read, was very popular in her day. Her
given name was Ada Ellen Bayly, and

she formed her pen name using letters from her real name. See EDWINA.

VARIANT **Edina**

★ Edna O'Brien (1932–), Irish novelist

★ Edna Ferber (1885–1968), US writer

☆ Edina Monsoon, principal character in the television series *Absolutely Fabulous*

Edoardo *see* Edward

Edom *m*

In the Bible Edom, the Hebrew for 'red', was the alternative name of ESAU. Since Esau seems to mean 'hairy', both names appear to come from the story that he was born covered with red hair. He famously sold his birthright to his younger twin 'for a mess of pottage'. The name was common in Scotland, particularly in the Middle Ages, where it was regarded as a variant of ADAM.

☆ *Edom O' Gordon* is a traditional Scottish Border ballad that may reflect the true atrocities of one Adam Gordon

Édouard *see* Edward

Edred *m*

An Anglo-Saxon name formed from *ead*, 'fortunate, prosperous' and *raed*, counsel'. It was the name of a rather obscure 10th-century king of England, and was one of the old names revived in the 19th century.

☆ Edred Arden is the hero of E Nesbit's 1908 children's novel *The House of Arden*, the popularity of which kept the name alive in the early 20th century

Edric *m*

An Anglo-Saxon name formed from *ead*, 'fortunate, prosperous', and *ric*, 'power, rule'. The name was not uncommon among the Anglo-Saxons, and was revived in the 19th century along with similar names.

★ 'Wild Edric' is an 11th-century Shropshire folk hero, said to have fought the Normans after the invasion. There were a number of Edrics living in that area at the time who may have been the source of the stories

☆ Edrik is a character in Frank Herbert's 1969 cult novel *Dune Messiah*

Edsel *m*

This rather obscure name is a variant of *Etzel*, a name found in Germanic legend which seems to be from *adal*, 'noble'. The most famous bearer was Edsel Ford (1893–1943), only son of Henry Ford who founded the Ford motor company. In the late 1950s Ford launched a new car named after Edsel, but it was a spectacular failure which, according to folk history, was partly due to its peculiar name. This failure inflicted a blow that this already obscure name is unlikely ever to recover from.

Eduard, Eduarda, Eduardo, Edvard *see* Edward

Edvige *see* Hedwig

Edvin *see* Edwin

Edward *m*

This is by far the most successful of the Anglo-Saxon *Ed-* names. Edward was the name of two royal saints. The lesser-known is Edward the Martyr (c.963–78), whose murder was actually political, but who came to be venerated as a saint. The more important one is Edward the Confessor (c.1002–66), whose death without heirs precipitated the Norman Conquest. He was particularly venerated by King Henry III, who named his son Edward, who was in turn followed as king by two more Edwards, so that there was an Edward on the throne of England from 1272 to 1377. This meant the name was firmly established in the stock of English names, further boosted by its continued use as a royal name. The name is formed from *ead*, 'fortunate, prosperous', and *weard*, 'guard'.

PET FORMS **Ed, Eddie, Eddy, Ned(die), Ted(dy), Teddie** • VARIANTS *Irish* **Eadbhárd** *Scots Gaelic* **Eideard, Eudard** *Dutch, German* **Eduard** *French* **Édouard** (m), **Éduarde, Éduardine** (fs) *Hawaiian* **Ekewaka** *Italian* **Edoardo** *Portuguese* **Eduardo, Duarte** (m), **Eduarda** (f) *Scandinavian* **Edvard** *Spanish* **Eduardo, Lalo**

Edwige *see* **Hedwig**

Edwin *m*
Edwin, King of Northumbria was an early convert to Christianity, thanks to the influence of his wife Ethelburga, and was baptized in 627. After dying in battle against pagans five years later, he came to be venerated as a martyr. His name is formed from the Old English *ead*, 'fortunate, prosperous', combined with *wine*, 'friend'. The name was popular on both sides of the Atlantic in the later 19th century, and remained in the top 100 boys' names in the USA until 1941. It has been in the top 200 names for all but one year since then.

PET FORMS **Ed, Eddie, Eddy, Ned(die), Ted(dy), Teddie** • VARIANTS **Edwyn** *Scandinavian* **Edvin**

★ Edwin 'Buzz' Aldrin (1930–), US astronaut, the second man to walk on the moon

Edwina *f*
The feminine form of EDWIN, this name only dates from the 19th century. In at least one case it has also acted as a compromise feminine of EDWARD, as Edwina Ashley (1901–60), later Lady Mountbatten, was named after King Edward VII, who had originally wanted her called *Edwardina*.

VARIANTS **Edwe(e)na, Edwyna** *Hungarian* **Edina**

★ Edwina Currie (1946–), English politician and writer

Edyn *see* **Eden**

Edyth *see* **Edith**

Efa *see* **Eva**

Effie *f*
This is an independent name derived from a short form of EUPHEMIA, HEPHZIBAH and, occasionally, EVELYN. It has particular associations with Scotland, where it was used as an anglicization of the Gaelic name *Oighrig* or *Aifric* meaning 'speckled one'. In the UK it was well used in the 19th century and into the early 20th, but is rare in the USA.

★ Euphemia 'Effie' Gray (1828–97), wife of art critic John Ruskin; model and later wife of Pre-Raphaelite artist John Everett Millais

Efimia *see* **Euphemia**

Efraim, Efraín *see* **Ephraim**

Efthymia *see* **Euphemia**

Egan *m*
This is an Irish name, either an anglicization of the name *Aogán*, a pet form of AODH, or else taken from the surname derived from this name.

Egbert *m*
This is the modern form of the Old English name *Ecgbeoht*, formed from *ecg*, 'edge, blade', and *beorht*, 'bright, famous'. It was a common name in Anglo-Saxon England, bearers including two saints and a king of Wessex, but fell out of use after the Norman Conquest. There was a revival in use in the 19th century, but the name is now rare and regarded as comic.

VARIANTS *German* **Ecbert, Eckbert**

Egidio *see* **Giles**

Egil *m*

A Scandinavian name derived from the word for 'sword, edge'. It was a common name in early Scandinavian culture, particularly in Iceland, where Egil One-Hand was hero of his own saga.

VARIANT **Eigil**

Eglantine *f*

The French name for a wild rosehip is *aiglant*, giving the word *aiglentine* for the briar rose, which became eglantine in English. The French name ultimately comes from Latin *acus*, 'needle', referring to the plant's thorns. The name was in use in the Middle Ages, with strong romantic associations, and has been in occasional use ever since.

☆ Madame Eglantyne is the unsuitably named Prioress in Chaucer's *Canterbury Tales*

☆ Eglantine Price is an apprentice witch in *Bedknobs and Broomsticks*, a 1971 film based on Mary Norton's books

Egon *m*

This was originally a short form of various old Germanic names containing the element *egin* or *egil* meaning 'edge, blade'.

★ Egon Schiele (1890–1918), Austrian painter

★ Egon Ronay (1915–), Hungarian-born author of British food guides

☆ Egon Spengler, scientist in the *Ghostbusters* series of films

Ehrin *see* **Aaron**

Ehud *m*

This is a Jewish name, belonging to a minor biblical character (Judges 3.15–26). It is variously interpreted as meaning 'pleasant, sympathetic' or 'united'.

★ Ehud Olmert (1945–), Israeli prime minister

Eibhear *m*

This is the name of at least three individuals found in the traditional stories of the origins of Ireland. Eibhear Scott was the great-grandson of Scota, daughter of the pharoah Nectanebus, who was said to have given her name to the Scots (ie Irish) race.

VARIANTS **Eibhir, Eber, Heber**

Eibhlin *see* **Eileen, Evelyn**

Eiddwen *f*

This is a modern Welsh name which comes from either *eiddun*, 'fond', plus the common name ending *(g)wen*, 'fair, blessed', or the name of a lake in Ceredigion. It may be that the ending of the lake's name made it suitable as a personal name. In Welsh 'dd' is pronounced like 'th' in the English word 'this'.

★ Eiddwen Harrhy (1949–), Welsh opera singer

Eideard *see* **Edward**

Eifion *m* Eifiona *f*

In Welsh tradition Eifion, grandson of King Cunedda, gave his name to the district near Pwllheli still known today as Eifionydd.

Eigil *see* **Egil**

Eigra *f*

This is the traditional name in Welsh of the mother of King Arthur, which appears in forms such as *Igerna* in better-known early Latin texts, for example Geoffrey of Monmouth's *History of the Kings of Britain*.

VARIANT **Eigr**

★ Eigra Lewis Roberts (1939–), Welsh-language author

Eike *mf*

A Geman name, originally a short form of names beginning *Egi-* or *Agi-*, derived from the Old High German *ecka* meaning 'point [of a weapon]'.

Eileen *f*

This is one of two anglicized forms
of the Irish name *Eibhlin* or *Aibhlin*,
the other form being EVELYN, or more
properly *Evlin*. The two forms arose
because there are regional variations
in the way that 'bh' is pronounced
in Irish; it is usually a 'v' sound, but
can be silent. While some in Ireland
like to link the name to the Irish
word *aoibheann*, meaning 'pleasant,
beautiful, radiant', and spell the name
Eibhleann, most regard the name as
an Irish form of AVELINE, of unknown
meaning. Aveline was a popular name
among the Normans, who took it
with them to Ireland where it became
Aibhilin, shortened to *Eibhlin*. Some
regard *Aileen* as a variant of Eileen,
while others see it as a form of HELEN or
ELEANOR, as EILIDH is.

VARIANT **Eilin**

Eilian *mf*

St Eilian is a Welsh saint who is
supposed to have come to Anglesey
from Rome in the 6th century. A
church dedicated to him still stands
where he is supposed to have built his
oratory in the parish of Llaneilian, as
well as a miracle-working well that
bears his name.

VARIANT **Eilean**

Eilidh *f*

This is the Scots Gaelic form of ELLIE,
and since this is a derivative of the
names often glossed as a Scottish form
of HELEN or ELEANOR, although it now
counts as an independent name. It is
a modern name which has become
increasingly popular in Scotland.

VARIANTS **Ailie, Eiley**

Eilís, Eilish *see* **Ailish, Elizabeth**

Eiluned *see* **Eluned**

Eilwen *f* Eilwyn *m*

The exact meaning of these Welsh
names is not certain. The second
element is the familiar *(g)wen/(g)wyn*
meaning 'fair, blessed, holy', but the
first element can be interpreted as
coming from either *ael*, 'brow', or
possibly *ail*, 'just like'.

Eimer *f*

This is an Irish name of unknown
meaning. In Irish mythology it was the
name of Cuchullain's long-suffering
wife, who was said to be endowed
with the 'six gifts of womanhood',
which to the saga writers consisted of
beauty, a gentle voice, sweet words,
wisdom, needlework and chastity. The
name was revived in the 20th century
and has been one of the more popular
Irish names.

VARIANTS **Emer, Eimear** *Scots Gaelic* **Eimhir**

★ Eimear Quinn, Irish singer

☆ The Scots Gaelic poet Sorley MacLean
   published a collection called *Poems
   to Eimhir*

Einar *m*

This is a popular Scandinavian name
formed from the Norse elements
einn, 'one', and *herr*, 'warrior'. The
name seems to have links with the
ancient *einherjar*, the term used for the
warriors fallen in battle who receive
their reward in Valhalla.

Éinin *f*

Pronounced 'AY-neen' (the first syllable
rhyming with 'hay'), this is a recent
name formed from the Irish *ean*, 'bird',
and meaning 'little bird'.

Einion *m*

This is an ancient Welsh name
meaning 'anvil', perhaps indicating
endurance or solid strength. It is a
name that appears frequently in old
records in a wide variety of spellings,
suggesting that several names may
have fallen together to create the
modern form. Einion Yrth ('the
Impetuous') was the son of Cunedda, a

king in the north of Britain. The family is said to have moved to North Wales in the 5th century to defend it from invasion.

PET FORM **Einwys** • VARIANTS **Eynon, Einon**

Einrí see **Henry**

Eira f
The Welsh for 'snow'.

Eireann see **Erin**

Eireen, Eirene see **Irene**

Eirian mf
Eirian is a Welsh word meaning 'bright, beautiful', but it is possible that the name is actually from *arian* meaning 'silver'. Indeed it has been suggested that a number of the Welsh *Eir-* first names that are usually interpreted as coming for *eira*, 'snow', may originally have been from *arian*. Eirian is sometimes said to be exclusively feminine, but this is not the case. However, the variants *Eirana, Eirienell, Eirianedd*, 'brightness', and *Eirianwen*, compounded from Eirian and *(g)wen* 'fair, white', are exclusively feminine.

Eirik, Eirik see **Eric**

Eiriol f
A Welsh name, meaning 'snowy'.

Eirlys f
A Welsh name, meaning 'snowdrop'.

Eirnin see **Ernan**

Eirwen f **Eirwyn** m
A Welsh name formed from *eira*, 'snow', and *(g)wen* or *(g)wyn*, 'fair, white, blessed'.

VARIANT **Eirawen**

Eiry f
A Welsh name that can either be from *eira*, 'snow', or serve as a short form of *Eirianwen*, a feminine form of EIRIAN.

Eistir see **Esther**

Eitan see **Ethan**

Eithne f
This is a common name in early Irish tradition, with at least nine saints called Eithne, including one who was mother of St Columba; the name is also found in royal families. One legendary Eithne was a member of the supernatural Tuatha Dé Danaan, a divine race of Celtic mythology, but was declared a Christian after her guardian demon was found to have been replaced by a guardian angel. The name has a variety of pronunciations including 'AIN-ya', 'EN-a', 'ET-na' and 'ETH-na', and comes from the word meaning 'kernel' which, as the heart of the nut, was a term of praise among Irish bards.

VARIANTS **Eitna, Ena, Ethna, Etna, Ethenia, Enya, Ethni**

★ Enya (Eithne Ni Bhraonain) (1961–), Irish singer

Ekaterina, Ekaterini see **Catherine**

Ekewaka see **Edward**

Elaine f
The source of this name is the Old French form of HELEN, of which the modern form, *Hélène*, with its silent initial 'H', has almost the same pronunciation as Elaine. In Arthurian legend Elaine is the maiden who is magically forced to lie forever in a bath, 'naked as a needle' in Malory's words, until rescued by Lancelot. She falls in love with her rescuer, tricks him into sleeping with her, and so becomes the mother of Galahad. It has, however, been suggested that as *elain* is the Welsh for 'fawn', and as most Arthurian names are Celtic, her name should be derived from this.

PET FORM **Lainey** • VARIANTS **Elain, Elayne, Elaina**

Elazar see **Eleazar**

Elda *see* **Hilda**

Eldon *m*

A surname from a place name, reused as a first name. The place name in turn comes from an Old English first name, ELLA, also found in ELTON. Eldon means 'Ella's hill'.

VARIANT **Elden**

★ Eldon Griffiths (1925–), English politician

★ Eldon Thompson (1974–), US author

Eldred *m*

Eldred comes from the Old English name *Ealdred*, formed from *eald*, 'old, mature', and *raed*, 'counsel'. It was the name of an 11th-century archbishop of York, and was generally well used by Anglo-Saxons. It was quietly revived in the 19th century; in recent years it has been more frequently used in the USA than in the UK.

FEMININES **Eldreda, Dreda** • VARIANT **Aldred**

★ Eldred Gregory Peck (1916–2003), US actor better known as Gregory Peck

Eldridge *m*

Eldridge is a first name taken from a surname. The surname comes from the same Old English name as ELDRED. The name is most frequently found in the USA and dates back to 1636 when two brothers, Robert and Samuel Eldredge or Eldrige – their records spell the name either way indiscriminately – arrived from England, one settling in Cape Cod, the other in Virginia.

★ Eldridge Cleaver (1935–98), US author, activist and Black Panther

Eleanor *f*

This name first appears in south-west France in the form *Alienor*, which makes the traditional interpretation of it as a form of HELEN difficult, although Helen may have affected later forms. It is more likely to have started out as some Germanic name formed from the element *ali* meaning 'other, stranger'.

The name came to England in 1156 when Eleanor of Aquitaine married King Henry II. There were two more queens of England with the name in succeeding generations: Eleanor of Provence, wife of Henry III, and Eleanor of Castile, wife of Edward I, attesting to the popularity of the name in Europe. It has remained steadily popular in various forms ever since, and has been prominent among the names chosen for girls in recent years.

PET FORMS **Ellie, Ellen, Leonora, Nell, Nelly, Nora** • VARIANTS **Elinor, Elenor, Elenora** *French* **Éléonore** *German* **Eleonore** *Italian* **Eleonòra**

★ Eleanor Roosevelt (1884–1962), US First Lady

★ Elinor Glyn (1864–1943), British novelist

☆ Elinor Dashwood in Jane Austen's novel *Sense and Sensibility* (1811)

Eleasha *see* **Elisha**

Eleazar *m*

A biblical name meaning 'God is my help', found in the Old Testament as the name of a son of Amos (Exodus 6.23) who becomes the second high priest of Israel, as well as of a number of other people. In the New Testament it takes the form LAZARUS.

VARIANTS **Eliezer, Elazar**

Electra *f*

The Greek *elektor*, 'brilliant', seems to be the origin of this name, although there are ancient Greek puns which imply that it comes from *a*, 'not', and *lectron*, 'married'. In Greek mythology Electra is the daughter of Agamemnon and Clytemnestra, who gets involved in a nasty tangle of duty and revenge when her mother murders her father.

VARIANT *Italian* **Elettra**

☆ Elektra King is a character in the James Bond film *The World is Not Enough* (1999)

Eleisha *see* **Elisha**

Elen *see* **Elin, Ellen**

Elena, Eleni *see* **Helen**

Éléonore *see* **Eleanor**

Eleri *f*
A popular Welsh name, this is found
as the name of a 5th-century princess.
Its meaning is not known, and it is
probably a coincidence that Eleri is
also the name of a Welsh river.
VARIANT **Teleri**

Elesha *see* **Elisha**

Elfrida *f*
This is the Latinate form of the Old
English *Aelfthryth*, formed from the
elements *aelf*, 'elf', also found in the
name ALFRED, and *thryth*, 'strength'.
It was a well-used noble name in
Anglo-Saxon England, belonging to
a daughter of King Alfred and to the
mother of Ethelred the Unready. The
8th-century hermit saint known as St
Alfrida may also have been an Elfrida.
The name died out after the Norman
Conquest, but was revived in the 19th
century.
PET FORM **Frida** • VARIANTS **Elfreda** *German*
Elfriede, Freda, Friede
★ Elfrida Vipont (1902–92), English
   headmistress and children's author,
   who wrote the infants' classic *The Bad
   Baby and the Elephant*
☆ Elfrida Arden is the heroine of E
   Nesbit's 1908 children's novel *The
   House of Arden*

Eli *m*
A Hebrew name, found in the Bible
as the name of the high priest who
raised the prophet Samuel after he was
dedicated as an infant to the Temple
in Jerusalem (1 Samuel 4). The name
was taken up with enthusiasm by the
Puritans in the 19th century, and was
taken by them to the USA where it

remained in regular use into the early
20th century. It is currently undergoing
a revival, along with similar-sounding
Hebrew names. The name comes from
the Hebrew for 'high, ascension'. There
is a second Hebrew name, transcribed
the same way in Roman letters but
spelt slightly differently in Hebrew,
which means 'my God'. Eli can also be
used as a short form of names such as
ELIJAH and ELISHA.
VARIANTS **Ely** *Greek (New Testament)* **Heli**
★ Eli Whitney (1765–1825), US inventor
   of the cotton gin
★ Eli Wallach (1915–), US actor

Eliana[1] *f*
This is the Spanish and Italian form of
the Roman family name, *Aelianus* in
the masculine, *Aeliana* in the feminine.
This Roman name in turn seems to
have come from the Greek word for
the sun, *helios*. The name has been
growing in popularity in recent years.
MASCULINE **Elian** • PET FORM **Lina** • VARIANTS
Elliana *French* **Éliane**

Eliana[2] *m*
This is a modern Hebrew name, which
first came into use in Israel, meaning
'my God has answered'.

Elias *m*
This is the form of the Hebrew name
ELIJAH used in the New Testament. Its
popularity in the past can be seen
from the fact that it is the source of
both the surnames ELLIS and ELLIOT. It
is once again increasing in frequency,
and has been particularly popular in
Scandinavian countries in recent years.
VARIANTS *Arabic* **Ily(a)as** *French* **Élie** *Hebrew*
Eliyahu *Polish* **Eliasz** *Romanian* **Ilie** *Russian*
Ilia, Ilya

Eliezer *see* **Eleazar**

Eligius *m*
Eligius is a Late Latin name formed
from the same root as the word 'elect'.

It was a popular name among the early Christians, and St Eligius was 7th-century Frenchman who was a goldsmith, king's councillor and missionary to Flanders. He is the patron saint of metalworkers and those who care for horses. While now rather obscure, he was a popular saint in the Middle Ages. Writing some time around 1380, Chaucer, in *The Canterbury Tales*, says of his Prioress 'Her greatest oath was "By Saint Loy"', showing the common medieval form of the name. The name is rare among English speakers, but found in other language groups.

VARIANTS *French* **Eloi** *Italian* **Eligio** *Polish* **Eligia** (f), **Eligiusz** (m) *Spanish* **Eloy, Eligia, Ligia** (fs)

Elijah *m*
This is the standard English form of the Old Testament Hebrew name *Eliyyahu*, 'My God is Yahweh'. In the New Testament it appears in the Greek form ELIAS (under which variants from other countries are listed). Elijah was a prophet whose exploits are told in the two biblical books of Kings, and who is said not to have died, but to have been carried up into Heaven in a fiery chariot. In recent years the name has had a major revival worldwide, but particularly in the USA, where it has always been more common than elsewhere, and where it is now in the top 30 names for boys.

PET FORM **Lige**
★ Elijah Wood (1981–), US actor

Elika *see* **Erica**

Elin *f*
The Welsh form of HELEN and one of the few Welsh names that has been in continuous use in Wales from the Middle Ages, most old Welsh names now in use being 19th century revivals. Some uses may be a respelling of the

related ELLEN, and the name can also be a Scandinavian form of Helen.
VARIANT **Elen**

Elined *see* **Eluned**

Elinor *see* **Eleanor**

Eliot *see* **Elliot**

Elisa *see* **Elise**

Elisabeth, Élisabeth *see* **Elizabeth**

Elise *f*
This is a French pet form of ELIZABETH, that has spread to many other languages. It was well established in France (in the form *Élise*) in the 17th century, where it was particularly common as a theatrical name, and became established as an English name in the 19th century.
VARIANTS **Elisa, Elissa, Ellisa, Ellissa, Elyse**

Elish *see* **Ailish**

Elisha[1] *m*
Elisha is a Hebrew name, a contraction of *Elishu'a*, meaning 'God is salvation'. Elisha, in the Old Testament, was the successor of ELIJAH. The name more likely to be found in the USA than in other English-speaking areas. It was used there regularly in the 18th and 19th centuries, all but disappeared in the middle of the 20th century, but is slowly coming back into use.
VARIANTS **Elishah** *French* **Élisée** *Italian, Spanish* **Eliseo** *Russian* **Yelisei**

Elisha[2] *f*
Although this is often analysed as a feminine use of ELISHA[1], this name is so variable that it seems more likely that it started out as a blend of ELISE, ALICIA, and related names. The existence of a feminine-sounding masculine name may merely have encouraged its development.
VARIANTS **Eleasha, Eleisha, Elesha, Elicia, Ellisha**

Elissa *see* **Elise**

Elisud *m*
This is an old Welsh name from *elus*, 'kind'. It was anglicized as ELLIS.

Elita *f*
This is generally interpreted as deriving from the French vocabulary word *élite*, but as it is most commonly found in the Americas and other Spanish-speaking areas, it seems most likely that it started out as a pet form of names such as *Carmelita* and *Angelita*, themselves pet forms of CARMEL and ANGELA, and that the vocabulary word merely served to reinforce usage. However, the vocabulary word does link the name to ELIGIUS, as they come from the same root.

Eliza *f*
A pet form of ELIZABETH, first used as an independent name as early as the 16th century, and particularly popular between the 18th and 19th centuries.
VARIANTS **Elisa**, **Elyza**
☆ Eliza Doolittle in George Bernard Shaw's 1913 play *Pygmalion*, and in the musical based on it *My Fair Lady* (1956, filmed 1964)

Elizabeth *f*
This is the English spelling of the name that appears in the New Testament as *Elisabeth*, the form used in most other European languages. This in turn is a form of the Hebrew name *Elisheva*, 'God is my oath', found in the Old Testament as the name of the mother of Aaron. In the New Testament, Elizabeth is the cousin of the Virgin Mary and mother of John the Baptist. When they meet when both are pregnant, Elizabeth recognizes that Mary is to be the mother of the Messiah and greets her with the words 'Blessed art thou among women, and blessed is the fruit of thy womb' (Luke 1.42). This sympathetic and significant role in the Christian story, combined with the importance of her son, meant that Elizabeth's name was widely adopted throughout Christendom. However, it did not become really popular in England until the reign of Queen Elizabeth I (1533–1603). Thereafter it was in regular use in the royal family and in the general population, and for many years was one of the most popular English names for girls. As a result of this widespread popularity, the name has evolved innumerable variants, many of which are used as independent names. For the sake of brevity, those that are given under other headwords are not listed here.
PET FORMS **Liz(ie)**, **Bet**, **Betty**, **Bess**, **Bessie**, **Beth**, **Buffy**, **Ebeth**, **Elise**, **Elsa**, **Libby**, **Lily**, **Lilibeth**, **Lisa**, **Lisbeth**, **Lisabeth**, **Lizbeth**, **Tetty** • VARIANTS **Elsbeth** *Irish* **Eilis** *Manx* **Eliasaid** *Scots Gaelic* **Ealasaid**, **Beileag** *Scottish* **Elspeth**, **Elspie**, **Elsie** *Welsh* **Elisabeth**, **Bethan**, **Betsan** *Dutch* **Els**, **Liesbeth**, **Liesja** *French* **Élisabeth**, **Babette**, **Lisette** *German* **Bettina**, **Ilsa**, **Ilse**, **Lies(e)(l)**, **Liesa**, **Lili**, **Lilo**, **Lotte**, **Lys** *Greek* **Elisavet** *Hawaiian* **Elikapeka** *Italian* **Elisabetta** *Portuguese* **Elisabete** *Russian* **Elizaveta**, **Lizaveta**, **Yelizaveta** *Scandinavian* **Elisabet**, **Elsa**, **Else**, **Lis** *Spanish* **Isabel**

Elkan *m*
Elkan is a mainly Jewish name; it is a shortening of *Elkanah*, 'possessed by God'.
★ Elkan Allan (1922–2006), English television producer and author, responsible for such television series as *Ready Steady Go!* and *Batman*

Elke[1] *f*
A feminine form of ELKAN.

Elke[2] *f*
Now an independent name, this was

originally a German pet form of ALICE, and of the related ADELAIDE.

VARIANT **Elkie**

★ Elke Sommer (1940–), German actress

★ Elkie Brooks (1945–), English singer

Ella *f*

This is a Germanic name introduced into English by the Normans. Although its origin is not certain, it is thought to have started out as a pet form of names containing the element *ali*, 'other, stranger', found in names such as ELEANOR. It is still used as a pet form of Eleanor as well as of *Isabella* (see ISABEL). It was widespread in the middle of the 19th century, then went through a quiet period, but is currently one of the most popular names in the English-speaking world. It is a common first element in compound names, with combinations such as *Ella-May* or *Ella-Jane*, a trend which was also found in the 19th century.

★ Ella Fitzgerald (1917–96), US jazz singer

Ellair *m*

A Scottish name, now very rare. A person who acted as a butler or steward could, in the past, be called a cellarer, ie someone with access to the contents of a cellar. This became *Ceallair* in Gaelic. When *Mac*, meaning 'descendant of', was put in front of this name the two 'c's were run together, and the name Ellair evolved.

VARIANT **Ellar**

Elle, Ellie *f*

Like ELLA, these names are currently widely popular. They too started out as pet forms of any name beginning *El-*. Elle was little used until the Australian supermodel Elle Macpherson (given name Eleanor) became famous. Ellie, like Ella, is a popular first element in compound names.

VARIANTS **Elli, Elly**

Ellen *f*

Ellen was originally a form of HELEN with the 'h' dropped, but is now more closely associated with ELEANOR. It came into use as an independent name in the 16th century, was revived again in the 19th and again in the 20th. It has strong associations with Scotland and Ireland, and is currently most popular in these regions.

PET FORMS **Ellie, Nell, Nelly, Nellie**

• VARIANTS *Welsh* **Elen, Elin** *Scandinavian* **Elin**

★ Dame Ellen MacArthur (1977–), English yachtswoman

★ Ellen DeGeneres (1958–), US comic actress

Ellery *mf*

This is a surname, derived from the first name HILARY, reused as a first name.

☆ Ellery Queen, US detective, originally created by Daniel Nathan and Manford Lepofsky in 1929

Elli *see* Ailbe

Elliana *see* Eliana

Ellie *see* Elle

Elliot *mf*

This was originally a Norman surname, derived from a pet form of *Élie*, the French variant of the first name ELIAS, 'My God is Yahweh'. It is only recently that it has come to be used for girls as well as for boys.

VARIANTS **Eliot, Elliott**

★ Elliott Gould (1938–), US actor

☆ Elliot Read, major character in the television series *Scrubs*, who has influenced the use of the name as a feminine since the show started in 2001

Ellis *mf*

Ellis is a surname, reused as a first name, which comes from the name

ELIJAH, 'My God is Yahweh', so shares a source with ELLIOT. In Wales it is used as an anglicized form of ELISUD. Use of Ellis is increasing, particularly as a girl's name, perhaps because of the popularity of ELLIE or the similarity of its sound to ALICE.

VARIANTS **Ellice, Ellyce**

★ Ellis Peters (1913–95), pen name of the English author Edith Pargeter who wrote the *Cadfael* series of novels

Ellisa *see* **Elise**

Ellisha *see* **Elisha**

Ellissa *see* **Elise**

Elma *f*

The origin of this name was probably as a pet form both of *Wilhelmine*, a Germanic feminine of WILLIAM, and of names ending in *-elma* such as *Findelma* or *Anselma* (see ANSELM). It was subsequently analysed as a blend of ELIZABETH and MARY, and as a feminine of ELMER. Use has mainly been confined to the USA.

Elmer *m*

This is the modern form of the Old English *Aethelmaer*, 'noble and famous', also the source of *Aylmer*. It became a surname which was taken to the USA. The fame of two bearers, Jonathan and Ebenezer Elmer, prominent in the American Revolution, led to its adoption as a first name there. The similar-sounding German name *Elmar* is different, being from a Germanic element meaning 'point of a weapon' combined with the element meaning 'fame'.

☆ Elmer Fudd, enemy of Bugs Bunny in the cartoon series, with whom the name is now strongly identified

Elmira *f*

The history of this name is obscure. It looks Spanish, although it is best attested from the USA. One theory

is that it is formed from the Arabic *amirah*, 'princess'. Another, slightly more convincing suggestion, is that it is a contraction of *Edelmira* which is a Spanish feminine of *Adelmar*, a Germanic name formed from elements meaning 'noble' and 'famous'. The story of the naming of the city of Elmira in upstate New York suggests that the name has a long history in the USA. The story varies but, according to the city's official website, the name was chosen in 1828, and 'although the origins are disputed, the most frequently told version of the story suggests the following: during a meeting at Nathan Teal's Tavern to discuss a new name, Elmira Teal, the young daughter of the tavern owner, made her presence known by running in and out of the meeting room while her mother repeatedly called her name. Hearing the repeated calls to young Elmira, someone at the meeting suggested the town should be named Elmira, to which everyone agreed'.

VARIANT **Almira**

☆ Elmyra Duff is the horrible, animal-molesting little girl in the children's cartoon series *Tiny Toons*. Her name is a play on that of Elmer Fudd, whose role she takes in this spin-off series

Elmo *m*

This is an Italian form of a Germanic name formed from *helm*, 'helmet, protection'. It is also used as a pet form of ERASMUS. St Elmo or Erasmus is the patron saint of sailors, and the mysterious atmospheric phenomenon known as St Elmo's fire is said to be a sign of his protection.

☆ Elmo is a red, furry and sometimes difficult character from the children's television series *Sesame Street*

Elodie *f*

This name was probably originally Visigothic, formed from the elements *ali*, 'foreign, other', also found in ELEANOR, and *od*, 'prosperity, riches, blessings', which occurs as *ead* in Old English and gives us so many *Ed-* names. St *Elodia* or *Alodia* was a Spanish martyr, killed in the 9th century alongside her sister Nunilo. Élodie, the French form of the name, has been popular in France since the 1990s, and is spreading to other countries.

VARIANTS **Elody** *Spanish* **Elodia**

Eloi *see* **Eligius**

Eloise *f*

There are various theories as to the origin of this name. The one that links the name to the Greek *helios*, 'sun', is not convincing, as the name appears in England in the 11th century as a Norman-French name, in the form *Helewise*, and the Normans are not known for creating names based on Greek. Much more likely is that it is a Germanic name. It has been used as a feminine form of LOUIS, via the Provençal form of the name *Aloys*; *Aloyse* in the feminine. This may have been the source, or it may have influenced the development of the name. Another possible origin is that it is a different Germanic name formed from the elements *hail*, 'robust, healthy' (which comes from the same root), and *wid*, 'wood'. Whatever its origin, the most famous bearer of the name dates from the 12th century. The passionate and highly intelligent *Heloise* (the Old French form of the name) fell in love with her tutor and foremost scholar of the age, Peter Abelard. Their tragic story, revealed in the letters they exchanged which still survive, has been told in many literary forms. Eloise has been undergoing something of a revival in recent years.

VARIANTS **Eloyse, Elouise, Heloise** *French* **Héloïse, Éloïse**

☆ *La Nouvelle Héloïse* ('The New Heloise') was a successful 1761 novel by Jean-Jacques Rousseau, which led to a revival of interest in the name

Eloy *see* **Eligius**

Elroy *m*

This is normally interpreted as a variant form of LEROY, but it could perhaps be a variant of the surname *Elray*, derived from the name HILARY.

PET FORM **Roy**

★ James Elroy Flecker (1884–1915), English author, known to his family as Roy

Els *see* **Elizabeth**

Elsa *f*

This was originally a German pet form of ELIZABETH, but is now used as an independent name. The name was given a high profile in the 1950s and 60s as the name of a lioness that featured in Joy Adamson's book *Born Free* and in the 1966 film adaptation of it.

VARIANT *Scandinavian, German* **Else**

★ Elsa Lanchester (1902–86), English actress, famous for playing the Bride of Frankenstein

Elsbeth, Else *see* **Elizabeth**

Elsie *f*

ELSPETH, a Scottish form of ELIZABETH, developed a pet form *Elspie*, which in turn was shortened to Elsie. The name spread beyond Scotland and was quite widely used in the 19th century, but since the 1920s has retreated to Scotland again.

PET FORM **Else** • VARIANT **Elsi**

☆ Elsie Tanner in the long-running television soap opera *Coronation Street*

Elspeth *f*

This is a Scottish contraction of the name ELIZABETH. Sir Walter Scott used the name in at least three of his novels,

thereby introducing it to a wider public, and it was well used in the later 19th and earlier 20th century in the UK, although it has never had a significant impact on the USA. It is no longer in fashion, even in Scotland.
PET FORMS **Elspie, Elsie** • VARIANTS **Elsbeth, Elspet**
★ Elspeth Huxley (1907–97), Kenyan-born English writer

Elton *m*
This is a transferred use of the surname, which means 'Ella's settlement'. *Ella* was an Anglo-Saxon masculine name, probably a short form of a name containing the element *aelf*, 'elf', found in names such as ALFRED.
★ Sir Elton John (1947–   ), English singer-songwriter, whose popularity spread the name to the general public
★ Elton Dean (1945–2006), English saxophone player. Elton John, then performing under his real name, Reginald Dwight, was in the band Bluesology with Dean and the singer Long John Baldry, and is said to have created his stage name from their names

Eluned *f*
This is an old Welsh name which may be from the Welsh *eilun*, 'idol, icon'. In the 12th century the French writer Chrétien de Troyes used the name in the form *Lunete* for the heroine of one of his Arthurian stories, and from this the name developed the form LYNETTE. The Welsh saint *Eiliwedd* is also known as St Eluned or *Eiluned*. She was said to be a 5th-century princess who was beheaded by a suitor when she preferred to become a bride of Christ rather than marry him. A miraculous well appeared where she was beheaded.
VARIANTS **Luned, Lunet, Eiluned, Elined**

Elva *see* **Ailbe**

Elvin *see* **Alvin**

Elvina *f*
This appears to be a variant of *Alvina*, the feminine of ALVIN. The name was used in the USA from the 19th century until about 1930, nearly as often in its pet form as in its full form, and shows faint signs of a comeback, particularly in France.
MASCULINE **Elvin** • PET FORM **Elvi(e)**

Elvira *f*
This is a Germanic name that was taken to Spain by the invading Visigoths in the Dark Ages. It is probably compounded from the elements *ali*, 'other, foreign', as in ELEANOR, and *wer*, 'true'. It was popular in the Middle Ages in Spain, but did not spread to English speakers until the 19th century. It was regularly used in the USA into the 1930s, but then gradually declined and was little used after the 1980s. It is, however, currently popular in Scandinavia.
PET FORM **Elva**
☆ Elvira is the heroine of Mozart's opera *Don Giovanni*
☆ Elvira is the name of the ghost in Noel Coward's 1941 play *Blithe Spirit*
☆ *Elvira Madigan* was an influential 1967 Swedish film

Elvis *m*
Although this name is so closely identified with the singer Elvis Presley (1935–77), it was by no means unique to him. In the year he was born, 49 boys were given the name, but in surrounding years the name was often given to more than 100. The name occurs from the 1880s, when records first become available. There have been numerous suggestions as to where it comes from. It has been suggested it could be a form of *Alvis*, a name of Old Norse origin meaning 'all wise' that had about the same

popularity as Elvis in the late 19th and first half of the 20th century. An alternative is that it is a form of either the surname *Elwes*, which comes from ELOISE or of *Elwin* which comes from ALVIN. Among the most probable theories is that it is a form of the Irish name AILBE, pronounced 'al-by' or 'al-vy'. This name, used for both sexes, regularly appears as a feminine *Elva*, and is found as Elvis, the name of a saint in Wales. What can no longer be accepted is the view that it was a name invented for Presley's father whose middle name it was.

★ Elvis Costello (1955–   ), English singer-songwriter

Elvy *see* **Ailbe**

Elwin *see* **Alvin**

Elwyn *m*
This name is found in both Ireland and Wales, but its origin is obscure, and it is not even certain if the Welsh and Irish forms are of the same name.
VARIANT **Elwin**
★ Elwyn Jones (1909–89), Welsh former Lord Chancellor

Ely *see* **Eli**

Elyse *see* **Elise**

Elyza *see* **Eliza**

Emalie *see* **Emily**

Emanuel, **Emanuele** *see* **Emmanuel**

Ember *f*
A vocabulary word that has recently become fashionable as a first name, although some uses may be as a respelling of AMBER. It is occasionally found for boys.

Emelia, **Emelie**, **Emely** *see* **Emily**

Emer *see* **Eimer**

Emerald *f*
Emerald is an unusual first name, which has been used occasionally since the 19th century, but which has never been as popular as its Spanish equivalent ESMERALDA. The most famous bearer of the name, Emerald Cunard (1872–1948), chose it for herself; she was born Maud Alice Burke, and only began calling herself Emerald in the 1920s at the height of her fame as a hostess.

Emeric, **Emerick** *see* **Imre**

Emerson *m*
A transferred use of the surname, from the medieval first name *Emery*, formed from *amal*, 'bravery, vigour' and *ric*, 'rule, power'. See also AMERICA.
★ Emerson Fittipaldi (1946–   ), Brazilian racing driver

Emery, **Emory** *see* **America**

Emil *m*
This name comes from the Latin family name of *Aemelius* which is thought to come from *aemulus* meaning 'rival'. The name has always been more popular on the Continent than with English speakers, but use has been growing in the UK in recent years. See also EMLYN.
VARIANTS **Emile** *French* **Émile**, **Émilien** *Italian, Spanish* **Emilio**, **Emiliano** *Russian* **Yemelyan**
★ Émile Zola (1840–1902), French author
☆ *Emil and the Detectives* (1929) is a classic children's novel by Erich Kästner

Emilia *see* **Amelia**

Emily *f*
This is the feminine equivalent of EMIL, from the Latin *Aemelia*. It was introduced to the general public in the 14th century, by Chaucer's *The Knight's Tale*. There the name appeared as *Emelye* and was a translation of

Emilia, which is the form it takes in Chaucer's source, Boccaccio's *Teseida*. The name first became really popular in the 18th century, when it ousted AMELIA, a name derived at least in part from the same source. There is considerable overlap between variants of EMILY, Amelia, EMMA and EMMELINE. Emily has enjoyed worldwide popularity in recent years, having been at one time the most frequent choice for girls not only in England and the USA, but also in Canada, Sweden and other countries.

PET FORMS **Em, Emmi(e), Emmy, Milly**
• VARIANTS **Emilie, Emelie, Emalie, Emelia, Emely, Emilee, Emillie, Emilly**
★ Emily Brontë (1818–48), English author
★ Emily Dickinson (1830–86), US poet

Emir, **Emire** *see* **Amir**

Emlyn *m*
This is a Welsh name of confused origin. It could be from the same source as EMIL, but Emlyn is also a Welsh place name in Dyfed, and many bearers identify the name with this source. The place name is very old and may be formed from *am*, 'surrounding', and *glyn*, 'valley'.
★ Emlyn Williams (1905–87), Welsh actor and writer
★ Emlyn Hughes (1947–2004), English footballer

Emma *f*
Emma is a very old Germanic name, recorded from at least the 7th century. It seems to be a short form of names compounded from the element *erm(in)* or *irm(in)*, 'whole, entire, immense, universal', found in names such as ERMINTRUDE and IRMA. It was very popular in the Middle Ages, and is once again widespread in many countries, sharing top billing with EMILY.
★ Emma, also known as *Aelgifu* (d.1052),

was wife of two kings of England and mother of King Edward the Confessor
☆ Emma Peel, character in the television series *The Avengers*
☆ Emma Geller-Greene, daughter of Rachel and Ross in the 1990s television series *Friends*. The choice of Emma as a name for this character has been cited as the reason for the revival of the name in the USA

Emmanuel *m*
Spelt Emmanuel in the New Testament and *Immanuel* in the Old Testament, this is a Hebrew term, meaning 'God with us', used for the Messiah prophesied by Isaiah.
PET FORM **Manny** • VARIANTS *French* **Emmanuelle** (f) *German* **Emanuel**, **Immanuel** *Greek* **Emmanouil** *Italian* **Emanuele** *Portuguese* **Manoel** (m), **Manoela** (f) *Spanish* **Manuel, Manolo** (ms), **Manuela, Manola, Manuelita** (fs)

Emmeline *f*
A name introduced by the Normans which comes from the same root as EMMA, a Germanic element meaning 'entire, whole, universal'. It was one of the medieval names revived in the 19th century. Modern use is usually with reference to its most famous bearer, the suffragette Emmeline Pankhurst (1858–1928).
VARIANT **Emmaline**

Emmeric, **Emmerich** *see* **Imre**

Emmet *m*
In the Middle Ages the name EMMA developed a pet form *Emmot* or *Emmet*, which in turn became a surname. This surname is used in Ireland as a first name to commemorate Robert Emmet, who led a rebellion against the British in 1798 and was executed in 1803.

Emrys *m*
This is the Welsh equivalent of AMBROSE.

The military leader and supposed uncle to King Arthur, known as Ambrosius Aurelianus, is called Emrys Wledig in Welsh tradition. He was a real person, living in the 5th century, as he is mentioned by name in a contemporary work by Gildas. In some traditions the wizard Merlin is known as Merlin Emrys.

Emmi, Emmie, Emmy *see* **Emily**

Emyr *m*
A Welsh name meaning 'ruler, king'.

Ena *f*
A multi-sourced name, this started out as either a pet form of names ending in *-ena* (compare INA), or as an anglicized form of EITHNE or ENAT. However, the cause of the name's popularity was poor handwriting. One of Queen Victoria's granddaughters was to be christened Victoria Eugénie Julia Eva, but the clergyman performing the christening misread the names supplied on a handwritten slip of paper, and called her Ena. The Princess, who lived 1887–1969, was always known as Ena, and after she became queen of Spain the name spread, although it is now out of favour.
☆ Ena Sharples, battle-axe character in the early years of the television soap opera *Coronation Street*

Enat *f*
Enat is the Irish feminine equivalent of AIDAN, 'little fire'. It is by no means as common as the popular masculine form and is sometimes transformed into ENA or ENID.
VARIANT *Irish* **Aodhnait**

Enda *mf*
This Irish name comes from *ean* meaning 'bird'. St Enda was a 6th-century warrior king who gave up his throne after the death of his fiancée,

and who is said to have founded ten monasteries on the Aran Isles.
VARIANT *Irish* **Éanna**
★ Enda Walsh (1967–), Irish playwright

Endre *see* **Andrew**

Enea, Eneas, Enéas *see* **Aeneas**

Enfys *f*
This is a modern Welsh name, taken from the vocabulary word for 'rainbow'. It is pronounced 'EN-viss', and has been recorded as a masculine name.

Engelbert *m*
This was the name of a 13th-century archbishop of Cologne who became a saint, not so much because of the holiness of his life – he was appointed through family influence and was more a statesman than a religious man – but because he was assassinated by a disgruntled relative. The second element of the name is the common Germanic element *berht*, 'bright', but there is little agreement about the source of the first. Among the theories is that it is from *Ingel* from the pagan god Ing; *Angel* 'Angle' found in England; *engel* 'angel'; or *ang* 'point of a sword'. The same element, but distorted over time, occurs in the medieval French name *Enguerrand* (earlier *Engilramn* or *Angilramn*) where the second element is *hramn*, 'raven'.
VARIANT **Ingelbert**
★ Engelbert Humperdinck (1854–1921), German composer
★ Engelbert Humperdinck (1936–), stage name adopted by the English singer Arnold Dorsey

Enid *f*
This is a Welsh name of uncertain origin, but most often analysed as being from *enaid*, 'soul', although *enit*, 'woodlark', has also been suggested. In Arthurian legend, Enid is the meek but

brave and long-suffering wife of the great knight GERAINT. It was Tennyson's retelling of their story in his *Idylls of the King* in 1859 which popularized the name among the general public in the 19th century.

★ Enid Blyton (1897–1968), English children's author

Enis *see* **Ennis**

Ennio *m*
Ennio is the modern Italian form of the Roman family name *Ennius*, of unknown meaning. Quintus Ennius, who lived in the 3rd to 2nd century BC, was one of the greatest of the early Latin poets.

★ Ennio Morricone (1928–), Italian composer, known for his film scores

Ennis *mf*
This is from the Gaelic *innis* (see INNES) meaning 'island'. It is found as a surname, and is also the name of a town, built on an island, in County Clare.

VARIANT **Enis**

☆ Ennis Del Mar, principal character in the film *Brokeback Mountain* (2005) adapted from the story by Annie Proulx

Enoch *m*
This is a biblical name of uncertain meaning, but it is probably 'dedicated, thoroughly schooled'. In the Bible Enoch is said to have lived 365 years and then to have been translated to heaven while still alive. The apocryphal books of Enoch describing his visits to heaven are a major source of angel lore. The name was used from the 17th century, but is now rare.

VARIANTS *Hebrew* **Chanoch** *Scandinavian* **Enok**

★ Enoch Powell (1912–98), English politician and academic

☆ Enoch Arden, a fisherman in the eponymous 1864 poem by Tennyson

Enola *f*
All sorts of stories, none of them entirely satisfactory, have grown up to explain this name since it sprang to public attention in 1945 in the form *Enola Gay*, the name of the plane that carried the atom bomb dropped on Hiroshima. The plane was named after the pilot's mother. There is a story that it is a Native American name for the magnolia tree, but no one has ever produced the evidence for this. Another story points out that Enola is 'alone' reversed. Yet another claims it comes from a novel, which would be convincing if anyone could cite which novel. All that is known for sure is that it has been in use in the USA since at least the 1880s, and its mild popularity peaked in the 1900s to 1920s. It is a place name as well as a first name. The first name has been linked to French-speaking Louisiana, but uses as a place name include one in Arkansas and one in Pennsylvania. Both have local legends which say they were named after the small daughter of a founder, and alternative ones that cite the 'alone' story, the Pennsylvanian one referring to a solitary telegraph pole.

☆ Enola is the name of the central child in the 1995 film *Waterworld*

Enos *m*
In the Bible Enos is the name of one of the grandsons of Adam. The name means 'mankind' in Hebrew. It was used in the USA from the 19th century until about 1920.

VARIANT **Enosh**

☆ Enos Strate is the name of the Deputy Sheriff in the 1970s television series *The Dukes of Hazzard*

Enrico, **Enrique** *see* **Henry**

Enya *see* **Eithne**

Enzo *m*
This is an Italian name of two possible

origins, the first as a pet form of names ending -*enzo*, such as *Lorenzo* (LAWRENCE) and *Vincenzo* (VINCENT); the second as an Italian form of the German name HEINZ, which is a diminutive of Heinrich, the German form of HENRY. Probably the two have reinforced each other. It may seem odd to have a German name in Italy, but parts of Italy were controlled by the German-dominated Holy Roman Empire in the Middle Ages, and Enzo was the name of a king of Sardinia born in 1224, who was the illegitimate son of the German Emperor Frederick II. In recent years the name has been very popular in France, being the most frequent choice for boys in 2004.
FEMININE **Enza**
★ Enzo Ferrari (1898–1988), Italian founder of the Ferrari motor company

Eoghan *m*
Although in the past this was considered to have the same meaning as EUGENE, by which it was often translated, it is now generally thought that the first syllable is based on the Gaelic *iúr*, 'yew', with the second still interpreted as 'born', as in Eugene. The name is used in both Scotland and Ireland, and has two pronunciations. One is 'oh-in', in which case the name can also appear as OWEN, the other is 'yew-en', in which case the name can appear as EUAN and its variants. There is tremendous overlap between these and similar names. The Northern Irish area of County TYRONE comes from this name, for in Irish it is *Tir Eoghan*, 'Land of Eoghan'
VARIANTS **Eóghan, Euan, Ewan, Ewen, Evan, Eoan, Eoghain, Owen**
★ Eoghan Roe (the Red) O'Neill (c.1590–1649), defeated the English at the Battle of Benburb in 1646

Eoin, Eòin *m*
Pronounced 'ow-in', and thus barely distinguishable from EOGHAN, this is one Irish form of JOHN, the other being SEAN. It shares with Eoghan the anglicized form OWEN. The two different forms of John developed because they come from different sources. Eoin represents the Irish form of the Latin name *Iohannes*, which would have been familiar from the Bible. Sean, on the other hand, is the Irish form of *Jean*, the variant of the name spread by the French-speaking Normans.
★ Eoin Colfer (1965–), Irish children's author

Ephraim *m*
This is a biblical name, meaning 'fruitful'. It was the name of one of Joseph's children, 'and the name of the second called he Ephraim: For God hath caused me to be fruitful' (Genesis 41.52). It started to be used by English speakers in the 16th century, and became more popular in the 18th and 19th centuries, but is now mainly restricted to the Jewish communities.
VARIANTS *French* **Éphrem** *Hebrew* **Efraim** *Russian* **Yefrem** *Spanish* **Efraín** *Yiddish* **Evron**

Eppie *f*
A pet name for those called EUPHEMIA, HEPHZIBAH or ESTHER. It was particularly used in Scotland in the 19th century, but is now rarely found.
☆ Eppie Dean in Sir Walter Scott's 1818 novel *The Heart of Midlothian*
☆ Eppie is the orphan child whose innocence and humanity redeems the miser Silas Marner, in George Eliot's 1861 novel of that name

Erasmus *m*
This name comes from the Greek *erasmos*, 'loved'. St Erasmus, also known as St ELMO, was a 3rd-century martyr who is the patron saint of

sailors. The name is most likely to be found in Scandinavia and Estonia.
PET FORM **Elmo** • VARIANT *Scandinavian* **Rasmus**
★ Desiderius Erasmus, commonly known as Erasmus (c.1466–1536), Dutch humanist scholar and theologian
★ Erasmus Darwin (1731–1802), English physician and poet

Erastus *m*

Erastus is closely related to ERASMUS, being from the Greek *erastos*, 'beloved'. This was the name of a companion of St Paul who is mentioned several times in the New Testament. It too was taken up by a theologian, although one less famous than Erasmus – the Swiss Thomas Erastus (1524–83).
PET FORM **Rastus**

Ercole *see* **Hercules**

Erhard *m*

A German name, formed from the elements *era*, 'honour, respect', and *hard*, 'brave, hardy'. Despite his German name, St Erhard was a 7th-century missionary who is said to have come from Ireland, in common with so many who converted the Germans.

Eric *m*

The Old Norse name *Eirikr* has a first element that is either from *ei*, 'ever, always', or from *einn*, 'one, single'. The second element is more easily dealt with as it is *rikr*, 'rule, power', the Old Norse equivalent of the *ric* element so common in Germanic names such as RICHARD and FREDERICK. St Eric Jedvarsson of Sweden died fighting the Danes and was made the national saint, despite the fact that he had murdered his way to the Swedish throne. The name seems to have been brought to Britain by Viking raiders, and reintroduced by the Normans who had it from their own Viking heritage. However, it was

not common until the 19th century, when use was encouraged by Dean Farrar's pious boys' book *Eric, or Little By Little* (1858).
PET FORMS **Rick, Ricky, Rikki** • VARIANTS **Eri(c)k** *Danish* **Jerrik** *French* **Éric** *German* **Erich** *Norwegian* **Eirik** *Portuguese* **Érico** *Swedish* **Eïrik, Jerk(er)**
★ Erik the Red (10th century), navigator and explorer, who discovered Greenland
★ Eric Carle (1929–), US children's author and illustrator, author of *The Very Hungry Caterpillar*
☆ Eric Cartman, in the cartoon television series *South Park*

Erica *f*

This name serves both as a feminine form of ERIC, and as a flower name, as it is the Latin for HEATHER. It dates only from the 18th century. The name was a popular choice in the USA in the 1990s.
PET FORM **Rikki** • VARIANTS **Eri(c)ka, Arica, Erykah** *Hawaiian* **Elika**
★ Erica Jong (1942–), US author

Érico *see* **Eric**

Erin *f*

The Irish word *Éirinn* means 'of Eire', Eire being the Irish name for the country otherwise known as Ireland. Erin has long been a poetic term for Ireland, and it seems to have been Irish expatriates who turned it into a first name. It was in use in the USA by the 1880s, and seems then to have spread to Canada and Australia. It was popular in Britain from the 1970s, but the Irish themselves were slow to take it up, although it is currently widespread there. The root of the word is very old, having been recorded as the name of the island by the 1st century BC. Erin is occasionally found as a masculine name, in which case it may be a respelling of AARON.

VARIANTS **Erinn, Eryn(n), Erina, Eireann, Aryn**
★ Erin Brokovich (1960–), US rights campaigner and television presenter
★ Erin O'Connor (1978–), English model

Ermanno *see* **Herman**

Ermengard *f*
This is a German name formed from *erm(en)*, 'whole, entire', and *gard*, 'enclosure'.
VARIANTS **Irma, Ermgard, Irm(en)gard, Irmingard**

Ermine *f*
This is either the vocabulary word for the white and black fur worn by peers, or else a variant of the German name *Hermine*, a feminine form of HERMAN. The fur, which comes from the stoat, gets its name from the medieval Latin for stoat, *armenius mus*, 'Armenian mouse'. As a first name Ermine is rare, and seems to have been most used around the turn of the 19th to 20th century.

Erminie *see* **Hermine**

Ermintrude *f*
This name is formed from the Germanic elements *ermin* or *irmen*, 'universal, entire', found in EMMA, and either *traut*, 'beloved', or *thruth*, 'strength'. The name was brought to England by the Normans, but is now very rare.
PET FORM **Trudy** • VARIANTS **Ermyntrude** *German* **Ermentraud(e), Ermtraud, Irmentrud, Irmtr(a)ud**
☆ Ermintrude the cow, in the children's television series *The Magic Roundabout*

Ernan *m*
Ernan or *Ernin* is an Irish name, prominent among the names of the early saints. St Ernan is the patron saint of Tory Island, while St Ernin Cass ('the curly haired') is patron saint of Leighlin, and shares his name with at least ten other saints. The name probably comes from the Irish word *iarn*, 'iron'.
VARIANTS **Ernin** (mf) *Irish* **Earnán, Eirnin** (mf)

Ernest *m*
The Old High German word *eaornost* was a technical term used to mean 'a battle to the death' or 'serious business'. It does, however, share a root with the English vocabulary word 'earnest', the sense of which has weakened over the years. The name was not introduced to English speakers until the 18th century, when George I, then merely Elector of Hanover, was invited to take the throne of Britain, and brought with him many new German names. In Britain it was popular into the early years of the 20th century, but is now out of favour. In the USA its popularity lasted much longer, and it is still in regular use.
PET FORM **Ern(ie)** • VARIANTS **Earnest** *German* **Ernst** *Italian, Spanish* **Ernesto**
★ Ernie Wise (1925–99), English comedian
★ Ernest Hemingway (1899–1961), US author
☆ *The Importance of Being Earnest* (1895) is a comedy that centres on the name Ernest and has influenced its comic reputation in the UK, while Hemingway has given it a more rugged reputation in the USA

Ernestine *f*
A feminine form of ERNEST. It was introduced in the 19th century and, like the masculine form, it has had longer success in the USA than in the UK.
VARIANTS **Ernestina, Ernice** *German* **Erna** *Italian, Spanish* **Ernesta**

Errol *m*

The earls of Erroll, hereditary High Constables of Scotland, are among the most prominent members of the Scottish aristocracy. In the past the name was also spelt Errol. It was probably from them that Frances Hodgson Burnett got the name of Cedric Errol, the upright boy from the USA who finds himself *Little Lord Fauntleroy* (published in 1885). The name became world famous in the 1930s with the success of the Australian film actor Errol Flynn. It is now most likely to be found in the West Indies and among African Americans.

VARIANTS **Erroll, Erol**

Ertha, Erthel *see* Eartha

Ervyn, Erwin *see* Irvine

Erykah *see* Erica

Eryn, Erynn *see* Erin

Esau *m*

According to the biblical book of Genesis, Esau was the name of the elder of the twin brothers born to ISAAC, who was tricked out of his inheritance by his brother JACOB. Esau comes from the Hebrew for 'hairy', a name given to the biblical Esau because he was born covered in red hair. The name was occasionally given in earlier centuries, but is now very rare. See also EDOM.

Esdras *see* Ezra

Esme *mf* Esmee *f*

The French name *Esmé* comes from the Old French word for 'loved, esteemed'. It came to Britain through the French-born Esmé Stewart, Seigneur d'Aubigny, who was a cousin and favourite of the boy-king James VII of Scotland, and the name has remained particularly associated with Scotland.

The name was sometimes respelt *Aimé* or *Aymé*, as if from the French verb *aimer*, so that there is some overlap with AMY. The name started being used for girls in the 18th century, and is now mainly female, and usually written without the accent. The name also functions as a pet form of ESMERALDA.

VARIANTS **Esma** *Scottish* **Edme**

☆ *For Esmé – with Love and Squalor* is a 1953 collection of short stories by J D Salinger

Esmeralda *f*

This is the Spanish for EMERALD. The main inspiration for its use is Victor Hugo's 1831 novel The *Hunchback of Notre Dame* (*Notre Dame de Paris*) where it is the name of the gypsy girl loved by Quasimodo.

PET FORM **Esme** • VARIANTS **Esmerelda, Esmaralda**

☆ Esmerelda (Esme) Weatherwax, witch, in Terry Pratchett's *Discworld* novels

Esmond *m*

There was an Old English name Esmond, formed from *east*, 'grace', and *mund*, 'protection', but this died out in the Middle Ages. It was revived in the 19th century. This was a time when many Old English names were revived, but in this case the success of *The History of Henry Esmond*, an 1852 novel by Thackeray, may have been influential. Esmond is now rare as a first name, although not uncommon as a surname.

VARIANT **Esmund**

★ Esmond Romilly (1918–41, English campaigner married to Jessica Mitford

Esperance *see* Hope, Speranza

Esperanza, Espérance *see* Speranza

Essa *see* Esther, Jesus

Estachio *see* Eustace

Estavan, Esteban *see* Stephen

Estefanía *see* **Stephanie**

Estelle *f*
Estelle is an Old French form of the Latin STELLA meaning 'star'. This form died out, ousted by *Étoile*, which has occasionally been used as a first name in France.
VARIANTS **Estella** *Spanish* **Estrella, Estela, Marianela** (a blend of Maria and Estela)
☆ Estella is the name of the girl brought up by Miss Havisham to punish men, in Dickens's *Great Expectations* (1861)

Ester *see* **Hester**

Estevão *see* **Stephen**

Esther *f*
In the Bible, Esther is the wife of King Ahasuerus of Persia who, by her bravery and quick thinking, saves numerous Jews subjected to persecution. Her Hebrew name is HADASSAH, meaning both 'myrtle' and 'bride', and it is implied that Esther is a translation of this. However, the name seems more likely to be either derived from the Persian *setareh*, 'star', or else to be a form of the name *Ishtar*, the Babylonian goddess of love and fertility, which would suit Esther's beauty. From the early Middle Ages, in Jewish communities, Esther was given to girls born during the period of Purim, the feast that celebrates the biblical Esther's achievements. The name was taken up by the Puritans in the 17th century, and despite the exotic story behind the name, retained a Puritan image for some time.
PET FORMS **Ess(ie), Essa, Eppie, Ettie, Etty** • VARIANTS **Hester, Esta** *Irish* **Eistir** *Hungarian* **Eszter** *Russian* **Yesfir** *Scandinavian* **Ester**
★ Esther Williams (1923–), US swimming champion turned film star
☆ Esther Summerson, heroine of Dickens's 1853 novel *Bleak House*
☆ Esther Waters, eponymous heroine

of George Moore's 1894 novel of working-class struggle

Estrid *see* **Astrid**

Esyllt *see* **Isolde**

Eszter *see* **Esther**

Etain *f*
In the Irish myth of *The Wooing of Etain*, Etain is a beautiful woman with whom the god Midir the Proud falls in love and marries, only for her to be persecuted by his jealous first wife. This presumably explains why the name is derived from Irish *et*, 'jealousy'. In 1914 an opera based on this story, *The Immortal Hour* by Rutland Broughton, was a success and caused a brief period of interest in the name, but it is now little used, even in Ireland.
VARIANTS **Étain, Éadaoin, Eadan**

Etel, Etelka *see* **Ethel**

Ethan *m*
Ethan is the name of a number of characters in the Bible and comes from the Hebrew for 'firmness'. Like other Old Testament names it came into use in the Reformation, but was one of those less commonly used. Recently, however, it has become extremely popular on both sides of the Atlantic.
VARIANTS **Ethen** *Hebrew* **Eitan**
★ Ethan Allen (1738–89), leader of the Green Mountain Boys of Vermont, who fought in the American Revolution
★ Ethan Hawke (1970–), US actor and film director
☆ Ethan Frome, eponymous hero of a 1911 novel by Edith Wharton

Ethel *f*
Old English *aethel*, 'noble', was a common element in Anglo-Saxon names for both sexes. Ethel is a shortening of names beginning with this element which was revived

in the 19th century, and remained popular into the early part of the 20th, although it is little used today. Two popular novels prominently featuring Ethels helped the spread of the name: Thackeray's *The Newcomes* (1855) and C M Yonge's *The Daisy Chain* (1856).

PET FORM **Eth** • VARIANTS Hungarian **Etel**, **Etelka**

★ Ethel Merman (1909–84), US singer and actress

★ Ethel Barrymore (1879–1959), US actress

☆ Ron Glum and his long-term fiancée Eth in the long-running 1950s radio show *Take It from Here*

Ethelbert *m*

This is an Old English name, more properly spelt *Aethelbert* or *Aethelbeorht*, formed from the elements *aethel*, 'noble', and *berht*, 'bright', and thus the Old English equivalent of ALBERT. It was the name of three Anglo-Saxon kings, two of whom became saints: St Ethelbert of Kent, who welcomed St Augustine to Canterbury when he was sent to convert the English, and St Ethelbert of the East Angles to whom Hereford Cathedral is dedicated, despite the fact that his assassination seems to have been for political rather than religious reasons. The name was revived on both sides of the Atlantic in the 19th century, but is very rare today.

FEMININE **Ethelberta** • PET FORM **Bert(ie)**

★ Ethelbert Nevin (1862–1901), US pianist and composer

☆ Ethelbert Stanhope in Anthony Trollope's 1857 novel *Barchester Towers*

☆ Ethelberta Chickerel in Thomas Hardy's 1876 novel *The Hand of Ethelberta*

Etheldreda *see* **Audrey**

Ethelred *m*

This is the modern form of the Old English name *Aethelraed*, formed from the elements *aethel*, 'noble', and *raed*, 'counsel'. The modern form of the name of the 11th-century king, known as Ethelred the Unready, is an unsuccessful attempt to translate the original pun of his Old English name *Aethelraed unraed*, meaning something like 'noble counsel the uncounselled' or 'ill-advised'.

Ethenia, **Ethna**, **Ethni** *see* **Eithne**

Étienne *see* **Stephen**

Etna *see* **Eithne**

Etta *see* **Harriet**, **Yetta**

Ettie *see* **Esther**, **Hester**

Ettore *see* **Hector**

Etty *see* **Esther**, **Hester**

Euan, **Ewan** *m*

These are anglicized forms of the Scots Gaelic name EOGHAN, initially used in Scotland but now, although they still have a Scottish flavour, found in other parts of the British Isles. Currently Euan is the slightly more popular form in Scotland, but both variants are well used.

VARIANTS **Ewen**, **Evan**, **Owen**, **Ewing**

★ Ewan McGregor (1971–   ), Scottish actor

Eubh, **Eubha** *see* **Eva**

Eudard *see* **Edward**

Eudocia *f*

This is the English form of the Greek names *Eudoxia*, 'good reputation', and *Eudokia*, 'comfort'. St Eudokia, or Eudocia, of Heliopolis was a 1st-century courtesan who was converted to Christianity when she heard a monk singing prayers, and was later beheaded for her faith. Her name was popular among the Byzantine aristocracy, and passed through dynastic marriages to other countries, including Russia, where another bearer of the name also became a saint, known as St Eudoxia of Moscow. The name has occasionally been used further west, but is now very rare.

VARIANTS *French* **Eudoxie** *Russian* **Avdotya**

Eudora *f*

This name can be analysed as formed from the Greek elements *eu*, 'good', and *doron*, 'gift', but seems to be a 19th-century creation, so may come directly from a blend of modern name elements. It was mainly used in the USA. It was most popular in the 1880s, and has been virtually abandoned since the end of the 1920s.

★ Eudora Welty (1909–2001), US author
☆ Eudora Addams is the grandmother in the cartoons and films of *The Addams Family*

Eufane, Eufemia *see* Euphemia

Eugene *m*

This is the English form of the Greek name *Eugenios*, 'well-born, noble', compounded from *eu*, 'good, well' and *genos*, 'birth, origin'. The name spread through the popularity of a number of early saints. In Gaelic-speaking areas the name was used to translate a number of local names, including EOGHAN, EOIN and AODH. In modern use it is more likely to be found in the USA than in the UK.

PET FORM **Gene** • VARIANTS *Welsh* **Owen** *French* **Eugène** *German* **Eugen** *Italian, Spanish* **Eugenio, Geno** *Russian* **Yevgeni**

★ Eugene O'Neill (1899–1953), US playwright
★ Yevgeni Yevtushenko (1933–), Russian poet

Eugenie *f*

The Empress Eugénie of France (1826–1920) was born, to give her her remarkably full name and titles, Doña María Eugenia Ignacia Augustina de Palafox de Guzmán Portocarrero y Kirkpatrick, 18th Marchioness of Ardales, 18th Marchioness of Moya, 19th Countess of Teba, 10th Countess of Montijo and Countess of Ablitas. She married the Emperor Napoleon III in 1853, and fled to England in 1870 when Napoleon was defeated and later deposed in the Franco-Prussian War. She became great friends with Queen Victoria – they called each other 'sister' and even shared the same dress designer. The Empress's name was given to one of Queen Victoria's granddaughters, Princess Victoria Eugénie of Battenberg, and Prince Andrew's daughter Eugénie (b.1990) was also named after her.

Eulalia *f*

This name comes from Greek *eulalos*, 'talking well' or 'good speaking', but was the name of a 4th-century Spanish martyr, who became the patron saint of Madrid. Although it was popular in the Middle Ages, it is now rarely used.

PET FORMS **Eula, Lal(ie), Lally** • VARIANTS **Eulalee** *French* **Eulalie** *Spanish* **Olalla** (variant)

Eumann *see* Edmund

Eunan *see* Adamnan

Eunice *f*

This name comes from the Greek name formed from *eu*, 'good', and *nike*, 'victory'. The pronunciation has gone through changes over the centuries. The Greek would have pronounced all the letters and used a hard 'k' sound. When it was first adopted into English in the 17th century it would have been pronounced with three syllables and a soft 'c', as 'you-ny-see', but this pronunciation has now been almost entirely superseded by 'you-nis' or 'you-nees'. The name can be given a Christian interpretation and, as it is given in the Bible as the name of the mother of Timothy, who introduced him to Christianity (2 Timothy 1.5), it was adopted by the Puritans with some enthusiasm. It had another peak in the 1920s, but is now rare.

VARIANT **Unice**

Euphemia *f*

This name comes from the Greek element *eu*, 'well, good', combined with *phenai*, 'to speak'. It was the name of a number of early saints, including one who was burned at the stake in AD 307. It was in use by English speakers by the 12th century and continued in use, particularly in the 16th and 17th centuries, and was revived in the 19th century. In the Scottish Highlands it had a particular role, as the English form of the Gaelic *Oighrig* (see EFFIE). There it is primarily found in its pet forms.

PET FORMS **Effie, Eppie, Phemie, Fanny, Phebe, Phoebe** • VARIANTS *Scottish* **Eufane** *French* **Euphémie** *Greek* **Efthymia, Efimia** *Italian, Spanish* **Eufemia** *Russian* **Yefim, Fima** (ms)

★ Euphemia Allen (c.1861–1949), British composer of the tune 'Chopsticks', published under the name Arthur de Lulli

Eurfron *f*

This is a Welsh name, formed from the common name elements *eur*, 'gold, golden', and *bron*, 'breast'. The legendary Tegau Eurfron was praised by the ancient bards for her chastity.

MASCULINE **Eurfyn**

Euron *f*

This is a Welsh name meaning 'golden', based on the word *eur*, 'gold'. In Welsh tradition it was the name of a beautiful enchantress, and in the 15th century the poet Llywelyn ap y Moel addressed his love poetry to a girl of this name. There are many

related names in Welsh formed from *eur*.

MASCULINE **Eurion** • VARIANTS **Auron, Euriona**

Euronwy *f*

Another Welsh name based on *eur*, 'gold', Euronwy, together with CERIDWEN and EURON, was, according to Welsh tradition, 'one of the three legendary enchantresses of the Island of Britain'. She, or a namesake, appears in other records as the daughter of a 6th-century ruler in northern Britain, and the same person appears in the story of OLWEN under the related name of *Euneit*, where she is described as one of the 'gold-torqued women' of Britain.

Eurwen *f*

A Welsh name formed from *eur*, 'gold', and *(g)wen*, 'white, holy, pure, fair', so can be interpreted as 'gold and fair'.

MASCULINE **Eurwyn**

Eusebius *m*

The Greek name *Eusebios*, Eusebius in Latin, comes from *eusebes*, 'pious', which is formed from *eu*, 'good', and *sebein*, 'to worship'. There were several early saints of this name, including a prominent theologian.

VARIANTS *French* **Eusèbe** (m), **Eusébie** (f) *Italian, Spanish* **Eusebio**

Eustace *m*

The Greek name *Eustachys*, formed from *eu*, 'good', and *stakhus* which could mean either 'grapes' or 'corn', so that the name is usually interpreted as meaning 'fruitful'. It became *Eustachius* in Latin. It came to English via the French *Eustache*, which explains its differences from the original Greek. St Eustace is supposed to have lived in the 2nd century AD and to have been converted to Christianity after having a vision of a stag with a cross between its antlers. This was a common subject in art, and the name was widespread in the Middle Ages. It became popular again in the 19th century, but is now rare.

PET FORM **Stacey** • VARIANTS *Italian* **E(u)stachio** *Spanish* **Eustaquio**

Eva *f*

This is currently as popular as, and in some areas more popular than, the traditional English form of the name, EVE, in the English-speaking world. It is both the Latin form, and also the standard form in many other languages. In Ireland it acts as an English spelling of AOIFE.

PET FORM **Evita** (Spanish) • VARIANTS *Scots Gaelic* **Eubha** *Welsh* **Efa**

Evadne *f*

Evadne is the name of two characters in Greek mythology, one of whom was considered an exemplary wife. The meaning of the name is not known, although the first element is thought to be *eu*, 'good'. The name has been in use among English speakers since the 17th century, but apart from a certain amount of interest in the 19th century, has always been rare.

Evalin, **Evalina**, **Evaline**, **Evalyn**, **Evalyne**, **Evalynn**, **Evalynne** *see* **Evelyn**

Evan *mf*

Evan is a name that can come from a number of different sources. It can be from either a Welsh form of JOHN, *Iefan* (see IEUAN), in which case it is also a common Welsh surname; a Scottish form of EUAN; or a short form of *Evangelos* (see EVANGELINE). Some feminine forms can be variants of the name EAVAN.

★ Evan Rachel Wood (1987–), US actress, who has given publicity to the name as a feminine

Evander *m*

This is a Greek name, originally formed from the elements *eu*, 'good', and *aner, andros*, 'man', also found in ALEXANDER. As with other names from Greek beginning Ev-, the change from Greek to Latin use accounts for the 'v' rather than 'u' form. The legendary Evander was a Greek who founded a city on the site where Rome was later to stand. The name is not common, but in the past was used in Scotland to anglicize *Iomhvair* (also found as IVOR), particularly among the MacIver clan where the form distinguished the first name from the last.

★ Evander Holyfield (1962–), US boxer

Evangeline *f*

Although the Greek masculine name *Evangelos* is ancient, the feminine form was only popularized by the 1848 poem 'Evangeline', by the US poet Longfellow. It tells the story of a French-Canadian (Cajun) girl expelled to Louisiana after the British took control of Canada, and her search for the lover from whom she has been separated. There has been some debate as to whether Evangeline was already a rare Cajun name or if it was invented by Longfellow. The name comes from the Latin *evangelium*, 'gospel', formed from the Greek *euangelion* (from *eu*, 'good', plus *angelma*, 'messages'), combined with the French feminine name ending *-ine*. It is thus, as its name suggests, related to ANGELA.

PET FORMS **Eva, Evie** • VARIANT **Evangelina**

★ Evangeline Booth (1865–1950), daughter of the founder of the Salvation Army, William Booth, who later ran the Army in the USA

Evaristus *m*

A name formed from the Greek *Euarestos*, derived from *eu*, 'good', and *areskein*, 'to please', so usually glossed as 'pleasing'. The name is very rare in England, but is used in other languages.

VARIANTS *French* **Évariste** *Italian, Spanish* **Evaristo**

Eve *f*

The name of the biblical first woman is *Havva* in Hebrew, thought to come from *hayya*, 'living'. It became EVA in Latin and Eve in English. The name is currently popular as Eve, Eva and *Evie*.
PET FORM **Evie** • VARIANT *Scots Gaelic* **Eubh**

Evelyn *mf*

The history of this name is disconcertingly circular. The masculine use comes from the surname, and seems to be a product of the later 19th century. However, the surname derives from the old feminine name AVELINE. As a feminine it can also come from the surname, or more directly from the anglicized form of the Irish *Aibhlin* or *Eibhlin* (see EILEEN), an Irish form of Aveline. The history of the feminine name is complicated by the possibility of analysing it as a blend of Eva and Lynn, and by earlier use of the name *Evalina*. This was used by Fanny Burney as the eponymous heroine of her 1778 novel, and it is not known how she intended the name to be interpreted. Evelyn was popular into the 1920s, but then went out of favour, although there are signs that it may be coming back into favour alongside EVE.
PET FORMS **Eve, Effie, Evie** • VARIANTS **Eveline, Evelyn(n)(e), Evalyn(n)(e), Evalin(e), Eveleen, Evlin, Evleen**

- ★ Evelyn Waugh (1903–66), English author, whose first wife was also called Evelyn
- ★ Dame Evelyn Glennie (1965–), Scottish percussionist

Everard *m*

This was originally an Old English name from *eofor*, 'boar', and *hard*, 'brave'. Various forms of the name, from the same Germanic roots, existed on the Continent (see EBERHARD). The English surname *Everett* is another form of the name.
VARIANTS *French* **Évrard** *German* **Eberhard, Ebbe** *Spanish* **Eberardo**

Everilda *see* Averil

Evert *see* Eberhard

Evie *see* Evangeline, Eve, Evelyn

Evita *see* Eva

Evleen, Evlin *see* Evelyn

Evonne *see* Yvonne

Évrard *see* Everard

Evron *see* Ephraim

Ewart *m*

This Scottish surname is used in honour of the politician William Ewart Gladstone (1809–98). As a surname it can come either from someone who was a ewe-herder, from a place name, or from a Norman form of EDWARD.

Ewen *see* Euan, Eoghan

Ewing *see* Euan

Eynon *see* Einion

Ezekiel *m*

The Hebrew name *Yechezqel* means 'God strengthens', and was the name of a major prophet in the Old Testament. It was only quietly used in the 20th century, but use has increased markedly in the 21st.
PET FORM **Zeke** • VARIANTS *Spanish* **Ezequiel** *Yiddish* **Yechezkel, Haskel**

Ezra *m*

Ezra means 'help' in Hebrew. It was one of the many Old Testament names taken up in the 17th century. In the New Testament the name appears as *Esdras*. It has always been used in the USA, if quietly, but in recent years there has been a noticeable increase in use.
- ★ Ezra Pound (1885–1972), US poet

F

Faaiz *see* **Faiz**

Faas *see* **Boniface**

Faatimah *see* **Fatima**

Fabia *f* **Fabian** *m*
The Roman family name *Fabius*, probably from the Latin *faba* meaning 'bean', developed a form *Fabianus*, giving us Fabian, while Fabia comes directly from Fabius. These names spread through Europe via the Church. There was a 3rd-century pope called Fabian, said to have been elected after a dove settled on his head, who was martyred in the Decian persecutions, and another St Fabian martyred in North Africa. Another saint shows a feminine elaboration of the name – St *Fabiola*, a 4th-century Italian who founded a hostel for pilgrims in Rome.
VARIANTS *French* **Fabien**, **Fabienne** *Italian* **Fabiano** *Italian, Spanish* **Fabio**, **Fabiana**
★ Queen Fabiola (1928–   ), Spanish-born Belgian queen

Fabrice *m*
This is the French form of a name derived from the Latin *Fabricius* meaning 'craftsman'.
VARIANTS *Italian* **Fabrizio** *Spanish* **Fabricio**

Fachtna *mf*
An Irish name, most often used as a masculine name, which probably comes from the Irish word for 'hostile, malicious'. It was the name of a 6th-century saint, more usually known as St *Fachnan*. In the past it was anglicized as FESTUS.

Faddei, **Faddey** *see* **Thaddeus**

Fadi *m* **Fadia** *f*
This is an Arabic name meaning 'ransomer, redeemer', a term used by Muslims for Christ.

Fadile *mf* **Fadila** *f*
Fadile is from the Arabic for 'virtuous, excellent', while the feminine Fadila comes from the related noun meaning 'moral excellence, virtue'.
VARIANTS **Fadil**, **Fadl(e)**, **Fazil**, **Fazila**, **Fadheela**

Fae *see* **Faye**

Faedra *see* **Phaedra**

Faelan *see* **Faolan**

Fahd *m*
Fahd is an Arabic name. The general meaning refers to one of the smaller big cats, the name being glossed variously as cheetah, leopard, lynx or panther.
VARIANTS **Fahad**, **Fahed**
★ Fahd ibn Abd al-Aziz al-Saud (1923–2005), king of Saudi Arabia

Fahim *m* **Fahima** *f*
An Arabic name meaning 'quick-witted'. Related names are *Faheem*, *Faheema*, 'intelligent, learned, judicious', and *Fahmi*, *Fahmida* meaning 'intelligent, intellectual'.
VARIANT **Faheemah**

Faïçal *see* **Faisal**

Faidra *see* **Phaedra**

Faisal *m*
Although this Arabic name is usually glossed as meaning 'judge', it is actually derived from the word for

a sword. This is because a good judge is one who can separate right from wrong, ie one who can discern (another word that goes back to the idea of cutting in two).

VARIANTS **Faysal, Feisal, Faizal** *French* **Fayçal, Faïçal**

★ Faisal ibn Abd al-Aziz (1905–75), king of Saudi Arabia

Faith *f*

This was one of the virtue names introduced in the 16th century and popular in the 17th, when, along with *Faithful*, it could be used for either sex. It was regularly used in the later 19th century, and in the last decade has been a popular choice on both sides of the Atlantic. Faith and one of the other virtue names, particularly HOPE, is a popular choice for twins.

PET FORMS **Fay, Faye**

Faivish *m*

Although this is a Jewish name, its origin seems to be Greek, and it is the Yiddish form of the name *Phoibus* or PHOEBUS, 'bright, pure', one of the titles of Apollo.

PET FORMS **Fayvel, Feivel** • VARIANTS **Feibush**

Faiz *m* **Faiza** *f*

This is an Arabic name usually meaning 'victor, winner', although Faiz can also be a spelling of *Fayz*, which means 'liberality'.

VARIANTS **Faaiz, Faizah**

Fajr *mf*

An Arabic name meaning 'dawn', as well as 'beginning, start'.

VARIANTS **Fajar, Fajer**

Fakhri *m* **Fakhriyah** *f*

An Arabic name from a word meaning 'proud (for a good reason), elegant, glorious'.

VARIANT **Fakriyya**

Fallon *mf*

Mainly used for girls, Fallon is from an Irish surname meaning descendant of *Fallamhan*, a name meaning 'leader'. It was mainly used in the 1980s when the name was receiving exposure on television.

VARIANT **Falyn**

☆ Fallon Carrington, character in the television series *Dynasty*

Fancy *see* **Frances**

Fanny *f*

Fanny was very popular in the 18th and 19th centuries, both as a pet form of FRANCES or, more rarely, EUPHEMIA and as an independent name. It was taken up enthusiastically in France, where it can also be a pet form of STEPHANIE. The name is now rare because of the associations with the slang vocabulary word.

VARIANT **Fannie**

★ Fanny Burney (1752–1840), English novelist and diarist

Fantine *f*

Fantine is a French name, derived from *enfant*, 'child'. It is very rare, but famous as the name of the mother of Cosette in Victor Hugo's 1862 novel *Les Misérables*.

Faolan *m*

An early Irish name borne by both legendary warriors and a number of saints, one of whom was a missionary to Scotland, where the name became *Fillan*. Faolan is pronounced something like 'fwail-awn' and is a pet form of *faol*, 'wolf'.

VARIANTS **Phelan, Fillan, Foillan, Faelan**

Farah *mf*

This is an Arabic name meaning 'joy'. There is a related pair of names *Farih* (m) and *Fariha* (f) defined as 'happy', a meaning shared by the associated *Farha(a)n* and *Farhana*.

VARIANT **Farrah**

Faraj *m*
An Arabic name from a word meaning 'improvement', or 'a remedy', comfort for something that upsets a person.
VARIANT **Farag**

Fares *m*
This is an Arabic name, meaning 'horseman, knight', with a strong association with chivalry. It is widely used throughout the Arabic world.
VARIANT **Faris**

Farid *m* **Farida** *f*
An Arabic name meaning 'unique, unrivalled, matchless'. The feminine form also has the sense of 'a precious gem'.
VARIANT **Fareed**
★ Farid al-Din (c.1142–c.1220), Persian poet

Farouk *m*
An Arabic name meaning 'distinguisher', used to indicate someone who is an effective judge.
VARIANTS **Faruq, Farooq**
★ Farouk I (1920–65), king of Egypt

Farquhar *m*
This is a Scottish name, found as both a surname and a first name. It is the anglicized form of *Fearchar*, a Gaelic name meaning 'dear man'. The name is old; Feachar Fada or Farquhar the Tall was a 7th-century Scottish leader, sometimes called king.

Fathih *m* **Fathiha** *f*
This Arabic name is of slightly obscure origin, but probably comes from a term meaning 'one who wins repeated victories'.
VARIANT **Fathiy(y)a**

Fatima[1] *f*
This name is popular throughout the Arabic world as it belonged to the Prophet Muhammad's favourite daughter, the mother of Hassan and Hussein, as well as to several other members of his family. The meaning of the name is quite complicated. The word applies either to a child who has just been weaned, or to the mother who weans it, and so implies a good mother. The word also contains the idea of abstinence, and so indicates someone who avoids forbidden things and is chaste. Being so widespread – it has been described as the most popular Muslim girl's name – it takes numerous forms.
PET FORMS **Fatouma, Fatoumata** • VARIANTS **Fat(h)ema, Fatama, Fathima, Faatimah, Fatimah, Fatma(h)**

Fatima[2] *f*
Mainly Portuguese name, taken from Our Lady of Fátima, a town in Portugal where three children had a vision of the Virgin Mary in 1917. According to legend the town gets its name from a Moorish princess called Fatima (see FATIMA[1]) who was captured, converted to Christianity and married the local count.

Faustine *f*
The Roman *faustus* or *fausta* means 'lucky, fortunate'. The Roman general and dictator Lucius Cornelius Sulla (c.138–78 BC) added FELIX, 'happy, fortunate', to his name, as he regarded himself as being particularly blessed by good fortune. He gave the names *Faustus* and *Fausta* to his twin children. From these the Latin name *Faustinus* developed, and Faustine became the French feminine.
VARIANTS *French* **Faustin** (m) *Italian* **Faustina, Faustino, Fàusto** *Spanish* **Fausto**
★ Johann Georg Faust (c.1480–1540), German scholar thought to be the inspiration for the legendary magician known as Faust or Faustus
☆ 'Faustine' is a famously decadent 1866 poem by Charles Algernon Swinburne,

said to have been written to settle a bet as to who could find most rhymes for the name

Fauzi *see* **Fawzi**

Fawn *f*
This is the vocabulary word for a young deer used as a first name. It has been in use since the 19th century, but has never been particularly popular, having been most common in the 1960s–80s.
VARIANT **Fawna**

Fawzi *m* **Fawziyya** *f*
The Arabic word *fawz*, triumph, victory', gives us this name meaning 'triumphant, victorious', as well as *Faw(w)az*, for someone who is repeatedly victorious and *Fawz*, 'victory' (mf).
VARIANTS **Fauzi, Fawziy, Fawziya**

Fayçal *see* **Faisal**

Faye *f*
This can be both a pet form of FAITH and an independent name. It appears to be the medieval term meaning 'fairy' used as a first name. This was familiar from the later Middle Ages, and known from the name of Morgan le Fay, evil sister of King Arthur. The name has been used, originally in the form *Fay*, since the later 19th century. It was used for a character by the novelist Ouida in 1872 and, as she was very popular and has a record of having popularized names, it may be that it was introduced or popularized by her.
VARIANTS **Fay, Fae**
★ Faye Dunaway (1941–   ), US actress

Faysal *see* **Faisal**

Fayvel *see* **Faivish**

Fayz *see* **Faiz**

Fazil, Fazila *see* **Fadile**

Feachar *see* **Farquhar**

Fearghas *see* **Fergus**

Fearn, Fearne *see* **Fern**

Fechin *m*
An Irish name from *fiach* 'raven'. There were several early saints with this name.
VARIANT **Feichín**

Fedèle *see* **Fidel**

Fedelma *see* **Fidelma**

Federica *see* **Frederica**

Federico, Federigo *see* **Frederick**

Fedor *see* **Theodore**

Fedora *see* **Theodora**

Fedya *see* **Theodore**

Fee *see* **Felicity**

Feibush, Feivel *see* **Faivish**

Feichín *see* **Fechin**

Feidhel *see* **Felim**

Feidhelm *see* **Fidelma**

Feidhlimid *see* **Felim**

Feisal *see* **Faisal**

Felic *see* **Phyllis**

Felicity *f*
The Late Latin name *Felicitas*, 'happiness, good fortune', was borne by a 3rd-century Carthaginian martyr. This, combined with the strong sense that the happiness referred to has Christian connotations, led to the name becoming widespread in Europe, although curiously it has been little used in the USA until recent years. *Felice* was the standard medieval form of the name, well known as the beloved of the popular romantic hero, Guy of Warwick. There is some overlap

between variants of this name and those of PHYLLIS. See also FELIX, feminine forms of which are also listed below.

PET FORMS **Lis(sie)**, **Licia**, **Fee**, **Flick**
• VARIANTS **Felicia**, **Phylicia** *French* **Félicité**, **Félice**, **Felicienne** *German* **Felicitas**, **Felicie** *Italian* **Felìcita** *Polish* **Felicyta**, **Zyta**, **Felicja** *Spanish* **Felicidad**
★ Felicity Kendal (1946–   ), English actress

Felim *m*
An Irish name, interpreted as meaning 'ever-good'. It was the name of a number of medieval Irish kings, one of whom managed to combine his role as king of Munster with being bishop of Cashel. It is pronounced *fail-im*.
VARIANTS **Felimid**, **Phelim** *Irish* **Feidhlimid**, **Feidhel**

Felipa *see* **Philippa**

Felipe *see* **Philip**

Felix *m*
This is the Latin word for 'happy, blessed', adopted as a name by the Roman dictator Sulla (see FAUSTINE). The name is thus the masculine equivalent of FELICITY. There were a number of early saints of the name, it being popular with Christians as it carried the idea of happiness in the afterlife. The use of Felix as a traditional name for a cat is based on a joke. The Latin for a wildcat or tomcat (as well as for a ferret and various other small hunting animals) is *feles*, which has the inflected form *felis*, while Felix has the inflected form *felicis*, and the two were thought to be close enough to make a pun.
VARIANTS *French* **Félix**, **Fleicien** *Italian*, *Spanish* **Feliciano** *Russian* **Felicks**
★ Felix Mendelssohn (1809–47), German composer

Fenella *f*
This is the anglicized Scottish form of

the Gaelic name FINOLA, which means 'white shoulder'.
VARIANTS **Finella**, **Finola**
★ Fenella Fielding (1934–   ), English actress

Feodor, **Feodora** *see* **Theodore**

Feofil *see* **Theophilus**

Ferdinand *m*
This name started out as the Germanic name *Fridunand* formed from *frid*, 'peace', and *nand*, 'brave'. However, the ordering of 'r' plus vowel is unstable and the name appears as *Ferdenandus* in Latin. The name was taken by the Visigoths to Spain, and quickly became a traditional name in the ruling houses. It passed to southern Italy when the Spaniards came to rule there too, and underwent further sound changes. In southern dialects 'rn' easily becomes 'rr', which led to the forms *Ferrand* or *Ferrant*, often found used interchangeably with Ferdinand in early records, while in Spain there also developed forms with an initial 'H' instead of 'F'. The name does not seem to have reached England until the 16th century, with Mary I's Spanish husband Philip II.
PET FORMS **Ferd**, **Ferdie**, **Ferdy**, **Nandy**
• VARIANTS *French* **Fernand**, **Fernande** *Italian* **Ferdinando** *Spanish* **Fernando**, **Hernando**, **Fernán**, **Hernán**, **Nando**

Ferelith *f*
This Scottish name is strangely neglected by books on first names, but has been in use since at least the 10th century and is not uncommon, having long been used among the aristocracy and particularly by the Hamilton and Ramsay families. The name is a version of the old Irish name *Forblaith*, recorded from at least the 8th century. This is formed from elements *for*, 'very, super-, great', and *flaith*, 'princess, rule', and can be interpreted as

meaning either 'true princess' or
'sovereignty'.

VARIANT **Ferelyth**

★ Ferelyth Wills (1916–2005), English
sculptor

Ferenc *see* **Francis**

Fergal *m*
An Irish name from the Gaelic
elements *fear*, 'man', and *gal*, 'valour'.

VARIANT **Feargal**

★ Fergal Keane (1961–   ), Irish writer
and broadcaster

★ Feargal Sharkey (1958–   ), Northern
Irish musician

Fergus *m*
An Irish and Scottish name formed
from *fear*, 'man', and *gus*, 'valour,
vigour'. Fergus was the name of one
of the traditional trio of Scots from
northern Ireland who founded the
Scottish kingdom of Argyll in about
500 AD and there was also an 8th
century Irish bishop, St Fergus, who
was a missionary to Scotland.

PET FORM **Fergie** • VARIANT *Gaelic* **Fearghas**

Fern *f*
One of the plant names that came
into fashion in the later 19th century,
when it was particularly well used in
the USA. Fern is currently enjoying a
revival.

VARIANTS **Ferne, Fearn(e)**

★ Fern Britton (1957–   ), English
television presenter

★ Fearne Cotton (1981–   ), English
television presenter

Ferrer *m*
A Catalan Spanish surname, meaning
'blacksmith', used in honour of St
Vincent Ferrer (c.1350–1418).

Ferris *m*
This can either come from a surname,
originally a form of FERGUS or it can
be an Irish form of PETER. The name
travelled a long way from the original,

but comes via Norman French *Piers*,
which became *Piaras* in Irish, which
was then changed to Ferris.

☆ *Ferris Bueller's Day Off*, 1986 comedy
film

Fester *m*
A German dialect pet form of SILVESTER.

☆ Uncle Fester in the cartoons and films
of *The Addams Family*

Festus *m*
This was originally a Roman name
meaning 'steadfast'. Although it
appears in the biblical Acts of the
Apostles, it has never been particularly
common, but has been used in Ireland
as the English form of the names
FACHTNA and FECHIN.

VARIANT **Feste**

☆ Feste, the Fool in Shakespeare's *Twelfth
Night* (c.1601)

Ffion *f*
This is a Welsh name from the word
for 'foxglove', although some like to
regard it as the Welsh form of FIONA.
In Welsh a single 'f' is pronounced as
a 'v', while 'ff' is pronounced 'f', thus
Ffion is 'fee-on'. The name has been
one of the most popular for girls in
Wales for some years.

Ffleur, Fflur *see* **Flora**

Ffraid *see* **Bridget**

Ffransis *see* **Francis**

Ffyona *see* **Fiona**

Fiachra *m*
This is an Irish name, formed from
fiach, which can mean 'raven' or
'hunt', and *ri*, 'king'. It was the name
of a saint who was a missionary to
France in the 7th century. Because
horse-drawn taxis in 19th-century
France used to wait outside St *Fiacre's*
church in Paris, they acquired the
name 'fiacres'.

VARIANT *French* **Fiacre**

Fiammetta *f*
This is an Italian name, a pet form of *Fiamma* meaning 'flame', made famous as the name of one of Boccaccio's main characters in the *Decameron* (c.1350).
VARIANT **Fiametta**

Fidel *m*
The Latin names *Fidelis* or *Fidelius*, 'faithful', became the name Fidel in Spanish. Fidel is the best-known form, having become frequently used in honour of St Fidelis or Fidel, a 6th-century Spanish bishop. The name is rare among English speakers, although it is used among Spanish speakers in the USA.
VARIANTS *French* **Fidèle** *Italian* **Fedèle**, **Fidèlio** *Spanish* **Fidel(i)a** (f)
★ Fidel Castro (1927–   ), Cuban president

Fidelma *f*
A traditional Irish name of unknown meaning that dates back to at least the 5th century. One bearer was among St Patrick's first converts.
PET FORM **Delma** • VARIANTS **Fedelma** *Irish* **Feidhelm**

Fife *m*
The name of the ancient Scottish kingdom and modern region, used as a first name. The kingdom was named after its legendary founder *Fib*.
VARIANT **Fyfe**

Fifi *f*
This started out as a French nursery form of the name JOSEPHINE, although it is also found occasionally as a pet form of names such as FIONA or SOPHIE. Because of its image as being very French and very 'fluffy', it is more usually found in fiction or for pets than as a personal name.

Filbert *see* **Philbert**

Filemón *see* **Philemon**

Filib, Filip *see* **Philip**

Filibert, Filiberto *see* **Philbert**

Filipa, Filippa *see* **Philippa**

Filipe, Filipp, Filippo *see* **Philip**

Fillan *see* **Faolan**

Filomena *see* **Philomena**

Fima *see* **Euphemia**

Fin *see* **Finn, Phineas**

Fina *see* **Fíona, Seraphina**

Finbar *m*
Finbar was the name of a king of the fairies in Irish mythology as well as, more importantly, the name of the patron saint of the city of Cork. It may be that these two got somewhat confused, as many supernatural events are ascribed to St Finbar, such as the story that he crossed the Irish Sea on horseback, and that the sun did not shine for two days after his death. The name is formed from the elements *fionn*, 'white, fair', and *barr*, 'head', so is one of the many names that derive from someone's colouring. Finbar is the main source of the name BARRY.
PET FORMS **Barry, Barr(a), Bairre** • VARIANTS **Fin(n)bar(r)** *Irish* **Fionnbarr, Fionbharr**

Findlay *see* **Finlay**

Finean *see* **Finnian**

Finella *see* **Fenella**

Fingal *m*
Fingal is a Scots Gaelic name formed from *fionn*, 'fair, white', and *gall*, 'stranger', and was originally given to Viking raiders. It is said that it was initially applied to the blonder Norwegian and Icelandic Vikings, while the darker Danes were called the *Dub* ('dark') *gall* (see DOUGAL). In the

18th century, the name became widely known through the highly fashionable epic poems of James Macpherson, who recreated the ancient legends of the Gaels, giving the role played by FINN in the Irish epic to his character Fingal. The famous Fingal's Cave gets its name from these stories.

PET FORM **Fin(n)** • VARIANTS **Fingall** *Scots Gaelic* **Fionghall**

Finlay *m*

A popular Scottish first name derived from the Gaelic *Fionnlagh* formed from *fionn*, 'white, fair', and *laogh*, 'warrior, hero'. Fionnlagh seems to have been modified by another local name, formed from FINN and the Old Norse *leiker*, 'battle'.

VARIANTS **Fin(n)dlay, Fin(n)(d)ley, Fin(n)(d)lie**

Finn¹ *m*

Finn, from the Irish for 'white, fair', is the name of one of the greatest Irish heroes, Finn MacCool. In sagas he is a mighty warrior, but in folklore he is a giant, and there is a distinct comic element in the stories told about him. The name is currently popular in Ireland. It can also act as a pet form of FINBAR and similar names.

VARIANTS **Fynn** *Irish* **Fionn**

Finn² *see* Phineas

Finnabhair *see* Guinevere

Finnian *m*

This is a pet form of FINN and related names. There were a number of early saints with the name, one of whom may have been the same person as St FINBAR.

VARIANTS **Finian, Finnan, Fiinean, Finnen** *Irish* **Finénn, Fionnán**

☆ Finian McLonergan in the 1947 stage musical, and 1968 film, *Finian's Rainbow*.

Finola *f*

This is the anglicized form of the Irish name *Fionnuala* meaning 'white shoulder'. According to Irish legend she was one of the three children of Lir who were turned into swans by their jealous stepmother, but later released from the spell by the sound of the Mass bell when St Patrick brought Christianity to Ireland. Having been enormously popular a generation ago, the name is now out of favour in Ireland. It is pronounced 'fin-OO-la' or 'fin-OH-la'. In Scotland the name is anglicized as FENELLA.

PET FORM **Nuala** • VARIANTS **Fionnu(gha)la, Finella**

Fintan *m*

Formed from the Irish words *fionn*, 'white', and *tine*, 'fire', this name belonged to 74 Irish saints.

VARIANTS *Irish* **Fiontan, Fionntán**

Fion *see* Finn

Fiona¹ *f*

Formed from the Gaelic *fionn*, 'fair, white', the origin of the masculine FINN, this name seems to have been invented by James Macpherson (1736–96) for his Ossianic poems depicting ancient life in Gaelic Scotland. It was further popularized by the success of the poems of 'Fiona Macleod' (pen name of William Sharp, 1855–1905). It was widespread in Britain in the 1960s, but then fell out of favour, although it shows signs of coming back into use in its native Scotland. In the USA it was all but unknown until the 1990s, since when it has rapidly increased in popularity.

PET FORM **Fi** • VARIANTS **Fionna, Fion(n)ah, F(f)yona**

Fíona² *f*

Fíona is an early Irish name, a Gaelicization of the Latin *vinea* meaning 'vine'.

VARIANT **Fina**

Fionbharr *see* **Finbar**

Fionghall *see* **Fingal**

Fionn *see* **Finn**

Fionnán *see* **Finnian**

Fionnbarr *see* **Finbar**

Fionntán *see* **Fintan**

Fionnula, Fionnughala *see* **Finola**

Fiontan *see* **Fintan**

Fiorella *see* **Flora**

Firdos *mf*
An Arabic name from *firdaws*, 'paradise'. The related name *Firdausi*, 'heavenly', is famous as being that of the great Persian poet Abdul Qaaasim Mansur Firdausi (940–1020), author of the epic *Shahnama* ('The Book of Kings').

Firoz *m*
An Arabic name, meaning 'victorious'.
VARIANT **Firus**

Flann *m*
This is the Irish name for 'blood red'. *Flannan* comes from the pet form of this name. The related *Flannery* means 'red valour' and is used for both sexes, as its best-known bearer, the US author Flannery O'Connor (1925–64), was female.
★ Flann O'Brien, pen name of Brian O'Nolan (1911–66), Irish writer

Flavia *f*
This is a Roman family name from the Latin *flavus*, 'golden, tawny', which would originally have been given to someone with blond hair. There were many early saints with the name, and it was famous as the family name of numerous 1st-century Roman emperors. It has been used by English speakers since the 16th century, but has never been common.

It is, however, one of the stock names in Italy, and other countries use both masculine and feminine variants of the name.
VARIANTS *French* **Flavie, Flavienne** (fs), **Flavien** (m) *Spanish, Italian* **Flavio**
☆ Princess Flavia is the heroine of Anthony Hope's 1894 novel *The Prisoner of Zenda*

Fleicien *see* **Felix**

Fleur *f*
This is the French word for 'flower'. Although it was recorded from the Middle Ages, its use as a modern first name was introduced by John Galsworthy, who used the name for a character in his series of novels, published between 1906 and 1922, known as the *Forsyte Saga*. Fleur had another resurgence of popularity when the novels were adapted for a very successful television series in the late 1960s. Other names with the same meaning are listed under FLORA.
VARIANTS **Fleurette, Fleurine, Florine**
★ Fleur Adcock (1934–), New Zealand-born British poet

Flick *see* **Felicity**

Flin, Flinn *see* **Flynn**

Flip *see* **Philip**

Floella *f*
A modern name which seems to have come into use in the mid-20th century, apparently as a blend of names with these sounds.
★ Floella Benjamin (1949–), Trinidad-born British television presenter

Flora *f* **Florian** *m*
Flora was the Roman goddess of flowers and spring, her name coming from the Latin word *flos* (inflected for *floris*) meaning 'flower'. The name Flora came to England from Scotland, where it was used to anglicize the

Gaelic *Fionnaguala* (see FINOLA). The romantic story of Flora (really Finola) Macdonald helping Bonnie Prince Charlie escape in 1746 helped to popularize the name. From the Latin Flora also developed the Roman family names *Florus* and *Florianus*. The latter gives us Florian, the name of a 3rd-century saint, now rare in English, but popular in German- and French-speaking areas. Flower itself has occasionally been used as a first name in English, and other languages also have names meaning flower which are given below, except for the French variants listed under FLEUR.

PET FORMS **Flo, Florrie** • VARIANTS **Floretta, Florentina** *Welsh* **Ffl(e)ur** *Dutch* **Floor, Floortje** *Italian* **Fiorella** *Spanish* **Flor**

Florence *f*

There was a Late Latin name *Florentius* (m), *Florientia* (f), which was the source of Florence, and was used in England in the Middle Ages for both sexes. It then died out, although its descendants are still used in other countries. The name was revived in the 19th century in honour of Florence Nightingale (1820–1910), who was named after her birthplace, the Italian city of Florence.

PET FORMS **Flo, Floss(ie), Florrie, Floy** • VARIANTS (MASCULINE) *French* **Florent** *Dutch* **Floris** *German* **Florenz** *Italian* **Florencio** *Russian* **Florenti**

Florine *see* Fleur

Floyd *m*

A version of the Welsh name LLOYD, 'grey', altered because of the difficulty non-Welsh speakers have in pronouncing the Welsh 'll' sound.
★ Floyd Patterson (1935–2006), US boxer

Flynn *m*

This is an Irish surname, meaning 'descendant of FLANN'. It has been used as a first name particularly in Australia,

no doubt in memory of the flamboyant Australian actor Errol Flynn (1909–59), and is making its mark elsewhere.
VARIANTS **Flyn, Flin(n)**

Foillan *see* Faolan

Folant *see* Valentine

Folke *see* Fulk

Foma *see* Thomas

Fons, Fonsie, Fonz, Fonzie, Fonzo *see* Alphonse

Forbes *m*

This is a Scottish surname used as a first name. The name comes from a district in Aberdeenshire which gets its name from Gaelic *forba*, 'fields'. It is still mainly confined to Scotland.
★ Forbes Burnham (1923–85), president of Guyana

Forrest *m*

This is a surname used as a first name, mainly in the USA. In the South it commemorates the Confederate General Nathan Bedford Forrest (1821–77).
VARIANT **Forest**
☆ Forrest Gump, eponymous hero of the 1994 film adapted from a 1986 novel by Winston Groom

Fouad *m* Fouada *f*

This is the Arabic for 'heart' which has strong spiritual overtones.
VARIANTS **Fuad, Fuada**
★ Fuad I (1868–1936), sultan who became the first independent king of Egypt

Frances *f*

This is now the standard feminine form of the name FRANCIS. However, until the 17th century the *-es* or *-is* endings were used interchangeably for both sexes, and the *-is* ending continued to be used occasionally for girls for some time afterwards. Frances was

very popular in the 19th century, but
has more recently lost its place to the
Italian form *Francesca*.

PET FORMS **Fanny**, **Fran(nie)**, **Fannie**,
Francie, **Fancy**, **Frankie** • VARIANTS *Dutch,
Scandinavian* **Frans** *French* **Françoise**,
France, **Francine**, **Francette** *German*
Franziska, **Franzi** *Italian* **Francesca**,
Franca *Polish* **Franciszka** *Portuguese*
Francisca, **Chica** *Spanish* **Francisca**, **Paca**,
Paquita

★ St Francesca Xavier Carbrini (1850–
  1917), nun and social worker, who in
  1946 became the first US citizen to be
  made a saint
★ Frances de la Tour (1944–), English
  actress

Francis *m*

In 12th-century Assisi, a young
man called Giovanni Bernadone
(c.1181–1226) was so keen on French
culture and fashion that his friends
nicknamed him *Francesco*, meaning
'little Frenchman'. This man later gave
up such worldly interests and became
more widely known as St Francis of
Assisi. His importance and cult have
spread the name worldwide. The
history of the name is further discussed
under FRANK.

PET FORMS **Frank**, **Frankie** • VARIANTS *Irish*
Proinsias *Welsh* **Ffransis** *Dutch* **Frans**
French **François**, **Francisque** *German*
Franz, **Franzi** *Hungary* **Ferenc** *Italian*
Francesco, **Franco** *Polish* **Franciszek**
Portuguese **Francisco**, **Chico** *Spanish*
Francisco, **Curro**, **Paco**, **Pancho**, **Paquito**

★ St Frances Xavier (1506–52), Spanish
  missionary to the East Indies, Japan
  and China
★ Francis Bacon (1561–1626), English
  philosopher, scientist and statesman
★ Francis Bacon (1909–92), British artist

Frank *m*

The group of tribes known to history
as the Franks thought that they were
named after the type of spear they

carried. In the 5th century they began
a series of emigrations from their lands
to the north of the Rhine, including
the invasion of the region that is
now France, which took its name
from them. The Franks took control
of the upper levels of society in their
conquered lands, and the word Frank
soon came to mean 'free' and later,
'liberal, open'. Nowadays Frank is
given as a first name, but is mainly
found as a short form of FRANCIS, or
sometimes FRANKLIN, while *Frankie* is
also used for FRANCES.

PET FORM **Frankie** • VARIANT **Franck**

Franklin *m*

In the Middle Ages, franklin was a
technical term for a free landowner,
usually a prosperous farmer (see
FRANK). This term became a surname,
and in turn a first name. The name is
mainly used in the USA, inspired by
the statesman and scientist Benjamin
Franklin (1706–90), and by the
president named after him, Franklin D
Roosevelt (1882–1945).

PET FORM **Frank**

Fraser *m*

This is an aristocratic Scottish surname
of unknown origin. The name is
associated with the strawberry plant
which the family adopted as its
heraldic symbol. This is because the
French name for the plant – *frasier* –
sounded like the surname, and such
puns were popular in heraldry, but
there is no known connection between
the two. The name is mainly confined
to Scots and those of Scottish descent,
and has been popular in Scotland for
some years.

VARIANTS **Frazer**, **Frasier**, **Frazier**

★ Fraser Fifield (1976–), Scottish
  musician
☆ Frasier Crane, principal character in
  the television series *Frasier*

Fraya *see* **Freya**

Fred *mf*
Usually a short form of FREDERICK
or ALFRED, as well as other names
containing the sound, but sometimes
found as a pet form of girls' names
beginning *Fr-*, such as FREDA and
FREDERICA, or of WINIFRED.
PET FORM **Freddie**

Freda *f*
This was originally a pet form of Old
English names revived in the 19th-
century, such as ELFRIDA or *Alfreda* (see
ALFRED), or of names like WINIFRED and
FREDERICA. It subsequently became an
independent name, and could function
as a feminine equivalent of FREDERICK.
VARIANTS **Frieda, Friede, Frida**

Frederica *f*
This female form of FREDERICK was
introduced to England from Germany
at the same time as its masculine form.
An early bearer of the name was the
Princess Frederica Charlotte of Prussia
(1767–1820), who in 1791 married
Prince Frederick, Duke of York and
Albany, and second son of George III.
PET FORMS **Fred(die), Freda** • VARIANTS
German **Fritzi, Rica** *Italian* **Federica**
Scandinavian **Fredrika, Rika**

Frederick *m*
The Normans introduced this name
to England, but it failed to catch on
and soon disappeared. However, it
reappeared quietly in the 17th century,
and was popularized in the 18th when
the German Hanoverian family came
to the throne and introduced many
German names to the common stock.
The name is formed from the elements
fred or *frid*, 'peace', and *ric*, 'rule'. The
pet form *Freddie* is currently a more
popular choice than the full form.
PET FORMS **Fred, Freddy, Freddie** • VARIANTS
Frederic, Fredric *Dutch* **Frederik, Freek,
Frits** *French* **Frédéric** *German* **Friedrich,**

Fritz, Rike *Italian* **Federico, Federigo**
Scandinavian **Frederik, Fredrik, Rikke**
★ Frederick Forsyth (1938–   ), English
author
★ Frederic Raphael (1931–   ), US-born
British author

Freya *f*
This is the name of the Scandinavian
goddess of love, beauty and fertility.
The origin of the name probably lies
with the same root as the German
word *frau*, 'woman'. The name was
a traditional one in Norse-influenced
Shetland, but its current popularity
probably stems from the indomitable
Dame Freya Stark (1893–1993),
explorer and writer, who made a
tremendous impact on the public
when she was televised still travelling
in wild regions in her eighties.
VARIANTS **Fraya, Freia, Fre(y)ja** *Norwegian*
Frøya

Frida *see* **Freda, Elfrida**

Frieda *see* **Freda**

Friede *see* **Elfrida, Freda**

Frits, Fritz *see* **Frederick**

Fritzi *see* **Frederica**

Frona *see* **Sophronia**

Frøya *see* **Freya**

Fuad, Fuada *see* **Fouad**

Fuchsia *f*
Pronounced 'fyou-sha', this plant
name has been used quietly but
regularly since at least the beginning
of the 20th century, despite its difficult
spelling. The flower gets its name from
the German botanist Leonard Fuchs
(1501–66), after whom it was named
in the early 18th century. The plant
was first extensively cultivated in the
Victorian period.
☆ Fuchsia is the sister of Titus Groan,

in Mervyn Peake's *Gormenghast* trilogy (1946–59)

Fulk *m*

This Germanic name was introduced to England by the Normans. It comes from the word *volk*, 'people, tribe, folk'. It was widespread in Europe in the Middle Ages, and was a traditional name for the counts of Anjou. It gradually died out in England, but was kept alive in the Greville family, whence it has occasionally been used by others.

VARIANTS **Fulke** *Scandinavian* **Folke**

★ Sir Fulke Greville (1554–1628), English poet, dramatist and statesman
☆ Fulk Fitzwarren, at least semi-fictional medieval landowner turned outlaw, ~ whose story is similar to that of Robin Hood

Fulton *m*

A Scottish surname, probably from a place name, which is occasionally used as a first name.

★ Fulton Mackay (1922–87), Scottish actor

Fulvia *f*

From the Roman family name *Fulvius*, which comes from the Latin *fulvus*, 'tawney', which would originally have described a blond or redhead (compare FLAVIA). A famous Roman Fulvia was a wife of Mark Antony. The name is more likely to be found in Italy than among English speakers.

MASCULINE **Fulvio**

Fyfe *see* **Fife**

Fynn *see* **Finn**

Fyodor *see* **Theodore**

Fyona *see* **Fiona**

G

Gabir, Gabr see **Jabir**

Gabriel *m* **Gabrielle** *f*
It is not clear whether the name
Gabriel should be analysed as
composed of the Hebrew *gheber*,
'man', or *gabar*, 'strong', combined
with *el*, 'god', and therefore the name
is variously interpreted as meaning
'man of God' or 'my strength is God'.
In the Bible, the angel Gabriel is the
messenger of God and intermediary
between God and man. He appears to
Daniel in the Old Testament (Daniel
8.16; 9.21), and in the New Testament
to Zacharius (Luke 1.19; 26.27), and
to Mary to announce her pregnancy
(Luke 1.2). In Islamic tradition Gabriel
is the angel who dictated the Koran
to the Prophet Muhammad. Gabriel
was used regularly by English speakers
from the 18th century until the start
of the 20th, but then dropped out
of favour. However, it is currently
enjoying a worldwide popularity for
both sexes. The most usual feminine
form is the French *Gabrielle*, although
the Italian *Gabriella* comes a close
second.
PET FORMS **Gabe, Gabbie, Gabby, Abbi,
Abbie, Abby, Gay, Brielle** ● VARIANTS
Arabic **Jabril, Jibril** *German* **Gabriele** (m),
Gabi (mf) *Hebrew* **Gavriel** *Hungarian*
Gabor *Italian* **Garbriele** (m) *Polish,
Portuguese* **Gabriela** *Yiddish* **Gavrel**
★ Gabriel Byrne (1950–ʺ), Irish actor
★ Gabrielle (1970–ʺ), English singer

Gae see **Gay**

Gaea see **Gaia**

Gael *mf* **Gaelle** *f*
There are two theories as to the origin
of this French name, although both
agree that its roots are Breton. Breton
is a minority Celtic language in France,
spoken by few even in Brittany, but
its naming traditions are still vigorous
and have been influential in the rest
of France for some years. *Gaël* may
be a shortening of the Breton name
Judicaël, meaning 'generous leader',
reinforced by the fact that Gaël is also
a place name in the area where St
Judicaël had a monastery. Alternatively,
the name be a shortening of *Gwenaël*,
the name of another Breton saint,
which is composed of the elements
gwenn, 'white, fair, pure', and *hael*,
'generous'. Gaël began to be used
significantly in France in the 1960s,
with *Gaëlle* appearing in the 1980s.
In some cases, however, Gael may be
a use of the ethnic name, or even a
respelling of GAIL.
★ Gael Garcia Bernal (1978–ʺ),
  Mexican actor and film director

Gaenor see **Gaynor**

Gaetano *m* **Gaetana** *f*
St Gaetano (or *Cajetan*) is the patron
saint of Naples, and this name is
particularly associated with southern
Italy. St Gaetano lived in the 16th
century and helped the poor of Naples.
One of his projects was to establish
not-for-profit pawn shops, which
might be considered the forerunner
of modern credit unions. The name
comes from the Latin *Caietanus*,
'person from Caieta', Caieta being
the Roman name for what is now

the southern Italian city of Gaeta. According to legend, this in turn was named after Aeneas's nurse, Caieta, who died there.

VARIANTS *French* **Gaëtan, Gaétan, Cajé, Gaëtane** *German* **Kayetan** *German, Polish* **Kajetan** *Portuguese* **Caetano** *Spanish* **Cayetano**

Gafar *see* Jafar

Gage *m*
This is a surname from an occupation, used either for someone whose job was to gauge or measure something, or for a moneylender who took pledges (French *gage*). Curiously, the name came into use for boys in the USA in 1989, the year a horror film called *Pet Sematary* (based on a Stephen King novel of 1982) appeared. In the film, the name was given to a monstrous zombie child. Gage has been increasingly popular in subsequent years.

VARIANTS **Gaige, Gauge**

Gaia *f*
This is the name of Mother Earth in Greek mythology, which comes from the Greek *ge*, 'earth', and is thus related to GEORGE. It does not seem to have been used before the middle of the 20th century.

VARIANT **Gaea**

Gaige *see* Gage

Gail *f*
Originally a short form of ABIGAIL, this began to be used as an independent name in the 1930s and was at its most popular in the middle of the 20th century. It is now out of favour.

VARIANTS **Gayle, Gale**

★ Gail Porter (1971–), Scottish television presenter

Gaius *see* Caius

Gala *see* Galina

Galahad *m*
Galahad is the name of the pure, perfect knight who achieves the Holy Grail in Arthurian romance, and was also the name of his father before it was changed to Lancelot. As with so many Arthurian names it is difficult to track down its original form, for such names have often passed through more than one language in their transition from Celtic source to French romance to English form. It has been suggested that this name may be formed from the same roots as Welsh *gwalch*, literally 'hawk', but used metaphorically to mean 'hero' and *cad*, 'hero'. Because it is such a difficult name to live up to, it is rarely given in real life.

VARIANT *Welsh* **Galâth**

Gale *see* Abigail, Gail

Galen *m*
This is the name of the 2nd-century AD physician used as a first name. It is the Latin form of a Greek name derived from *galene* meaning 'calm'. The name is regularly used in the USA, occasionally for women.

★ Galen Strawson (1952–), English philosopher and critic

☆ Dr Galen is the assistant of Dr Zaius in the *Planet of the Apes* films

Galfrid *m*
Although this looks like an Old English name it is, like *Alured* (see ALFRED), a more recent coinage formed from a misunderstanding of Latin documents. In this case scribes writing Latin had turned GEOFFREY into *Galfridus*, which was mistakenly interpreted as being Latin for a name, Galfrid. The name seems to have come into use in the beginning of the 18th century, and was used in the 19th, but is now virtually extinct.

PET FORM **Gal**

Galia *f*
This is the Hebrew for 'wave', pronounced 'gah-lyah'. The form *Gal* can be used for either sex.
VARIANT **Galit**

Galila *see* **Jalal**

Galilea *f*
This is the Spanish form of the biblical place name *Galilee* (also used as a first name). Use has recently spread from Mexico to the USA.
VARIANT *Italian* **Galileo**
★ Galileo Galilei (1564–1642), Italian astronomer

Galina *f*
Galina is a Russian name which probably comes from the Greek *galene*, 'calm, serene', and so is a female equivalent of GALEN. The pet form *Gala*, also used as an independent name, can be derived from a form of HELEN.
PET FORMS **Gala, Galya** • VARIANT *Polish* **Halina**

Gallagher *m*
This is the Irish surname used as a first name. The surname means 'descendant of *Gallchobhar*', a traditional name formed from *gall*, 'stranger, foreign', and *cabhair*, 'help'.

Gamal *see* **Jamil**

Gamaliel *m*
This is a biblical name interpreted as meaning 'benefit of God'. It was the name of a prince in the Old Testament, and a teacher of St Paul in the New Testament. It is well represented among prominent rabbis in the first few centuries AD and is the name of an angel in the Kabbalah tradition. It was used from the 15th century and taken up by Puritans in the 17th century, but is now rare.
★ Warren G Harding (1865–1923), 29th US president, had Gamaliel as his middle name

Gamil, Gamila *see* **Jamil**

Ganesh *m*
This is the Sanskrit for 'lord of hordes' formed from *gana*, 'horde', and *isha*, 'ruler, lord'. It was originally linked with the god Shiva, but is now associated with his son by Parvati. Statues of Ganesh usually show him as a tubby man with an elephant's head, and he is considered the god of wisdom and good luck.
VARIANT **Ganesha**

Garbriele *see* **Gabriel**

Gardenia *f*
An unusual flower name, in occasional use since the 19th century. The plant was named in honour of the Anglo-American botanist Alexander Garden (1730–91).

Gareth *m*
A somewhat mysterious Arthurian name, which only appears in the 15th century in Sir Thomas Malory's *Le Morte D'Arthur*. It looks Celtic, and Malory may have based it on an earlier name. Some like to link it to the Welsh word *gwaraidd*, 'gentle', which suits one aspect of Malory's fictional character, or it may be a form of GERAINT. It was very popular in Wales in the 20th century, and was also common outside Wales particularly in the mid-20th century, although it is now somewhat in decline.
PET FORMS **Gary, Gaz, Garth**
★ Gareth Hunt (1942–2007), English actor
★ Gareth Gates (1984–), English singer

Garfield *m*
This is a surname, originally a place name, used as a first name. The place name is formed from the Old English *gar*, 'triangle, gore', and *feld*, 'open

country, field'. It is mainly found in the USA, and probably came into use in honour of President James A Garfield who was assassinated in 1881.

PET FORMS **Garry**, **Gary**

★ Sir Garfield 'Gary' Sobers (1936–), West Indian cricketer

☆ Garfield is the name of the cat in Jim Davis's cartoon strip

Garmon *m*

Garmon is the Welsh form of the name of St *Germanus* of Auxerre (see GERMAIN), a 5th-century Gallo-Roman sent to convert the British from the Pelagian heresy. During the course of his mission, he managed to achieve a bloodless victory over invading Picts and Saxons.

Garpar *see* Gaspard

Garret *m*

This is originally an Irish name, although it has been regularly used in the USA in recent years. It is a surname, derived from GERALD and GERARD, used as a first name. It is also used in Ireland as the anglicization of *Geraóid*, the Irish form of Gerald, taken directly from the Old French form *Geraud*.

PET FORMS **Gary**, **Garry** • VARIANT **Garrett**

★ Garret FitzGerald (1926–), prime minister of Ireland

Garth *m*

The Old Norse *garthr*, 'enclosure', became the northern dialect word 'garth' for a yard or garden. This in turn became a surname which is now a first name. Although it was in use by the early 20th century, what really established the name was the international success of the strip cartoon *Garth*, about a time-travelling all-action superhero, which first appeared in the *Daily Mail* in 1943 and ran until 1997. Garth is also used as a pet form of GARETH.

★ Garth Brooks (1962–), US country singer

★ Garth Nix (1963–), Australian children's writer

Garvan *m*

This is the anglicized version of the traditional Irish name *Garbhán*, a pet form of the word *garbh*, 'rough'. There were several early saints of the name, including one who founded a church near what is now Dungarvan in County Waterford.

VARIANT **Garvin**

Gary *m*

When the budding actor Frank Cooper was looking for a stage name his agent, Nan Collins, suggested her home town of Gary, Indiana. When Gary Cooper became a famous film star the name spread. The town was named after Elbert H Gary, chairman of the United States Steel Corporation which had founded it in 1906. The town is pronounced with the 'a' having the sound of 'air', but the pronunciation of the vowel in the name was shortened, hence the common respelling, *Garry*. The name also serves as a pet form of GARETH.

PET FORM **Gaz** • VARIANTS **Garey**, **Garry**

★ Gary Oldman (1958–), English actor

★ Gary Lineker (1960–), English footballer

Gaspard *m*

This is the French form of CASPER. The final 'd', found only in the French form of the name, seems to have derived from association with the *-ard* endings of the many names from Germanic *hard*, 'brave'. See also JASPER.

VARIANTS **Garpar**, **Gasparine** (f)

Gaspare, Gasparo *see* Casper

Gaston *m*

Gaston is a French name from the Germanic word *gast* which meant both 'guest' and 'stranger'. It was the name of a 6th-century bishop who was a missionary to the Franks. This led to it being very well used by the aristocracy of the early Middle Ages, and the name was revived in the 19th century, although it is now rarely given in France.

VARIANT *Italian* **Gastóne**

Gauge *see* **Gage**

Gaurav *m*

This is the Hindi word for 'pride, honour, respect' used as a first name.

VARIANTS **Gourav**, **Gorav**

Gauri *f*

This is a Hindu name meaning 'white, fair' and is one of the titles of the goddess PARVATI.

VARIANT **Gowri**

Gautam *m*

This Indian name owes its popularity to *Gotam* having been the name of the Buddha, for it means 'descendant of Gotam'. Gotam or *Gotama* means 'the best cow' from the Sanskrit *go*, 'cow, ox', and *tama*, 'best'.

VARIANT **Gotama**

Gautier *see* **Walter**

Gavin *m*

This is the Scottish form of the name *Gawain*. The name of this knight of the Round Table has a confused history. Gawain appears in early Welsh literature as *Gwalchmai*. The first element, *gwalch*, means 'hawk' but was also used to describe the qualities of a hero. The *mai* element has never been satisfactorily interpreted. Proposed meanings have included 'May', 'of the plains', 'fierce' and 'pure, light'. The name passed into French Arthurian literature (possibly via Breton) where it appears as *Gauvain*. It is difficult to explain the difference in the ending, but it is possible that if

mai had the meaning 'pure, light' it could have been translated into Breton as something like *Gwalch(g)wyn*, incorporating the common name element *(g)wyn*, 'white, pure, fair', found in so many Welsh names. Whatever happened, Gauvin became Gawain in England, and Gavin in Scotland, although forms of the name were very unstable throughout the Middle Ages. Thereafter Gavin was restricted to the north of England and Scotland until the 20th century when it became widely used by English speakers, although it has retained its Scottish associations.

VARIANTS **Gawayne**, **Gawan**

☆ Gavin Shipman in the sitcom *Gavin and Stacey*

Gavrel, Gavriel *see* **Gabriel**

Gawain, Gawan, Gawayne *see* **Gavin**

Gay *f*

This name, taken from the vocabulary word, became popular in the 1930s but went into steep decline when the meaning of the word changed in the 1960s. It has also been used as a pet form of GAIL, and in Ireland is found as a masculine short form of GABRIEL.

VARIANTS **Gaye**, **Gae**

★ Gay Search, British gardener

Gayle *see* **Abigail, Gail**

Gaylord *m*

This is a surname, a form of the French *Gaillard* meaning 'high-spirited' or 'dandy'. The Gaylord family was a prominent one on the east coast of the USA, and the surname had become a first name by 1769, the year that Gaylord Giswold, later a successful politician, was born. He appears to have been named after his paternal grandmother who was born Esther Gaylord. The name, which is mainly confined to the USA, fell out of favour with parents in the late 1950s, but up until then it had been used regularly, and still survives in the USA as the name of a chain of hotels, a place name, and in manufacturing.

★ Gaylord Perry (1938–), US baseball player

★ Gaylord Nelson (1916–2005), US politician and conservationist, founder of Earth Day

☆ Gaylord Ravenal is the lead role in the musical *Show Boat* (1927), written by Jerome Kern and Oscar Hammerstein

Gaynor *f*
This is a contracted form of GUINEVERE, in use since at least the mid-15th century.
VARIANT **Gaenor**

Gaz *see* **Gareth, Gary**

Gearalt, Gearoid, Gearóid *see* Gerald

Gearoidin *see* **Geraldine**

Ged *m*
Now used as an independent name, this was originally a pet form of GERALD or GERARD.

★ Ged Peck (1947–), English guitarist

★ Gérard Houllier (1947–), French football manager, was nicknamed Ged by the fans at Liverpool FC during his time with the club

Geena *see* **Gina**

Geert *see* **Gerard**

Geertje, Geertruida *see* **Gertrude**

Geeta *see* **Gita**

Geetanjali *see* **Gitanjali**

Gellert *see* **Gerard**

Gelo *see* **Angel**

Geltrude *see* **Gertrude**

Gemma *f*
This is the Italian word for 'gem, jewel'. Use increased outside Italy after St Gemma Galgani (1878–1903) was canonized in 1940. She was a sickly orphan who spent her short life in hard domestic service, but had visions and received the stigmata. The name was one of the most popular for girls in England in the 1980s.
PET FORM **Gem** • VARIANT **Jemma**

★ Gemma Donati married the Italian poet Dante in 1285

★ Gemma Craven (1950–), Irish-born British actress

Gena *see* **Gina, Regina**

Gene *mf*
As a masculine form this was originally short for EUGENE. The name is most often found in the USA; as a feminine form it is a respelling of JEAN.

★ Gene Tierney (1920–91), US actress

★ Gene Hackman (1930–), US actor

★ Gene Pitney (1940–2006), US singer-songwriter

Genesis *f*
This name has become increasingly popular in the USA since the late 1980s, and was ranked 139 in the list of most popular girls' names in 2007. The biblical book of Genesis comes from the Greek word for 'beginning'. Its popularity may owe something to its echoing of other names and its ability to be abbreviated to JENNY.

Geneva *f*
An name which may be either a use of the city name; a form of *Genevra*, the Italian for GENEVIEVE; or a Germanic form of JUNIPER. It has mainly been used in the USA where it was well established in the later 19th century, and spent the first 40 years of the 20th century in the top 200 feminine names.

Genevieve *f*

Geneviève is the French form of the name that appears in 5th-century Latin texts as *Genovefa*. The origin of the name is uncertain, but it may be linked with the Celtic *gen*, 'people'. The 5th-century St Genevieve is the patron saint of Paris, as she is credited with leading the citizens in their resistance to the invading Franks and Huns when they threatened the city. There is another, largely mythical, saint with this name, St Genevieve of Brabant, supposedly a 10th-century woman accused of adultery, who was forced to live in hiding in the forest, where she had her baby, until at last her husband recognized his mistake. This story was the subject of much creative interest in the 19th century, with Schumann writing a piece on her in 1850 and Offenbach a comic opera in 1859. This helped popularize the name in France at the time. For British people over a certain age, the name is most strongly linked to the 1953 film *Genevieve* when it was the name of a vintage car.

PET FORMS **Ginette, Ginetta, Jenny**
• VARIANTS *Italian* **Genovèffa** *Spanish* **Genoveva, Ginevra**
★ Geneviève Bujold (1942–), French-Canadian actress

Geni *see* Jean

Genine *see* Janine

Genista *f*

A rare name, taken from the Latin for the broom plant. The same name is found in the Plantagenet royal line, derived from the full Latin form *planta genesta*, 'broom plant'. This arose from the founder's use of a sprig of broom as his distinguishing mark in battle.

PET FORM **Jenny**
★ Baroness Genista (Jenny) McIntosh (1946–), English arts administrator and life peer

Gennadi *m*

This is the Russian form of the Greek name *Gennadios*. The origin of this name is disputed. It has been linked to the Greek *gennadas*, 'noble, generous', or it may have started out as a pet form of names such as *Diogenes*, 'born of Zeus', or *Hermogenes*, 'born of Hermes'. There is a popular Eastern Orthodox saint called Gennadi, one of many sharing the name.

VARIANTS **Gennady, Gennadiy**
★ Gennadi Gerasimov (1930–), Russian politician

Gennaro *m*

This is a popular name in southern Italy, as St Gennaro is the patron saint of Naples. His name comes from the Latin *Januarius*, 'January', which in turn derives from *Janus*, the Roman god of beginnings.

VARIANT *Spanish* **Jenaro**

Gennine *see* Janine

Geno *see* Eugene

Geoffrey *m*

This is a Germanic name introduced to England at the Norman Conquest. Its exact origin is disputed; it may be a respelling of GODFREY, or it may be a separate name that shares the same ending *frith*, 'peace'. There are so many different spellings of early forms of the name that it is impossible to tell if the first element was *Gaut*, 'goth'; *gawia*, 'territory'; *walah*, 'stranger'; or *gisel*, 'pledge, hostage'. It is quite possible that a number of names have fallen together to form this one. Geoffrey was popular throughout the Middle Ages and was revived in the 19th century, remaining in regular use until the middle of the 20th century. In the USA interest arrived later and peaked in the 1970s and 80s.

PET FORMS **Geoff, Jeff** • VARIANTS **Jeff(e)rey** *Irish* **Siothrún, Seathrún, Sheary** *Scots*

Gaelic **Goiridh** *Welsh* **Sieffre** *French*
Geoffroy, Geoffroi, J(e)offroy, J(e)offrey

★ Geoffrey Chaucer (c.1345–1400),
   English writer

★ Geoffrey Boycott (1940–   ), English
   cricketer

George *m*

This is the English form of the Greek
name *Georgios*, which in turn comes
from *georgos*, 'farmer' or literally
'earth worker', being formed from *ge*,
'earth', and *ergein*, 'to work'. There are
a number of Eastern Orthodox saints
of the name, including the famous
dragon slayer whose very existence is
now doubted. Despite this, St George
is the patron saint of England, Russia,
Georgia, Malta and Greece. Edward
III dedicated the Order of the Garter
to him, which is how he became
the patron of England. Nevertheless,
the name was not common in the
Middle Ages, and only entered the
general stock of names in the 15th
century. It became really popular in
18th century, when there were four
Hanoverian kings of the name (a fact
that discouraged use in the USA),
and many prominent bearers. The pet
form *Geordie* is distinctively northern
English and Scottish, so much so that it
became a nickname for Tynesiders.
PET FORMS **Georgie, Georgy, Geordie**
• VARIANTS *Irish* **Seoirse** *Scots Gaelic*
Deòrsa, Seòras *Welsh* **Siôr, Siors, Siorus**
Cornish **Jory** *Czech* **Jiří** *Dutch* **Joris, Joeri,
Jurgen** *French* **Georges** *German* **Georg,
Jörg, Jürgen** *Greek* **Georgios, Y(i)orgos**
Italian **Giorgio, Giorgino** *Polish* **Jurek,
Jerzy** *Russian* **Georg(i)y, Georgy, Yegor,
Yuri(y)** *Scandinavian* **Göran, Örjan,
Jör(a)n, Jørgen, Jorck, Jurian** *Spanish*
Jorge, Jordi

★ George Washington (1732–99), first
   president of the USA

★ George H W Bush (1924–   ), 41st
   president of the USA

★ George W Bush (1946–   ), 43rd
   president of the USA

Georgia, Georgiana, Georgina *f*

These are the three commonest of
the many feminine forms of GEORGE.
Georgina seems to have been the first,
introduced to Scotland in the 18th
century by anti-Jacobites (the Jacobites
may well have called their daughters
Jamesina, or one of the other Scottish
feminines for JAMES). This was closely
followed by Georgiana. Although there
was a 5th-century French saint called
Georgia, the name does not seem to
have been used by English speakers
until the later 19th century, although it
is now the most popular of the three.
Other feminines of George are listed
below, under variants.
PET FORMS **Georgie, Georgi, Georgy,
George** • VARIANTS **Georgette, Georgine,
Georgene, Georgeana**

★ Georgia O'Keeffe (1887–1986), US
   painter

★ Georgette Heyer (1902–74), English
   novelist

Ger *see* Jerry

Geraint *m*

This popular Welsh name presents
something of a problem. It first appears
in Latin as *Gerontius*, which was a
well-established Roman name, derived
from Greek *Gerontios*, 'old man'.
However, there is some reluctance
to see the name as derived from
this, even though we have records
of a Roman general who was born
in Britain, and who died in AD 411,
called Gerontius, and Geraint regularly
appears in Latin texts as Gerontius.
Geraint was the name of a real king of
Dumnonia (the south-west peninsula
of Britain) who died in 710; we even
have a surviving letter written by him.
It is also the name of one of King
Arthur's knights, who may be based

on this king and who is prominent in Welsh legend. There is another Geraint who died at the Battle of Llongborth in 530, and the legendary Arthurian figure may be a combination of the two.

★ Sir Geraint Evans (1922–92), Welsh baritone

Gerald *m*

This is one of the Germanic names brought to England by the Normans. It is formed from *ger*, a variant of *gar* meaning 'spear', and *wald*, 'rule'. There has always been considerable overlap between Gerald and GERARD. The name was popular in the early Middle Ages, but then fell out of favour and was little used except in Ireland. There it was widespread, having been introduced by the Norman invaders who were led by the 'sons of Gerald' or the 'Fitzgeralds' as they became known, using the Norman French form. This gave the name further aristocratic status. Outside Ireland, the name experienced a revival in the 19th century and was well used during the 20th, particularly in the USA where it remained in the top 100 names for most of the first 70 years of that century.

PET FORMS **Jerry, Ger(ry), Ged** • VARIANTS **Jerald, Jer(r)old, Ger(r)old, Jarrett, Gerrald** *Irish* **Garret, Gearoid, Gearalt** *Welsh* **Gerallt** *Dutch* **Gerolt** *French* **Géraud, Gérald** *German* **Gerhold** *Italian* **Giraldo** *Spanish* **Geraldo**

★ Gerald Ford (1913–2006), 38th president of the USA
★ Gerald Durrell (1925–95), English writer and naturalist

Geraldine *f*

In Ireland the Fitzgeralds (see GERALD above) were also known collectively as the Geraldines. One branch of the Geraldines, the earls of Kildare, fell into disgrace when a son of the family tried to rebel against English rule. However, one of the daughters, Lady Elizabeth Fitzgerald, who through her mother was a cousin of the English king, Henry VIII, was allowed to join the household of the Tudor princesses Mary and Elizabeth, no doubt in a position between employee and hostage. While there, in about 1540, she was seen by the Earl of Surrey, a family friend and poet, who wrote a sonnet in her praise, addressing her as 'the Fair Geraldine' – less romantically, she is Garrett (see GARRET) in another poem. Although this marked the first use of Geraldine as a personal name, it was not until the 18th century that it became popular.

PET FORMS **Geri, Gerie, Gerri, Gerrie, Gerry** • VARIANT *Irish* **Gearoidin**

Gerard *m*

This name, brought to Britain by the Normans, is formed from the Germanic elements *gar, ger*, 'spear', and *hard*, 'brave'. Its history is muddled with that of GERALD, and the two were often used interchangeably, although Gerard was the more frequent form in the Middle Ages. It was among the medieval names revived in the 19th century, but went into decline after the 1950s, although there are slight signs that it may be making a comeback.

FEMININE **Geradine** • PET FORMS **Ger(ry), Jerry, Ged** • VARIANTS **Gerrard, Jerrard** *Irish* **Garret, Gearóid** *French* **Gérard, Girard, Gérarde** (f) *German, Dutch* **Gerhard(t), Geert** *Hungarian* **Gellert** *Italian, Spanish* **Gerardo**

★ Gerard Manley Hopkins (1844–89), English poet
★ Gerard Hoffnung (1925–59), German-born British musician and cartoonist
★ Gérard Depardieu (1948–), French film actor

Gerasim *m*
This is the Russian form of the Greek *Gerasimos*, derived from *geras* which can mean either 'old' or 'honour'. It is thus linked to GERAINT and to *Gerontius*, 'old man', and the German *Gereon* from the same root. St Gerasimos was a 5th-century hermit revered in the Eastern Orthodox Church.

Géraud *see* **Gerald**

Gerda *f*
Gerda is the modern form of the Old Norse *Gerd*, the name of the goddess of fertility. Gerda also acts as feminine form of the German and Dutch name *Gerhart* (see GERARD).
VARIANT **Gerde**
☆ Gerda is the name of the heroine of Hans Christian Andersen's 1846 story *The Snow Queen*

Geri, **Gerie** *see* **Geraldine**

Germain *m* **Germaine** *f*
Although the masculine form of this name is rare among English speakers, it is well used in other countries. There have been several saints called Germain, including a 6th-century bishop of Paris after whom the famous district of Saint-Germain-des-Prés was named. Although the name is sometimes interpreted as deriving from the ethnic name *German*, its origin lies in the Latin *germanus*, 'close relative, brother'. There is also a famous female French saint, St Germaine Cousin (1579–1601), who was mistreated by her stepmother, and sent out from a young age to look after the sheep. It is said that she took some bread to give to one even poorer than herself, and her stepmother accused her of stealing. When she was made to open her apron where the bread lay hidden, it was revealed to be full of spring flowers instead. Germaine, particularly in the variant *Jermaine*, is sometimes used as a masculine name.
VARIANT **Jermaine**
★ Germaine Greer (1939–   ), Australian feminist and author
★ Jermaine Jackson (1954–   ), US singer

Gerolamo, **Gerome**, **Geronimo** *see* **Jerome**

Gerontius *see* **Geraint**, **Gerasim**

Gerri, **Gerrie** *see* **Geraldine**

Gerry *see* **Jerry**

Gertrude *f*
A Germanic name formed from *ger*, 'spear', and *thruth*, strength, this was the name of a 13th-century mystic, sometimes called Gertrude the Great, who entered a nunnery at the age of five and remained there until her death. The name only came into use in England in the later Middle Ages. It may have been introduced by immigrants from the Low Countries who came to work in the cloth trade. They revered St Gertrude of Nivelles, a 7th-century saint around whom a large body of folklore accumulated. It was one of the many medieval names revived in the 19th century, but is currently out of fashion, although forms of TRUDY are sometimes used. The German name *Gertrun*, from *ger* and *run*, 'rune, magic', is related.
PET FORMS **Gert(ie)**, **Tru**, **Trudy** • VARIANTS *Dutch* **Geertruida**, **Geertje**, **Truus** *German* **Gertr(a)ud** *Italian* **Geltrude** *Polish* **Gertruda** *Portuguese* **Gertrudes** *Spanish* **Gertrudis**
★ Gertrude Lawrence (1898–1952), English actress
★ Gertrude Stein (1874–1946), US writer and patron of the arts
☆ Gertrude is the name of Hamlet's mother in Shakespeare's play

Gervase *m*
Despite the fact that this was a popular

name in the Middle Ages, we have no clear idea where it comes from. In AD 386 St Ambrose of Milan had a 'presentiment' that the bodies of two forgotten martyrs, saints *Protase* and Gervase, would be found in Milan, and when a search was conducted the bodies were duly found. The two then became popular saints, even though nothing was known about them. The name Protase, which did not catch on, appears to be Greek, derived from *protos*, 'first', but it is difficult to find a convincing Greek source for Gervase. Attempts have been made to link the name to the Germanic *ger* names, but it seems unlikely that they would be in use at that time and linked to early Christians. The popularity of the name in the past is attested by the English surnames JARVIS and *Jervis* which come from it, and which are sometimes used as first names.

VARIANTS *French* **Gervais** *German* **Gervas** *Italian, Spanish* **Gervasio**

☆ Gervase Fen is the hero of the classic detective stories by Edmund Crispin

Gethin *m*
This is a Welsh name, meaning 'dark, swarthy'.
★ Gethin Jones (1978–), television presenter
★ Gethin Jenkins (1980–), Welsh international rugby player

Ghassan *m*
This is an Arabic name, from the word for 'youth, vigour', that also belonged to an Arabian tribe which died out in the 6th century.

Ghazala *f*
An Arabic name, taken from the vocabulary word 'gazelle'.
VARIANT **Ghazal**

Ghazi *m*
An Arabic name, meaning 'conqueror, hero', which was the title of the

Mughal emperor Aurangzeb who ruled 1658–1707.

Ghislane *f*
This is the feminine form of the old French *Ghislain*, the name of an obscure and probably legendary saint. It comes from the Germanic *gisil* or *gisel*, 'pledge, hostage'; this developed a pet form *Gislin*, which was then turned into *Gislenus* in Latin texts, finally becoming Ghislain in French. Because of the twists and turns of medieval inflexions and spelling, it is essentially the same name as GISELLE. The name, in which the 's' is silent, has never been very common, but was briefly fashionable in France in the 1950s.
VARIANT **Gislaine**

Giachetta *see* James

Giacinta *see* Jacinta

Giacobbe *see* Jacob

Giacomo *see* Jacob, James

Giambattista *see* Baptist

Gianna *see* Jane

Gianni, Giannino *see* John

Gideon *m*
This is a biblical name, which can be interpreted either as 'he who cuts down' or as 'having a stump for a hand', meanings that are both appropriate for the judge and war-leader described in the book of Judges. The name was used by the Puritans in the 16th century, and has had something of a revival in recent years.

Gigi *f*
This French name, made famous by the 1944 novel by Colette which was filmed in 1958, was originally a pet form of the French feminine of GILBERT,

Gilberte. It can also be used in France for *Georgine* (GEORGINA) and VIRGINIA.

Gila *see* **Giselle**

Gillanders *m*

This is the first of a list of Scots Gaelic religious names beginning with *gille* meaning 'servant, devotee of'. Once standard Highland names, they are now rarely given, although many are still very much present as surnames. This list includes *Gillanders* or *Gillandreis*, 'servant of St Andrew', *Gilbride*, 'servant of St Bridget', *Gillecalum*, 'servant of St Columba', *Gillemartin*, 'servant of St Martin', *Gilleonain*, 'servant of St Adamnan', and *Gilmore* or *Gilmour*, 'servant of Mary'. *Gillespie* is the anglicized form of the Scots Gaelic *Gilleasbaig*, 'servant of the bishop'. It was regularly 'translated' as ARCHIBALD, for reasons which are obscure, although it has been suggested that there was an association made between the *bald* element of Archibald and the tonsure likely to be worn by a bishop's servant. *Gillies* comes from *Gille Iosa*, 'servant of Jesus'. Because Celtic languages tend to have two different forms of the name JOHN both GILZEAN and GILL'EOIN mean 'servant of St John'. This latter also appears as *Filian*, *Gilleon*, *Gillian* or *Gellion*. The 'g' in all cases is hard.

Gilbert *m*

A Germanic name formed from *gisil*, 'pledge, hostage', and *berht*, 'bright', which was introduced to Britain by the Normans. A descendant of one of William the Conqueror's soldiers was born at Sempringham in 1083, and grew up to be a monk. Now known as St Gilbert of Sempringham, he founded an order of monks and nuns still known as the Gilbertines.

Gilda *f*

This originally Italian name started out as a pet form of names such as *Ermengilda*, the Italian form of *Herminigild*, a Germanic name formed from *ermin* or *irmin*, 'entire, total' (see IRMA), and *gild*, 'sacrifice'. This old name was brought to public attention in 1851 by Verdi's opera *Rigoletto*, set in the Middle Ages, in which Gilda is the name of the heroine. This led to its spread to other languages, including English.

☆ *Gilda* was a 1946 film starring Rita Hayworth as a femme fatale

Gildas *m*

This is the name of a 6th-century Welsh saint, known as Gildas the Wise, who wrote many works including one of the few contemporary accounts of British history of that time. He is also said to have been a missionary, although the accounts of his life are so embroidered it is difficult to winnow out the truth. He is credited with founding a monastery in Brittany, where the name has traditionally been used, and from where it spread to other parts of France.

Giles *m*

This name has gone through considerable changes from its Greek original *Aigidios*, formed from *aigidion*, 'kid, young goat'. Aigidios became *Aegidius* in Latin, then in French lost its initial vowels to become *Gides*, before finally the 'd' was transformed into an 'l'. The traditional legend of St Giles says that he was a Greek hermit who, appalled by the publicity associated with his healing the crippled, fled to St Gilles in Provence. Although not particularly popular in the Middles Ages, the name was well used in Scotland, where there are also records of *Aegidia* or *Egidia* used as a feminine name. However, it is probable that these were merely formal written versions and that, in everyday speech,

Giles would have been used for both sexes. The name is rare in the USA, where it is thought of as typically British.

VARIANTS **Gyles**, *Dutch, Scandinavian* **Gillis** *French* **Gilles** (m), **Gilette** (f) *Italian* **Egidio** *Spanish* **Gil**

★ Giles Gilbert Scott (1880–1960), English architect
★ Gyles Brandreth (1948–   ), English politician, writer and television presenter
☆ The traditional term 'Farmer Giles' is taken from Robert Bloomfield's poem of 1800 'The Farmer's Boy'

Gillespie *see* **Archibald, Gilanders**

Gillian *f*
This is a feminine form of JULIAN. It came into use in the Middle Ages, when there was no distinction between masculine and feminine forms, and only evolved as an independent name in the 17th century. In the past, Gillian or *Gill* was so popular that it became a generic term for a female, just as JACK did for a male, and is still used as a technical term for the female of some species.

PET FORMS **Gill(ie), Jill** • VARIANT **Jillian**

★ Gillian Cross (1945–   ), English children's author
★ Gillian Anderson (1968–   ), US actress

Gina *f* **Gino** *m*
Gina is both an Italian and English name, which started out as a pet form of names ending in *-gina* such as GEORGINA and REGINA, or of names like VIRGINIA. *Giana* is not a variant but an Italian form of JANE. There is also some overlap with forms of JEAN. Similarly Gino, only occasionally found outside Italian contexts, was a pet form of names ending in *-gino* or of names such as *Giacomo* (see JAMES).

VARIANTS **Gena, Geena**

★ Gina Lollobrigida (1927–   ), Italian actress
★ Geena Davis (1957–   ), US actress

Ginetta, Ginette *see* **Genevieve, Virginia**

Ginevra *see* **Genevieve**

Ginger *mf*
As a masculine name, this is nearly always a nickname for someone with red hair (compare names such as RORY), but for girls it can also be a pet form of VIRGINIA.

★ Ginger Rogers (1911–95), US dancer and actress
★ Peter 'Ginger' Baker (1939–   ), English musician

Ginnie, Ginny *see* **Virginia**

Gioacchino, Gioachino *see* **Joachim**

Gioconda *f*
The Italian for 'happy'. It was the name of a 5th-century saint, but is best-known as the alternative name of Leonardo's painting *Mona Lisa*.

Gioele *see* **Joel**

Giordano *see* **Jordan**

Giorgino, Giorgio *see* **George**

Giovanna *see* **Jane**

Giovanni *see* **John**

Gipsy *see* **Gypsy**

Giraldo *see* **Gerald**

Girard *see* **Gerard**

Girolamo *see* **Jerome**

Giselle *f*
This French name comes from *gisel*, 'pledge, hostage', and is another form of the name GHISLANE. There are traces of a masculine version of the name, which has long fallen out of use. The

feminine was kept in the stock of names thanks to the Blessed Giselle, who was born in 985 and married off at a young age to the King of Hungary, whom she helped to convert his country to Christianity. It may be that it started out as a description of the bearer's status, as it was common practice for children to be raised in other nobles' courts as a pledge of their parents' good behaviour, and for alliances to be sealed by marriage. An example of this happened in 911 when Giselle, the daughter of Charles the Simple of France, was married to Rollo of Normandy. He had taken control of her father's lands by force, and the marriage was made as part of the peace treaty that recognized Rollo's position as ruler of those lands. The name was a common one in the 9th to 10th centuries in France, but then was used only quietly until 1841, when the success of Adolphe Adam's ballet *Giselle* introduced the name to a much wider range of countries, and this is when it started to be used by English speakers. The name is currently most often found in South America.

VARIANTS **Gisele** *French* **Gisèle** *German* **Gisela, Gisa, Gila** *Italian* **Gisella** *Scandinavian* **Gislög, Gislaug**

★ Gisele Bündchen (1980–), Brazilian model

Gislaine *see* Ghislane

Gita *f*

This is the Sanskrit word for 'song' used as a first name. The name has strong religious connotations, particularly in the title of the major Hindu religious text the *Bhagavad Gita*.

VARIANT **Geeta**

Gitanjali *f*

This is the Sanskrit for 'an offering of songs', usually used with reference

to prayer. It is also the title of an anthology of poems by Rabindarath Tagore which caused a great stir when published in translation in 1913. See also ANJALI.

VARIANTS **Geetanjali, Gitanjoli**

Githa *see* Gytha

Gitta, Gittan *see* Bridget

Giuditta *see* Judith

Giulia *see* Julia

Giuliano *see* Julian

Giulietta *see* Juliet

Giulio *see* Julian

Giuseppe *see* Joseph

Giuseppina, Giuseppa *see* Josephine

Giustina, Giustino *see* Justin

Gjord *see* Godfrey

Gladys *f*

This is a Welsh name of uncertain origin; it may perhaps be a feminine of *gwledig*, an old term for a ruler of a *gwlad*, which is now used to mean a country but which previously meant 'territory'. Another tradition makes the name an old British form of CLAUDIA. Much of this rests on a reference by the Latin poet Martial to a friend Pudens, who had a wife 'Claudia, the foreigner from Britain'. It is an old name: one 13th-century manuscript gives it as the name of the 5th-century princess, 'of very noble lineage, most beautiful to behold and clad in silk', who was the mother of St Cadfan. It was one of the top three Welsh names for females between the 13th and 17th centuries. It spread to the general British population and to other countries in the 19th century and was particularly popular in the 1930s.

PET FORM **Glad** • VARIANTS *Welsh* **Gwladus,
Gwladys**
★ Dame Gladys Cooper (1888–1971),
English actress
★ Gladys Knight (1944–   ), US singer

Glaw *mf*
A modern Welsh name, from the
vocabulary word for 'rain'.

Glen *mf*
The Gaelic word *gleann*, 'valley',
became 'glen' in general Scottish use.
It has been widely used outside the
country, particularly in the USA. Use
as a female name is comparatively
recent. See also GLYN.
FEMININES **Glenna, Glenne** • VARIANT **Glenn**
★ Glenn Gould (1932–82), Canadian
pianist
★ Glenn Close (1947–   ), US actress

Glenda *f*
This name is something of a puzzle. It
appears to be formed from the Welsh
elements *glan*, 'pure, clean', and *da*,
'good', but there is some evidence that
the name was first used in the USA,
where it features in the name charts in
1911. It may therefore be a blend of
other names, or represent a feminine
of GLEN, which was well established by
this time. The apparent variant *Glinda*
is even earlier, appearing in L Frank
Baum's children's book of 1900, *The
Wizard of Oz*, as the name of the good
witch. Glinda attracted a brief flurry of
interest in the USA, around the mid-
20th century.

Glenys *f*
This is a fairly recent Welsh name, of
somewhat uncertain origin, but most
likely formed from *glan*, 'pure, holy',
combined with the *-ys* ending found in
many Welsh feminine names.
PET FORM **Glen** • VARIANTS **Glen(n)is,
Glenice**
★ Glenys Kinnock (1944–   ), Welsh
politician

Glesni *f*
This name comes from the Welsh word
for 'blue'.

Glinda *see* **Glenda**

Gloria *f*
This is the Latin word for 'glory' and
is prominent in the Latin Mass. It does
not seem to have been used in English
until George Bernard Shaw gave it to a
character in his 1898 play *You Never
Can Tell*. However, Queen Elizabeth
I had been addressed as *Gloriana*,
and names such as *Gloriande* and the
masculine *Gloriant* are found in French
medieval romance.
VARIANT **Glory**
★ Gloria Swanson (1897–1983), US
actress
★ Gloria Estefan (1957–   ), Cuban-born
US singer

Glyn, Glyndwr *m*
This is the Welsh word for 'valley',
and thus the equivalent of the Scottish
GLEN. The longer name Glyndwr has
the added element *dŵr*, meaning
'water'. This has two stresses in Welsh.
If written Glyndŵr, the stress is on the
second syllable; if written Glyndwr,
it is on the first. In both cases the 'w'
is pronounced as 'oo'. The name is
anglicized as *Glendower*, and it is
shortened to Glyn.
VARIANT **Glynn**
★ Glyn Daniel (1914–86), Welsh
archaeologist and television
personality

Gobind *m*
This popular Indian name comes from
the Sanskrit *go*, 'cow', and *vinda*,
'finding'. The original cow finder was
the god *Indra*, but the name is now
more strongly associated with KRISHNA.
VARIANTS **Gobinda, Govinda, Govind**

Gobnet *f*
This is the name of an Irish saint

who is particularly associated with beekeeping. It has been linked to the word *gob*, 'mouth', but is more probably from *goba*, 'smith', which is also the source of the masculine name *Gobbán*.

VARIANTS **Gobnait, Gobnat, Gobinet**

Godfrey *m*

This is the Norman-French form of a Germanic name created from the elements *god*, 'God' (or possibly from 'good'), and *frith*, 'peace'. It was found in Anglo-Saxon England as *Godfrith* but, apart from rare 19th-century revivals, this was ousted by the Norman-French form. The name overlaps with GEOFFREY, and medieval bearers can often appear in documents with the two names used interchangeably. Although Godfrey was used in the 19th and early 20th century it is now rare.

VARIANTS *Irish* **Gofaridh** *Scots Gaelic* **Goraidh** *Dutch* **Godfried** *French* **Godefroy** *German* **Gottfried** *Italian* **Goffredo** *Scandinavian* **Gottfrid, Gjord, Gyrd, Jul** *Spanish* **Godofredo**

Godiva *f*

The legend of Lady Godiva is so well known (even if the fact that her naked ride was done to force her husband to reduce taxes on the poor is not so often recalled), that it is difficult to remember that Godiva is the written Latin form of an Old English name, which would have been something like *Godgyfu*, from elements meaning 'God' and 'gift'. The associations with Lady Godiva and with the well-known chocolate brand are so strong that the name is rarely given to a child.

Godric *m*

This name, formed from *god*, 'God', and *ric*, 'ruler', was the name of a very important East Anglian saint, who features in a long Old English poem.

Consequently the Normans, who had no equivalent name, considered it typically English; when they wanted to mock Henry I (r.1100–35), for his English sympathies, and his wife Matilda, who was descended from the pre-Conquest English ruling family, they nicknamed them Godric and GODIVA. The final 'c' in the name should be pronounced with a 'ch' sound, but on the rare occasions it is revived it is also found pronounced with a hard 'c'.

☆ Godric Gryffindor is the founder of Gryffindor House in the *Harry Potter* books, by J K Rowling

Godwin *m*

This is an Old English name formed from the elements *god*, 'God', and *wine*, 'friend'. It was the name of the father of the King Harold defeated by William the Conqueror, and also of a Belgian saint. It continued in use among the English after the Norman Conquest, which is why it is now a not-uncommon surname. Modern uses are likely to be from this surname.

VARIANT **Goodwin**

Gofaridh, Goffredo *see* Godfrey

Goiridh *see* Geoffrey

Golda, Goldie *f*

Golda is a Jewish name from the Yiddish for 'gold'. Goldie is either a pet form or translation of this name, sometimes used independently, or as a nickname for a blonde. It can also be found as a pet form of the name MARIGOLD.

VARIANT **Golde**

★ Golda Meir (1898–1978), Israeli prime minister

★ Goldie Hawn (1945–), US actress

Gonzalo *m*

This is a Spanish name used by Hispanic Americans. Its origins, however, are Germanic, having been brought to Spain by invading Visigoths. It appears in early Latin records as *Gundisalvus*, which allows us to reconstruct the first element as deriving from *gund*, 'war', but the origin of the second half is obscure.

☆ Gonzalo is a character in Shakespeare's *The Tempest*

Goodwin *see* **Godwin**

Gopal *m*
This is from the Sanskrit for 'cow protector', one of the titles of the god KRISHNA.
VARIANTS **Gopala, Gopalkrishna**
★ Gopala (reigned c.750–70), founder of the Pala dynasty of Bengal

Goraidh *see* **Godfrey**

Goran, Göran *see* **George**

Gorav *see* **Gaurav**

Gordon *m*
This is a surname used as a first name. It has strong Scottish associations, being a prominent clan name, but the place name could come from either Scotland or Normandy. It spread from being a limited Scottish name to one used throughout the UK in the 19th century, when it was given in honour of General Charles Gordon (1833–85), popularly known as 'Gordon of Khartoum'.
PET FORMS **Gordy, Gordie** • VARIANT **Gorden**
★ (James) Gordon Brown (1951–), Scottish MP, British prime minister
★ Gordon Ramsay (1966–), Scottish chef and television personality

Gormlaith *f*
A traditional name in Ireland and Scotland formed from the Gaelic words *gorm*, 'illustrious, splendid', and *flaith*, 'lady, princess'. It is pronounced 'GORM-leh' or 'GORM-la'.
VARIANTS **Gormla, Gormelia**

Goronwy *m*
A traditional Welsh name which appears as *Gronw* in the medieval *Mabinogion* stories. It was revived in the mid-18th century by the Welsh bardic movement, when Goronwy Owen took it as his bardic name, modelling it on that of the medieval bard Goronwy Ddu.
VARIANTS **Gronw(y)**

Gösta *see* **Gustav**

Gotama *see* **Gautam**

Gottfrid, Gottfried *see* **Godfrey**

Gottlieb *m*
A German name formed in the 17th century from the German *Gott*, 'God', and *lieb*, 'love'. It is a translation of the more widely used name THEOPHILUS, and Mozart's middle name AMADEUS translates as Gottlieb in German.

Gourav *see* **Gaurav**

Govind, Govinda *see* **Gobind**

Gowri *see* **Gauri**

Goyo *see* **Gregory**

Grace *f*
This is one of the virtue names introduced by the Puritans, although modern users probably associate it more with the physical attributes rather than the religious ones. As it shares a meaning with ANNA or HANNAH, it may sometimes have been used as a translation of these. It is currently very popular worldwide, both in its basic form and in its pet form, which is also being increasingly combined with other names.
PET FORM **Gracie** • VARIANTS **Grayce, Gracilia** *Dutch* **Gratia** *French* **Grâce, Gracieuse** *Italian* **Graziella, Gràzia** *Spanish* **Gracia, Graciela**
★ Grace Darling (1815–42), English lighthouse keeper's daughter whose

heroic rescue of shipwrecked sailors led to an increase in the use of her name

★ Dame Gracie Fields (1898–1979), English variety artist and singer

Grady *mf*

An Irish surname which is more common in the USA, where it was regularly used from the 19th to the mid-20th century. Thereafter it faded but did not disappear, and has recently come back into fashion. It is only occasionally used for girls. As a surname it comes from *Ó Grádaigh*, 'descendant of Grádaigh', with Grádaigh meaning 'noble' in Gaelic.
VARIANT **Graidi(e)**

Graham *m*

Although this is famous as a Scottish clan name, it was only taken to Scotland in the 12th century by the ancestor of the clan, William de Graham. He came from Grantham in Lincolnshire, which appears in the form Graham in the Domesday book, and which probably means 'gravelly settlement' from *grand*, 'gravel' (hence the various spellings), and *ham*, 'settlement'. Scottish emigrants took the name with them to the colonies in the 19th century, where it flourished, particularly in Canada. In the UK it was notably popular in the middle of the 20th century, but is now only moderately used, even in Scotland.
PET FORM **Gram** • VARIANTS **Graeme, Grahame**

★ Graham Greene (1904–91), English writer

★ Graeme Garden (1943–), Scottish-born comedian

Grainne *f*

This is an ancient Irish name, once that of a harvest goddess, but best-known in legend as the beautiful but doomed lover of DERMOT. It has

been used steadily since early times, and its most famous real-life bearer was Grainne Ni Mhaille, known to her Elizabethan opponents as Grace O'Malley, and now sometimes referred to as 'The Pirate Queen'. So great is her current popularity that *Granuaile*, an elided form of her full name, is now an independent name in Ireland. Grainne is pronounced 'graw-nya'. Its origin is unclear, but given the ancient connection with fertility, the Irish word *gran*, 'grain, corn', is the most likely.
VARIANTS **Grania, Granya** *Irish* **Gráinne**

Gram *see* **Graham**

Grant *m*

A surname used as a first name, derived from the French *grand*, 'big, tall', which probably started out as a nickname. The surname was taken to Scotland by Norman nobles in the 13th century, and is particularly associated with the country. As a first name it is still moderately popular in Scotland, but elsewhere had peaked by the end of the 20th century. Use in the USA is frequently linked with commemorating President Ulysses S Grant (1822–85).

☆ Grant Mitchell in the television soap *EastEnders*

Granville *m*

This was originally a Norman surname from a place called *grand ville*, 'large town'. In England it became an aristocratic surname, and was part of the trend for using such surnames as first names in the 19th century. It has never been particularly popular. See also GREVILLE.
VARIANT **Grenville**

★ Granville Hicks (1901–82), US literary critic, teacher and novelist

☆ Granville is a character in the television sitcom *Open All Hours* (1976–85)

Gratia *see* **Grace**

Gratien *m*
The Roman Emperor *Gratian* (Latin *Gratianus*) got his name from the Latin word *gratus*, 'pleasing'. The name entered the stock of French names via a 4th-century saint and also a 12th-century monk, whose editorial work on canonical texts was still in use in the 20th century. The name is now rare.
VARIANTS *Italian* **Graziano** *Spanish* **Graciano**

Grayson *mf*
Despite its apparent relationship to the vocabulary word, this surname actually comes from the Old English *greyve*, 'steward'. It has been growing steadily in popularity in the USA as a first name for boys since the 1990s, and is occasionally given to girls.
★ Grayson Perry (1960–), English artist

Gràzia, Graziella *see* **Grace**

Gréagóir *see* **Gregory**

Greer *f*
This is a Scottish surname, from a shortening of *Gregor* the local form of GREGORY, which has appeared as a rare first name since the Middle Ages. It was brought to public attention by the US actress Greer Garson (1908–96), and has recently appeared as a fashionable name, chosen by celebrities for their children.
VARIANT **Grier**

Gregory *m*
This name comes via Latin from the Greek *Gregorios*, 'watchful, vigilant'. As the Bible instructed them to 'be sober, be vigilant' (1 Peter 5.8) the name was taken up with enthusiasm by early Christians. There were many prominent early saints with the name; consequently it spread throughout the Christian world and was borne by 16

popes. The first of these, St Gregory the Great, is the most significant in England, as it was he who sent St Augustine of Canterbury to convert the English to Christianity. *Gregor*, the Scottish form of the name, is currently popular in Scotland. See also GREER.
PET FORMS **Greg(g)** • VARIANTS *Irish* **Gréagóir** *Scottish* **Gregor, Griogair, Greig** *Welsh* **Grigor** *French* **Grégoire** *German* **Gregor** *Greek* **Gregorios** *Italian* **Gregorio** *Polish* **Grzegorz** *Russian* **Gregori(y), Grigory, Grisha** *Spanish* **Gregorio, Goyo** *Scandinavian* **Greger(s)**
★ Gregory Peck (1916–2003), US actor
★ Greg Rusedski (1973–), Canadian-born British tennis player

Grenville *see* **Granville**

Greta, Gretel *f*
Greta was originally a Scandinavian and German pet form of *Margareta*, while Gretel was a pet form of *Grete*, in turn a diminutive of MARGARET. Greta spread to the rest of the world thanks to the fame of Swedish film star Greta Garbo (1905–90).
PET FORM **Gretchen** • VARIANT **Gretta**
☆ Gretel is the girl in the folk tale *Hansel and Gretel*
☆ Gretchen is the wronged girl in Goethe's *Faust*

Greville *m*
This is an aristocratic surname, being the family name of the earls of Warwick, which has been recorded as a first name since the 17th century. The surname comes from Gréville in the La Manche district of France and is Norman in origin. It has never been widely used. Compare GRANVILLE.
★ Greville Janner, Baron Janner of Braunstone (1928–), Welsh Labour politician and president of the Board of Deputies of British Jews

Grier *see* **Greer**

Griffin *m*

This is a modern US name, which has been increasingly popular there since the 1980s. There are earlier uses, dating from the 19th century. These cases are probably taken from the surname, which is a variant of GRIFFITH from the medieval Latin form *Griffinus*, but more recent uses probably relate as much to the mythical animal as to the surname.

PET FORM **Griff** • VARIANT **Griffyn**

Griffith *m*

This is the anglicized form of an old Welsh name, *Gruffudd* (the 'dd' is pronounced 'th'). The first part of the name is obscure, but the second half means 'lord'. It has long been popular in Wales, having been made famous by Gruffydd ap Llewelyn, who was ruler of all Wales until he was defeated by the English in 1063. The short form *Griff* is also found as an independent name.

PET FORM **Griff** • VARIANTS **Gruffud, Griffudd, Gruffydd** *Welsh pet forms* **Guto, Gutun, Gutyn**

★ Griff Rhys Jones (1953–), Welsh actor, writer and comedian

Grigor, Grigory, Griogair *see* Gregory

Griselda *f*

This is a Germanic name made up of the elements *gris*, 'grey', and *hild*, 'battle'. It was well used in the Middle Ages, and is best-known from that period because of 'Patient Griselda', the long-suffering wife in a story told first by Boccaccio, and then adapted into English by Chaucer. Its pet form is probably now more familiar.

PET FORM **Zelda** • VARIANTS *Scottish and northern English* **Griz(z)el** *Yiddish* **Zelde**
☆ Griselda Grantly, later Lady Dumbello in Anthony Trollope's *Chronicles of Barsetshire*

Grisha *see* Gregory

Gro *f*

This Scandinavian name is probably from the Old Norse *groa*, 'to grow', although another theory links it to the Celtic *gruach* meaning 'woman'.

★ Gro Harlem Brundtland (1939–), Norwegian prime minister and environmentalist

Gronw, Gronwy *see* Goronwy

Grover *f*

This is a surname, originally for someone who lived near a grove, used as a first name. It is used primarily in the USA, inspired by President (Stephen) Grover Cleveland (1837–1908).

☆ Grover is a *Sesame Street* character

Gruffud, Gruffudd, Gruffydd *see* Griffith

Grzegorz *see* Gregory

Guadalupe *fm*

This is the name of a Spanish convent with a famous image of the Virgin Mary. In the 16th century a Mexican man had a vision of the Virgin of Guadalupe, which led to the cult being particularly popular in Mexico. The Virgin of Guadalupe is the patron of Mexico and, some would say, of the Americas. Consequently the name is particularly popular in Mexico, and is well used by Spanish speakers throughout the Americas. It is mainly feminine in use.

PET FORMS **Lupe, Lupita**

Gualter, Gualtiero *see* Walter

Gudrun *f*

Gurdrun, formed from the Old Norse elements *guth*, 'god', and *run*, 'rune, secret learning', features in a number of early Germanic stories and Icelandic sagas, and is still a popular name in

Iceland. Its use in Wagner's *Ring Cycle* has led to some use outside its native area.

PET FORM **Guro**

☆ Gudrun Brangwen in D H Lawrence's *The Rainbow* (1915) and *Women in Love* (1920)

Guenevere *see* **Guinevere**

Guglielmo *see* **William**

Guido *see* **Guy**

Guillaume, Guilherme *see* **William**

Guillermo *see* **William**

Guinevere *f*
This is the medieval French form given to the Welsh *Gwenhwyfar*, the traditional name of King Arthur's wife. Indeed in early Welsh mythology, Arthur is said to have been married to three women successively, each bearing this name. There is general agreement that the first element of the name is the Welsh *gwen*, 'fair, white, holy', and the majority view is that the second element is *hwyfar*, 'smooth, soft, yielding'. However, those keen to link Arthurian texts with pre-Christian beliefs have found meanings such as 'spirit', 'enchantress' and 'wave' in the second part. It is not a common name, but is important as the source of both GAYNOR and the popular JENNIFER.

PET FORMS **Gwen, Gwenny** • VARIANTS **Guenevere** *Irish* **Finnabhair**

Guiomar *see* **Xiomara**

Gull *f*
This is a Scandinavian first name derived from the pet forms of Old Norse names from *guth*, 'god', or *gull*, 'gold'. It is most commonly found today in compound names such as *Gull-Britt*.

Gullan *see* **Gunnar**

Gulzar *mf*
Gul, also used as an independent name, is the Persian for 'rose', with Gulzar meaning 'rose garden'. There are a number of Arabic names based on *gul*, such as *Gulistan* and *Gulshan*, synonyms for 'rose garden', and *Gulisar*, 'rose petal'. Gulzar is mainly feminine, but masculine in India.

VARIANT **Gulzaar**

Gunnar *m* **Gunhilda** *f*
These are the most prominent of a group of names formed from the Old Norse element *gunnr* meaning 'strife'. Gunnar combines this element with *arr*, 'warrior', while Gunhilda uses the Latinate form of *hildr*, 'battle', which is often found in its pet form *Gunilla*. Gunnar is an old name, having belonged to the husband of Brunhilda in the *Nibelungenlied*. Other masculine names based on *gunnr* are *Gunnbjorn*, 'bear', and *Gunnleif*, 'descendant'. Feminines include *Gunnborg*, 'fortification', and *Gunnvor*, 'cautious'.

PET FORMS **Gunne** (mf), **Gullan, Gunn** (fs) • VARIANTS **Gunilla, Gunhild, Gunvor, Gunver, Gunder** *German* **Günt(h)er**

Gurdeep *mf*
This is a Sikh name formed from *gur*, 'guru, teacher', and *deep, dip*, 'light', and so is interpreted as meaning 'enlightened by the guru'.

VARIANT **Gurdip**

Gurinder, Gurvinder *mf*
Sikh names, meaning 'lord, guru'.

★ Gurinder Chadha (1960–   ), Kenyan-born British film director

Guro *see* **Gudrun**

Gus *m*
This is a pet form of names such as ANGUS, AUGUSTINE and GUSTAV. Gussie acts as a feminine form of AUGUSTA.

Gusta *see* **Augustine**

Gustav *m*
A Scandinavian name of somewhat obscure origin. The old form is *Gotstaff*, the first half of which may be from *Gautr*, 'Goth', or possibly *got*, 'god'. The second half is generally accepted to be *stafr*, 'staff'. It is a traditional name in the Swedish monarchy, having belonged to Gustav Vasa who led the Swedish fight for independence from Denmark, and eventually became Gustav I in 1521. The Spanish form of the name is currently popular among Hispanics in the USA.

PET FORM **Gösta** • VARIANTS **Gustavus, Gustaf** *French* **Gustave** *Spanish* **Gustavo**
★ Gustav II Adolf (1594–1632), king of Sweden, known as 'The Lion of the North'
★ Gustav Holst (1874–1934), English composer

Guthrie *m*
A Scottish and Irish surname that can come from various sources, which is occasionally used as a first name, particularly in Scotland.
☆ Guthrie Featherstone, character in John Mortimer's books and television series about *Rumpole of the Bailey*

Guto, Gutun, Gutyn *see* **Griffith**

Guy *m*
This name goes back to an old Germanic name *Wido*. It is unclear if this represents *witu*, 'wood', or *wit*, 'wide'. It was introduced into English via Norman French, which explains the change from 'w' to 'g' (compare WILLIAM and its French form *Guillaume*). The name had been popular in the Middle Ages but became virtually unusable after Guy Fawkes made it notorious. It was revived in the 19th century, but has only been quietly used since the 1920s.

VARIANT *Spanish, Italian* **Guido**

★ Guy de Maupassant (1850–93), French author
★ Guy Ritchie (1968–), English film director
☆ Guy of Warwick was the hero of a very popular medieval romance
☆ *Guy Mannering* (1816), a novel by Sir Walter Scott, which helped to revive the name

Gwalchmai *see* **Gavin**

Gwalter *see* **Walter**

Gwatcyn *see* **Walter**

Gwawr *f*
A modern Welsh name from the vocabulary word for 'dawn'. It is pronounced 'GOO-er' or 'gwar' depending on which part of the country you come from.

Gwen *f* **Gwyn** *mf*
Originally pet forms of the numerous Welsh names formed from *gwen*, *gwyn*, 'white, pure, blessed, holy', now used as independent names. Gwen is also a pet form of GUINEVERE, while Gwyn is also found as a pet form of names such as GWYNETH.

PET FORM **Gwenno** • VARIANTS **Gwin, Win(n)** *French (Breton)* **Gwenn** (mf)
★ Gwen Stefani (1969–), US singer
☆ Gwyn ap Nudd is the king of the underworld in Welsh folklore

Gwenael *see* **Gael**

Gwenant *see* **Gwynant**

Gwenda *f*
A Welsh first name formed from *gwen*, 'fair, blessed', and *da*, 'good'. It is also used as a pet form of GWENDOLEN.

Gwendolen *f*
This Welsh name is formed from *Gwen* and *dolen*, 'ring, bow'. Some see this as a reference to the circle of the moon and a possible link to a moon goddess. The name occurs in various contexts

in early Welsh tradition, for example as the name of the mother of the magician Merlin. It became popular among English speakers in the later 19th century and peaked in popularity in the 1920s.

VARIANTS **Gwendolyn(e)**, **Gwendoline**

☆ Gwendolen Fairfax, character in Oscar Wilde's *The Importance of Being Earnest* (1895)

Gweneira *f*
A Welsh name formed from *gwen* 'white' combined with *eira* meaning 'snow'; the Welsh equivalent of 'Snow White'.

VARIANT **Gwyneira**

Gweneth *see* **Gwyneth**

Gwenfrewi *f*
A Welsh name formed from *Gwen* and *frewi*, 'reconciliation'. It was the name of a 7th-century saint. There are many legends about her, including the story that she was killed and then restored to life, after which she rewarded the saint who revived her by making him a wind- and waterproof cloak. See also WINIFRED.

VARIANTS **Gwenfrewy**, **Gwenffrewi**

Gwenfron *f*
A Welsh name formed from *gwen* 'white, fair' and *bron*, 'breast', an alternative to BRONWEN.

Gwenhwyfar *see* **Guinevere**

Gwenith *see* **Gwyneth**

Gwenllian *f*
A Welsh name formed from *gwen* 'white, fair' and *lliant*, 'flood, foam', probably used to indicate fairness. The name was one of the most popular in medieval Wales.

★ Gwenllian ferch Llywelyn (d.1337), only child of Llywelyn ap Gruffydd, last Welsh prince of Wales, who has

become something of a symbol of the oppression of the Welsh

★ Gwenllian ferch Gruffydd (1097–1136), beautiful princess who was also a military leader against the Norman invasion of Wales

Gwennant *see* **Gwynant**

Gwenneth *see* **Gwyneth**

Gwil, Gwilim, Gwillym, Gwilym *see* **William**

Gwin *see* **Gwen**

Gwinifred *see* **Winifred**

Gwladus, Gwladys *see* **Gladys**

Gwydion *m*
The name of a magician, son of the goddess Don in the medieval Welsh *Mabinogion*. Its meaning is obscure, but 'to speak poetry' has been suggested.

★ Gwydion Brooke (1912–2005), Welsh bassoonist

★ Gwydion Pendderwen (1946–82), US neopagan writer

Gwydyr *see* **Victor**

Gwyn *see* **Gwen**

Gwynant *m*
A Welsh name derived from *gwyn*, 'white, fair', and *nant*, 'stream'. Llyn Gwynant is a lake in Snowdonia.

FEMININES **Gwenant**, **Gwennant**

Gwyneira *see* **Gweneira**

Gwyneth *f*
Despite its wide use, the meaning of this name is doubtful. It could be from the Welsh district name Gwynedd (probably from *gwen*, 'white, fair'), or it may derive from the vocabulary word *gwynaeth*, 'luck, happiness'. It seems to have originated with Gwyneth Vaughan, the pen name of the popular novelist Annie Harriet

Hughes (1852–1910). The name is further complicated by *Gwenith* which can either be a variant of Gwyneth or may come from the Welsh vocabulary word for 'wheat', used as a term of praise, much as 'the cream of...' is in English.

VARIANTS **Gwynedd, Gwynneth, Gweneth, Gwenneth**

★ Gwyneth Paltrow (1972–   ), US actress

Gwynfor *m*

Welsh name derived from *gwyn*, 'white, fair', and *mawr*, 'great, large'. It is a common Welsh place name.

VARIANT **Wynfor(d)**

★ (Richard) Gwynfor Evans (1912–2005), Welsh politician

Gwythyr *see* **Victor**

Gyles *see* **Giles**

Gypsy *f*

This name, from the vocabulary word with all its romantic associations, has been used as a first name since at least the late 19th century, although it has never been widespread. The word comes from a corruption of 'Egyptian',

although the Romany people actually come from northern India. Some now regard the term Gypsy as politically incorrect. Gypsy is often found combined with Rose, as in the famous Gypsy Rose Lee (Rose Hovick, 1911–70) actress, burlesque dancer and writer, about whom the musical *Gypsy* was written.

VARIANTS **Gipsy, Gypsie**

★ Gypsy Abbott (1896–1952), silent film star who may have introduced the name to the general public

Gyrd *see* **Godfrey**

Gytha *f*

An Old English name based on *gyth*, 'strife', and probably a shortening of a longer name. It was the name of both the mother and a daughter of Harold Godwinson, last Saxon king of England. The name was revived in the 19th century along with so many other Anglo-Saxon names, but never became popular.

VARIANT **Githa**

☆ Gytha 'Nanny' Ogg, so much more than just a witch, in Terry Pratchett's *Discworld* novels

H

Haadiyah *see* **Hadiya**

Haafiza *see* **Hafiz**

Haakim *see* **Hakim**

Haakon *see* **Håkon**

Haamed, Haameda *see* **Hamid**

Haashim *see* **Hashim**

Habakkuk *m*
This is from the Hebrew for 'embrace', it was borne by one of the minor prophets who gave his name to a book of the Bible. It was in use, quietly, between the 17th and the 19th centuries.
VARIANT **Habacuc**

Habib *m* **Habiba** *f*
These come from the Arabic word for 'darling, dear' and are popular names in the Muslim world. Habib has sometimes been anglicized as HAPPY.
VARIANTS **Habeeb, Habibah**
★ Habib Bourguiba (1903–2000), president of Tunisia
★ Dr Habiba Sarabi (1956–), Afghan campaigner for women's rights, first female provincial governor

Hacon *see* **Håkon**

Hadassah *f*
According to the Bible (Esther 2.7) Hadassah, 'myrtle', was the Jewish name of ESTHER, changed to hide her ethnicity from the Persian king when she was taken into his harem. It has been revived to join the stock of Jewish names in recent times.
PET FORM **Dassah** • VARIANTS **Hadas(s)a(h)**

Haden *see* **Hayden**

Hadi *m* **Hadia** *f*
This is the Arabic for 'leader, guide'. It is one of the names of Allah.
VARIANTS **Had(i)ya**

Hadil *f*
This is an Arabic name from the vocabulary word for the sound of a cooing pigeon.
VARIANT **Hadeel**

Hadiya *f*
An Arabic name meaning 'gift'. The masculine form, *Hadaya*, means 'gifts'.
VARIANT **Haadiyah**

Hadjar *see* **Hajar**

Hadrian *see* **Adrian**

Hadyn *see* **Hayden**

Hafiz *m* **Hafiza** *f*
Arabic names from the vocabulary word for 'guardian, custodian'. The names were originally honorifics given to people who had memorized the entire Koran.
VARIANTS **Haafiza, Hafeez**

Hafsa *f*
This is a name of disputed and obscure meaning. Some interpret it as meaning 'motherliness', some as 'gathering', while others make no attempt to explain it. It is a popular Muslim name because it was borne by one of the Prophet Muhammad's wives.
VARIANTS **Hafsah, Hafza, Hafswa**

Hagar *see* **Hajar**

Hagen, Hagun *see* **Håkon**

Haibah *see* **Hiba**

Haidar *m*
This is the Arabic for 'lion'. *Haidar Allah* was a name given to the Prophet Muhammad's son-in-law, Ali.
VARIANTS **Haider, Hayder**

Haidee *f*
This name was created by the poet Byron for the beautiful, innocent Greek girl with whom the young Juan falls in love, in his satiric epic *Don Juan*. It is probably based on the Greek *aidos* meaning 'modest', and is pronounced 'HAY-dee'. It is occasionally used as a respelling of HEIDI.
☆ Haydée, a French variant, is the name of the girl rescued from slavery by the Count of Monte Cristo, in the 1844 novel by Alexandre Dumas

Haiden, Haidyn *see* **Hayden**

Hailey, Hailie, Haillie *see* **Hayley**

Haim *see* **Chaim**

Hajar *f*
This is the name of the mother of Ishmael, the patriarch of the Arab race. In Islamic tradition Hajar was Abraham's second wife; when she gave birth to her son friction arose between her and the barren Sarah, and it was necessary to separate the two women. In the Old Testament, where a different version of her story is told, she appears as *Hagar*, a form also found among Arabs. In Hebrew, Hagar is interpreted as meaning 'flight'. The interpretation of the Arabic name is less clear, but it may be from *hajara*, the Arabic equivalent of the Hebrew word, meaning 'to flee, emigrate'. This is certainly the most popular explanation, as her name often appears in the form *Hajara*, reinforced by the fact that a re-enaction of part of her story is an important element of the

Hajj pilgrimage, which gets its name from the same root.
VARIANTS **Hadjar, Hajra, Hajrah, Hajjra, Hajjrah**

Hakim *m*
This is from the Arabic for 'wise, judicious'. The *All-Wise* is one of the titles of Allah. The variant *Akeem* is particularly found in Nigeria and among African Americans.
FEMININE **Hakeema** • VARIANTS **Hakeem, Haakim, Akeem**

Håkon *m*
This is a Scandinavian name from the Old Norse *Háon*, formed from *ha* which can be interpreted as either 'horse' or 'high', and *konr* meaning 'son'. The name has been prominent in the Norwegian royal family.
VARIANTS **Haakon, Hagen, Hagun** *Scottish* **Hacon**

Hal *see* **Harold, Henry**

Hala *f*
An Arabic name, from the word to describe the halo that sometimes appears around the moon.

Halarien *see* **Hilary**

Halim *m* **Halima** *f*
From the Arabic for 'patient, tolerant, clement', this is one of the names of Allah.
VARIANTS **Haleem, Haleema**

Halina *f*
This well-used Polish name is probably a variant of GALINA, perhaps influenced by HELEN.

Halle[1] *m*
This is a Scandinavian name, originally a pet form of names such as *Halldor* (from Old Norse *hallr*, 'rock', and *thorr*, the name of the thunder god Thor) and *Hallstein* (from *hallr* and *steinn*, 'stone').

Halle² f
This name was introduced to the general public by the US film actress Halle Berry (b.1968). She is said to have been named after the Halle Brothers department store. The name is pronounced 'halley'.
VARIANTS **Halley, Hallie** (it is not always possible to distinguish between variants of this name and of, **Hayley**)

Ham see Abraham

Hamdi m
This is an Arabic name, from the word meaning 'engaged in praising Allah'.

Hamid m Hamida f
Hamid is an Arabic name from the vocabulary word meaning 'praiseworthy, commendable'. It is one of the names of Allah. There are a number of closely related names based on the root meaning 'praise', all with strong religious connotations. As well as *Hamdi* 'praising', these include *Haamad* (m) and *Haamida* (f), 'praiser'; *Hamad*, 'much praising'; *Hamd* (m) and *Hamda* (f), 'praise'; and *Hamdani* (m) and *Hamdan* (f), 'much praise'. Hamdan is also the name of a tribe in Arabia, and the Hamdani dynasty ruled al-Jazira and Syria throughout the 10th century. This group of names is widely popular in the Muslim world.
VARIANTS **Haamed, Hammad, Ham(m)ud, Haameda, Hamideh**

Hamilcar m
Hamilcar Barca was a 3rd-century BC Carthaginian general, who was the father of the more famous HANNIBAL, and who is said to have raised his children to be implacable enemies of Rome. The name, which has come down to us via Latin, is formed from the Phoenician *hi*, 'friend, son', and *Melqart*, the name of a Carthaginian god. Surprisingly, considering the damage done to Rome by Hamilcar's son, the name is most likely to be found in its Italian form.
VARIANTS *Italian* **Amilcare** *Portuguese, Spanish* **Amilcar**

Hamish m
This is a Scottish form of JAMES. Gaelic languages have no 'j' sound, and so the usual form of James is SEAMUS and its variants. In Scots Gaelic this becomes *Sheumais* in the vocative, the case normally used when addressing someone, with the final 's' sound softened. Hamish developed from this. Although the name is found in other countries, it still has strong Scottish associations, and is currently well used there.

Hamna f
An Arabic name from the word for 'black grape'. It was borne by one of the sisters-in-law of the Prophet Muhammad.
VARIANT **Hamnah**

Hampus see John

Hamza m
Hamza was the name of the Prophet Muhammad's uncle. It is usually interpreted as deriving from the Arabic *hamuza*, 'strong, steadfast', which is an epithet of lions, a meaning that is sometimes given for the personal name.

Hana f
A popular Arabic name meaning 'happiness, bliss'. There is some overlap with the English name HANNAH.

Hanan f Hannan m
This is an Arabic name, meaning 'compassionate, tenderness, warm-heartedness', and is one of the titles of Allah.
VARIANT **Hanaan**
★ Hanan Ashrawi (1946–), Palestinian scholar and politician

Hani *m* Haniya *f*

An Arabic name meaning 'happy, delighted'.

VARIANTS **Hany**, **Haneeah**, **Hania**, **Haniy(y)a(h)**

Hank *m*

Hank, now an independent name or a pet form of HENRY, started out as a pet form of John. John came into English in two different forms, which explains why there are so many variants in the Celtic languages (see JOHN). The form John comes from Latin *Iohannes*, but JACK and Hank come from the medieval French form *Jehan*, source of modern French *Jean*. A pet form was created by dropping the first syllable of *Jehan*, giving *Han*, and then the old English diminutive ending -*kin* was added, giving *Hankin*. However, this was wrongly analysed as *Hank* with the French diminutive ending -*in*, thus producing the name Hank. The switch from John to Henry came about again through French influence, just as it affected the development of HARRY. The nasalized French pronunciation of *Henri*, sounding more like '-an' in the middle, explains why *Han*- was thought of as belonging with Henry. Hank is particularly used in the USA.

★ Hank Williams (1923–53), US country singer
★ Hank Azaria (1964–), US actor and voiceover artist for the television series *The Simpsons*

Hanke *see* John

Hannah *f*

This is an Old Testament name meaning 'He (God) has favoured me', and is thus equivalent to the New Testament ANNA or ANNE. In the Old Testament it is the name of the mother of the prophet Samuel. The name Anne has been closely associated with the mother of the Virgin Mary, and so after the Reformation, with the reaction against names associated with saints, the form Hannah was adopted as a replacement for what had been a very popular name. Hannah fell out of favour in the early 20th century, but has become very popular again in the last 25 years.

VARIANTS **Hana** *Hebrew* **Hanna** *Scandinavian* **Hanna**, **Hanne** (also a pet form of *Johanna*, see Joanna) *Yiddish* **Hena**

Hanne *see* Jane

Hannes *see* John

Hannibal *m*

This name comes from the Latin form of the Carthaginian *Hanni Ba'al*, 'grace of Baal', Baal being a god's name simply meaning 'Lord, King'. Hannibal was the name of the brilliant military strategist and son of HAMILCAR, brought up to be the enemy of Rome. Having invaded Italy via the Alps, he came very close to destroying the nascent Roman Empire in the 3rd century BC. Because Hannibal famously brought elephants with him, the name has frequently been used for elephants kept in circuses and zoos. For humans, the name has been recorded among English speakers since at least the 16th century (and from the 13th in France) and is said to have been a traditional name in Cornwall. It is still regularly given in Italy, but among English speakers is now more often found in fiction. Hannibal's brother's name, *Hasdrubal*, 'Baal helps', is also found in Italian and Spanish.

VARIANTS *Italian* **Anibale** *Spanish* **Anibal** *Italian, Spanish* **Asdrubale**

★ Annibale Carracci (1530–1609), Italian painter
☆ Dr Hannibal Lecter, murderer in the Thomas Harris 1988 novel and 1991 film *The Silence of the Lambs*

☆ John 'Hannibal' Smith, leader of the A-Team in the 1980s television series

Hans *see* **John**

Hansine *see* **Jane**

Happy[1] *f*
A 20th-century name, formed from the vocabulary word.

Happy[2] *m*
This is sometimes found as a masculine name, particularly in the USA where it is usually a result of immigration officials misunderstanding the Arabic HABIB.

Hari *m*
A Sanskrit colour name, with no exact correspondence in English, but covering shades including brown, yellow and tawny. It is also used as a name for animals with these colourings, including monkeys, lions and horses, and is particularly given to the horses of Indra. The word is also a title of both the gods Vishnu and Krishna, and in Sikh names takes the simple meaning 'God'.
VARIANT **Harikrishna**

Harinder *m*
An Indian name, particularly used by Sikhs, formed from HARI combined with the name of the god Indra.
VARIANT **Harenda**

Harish *m*
An Indian name meaning 'lord of the monkeys' formed from Sanskrit *han*, 'monkey', and *isha*, 'lord'. It is one of the titles of the god Vishnu.

Harjit *m*
A predominantly Sikh name meaning 'victory of god'.
VARIANT **Harjeet**

Harlan *m*
This surname, meaning 'hare-land', came into use in the USA as a first name in honour of Judge John Marshall Harlan (1833–1911), a great defender of civil rights. It has been little used since the 1980s, but the feminine form has been common in Canada.
FEMININE **Harleen**
★ Harlan Ellison (1934–), US science fiction writer

Harley *mf*
A surname, formed from the Old English *hara*, 'hare', and *leah*, 'clearing', now used as a first name. It is mainly found in the USA (although it is appearing increasingly in the UK), and has been used as a masculine name since the 19th century. It has only been regularly chosen for girls since the 1990s, but is now more common among girls than boys. The high status of the Harley Davidson motorcycle is thought to have influenced the spread of the name.
VARIANTS **Harlee, Harleigh, Harli(e)**

Harminder *mf*
This is a Sikh name meaning 'house of God'. Harminder Sahib is another name for the Golden Temple, the most important shrine of the Sikhs.
VARIANT **Harmander**

Harmony *f*
This is the vocabulary word that has been given as a first name since at least the 1970s, and is now in regular use in the USA. There is a growing trend for names with musical links such as ARIA and MELODY.
VARIANT **Harmoni(e)**
★ Harmony Korine (1973–), US film director (a rare example of the masculine use of the name)
☆ Harmony, Symphony, Melody, Rhapsody and Destiny were the 'angel' pilots in the 1960s television puppet series *Captain Scarlet and the Mysterons*. All their names have now come into use as given names

Harold *m*
An Old English name, formed from the elements *here*, 'army', and *weald*, 'ruler'. It was a traditional name among Scandinavian ruling families in the Middle Ages. In Britain it is strongly associated with Harold Godwinson, the last English king of England, defeated by William the Conqueror in 1066. It is, therefore, hardly surprising that it was scarcely used after the Conquest, until there was a major revival in the 19th century. It cannot have died out entirely, as there is an English St Harold about whom almost nothing is known, other than that he is supposed to have been killed while still a child in 1168. However, WALTER, a French Germanic name formed from the same elements in reverse order, was very popular in the Middle Ages. In the USA, between World War I and the early 1930s, Harold was occasionally used for girls. There, it remained one of the most popular boys' names throughout the 20th century, and is still more likely to be used in the USA than in the UK.
PET FORMS **Hal, Harry** • VARIANTS *German, Scandinavian* **Harald** *Italian* **Aroldo**
★ Harold Macmillan (1894–1986), English statesman and prime minister
★ Harold Pinter (1930–2008), English playwright
☆ Byron's poem based on his travels in the eastern Mediterranean, *Childe Harold's Pilgrimage* (1812–18), probably influenced the popularity of the name

Harpal *mn*
This is a mainly Sikh name based on the Sanskrit for 'One protected by God'.

Harper *mf*
This is an occupational surname, now used as a first name. It is mainly given to girls, as it came to public attention when Harper Lee (Nelle Harper Lee, b.1926) published her novel *To Kill a Mockingbird* (1960).

Harpreet *mf*
This is a mainly Sikh name based on the Sanskrit for 'God's love'.

Harri *see* **Henry**

Harriet, Henrietta *f*
Harriet is the feminine equivalent of HARRY, having developed from the more formal Henrietta. However, unlike Harry, which until recently was only a pet form of Henry, Harriet has long been an independent name. The name was introduced to England when Charles I married the French princess known formally as Henrietta Maria , but in her lifetime more familiar as *Henriette* Marie, who was named after both her parents. Henriette rapidly became Hariet(te) in common use. The name fell out of fashion in the early 20th century, but has recently become popular once again.
PET FORMS **Harrie, Hattie, Hat(ty), Hetty, Etta** • VARIANT **Harriette**
★ Harriet Martineau (1802–76), English writer
★ Harriet Beecher Stowe (1811–96), US writer and abolitionist
☆ Harriet Smith in Jane Austen's 1816 novel *Emma*
☆ Harriet Vane in Dorothy L Sayer's 1930s novels featuring Lord Peter Wimsey

Harris *m*
This is a common surname meaning 'descendant of HARRY'. However, since it is currently particularly popular in Scotland, it may be part of the trend there for using local island names as first names.

Harrison *m*
A surname meaning 'son of HARRY'. It has been recorded since the 19th

century, particularly in the USA, where it is thought presidents William H Harrison (1773–1841) and Benjamin Harrison (1833–1901) may have influenced its use. More recently, the fame of the US actor Harrison Ford (1942–) has spread the name.

★ (William) Harrison Ainsworth (1805–82), English historical novelist
★ Sir Harrison Birtwistle (1934–), English composer

Harry *m*
This was the standard medieval pet form of the name HENRY. It arose because Henry was introduced with the Norman Conquest in the French form *Henri*. The French nasalized pronunciation of the '-en' caused the 'n' to be dropped by the English, producing *Herry* or Harry. Harry is also used as a pet form of HAROLD. The name has been widely popular in recent years, more so than its more formal original. This is ascribed to the choice of Henry for the Prince of Wales's second son (b.1984), more commonly known as Prince Harry, and to the international success of the Harry Potter novels.

Harun *m*
This is the Islamic equivalent of AARON. In the Koran, as in the Old Testament, he is the brother of Mousa (Moses).
VARIANTS **Haroun, Haroon**

★ Harun al-Rashid ('the Rightly Guided') (766–809), 'Abbasid caliph featured in the *Arabian Nights*

Harvey *m*
This was originally a Breton name, *Haerviv*, which became *Hervé* in French. Its exact origin is disputed, although it is agreed that the general sense is that of a strong, vigorous warrior. The first element is interpreted as coming from *haer*, 'battle', or from *hoiarn*, 'iron', while the second half

could be *vy*, 'worthy', or *viv* (modern French *vif*), 'lively'. It was an important name in Brittany, as it was borne by a local 6th-century saint, and was brought to England by William the Conqueror's soldiers, many of whom were Breton. It was popular in the earlier Middle Ages, but declined later in the period, although it survived as a surname. Since it was an aristocratic surname, its revival in the 19th century was probably linked to the general taste in such names at the time. Harvey is currently popular in the UK, but little used in the USA.
PET FORMS **Harv, Harve** • VARIANTS **Harvie** *French* **Hervé**

★ Harvey Firestone (1868–1938), US founder of Firestone Tyres
★ Harvey Keitel (1939–), US actor
☆ Harvey is the eponymous imaginary rabbit in the 1944 play by Mary Chase, and in the subsequent film adaptation

Hasan *see* **Hassan**

Hashim *m*
This was the name of the great-grandfather of the Prophet Muhammad. It is thought to come from the Arabic *hashama*, 'he breaks', referring to the breaking of bread, because he provided food at the temple then at the Ka'ba.
VARIANTS **Haashim, Hashem**

Hasim *m*
An Arabic name, meaning 'decisive, defining'. *Hatim* has the same meaning.

Haskel *see* **Ezekiel**

Hassan *m*
Strictly speaking *Hasan* with one 's' is an Arabic name meaning 'handsome, excellent', and Hassan, with its double 's' means 'beautifier', both being derived from the root *hasuna*, 'to be good'. In practice in the West,

they are used interchangeably, with Hassan occurring more frequently. The name is a popular one, particularly among Shiites, in honour of Hassan and HUSSEIN, the two grandsons of the Prophet. They were the children of the Prophet's daughter Fatima and his cousin Ali, and are regarded as martyrs by Shiites. Twins are often given their names.

FEMININE **Has(s)ana** • VARIANT **Hasan**

Hat, Hattie, Hatty see Harriet

Havelock m

The name Havelock appears in the Middle Ages as the hero of the romance, *Havelok the Dane*, which, despite its foreign hero, is really a work of English nationalism. The name, which seems to be from the Old Norse *Hafleikr*, from *haf*, 'sea', and *leikr*, 'sport, play', was also used in real life, and so became a not uncommon surname. Some, however, claim the name is a Welsh form of OLIVER. The occurrence of Havelock as a first name in the 19th century was not, however, due to the fashion for reviving medieval names, but in honour of Major-General Sir Henry Havelock (1795–1857). He was an outstanding soldier whose death in the Indian Mutiny made him a national hero. He was popular with his troops, both for his bravery and, among some at least, his concern for their moral welfare arising from his strong religious convictions. This popularity led not only to a statue of him raised by public subscription and a generous pension voted to his family by Parliament, but to the adoption of his surname as a first name in Victorian England. The name is pronounced with three syllables, the 'e' being sounded.

★ Havelock Ellis (1859–1939), English physician and writer

☆ Havelock Vetinari, Patrician of Ankh-Morpork, in Terry Pratchett's *Discworld* novels

Hayden mf

This name has caused much confusion and puzzlement. It appears to have originated in Wales, and was certainly regarded as a Welsh masculine name until the later 20th century, when it spread through the English-speaking world and came to be used for both sexes. It is currently popular for both sexes in the USA and Australia, and is growing in popularity in the UK. The problem is that no one is quite sure where it comes from. Some people have identified it as a Welsh form of AIDAN. Others regard *Haydn* as the root and see it as being used by the music-loving Welsh in honour of the Austrian composer Josef Haydn (1732–1809), whose name comes from a form of the word 'heathen'. Less romantic is the suggestion that it is a use of a surname, either *Haddon*, 'hill covered with heather', or *Heydon*, 'hay meadow'.

VARIANTS **Haydn, Haden, Haiden, Hadyn, Haidyn, Haydyn**

★ Hayden Christensen (1981–), Canadian actor

★ Hayden Panettiere (1989–), US actress

Hayder see Haidar

Hayley f

This popular name comes from a surname, which is based on a place name, Hailey in Oxfordshire, meaning 'hay meadow'. It seems to have been coined for, and was certainly introduced to the general public by, the English actress Hayley Mills (b.1946), who was named after her mother, Mary Hayley Bell. There is now some overlap between forms of this name and HALLE.

VARIANTS **Hailey, Hailie, Haillie, Hayleigh, Haylie**

★ Hayley Westenra (1987–ㅤ), New Zealand soprano

Haym *see* **Chaim**

Hazel *f*
One of the many plant names adopted as first names in the 19th century. It may have originated in the USA, and was certainly particularly popular there from the late 19th century through to the 1930s. Having been out of favour internationally for some years, it currently shows signs of coming back into fashion. It is sometimes used with reference to eye colour.
★ Hazel Blears (1956–ㅤ), English politician
★ Hazel Dickens (1935–ㅤ), US bluegrass singer
☆ Hazel is the name of one of the rabbits in the 1972 Richard Adams novel *Watership Down*, a rare example of a masculine use

Heath *m*
This name serves as a masculine equivalent of HEATHER, being a synonym for the plant name. It can also be a shortening of *Heathcliff* ('dweller by a heather cliff'), as in the case of Australian actor Heath Ledger (1979–2008), whose fame increased public awareness of the name. Heathcliff is best-known as the brutal but romantic hero of Emily Brontë's 1847 novel, *Wuthering Heights*.

Heather *f*
This 19th-century plant name was particularly popular in the USA in the final quarter of the 20th century. It is now most likely to be found in Scotland, with which the heather plant is closely associated, and has been steadily used there since its introduction. See also ERICA.
★ Heather Mills (1968–ㅤ), English former model and former wife of Sir Paul McCartney

Heaven *f*
This vocabulary word has been used as a first name since at least the 1970s, but only came into more general use in the USA in the 1990s. *Haven*, although an independent vocabulary word, is sometimes used as a variant. Heaven is frequently found combined with forms of LEE.
VARIANT **Heavenly**

Hebe *f*
An ancient Greek name from *hebos*, 'young'. In Greek mythology, Hebe was the goddess of youth and cup-bearer to the Olympian gods. The name does not seem to have been used by English speakers before the 19th century, and its occasional modern use may be linked as much to the popular flowering garden shrubs as to the myth.
☆ Hebe is the name of a character in Gilbert and Sullivan's operetta *HMS Pinafore*

Heber *m*
This is a Hebrew name meaning 'enclave', which is borne by a number of minor Old Testament characters. It has been used in Ireland as a 'translation' of the Gaelic name EIBHEAR.

Hector *m*
This is a Greek name with strong Scottish associations. In the Greek legends of the Trojan War, Hector was a prince and mightiest warrior of Troy. His name is probably derived from Greek *ekhein*, 'to restrain, hold fast', which came to indicate 'defending', and was one of the titles of Zeus. The name came to Scotland as an 'English' version of the Gaelic name EACHANN, and is still often used there. It is also currently enjoying increasing popularity in the USA, where it has long been in regular use.

PET FORMS **Hec(k)(ie)** • VARIANTS *Italian* **Ettore** *Portuguese* **Heitor**

★ Hector Berlioz (1803–69), French composer

☆ Hector Zeroni ('Zero') in Louis Sachar's 1998 novel *Holes*

☆ *Hector's House* was a popular children's television puppet show in the 1960s and 70s in which Hector was a dog

Hedda *see* **Hedwig**

Hedley *m*

A surname that was used as a first name from the late 19th to early 20th century, but is now rare. It comes from a place name meaning 'clearing where heather grows'.

Hedwenn *f* **Heddwyn** *m*

These are Welsh names formed from *hedd*, 'peace', and the common Welsh name ending meaning 'fair, white, blessed'. They date from the late 19th or early 20th century. The masculine form was popularized by Ellis Humphrey Evans, who used *Hedd Wyn* as his bardic name, and was posthumously awarded the Bardic Chair at the 1917 National Eisteddfod, after his death in World War I.

Hedwig *f*

A German name formed from the elements *hadu*, 'struggle, contention', and *vig*, 'war'. It was a popular name in northern Europe from the 19th to early 20th century, but is now considered old-fashioned. In German the 'w' is pronounced with a 'v' sound. AVIS may be a related name.

PET FORMS **Hedy**, **Hedda** • VARIANTS *French* **Edwige** *Italian* **Edda**, **Edvige** *Scandinavia* **Hedda**, **Hedvig**

★ Hedy Lamarr (1913–2000), Austrian-born US actress

☆ Hedda Gabler, eponymous heroine of Ibsen's 1890 play

☆ Hedwig is Harry Potter's owl in J K Rowling's books

Hefin *m* **Hefina** *f*

Modern Welsh names, based on *haf* meaning 'summer'.

Hege *see* **Helga**

Heida *see* **Adelaide**

Heidi *f*

This is a Swiss pet form of *Adelheid*, the German form of ADELAIDE. It was made famous by Johanna Spyri's children's novel *Heidi* (1881) which was made into a film, starring Shirley Temple, in 1937. The film was the biggest box-office draw of the 1930s, after which Heidi entered the stock of names in the USA. It was particularly popular there in the 1970s.

VARIANTS **Heide(e)**, **Heidy**

★ Heidi Klum (1973–), German model

Hein, Heinrich *see* **Henry**

Heinz *m*

This is a pet form of the German *Heinrich* (HENRY), now used as an independent name. Similar pet forms are *Heini* and *Heike*.

★ Heinz Wolff (1928–), German-born British bioengineer

Heitor *see* **Hector**

Heledd *f*

Pronounced with the final 'dd' as in 'then', this is an old Welsh name of unknown meaning. It was borne by a 7th-century princess, and a poem in which she is portrayed lamenting the death of her brother, Cynddylan, is one of the gems of early Welsh poetry.

VARIANT **Hyledd**

Helen *f*

In Greek legend, this name was borne by the beautiful, semi-divine woman whose abduction triggered the Trojan War. The origin of the name is obscure, but it is often interpreted as something like '(sun)light, ray', or 'warmth', and linked to the Greek *helios*, 'sun'. However, despite her fame, it was not this Helen who spread the name widely though Europe, but rather St Helen or *Helena*, the mother of the Emperor Constantine. St Helen is credited with having found the True Cross in about AD 325. Although she was actually born in Turkey, British legend has it that she was a British princess. The name was immensely popular in medieval Europe, and developed innumerable variants including EILEEN, ELAINE, ELEANOR, ELLEN, ILONA, LENA and their variants. Indeed, Helen has so many variants and pet forms, that it is often a subjective judgement as to where the division lies between them and independent names.

VARIANTS **Helena** *Irish* **Léan(a)** *Dutch* **Heleen, Heleentje** *French* **Hélène** *German* **Helene, Alena, Leni** *Greek* **Eleni** *Hungarian* **Ilona, Ili, Ilka** *Italian, Spanish* **Elena** *Russian* **Yelena, Alyona** *Scandinavian* **Helene** *Spanish* **Ileana**

Helga *f*
This is a Scandinavian name meaning 'prosperous, healthy' from the same Germanic root as the English 'hale'. The name was later reinterpreted as deriving from *heilagr*, 'holy'. See also OLGA.

MASCULINE **Helge** • VARIANTS **Hege, Hella, Helle, Helje**

Heli *see* **Eli**

Heliose *see* **Eloise**

Helma, Helmi, Helmine *see* **Wilhelmina**

Helmut *m*
A German name from the Old German *helm*, 'helmet, protection', and *muot*, 'spirit'.

VARIANT **Helmuth**
★ Helmut Kohl (1930–), German statesman

Heloise, Héloïse *see* **Eloise**

Hema *mf*
This is an Indian name from the Sanskrit for 'gold, golden'.

VARIANT **Hem** (m)

Hena *f*
An Arabic name meaning 'henna, camphor'. See also HANNAH.

VARIANT **Hinna**

Henry *m*
The Old Germanic name *Haimric*, formed from elements meaning 'home' and 'rule, power', became *Henri* in French. It was brought to England by the conquering Normans, and has been one of the core masculine names ever since. The natural English pronunciation of the French name was HARRY, and it was not until the 17th century that the influence of the Latin form, *Henricus*, introduced a split between the formal Henry and the diminutive Harry. In the Middle Ages, *Hal* developed as a pet form of Harry. The 'r' sound is one of the least stable in English – standard pronunciation has dropped it at the end of many words, and it is the sound that is most problematic for some English speakers, who replace it with a 'w'. There is a regular pattern of using 'l' for 'r' in pet forms which is still in operation: Molly had developed from Mary by the 17th century; Sally from Sarah by the 18th; while Tel from Terry and Del from Derek are much more recent. Harry has, in recent years, reasserted itself as the dominant form of the name. For *Henriette* or *Henrietta* see HARRIET.

PET FORMS **Harry, Hank, Hal** • VARIANTS *Irish* **Einrí, Anraí** *Scots Gaelic* **Eanraig** *Welsh* **Harri** *Dutch* **Hendrik, Hein, Henk** *French* **Henri** *German* **Heinrich, Heinz, Henrik,**

Hinrich, Henning *Italian* Enrico, Rico, Enzo, Arrigo *Polish* Henryk *Portuguese* Henrique *Scandinavian* Hen(d)rik *Spanish* Enrique

Hephzibah *f*

A Hebrew name meaning 'my delight is in her'. Although in the Old Testament it is borne by the wife of King Hezekiah, its adoption in the 17th century comes from its use by the prophet Isaiah as an allusive term for Israel. The name is now very rare, and is usually pronounced with the 'ph' as 'p' rather than 'f'.

PET FORMS **Eppie, Effie, Hepsie, Heps(e)y**
• VARIANT **Hepzibah**
★ Hephzibah Menuhin (1920–81), US pianist

Herbert *m*

This is an old Germanic name formed from the elements *hari*, 'army', and *berht*, 'bright'. The name first appeared in British history in the 6th century when *Charibert*, King of Paris (the Germanic 'h' regularly became 'ch' in early Latin forms of names) married his daughter to the pagan Ethelbert of Kent. This brought Christians to Kent, and made it possible for St Augustine to have a safe base in Canterbury when he arrived to convert the English in 597. The name was quite popular in the Middle Ages, as shown by its frequency as a surname. Thereafter it died out, but was revived in the 19th century, probably as part of the trend to use aristocratic surnames, as Herbert was the family name of the earls of Pembroke. In the early 20th century, in the UK, it developed the slang sense of an inconsequential or stupid person, and fell out of favour. However, it remained among the most popular of masculine names in the USA into the middle of the 20th century.

PET FORMS **Bert, Herb, Herbie** • VARIANTS

French **Herbertine** (f) *German* **Heribert** *Spanish, Portuguese* **Her(i)berto**
★ Herbert George Wells (1866–1946), English author
★ Herbert Hoover (1874–1964), 31st president of the USA

Hercules *m*

This is the Latin form of the Greek *Herakles*, 'glory of Hera'. It was the name of the semi-divine hero, famous for his twelve labours. It has been in use among English speakers since the 16th century, but has always been rare. In Scotland it has been recorded as an anglicization of the Gaelic name *Athairne* (a rare name of uncertain origin) and of the Norse *Hacon* (see HÅKON).

VARIANTS *French* **Hercule** *Italian* **Ercole** *Spanish* **Heraclio**
★ Sir Elton Hercules John (1947–   ), English pop singer, songwriter and pianist
☆ Hercule Poirot in Agatha Christie's detective novels

Hereward *m*

An Old English name formed from the elements *here*, 'army', and *weard*, 'guardian', this was famously borne by an East Anglian, Hereward the Wake, who led local resistance to the Norman Conquest. As such it was quietly revived in the 19th century, but is now very rare.

Herman *m*

A Germanic name from the element *hari*, 'army', combined with 'man'. It was introduced to England by the Normans, continued in use into the 17th century, and was revived in the 19th. It was particularly popular in the USA, which is attributed to the influx of German immigrants. In Germany itself the name has a distinctive history. By the Renaissance it had been identified with the name of the

German tribal leader *Arminius* (the source of the German name *Armin*, see ARMAND), who defeated the Romans so comprehensively at the Battle of the Teutoburg Forest in AD 9. Whether or not this is correct – some would derive the name from *irmin*, see HERMINE below – Herman(n) became associated with German nationalism, and was particularly popular during the 19th century when the German states were united in one country.

FEMININES **Hermine, Ermine** • VARIANTS *German* **Hermann** *Italian* **Ermanno**

★ Herman Melville (1819–91), US novelist
★ Hermann Goering (1893–1946), German Nazi politician

Hermia *f*

This is a feminine form of the name of the Greek god *Hermes*. It was used by Shakespeare for one of the lead female roles in *A Midsummer Night's Dream*, but has never been as popular with parents as some of the other Shakespearean character names.

Hermine *f*

Although this name functions as a feminine form of HERMAN, it seems to represent the falling together of a number of different names. It is very rare in English, but is used in France and Italy in various forms. There is a Germanic name *Ermine* or *Irmine*, formed from the element *erm* or *irm* meaning 'entire, great, total', which may also lie behind the name *Arminius*, and which is found in names like EMMA. Another strand to the name is found in the Roman family name *Herminius*, which gives *Herminia* in the feminine, and which was in use as a name in Renaissance Italy in the form *Erminia*. This was made famous by Torquato Tasso, when he used it for a Saracen princess in his 1580 epic *Jerusalem Delivered*. Finally the

high status of ermine fur (ermine and Hermine are pronounced the same way in French), may have influenced the French use of the name. Ermine gets its name from the Latin *arminius mus*, 'Armenian mouse'.

VARIANTS **Ermine, Erminie**

Hermione *f*

Like HERMIA, this is a feminine form of the name of the Greek god *Hermes*, but unlike Shakespeare's Hermia, it is also a genuine ancient Greek name, traditionally borne by the daughter of Helen of Troy and her legitimate husband Menelaus. Even earlier, it was the name of the wife of Cadmus, in Greek mythology the founder of the city of Thebes. Shakespeare introduced Hermione to the fund of English names, by using it for the patient and long-suffering wronged wife in *A Winter's Tale*. It was taken up in the late 19th and early 20th century, and is still quietly but regularly used.

★ Hermione Baddeley (1906–86), English actress
★ Hermione Gingold (1897–1987), English actress
☆ Hermione Granger, key character in the *Harry Potter* books by J K Rowling

Hernán, Hernando *see* Ferdinand

Hero *f*

Yet another ancient Greek name introduced into English use by Shakespeare. In the Greek myth Hero was the beloved of LEANDER, who swam across the Hellespont every night to be with her, until one night he was drowned during a storm. The legend was a popular one in Renaissance England and was turned into verse by Christopher Marlowe. Shakespeare gave the name Hero to the wronged woman in *Much Ado About Nothing*, and it has been used occasionally since at least the 19th century.

Hershel *m*
A Yiddish name, originally a pet form of *Hirsh*, from the vocabulary word meaning 'hart, deer'. The feminine equivalent is *Hinde*.
VARIANTS **Hirsch, Herschel, Heshel, Heshi**

Hervé *see* **Harvey**

Heshel, Heshi *see* **Hershel**

Hester *f*
This is a variant of the biblical name ESTHER. The two forms were interchangeable for some time from the Middle Ages onwards, but are now regarded as separate names.
PET FORMS **Hettie, Hetty, Ester, Ettie, Etty**
★ Lady Hester Stanhope (1776–1839), English traveller and eccentric
☆ Hester Prynne, heroine of Nathaniel Hawthorne's 1850 novel *The Scarlet Letter*

Hettie, Hetty *see* **Harriet, Hester, Mehitabel**

Heulwen *f*
A Welsh name, currently widespread, meaning 'sunshine'. The related *Heulog*, 'sunny', is used for both sexes.

Hevel *see* **Abel**

Hew, Hewie *see* **Hugh**

Hezekiah *m*
An Old Testament name from the Hebrew for 'God strengthens', borne by one of the kings of Judah. It was adopted as an occasional name by the Puritans, who took it with them to the USA. It was in regular use there in the 19th century and survived into the 1920s. Thereafter it disappeared, but is just beginning to make a comeback, as part of a trend among certain communities for using biblical names.

Hiba *mf*
An Arabic name meaning 'gift'.
VARIANT **Haibah**

Hieronymous, Hieronymus *see* **Jerome**

Hilal *mf*
An Arabic name meaning 'crescent, new moon', the symbol of Islam.

Hilary, Hillary *mf*
This is the English form of the Latin name *Hilarius*, from *hilaris*, 'cheerful'. It was widely adopted in honour of the 4th-century writer and theologian St Hilary of Poitiers. Until the 19th century it was predominantly a masculine name, but is now rare for men. The spelling Hillary is the usual one in the USA, and has begun to appear more in the UK since politician Hillary Clinton came to the fore. ELLERY, a surname which comes from Hilary, is sometimes used as a first name.
PET FORMS **Hill(ie), Hilly** • VARIANTS **Hilarie, Hilaria** *Welsh* **Ilar** (m) *French* **Hilaire, Hilarion, Halarien** (ms), **Hilairie** (f) *Italian* **Ilaria, Ilario** *Russian* **Ilari, Illarion**
★ Hilary Mantel (1952–), female English novelist
★ Hilary Benn (1953–), male English politician
★ Hilaire Belloc (1870–1953), French-born British writer

Hilda *f*
This is a Germanic name, found on the Continent and in England, derived from the word for 'battle'. It was probably originally a short form of a name containing this element. It had died out by the end of the 14th century, but was strongly revived in the 19th century, in honour of St Hilda of Whitby (614–80). She was a learned abbess who was in charge of a joint monastery of nuns and monks, and was an adviser of kings and bishops. This made the name popular with those who supported a greater role for women and explains why her name comes up so often in educational

contexts. The name is not much used now.

VARIANTS **Hylda** *Dutch, German* **Hilde** *Italian* **Elda**

★ Hylda Baker (1905–86), English actress
☆ Hilda was the name of one of the Valkyries
☆ Hilda was the name of Rumpole's battle-axe wife in John Mortimer's books and television series about *Rumpole of the Bailey*

Hildebrand *m*

This is a German name formed from *hild*, 'battle, war', and *brand*, sword'. It was borne by an 11th-century saint, who became Pope Gregory VII, as well as by a major character in medieval German legendary literature.

PET FORM **Hildy**

☆ Hildy Johnson, reporter in Ben Hecht and Charles MacArthur's 1928 play, *The Front Page*, and in the subsequent film adaptations

Hildegard *f*

From the Germanic elements *hild*, 'battle', and *gard*, 'enclosure, garden'. It was a popular name in the early Middle Ages. Its most famous bearer is probably St Hildegard of Bingen (1092–1179), an extraordinary woman who combined her role as abbess of a large convent, with being a writer of politically influential letters, a scientist, a poet, a mystic, a theologian and the composer of some of the most admired music of the period.

PET FORM **Hildy** • VARIANT **Hildegart**

Hillary *see* Hilary

Hillel *m*

A Hebrew name from *halal*, 'praise'. It is briefly mentioned in the Old Testament, but its popularity comes from Hillel the Elder of Babylon, a famous and influential 1st-century BC rabbi.

Hind *f*

An Arabic name of unknown meaning, used because it was borne by one of the wives of the Prophet.

Hinde *see* Hershel

Hinna *see* Hena

Hinrich *see* Henry

Hippolytus *m*

The Latin form of the Greek *Hippolytos*, 'freer of horses', formed from *hippos*, 'horse' and *luein*, 'to free'. In Greek mythology Hippolytos was the son of Theseus and the Amazon Queen Hippolyta. When he rejected his stepmother PHAEDRA's advances she accused him of rape; he was cursed by his father and subsequently died in a chariot accident. However, the name's popularity in Roman Catholic countries comes from the 2nd-century theologian St Hippolytus.

VARIANTS *French* **Hippolyte** *Italian* **Ippolito** *Spanish* **Hipolito**

Hiram *m*

In the Old Testament, this name is borne by the king of Tyre who supplies both David and Solomon with rich materials to build the Temple at Jerusalem. Views are divided as to whether it is a Phoenician name of unknown meaning, or a shortening of the Hebrew *Ahiram*, 'my brother is exalted'. The name has been more common in the USA than the UK.

VARIANTS **Hyram, Hyrum**

★ Hiram Revels (1822–1901), first African-American senator in the USA
★ Hyrum Smith (1800–44), brother of Joseph Smith, founder of the Latter Day Saints (Mormons)

Hirsch *see* Hershel

Hob *see* Robert

Hodge *see* **Roger**

Holden *m*
A surname from the Old English meaning 'deep valley', which came into use as a first name after being given to the narrator of J D Salinger's 1951 novel *The Catcher in the Rye*. Salinger is said to have created the name Holden Caulfield after he saw a poster advertising a film starring the actors William Holden and Joan Caulfield.

Holly *f*
This is one of the plant names introduced at the turn of the 20th century. It is currently a widely popular name, and is often given to girls born around Christmas. It is very occasionally a masculine name, as in the character of Holly Martins in Graham Greene's *The Third Man*.
VARIANT **Holli(e)**
★ Holly Hunter (1958–   ), US actress

Homer *m*
This ancient Greek name is of uncertain origin, although its original form *Homeros* is identical with the vocabulary word for 'hostage'. It came into use among English speakers in the early part of the 19th century, and was very popular in the late 19th century in the USA, where there was a strong trend for naming children in honour of outstanding writers (compare MILTON, VIRGIL). Nowadays it is firmly associated with the accident-prone Homer Simpson in the cartoon television series *The Simpsons*.

Honey *f*
A pet name based on the vocabulary word, which is being used increasingly as a given name, particularly since celebrity chef Jamie Oliver gave it to one of his children.
VARIANT **Honie**
☆ Honey Wilkes is Ashley Wilkes's sister

in Margaret Mitchell's 1936 novel *Gone with the Wind*
☆ Honeychile Ryder, known as Honey, is a character in Ian Fleming's *Dr No* and in the 1962 film of the novel

Honoria, Honor *f*
Names based on the word 'honour' date back to ancient Rome; Emperor Theodosius the Great was voted the name *Honorius* as a title, and his niece became known as Honoria. There are a number of early saints with names such as Honorius and *Honoré* (the modern French masculine). Honor or *Honour* was used by the Puritans for both sexes. See also YNYR, ANEURIN.
VARIANTS *Irish* **Ónora, Nora, An(n)ora**
French **Honorine, Honorée** *Italian* **Norina**
★ Honor Blackman (1925–   ), English actress whose fame has made this the standard form of the name in the UK
★ Honoré de Balzac (1799–1850), French author
☆ Honoria Glossop in P G Wodehouse's *Jeeves* novels

Hopcyn *see* **Robert**

Hope *f*
When this name was introduced by the Puritans as one of their virtue names, along with the related *Hopeful*, it was given to both sexes but is now exclusively female. It's a popular choice for twins when used alongside one of the other virtue names, particularly FAITH. The French equivalent, *Espérance*, is used by French speakers.

Horace *m*
The Latin family name *Horatius* – sometimes found as an English first name – is of unknown, possibly Etruscan, origin. There were two famous bearers of the name. The first was the semi-legendary early Roman hero celebrated in Macaulay's 1842 poem 'How Horatius Kept the

Bridge'. The second was the poet Quintus Horatius Flaccus (65–8 BC), better known in English by the name of Horace. It was his fame that was most instrumental in spreading the name. It is found in Italian as *Orazio*, and this influenced the alternative form *Horatio*, most famously borne by Horatio Nelson (1758–1805). His daughter, *Horatia*, is a rare example of the feminine form. Horace was very popular in the 18th and 19th centuries, but is little used today.

PET FORM **Horry**

★ Sir Horace Walpole (1717–97), English writer

★ Horatio Herbert Kitchener (1850–1916), Irish-born British soldier and statesman

☆ Horatio Hornblower, hero of the series of maritime novels by C S Forester

Horst *m*

A German name which is either an alteration of *Horsa*, 'horse', the traditional name for the leader of the invading Anglo-Saxons, or derived from a word meaning 'wood, thicket'.

Hortense *f*

The French form of the feminine of the Roman family name *Hortensius*, from *hortus*, 'garden', also the source of the word 'horticulture'. Although in use by the 17th century, both in the UK and France, the name was most common in the 19th century.

VARIANT **Hortensia**

Hosanna *mf*

This is from the Hebrew for 'God save us'. Although the name has been in use since at least the 13th century, it peaked with the Puritans and has never been common.

VARIANTS **Hosannah** *French* **Osanne, Ozanne**

Hosea *m*

This is the standard English form of the Hebrew name *Hoshea*, 'salvation'. Hosea is a minor prophet of the Old Testament, and so was one of the names available to the Puritans. It was not uncommon in the USA in the 19th century and is still in occasional use. JOSHUA is a related name.

Hosni *see* **Husni**

Houston *m*

The name of this Texan city has been quietly used as a first name in the USA since the 1980s, but without ever gaining the popularity of its neighbour DALLAS. Houston was named after Sam Houston (1793–1863), first president of the Republic of Texas.

Howard *m*

This is the surname of the dukes of Norfolk, which probably came from a Scandinavian name meaning 'high warden', used as a first name. Like many other aristocratic surnames, it came into general use as a first name in the 19th century. It was particularly well used in the USA and remained in the top 100 boys' names from the late 19th century until the middle of the 20th. The pet form *Ward* can also be an independent name, derived from a surname meaning 'guard'.

PET FORMS **Howie, Ward**

★ Howard Hughes (1905–76), US millionaire

Howel, Howell *see* **Hywel**

Hoyt *m*

A surname, probably from a Middle English word meaning 'stick', which may originally have been a nickname for someone thin. It has been quietly but regularly used as a first name in the USA since at least the 19th century.

Hubert *m*

The Germanic name *Huguberht* was formed from the elements *hugu*, 'thought, mind', and *berht*, 'bright, famous', and became Hubert in French. It was very popular with the Normans, who introduced it to England, probably because they were keen on hunting and had a particular affection for the patron saint of their sport, St Hubert (665–727).

PET FORMS **Hugh, Bert, Bertie**

★ Hubert Humphrey (1911–78), US politician

Huda *mf*

Huda is an Arabic name meaning 'right path or guidance'.

★ Huda al-Sha'rawi (1879–1947), Egyptian campaigner for women's rights

Hudes *see* Judith

Hugh, Hugo *m*

This is a Germanic name which comes from *hug*, 'heart, mind, spirit'. It probably started out as a pet form of a longer name, as it was popular with the Frankish aristocracy who usually used two-part names. The Normans brought the name to England, where it became popular, but it died out in the 16th century only to be revived, along with other medieval names, in the 19th. Currently, the alternative form Hugo is the more likely to be used by English speakers, and has been common on the Continent in recent years. In Gaelic-speaking areas Hugh has been used to translate AODH and sometimes EOGHAN and UISDEAN.

PET FORMS **Hewie, Huey, Hughie, Shug(gie)** (Scottish) • VARIANTS **Hugina** (f) *Welsh* **Huw, Hew** *French* **Huges** (m), **Hug(u)ette** *Italiana* **Ugo, Ugolin**

★ St Hugh of Lincoln (c.1135–1200), English prelate, usually depicted in art with his pet swan, which would nestle with its head up Hugh's sleeve but attack anyone else

★ Huw Wheldon (1916–86), Welsh broadcaster

Hùisdean *see* Hugh, Uisdean

Hulda[1] *f*

A Scandinavian name, from *huld* meaning 'sweet, lovable'.

Hulda[2] *f*

A Hebrew name, meaning 'weasel, mole, rat', used because it was the name of a prophetess who warned Josiah of the destruction of Jerusalem (2 Kings 22).

VARIANTS **Huldah, Chulda**

Humayra *f*

This is an Arabic word, 'red', used because it was an alternative name for the Prophet's wife AISHA.

VARIANTS **Humaira, Humeira**

Humbert *m*

This Germanic name was formed from the elements *hun-*, meaning 'bear-cub' and, by extension, 'warrior', and *berht*, 'bright, famous'. Although it was introduced by the Normans it has never been much used in the UK, but was common in Italian ruling families.

VARIANTS *Italian* **Umberto** *Spanish, Portuguese* **Humberto**

★ Umberto Eco (1932–   ), Italian scholar and author

☆ Humbert Humbert, narrator, and lover of Lolita in Vladimir Nabokov's 1955 novel *Lolita*

Humeira *see* Humayra

Humphrey *m*

A Germanic name formed from the elements *hun-*, meaning 'bear-cub' and, by extension, 'warrior', and *frith*, 'peace'. The original spelling would have been with an 'f'; the 'ph' was introduced to make it look more like a classical name.

PET FORMS **Hump(ie), Humph** • VARIANTS **Humphry, Humfr(e)y** *Welsh* **Wmffre**

★ Humphrey Bogart (1899–1957), US actor

★ Humphrey Lyttleton (1921–2008),

English jazz trumpeter, cartoonist and broadcaster

Hunter *m*
An occupational surname, used as a first name. It has been popular in the USA in recent years.
★ Hunter Davies (1936–), Scottish author and journalist
★ Hunter S Thompson (1937–2005), US gonzo journalist

Husni *mf*
An Arabic name meaning 'excellence'.
VARIANT **Hosni**
★ Hosni Mubarak (1928–), president of Egypt

Hussein *m*
This Arabic name, originally a pet form of HASSAN, is an important one for Shiites as it was borne by the grandson of the Prophet who was their third imam.
FEMININE **Husayna** • VARIANTS **Husayn, Hus(s)ain**

Huw *see* **Hugh**

Hyacinth *mf*
This was originally a masculine name, *Hyakinthos* in Greek, borne by a youth beloved by the god Apollo in Greek mythology. When the god accidentally killed him, a flower (not the modern hyacinth) sprang from his blood. It was also borne by a popular 3rd-century saint, which spread the use of the masculine name in the early years of Christianity. In the 19th century it was reintroduced to English speakers as a feminine name (although there was an Italian female saint called Hyacinth in the 17th century), this time as part of the trend for flower names. See also JACINTA.
PET FORMS **Hy, Cynth, Sinty** • VARIANT French **Hyacinthe**
☆ Hyacinth Bucket, snobbish wife in the

1990s television series *Keeping Up Appearances*

Hylda *see* **Hilda**

Hyledd *see* **Heledd**

Hyman *m*
An alteration of *Hyam* (see CHAIM) from the Hebrew *hayyim*, 'life'. Traditionally, it was added to a very ill person's name in the hope of aiding recovery.
PET FORM **Hymie** • VARIANT **Hymen**
☆ Hyman Kaplan, anti-hero of the series of humorous books by Leonard Q Ross (Leo Rosten), about a language nightclass

Hypatia *f*
A Greek name from *hypatos*, 'highest'. It was famously borne by Hypatia of Alexandria, a 5th-century BC woman renowned as a mathematician, philosopher and astronomer, who was consequently murdered by a Christian mob. Charles Kingsley published a novel about her in 1853, which led to occasional use of the name.
PET FORM **Patsy**

Hyram, Hyrum *see* **Hiram**

Hywel *m*
This is a Welsh name meaning 'conspicuous, eminent'. It was a popular medieval name, found from at least the 9th century, which was revived in modern times. King *Hoel* of Brittany, who appears in Arthurian legend as King Arthur's relative and ally, is an early example of the name. Depending on where in Wales it is used, Hywel can be pronounced 'huwel' or 'howel'.
PET FORM **Hywyn** • VARIANTS **Howel(l)**
★ Hywel Bennett (1944–), Welsh actor
☆ *Howl* in Diana Wynne Jones's 1986 novel *Howl's Moving Castle* (made into an animated film in 2004), is really a *Howell*

I

Iagan *see* **Aidan**

Iago *m*
This is a form of the name JAMES found in Wales and parts of Spain (compare SANTIAGO). The initial 'I' comes from the old spelling and pronunciation of the Latin form of James, *Iacomus*. Iago was in use in Wales by the 7th century.
★ Iago ap Ieuan (1833–1902), Welsh composer of the tune of 'Hen Wlad fy Nhadau' ('Land of my Fathers')
☆ Iago, villain of Shakespeare's *Othello* (1603/4)

Ian, Iain *m*
Ian is the Scottish form of JOHN. It does not seem to have been used in Scotland before the 19th century, and was widely popular outside the country in the 20th. The Gaelic spelling, *Iain*, is currently the more common in Scotland. Ian is now occasionally found used as a feminine, sometimes as *Iana*.
★ Sir Ian McKellen (1939–   ), English actor
★ Iain Banks (1954–   ), Scottish author

Iannis *see* **John**

Ianthe *f*
This name, pronounced 'eye-an-thi', is derived from the classical Greek words *ion*, 'violet', and *anthos*, 'flower'. In Greek mythology it was the name of a sea nymph. It was in use on the English stage in the 17th century, and had a brief flurry of popularity in literary circles in the 19th century, appearing in poems by Byron, Shelley and Walter Savage Landor. Shelley also chose it for his daughter in 1813.

VARIANT **Iantha**

Ianto *m*
This is a Welsh name, originally a diminutive of IEUAN which is a Welsh form of JOHN.
☆ Ianto Jones, character in the television series *Torchwood*

Iarlaith *m*
This is an Irish name pronounced 'EE-AR-la'. The second element seems to be from the Irish *flaith*, 'lord', but the meaning of the first part in unknown. The name is primarily found in the district of Galway, where it is borne by a local saint. It is anglicized as *Jarlath*.
VARIANT **Jarlath**

Ib *mf*
As a masculine, Ib is a Danish first name, perhaps originally a pet form of JACOB. As a feminine, it is an old pet form of ISOBEL.
PET FORMS **Ibby, Ibbie**

Ibrahim *m*
Ibrahim is the Arabic equivalent of ABRAHAM. It is derived from the Arabic *abu*, 'father', and *rahim*, 'kind'.
VARIANTS **Ibraheem, Ebrahim**

Ichabod *m*
Pronounced with the 'ch' as a 'k', this has always been a rare name, although it was used by the Puritans. It appears in the Old Testament as the name of the grandson of ELI and son of PHINEAS. It comes from the Hebrew meaning 'where is the glory?', and was given to the child because he was born on the day that the Philistines captured the Ark of the Covenant. As

a distinctively Puritan name, it was used by Washington Irving for Ichabod Crane, the main character in his story *The Legend of Sleepy Hollow* (1820), set in Connecticut. There was also a real Ichabod Crane, who was a New England colonel in the US army; Irving is thought to have met him and borrowed his name.

Ida *f*

A Germanic name, brought to England by the Normans, which probably comes from *id*, 'work, labour'. It was among the many medieval names revived in the 19th century, particularly after it was used by Tennyson in his 1847 poem *The Princess*, a work that was taken by Gilbert and Sullivan as the basis of their comic opera *Princess Ida* in 1870. The name is not much used by English speakers at present, but is still popular in Scandinavia. Some may have used the name as a short form of IDONEA, and in Ireland Ida is occasionally found as an English form of the Irish *Ide* or *Ita*, a saint's name which may come from the word *ita* meaning 'thirst'.

★ Ida Lupino (1918–95), English-born US film actress and director

Idonea *f*

This name, which is pronounced 'eye-DOH-nee-a', is particularly associated with north-east England, as befits its Old Norse ancestry. It comes from the name of the Old Norse goddess *Ithunnr*, often found in the Latinate form *Iduna*, who was in charge of the apples that kept the gods young. The name probably comes from *ith*, meaning 'again', although it may derive from the same root as IDA. Iduna became *Idony* in the Middle Ages, a popular name in the 11th and 12th centuries, which appears as Idonea in official documents, perhaps under the influence of the Latin word *idonea*, 'suitable'.

VARIANT **Idonia**

Idris[1] *m*

In Welsh, Idris is an ancient name formed from the elements *iud*, 'lord', and *ris*, 'ardent'. In Welsh tradition Idris the Giant was an astronomer who used to observe the heavens from the mountain known as Cader Idris ('Idris's Chair'). It is said that anyone who spends the night there will find death, madness or poetic inspiration. The name was popular in the Middle Ages and was revived in the 19th century.

Idris[2] *m*

In Arabic, Idris is the name of the 'true man, a prophet' known as ENOCH in the Old Testament.

VARIANTS **Idries, Idrees**

★ Idris I (Idris ibn Abdullah) (d.791), founder of the Idrisid Dynasty of Morocco
★ Idries Shah (1924–96), Indian-Afghan Sufi author

Idwal *m*

An ancient Welsh name, prominent in princely houses from the 7th century through to the 11th, particularly in the kingdom of Gwynedd. It comes from the elements *iud*, 'lord', and *(g)wal*, 'wall, rampart'.

★ Idwal Foel (the Bald) (d. 942), ruler of Gwynedd
★ Idwal Jones (1887–1964), Welsh author who wrote novels and non-fiction about California. Roughly contemporary with him, although slightly younger, was a Welsh humorist of the same name

Ieasha *see* **Aisha**

Iefan *see* **John**

Iesha *see* **Aisha**

Iestin, Iestyn *see* **Justin**

Ieuan *m*

This is a Welsh form of JOHN, derived from the Latin form *Johannes*, while the alternative form of John, *Siôn*, comes from the French *Jean*. Confusingly, Ieuan also appears as *Iefan*, and is then shortened to *Ifan*. This is the source of the surname EVAN. IANTO is a pet form. A further variant, *Ioan*, is found in the Welsh Bible.

VARIANTS **Iwan, Ioan**

★ Ioan Gruffudd (1973–   ), Welsh actor

Ifor *m*

An old Welsh name of unknown meaning. Since it is pronounced in the same way as IVOR it is sometimes anglicized in this form, although the two names are unrelated.

Iftikhar *m*

An Arabic name, meaning 'pride', which is also found in the fuller form *Iftikharuddin*, 'pride of the religion'. The name is particularly popular in Pakistan.

★ Iftikhar Ali Khan, Nawab of Pataudi (1910–52), cricketer who both captained the Indian team and played for England

★ Iftikhar Muhammad Chaudhry (1948–   ), Chief Justice of Pakistan

Ignatius, Inigo *m*

Ignatius is a version of the Latin family name *Egnatius*, which is of unknown origin, possibly Etruscan. It was altered to Ignatius under the influence of the Latin *ignis*, fire. It is chiefly used today in honour of the Spanish saint, Ignatius Loyola (1491–1556), although there were also earlier saints called Ignatius. In the Middle Ages the name was popular enough in Spain to develop a shortened form, Inigo, which was Loyola's birth name. This came to England in the 16th century, when Mary I married Philip of Spain, and Spanish names briefly became fashionable, particularly among devout Catholics. One such bearer of the name was Inigo Jones, who

passed it on to his more famous son (1573–1652), the architect, who in turn bestowed the name on his son. Inigo Jones's association with Wales led to the name being used there, but it has not been common since the 17th century, although there has been some interest in the name in recent years.

PET FORM **Iggy** • VARIANTS *Dutch* **Ignaas** *French* **Ignace** *German* **Ignatz** *Italian* **Ignazio** *Polish* **Ignacy** (m), **Ignacja, Iga** (fs) *Spanish* **Ignacio, Nacho, Nacio** *Russian* **Ignati**

Igor *m*

This is a Russian variant of the Scandinavian name IVOR. It was taken to Russia in the 9th century by the Rus, the Scandinavian settlers who gave Russia its name.

VARIANT **Ygor**

★ Igor Stravinsky (1882–1971), Russian-born US composer

☆ Igor has become the traditional name of the sinister servant in the horror genre, particularly material based on *Frankenstein* or *Dracula*. The name is not found in the original written works, but seems to have been introduced in 1930s films

Ike *see* **Isaac**

Ilan *m* **Ilana** *f*

A modern Hebrew name meaning 'tree'.

Ilar, Ilari, Ilaria, Ilario *see* **Hilary**

Ileana , Ili *see* **Helen, Ilona**

Ilia, Ilie *see* **Elias**

Iliana *see* **Ilona**

Ilka *see* **Helen, Ilona**

Illarion *see* **Hilary**

Illiam *see* **William**

Illtyd *m*
This is a Welsh name formed from *il*, 'multitude', and *tud*, 'land'.
VARIANT **Illtud**
★ St Illtyd was a 6th-century saint who founded the monastery at Llantwit Major (the place name being a corruption of Llan-Illtud, 'Church of Illtud')

Ilma *see* **Wilhelmina**

Ilona *f*
Ilona is a form of HELEN used in a number of European languages including German, Hungarian and Polish.
PET FORMS **Ilonka, Ili, Ilka** (Hungarian)
• VARIANTS *Romanian, Spanish* **Ileana** *Spanish* **Iliana**

Ilsa *see* **Elizabeth**

Ilse *f*
A German form of ELIZABETH.
VARIANT **Ilsa**
☆ Ilsa Lund, heroine of the 1942 film *Casablanca*

Ilya, Ilyaas, Ilyas *see* **Elias**

Imad *m*
An Arabic name meaning 'pillar'.

Iman *mf*
An Arabic name meaning 'faith'. See also AMIN.
VARIANTS **Imaan, Imani, Imen**
★ Iman (1955–), Somalian-born supermodel

Imelda *f*
This is the Italian form of the Germanic name *Irmhild*, formed from the elements *irmin* or *ermin*, 'whole, entire', and *hild*, 'battle'. It came into more general use in honour of the 14th-century saint, Imelda Lambertini. It is mainly used in Italy, Spain and, among English speakers, in Ireland.

★ Imelda Marcos (1929–), former First Lady of the Philippines
★ Imelda Staunton (1956–), English actress

Imen *see* **Iman**

Immaculata *f*
Taken from the Latin title of *Maria Immaculata*, given to the Virgin Mary with reference to the Immaculate Conception, this name is mainly found among English speakers in Ireland, sometimes in the form Mary Immaculata.
VARIANTS *Italian* **Immacolata** *Spanish* **Immaculada**

Immanuel *see* **Emmanuel**

Immy *see* **Imogen**

Imogen *f*
This name probably first appears in the 11th-century *History of the Kings of Britain*, by Geoffrey of Monmouth, as *Ignoge*, wife of Brutus, the mythical first king of Britain. By the 16th century, Ignoge has become 'fayre *Inogene* of Italy' in Spenser's *Faerie Queene*. In Holinshed's *Chronicles*, which Shakespeare used as the source of his play *Cymbeline*, she appears as *Innogen*. This was probably the form that Shakespeare originally used, for someone who saw an early production of the play gives the name as *Inogen*. However, when the play was first printed in 1623 the 'nn' seems to have been misread as 'm', for the name appears there as Imogen. There have been various suggestions as to the name's meaning, most of which centre on the role of Cymbeline's daughter, ignoring the Ignoge form, and the fact that she was supposed to be Greek. There is a record from c.1000 of a Breton lady called *Ynoguen*, which could be the same name. In this case the second element may be the same

as the Welsh *gwen*, 'white, fair'. The form Innogen has been linked to Latin *innocens*, 'innocent', but the most popular explanation links the name to the Gaelic *inghean* meaning 'daughter, maiden, girl'. The name has been popular in the UK in recent years.

PET FORM **Immy** • VARIANT **Imogene**
★ Imogen Holst (1907–84), English composer and conductor
★ Imogen Stubbs (1961–), English actress

Imre, Emeric *m*

Imre is the Hungarian form of the German Emeric. The name is popular in Hungary thanks to St Imre, an 11th-century prince who died young and was canonized for his piety. The name was sometimes Latinized as *Henricus*, which has led to it being regarded as a form of HENRY, but it is more likely that Imre (pronounced as if there is an acute accent on the 'e') and Emeric come from the Germanic elements *amal*, 'work' (or possibly *heim*, 'home'), and *ric*, 'rule', and are the same as *Almeric*, source of AMERICA.

VARIANTS **Emmeric, Emerick, Emmerich**
★ Imre Nagy (1895–1958), Hungarian prime minister deposed by the Russian invasion in 1956
★ Imre Kertész (1929–), Hungarian author who won the Nobel Prize for Literature in 2002
★ Emeric Pressburger (1902–88), Hungarian screenwriter, director and producer

Ina *f*

A name with several sources. It can be a short form of any name ending in *-ina*; it can be a variant of ENA; or in Ireland it can be a saint's name, also found as *Aghna*, perhaps an Irish form of AGNES.

Inara *f*

This can come from the Arabic for 'ray of light, illumination'. It has

started to be used outside the Arabic-speaking world under the influence of the character of Inara Serra, from the television series *Firefly*.

VARIANT **Inaara**

Inaya *f*

An Arabic name meaning 'concern, solicitude'.

VARIANTS **Inaaya, Inayah**

Inci *f*

A Turkish name meaning 'pearl'.

Indeg *f*

In early Welsh literature, Indeg is the name of one of the great beauties at King Arthur's court and, some say, Arthur's mistress. So great was her fame that she became the standard of beauty in Welsh poetry.

Inderjit *mf*

This is an Indian name, derived from the name of the god Indra combined with the Sanskrit element *jit*, 'conqueror', indicating 'conqueror of Indra'. In the *Ramayana* it is the name of the son of the demon king Ravana. A related masculine name is *Inderpal*, from Indra and *pala*, 'protector'. Both names are particularly used by Sikhs.

India *f*

The name of the country (which comes from the River Indus) used as a first name. It was first introduced to the general public as a given name in Margaret Mitchell's 1936 novel *Gone with the Wind*, set during the American Civil War. However, it only came into common use much later, in part publicized by the model India Hicks. In her case she was named after the country because her grandfather, Lord Mountbatten, had been the last viceroy of India.

PET FORMS **Indi(e), Indy**

Indiana *mf*

Although best-known from the *Indiana*

Jones movie franchise, Indiana is more often used as a feminine rather than a masculine name. It is borne by a female character in Fanny Burney's 1796 novel *Camilla*, and was used as an occasional feminine name in the USA in the 19th century. Currently, it is quietly but regularly used.
PET FORMS **Indi(e)**, **Indy**

Indigo *mf*
An uncommon name given a certain amount of publicity after it was chosen by some people in the media for their children. The colour gets its name from INDIA, being a dye first produced there.

Indira *f*
An Indian name from the Sanskrit word for 'beauty, splendour'. It is one of the names of the goddess LAKSHMI.
★ Indira Gandhi (1917–84), assassinated prime minister of India

Indra *m*
The name of the Hindu god of the sky and rain who, like the Greek Zeus, uses the thunderbolt as his weapon. The origin of the name is unclear, but may come from the Sanskrit for 'possessing raindrops'.

Ineke *see* Ingrid

Ines, Inés *see* Agnes, Innes

Ingelbert *see* Engelbert

Ingram *m*
This is an old first name which became a surname, which was then turned into a first name again. The Normans brought with them the name *Engelram*, of which the second element is the Germanic *hramm*, 'raven'. The first element is probably the name of the Norse fertility god *Ing* (compare INGRID), but may be the ethnic name *Engel*, 'Angle'. The name remained in use into the 17th century – for example Ingram Frizer, who died in

1627, was implicated in the murder of Christopher Marlowe – and was revived in the 19th century.

Ingrid *f*
This is a Scandinavian name derived from the Norse god of fertility, *Ing*, combined with either the element *frithr*, 'beautiful', or *rida*, 'ride'. Related feminine names, rarely used outside Scandinavia, include *Ingeborg* (Ing + *borg*, 'fortification'), *Ingegerd* or *Ingegard* (Ing + *garthr*, 'enclosure'); masculines are *Ing(e)mar* (Ing + *maerr*, 'famous'), and *Ingvar* or *Yngvar* (Ing + *arr*, 'warrior').
PET FORMS **Inge**, **Inga**, **Inka**, **Ineke**, **Inger** (fs)
★ Ingrid Bergman (1915–82), Swedish film star
★ Ingmar Bergman (1918–2007), Swedish film director

Inigo *see* Ignatius

Inka *see* Ingrid

Innes *mf*
This Scottish name can have two sources: it can either be a phonetic spelling of the Gaelic pronunciation of the name ANGUS and the surname that comes from this, or it can be from the Gaelic *inis*, 'island', which is also the name of a district and barony in Moray. It has traditionally been a masculine name, which is currently popular in Scotland. More recently it has started to be used occasionally as a feminine name, perhaps influenced by *Ines*, the Spanish form of AGNES.
VARIANTS **Ines**, **Innis**
★ Brigadier General Innis Doyle (1873–1919), less famous brother of the author Sir Arthur Conan Doyle

Innocent *m*
This name is widely known as that of 13 popes, but is little used by English

speakers. It comes from the Latin *innocent*, 'without harm, innocent'.

VARIANTS *Italian* **Innocenzo** *Russian* **Innokenti**, *Kenya Spanish* **Inocencio**

Ioan *see* **Ieuan**

Ioanna *see* **Joanna**

Ioannes, **Ioannis** *see* **John**

Iobhar *see* **Ivor**

Iokua *see* **Joshua**

Iolanda, **Iolande**, **Iolante** *see* **Yolanda**

Iole, **Iolanthe** *f*
Iole is the Greek word for 'violet', and in mythology was the name of a Greek princess with whom Hercules fell in love. Iolanthe is usually analysed as deriving from *iole* and *anthos*, 'flower', and described as a modern name, but it is found in medieval French as a variant of YOLANDA, and the two names seem to have influenced each other. In Wales, the form *Iola* can also be a feminine of IOLO. Iole is pronounced with three syllables, but use varies as to whether the stress is on the first or second syllable.

VARIANT **Iola**

☆ Iolanthe, eponymous heroine of Gilbert and Sullivan's 1882 comic opera

☆ Iola Morton, girlfriend of Joe Hardy, in the long-running US series of children's detective books *The Hardy Boys*

Iolo *m*
A Welsh name which comes from a pet form of IORWORTH, although it is sometimes regarded as a form of JULIUS.

VARIANT **Iolyn**

★ Iolo Goch ('the Red') (c.1320–c.1398), prominent Welsh poet, noted for his poems in praise of Owen Glendower

★ Iolo Morgan (1747–1826), poetic name of Edward Williams, Welsh poet,

antiquarian and literary forger, who refounded the bardic tradition in Wales

Iomhvair *see* **Ivor**

Ion *m* **Iona¹** *f*
Welsh names, from *Ionawr*, 'January'. Ion is also a Romanian form of JOHN.

Iona² *f*
This is the name of the Scottish island, famous for its religious foundation and as the burial place of Scottish kings, used as a first name. It seems to have come into use in the late 19th century, and only spread from Scotland comparatively recently.

★ Iona Opie (1923–), English researcher on childhood, folklore and children's literature

Ionatán *see* **Jonathan**

Ione *f*
This name is based on the Greek for 'violet'. It features in a minor way in Greek literature, being borne by one of the Nereids, the daughters of Ocean, in the writings of Apollodorus of the 2nd century BC. In 1834, the name was used by Edward Bulwer-Lytton for the heroine of his highly successful novel *The Last Days of Pompeii*. He took it either directly from *ione* or from the Ionians, an ancient Greek people who inhabited Athens which was also known as Ion, 'the city of the violet crown' (compare DORIS). Ione was taken up as a first name after the publication of Bulwer-Lytton's book. The name is pronounced with the syllables 'eye-oh-nee'. See also IOLE.

★ Ione Skye (1970–), English-born US actress

Iorworth *m*
A Welsh name based on *ior*, 'lord', and *berth*, 'handsome', found in the early genealogies of the kings of Powys. It came to be thought of as the Welsh

equivalent of EDWARD, although the names are unconnected.

PET FORM Iolo • VARIANT Yorath

Iosif see **Joseph**

Ippolito see **Hippolytus**

Ira m
An Old Testament name from the Hebrew for 'watchful'. It was borne by one of King David's priests. The name was taken up by the Puritans in the 17th century, despite the fact that it is easily mistaken for a female name, and taken by them to the USA. In Russia Ira is a pet form of IRENE.

★ Ira Gershwin (1896–1983), US lyricist
★ Ira Levin (1929–2007), US author

Irene f
Irene (originally *Eirene*) was the Greek goddess of peace, which is also the meaning of her name. In the past, Irene was usually pronounced in the Greek manner, with three syllables 'eye-ree-nee', but the two-syllable 'eye-reen' is now the norm. The name spread, particularly in the Christian Orthodox East, because it belonged to a number of saints, one of whom, Irene of Athens (c.752–803), managed to become a saint despite being the first woman to rule as emperor of Constantinople in her own right, in part through murdering her own son. There is a masculine equivalent, meaning 'peaceable', which is not used by English speakers, but which appears as *Iréné* in French, *Ireneus* in Dutch and *Irinei* in Russian.

PET FORMS René, Renie • VARIANTS Irena *Irish* Eireen *French* Irène *Russian* Irina, Irinei, Ira

Irial m
An early Irish name of unknown meaning which has been revived in modern times. The stress is on the first syllable.

Irina, Irinei see **Irene**

Iris f
In Greek mythology, Iris is the goddess of the rainbow, which she used as a bridge from heaven to earth to carry messages for the gods. In the 16th century the name was given to the flower because it came in so many colours. Use as a first name dates from the 19th century and was probably taken from the flower, as flower names were fashionable at that time.

★ Iris Murdoch (1919–99), Irish novelist and philosopher

Irish see **Catherine**

Irma f
This was originally a pet form of names such *Irmengard* (see ERMENGARD) or *Irmentrud* (see ERMINTRUDE).

☆ Irma, the stereotypical 'tart with a heart', in Billy Wilder's 1963 film *Irma la Douce*

Irmengard, Irmgard see **Ermengard**

Irmhild see **Imelda**

Irmingard see **Ermengard**

Irmtraud, Irmtrud see **Ermintrude**

Irvine, Irving m
These names can have two different origins. One is as a variant of the German name *Erwin* formed from *era*, 'honour', and *win*, 'friend'. The other is as a Scottish surname taken from place names meaning 'fresh water'. Irving is particularly found in the USA where it has been adopted as a naturalized form of the Jewish name ISRAEL.

VARIANTS Irvin, Ervyn

★ Irving Berlin (1888–1989), Russian-born US songwriter

Irwin m
This is either another variant of *Erwin* (see IRVING, above) or from the English surname, which is derived from an Old English name composed of *eofor*,

'boar', the symbol of warriors and the god Frey, and *wine*, 'friend'.

★ Irwin Shaw (1913–84), US writer

Isa *see* **Jesus**

Isaac *m*
This is a biblical name borne by the son of Abraham, whom Abraham believed he had been ordered by God to sacrifice, until a ram was finally offered in the son's place. The name may originally be pre-Hebrew, but it is usually linked to the Hebrew for 'he laughed' because, according to the story, Abraham laughed at the idea that he and Sarah would have a son in their old age. It was used in the Middle Ages and by the Puritans, and in recent years there has been a surge of interest in the name, with it getting into the top 50 choices for boys in many parts of the world.

PET FORMS **Ike, Zac, Zack** • VARIANTS **Izaak** *Arabic* **Ishaq** *German, Russian* **Isaak** *Hebrew* **Yitzak, Itzhak** *Scandinavian* **Isak** *Yiddish* **Itzik, Itzl**

★ Sir Isaac Newton (1642–1727), English scientist and mathematician
★ Isaac Asimov (1920–92), Russian-born US scientist and writer

Isabel, Isobel *f*
Isabel, or Isobel (neither is more 'correct' than the other, and the relative popularity of the two forms varies over time), may seem a long way from ELIZABETH, but is the same name. In the early Middle Ages in Provence, and later in the rest of France and in Spain, the first syllable, which sounded like the article *el*, was dropped to produce the form *Isabeth*, which was then altered in French to *Isabeau*. However, probably because this seemed too masculine an ending (*beau* being the French masculine for 'fair, handsome') it was further changed to Isabel. The name had reached England by the early 13th century. For generations during the Middle Ages, Isabel and Elizabeth were interchangeable.

PET FORMS **Is, Izzie, Izzy, Bel, Bella, Ella, Ib(bie), Tibby** (archaic) • VARIANTS **Isabelle, Isabella, Isobelle, Isobella, Izabel(le), Ysabel, Ysobel** *Irish* **Sibéal** *Scottish* **Beileag, Isbel, Iseabail, Ishbel**

Isadora *see* **Isidore**

Isaiah *m*
Isaiah, meaning 'God is salvation', is the name of one of the major prophets in the Old Testament. It was taken up by English speakers during the Reformation. In the USA, where the name is currently very popular, it is usually pronounced with the middle syllable as 'zay' or 'zee', but in the UK it is usually pronounced with the vowel as in the word 'I'.

VARIANTS **Isai, Isaias, Isiah**

Isambard *m*
This name, kept alive by the fame of the great Victorian engineer Isambard Kingdom Brunel (1806–59), is an Old Germanic name perhaps formed from the elements *isan*, 'iron', and *berht*, 'bright'. It came to England with the Normans, usually in the form *Isembert* or *Imbert*, but is now very rare, except in the surnames that derive from it. Brunel was christened with the middle name of his French father.

Isandro *see* **Lysander**

Isbel, Iseabail *see* **Isabel**

Iser *see* **Israel**

Iseult, Iseut *see* **Isolde**

Isha *mf*
An Indian name from the Sanskrit meaning 'Lord, Protector'.

Ishaq *see* **Isaac**

Ishbel *see* **Isabel**

Ishmael *m*
This is the biblical form of the Hebrew *Yishmael*, 'God will harken'. In the Old Testament he is the son of Abraham by his maidservant Hagar. In Arabic tradition, in the form *Ismail*, he is celebrated as the founder of the Arab nation.
VARIANTS *Arabic* **Ismail, Ismaeel** *French* **Ismaël**
★ Ismail Kadaré (1936–), French-based Albanian novelist

Ishtiaq *m*
An Arabic name meaning 'wish, desire, yearning'
VARIANT **Ishtiyaq**

Isiah *see* **Isaiah**

Isidore *m* **Isadora** *f*
Isidore was originally a Greek name meaning 'gift of the goddess Isis', combining *Isis* with the element *doron*, 'gift'. Worship of the Egyptian goddess was transferred from Egypt to Greece early on, and eventually spread throughout the Romanized world. Despite its pagan origins, it was well used in early Christian communities, notably by St Isidore of Seville, a 6th-century scholar whose encyclopedia preserved much classical knowledge through the Middle Ages. In the later Middle Ages, Isidore came to be thought of as a typically Jewish name, as it was used to Westernize the Jewish ISAIAH. Although the regular feminine form of the name is *Isidora*, Isadora has now become the more common spelling, probably under the influence of US dancer Isadora Duncan (1878–1927).
PET FORMS **Izzy, Izzie** (mf), **Dora** (f)
• VARIANTS *German, Russian* **Isidor** *Italian, Spanish* **Isidoro** *Polish* **Izydor**

Iskander *see* **Alexander**

Isla *f*
Isla is the old spelling, reflecting the

pronunciation, of the Hebridean island of Islay. It was in occasional use as a first name from the middle of the 19th century. Although it has spread outside Scotland, it is still more likely to be used there, where it is currently among the most popular choices for girls.

Isleen *see* **Aisling**

Islwyn *m*
This is a Gwent place name formed from the Welsh *is*, 'below', and *llwyn*, 'grove'. It was introduced to the stock of Welsh names by the local poet William Thomas (1832–78) who took it as his bardic name.

Ismaeel, Ismaël, Ismail *see* **Ishmael**

Ismat *mf*
An Arabic name from the word for 'purity, chastity'.
VARIANTS **Isma, Ismet**

Ismay *f*
Despite this name being recorded from as early as the 13th century, its history is not known, although it has been claimed as both a Gaelic name and a variant of ESME.
VARIANT **Ismey**

Ismene *f*
This unusual name, pronounced with three syllables, is borne by one of the daughters of Oedipus and Jocasta in Greek mythology. The origin of her name is uncertain, but it may be from Greek *isme*, 'knowledge'. See also ANTIGONE.

Isobel, Isobella, Isobelle *see* **Isabel**

Isolde *f*
Neither the meaning nor the original form of this name is clearly known. There is no doubt, however, of the widespread fame of the tragic love story of how TRISTAN (another widely variable name) was sent to fetch the

beautiful Isolde from Ireland, and how the two young people mistakenly drank the love potion that was meant for the wedding night of Isolde and Mark.

The name was not uncommon in the Middle Ages, then largely dropped out of use until revived in the 19th century along with other medieval names.

VARIANTS **Iseu(l)t**, **Isolda**, **Yseu(l)t** *Welsh* **Esyllt**

Isra *f*

From the Arabic for 'night journey', used with reference to the famous night journey of the Prophet from Mecca to Jerusalem.

VARIANT **Israa**

Israel *m*

Israel was originally the name, meaning 'he who strived with God', given to the patriarch Jacob after he wrestled with an angel (Genesis 32.28) which was subsequently taken as an ethnic name by his descendants. Israel has always been popular among Jews, was adopted by the Puritans and then reverted to being a mainly Jewish name again, although there is currently renewed interest in the USA.

PET FORMS **Izzy**, **Izzie** • VARIANTS *Yiddish* **Iser**, **Issur**

Issa *see* **Jesus**

Issur *see* **Israel**

Istvan *see* **Stephen**

Ita *see* **Ida**

Italo *m* Itala *f*

An Italian name meaning 'Italian'. In Roman legend *Italus* was the legendary ancestor after whom the country was named.

★ Italo Calvino (1923–85), Italian writer

Itzhak, Itzik, Itzl *see* **Isaac**

Iúile *see* **Julia**

Ivan *m* Ivana *f*

Ivan is the Russian equivalent of JOHN. The name became synonymous with 'Russian' during the Cold War.

FEMININE **Ivanna** • PET FORMS **Van**, **Vanya**

★ Ivan Turgenev (1818–83), Russian author

★ Ivana Trump (1949–), Czech-born skier, model and businesswoman

☆ *Uncle Vanya* is an 1896 play by Anton Chekhov

Ives *see* **Yves**

Ivo *m*

This is the German, and occasionally English, form of the French name YVES, taken from the Latin form of the name.

VARIANT **Ivon**

Ivonne *see* **Yvonne**

Ivor *m*

This is the English spelling of the Scandinavian *Ivar(r)*. In Old Norse this was *Yherr*, formed from *yr* meaning 'yew' and, by extension, 'bow', and *herr*, 'army'. It is sometimes also used as an English form of the Welsh name IFOR.

VARIANTS *Irish* **Iobhar** *Scottish* **Iomhvair**

★ Ivor Novello (1893–1951), Welsh composer and actor

☆ *Ivor the Engine*, 1960s and 70s children's cartoon set in Wales

Ivy *f*

One of the many plant names introduced in the 19th century. Its popularity peaked in the 1920s, but it fell out of favour in the later 20th century. There are faint signs of a revival of interest in the name, along with other names from the period.

Iwan *see* **Ieuan**

Izaac, Izaak *see* **Isaac**

Izabel, Izabelle *see* **Isabel**

Izydor *see* **Isidore**

Izzy, Izzie *see* **Isabel**, **Isidore**, **Israel**

J

Jaabir *see* **Jabir**

Jaap *see* **Jacob**

Jabez *m*
This is a biblical name meaning 'sorrowful'. Of the original bearer, we are told in 1 Chronicles 4.9 'his mother called his name Jabez, saying, Because I bare him with sorrow'. The name was used by the Puritans in the 17th century, but is now rare, although it has recently been brought to the attention of Evangelicals through Bruce Wilkinson's controversial book *The Prayer of Jabez: Breaking Through to the Blessed Life*. It has been suggested that the original form of the name was *Jazeb*, and this too is sometimes used.
☆ Jabez Stone in Stephen Vincent Benét's 1937 short story *The Devil and Daniel Webster*

Jabir *m*
This Arabic name means 'comforter, one who gives help in time of trouble or need'. Closely related is *Jabr*, 'consolation'.
VARIANTS **Jaabir, Jabber, Jaber, Gabir, Gabr**
★ Jabir ibn Hayyan (c.721–c.815), Arab alchemist, known in the medieval West as *Geber*, often called 'the father of chemistry'

Jabril *see* **Gabriel**

Jace, Jacen *see* **Jason**

Jacinta *f*
This is the Spanish form of HYACINTH, now found among English speakers, particularly in Ireland and the USA. There are masculine equivalents in other languages, such as the Spanish *Jacinto* and the Polish *Jacek* or *Jach*.
VARIANTS **Jacintha, Jacint(h)(e)** *Italian* **Giacinta**

Jack *m*
Jack, now an immensely popular independent name, started out as a pet form of JOHN. John once had the alternative pronunciation of JAN (imagine a West Country pronunciation of the name), and this developed a pet form in the Middle Ages of *Jankin* (source of the surname Jenkins). This in turn was shortened to *Jakin*, and eventually the *-in* dropped to give Jack. The long-term popularity of the name can be seen from the number of terms based on it that have entered the English language; from the jack used to raise a car, to the lowest value court card and to phrases such as 'Jack-of-all-trades'. There is sometimes confusion about the history of the name caused by the similarity between Jack and *Jacques*, the French form of JACOB/JAMES. Jack became the most popular name given to boys in England and Wales in 1995 and has remained at the top ever since. It has also been well used in other English-speaking countries.
PET FORMS **Jackie, Ja(i)kie** • VARIANTS **Jac** *Scottish* **Jock, Jockey, Jockie**
★ Jack (John F) Kennedy (1917–63), 35th president of the USA
★ Jack Kerouac (1922–69), US novelist
☆ Jack Bauer, lead character in the television series *24*

Jackie *mf*
A pet form of JACK or JACQUELINE or JACKSON regularly used as an

independent name. The main alternative feminine forms are listed under Jacqueline.

VARIANT **Jacky**

★ Jackie Collins (1941–), English author
★ Sir Jackie Stewart (1939–), Scottish racing driver

Jackson m

This is a surname, meaning 'son of Jack', used as a first name. It has been given regularly in the USA since the 19th century, perhaps influenced by Andrew Jackson, 7th US president, or the Confederate General 'Stonewall' Jackson, and is currently very popular there, outperforming even JACK. It is now occasionally being given to girls.

PET FORMS **Jack(ie)**, **Jax** • VARIANT **Jax(s)on**

★ Jackson Pollock (1912–56), US artist
★ Jackson Browne (1948–), US singer-songwriter

Jacob, Jake m

Although they look so different Jacob and JAMES are actually the same name. They both come from the biblical Hebrew *Yaakov*. This became *Iakobos* in the Greek of the New Testament and *Jacobus* in Latin 'J' originally being the form that 'i' took as a capital letter). Then an alternative Latin spelling, *Jacomus*, developed and this became James in English when the second syllable was dropped. The two forms provided a useful distinction between the Old Testament patriarch Jacob, and the New Testament apostles called James. The original meaning of the name is obscured. It may have been a form of a name meaning 'may God protect', but the story that Jacob was born holding on to the heel (Hebrew *aqeb*) of his elder twin Esau, and the fact that he later supplanted his brother's right to inherit (Hebrew *aqab*, 'to usurp'), may have led to the idea that the name means 'supplanter'.

Jacob was one of the Old Testament names adopted in the 16th century, and there has been a strong revival of interest in recent years, particularly in its pet form Jake. There are feminine forms of the name, including *Jacoba*, *Jacobine* and particularly *Jacobina*. These are very rare now, but were used in the 18th century, particularly in Scotland where there is a tradition of such feminizations, to indicate family support for the Jacobite cause.

PET FORMS **Jake**, **Jeb** • VARIANTS *Cornish* **Jago** *Welsh* **Iago** *Arabic* **Yaqub** *Dutch* **Jaap**, **Jakob(us)**, **Kobus**, **Cobi** *French* **Jacques** *German* **Jakob** *Hebrew* **Yakov**, **Akiva** *Italian* **Giacobbe**, **Giacomo**, **Jacopo** *Polish, Czech* **Jakub** *Russian* **Yakov** *Spanish, Portuguese* **Jacobo** *Yiddish* **Kapel**

★ Sir Jacob Epstein (1880–1959), British sculptor, born in New York
★ Jake (Jacob) Gyllenhaal (1980–), US actor
☆ Jacob Marley in Charles Dickens's *A Christmas Carol* (1843)

Jacomina *see* Jacomina *see* **James**

Jacqueline f

This is the standard feminine equivalent of JAMES/JACOB derived from the French masculine form of the name, *Jacques*. Although it was already a well-established name, it became particularly popular in the 1960s, probably influenced by Jacqueline Kennedy Onassis (1929–94), and developed a number of variant forms which were widely used.

PET FORMS **Jackie**, **Jack(y)**, **Jacki**, **Ja(c)qui(e)**, **Jak(k)i**, **Jaci** • VARIANTS **Jacalyn**, **Jacalin(e)**, **Jaclyn**, **Jaqueline**, **Jacquelyn**, **Jackeline**

★ Jacqueline Bisset (1944–), English actress
★ Jacqueline du Pré (1945–87), English cellist

Jacques *see* **James**

Jacquetta *f*
A feminine form of *Jacques*, the French for JAMES/JACOB, which probably evolved from the Italian form *Giachetta*. It was widely used in the Middle Ages, but in modern times has never been as popular as the alternative feminine JACQUELINE.
VARIANTS **Jaquette**, **Jaquenetta**

Jacy *mf*
A modern name which probably originated from a number of sources, including the initials J C, a pet form of JACQUELINE, and *Jace*, the short form of JASON. It is more often feminine than masculine.
VARIANTS **Jasie**, **Jaci(e)**, **Jaycee**, **Jaycie**
☆ Jacy Farrow in the 1971 film *The Last Picture Show*

Jade *f*
This popular jewel name only came to public attention in 1971 when it was chosen by Mick and Bianca Jagger for their first child. It grew in popularity until the 1990s, since when it has declined somewhat, although it is still well used. It might not have caught on so readily with the public if they had been more aware of the fact that the name comes from the Spanish for 'bowels'. In its full form the Spanish name for the gemstone is *piedra de ijada*, 'stone for the bowels or flank', from the belief that it could cure colic. This became *l'ejade* and then *le jade* in French, from whence it came into English as jade. In the USA, the elaboration *Jada* is currently more popular as a first name than the simple form. The Mexican *Yadira* or *Jadira* may be a form of this name. Variants such as *Jadine* shade imperceptibly into forms of JADEN. Jade is occasionally used as a masculine name.
VARIANTS **Jayde**, **Jaid(e)**, **Jayda**, **Jaida**
Spanish **Jadira**

★ Jada Pinkett Smith (1971–), US actress

Jaden *mf*
Although Jaden has sometimes been linked to the minor Old Testament name *Jadon*, variously interpreted as 'thankful' or 'he will judge' in Hebrew, it seems more likely that it is a modern coinage. Originally it was a masculine name which appeared in the USA in the 1990s, probably as a form of the popular JADE, combined with the widespread *-aden* ending which is currently part of the majority of popular masculine names there. It was given publicity as the name chosen by several celebrities for their children, and rapidly developed numerous variants and became used for both sexes.
VARIANTS **Jaiden**, **Jayden**, **Jadon**, **Jaeden**, **Jadyn**

Jaeden *see* **Jaden**

Jael *f*
In the Bible this is the name of a Hebrew woman who saves her nation by killing the captain of the Canaanite army. The name comes from Hebrew *ya'el*, 'mountain goat'.
VARIANT **Yael**

Jafar *m*
An Arabic name from the vocabulary word for 'spring, stream'.
VARIANTS **Gafar**, **Jaffer**, **Jaffar**

Jafet *see* **Japheth**

Jagannath *m*
Jagannath is one of a number of Indian names based on the Sanskrit *jagat*, 'worth', in this case combined with *natha*, 'lord'. Others include *Jagdish* (*jagat* plus *isa*, 'ruler') and *Jagjit*, 'conqueror of the world'.

Jagienka, Jagna, Jagusia *see* **Agnes**

Jago *see* **Jacob**

Jahan *f* Jahangir *m*

Jahan comes from the Persian for 'world', with Jahangir meaning 'holder of the world'. The Mughal emperor Jahangir (1569–1627) was married to the empress Nur Jahan (1577–1645). Their love for each other was famous, and Nur Jahan was one of the most powerful and influential women to rule on the Indian subcontinent.

Jai *see* **Jay**

Jaid, **Jaida**, **Jaide** *see* **Jade**

Jaiden *see* **Jaden**

Jaikie *see* **Jack**, **James**

Jaime, **Jaimee**, **Jaimie** *see* **James**, **Jamie**

Jair, **Jairo** *see* **Yair**

Jaison *see* **Jason**

Jake *see* **Jacob**

Jaki *see* **Jacqueline**

Jakie *see* **Jack**

Jakki *see* **Jacqueline**

Jakob, **Jakub** *see* **Jacob**

Jalal *m* Jalila *f*

Jalal is an Arabic name meaning 'great, exalted, magnificent'. Jalila, the feminine equivalent, means 'honourable, exalted'.
VARIANT **Galila**

Jaleesa *see* **Whitley**

Jalen *mf*

Jalen is a modern name popularized in the 1990s by the fame of US basketball player Jalen Rose (b.1973). In his case the name is a blend of his father's name JAMES and that of his uncle LEONARD (Len).

Jameel, **Jameela**, **Jameelia** *see* **Jamil**

James *m*

James is the New Testament form of the name which appears in the Old Testament as JACOB (where the early history of the name is given). James came to prominence in Britain in 1424, when the Stuart king James I came to the throne of Scotland. Thereafter it had strong royal associations, particularly after James VI of Scotland became James I of England in 1603. The last Stuart king of England, James II, was deposed in 1688 because he was a Catholic, and for some time afterwards the giving of the name was linked with Catholicism and support of the Jacobites (from the alternative form of the name) who fought for the return of the Stuart kings. In Scotland this association was particularly strong with the use of the feminine form *Jamesina*. However, once the fear of rebellion had died down the name returned to favour and by the early 19th century was firmly re-established as part of the basic stock of English first names. It is currently popular in most English-speaking areas, with JAMIE, which has replaced JIM as the normal pet form, well used as an independent name.
PET FORMS **Jamie**, **Jim(my)**, **Jimmie**, **Jem**, **Jazz** • VARIANTS *Gaelic* **Seumas** *Irish* **Seamus** *Scottish* **Hamish**, **Jaikie** *Welsh* **Iago** *Dutch* **Jaume** (m) **Jacomina** (f) *French* **Jacques** *Italian* **Giacomo** (m), **Giachetta** (f) *Spanish* **Jaime**, **Diego**

Jameson *m*

A surname, meaning 'son of James', sometimes found as a first name, particularly in the USA.
VARIANTS **Jamison**, **Jim(i)son**

Jamie *mf*

As well as being a pet form of JAMES, often given as a name in its own right, Jamie has been used as a female first name since at least the 19th century, primarily in the USA. It was very popular there in the 1970s to 90s. It is not infrequently combined in the form *Jamie-Lee* and its variants, probably under the influence of the actress Jamie Lee Curtis (b.1958), who brought the name to a wider public.

VARIANTS **Jaim(i)e, Jamey, Jaimee, Jamee**

☆ Jamie Sommers, the Bionic Woman in the 1970s television series

Jamil *m* Jamila *f*

An Arabic name that comes from the word for 'handsome, beautiful'. Jamil, often appearing in the form *Jamal*, is one of the Arabic names that have been popular with African Americans. *Jamar*, used in the USA since the 1970s, is probably a development of this, perhaps blended with LAMAR. There is a related Arabic name Jamal which means 'good looks, beauty'.

VARIANTS **Jamal(a), Djamil(a), Jamil(i)(a), Gamil(a), Jameel(a), Jamil(l)ah, Jamelia, Gamal, Gamil**

★ Jamelia (1981–), English singer-songwriter

Jan *mf* Jana *f*

As a girl's name Jan is a pet form of any name that begins with *Jan*, such as JANET. As a boy's name it represents an old or West Country variant of JOHN, as well as being the form of the name used in some European countries. Jana, although it is the equivalent of JANE in several European languages, is probably, like *Janae*, a modern coinage in English. Jana and Janae can be seen as elaborations of Jan or variants of names such as JANE. *Janna* can also be a Muslim feminine name meaning 'garden, paradise'.

VARIANTS **Janna, Janae**

Janant *see* Jay²

Jancsi *see* John

Jancis *f*

A 20th-century name, usually analysed as a blend of JAN and FRANCES. It may have been the invention of Mary Webb who used it as a typically rustic name in her 1924 novel *Precious Bane*, a sub-Hardyesque novel of passion and angst among the peasantry that was immensely popular in its day, and ruthlessly parodied by Stella Gibbons in her 1932 comic novel *Cold Comfort Farm*.

★ Jancis Robinson (1950–), English wine writer

Jane *f*

Jane is, alongside such names as JEAN and JOAN, a feminine form of JOHN. The Latin form of the name *Johanna*, became *Jehane* in medieval French (later *Jeanne*). This became Jane in English. It was in use by the later Middle Ages, and by the 16th century was replacing other forms of the name to become a lastingly popular core name. However, by the 19th century it had become a rather lacklustre choice, and was associated with 'plain Jane' housemaids and mousy characters such as Charlotte Brontë's meek Jane Eyre. There was something of a revival of the name in the first part of the 20th century, but it is once again only quietly used, although it is sometimes found in combinations such as *Sarah-Jane*, and lies behind a number of more popular choices.

PET FORMS **Janey, Janie, Jaynie, Jenny**

• VARIANTS **Jayne, Jana, Janet, Jean, Joan** *Irish* **Síne, Sheena** *Scots Gaelic* **Sìne, Sheena** *Welsh* **Siân** *Dutch* **Johanna, Janna** *French* **Jeanne** *German* **Johanna, Hanne, Hansine** *Italian* **Giovanna, Gianna** *Scandinavian* **Johanna, Jonna, Jensine** *Spanish* **Juana, Juanita**

Janelle *f*

A modern elaboration of JANE.

VARIANT **Jenelle**

Janessa *f*

A modern coinage based on JANE

blended with the feminine ending
-*essa*.

Janet *f*
This was originally a pet form of
JANE, formed by adding the standard
diminutive ending -*et(te)*. It was
widely used in the Middle Ages, after
which it became far less common in
England, but remained widespread
in Scotland and came to be thought
of as a typically Scottish name. It was
revived in the 19th century and was
popular in the first half of the 20th,
so much so that the standard early
reading texts used Janet and John as
the names of their typical children.
Since the 1960s it has become less
popular and is now only quietly used.
PET FORMS **Jan**, **Jenny**, **Jennie**, **Jinty**, **Netta**,
Jessie, **Jes** • VARIANTS **Jana**, **Janette**,
Janetta, **Jannet(te)** *Irish* **Sinead**
- ★ Janet Suzman (1939–), South African
  actress
- ★ Janet Jackson (1966–), US singer-
  songwriter

Janice *f*
An elaboration of JANE, which seems
to have been coined, perhaps by
blending Jane with ALICE, by the
US novelist Paul Leicester Ford for
his novel *Janice Meredith* (1899).
Although this is set during the time
of the American Revolution, the
name was not in use then, although it
rapidly came into circulation after the
publication of the novel.
VARIANT **Janis**
- ★ Janice Dickinson (1955–), US
  model, television personality and
  author
- ★ Janis Joplin (1943–70), US rhythm and
  blues singer

Janika *see* **John**

Janine *f*
This is the anglicized form of the
French *Jeannine*, a pet form of *Jeanne*,

feminine equivalent of JOHN. See also
JEAN.
PET FORM **Jan** • VARIANTS **Jannine**, **Jan(n)ina**,
Jean(n)ine, **Gen(n)ine**

Janna *see* **Jan**

Jannike *see* **Joanna**

János, **Janusz** *see* **John**

Japheth *m*
Japheth, from the Hebrew *Yapheth*
meaning 'enlargement, expansion',
appears in the Old Testament as one of
the sons of Noah whose descendants
repopulated the earth after the Flood.
It was taken up by Puritans in the 17th
century, but is not used much now,
although it has a certain currency
among US fundamentalists.
VARIANTS **Jap(h)et(h)** *Spanish* **Jafet**

Japhtha *see* **Jephthah**

Japonica *f*
This is one of the more unusual plant
names. Japonica is simply the Latin for
'of Japan'. In the early 19th century
the word was used for the camellia
(Latin *Camellia japonica*), but was later
adopted as the English name for the
plant commonly known as Japanese
quince (*Chaenomeles speciosa*).

Jaqueline, **Jaqui**, **Jaquie** *see*
Jacqueline

Jared *m*
The Old Testament name Jared
(from the Hebrew *yeredh*) means
'descendant', although it has often
been interpreted as meaning 'rose'.
The original bearer appears as the
father of Enoch, although all we are
told about him is that he lived for 962
years. Jared was particularly popular
in the USA from the mid-1970s until
the early 2000s, and consequently
developed a wide variety of spellings.
The occasionally-found *Jaron* should
probably be regarded as a modern

variant, while the variant *Jarrod* can also be from a surname derived from GERALD.

VARIANTS **Jarred, Jar(r)od, Jer(r)ed**

★ Jared Diamond (1937–   ), US physiologist and ecologist

Jarlath *see* **Iarlaith**

Jaroslaw *m*

Pronounced *yarroslav*, this is a Polish name formed from two popular Slavic elements: *jaro*, 'spring', and *slav*, 'victory'. Similar names are *Jaromierz*: *jaro* plus *meri*, 'grace, favour'; *Jaropelk*: *jaro* plus *pelk*, 'people'; and *Jaromil*: *jaro* plus *milo*, 'grace, favour', which has a feminine *Jarmila*. They all share the same pet forms.

FEMININE **Jaroslawa** • PET FORMS **Jarek** (m), **Jarka** (f) • VARIANT *Russian* **Yaroslav**

Jarred *see* **Jared**

Jarrett *see* **Gerald**

Jarvis *m*

A surname, derived from GERVASE, used as a first name.

VARIANT **Jervis**

★ Jarvis Cocker (1963–   ), English singer-songwriter

Jasie *see* **Jacy**

Jasminder *f* **Jaswinder** *m*

This name, which combines the name of the god Indra with that of his thunderbolt, literally means 'Indra of the thunderbolt' but is often interpreted as 'Lord's Glory'.

VARIANT **Jasvinder**

Jasmine *f*

This is currently one of the most popular flower names. The sweetly scented jasmine gets its name from the Persian word for the flower, *Yasmin*, a name widely familiar from *The Arabian Nights*. It came into English with spellings beginning *Je-*, hence early forms such as *Jessamine, Jessamyn* and

Jessamy. The latter came to mean a fop or effeminate man, from the use of jasmine as a perfume. The name was not common in the 19th century, but was used from the beginning of the 20th, and its more recent popularity has spawned numerous variants.

PET FORMS **Jas(s), Jazz, Min** • VARIANTS **Jasmin, Jasmina, Jasmyn, Jazmin(e)** *Arabic* **Yasmin, Yasmeen, Yasim**

Jason *m*

In Greek mythology Jason, *Iason* in the original Greek and pronounced with an initial 'ya' sound, was the hero of the Argonauts' mission to retrieve the Golden Fleece from Colchis. The name is thought to come from the Greek word *iasthai*, 'to heal'. However, Jason came into the common stock of Western names not from Greek mythology but from the New Testament, where someone called Jason provides hospitality to St Paul when he visits Thessalonika. This early Christian was probably Jewish, for Jason was regularly used by Mediterranean Jews as a more familiar form of JOSHUA. Moreover, in the 17th century when the name came into use in England, Jason was believed to be the name of the author of the biblical book *Ecclesiasticus*. Jason became very popular in the 1970s.

PET FORMS **Jase, Jace, Jay(ce)** • VARIANTS **Jacen, Jaison, Jasen, Jayson, Jaysen**

★ Jason Robards Jr (1922–2000), US actor

★ Jason Donovan (1968–   ), Australian actor and singer

☆ Jason Bourne is the eponymous hero of the 'Bourne' trilogy of films

Jasper *m*

This is the English form of the name CASPER (where other variants are listed), in Christian tradition given to one of the 'Three Wise Men' or Magi. The link between the two can be found in the French form GASPARD. The name, which is usually interpreted as deriving from the Persian for 'treasure keeper', was introduced to England from the Low Countries in the Middle Ages. The name of the precious stone, although it too comes from Persian or a related language, is unconnected.

PET FORMS **Jas(s)**, **Jaz(z)** • VARIANT Dutch **Jesper**

★ Jasper Johns (1930–), US artist
★ Jasper Conran (1959–), English fashion designer

Jasvinder, Jaswinder see Jasminder

Jaume see James

Javed m
A Muslim name meaning 'eternal, perpetual' from the Persian jawid.
VARIANT **Javaid**

Javier see Xavier

Javon m
A modern US name with many variants, which is probably simply a combination of fashionable sounds. There have been attempts to interpret variants such as Jevon as deriving from a surname, or to link Javan with the biblical name of one of the grandsons of Noah, but since the name only appeared in the 1970s, this seems unlikely.
VARIANTS **Javan**, **Javion**, **Javin(e)**, **Javonne**, **Jayvion**, **Jayvon**, **Jevon**

Jawad m
An Arabic name meaning 'generous, open-handed'. It was the nickname of Imam Taqi (810–35), 9th imam of the Shiites.

Jax, Jaxon, Jaxson see Jackson

Jay¹ mf Jaya¹ f
This was probably originally a pet form of any name beginning with 'J' now used as an independent name. It appears to have come into

general use in North America in the 19th century, but is now well used throughout the English-speaking world, mainly as a masculine name, with Jaya an occasional feminine form. The development of Jay in the USA may have been influenced by the founding father John Jay (1749–1825).

★ Jay (Jason) Gould (1836–92), US millionaire railroad developer
★ Jay (John) McInerney (1955–), US author
☆ Jay Gatsby in F Scott Fitzgerald's 1925 *The Great Gatsby*

Jay² m Jaya² f
An Indian name from the Sanskrit jaya, 'victory'. Jaya also forms the basis of a number of other names, notably Jayakrishna (m), 'victorious Krishna'; Janant (m) and Jananti (f), 'victory'; Jayashanka (m), 'victorious Shiva'; Jayshree or Jayashri, 'goddess of victory'; and Jaywant, 'possessing victory'.
VARIANT **Jai**

Jay³, Jayce see Jason

Jaycee, Jaycie see Jacy

Jayda see Jade

Jaydan, Jayden see Jaden

Jayde see Jade

Jayne, Jaynie see Jane

Jaysen, Jayson see Jason

Jayvion, Jayvon see Javon

Jaz see Jasper

Jazeb see Jabez

Jazmin, Jazmine see Jasmine

Jazz mf
Although occasionally given as an independent name, this is usually a pet form of names beginning Ja(s), particularly JASMINE in the feminine,

and JASPER and JAMES in the masculine. The latter comes from the old written abbreviation for James, *Jas*.

VARIANT **Jaz**

Jean, Jeanette *f*

This is the English form of the French *Jeanne*, which is the feminine of *Jean*, the French equivalent of JOHN. The medieval French form *Jean(ne)* was brought to England and developed into both JANE and Jean. By the end of the Middle Ages Jean had become primarily a Scottish name, and often appears in literature as typically Scottish. The interest in all things Scottish in the 19th century helped reintroduce the name to wider use. It was particularly popular in the UK in the 1930s, and spent most of the first 60 years of the 20th century in the top 100 names in the USA, but is now little used, even in Scotland. Jeanette is a pet form that shades into JANET.

PET FORMS **Jean(n)ie, Geni** • VARIANTS **Jenette, Jeanna**

Jean-Baptiste *see* Baptist

Jeanine *see* Janine

Jeanne *see* Jane

Jeannine *see* Janine

Jeannot *see* John

Jeb *m*

Jeb is usually a US name which can be from a number of sources. It is sometimes used a pet form of JACOB, or of *Jebediah*, a not unusual variant of JEDEDIAH. In the Southern states of the USA it came into use in memory of James Ewell Brown Stuart (1833–64), a Confederate General usually known as Jeb Stuart from his initials. It can still be found as a nickname for anyone with the initials J E B.

★ Jeb Bush (John Ellis Bush) (1953–),

governor of Florida and younger brother of President George W Bush

Jebediah *see* Jedediah

Jed *see* Andrew

Jedediah *m*

This is an Old Testament name meaning 'beloved of God', given to Solomon by the prophet Nathan. It was taken up by the Puritans in the 17th century who took it to the USA where it became firmly entrenched. The pet form is now more often used than the full one.

PET FORMS **Jed** (also a Polish form of Andrew) **Jeb** • VARIANT **Jebediah**

Jedrzej *see* Andrew

Jef *see* Joseph

Jeff, Jefferey, Jeffrey *see* Geoffrey

Jefferson *m*

This is the surname of US President Thomas Jefferson used as a first name. The surname means 'son of Jeffrey' (see GEOFFREY).

★ Jefferson Davis (1808–89), president of the Confederate States of the USA

★ William Jefferson Clinton (Bill Clinton) (1946–), 42nd president of the USA

Jehoshaphat *m*

This name, meaning 'God has judged', belonged to one of the kings of Judah (2 Samuel 7.16). It is extremely rare as a given name, although there is a Polish variant, *Jozofat*, so presumably it is recorded in Poland. However, it is kept in the public mind by the expression 'jumping Jehoshaphat', used as a mild expletive since at least the middle of the 19th century.

★ George Jehoshaphat Mountain (1789–1863), bishop of Quebec

Jelena *f*

Jelena is a Slavic form of the name HELEN.

PET FORM **Jelka** • VARIANT *Russian* **Yelena**

Jelle *see* William

Jem *m*
A pet form of JAMES (reflecting the old pronunciation of the name) or JEREMY, occasionally found as an independent name.
PET FORM **Jemmy**

Jemima *f*
In the Old Testament Jemima is the eldest of the three daughters of Job famous for their beauty, the others being KEZIAH and *Kerenhappuch* (see KEREN). The name was taken up by the Puritans and has remained in use ever since. It is usually interpreted as meaning 'dove', although 'fair as the day' is an alternative interpretation.
PET FORM **Mima**
★ Jemima Khan (1974–), English socialite
☆ Aunt Jemima, a brand name in the US food industry particularly known for pancake mixes, dating from the 19th century. The term 'Aunt Jemima' is also used in the USA as a feminine equivalent of 'Uncle Tom'

Jemma *see* Gemma

Jenaro *see* Gennaro

Jenelle *see* Janelle

Jenette *see* Jean

Jenna *f*
A variant of JENNIFER, which was in use by the early 20th century, but only became widespread in the 1970s.
VARIANTS **Jena, Jennah, Jennae**
★ Jenna Bush (1981–), daughter of President George W Bush, named after her grandmother (b.1919)
☆ Jenna Wade in the television series *Dallas*, played by Priscilla Presley, from 1983 to 1988

Jennie *see* Janet

Jennifer *f*
This was originally a Cornish form of GUINEVERE. Although there are rare occurrences of the name outside the county by at least the mid-18th century, it appears to have been introduced to the general public by the character of Jennifer Dubedat in the 1905 play *The Doctor's Dilemma* by George Bernard Shaw, who had a liking for unusual names in his plays. The name increased in popularity through the early years of the 20th century and started to become really popular in the UK in the 1940s. In the USA the name came into use rather later, but then climbed rapidly and was the most popular choice for girls for 14 years from 1970.
PET FORM **Jenny** • VARIANTS **Jenna, Jenifer**

Jenny *f*
Although this is now thought of as a pet form of JENNIFER, before the 20th century it was a pet form of JEAN, JANE or JANET and was used in this way from the Middle Ages.
PET FORM **Jen** • VARIANTS **Jen(n)i, Jenna**
☆ Jenny was a traditional name for the wren. Dickens used the name Jenny Wren in his 1865 novel *Our Mutual Friend*, and the character was celebrated in a 2005 song by Paul McCartney

Jens *see* John

Jensen *m*
Jensen is a surname, the Scandinavian equivalent of Johnson, 'son of John', used as a first name. It is also the name of an elite brand of car, and so fits in with the growing trend to use exclusive brand names as first names. It was brought to the attention of the general public by English racing driver Jensen Button (b.1980). It is occasionally found used for girls.
VARIANTS **Jenson, Jensyn**

Jensine *see* **Jane, Joanna**

Jeoffrey, Jeoffroy *see* **Geoffrey**

Jephthah *m*
This is the English form of the Hebrew *Yiphtah*, meaning 'He [God] opens' with reference to the birth of a first child. This explains why, when the name was occasionally used by Nonconformists in the past, it was usually given to a first-born.
VARIANTS **Japhtha, Jeptha**

Jerald *see* **Gerald**

Jered *see* **Jared**

Jeremiah *m*
The Hebrew name *Yirmiyahu*, 'God has appointed', became Jeremiah in the Old Testament. It was the name of a prophet who bewailed the fall of Jerusalem and threatened his people with God's wrath – hence the term 'jeremiad'. It was one of the names adopted by the Puritans in the 16th century, who took it with them to the USA. There it has been more popular than in the UK, and is currently enjoying considerable use, being more often chosen for children than its derivative JEREMY.
PET FORMS **Miah, Jer, Jerry, Jem** • VARIANTS **Jeramiah** *German* **Jeremias**

Jeremy *m*
Jeremy is the New Testament form of the name JEREMIAH. It has been used since the Middle Ages, but only entered the stock of really popular names in the 20th century. Influential in this was the success of a series of books about a boy called Jeremy, written by the well-known novelist Hugh Walpole, the first of which, *Jeremy*, was published in 1919. Popularity of the name peaked in the mid-20th century in the UK, and it is now rarely chosen. In the USA, Jeremy was little used before the mid-20th

century (although Jeremiah was), after which its popularity steadily grew and the name is currently in the top 100 choices for boys.
PET FORMS **Jerry, Je(r)ri(e), Jer, Jem**
• VARIANT *French* **Jérémie**
★ Jeremy Irons (1948–　), English actor
★ Jeremy Clarkson (1960–　), English journalist and broadcaster
☆ Jeremy Fisher, in Beatrix Potter's 1906 book *The Tale of Mr Jeremy Fisher*

Jerk, Jerker *see* **Eric**

Jermaine *see* **Germaine**

Jerold *see* **Gerald**

Jerome *m*
The Greek name *Hieronymous*, from *hieros*, 'holy, sacred', and *onoma*, 'name', became Jerome in English. It was a pre-Christian name, but entered the stock of names in Western Europe (in widely varied forms) because of the fame of St Jerome (*Eusebios Hieronymous Sophronios* in his native Greek), who in the 5th century translated the Bible into Latin from its original Hebrew and Greek. This Vulgate version of the Bible remained the basis for all biblical translations until recently. The Apache chief *Geronimo* was so called because this was the nearest Westerners could get to his true name *Goyathlay*.
PET FORM **Jerry** • VARIANTS **Gerome** *Dutch* **Jeroen** *French* **Jérôme** *German* **Hieronymus** *Italian* **Geronimo, Gerolamo, Girolamo** *Spanish* **Jeronimo**
★ Jerome K Jerome (1859–1927), English author of *Three Men in a Boat*
★ Jerome Kern (1885–1945), US songwriter
★ Hieronymus Bosch (c.1450–1516), painter, famous for his paintings of hell

Jerrard *see* **Gerard**

Jerred *see* **Jared**

Jerrell *m*
A modern US name, apparently a blend of JERRY and DARRYL or similar names.
VARIANTS **Jer(r)el(l)**, **Jerryl**

Jerrica *f*
A modern name, apparently a blend of JERRY and ERICA, mainly confined to the USA.

Jerri, Jerrie *see* Jeremy

Jerrik *see* Eric

Jerrold *see* Gerald

Jerry *mf*
Now often an independent name, this was originally a pet form of GERALD, GERARD, JEREMIAH, JEREMY, JEROME, and, in the feminine, GERALDINE.
PET FORMS **Jer, Ger** • VARIANTS **Gerry, Jeri**

Jerusha *f*
An Old Testament name, belonging to the wife of King Ussiah of Judah, meaning 'possession'. It was found among the Puritans from the 16th century, and was still used in the USA in the 19th century, but is now rare.
★ Jerusha Hess (1980–), US screenwriter

Jervis *see* Jarvis

Jerzy *see* George

Jes *see* Janet

Jesenia *see* Yesenia

Jesper *see* Jasper

Jess *see* Jesse, Jessica, Jessie

Jesse *mf*
This is the English version of the Hebrew name *Yishai*, 'God is', found in the Old Testament as the name of King David's father. He stands at the head of the family tree from which Jesus traced his descent through David. It was one of the many Old Testament

names taken to the USA by the Puritans, and it tends to be found more often there than in the UK. As a girl's name it is usually either a respelling of JESSIE or a pet form of JESSICA.
PET FORM **Jess**
★ Jesse James (1847–82), US Wild West outlaw
★ Jesse Jackson (1941–), US politician and clergyman

Jessenia *see* Yesenia

Jessica *f*
This name was created by Shakespeare for his play *The Merchant of Venice*. There it is borne by the daughter of the Jew Shylock, and is probably modelled on the name JESSE, rather than the other possibility, which is the obscure biblical name *Iscah*. This has become a candidate for the source because it can be found in Shakespeare's time in biblical translations as *Jesca*. Jessica did not enter the stock of names until it started to be used quietly in the 19th century – for example the painter Landseer's sister, a painter and engraver in her own right, who was born in 1807 was called Jessica – but it only came into general use in the early 20th century along with other Shakespearean names. Jessica became very popular in England in the late 1980s, has remained in the top few names for a number of years, and was the most popular choice for girls in 2005. In the USA, it hit the number one spot for several years in the 1980s and 1990s.
PET FORMS **Jess, Jesie, Jessie** • VARIANT **Jessika**
★ Jessica Mitford (1917–96), English writer
★ Sarah Jessica Parker (1965–), US actress

Jessie *fm*
As a female name this is either originally a Scottish pet form of JEAN or

JANET, or else a pet form of JESSICA. As a masculine form it can be a respelling of JESSE.

VARIANT **Jessye**

★ Jessye Norman (f) (1945–), US soprano

Jesus *m*

This is the New Testament form of the name JOSHUA. In Protestant countries, Jesus is usually considered too sacred to use as a first name, but it is well used in Catholic Spain and by Spanish speakers, who pronounce it 'hay-SOOS'.

FEMININE *Spanish* **Jesusa** • PET FORMS *Spanish* **Chucho, Chus, Chuy** • VARIANTS *Arabic* **Is(s)a, Essa**

Jet *mf* **Jetta** *f*

From the black semi-precious stone which gets its name, via the French *jaiet*, from the Latin *gagates*, '[stone] of Gagai', an ancient town in Asia Minor. Jetta can be either a feminine elaboration of this or, when pronounced with an initial 'y' sound, a Dutch pet form of HENRIETTA.

Jethro *m*

This is the English form of the Hebrew name *Yitro*, 'excellence, abundance', and in the Old Testament was the name of Moses's father-in-law. It was among the Old Testament names taken up by the Puritans, but is not much used today.

★ Jethro Tull (1674–1741), English agriculturist, whose name was borrowed by a rock group in the 1970s
☆ Jethro Larkin in the radio soap *The Archers*

Jevon *see* **Javon**

Jewel *f*

A name from the vocabulary word which came into use, along with many jewel names, in the 19th century.

VARIANT **Jewell**

★ Jewel Staite (1982–), Canadian actress

Jezebel *f*

In the Bible Jezebel, from the Hebrew meaning 'not exalted', was the name of the Phoenician wife of King Ahab who tried to turn him away from his faith. When Ahab's subjects rebelled, Jezebel dressed in her best and spoke to the people from a window (hence the use of the term for a forward woman). Elijah ordered that she be thrown from the window and left to be eaten by dogs. Despite this, the name is occasionally used in real life, although it is more common in fiction.

Jibril *see* **Gabriel**

Jill, Jilly *f*

Originally these were pet forms of GILLIAN, reflecting a variant spelling, *Jillian*. The expression 'Jack and Jill' for male and female was established by the 15th century.

VARIANT **Jilli**

★ Jill Murphy (1949–), English children's author
★ Jilly Cooper (1937–), English author

Jillian *see* **Gillian**

Jim, Jimmy *m*

Jim has been used as a short form of JAMES since the Middle Ages. Jim and Jimmy are now found as independent names.

VARIANT **Jim(m)i(e)**

★ Jim Carrey (1962–), Canadian-born US film actor
★ Jimmy Choo (c.1961–), Malaysian-born British shoe designer
★ Jimi Hendrix (1942–70), US rock guitarist and singer
☆ Jim Hawkins, boy hero of Robert Louis Stevenson's 1883 novel *Treasure Island*
☆ Jimmy Porter in John Osborne's 1956 play *Look Back in Anger*

Jimena *see* **Ximena**

Jimison, Jimson *see* **Jameson**

Jinny, Ginny *f*
Usually a variant of *Ginnie*, pet form of
VIRGINIA, but in the case of the fictional
Harry Potter character Ginny Weasley
it is a diminutive of *Ginevra*, the
Spanish form of GENEVIEVE.

Jinty *see* **Janet**

Jiochim *see* **Joachim**

Jiří *see* **George**

Jitendra *m*
An Indian name from the Sanskrit
meaning 'having conquered Indra'.
VARIANTS **Jitender, Jitinder**

Jo *fm*
Usually a feminine, this was originally
a pet form of names beginning *Jo-* such
as JOANNE and JOSEPHINE. It is also used
as a combining form in names like
Jo-Beth. As a masculine it is sometimes
found as a variant of JOE.

Joachim *m*
This is the traditional, non-biblical,
name of the Virgin Mary's father.
Joachim appears to be a variant
of either the Old Testament
Johoiachin, 'established by God',
which belonged to a king of Judah
defeated by Nebuchadnezzar, or the
name of the king's father *Jehoiakim*,
'raised by God'. The name varies in
pronunciation between languages.
In English it is 'O-a-kim', in German
it is pronounced with an initial *'yo'*
sound, while the Spanish form *Joaquin*
is pronounced 'wha-KEEN'. The latter
is currently the most prominent form
of the name, thanks to the fame of the
Puerto Rican-born US actor Joaquin
Phoenix (b.1974).
VARIANTS *Dutch, German* **Jochem** *German*
Achim, Jochen, Jiochim *Italian*
Gioa(c)chino *Portuguese* **Joaquim** *Russian*

Akim, Yakim *Scandinavian* **Joakim,
Jokum, Kim**

Joan, Joanne *f*
These names are among several old
feminine forms of JOHN (see also JANE,
JEAN). In this case the Latin *Io(h)anna*
became *Jo(h)anne* in Old French and
passed into English as both Joanne
(two syllables) and Joan. Joan was the
usual form of the name in the Middle
Ages, but thereafter was gradually
replaced by Jane, although it by no
means disappeared. It became popular
again in the early part of the 20th
century; St Joan of Arc was canonized
in 1920, followed in 1923 by George
Bernard Shaw's highly successful play
about her, both of which events may
have influenced the increase in use.
PET FORMS **Joani, Joni** • VARIANTS **Jo Anne**
Irish **Siobhan** *Scots Gaelic* **Siubhan**
Scottish **Johan** *Welsh* **Siwan**
★ Joan Crawford (1906–77), US film
actress
★ Dame Joan Sutherland (1926–),
Australian soprano

Joanna *f*
Joanna is a variant of JOAN derived
directly from the Latin *Io(h)anna*,
which in turn is taken from the Greek
form *Ioanna*. Joanna appears in the
New Testament as the name of both
the wife of King Herod's steward and
one of the women who supported
Christ while he was preaching. Early
uses are often spelt *Johanna*, but
Joanna did not become widely used
until the 18th century.
PET FORM **Jo** • VARIANTS **Jo(h)annah** *Greek*
Ioanna *Scandinavian* **Johanna, Jonna,
Jannike, Jensine**
★ Joanna Trollope (1943–), English
novelist
★ Joanna Lumley (1946–), English
actress

João *see* **John**

Job m

Job is the English form of the Hebrew *Iyyobh*, meaning 'persecuted, hated'. In the Old Testament Job is an upright man who proves his loyalty by refusing to curse God, despite all the troubles that the Adversary (Satan) is allowed to visit him with. His reward is to be restored to even greater prosperity.
PET FORMS **Joby, Jobie** • VARIANT *Arabic* **Ayub**

Jocasta f

A Greek name of unknown origin. It was borne by the mother, and later wife, of Oedipus, who killed herself when she discovered the incestuous relationship. Despite this, the name has been recorded in England since the late 15th century and continues to be used.

Jocelyn mf

When this name was brought to England by the Normans it was a masculine one. The Normans used the form *Joscelin* which was from the Germanic form *Gauzelin* or *Gautzelin*, a pet term for a member of a Germanic tribe, the Gauts, who may have been the same as the Goths. However, there seems to have been some confusion with pet forms of the name *Josse*. This was the French form of *Judoc* or *Jodoc*, probably from Celtic *jud*, 'chief'. *Josse* or *Judoc* was the name of a popular Breton saint. Jocelyn was revived in the 19th century and rapidly transferred to girls, particularly as it could be identified with names like JOYCE (which also derives from Josse) and analysed as Joyce plus LYN. It is now rare as a masculine name.
PET FORM **Joss** • VARIANTS **Joscelyn, Joselyn, Josceline, Joslyn**

Jochem, Jochen see **Joachim**

Jock, Jockey, Jockie see **Jack**

Jodoc see **Jocelyn**

Jody mf

Jody was introduced to the general public as a boy's name in Marjorie Kinnan Rawlings's Pulitzer Prize-winning novel, *The Yearling* (1938), and in the subsequent 1946 film adaptation, although it had already been used by Steinbeck for a boy in his novella *The Red Pony* (1933). As a masculine name it may have been a form of JOSEPH. It is now better known as a feminine name, when it is usually regarded as a variant of *Judy* (see JUDITH).
VARIANT **Jodi(e)**
★ Jodie Foster (1962–), US film actress
★ Jodie Marsh (1978–), English glamour model

Joe m

This is usually a pet form of JOSEPH, but can be from any name beginning *Jo-* and is increasingly used as an independent name.
PET FORM **Joey** • VARIANT **Jo**

Joel m Joelle f

These increasingly fashionable names come from the Hebrew name *Yoel*, formed from the elements *Yah(weh)* and *El*. These both mean 'God' and the implication is that this is the only God. There are a number of characters in the Old Testament called Joel, and it was among the many Old Testament names adopted by the Puritans and taken to the USA, where it has been more commonly used than in the UK. Joelle is a French feminine form which appears to be a 20th-century coinage.
PET FORM **Joe** • VARIANTS **Joella, Joely** *French* **Joël, Joëlle** *Italian* **Gioele**
★ Joel McCrea (1905–90), US actor
★ Joel Grey (1932–), US actor

Joep see **Joseph**

Joeri see **George**

Joffrey, Joffroy see **Geoffrey**

Johan *see* **Joan**

Johanna, Johannah *see* **Jane, Joanna**

John *m*
This is the English form of the Hebrew name *Johanan*, 'God is gracious'. It became *Ioannes* in the Greek of the New Testament and then *Io(h)annes* in St Jerome's Latin translation. This name was brought to England by the Normans in the form *Johan*, which was then shortened to John. The French-speaking aristocracy also introduced the French form *Jean* and the feminine equivalents (see JANE, JEAN, JOAN). When the name entered the Celtic languages it often developed two or more forms based on both the Latin and French variants. As these languages have no 'j' sound, the 'John' forms usually became names starting with a vowel, while the 'Jean' forms became names starting with 'S' (pronounced 'sh'), the nearest equivalent of the French 'je' sound (see examples under variants). John spread throughout the Christian world because it was borne by several important figures in early Christianity, including John the Baptist, the precursor of Christ; John the Apostle, one of Christ's disciples; the author of the Gospel of St John; and the author of the Book of Revelation. The name has been steadily popular since the Norman Conquest. It has usually been in the top twelve names for boys, and in the 17th century was borne by approximately one in three men. In the later 20th century it went through a quiet period, but is once more back in fashion. It is often now used in compounds, particularly *John-Paul*, both in imitation of this combination in other languages and in honour of two recent popes.
PET FORMS **Jack, Johnny, Johnnie, Jojo,**

Hank • VARIANTS *Cornish* **Jowan** *Irish* **Sean, Eoin** *Manx* **Ean** *Scottish* **Ian, Iain, Eòin, Seathan, Seocan** *Welsh* **Evan, Ianto, Iefan, Ieuan, Ioan, Siôn, Sioni, Sionyn, Jon** *Arabic* **Yahya** *Dutch* **Jan, Hans, Hannes, Joop** *French* **Jean, Jeannot, Yannic(k)** (Breton) *German* **Johann, Johannes, Hans, Hanke** *Greek* **Ioannis, Iannis, Ioannes, Yanni(s), Yiaanni(s)** *Hawaiian* **Keoni** *Hungarian* **János, Jancsi, Janika** *Italian* **Giovanni, Vanni, Gianni, Giannino, Nino** *Polish* **Jan, Janusz** *Portuguese* **João** *Russian* **Ivan** *Scandinavian* **Johan, Jon, Jens, Jan, Johan, Jöns, Hans, Hampus** *Serbian* **Jovan** *Spanish* **Juan, Juanito**

Johnathan *see* **Jonathan**

Joi, Joie *see* **Joy**

Jojo *see* **John, Joseph, Josephine**

Jokum *see* **Joachim**

Jolanda *see* **Yolanda**

Jolene *f*
This name appeared in the USA in the 1920s and was given publicity by the 1974 hit song 'Jolene' by Dolly Parton. It is assumed to be a blend formed from JO with the element *-lene* found in names such as MARLENE.
VARIANT **Joleen, Jolean**
★ Jolene Blalock (1975–), US actress known for her role in the television series *Star Trek: Enterprise*

Jolyon *see* **Julian**

Jon *see* **John**

Jonah, Jonas *m*
Jonah is from the Old Testament name, in Hebrew *Yonah*, meaning 'dove'. This appears as Jonas, the father of Simon Peter, in the New Testament. The Old Testament prophet, swallowed by a whale while trying to avoid God's commands, became a symbol of bad luck, and although the Puritans did use

Jonah, until recently, the more positive Jonas tended to be the preferred form.
VARIANTS *Arabic* **Yunus** *Hebrew* **Yonah**
★ Jonah Barrington (1941–), English-born Irish squash player
★ Jonah Lomu (1975–), New Zealand rugby union player
☆ Jonah Baldwin is the name of the child in the 1993 film *Sleepless in Seattle*. The character has been credited with a revival of interest in the name in the USA
☆ Jonas Quinn in the television series *Stargate SG-1*

Jonathan *m*
This Old Testament name, meaning 'gift of God' in the original Hebrew, is famous as the name of King David's close friend who was prepared to defy his father for David's sake, and for whom David composed some of his finest poetry as a lament for his death. It was in use in the Middle Ages and was a popular name among Puritans. They took it to the USA, where it was so common in the 17th and 18th centuries that the British used 'Brother Jonathan' as a nickname for Americans.
PET FORMS **Jon, Jonny, Jonty** • VARIANTS **Jonathon, Johnathan** *Irish* **Ionatán** *German, Scandinavian* **Jonatan** *Hebrew* **Yonatan, Yoni**
★ Jonathan Swift (1667–1745), Anglo-Irish clergyman and author

Jonelle *f*
A recent feminine form of JOHN, mainly confined to the USA.

Joni *see* Joan

Jonna *see* Jane, Joanna

Jonquil *f*
A flower name mainly used in the 1940s and 50s and now rarely given. Compare DAFFODIL.

Jöns *see* John

Jonty *see* Jonathan

Jools *see* Julia, Julian

Joop *see* John, Joseph

Joord *see* Jordan

Joos *see* Joseph, Justin

Joost *see* Justin

Jöran *see* George

Jorck *see* George

Jordan *mf*
The name of the River Jordan comes from the Hebrew word for 'to descend, flow down'. Because it was the river in which Christ himself was baptized, from the early Middle Ages Jordan water was prized for use in baptisms, and was brought back from the Holy Land for this purpose. It is thought that the name was introduced for boys so baptized. The name has been recorded in England from at least the 13th century. It came to be used as a feminine name only in the 20th century and for a while in the 1990s and 2000s it looked as if the feminine use was going to oust the masculine, but it is now back to being predominantly masculine. Some of its popularity as a male name in the USA may be influenced by the basketball player Michael Jordan.
PET FORMS **Jordy, Judd** • VARIANTS **Jorden, Jordyn, Jourdan, Jordon, Jordana, Jordanne** *Dutch* **Jordaan, Joord** *French* **Jordane, Jourdain** *Hebrew* **Yarden, Yardena** *Italian* **Giordano**
★ Jordan (1978–), English glamour model

Jordi, Jörg, Jorge, Jørgen *see* George

Joris, Jory *see* George, Marjory

Jörn *see* George

Jos, Joss *m*
Originally a pet form of names such as JOSEPH and JOSIAH, now given as an independent name.

Joscelin, Josceline, Joscelyn, Joselyn *see* **Jocelyn**

Joseph *m*
This is the English form of the Hebrew name *Yosef*, '[God] shall add [a son]'. The best-known Josephs in the Bible are the favourite son of Jacob, who was given the many-coloured coat and sold into slavery in Egypt by his jealous brothers, and the husband of the Virgin Mary. The fame of these two characters has spread the name throughout European languages, although it has only been really common among English speakers since the 17th century.
PET FORMS **Joe, Jojo, Jos(s), Josh** • VARIANTS *Irish* **Seosamh** *Scots Gaelic* **Seòsaidh** *Arabic* **Yusuf, Yous(s)ef, Yusef** *Dutch* **Josef, Jef, Joep, Joop, Jo(o)s, Sjef, Zef** *French* **José** *German* **Josef, Sepp(el)** *Hungarian* **József, Jóska, Józsi** *Italian* **Giuseppe, Beppe, Peppe, Peppi** *Polish* **Józef** *Russian* **Iosif, Osip** *Spanish* **José, Pepe, Pepito** *Yiddish* **Yussel, Yos(i), Yosel, Joske, Yoske**

Josephine *f*
A feminine form of JOSEPH, based on the French variant. English speakers began to use it in the 19th century.
PET FORMS **Fifi, Jo, Jody, Jojo, Josie, Josy, Josey, Posy, Posey** • VARIANTS **Josephina** *Irish* **Seosaimhn** *Dutch* **Jozefien** *French* **Josée, Josette, Josiane, Josianne, Josyane, Josèphe, Joséphine** *Italian* **Giuseppina, Giuseppa** *Polish* **Józefa** *Spanish* **Josefina, Pepita**

Joshua *m*
The Hebrew name *Yehoshua* means 'the Lord is my Salvation', and in the Old Testament was borne by a great general who succeeded Moses as leader of the Jewish exodus from Egypt. In the New Testament the name appears in two forms: JASON and JESUS, the latter representing the Aramaic form of the Hebrew name, *Yeshu'a*. Joshua is currently popular in the Anglophone world, both in its full form and in the short form *Josh*.
PET FORM **Josh** • VARIANTS *Arabic* **Yushua** *Hawaiian* **Iokua** *Hebrew* **Yehoshua, Yeshua** *French* **Josué** *Spanish* **Josue**

Josiah *m*
From the Hebrew *Yoshiyah*, 'God heals', this was the name of one of the kings of Israel, killed fighting the Egyptians at Megiddo. It entered the stock of names in the 17th century, then declined, but has become increasingly popular in the USA in recent years.
PET FORMS **Jos(s), Josh, Si** • VARIANT **Josias**
★ Josiah Wedgwood (1730–95), English potter
★ Josiah Spode (1754–1827), English potter

Josiane *see* **Josephine**

Jóska *see* **Joseph**

Joslyn *see* **Jocelyn**

Joss *see* **Jocelyn, Joseph, Josiah**

Josse *see* **Jocelyn**

Jourdain, Jourdan *see* **Jordan**

Jovan, Jowan *see* **John**

Joy *f*
This name, based on the vocabulary word, has been recorded from the 12th century. It was taken up by the Puritans as a response to the instruction to 'be joyful in the Lord', but rarely has such religious connotations today. It is also found as a pet form of JOYCE.
VARIANTS **Joi(e), Joya**
★ Joy Adamson (1910–80), Austrian-born British naturalist, who famously wrote

about her experiences with Elsa the lioness in *Born Free* (1960)

★ Joy Davidman (1915–60), US author and wife of C S Lewis

Joyce *mf*
This is the modern form of the Norman-French name *Josse* or *Josce* which is derived, via the Latin *Judocus*, from *Judoc* or *Jodoc*, itself probably a Breton name based on *jud*, 'chief' (see also JOCELYN). Many of William the Conqueror's followers were Breton, and they probably imported the name, which was strictly masculine at the time. The name had largely died out by the end of the 14th century, but there are sporadic occurrences from the 16th century in Puritan areas, where it is a female name. It has been suggested that this was linked to the Puritan use of JOY (the usual short form) or perhaps the word 'rejoice'. The name was revived for both sexes in the 19th century, but is now almost exclusively female, although the author Joyce Cary (1888–1959) kept an awareness of the masculine use alive. The name was popular around the 1920s, but is not much used today.

Józef *see* Joseph

Józefa, Jozefien *see* Josephine

József, Józsi *see* Joseph

Juan *see* John

Juana, Juanita *see* Jane

Juanito *see* John

Judah *m*
This is the Old Testament form of the Hebrew name *Yehudah*, 'praised'. It was the name of one of the twelve sons of Jacob whose tribe eventually founded the Kingdom of Judah. The name is mainly confined to Jewish communities, the New Testament JUDE being more common elsewhere.

VARIANTS **Yehudi, Yudel**

★ Baron Yehudi Menuhin (1916–99), US-born British violinist

☆ Judah Ben Hur in Lew Wallace's 1880 novel *Ben Hur*

Judd *see* Jordan

Jude *mf*
The translators of the New Testament were faced with a problem when dealing with the Hebrew name JUDAH. The normal Hellenized form is *Judas*, but this is so firmly associated with the hated Judas Iscariot that it was considered necessary to find an alternative for the other Apostle bearing the name, Judas Thaddaeus, so the name was shortened to Jude. Nevertheless, Jude has not, historically, been a popular name, and it is only in the last 50 or so years that it has had general currency. As a feminine name, Jude is usually a pet form of JUDITH.

★ Jude Law (1972–), English actor

☆ Jude Fawley in Thomas Hardy's 1895 novel *Jude the Obscure*. This, combined with the 1968 Beatles song 'Hey Jude', may have influenced modern use of the name

Judge *m*
This vocabulary word is more often a nickname than a given name, although it has been used on occasion as an independent name.

★ Judge Reinhold (1957–), US actor

Judicael *see* Gael

Judith, Judy *f*
In the Old Testament Judith – *Yehudhith*, simply meaning 'woman of Judea' or 'Jewess' – is the saviour of her people against the invading Assyrians, when she gets their lascivious general Holophernes drunk before beheading him with his own sword and then leading her people against his demoralized troops. It was one of the first Old Testament names

to become widely known among the Germanic aristocracy of Western Europe, being well established among the ruling families by the 9th century. However, it did not become widespread among English speakers until the 16th century. Before then it had been thought of as typically Jewish. More recently, it peaked in popularity between the 1940s and 1960s. The pet form Judy was being used as an independent name by the 17th century, and JODY is a modern offshoot.

PET FORMS **Judi(e)**, **Jude** • VARIANTS *German* **Jutta**, **Jutte** *Italian* **Giuditta** *Polish* **Judyta** *Scandinavian, Spanish* **Judit** *Yiddish* **Yehudit**, **Hudes**, **Yidel**, **Yutke**

★ Judith Weir (1954–), Scottish lecturer and composer
★ Judy Garland (1922–69), US singer and actress

Judoc *see* **Jocelyn**

Jul *see* **Godfrey**

Julia, Julie *f*
The Roman family of the Julii used Julia as the name of all their women, just as JULIUS was borne by all the men. The Julii had their own account of the origin of the name, claiming descent from the goddess Venus through her grandson *Julus* or *Iulus* (the letters are interchangeable in Latin). Julus was a term for the first fluffy growth of beard on a youth, and was given as a name to the ancestor of the Julii because he had killed his first man in battle while at this stage in his life. A more realistic explanation is that the name comes from the Latin *deus*, 'god', with the 'd' changed to a 'j' sound. There is a Julia mentioned in St Paul's Epistle to the Romans, and there were a number of early saints called Julia, but the name did not enter regular use among English speakers until classical names became popular in the 18th century.

Julie is both the French form of Julia and the English pet form, now well established as an independent name.

PET FORMS **Jools**, **Jules** • VARIANTS *Irish* **Iúile** *Italian* **Giulia** *Russian* **Yuli(y)a**

★ Julia Roberts (1967–), US film actress
★ Dame Julie Andrews (1935–), English singer and actress
☆ Julia in Sheridan's 1775 play *The Rivals*

Julian, Julius *m*
As has been stated under JULIA, the Roman family name of Julii probably comes from *deus*, the Latin for 'god', in a sound change from 'd' to 'j' which is also found in the name of the king of the gods, Jupiter, originally *deus pater*, 'god the father'. The Roman family name *Julianus* referred to a collateral branch of the family or someone otherwise connected with them. It was borne by the Roman emperor who tried to return the Empire to paganism, but this was counterbalanced by the fact that it was also the name of several saints, which made it possible to use Julian as a first name. In the Middle Ages Julian was used for both sexes, but later the feminine form was distinguished by being spelt GILLIAN. *Jolyon* is a variant from the north of England which spread to a wider audience after it was used for a character in John Galsworthy's series of novels known as *The Forsyte Saga* (1906–22).

PET FORMS **Jools**, **Jules** • VARIANTS **Julyan** *French* **Jules**, **Julien** *Italian* **Giulio**, **Giuliano** *Polish* **Juliusz**, **Julek** *Russian* **Yuli(y)** *Spanish* **Julio**

★ Julian Bream (1933–), English guitarist and lutenist
★ John Julius Norwich (1929–), English historian and travel writer
☆ Julian was the name of one of Enid Blyton's *Famous Five*

Juliana *f*
Although JULIAN was used for both

sexes in the Middle Ages, in Latin the female name was given a feminine ending and appeared as Juliana. This form was revived in the 18th century. In modern use the name is often analysed as JULIE combined with ANNE or ANNA, hence forms such as *Julieanne* and *Julieanna*.

★ Queen Juliana of the Netherlands (1909–2004)
★ Julianne Moore (1960–), US actress

Juliet *f*
Use of this name, based on an Italian pet form of JULIA, comes from the heroine of Shakespeare's play *Romeo and Juliet* (1596).

VARIANTS *French* **Juliette** *Italian* **Giulietta** *Polish* **Julita**

★ Juliet Mills (1941–), English actress
★ Juliette Binoche (1964–), French actress

June *f*
This name, from the calendar month, was one of a number of month names that came into use in the early 20th century. It had its peak in popularity in the 1930s. The month gets its name from the Roman goddess JUNO.

★ June Whitfield (1925–), English comic actress
★ June Carter Cash (1929–2003), country singer, wife of Johnny Cash

Junior *m*
This was originally a nickname, or a distinguishing element in the name of a son called after his father. It is now increasingly being given as an independent name.

Juniper *fm*
This is a modern plant name, most often used for women.

Juno *f*
Juno was the Roman queen of the gods, whose name may be based on a Latin word for 'young'. In Ireland it has been used to anglicize the Irish name *Úna*, otherwise anglicized as OONA.

★ Juno Temple (1989–), English actress
☆ Juno MacGuff in the 2007 film *Juno*
☆ Juno Daly in Sean O'Casey's 1924 play *Juno and the Paycock*

Jurek, Jurgen, Jurian *see* George

Jürgen *see* George

Justin *m* Justine *f*
Justus was a Roman name from the vocabulary word meaning 'just, fair'. This developed the forms *Justinus* and *Justina*, which became Justine in French. Since they were borne by several saints, these names quickly spread through Europe, for example *Iestin*, the Welsh form, has been in use since the 6th century.

VARIANTS **Justyn** *Welsh* **Iestyn** *Dutch* **Joos(t)** *French* **Juste** *Italian* **Giustina, Giustino** *Polish* **Justyn, Justyna** *Russian* **Ustinya, Yustina**

★ Justin Timberlake (1981–), US singer and actor
☆ Justine is the eponymous heroine of Lawrence Durrell's 1957 novel in his *Alexandria Quartet*. The novel is thought to have been influential in spreading the name

Jutta, Jutte *see* Judith

Juwairiyah *f*
This Arabic name means 'little damask rose' and was borne by one of the Prophet Muhammad's wives.

Jyoti *f*
A name from the Sanskrit *jyotis*, 'light'. It is occasionally used for boys.

K

Kabir *m*
An Arabic name meaning 'great, magnificent'. *Al-Kabeer*, 'The Great', is one of the titles of Allah.
VARIANT **Kabeer**

Kacey *f*
Either a variant of CASEY, or else a modern name based on the initials K C.
VARIANTS **Kacee, Kaci(e), Kacy, Kaycee**

Kacper *see* **Casper**

Kade *see* **Cade**

Kaden *see* **Caden**

Kadence *see* **Cadence**

Kadin *see* **Caden**

Kady *f*
A modern name that can be analysed as either a development of KAY (or Kay and DEE); a name made from the initials K D; a US regional pronunciation of KATY; or simply a combination of fashionable sounds.
VARIANTS **Kadi(e), Kadey, Kaid(e)y, Kaedy**

Kadyn, Kaeden *see* **Caden**

Kaedy *see* **Kady**

Kai¹ *m*
Originally a German and Scandinavian name, pronounced to rhyme with 'sky'. It represents either a form of the name CAIUS, or a pet form of any name beginning with 'K' or 'G', particularly *Gerhard* (see GERARD). See also KAI².
VARIANT **Kay**
☆ Kay is the name of the boy in Hans Christian Andersen's 1845 story *The Snow Queen*

Kai² *mf*
Kai is a Hawaiian name meaning 'big water, sea'. It is impossible to determine from the statistics whether it is this name or Kai¹ that has become so popular among English speakers in recent years, or even if the givers of the name make any distinction between the two. Kai is a common name in many languages, including Chinese (where it can mean, among other things, 'triumphant'). It has also been used extensively as a fantasy name in computer games, film, television and print, and the popularity of the name may well come from this. It is more often masculine than feminine. See also CAI and KAY.
VARIANT **Kaia** (f)

Kaiden *see* **Caden**

Kaidey, Kaidy *see* **Kady**

Kaila *see* **Kayla**

Kailash *mf*
An Indian name from the Sanskrit name of a mountain peak in the Himalayas, thought to be the paradise of the god Shiva and the home of the god of wealth.
VARIANT **Kailas**

Kailee, Kaileigh, Kaily *see* **Kayleigh**

Kailyn *see* **Kaylin**

Kain, Kaine *see* **Kane**

Kaitlin, Kaitlyn *see* **Caitlin**

Kajetan *see* **Gaetano**

Kale *see* **Cale**

Kaleb, Kalev *see* **Caleb**

Kalee *see* **Kayleigh**

Kali *f* **Kalidas** *m*
Kali, meaning 'the black one' in Sanskrit, is the name of the goddess who is Shiva's wife in her fierce aspect, when she represents time and change, and hence death and destruction. Kalidas means 'servant of Kali'. Some Western uses of Kali may represent respellings of CARLY or CALLIE.

Kalie *see* **Kayleigh**

Kalin *see* **Caoilainn**

Kallan *see* **Callan**

Kalli, **Kallie** *see* **Callie**

Kallum, **Kalum** *see* **Calum**

Kalvin *see* **Calvin**

Kalysta *see* **Callista**

Kamal *m*[1]
This is from the Arabic for 'perfection'. *Kamal-ud-Din* means 'perfection of religion'.
VARIANT **Kemal**
★ Mustafa Kemal Atatürk (1881–1938), Turkish general and statesman, known as the founder of modern Turkey

Kamal *m*[2] **Kamala** *f*
These Indian names come from the Sanskrit word both for 'pink' and, from its colouring, for the lotus flower. Kamala is also one of the names of the goddess LAKSHMI.

Kameron *see* **Cameron**

Kamil *m*[1] **Kamila** *f*
These come from the Arabic for 'perfect, complete, genuine'. *Al-Kamil*, 'the perfect', is one of the titles of Muhammad. Western uses of these names may represent variants of *Camille* and CAMILLA.
VARIANTS **Kamel**, **Kamil(l)ah**, **Kamla**
★ Mustafa Kamil (1874–1908), Egyptian

nationalist who fought for his country's independence

Kamil[2] **Kamilla** *see* **Camilla**

Kamran *m*
A Muslim name from the Persian for 'lucky, happy, fortunate'.

Kamron, **Kamryn** *see* **Cameron**

Kandace, **Kandi**, **Kandice**, **Kandy** *see* **Candace**

Kane *m*
An English form of the Irish name CATHAN, and a common Irish surname. It is also found as a variant of KEAN. Use has recently increased in the English-speaking world. See also CAIN.

Kanta, **Kanti** *f*
Kanta comes from the Sanskrit for 'desired, beautiful', while Kanti means 'beauty' and is one of the names of the goddess LAKSHMI.

Kapel *see* **Jacob**

Kara *see* **Cara**

Karaline *see* **Caroline**

Karam *m*
An Arabic name from the vocabulary word for generosity.

Kareem, **Kareema** *see* **Karim**

Karen *f*
This was originally a Danish pet form of *Katerina*, the Scandinavian form of CATHERINE. The name was taken to the USA by Scandinavian immigrants and then spread to the rest of the English-speaking world. It was particularly popular in the middle years of the 20th century.
PET FORM **Kaz** (mainly Australian) • VARIANT *Norwegian, Swedish* **Karin**

Karenza *f*
A Cornish name meaning 'loving' from *car*, 'love'.
VARIANTS **Carenza**, **Kerenza**, **Kerensa**

Karim *m* **Karima** *f*
An Arabic name, meaning 'generous'.
It is one of the Arabic names taken up
by African Americans, usually in the
form *Kareem*. See also ABDUL.
VARIANTS **Kareem, Kareema**
★ Kareem Abdul-Jabbar (1947–), US
basketball player

Karin *see* **Karen**

Karine *see* **Carreen**

Karis, Karisa, Karissa *see* **Carys,
Charis, Carissa**

Karita *see* **Charity**

Karl, Karla *see* **Carl, Carla**

Karli, Karlie, Karly *see* **Carly**

Karlton *see* **Carlton**

Karma *f*
The concept, from the Sanskrit for
'action, deed, effect', which lies
behind the cycle of cause and effect
in Indian religious thought. Karma
can also be an Arabic feminine name
meaning 'grapevine'.

Karmen *see* **Carmen**

Karol *see* **Carol**

Karolin, Karolina, Karoline *see*
Caroline

Karolyn, Karolynn *see* **Carolyn**

Karson *see* **Carson**

Karsten *see* **Christian**

Karys *see* **Carys**

Kasandra *see* **Cassandra**

Kasey *see* **Casey**

Kashi *m*
From the Sanskrit for 'shining', this is
a name for the sacred Hindu city of
Varanasi (Benares) used as a first name.
VARIANT **Kasi**

Kasia *see* **Catherine, Keziah**

Kasimir *see* **Casimir**

Kason *see* **Carson**

Kaspar, Kasper *see* **Casper**

Kassandra *see* **Cassandra**

Kassidy *see* **Cassidy**

Kasy *see* **Casey**

Kat, Katarina, Katarine, Katarzyna
see **Catherine**

Kate *f*
A pet form of CATHERINE, and related
names such as CAITLIN, which has been
in use since the Middle Ages.
PET FORMS **Katie, Katy** • VARIANTS *Irish* **Cáit**
Scots Gaelic **Ceit**

Katelijn, Katelijne *see* **Catherine**

Katelyn, Katelyne *see* **Caitlin**

Katerina *f*
A Russian, Greek and Scandinavian
form of CATHERINE, now occasionally
used by English speakers.
PET FORM **Karen** • VARIANT *Dutch, German,
Scandinavian* **Katrina**

**Katharina, Katharine, Katherine,
Katheryn** *see* **Catherine**

Kathleen *f*
An alternative anglicization of CAITLIN,
which was popular from the 1920s to
the 1960s.
PET FORMS **Kath, Kathy** • VARIANTS
Kathlene, Cathleen, Kathlyn
★ Kathleen Ferrier (1912–53), English
contralto
★ Kathleen Turner (1954–), US actress

Kathryn *f*
A 20th-century variant of CATHERINE.

Kathy, Katia *see* **Catherine**

Katie *see* **Kate**

Katina, Katinka, Katrien, Katrine

see **Catherine**

Katrina *see* **Catriona**

Katy *see* **Kate**

Katya *see* **Catherine**

Kavita *f*
An Indian name, from the Sanskrit for 'poem'.

Kay *f*
A pet form of any name beginning with a 'K' sound, most often CATHERINE, which is now used as an independent name. For masculine uses see under CAI and KAI.
VARIANT **Kai**
★ Kay Kendall (1926–59), English actress

Kaycee, Kayci, Kaycie *see* **Casey, Kacey**

Kaydence *see* **Cadence**

Kayetan *see* **Gaetano**

Kayla *f*
A name which started to appear in the USA in the late 1950s, and has been in the top 30 names there since the mid-1980s. The rapid increase in popularity in the 80s has been attributed to the appearance of the character of Kayla Brady Johnson in the long-running US soap opera *Days of our Lives*. It can be analysed as a blend of fashionable sounds, or as a shortening of MICHAELA (see MICHELLE). Kayla or *Keila* can also be a pet form of the Yiddish name *Kelila*, meaning 'crown of laurel'.
VARIANTS **Kaila, Kaylah**

Kayleigh *f*
A modern name, spelt in numerous ways, which became popular after the band Marillion had a hit song 'Kayleigh' in 1985. The name is formed from a blend of KAY and LEIGH, but is nevertheless often used in other combinations, like *Kayleigh-Anne*.

Variants can overlap with names such as CALLIE.
VARIANTS **Ka(y)lee, Ka(y)lie, Kaleigh, Calie, Kailee, Kaileigh**
☆ Kaylee Frye, ship's engineer in the television series *Firefly*

Kaylin, Kailyn *f*
A name that can be either a blend of KAY and LYN, or else a variant of *Keelin* (see KEELAN).

Kaz *see* **Karen, Casimir**

Kazia, Kazimiera, Kazimierz, Kazimir *see* **Casimir**

Keagan *see* **Keegan**

Kealan, Kealon *see* **Caolan**

Kean *m*
This is both a surname and an anglicized form of the Irish name CIAN, meaning 'enduring, ancient'.
FEMININE **Kean(n)a** • VARIANTS **Keane, Kian, Kane**

Keanu *m*
A Hawaiian name based on *anu*, 'coolness', and usually interpreted as meaning 'cool breeze'. The name was all but unknown outside Hawaii, until it was brought to wider attention by the US actor Keanu Reeves (b.1964).

Keavy *see* **Caoimhe**

Keefer *see* **Kiefer**

Keegan *m*
This is an Irish surname used as a first name. The surname comes from the Irish *MacAodhagain*, 'son of AIDAN'.
VARIANTS **Keigan, Keagan**

Keela *see* **Keeley**

Keelan, Keelin *mf*
While in theory it is possible to make a distinction between these two names, and to mark one as masculine and the other as feminine, in practice both forms are used for both sexes.

Strictly speaking, Keelan is an Irish surname from the Irish *O Ceilecachain*, 'descendant of the little companion', and originally masculine. Keelin is either an anglicization of CAOILAINN, 'fair and slender', or a form of CAOLAN, and originally feminine.
VARIANTS **Kellen, Kellan**

Keeley *f*
The origin of this name is unclear. It may derive from the Irish surname Keeley, which goes back to *caol*, 'slender'. Alternatively, it may be a variant of KEELIN or from the same root, or it may be linked with the Irish name *Cadhla*, 'beautiful, graceful', anglicized as *Keela* or *Kyla* (see KYLE). The name started to be used in the USA in the late 1950s, but there the spelling *Keely* is preferred.
VARIANT **Keely**
★ Keeley Hawes (1976–), English actress
★ Keely Smith (1932–), US jazz singer

Keelin *see* **Keelan**

Keenan *m*
An Irish surname now found as a first name, derived from the Irish name CIAN, 'old one, ancient'.
VARIANT **Kienan**

Kees *see* **Cornelius**

Keesha *see* **Keisha**

Keeva *see* **Caoimhe**

Keevan *see* **Cavan**

Keigan *see* **Keegan**

Keila *see* **Kayla**

Keilidh *see* **Ceilidh**

Keir, Kerr *m*
Keir is a variant of the Scottish and northern English surname Kerr, from the Old Norse place name *kjarr*, 'boggy ground'. Keir became well known through the Scottish politician,

Keir Hardie (1856–1915). In his case it was his mother's surname. Both names are mainly confined to Scotland.

Keira *f*
A respelling of *Kiera*, the anglicized form of the Irish name CIARA from *ciar*, 'black'. This has now become the dominant spelling of the name due, at least in part, to the success of English actress Keira Knightley (b.1985).
VARIANT **Kiera**

Keiran *see* **Ciaran**

Keisha *f*
This modern name, which first appeared in the USA in the 1960s, has been linked to a Central African language, such as Bobangi, where the word *nkisa* is said to mean 'favourite'. However, there is little evidence to support this, and the name is more likely to be a regional pronunciation of KEZIAH, or to have simply been invented. It peaked in popularity in the 1970s to 80s, and has mainly been used by African Americans. It is also found with the popular African-American prefix *La-* in forms such as *Lakeisha*.
VARIANTS **Keesha, Kesha, Kisha**

Keith *m*
The district of Keith in East Lothian probably gets its name from British *cet*, 'wood'. The district name became an aristocratic family name and was among the many, such as BRUCE and DOUGLAS, that were adopted as first names in the 19th century. Keith became particularly popular in the USA, where it was in the top 100 names for boys from 1946 to 1991.
★ Keith Waterhouse (1929–), English author
★ Keith Richards (1943–), English rock guitarist

Keiva *see* **Caoimhe**

Kekepania *see* **Stephanie**

Kelci *see* **Kelsey**

Kelila *see* **Kayla**

Kellan, Kellen *see* **Keelan**

Kelly *mf*
The Irish masculine name *Ceallach*, 'strife, war', which was borne by a number of Irish saints, became the surname Kelly. This was thought of as a typically Irish surname. As a masculine first name Kelly was being used in the USA, presumably by Irish immigrants, in the 19th century. It started being chosen as a feminine name there in the 1950s and was particularly popular from the 1960s to 90s. It is now rare as a masculine name. Like many such names, it was slow to be adopted in Ireland itself.
VARIANT **Kelley**
★ Dame Kelly Holmes (1970–), English athlete
★ Kelly Osbourne (1984–), English singer and television personality
☆ Kelly is the name of one of the 'little sisters' of the Barbie doll®

Kelsey *mf*
This is the surname, from an Old English personal name, used as a first name. It appears in records as a first name from the 19th century, but only came into regular use in the 1970s, initially as a boy's name. However, feminine use rapidly overtook the masculine, and it is now rarely chosen for boys.
VARIANTS **Kel(l)si(e), Kelci(e), Kelsy**
★ Kelsey Grammer (1955–), US actor

Kelvin *m*
This is the name of a river in Scotland, perhaps from the Celtic for 'narrow river', used as a first name. It came into use in the 1920s, perhaps influenced by the fame of the scientist Lord Kelvin of Largs (1824–1907).
VARIANT **Kelvyn**

★ Kelvin Mackenzie (1946–), English journalist and television presenter
☆ Kelvin Carpenter in the television soap *EastEnders*

Kemal *see* **Kamal**

Ken *m*
Short form of KENNETH, and of any name beginning with these letters, sometimes given as an independent name.

Kendall *mf*
A surname, from the English place name meaning 'valley of the river Kent', now used as a first name. The name was masculine when it first came into use at the beginning of the 20th century but, as so often happens, this has been overtaken by the later feminine use, although it is still occasionally used as a boy's name.
PET FORM **Ken** • VARIANTS **Kendal, Kendel(l), Kendyl(l)**

Kendra *f*
Kendra is usually glossed as a feminine variant of KENDRICK, but this ignores the fact that Kendra came into use in the USA in the 1940s, predating Kendrick by some 20 years, and that it has always been the more popular. It is more likely to be a blend of KEN and the ending of a name such as SANDRA.
VARIANT **Kendrah**
☆ Kendra Young, substitute slayer in *Buffy the Vampire Slayer*
☆ Kendra Saunders, comic superheroine known as Hawkgirl

Kendrick *m*
The surname, which can come from many sources, used as a first name, mainly in the USA. See also KENDRA.

Kenelm *m*
An Old English name formed from the elements *cene*, 'keen, brave', and *helm*, 'helmet'. It was borne by a 9th-century saint and was well used in the Middle Ages, but then went out of

fashion except among the Digby family who kept it alive.

★ Sir Kenelm Digby (1603–65), English diplomat and writer

Kennedy *fm*

The Irish name *Cinnéidigh* was formed from *ceann*, 'head', and *éidigh*, 'armoured, ugly, misshapen'. It was a nickname given to one of Brian Boru's nephews in the 10th century, because he had some sort of deformity. It developed into a widespread surname, most notably that of President John F Kennedy and his brother Robert. It started to be used as a first name for boys in 1960, when Kennedy was running for president, but then disappeared again a few years later. It reappeared in the early 1990s chosen for both sexes, but is now mainly feminine.

VARIANTS **Kennedi, Kenadie**

Kenneth *m*

This seems to be derived from a falling together of two Scots Gaelic names: *Cinead*, 'born from fire', and *Cainneach*, 'handsome'. The name spread from Scotland in the 20th century, and became very popular for a while, but is now in decline. See also KENZIE, MACKENZIE.

PET FORMS **Ken, Kenny** • VARIANT **Kennith**

★ Kenneth I or Kenneth MacAlpin (d.858), first king of the Picts and Scots
★ Kenneth Branagh (1960–), Northern Irish actor and director

Kent *m*

The county of Kent, in the south-east corner of England, gets its name from a Celtic word meaning 'edge, border'. Kent became a well-used surname which in turn was adopted as a first name. It was quite popular in the USA in the middle years of the 20th century.

☆ Kent Brockman, television anchorman in television cartoon *The Simpsons*

Kentigern *see* **Mungo**

Kenton *m*

Kenton is a place name which can have a number of meanings depending on its location, including 'king's settlement' and 'settlement on the river Kenn'. Use as a first name, which in some cases may have been influenced by US jazz pianist Stan Kenton (1911–79), comes from the surname derived from the place. The name has never been common, but has been brought to public attention through the character of Kenton Archer in the long-running radio soap *The Archers*.

PET FORM **Kent**

Kenya *f*

This is the name of the African country which has been regularly used as a first name since the 1960s, mainly by African Americans. The country gets its name from the snow-capped Mount Kenya, which is called *Kere Nyaga*, 'mountain of whiteness', in the local Kikuyu language. As a masculine name, Kenya is a Russian pet form of *Innokentiy* (see INNOCENT).

Kenzie *mf*

A shortening of MACKENZIE, 'son of KENNETH', which has been growing in popularity in recent years with many different spellings.

VARIANTS **Kenzi, Kenzy, Kenzeigh**

Keoni *see* **John**

Keren *f*

Keren is the usual form of the biblical name *Kerenhappuch*, 'horn [ie container] of kohl'. Keren can also mean 'ray [of light]' in Hebrew and, as it is now mainly Jewish (although it was one of the Old Testament names adopted by the Puritans), some may use it in this sense. Kerenhappuch was the name of one of the beautiful daughters of Job, the others being JEMIMA and KEZIAH. It is also sometimes found as a variant of KAREN.

VARIANTS **Ker(r)yn, Keran, Ker(r)in, Keron, Kerena, Kerina**

Kerensa, Kerenza see **Karenza**

Keri, Kerie see **Ceri, Kerry**

Kerith see **Cherith**

Kermit *m*
This is a surname used as a first name. The surname was originally the Irish *Mac Dhiarmaid*, 'son of DERMOT'. The name was not uncommon in the early years of the 20th century but is now rarely given, being most strongly associated with Kermit the Frog from *The Muppets*.

PET FORM **Kim**

★ Kermit Roosevelt (1889–1943), US entrepreneur and son of President Theodore Roosevelt. It was probably the choice of the name for him that helped its spread

Kerneels see **Cornelius**

Kerr see **Keir**

Kerri, Kerrie see **Kerry**

Kerrith see **Cherith**

Kerry *mf*
This is the name of the Irish county, which in Gaelic is *Chiarrai* meaning 'Ciar's people' (see CIARAN), used as a first name. It seems to have originally come into use as a first name in Australia, but rapidly spread to the rest of the English-speaking world. It is now more used for girls than boys, sometimes in combinations such as *Kerry-Anne*, and there is some overlap with CERI.

VARIANT **Ke(r)ri(e)**

Kerryn see **Keren**

Kerstin see **Christina**

Kesha see **Keisha**

Kester *m*
This is an old, mainly Scottish, form of CHRISTOPHER. Its occasional use in modern times may owe something to the success of Mary Webb's novel *Precious Bane* (see further under JANCIS), in which it is the name of the hero.

★ Kester Berwick (1903–92), Australian theatre actor and writer

Keturah *f*
In the Bible Keturah, whose name means 'incense, fragrance' in Hebrew, was the second wife of Abraham. The name has never been common, and is most likely to be found in the USA, particularly among Mormons.

Keva see **Caoimhe**

Kevan see **Cavan**

Kevin *m*
This is an Irish name, *Caoimhín* in the original Gaelic, which spread from Ireland to the rest of the world from the 1920s onwards. The older form of the name was *Coemgen*, formed from the Old Irish elements *coem*, 'comely, kind, gentle', and *gein*, 'birth'. It was borne by a prominent 6th-century Irish saint who founded a monastery at Glendalough, which became equally famous for its scholarship and the beauty of its location.

PET FORM **Kev** • VARIANTS **Kevan, Keven, Kevyn**

★ Kevin Keegan (1951–), English footballer and manager
★ Kevin Costner (1955–), US film actor and director

Keyana see **Kiana**

Keyne see **Ceinwen**

Keziah *f*
This is the Hebrew word for the cassia tree which, like its close relative CINNAMON, has a fragrant bark used both in cooking and in religious ritual. In the Bible Keziah was the name of one of the three daughters

of Job. Variants such as *Keshia* (with a pronunciation 'KAY-sh(i)a') may lie behind the name KEISHA.

PET FORMS **Kez, Kezzie, Kezzy, Kissie, Kissy** • VARIANTS **Kezia, Cassia, Kasia**

★ Keziah Jones (1968–), Nigerian guitarist and a rare example of a masculine use

☆ Kezia Walker in the television series *The Bill*

Kfir *m*

This is a modern Israeli name, from the Hebrew for 'lion cub'. Use has been growing since the 1980s.

Khadija *f*

This means 'premature child' in Arabic, but is a popular Muslim name as it was borne by Muhammad's first wife, the only one by whom he had children. She was the first woman to convert to Islam.

VARIANT **Khadijah**

Khalid *m* Khalida *f*

This is an Arabic name meaning 'eternal, immortal'.

VARIANTS **Khaled, Khaleda**

★ Khalid ibn-al-Walid (c.592–642), Arabian military leader known as 'the Sword of Islam' and said to be the first bearer of the name

Khalifa *m*

An Arabic name meaning 'successor' and the source of the English word 'caliph'.

Khalil *m*

An Arabic name meaning 'close friend'.

★ Khalil Gibran (1883–1931), Lebanese mystical writer, poet and artist

Khayri *m* Khariyya *f*

An Arabic name meaning 'charitable, benevolent'.

Khloe *see* Chloe

Kia *mf*

This is a modern name of uncertain origin, although it has been linked to the Maori greeting *Kia ora*, 'be well'. Kia can also be a Swedish pet form of *Kristina* (see CHRISTINA).

Kian *see* Cian, Kean

Kiana *f*

Kiana can have two sources. The first is the Hawaiian form of the name DIANA. The second, mainly used by African Americans, is a form of the name *Qiana*, a brand of silky fabric. In addition Kiana can be a Persian name meaning 'nature'.

VARIANTS **Kianna, Keyana**

★ Kiana Tom (1965–), Hawaiian-born exercise expert and actress, who popularized the name in the 1980s

Kiara *f*

A respelling of both CIARA and CHIARA, which came into use in the USA in the 1980s with the success of a singing duo of the name.

VARIANT **Kiar(r)a(h)**

☆ Kiara is a character in the 1998 Disney animation *Lion King II*

Kiefer *m*

This is a surname, originally the Dutch equivalent of COOPER, which came into use as a first name through the fame of actor Kiefer Sutherland. He was given the surname of a family friend.

VARIANT **Keefer**

Kienan *see* Keenan

Kiera *see* Ciara, Keira

Kieran, Kieren, Kieron *see* Ciaran

Kiki *fm*

Usually feminine, this is a pet form of any name beginning with a 'K'.

★ Kiki Dee (1947–), English singer

Kilian, Killian *see* Cillian

Kim *mf*

As a feminine this is usually a pet form of KIMBERLEY, sometimes given as an independent name. It is also a common Vietnamese name meaning 'golden'. The masculine name can have a number of sources. It can be a pet form of the names JOACHIM and KERMIT. Most often it is a nickname derived from, or direct use of, the name of the character in Kipling's 1901 novel *Kim*. The hero of this much-loved novel of Indian life is universally known as Kim, but his true given name is *Kimball*, a surname which can be derived from either the Welsh name *Cynbel*, meaning 'chief war', or the Old English name *Cynebald*, meaning 'royal boldness'.

PET FORMS **Kimmie, Kimi** • VARIANT **Kym**
★ Kim Philby (1911–88), Indian-born British double agent
★ Kim Basinger (1953–   ), US actress

Kimberley *f*
The town of Kimberley in South Africa was named after Lord Kimberley (1826–1902), whose title came from a place name interpreted as 'Cyneburga's field', Cyneburga meaning 'royal fortress'. Kimberley played an important role in the Boer War, and it was not unusual for soldiers in the 19th and early 20th centuries to name their children after the garrison town where they were born, or after a battle. Thus Kimberley had a brief life as a predominantly male name around the time of the Boer War. It was then revived in the middle of the 20th century as a feminine name and became enormously popular, particularly in North America where it is usually spelt without the final 'e'.

PET FORMS **Kim, Kimmy, Kimmie, Kimber** • VARIANTS **Kimberly, Kymberl(e), Kimberleigh**
★ Kimberly Williams (1971–   ), US actress

Kina *see* **Alexandra**

Kingsley *mf*
A surname from a place name

meaning 'king's field', now increasingly being used as a first name.

PET FORM **King** • VARIANTS **Kingsly, Kingslie**
★ Sir Kingsley Amis (1922–95), English novelist and poet

Kip *see* **Christopher**

Kira *see* **Kyra**

Kiran *mf*
This is an Indian name from the Sanskrit for 'ray of light', particularly referring to a moonbeam or a shaft of sunlight.

★ Kiran Desai (1971–   ), Indian novelist

Kiri *f*
This Maori name was introduced to the public by the New Zealand opera singer Kiri Te Kanawa (b.1944). The name is said to mean 'skin, bark, rind'.

Kirill *see* **Cyril**

Kirk *m*
A surname used as a first name from the northern dialect word for 'church'.

VARIANT **Kirke**
★ Kirk Douglas (1916–   ), US film actor

Kirsten, Kirsty *f*
Kirsten was originally a Scandinavian pet form of CHRISTINE, which is now widely used as an independent name. It is particularly popular in Scotland where the variant Kirsty developed, which has since spread to other countries.

VARIANTS **Kirstin, Kirstyn, Kirstie** *Scottish Highlands* **Chirsty** *Scots Gaelic* **Ciorstaidh, Ciorstag**
★ Kirsten Flagstad (1895–1962), Norwegian soprano
★ Kirsty MacColl (1959–2000), English folk singer-songwriter
★ Kirsty Young (1968–   ), Scottish journalist and news presenter

Kisha *see* **Keisha**

Kishan, Kishen *see* **Krishna**

Kissie, Kissy *see* **Keziah**

Kistna *see* **Krishna**

Kit *m*
A pet form of CHRISTOPHER sometimes
used as an independent name. See
also KITTY.
★ Kit Carson (1809–68), US frontiersman

Kitty *f*
A pet form of CATHERINE and its variants
such as KATHLEEN, sometimes given as
an independent name.
PET FORM **Kit**

Kizzie, Kizzy *see* **Keziah**

Klara *see* **Clara**

Klaas *see* **Claus**

Klasina *see* **Nicola**

Klaudia *see* **Claudia**

Klaus *see* **Claus, Nicholas**

Klava, Klavdiya *see* **Claudia**

Klazina *see* **Nicola**

Klemens *see* **Clement**

Klementyna *see* **Clementine**

Kliment *see* **Clement**

Knut *m*
A Scandinavian name from the
Old Norse word for 'knot', which
originated as a nickname for someone
stocky. The king of England known to
history as *Canute* was really a Knut.
VARIANTS **Knud, Knute**
★ Knute Rockne (1888–1931), US coach
of American football

Kobe *m*
This name has come into use through
the fame of the US basketball player
Kobe Bryant (b.1978), whose parents
chose it for him after seeing Kobe beef,
named after the Japanese city of Kobe,
on a menu. See also COBI.
VARIANTS **Kobi, Koby**

Kobus *see* **Jacob**

Kodee, Kodey, Kodi, Kodie, Kody
see **Cody**

Koenraad *see* **Conrad**

Kolby *see* **Colby**

Kole *see* **Cole**

Kolman, Koloman *see* **Columba**

Kolton *see* **Colton**

Kolya *see* **Nicholas**

Kondrat *see* **Conrad**

Koner, Konner, Konnor, Konor *see*
Connor

Koni, Konstancja *see* **Constance**

Konnie *see* **Connie**

Konrad *see* **Conrad**

Konstantin *see* **Constantine**

Konstanty *see* **Constant**

Konstantyn *see* **Constantine**

Konstanze *see* **Constance**

Koppel *m*
A Yiddish pet form of JACOB.

Kornel *see* **Cornelius**

Kornelia *see* **Cornelia**

Kort *see* **Conrad, Kurt**

Kostantyn, Kostya *see* **Constantine**

Koty *see* **Coty**

Kreine *f*
A Yiddish name from *kroine*, 'crown'.

Kris *see* **Chris**

Krishna *m*
From the Sanskrit *krsna*, 'dark, black',
this is the name of one of India's most
popular Hindu gods and a well used
first name.
VARIANTS **Kishan, Kishen, Kistna**

Krispin *see* **Crispin**

Kriss *see* **Chris**

Krissie, Krissy *see* **Chrissie**

Kristen *see* **Christian**

Kristin *see* **Christina, Christine**

Kristina *see* **Christina**

Kristine *see* **Christine**

Kristoffer, Kristopher *see* **Christopher**

Kryssa *see* **Christina**

Krystal *see* **Crystal**

Krystina, Krystyna, Krzystyna *see* **Christina**

Krysztian *see* **Christian**

Krzysztof, Krzyś *see* **Christopher**

Ksenia *see* **Xenia**

Kumar *m* **Kumari** *f*
These are Hindu names. Kumar means 'boy, son, prince' and is a name belonging to both Skanda, the son of Shiva, and Agni the fire god. Kumari is the feminine equivalent and is one of the names of Shiva's wife, Durga.
VARIANT **Kumara (m)**

Kurt *m*
Kurt was originally a German pet form of *Konrad* (CONRAD), which is now used as an independent name.
VARIANTS **Curt** *Dutch* **Kort**
★ Kurt Vonnegut (1922–2007), US writer
★ Kurt Cobain (1967–94), US singer and guitarist

Kye *see* **Kai**

Kyle *m* **Kyla** *f*
Kyle is a Scottish surname which comes from the Gaelic word *caol*, 'narrow', used of a strait or channel. It was occasionally used in the 19th century, but did not become common until the 1940s and has peaked much more recently. Kyle has also recently come into use for girls, perhaps as a pet form of KYLIE, but the form Kyla (see also KEELEY) is more frequent as a feminine.
VARIANT **Kylah**
★ Kyle MacLachlan (1960–), US actor

Kylian *see* **Cillian**

Kylie *f*
Kylie is said to be the word for 'boomerang' in the Aboriginal Noongar language, and was given as a childhood nickname to the Australian writer Kathleen Tennant (1912–88). She used it as a pen name and, as she was a very successful novelist, the name began to be used by other Australians. The huge success of the Australian actress and singer Kylie Minogue spread it to the rest of the world.

Kyllian *see* **Cillian**

Kym *see* **Kim**

Kymberl(e), Kymberl(e)y *see* **Kimberley**

Kyra *f*
This increasingly popular name is probably largely the product of modern invention using fashionable sounds, but can also be analysed in a number of different ways. Kyra can be seen as a feminine of CYRUS or of CYRIL from the Greek *kyria*, 'lady'. The similar name *Kyrie*, taken from the Christian prayer *Kyrie eleison* ('Lord have mercy'), comes from the same root as Cyril. Kyra and *Kira* can also be interpreted as anglicized spellings of the Irish name CIARA, just as CIARAN is found as *Kyron*. Alternatively, the source can be a fictional one, from the character of Kira Nerys in the television series *Star Trek: Deep Space Nine*.
VARIANT **Kira**

L

Laaiba, Laaibah *see* **Laiba**

Laban *m*
This is a biblical name from the Hebrew for 'white'. It was borne by the father of Jacob's wives Leah and Rachel, who were also sisters, and was taken up by the Puritans but never widely used.
★ Laban Ainsworth (1757–1858), US clergyman and hymn writer, said to have been the longest-serving pastor in US history, having worked in his parish from 1782 to 1858
☆ Laban Tall in Thomas Hardy's 1874 novel *Far From the Madding Crowd*

Labhoise *see* **Laoise, Louise**

Labhrainn, Labhras, Labhrás *see* **Laurence**

Lacey *fm*
Strictly speaking this is a surname, that of Norman aristocrats influential in Ireland, who originally came from Lassy in the Calvados region of France. It was used as a masculine first name from the Middle Ages until about the 1960s. In the 1970s, Lacey came into use as a feminine name in the USA, in this case having strong associations with the vocabulary word 'lace'. See also LADISLAS.
VARIANTS **Lacy, Laci(e)**
★ Lacey Chabert (1982–), US actress
★ Lacey Turner (1988–), English actress
☆ Lacey Rawlins (m) in Cormac McCarthy's 1992 novel *All the Pretty Horses*

Lachlan *m*
The old Gaelic term for Norway was *Lochlann*, 'land of the lochs', and this name is thought to have started out in the Scottish Highlands as a nickname for the many Norse settlers in the area. The name was exported by emigrants to Canada and Australia where it has been among the most popular names for a number of years. It is still regularly used in Scotland. The surname McLachlan, or McLoughlin, comes from this name.
FEMININE **Lachina** • PET FORMS **Lachie, Lockie, Lockey, Lachy, Lauchie**
• VARIANTS **Lachlann, Lochlan(n)** *Irish* **Lachlainn, Loughlin**
★ Major-General Lachlan Macquarie (1761–1824), Scottish soldier and highly successful governor of New South Wales, Australia, after whom the River Lachlan and other local features are named
★ Lachlan Murdoch (1971–), media executive son of Rupert Murdoch

Lachtna *m*
Meaning 'milk-like or -coloured' in Irish, this was the name of both the great-grandfather and a brother of the great Irish king Brian Boru, and thus became a traditional name in the O'Brien family. It is pronounced 'LOKHT-na'. It was sometimes anglicized as *Lucius* (see LUCIAN) in the past.

Laci *see* **Ladislas**

Lacreesha, Lacrisha *see* **Lucretia**

Ladislas *m*
This is the English form, derived via Latin from the Slavic *Vladislav* formed from *volod*, 'rule', and *slav*, 'glory'.

FEMININE **Ladislava** • VARIANTS **Ladislaus**
Hungarian **László**, **Laci** *Italian* **Ladislao**
Polish **Władysław**, **Włodysław**,
Władysława

Laela *see* **Layla**

Laetitia *see* **Letitia**

Lafayette *m*
This is the name of the Marquis of
Lafayette, the French general who
helped the Americans fight for
independence against the British, used
as a first name. It was common in the
USA in the 19th century, but seems to
have all but died out by the middle of
the 20th.
★ Lafayette Ronald (L Ron) Hubbard
(1911–86), US science fiction author
and founder of Scientology

Laiba *f*
An Arabic name meaning 'angel'.
VARIANT **La(a)ibah**

Laila, **Lailah** *see* **Layla**

Lainey *f*
A pet form of ELAINE and similar names
such as DELANEY, now used as an
independent name.
VARIANTS **Lainie**, **Lani**, **Lanie**, **Laney**,
Layney, **Laina**

Lajos *see* **Louis**

Lakeisha *see* **Keisha**

Lakshmi *fm*
This is the name of the Hindu
goddess of beauty, prosperity and
luck whose symbol is the lotus flower.
It means 'sign, mark, omen'. The
name is predominantly feminine but
is sometimes masculine. The male
equivalent is *Lakshman* or *Laxman*.
VARIANT **Laxmi**
★ Lakshmi Mittal (1950–), Indian
billionaire industrialist

Lal[1] *m*
Lal is the Sanskrit for 'to play, caress',
but is used to mean 'darling boy'.

Lal[2] *see* **Eulalia**

Lalage *f*
The Greek word *lalagein* means
'to babble, chatter'. From this, the
classical Latin poet Horace took the
name for a character in his *Odes*,
which were consciously imitating
Greek originals. Despite the rather
airheaded implications of the name,
it has been used regularly, if quietly,
since the 19th century. Lalage is also
the name of a species of tropical bird,
otherwise known as trillers.
PET FORMS **Lal(ly)**, **Lallie**

Lalie *see* **Eulalia**

Lalit *m* **Lalita** *f*
From the Sanskrit for 'playful,
charming, desirable'. In the story of
the god Krishna, Lalita is one of the
women cowherds associated with him.

Lally *see* **Eulalia**, **Lalage**

Lalo *see* **Edward**

Lamar *m*
This was originally a French surname
from a place in Normandy called *la
mare*, 'the pool'. It is a particularly US
name with Southern associations, and
has been in use since the 19th century.
It probably came into use through
a prominent Georgian family with
the name, whose members included
Mirabeau Buonaparte Lamar (1798–
1859), 2nd president of the Republic of
Texas, and Lucius Quintus Cincinnatus
Lamar (1825–93), Confederate
politician and associate justice of
the US Supreme Court. Lamar is one
of the names which lie behind the
development of *La-* as a masculine
prefix in African-American names.

Lambert *m*

A Germanic name formed from the elements *land*, 'land', and *beorht*, 'bright'. It came into general use as the name of a number of early saints, including one who was martyred in the 7th century after denouncing the Frankish king Pepin II for his adultery. It is little used today, except as a surname.

★ Lambert Simnel (c.1477–c.1525), pretender to the throne of England.

Lamorna *f*

This is a Cornish place name used as a first name (compare DEMELZA). The exact meaning of the place name is uncertain, but it may be a corruption of the Cornish for 'valley of the Mornow stream'. However, there is a local legend that it is named after a beautiful girl who was turned into a hare by a witch and then shot.

Lana *f*

Mainstream use of Lana as an independent name seems to have started with actress Lana Turner (Julia Turner), who made her first film in 1937. However, the name has been recorded in sporadic use by English speakers before Turner adopted it, and in these instances Lana may represent pet forms of either ALANA or SVETLANA.

VARIANT **Lanah**

Lance *m*

Although this name later became associated with the vocabulary word 'lance', and is often thought of as a short form of LANCELOT, it is derived from the Germanic name *Lanzo*, originally a short form of names formed from Germanic *land*, 'land', such as LAMBERT.

VARIANT **Launce**

★ Lance Percival (1933–), English comedian and actor
★ Lance Armstrong (1971–), US cyclist

Lancelot *m*

This name was first used for the greatest of King Arthur's knights in the 12th-century writings of Chrétien de Troyes. Chrétien may have simply invented it, but this has not stopped endless speculation as to its etymology. Most Arthurian names have Celtic roots, but no convincing Celtic root has been found for Lancelot. One attractive guess, given Lancelot's role as a servant of women, is that the name is based on the old French *ancel*, 'page boy, servant', with the pet-form ending *-ot* added.

VARIANT **Launcelot**

★ Lancelot Andrewes (1555–1625), English prelate and scholar, one of whose sermons inspired T S Eliot's 'Journey of the Magi'
★ Lancelot 'Capability' Brown (1715– 83), English landscape gardener
☆ Launcelot Gobbo in Shakespeare's *The Merchant of Venice* (1594/5)

Landon *m*

A surname from the Old English meaning 'long hill, ridge', which has become a very popular first name in the USA.

Laney, Lani, Lanie *see* **Lainey**

Lanta, Lanty *see* **Atalanta, Atlanta**

Lanzo *see* **Lance**

Laoise *f*

This popular Irish name, pronounced 'LEE-sha', presents some problems. It is most probably a form of the old name LUISEACH, based on the word 'radiance', and derived from *Lug*, the feminine of *Lugh*, the name of the god of light. However, it is also an Irish place name: County Laois is *Contae Laoise* in Irish Gaelic. This is the source of the masculine name *Laoiseach*, 'someone from Laois', and is pronounced the same way as the name Laoise. Laois

means 'the residence of the people of Lughaidh', with *Lughaidh* being another old name derived from the god Lugh. To complicate matters even further Laoise is sometimes described as the Irish form of LISA and LUCY, as it has much the same meaning, and even more frequently as the Irish form of LOUISE, which is properly *Labhaoise* and is also pronounced 'LEE-sha'; indeed Laoise may well function as a simplified spelling of Labhaoise.
VARIANT **Leesha**

Lara *f*
Lara is the Russian pet form of *Larissa*, a name of unknown origin. It was introduced to the English-speaking world with the heroine of Boris Pasternak's 1957 novel, *Dr Zhivago*, and its very successful 1965 film adaptation.

Laraine *see* Lorraine

Larch *f*
One of the less common plant names which has been used occasionally in modern times.

Larissa *see* Lara

Larrie, Larry, Lars *see* Laurence

Lassarina *f*
This is an Irish name formed from *lasair*, 'flame', combined with *fion*, 'wine'. The stress is on the third syllable.
VARIANTS **Lasrina** *Irish* **Lasairíone**

Lasse *see* Laurence

Laszlo, László *see* Ladislas

Lata *f*
From the Sanskrit word meaning 'tendril, climbing vine', and so used to indicate sinuousness or curves.

Latasha *f*
One of the more common of the many mainly African-American names combining *La-* with familiar name elements; in this case with *Tasha*, pet form of NATASHA. It can also be interpreted as a variant of LETITIA.

Lateisha *see* Letitia

Latif *m* Latifa *f*
These are Arabic names from a word meaning 'kind, gentle, well-mannered'. See also ABDUL.

Latisha *see* Letitia

Latoya *f*
Another of the primarily African-American names beginning with *La-*, this time combined with TOYA, a Mexican pet form of VICTORIA.
VARIANTS **Latoy, La Toya**
★ La Toya Jackson (1956–   ), US singer
★ LeToya Luckett (1981–   ), US singer, formerly with Destiny's Child

Lauchie *see* Lachlan

Launce *see* Lance

Launcelot *see* Lancelot

Laura *f*
This comes from the Latin word for the laurel tree, from which victory wreaths were made (compare DAPHNE). Although it was borne by a 9th-century Spanish martyr, the name is most strongly associated with the fictitious woman to whom the Italian Renaissance poet Petrarch addressed his love poetry, and use of the name is believed to have been inspired by her. The name has been used by English speakers since at least the 13th century.
PET FORMS **Laurie, Lori(e)** • VARIANTS **Laurel(le), Lora, Lorel, Lorinda** *Welsh* **Lowri** *French* **Laure, Laurette** *Italian* **Lauro** (m), **Lauretta** *Spanish* **Laurita**
★ Laura Ingalls Wilder (1867–1957), US

children's writer, author of the *Little House on the Prairie* books
★ Laura Ashley (1925–85), Welsh fashion designer

Lauraine *see* Lorraine

Laure, Laurel *see* Laura

Lauren *fm*
Lauren, falling halfway between LAURA and LAURENCE, seems to have been coined by the movie mogul Howard Hawkes for the actress Lauren Bacall (Betty Joan Perske) in 1944. Her first film, *To Have and Have Not*, released the same year, was a great success, and Lauren entered the US name charts the following year. However, the alternative form *Loren* has been in regular use as a masculine name since the 19th century, presumably from a surname or a pet form of Laurence, and Lauren may have been introduced as a feminine form of this. Subsequently, both forms have been used for both sexes, but there has been a tendency to keep the 'au' form predominantly feminine and the 'o' spelling predominantly masculine. Lauren is currently a popular girl's name on both sides of the Atlantic. There is some overlap between variants of Lauren and LORRAINE.
VARIANTS **Lauryn, Lauraine, Lorena, Laureen, Lo(r)rin, Loren**
★ Lauren Hutton (1943–   ), US model and actress
★ Lauryn Hill (1975–   ), US singer and actress

Laurence, Lawrence *m*
This name comes via French from the Latin *Laurentius*, 'man of Laurentum', an ancient town in central Italy. The name of the town may have come from the Latin *laurus*, 'laurel', thus linking the name to LAURA. It is widespread throughout the Christian world because of the fame of St Lawrence, a

3rd-century martyr. Sometimes known as St Laurence the Librarian – surely one of the few really famous members of that profession – he was in charge of the records and treasures of the early Church in Rome. He refused to hand over the Church's goods when they were demanded by the prefect of Rome, and presented the poor of Rome in their place saying that they were the Church's treasures. He is said to have been martyred on a gridiron, slowly roasted to death in an attempt to torture him into handing over the valuables. In the Middle Ages, the name was used for both genders.
PET FORMS **Larry, Larrie, Laurie, Lawrie, Lonnie** • VARIANTS *Irish* **Labhrás** see also LORCAN *Scots Gaelic* **Labhrainn** *Dutch* **Lars, Laurens, Lourens** *French* **Laurent, Laurentin** (ms), **Laurentine** (f) *German* **Lorenz, Laurenz, Lenz** *Greek* **Lavrentios** *Italian* **Lorenzo, Loris, Renzo** *Polish* **Laurencjusz, Lawrenty, Wawrzyniec** *Russian* **Lavrenti, Lavrent(i)y** *Scandinavian* **Lars, Lasse, Laurits, Lauritz** *Spanish* **Lorencio**
★ Sir Laurence Olivier (1907–89), English actor, producer and director
★ Lawrence Durrell (1912–90), English author

Lauryn *see* Lauren

Lavena *see* Lavinia

Lavender *f*
One of the many flower names that were introduced in the 19th century. The name of the plant comes ultimately from Latin *lavare*, 'to wash', because the plant was used to perfume water for washing.
☆ Lavender Brown in the *Harry Potter* books by J K Rowling

Laverne *mf*
Laverne is ultimately a French surname, derived from a place name based on the Gaulish *vern*, 'alder'.

The Laverne, or Lavergne, family was an aristocratic one in France who sent early settlers to Canada. Members of the family were expelled from Canada when the French lost territory to the British in 1755, and were among the Arcadian (Cajun) French who emigrated from Canada to Louisiana. The name was in use for both sexes in the USA by the later 19th century and continued in regular use into the 1970s. Since Laverne could also be analysed as from *La* plus *Vern*, pet form of VERNON (a French surname from the same root as Laverne), which was popular at the same time, Laverne is probably one of the most important contributers to the development of *La*- as a name prefix, in part through the development of *Lavon(ne)*, a variant form in use from the early 20th century. See also under LAVINIA.

VARIANTS **La Vern(e)**, **Lavern**

★ Laverne Baker (1929–97), US R&B singer

Lavinia *f*

This name comes from Roman mythology, in which Lavinia was the wife of Aeneas, ancestor of the Roman race. She was said to be a local princess whom he married when he arrived in Italy from Troy. The name was not used by the Romans, but was picked up in the Renaissance as part of the interest in classical names, and is recorded in England from the 17th century. It became more common in the 18th century after the success of a poem by James Thomson called 'Lavinia and Palemon' which was little more than a romantic reworking of the biblical story of Ruth and Boaz. In the 19th-century USA the name developed a number of variant forms.

PET FORMS **Vina**, **Vinia** • VARIANTS **Lavina**, **Lavenia**, **Lavon(i)a**, **Lavernia**

Lavrentiy, Lavrenty, Lavrenti,

Lavrentios, Lawrence, Lawrenty, Lawrie *see* **Laurence**

Lawson *m*

A surname, derived from 'son of Law(rence)' used as a first name. It has been particularly common in Australia due to the prominence of explorer William Lawson (1774–1850), and author Henry Lawson (1867–1922).

Laxmi *see* Lakshmi

Layla *f*

This is an Arabic name meaning 'night', but because it is also used for those things associated with a dark night, including wine, intoxication and sensuality, it is sometimes found glossed in these ways. The name has strong romantic associations in the Arab world from the story of Layla and Majnun, which is similar to *Romeo and Juliet*. The name was introduced into England as *Leila* by Lord Byron, who used it in *The Giaour* (1831) and again in *Don Juan*. The form Layla has become the dominant one since the release in 1970 of Eric Clapton's song 'Layla' and its repeated return to the music charts.

VARIANTS **Leila(h)**, **Leyli**, **Laila(h)**, **Leala**, **Lyla**

Layney *see* Lainey

Lazarus *m*

In the New Testament Lazarus is the brother of Martha and Mary, who is raised from the dead by Christ (John 11.1). The name is also borne by another New Testament character (the only one in a parable to be given a name), the poor leper who is contrasted with *Dives*, 'riches, rich man'. The name is a shortening of ELEAZAR, 'God is my help'. In English the name is rarely given, and is usually only used symbolically, but it is sometimes found in other languages.

VARIANTS *French* **Lazare** *Italian* **Lazzaro** *Russian* **Lazar**

☆ Lazarus Long is a recurrent character in the works of the US science fiction writer Robert Heinlein (1907–88)

Lea, Léa *see* **Leah, Lee**

Leaf *mf*
A modern plant name found occasionally.

★ The actor Joaquin Phoenix (1974–) temporarily took the first name Leaf to complement the nature-related names of his siblings, such as River Phoenix

Leagsaidh *see* **Lexie**

Leah *f*
In the biblical book of Genesis (29) Leah, through a trick on her father's part, becomes Jacob's first wife although it is her sister Rachel, whom he takes as his second wife, he really wants. Unsurprisingly, the marriage was not a happy one, although Leah was comforted by having many sons. The name was used by the Puritans, but was mainly Jewish until well into the 20th century. It has been a widely popular name in recent years.
VARIANTS **Le(e)a** *French* **Léa** *Italian, Spanish* **Lia**

Leala *see* **Layla**

Léan, Léana *see* **Helen**

Leander *m*
The Greek name *Leandros* was formed from *leon*, 'lion', and *andros*, 'of man', an appropriate name for the character in Greek mythology who is said to have swum the width of the Hellespont and back every night for assignations with his lover HERO who lived on the other side. He was drowned in a storm one night and his body washed up at the foot of the tower where Hero lived. There was also a 6th-century saint by

the name, which accounts for its entry into the stock of European names.
FEMININE **Leandra** • VARIANTS *French* **Léandre** *Italian* **Leandro**

★ Leander Paes (1973–), Indian tennis player

★ Leandra Cave (1978–), English triathlete

Leanne, Leeanne *f*
This can be analysed either as a combination of LEE and ANNE, or as a variant of LIANNE.
VARIANTS **Leean(n)a, Leighanne**

Lecia *see* **Alice**

Lee *mf*
This is a surname from the Old English *leah*, 'wood, clearing in a wood', used as a first name. It seems to have first become popular in the Southern States, used in honour of Confederate General Robert E Lee (1807–70), but has since become so widely used as to have lost association with him. The variant spellings are used for both sexes, but currently in the UK Lee is more usual for boys. For girls *Leigh* is quite often used in combinations such as *Leighann*.
VARIANTS **Lea, Leigh**

Leea *see* **Leah**

Leeana, Leeanna *see* **Leanne**

Leela *see* **Lila**

Lee Roy *see* **Leroy**

Leesha *see* **Laoise**

Leia *f*
This is the name of the princess in George Lucas's *Star Wars* films, probably based on the name LEAH. It has become firmly established in the stock of names since the films were first shown in the late 1970s.

Leif *m*
Originally a short form of
Scandinavian names using the element
liefr, 'descendant, heir'.
★ Leifur heppni Eiríksson (known as Leif
the Lucky) (fl.1000), Norse explorer
who settled Vinland in the New World

Leigh *see* **Lee**

Leighanne *see* **Leanne**

Leila, **Leilah** *see* **Layla**

Leilani *f*
A Hawaiian name, meaning 'heavenly
flowers'.

Lela *see* **Lila**

Leland *m*
This name first came to prominence
in the USA through tycoon Leland
Stanford (1824–93), who founded
Stanford University in memory of his
son Leland Stanford Junior (the correct
title of the University). The name,
originally a surname meaning 'fallow
land', was common in the USA in the
19th and early 20th centuries, and has
recently been revived, perhaps under
the influence of several uses in the
media. It is also spreading elsewhere.
★ Leland Hayward (1902–71), US film
producer

Lemuel *m*
This name means 'belonging to God'
and is borne by a minor king in the
Old Testament. It was taken up by the
Puritans, but is now very rare.
PET FORM **Lemmy**
☆ Lemuel Gulliver in Jonathan Swift's
1726 work *Gulliver's Travels*

Len *m*
Pet form of LEONARD, or any name
beginning *Len-*, sometimes found as an
independent name.

Lena *f*
This was originally a pet form of names
ending in *-lena*, particularly HELENA
(see HELEN). It is widespread on the
Continent, where it can be derived
from names such as *Yelena*, the
Russian form of Helena, or *Magdalena*,
a form of MADELEINE. The variants are
arrived at by similar routes. Lena began
to be used by English speakers as an
independent name in the 19th century.
VARIANTS **Lina**, **Leni**, **Lene**
★ Lena Horne (1917–   ), US jazz singer
and actress

Lenard *see* **Leonard**

Lenin *see* **Lennon**

Lenka *see* **Madeleine**

Lennard, **Lennart**, **Lennie** *see*
Leonard

Lennon *m*
There are two Irish names, *Leannán*,
'sweetheart', and *Lonán*, 'little
blackbird', that are both anglicized
as Lennon or *Lennan*. This anglicized
form then became a surname. Outside
Ireland at least, modern use of Lennon
as a first name is strongly associated
with musician John Lennon (1940–80),
particularly after rock singer Liam
Gallagher named his son Lennon in
1999, publicly stating that he did
so in honour of the Beatles singer.
The occasional use of *Lenin* as a first
name may, in modern times, represent
a variant of Lennon, although until
recently it would have been taken from
Vladimir Ilyich Lenin (1870–1924),
Russian politician and founder of the
Leninist branch of Communism.

Lennox *m*
This is a Scottish aristocratic title used
as a first name. The earls of Lennox
took their title from an area of land just
north of Glasgow. The meaning of the
place name is disputed.
PET FORM **Len(ny)** • VARIANT **Lenox**

★ Sir Lennox Berkeley (1903–89), English composer

★ Lennox Lewis (1965–), English boxer

Lenny *m*

This is usually a pet form of LEONARD, but can be found used for any name beginning *Len-*. It is now given as an independent name.

PET FORM **Len** • VARIANT **Lennie**

★ Lenny Henry (1958–), English comic actor

☆ Lenny Leonard, worker at the Springfield atomic plant in television cartoon *The Simpsons*

Lenore *f*

A variant of LEONORA, chiefly known from the poems of Edgar Allen Poe, particularly *The Raven* (1845). It has never been common, and is now associated with a brand of fabric softener.

Lenz *see* Laurence

Leo, Leon *m*

Leo is the Latin for 'lion'. It came into use in the late Roman period and was the name of several saints. It was also borne by 13 popes including Leo I, known as Leo the Great (c.390–461), who sent missionaries to Britain. It had come into use in Britain by the 13th century, but was never very common in the past, although well used in other countries. This was to some extent because Leo and Leon were more likely to be found among Jews than Gentiles. In recent years the names have become popular. Leo can also be used as a pet form of LEOPOLD.

VARIANTS *French* **Léo(n)**, **Lionel** *Italian* **Leone**, **Leonzio** *Polish* **Lew** *Russian* **Leonti**, **Leonty**, **Lev**, **Lyov**

★ Leo Amery (1873–1955), English politician and journalist

★ Leo McKern (1920–2002), Australian actor

Leofranc *m*

An Old English name formed from the elements *leof*, 'dear', and *ric*, 'rule, ruler'. It was borne by Lady Godiva's husband. The name was quietly revived in the 19th century.

PET FORM **Leo**

Léon *see* Leo

Leona, Leonie *f*

These are feminine forms of LEO, introduced to Britain in the 19th century, the first from Italy, the second from France. They have shared some of the recent popularity of Leo.

VARIANTS **Leotine**, **Leontyne**, **Leontia**, **Leonah**, **Leoni**, **Leone**, **Leola** *French* **Léontine** *Italian* **Leontina**

★ Leona Lewis (1985–), English singer-songwriter

★ Leontyne Price (1927–), US soprano

Leonard *m*

Leonard is based on the Germanic word for 'lion' combined with *hard*, 'brave, strong'. It was introduced by the Normans and was at its most popular in the 19th century in the UK, and in the early 20th century in the USA.

PET FORMS **Leo**, **Len(nie)**, **Lenny** • VARIANTS **Len(n)ard** *German* **Leonhard** *Italian, Spanish* **Leonardo** *Scandinavian* **Lennart**

★ Leonard Nimoy (1931–), US actor

★ Leonardo DiCaprio (1974–), US actor

Leonidas *m*

The name of the Spartan leader who died at the battle of Thermopylae was formed from the Greek *leon*, 'lion'. It was well used in the early centuries AD, and was borne by a number of saints, most notably the 3rd-century martyr St Leonides of Alexandria. The name has never been common among English speakers, but is regularly used in Russia in the form *Leonid*.

★ Leonidas Daskalides (1876–1954),

Turkish-Greek founder of the Belgian chocolate manufacturer, *Leonidas*
★ Leonidas Kavakos (1967–), Greek violinist

Leonora *f*
This is a mainly German and French variant of ELEANOR. Use by English speakers is likely to be influenced by the character of Leonora in Beethoven's opera *Fidelio*.
VARIANT **Leonore**

Leontia, Léontine, Leotine, Leontyne *see* Leona

Leopold *m*
Although this looks like one of the *leo* names, that is only because their influence has changed its original Germanic form, which was *luit*, 'people', combined with *bold*, 'brave, bold'. The name was little used in Britain until the reign of Queen Victoria, who called one of her sons Leopold, in honour of her uncle Leopold, King of the Belgians (1790–1865), to whom she was close.
VARIANT *Italian, Spanish* **Leopoldo**
★ Leopold Stokowski (1882–1977), US conductor
☆ Leopold Bloom in James Joyce's 1922 novel *Ulysses*

Leroy *m*
Originally a surname from the Old French for 'the king', which was probably originally given to servants of the king. It was popular in the USA in the 19th century and remained in regular use there until recently. In the UK it has mainly been used by those of Caribbean descent.
PET FORM **Roy** • VARIANTS **Lee Roy, LeRoy**

Lesia *see* Alice

Leslie, Lesley *mf*
This is a Scottish surname, probably from the Gaelic *leas cuilinn*, 'garden of hollies', used as a first name. The first recorded use of Lesley as a first name is found in the 18th-century poem 'Bonnie Lesley' by Robert Burns. There used to be a distinction between Leslie, masculine, and Lesley, feminine, but that distinction has now disappeared. Leslie is currently a popular choice for girls in the USA, but is out of favour in the UK, rarely chosen even in its native Scotland.
PET FORM **Les** • VARIANTS **Leslee, Lesleigh, Lezli(e), Lesli**
★ Leslie Howard (1893–1943), English actor
★ Leslie Nielsen (1926–), Canadian actor

Lester *m*
A respelling of the name of the town of Leicester, which became a surname and then a first name. The second part of the place name is the Old English *caester*, from the Latin *castra*, 'fort'; the first part probably represents the name of a local British tribe.
★ Lester Pearson (1897–1972), Canadian prime minister
★ Lester Piggott (1935–), English jockey

Letitia *f*
This is the standard modern spelling of the Latin name *Laetitia*, 'joy, happiness'. The name was used in the Middle Ages, usually in the form *Lettice*, which is still occasionally found. It was revived in the 18th century and became quite popular in the 19th. In the UK it is usually pronounced 'le-TISH-(i)a' with short vowel sounds, but in the USA, where it has been particularly popular among African Americans, it is often 'le-TEE-sha', and has developed many variants, including *Latisha*, thus making it one of the major influences on the formation of *La-* as a name prefix.
PET FORMS **Ti(e)sha, Ticia, Teesha, Letty**

• VARIANTS **Laetitia, Lateisha, Latisha**
Spanish **Leticia**

Lev *m*
As well as being the Russian version of
LEO, Lev is also a Jewish name from the
Hebrew word 'heart'.

Levi *mf*
Levi, from the Hebrew for 'attached',
appears in the Old Testament as the
third son of Jacob and Leah, and was
the ancestor of the only one of the
twelve tribes of Israel whose members
could become priests. The name was
quietly used among the Puritans, but
was mainly confined to Jews until the
20th century in the UK, although it
was more widespread in the USA. Its
recent increase in popularity, and even
more recent use as a feminine name,
is probably due to the influence of the
brand name of Levi jeans, made by
a company founded by Levi Strauss
(1829–1902).
VARIANT **Levy**

Lew *see* Leo

Lewis *m*
This is the English form of LOUIS, which
has been in use since the Middle
Ages and is currently popular. In
some cases it may be taken from the
surname (from the same source), and
in Scotland some uses may be after the
Isle of Lewis. In Wales it can be a form
of LLYWELYN.
PET FORM **Lew(ie)**

Lex *see* Alexander, Alexandra

Lexa *see* Alexandra

Lexie *f*
This is a feminine pet form of ALEXANDER,
which has recently become popular.
It is not new, having appeared by the
19th century in the Scottish Highlands,
where it probably represents a form of
Alecsina and other particularly Scottish

feminine forms. Elsewhere, it is from
ALEXANDRA or ALEXIS.
VARIANTS **Lexa, Lexi, Lexine, Lexy** *Scots
Gaelic* **Leagsaidh**

Lexus *see* Alexis

Leyli *see* Layla

Lezli, Lezlie *see* Leslie

Lia *f*
This is a pet form of any name ending
-*lia*. It is also the Italian and Spanish
form of LEAH.

Liadan *f*
This is an old Irish name, probably
based on *leath*, 'grey', and usually
glossed as 'grey lady'. It was the name
of two Irish saints and of a poet who
entered a nunnery, only to die of grief
at being separated from her lover.
☆ Liadan is the name of a character in
 Juliet Marillier's popular *Sevenwaters
 Trilogy* of historical fantasy novels

Liam *m*
This is an Irish form of the name
WILLIAM, which has become very
popular outside its native country.
★ Liam Neeson (1952–), Northern Irish
 actor
★ Liam Gallagher (1972–), English
 rock singer

Lianne *f*
This name was borne by an early
saint, but modern use comes from pet
forms of names ending in -*lian(ne)*,
particularly the French *Julianne*. It
is now regarded as an independent
name, sometimes as a variant of
LEANNE.
VARIANTS **Leanne, Liane, Lian(n)a**
★ Liane de Pougy (1869–1950), raised
 in a nunnery, she became a Folies
 Bergères dancer and France's most
 famous courtesan

Libby *f*
A pet form of ELIZABETH, now used as an independent name.
VARIANT **Libbi(e)**
★ Libby Purves (1950–   ), English author and radio presenter

Liberty *mf*
This is predominantly a feminine name, most common in the USA. It had a brief patriotic popularity at the end of World War I and then became rare until 2001, when it suddenly came back into fashion after the 9/11 attack on the World Trade Center.
☆ In the 1962 Western film *The Man Who Shot Liberty Valance*, Liberty Valance is the name of a male outlaw

Licia *see* **Felicity**

Lies, **Liesa**, **Liesbeth**, **Liese**, **Liesel**, **Liesja** *see* **Elizabeth**

Life *f*
According to Irish legend this was borne by a woman who gave her name to the River Liffey, which runs through Dublin. In fact, Life seems to have been the old name for the valley through which the river runs, and it is likely that this is the source of the river name. In Irish the river is called the *abha Lifi*, a name that James Joyce adapted for his character Anna Livia Purabelle in *Finnegans Wake* (1939).

Lige *see* **Elijah**

Ligia *see* **Eligius**

Lila¹ *f*
This is an Indian name from the Sanskrit word for 'play'.
VARIANT **Lela**

Lila² *f*
A name that can come from a number of sources, or may simply be used for its sound. It can be either a variant of LAYLA, via *Leila*; a variant of names such

as LILIAN and related names; or a variant of DELILAH. Lila is also the German for 'lilac'. However, the name is most often regarded as a variant of LILY.
VARIANT **Lilah**

Lilac *f*
An occasionally-used flower name. The plant name comes via the Arabic *lilak* from the Persian *nilak*, 'bluish', from *nil*, 'blue', connected with the Sanskrit name NILA.

Líle *see* **Lily**

Lili *see* **Elizabeth**, **Lily**

Lilian *f*
Although the origin of this disputed name was probably a pet form of ELIZABETH, it is now more often associated with LILY, from the Latin *lilium*. It has been in use in English since at least the 16th century and the Italian form is even earlier.
VARIANTS **Lillian** (the usual US form), **Lily-Ann** *Scottish* **Lil(l)ias** *French* (m), **Liliane** (f) *Italian, Spanish, Polish* **Liliana**
★ Lilian Gish (1893–1993), US actress
★ Lillian Hellman (1905–84), US writer

Lilibeth *see* **Elizabeth**

Lilith *f*
In Jewish tradition Lilith was the first wife of Adam who was rejected and replaced by Eve because she would not obey him. She then became a demon. The name can be interpreted as 'screech owl' or 'succubus'. It has been taken up by feminists – for example, it is the title of a Jewish feminist magazine –and the character of Lilith is now treated in fiction much more sympathetically than in the past. Some users may regard the name simply as an elaboration of *Lily*.
VARIANT **Lilit**
☆ Lilith Sternin was a character in the television series *Cheers* and its spin-off *Frasier*

Lilo *see* **Elizabeth**

Lily *f*
Lily probably started out as a pet form of ELIZABETH (and *Lili*, as in the song 'Lili Marlene', is still so used in German), but rapidly became associated with the flower, a symbol of purity in the Bible. Having been considered rather old-fashioned in the middle part of the 20th century, the name is currently very popular throughout the English-speaking world. It is often used in combination with another name. See also LILIAN. SUSAN is the Hebrew equivalent of Lily.
PET FORM **Lil** • VARIANTS **Lilly, Lillie, Lila, Lilla(h), Lilya, Lil(l)ia** *Irish* **Líle** *Welsh* **Lili, Lilwen**
★ Lily Allen (1985–), English singer
★ Lily Cole (1988–), English model
☆ Lily Potter, mother of Harry in the *Harry Potter* books by J K Rowling

Lina[1] *f*
A pet form of any name ending with *-lina*, such as CAROLINA or *Angelina*. It is now regarded as an independent name.

Lina[2] *f*
An Arabic name with a dual meaning; the word can mean 'soft, tender', and is also a type of palm tree.

Lina[3] *f*
An Indian name from the Sanskrit for 'absorbed, united'.

Lincoln *m*
This is a surname, derived from a place, used as a first name. The English city of Lincoln gets its name from the Latin *Lindum colonia*, a *colonia* being an official Roman settlement. The first part of the name probably comes from an ancient British (Celtic) word meaning 'pool', which also lies behind the name LINDSAY. Although in use as a first name as early as the 18th century,

it is now strongly associated with US President Abraham Lincoln (1809–65).

Linda *f*
A name which may have several different sources. As it does not appear to have been used before the 19th century, it probably comes from a shortening of names such as BELINDA. It could also be a shortening of names ending with the Germanic element *linde*, 'soft', such as ROSALINDA. It probably did nothing to hinder its popularity, particularly in the USA, that the name is also the same as the Spanish word for 'pretty'. Linda was particularly popular in the middle of the 20th century.
PET FORMS **Lin, Lyn, Lynn** • VARIANTS **Lynda, Lindi(e), Lyndi(e), Lindy**
★ Linda McCartney (1942–98), photographer and vegetarian
★ Linda Evangelista (1965–), Canadian model

Linden *fm*
Linden appears in the USA in the 19th century as a masculine name, in which case it probably comes from a surname. Occasional modern uses of the masculine are probably influenced by LYNDON (from the same root). As a feminine name it is probably a 20th-century coinage, and usually refers to the alternative name for the lime tree, the flowers of which are used in linden-blossom tea. No doubt use of the name was influenced by the popularity of LINDA.

Lindon *see* **Lyndon**

Lindsay *mf*
This is a place name meaning 'island of LINCOLN'. It was the surname of Sir Walter de Lindsey, who became a Scottish aristocrat, and thus Lindsay was available to join the list of aristocratic surnames adopted as first names in the 19th century. At first it

was mainly masculine, but rapidly came to be used for girls. Initially there was a distinction made between Lindsay, masculine, and other variants used as feminines, but now that the name is rarely masculine this distinction has gone.

PET FORMS **Lin, Lyn** • VARIANTS **Lin(d)sey, Linsay, Linzi(e), Lynsey, Linzee**

★ Lindsay Anderson (1923–94), Indian-born British stage and film director

★ Lindsay Lohan (1986–), US singer and actress

Lindy see Linda

Linford m

A common place name that became a surname, sometimes used as a first name. The place name can have various origins including the Old English *lin*, 'flax, linen' or *lind*, 'lime tree', combined with 'ford'.

VARIANT **Lynford**

★ Linford Christie (1960–), English athlete

Linnea f

A Swedish name which has spread to other countries, given in honour of the 18th-century Swedish botanist Carl von Linné, better known by the Latin form of his name, *Linnaeus*. He was responsible for devising the system for classifying plants that is still in use.

PET FORM **Nea** • VARIANT **Linnaea**

Linnet f

This is probably best regarded as a variant form of LYNETTE which has been influenced by the bird name linnet, although in some cases it may be taken directly from the bird name. The bird is so called because it eats flaxseed, *lin* in French.

☆ One of the ghost children in Lucy M Boston's classic children's story *The Children of Green Knowe* (1954) is called Linnet

Linnette see Lynette

Linsay, Linsi, Linsie see Lindsay

Linus m

This is the Latin form of the New Testament Greek name *Linos*, 'flax', perhaps indicating flaxen hair. The biblical Linus is mentioned by St Paul, and is possibly the same Linus who succeeded St Peter to become the second pope.

★ Linus Roache (1964–), English actor

★ Linus Torvalds (1969–), Finnish computer scientist who gave his name to LINUX

☆ Linus van Pelt is a character in Charles M Schulz's strip cartoon *Peanuts*. He first appeared in 1952, and was probably influential in the subsequent growth in use of the name

Lionel m

This was originally a medieval French pet form of LEON. It established itself quickly as an independent name and by the 14th century was in use by the English royal family in the person of Lionel, Duke of Clarence, Geoffrey Chaucer's first employer.

VARIANT *Italian* **Lionello**

★ Lionel Hampton (1908–2002), US jazz musician

★ Lionel Richie (1949–), US singer-songwriter

☆ Sir Lionel was one of the knights of King Arthur's Round Table

Lis see Felicity

Lisa f

This was originally a pet form of ELIZABETH, but from the second half of the 20th century has been a popular independent name.

VARIANTS *French* **Lise** *German* **Liese**

★ Lisa Stansfield (1966–), English singer

★ Lisa Marie Presley (1968–), US

singer-songwriter, only child of Elvis
Presley
☆ Lisa Simpson in the television cartoon
The Simpsons

Lisabeth, Lisbet, Lisbeth, Lisette
see **Elizabeth**

Lisha *see* **Alice**

Lissa *see* **Melissa**

Lissie *see* **Felicity**

Lita *see* **Angela**

Lito *see* **Angel**

Liùsaidh *see* **Lucy**

Liv *f*
Although this Scandinavian name
seems to have originated with the
Old Norse word *hlif*, 'protection', in
modern use it is associated with *liv*,
'life'. The name is also used as a pet
form of OLIVIA.
★ Liv Ullmann (1938–), Norwegian
actress
★ Liv Tyler (1977–), US actress, named
after Liv Ullmann

Livia *f*
Although there was a Roman family
name Livia, probably from *lividus*,
'bluish, leaden', the usual source of
this name is as a pet form of OLIVIA.
PET FORM **Liv(v)y** • VARIANTS **Liva, Livi(e)**

Liz, Lizaveta, Lizbeth, Lizzie *see*
Elizabeth

Lleucu *see* **Lucy**

Llew, Llewelyn, Llewela, Llewellyn
see **Llywelyn**

Llian, Llinos *f*
This Welsh name is both the word for
'linen' and, along with *Llio*, a pet form
of GWENLLIAN. Llinos is the vocabulary
word for the linseed-eating linnet, also
used as an image for a pretty woman.

Lloyd *m*
This is a Welsh surname, meaning both
'grey' and 'holy' used as a first name.
See also FLOYD.
VARIANTS **Lloyde** *Welsh* **Lwyd**
★ Lloyd Bridges (1913–98), US actor
★ Loyd Grossman (1950–), British-
based US cook and television
presenter

Llywelyn *m*
An ancient Welsh name of uncertain
origin. It may go back to the Old Celtic
Lugobelinus, a name associated with
the Celtic god of light, *Lug*. However, it
was early on associated with the word
llew, 'lion', and anglicized as LIONEL
or *Leoline*. It was an important name
in the medieval royal houses of Wales
and has remained in regular use.
FEMININES **Llewela, Llywela** • PET FORMS
Llew, Lyn, Lynn • VARIANTS **Llewel(l)yn,
Llywellyn**

Lochlan, Lochlann, Lockey, Lockie
see **Lachlan**

Lodewijk, Lodovico *see* **Ludovic**

Logan *mf*
There are a number of Scottish and
Irish place names called Logan,
from the Gaelic for 'little hollow',
most notably a town in Ayrshire. This
became a surname and then a first
name. It is more often used for boys
than girls, is currently very popular
as a masculine name throughout the
English-speaking world and is also well
used in France. Its prevalence may be
partly due to the popularity among
science fiction fans of *Logan's Run*, a
novel published by William F Nolan
and George Clayton Johnson in 1967,
which was subsequently twice filmed
and once turned into a television
series.
VARIANT **Logan(n)(e)**
☆ Wolverine, of the X-Men, is otherwise
known as Logan

Loinnir *f*
This is the Irish vocabulary word for 'brightness, brilliance, shimmering, radiance', which came into general use in Ireland after the politician Roisin McAliskey chose it for her daughter, born in prison. It is pronounced 'LUN-ir'.

Lois *f*
In the New Testament Lois is the name of the grandmother of Timothy. As the rest of her family have Greek names, it is thought that Lois is probably also from Greek, but the meaning of the name is not known. Lois was adopted by the Puritans who took it to the USA, where the name has always been more popular than in the UK, although interest in it has recently increased in the UK.
☆ Lois Lane is Superman's girlfriend

Lola, Lolita *f*
Lola was originally a Spanish pet form of DOLORES. Lolita was then a further pet form of this.
★ Lola Montez (1821–61), Irish-born US dancer, courtesan and power behind the throne of Bavaria
☆ Lolita Haze is the 'nymphet' lusted after by Humbert Humbert in Vladimir Nabokov's 1955 novel *Lolita*

Lona *see* **Moelwyn**

Lonan *see* **Lennon**

Lonnie *m*
A pet form of *Alonzo* (see ALPHONSE) and similar names, later used as an independent name.
PET FORM **Lon** • VARIANT **Lonny**
★ Lon Chaney (1883–1930), US actor
★ Lonnie Donegan (1931–2002), Scottish singer and guitarist

Lope *m*
A Spanish name, from the Late Latin *lupus*, 'wolf'. It was the name of several early saints.
VARIANT *French* **Loup**
★ Lope de Vega (1562–1635), Spanish dramatist and poet

Lora *see* **Laura**

Lorcan *m*
An Irish name, a pet form of the word *lorc*, 'fierce'. It is an important name in Irish history as the name of St Lorcan O Tuathail (1128–80), otherwise known as Laurence O'Toole. He was archbishop of Dublin at the time of the Norman invasion of Ireland and did his best to negotiate for the Irish.

Loredana *f*
This is a name apparently created by George Sand for a character in her 1833 novel *Mattea*. It achieved fame in a 1908 Italian novel by Luciano Zuccoli, *L'amore de Loredana*, and was taken up as a first name in Italy and later in Romania. It is thought the name may be based on the Venetian surname Loredan, which came from a place called Loreo, 'laurel grove'.

Lorel *see* **Laura**

Lorelei *f*
According to legend the Lorelei is a beautiful woman who sits on the Lorelei Rock in the Rhine and lures sailors to their deaths. The name is obscure, but may be made up of elements meaning 'to lure' and 'cliff'. The name is most likely to be found in France and the USA.
VARIANTS **Lorely, Lorelai**
☆ Lorelei Lee is the name of the heroine of Anita Loos's 1925 comic novel *Gentlemen Prefer Blondes*.

Loren, Lorena *see* **Lauren**

Lorencio, Lorenz, Lorenzo *see* **Laurence**

Loreto, Loretta *f*
Loreto is the name of the town in Italy where the Holy House of the Virgin is

supposed to have been miraculously transported from Nazareth by angels. It is given to Roman Catholic girls in the same way that titles of the Virgin Mary, such as DOLORES, are. Loretta seems to be a more obviously feminine form of the name modelled on *Lauretta* (see LAURA).

★ Loretta Young (1913–2000), US actress

Lori, Lorie *see* **Laura, Lorraine**

Lorin *see* **Lauren**

Lorinda *see* **Laura**

Loris *see* **Laurence**

Lorna *f* **Lorne** *m*
Lorna was a name invented by R D Blackmore for the heroine of his 1869 novel *Lorna Doone*. Although the novel is set in Devon, Lorna was actually the kidnapped daughter of the Marquis of Lorne, hence her name. Lorne, or Lorn, is a territory in Argyll, Scotland. The meaning of the name is not known, although it is accounted for by the legend that it came from a certain *Loarn mac Eirc* who ruled the region in the 5th century, and it has been suggested that his name is connected with the Gaelic for 'fox'. Lorne seems to have developed in Canada where there were not only many Scottish settlers but also a number of places called Lorne. Lorne seems only to have come into use in the early 20th century.

★ Lorna Luft (1952–), US actress and singer
★ Lorne Greene (1915–87), Canadian actor who popularized the name
☆ Lorne Greene is also the adopted name of a green demon in the television series *Angel*

Lorraine *f*
While it seems quite clear that this is the name of the French region used as a first name, there is little agreement

as to why. There is a theory that it is a Scottish surname which came into use as a first name in the 19th century. Some say that it is not used in France, except as a recent import, but others claim that it was given in the 19th century as a patriotic gesture after Lorraine was lost to the Prussians in the Franco-Prussian war. There are also claims that its popularity, if not its origin, stems from US soldiers bringing back the name from the trenches after World War I. This latter is somewhat contradicted by the fact that Lorraine is recorded in quiet use in the USA in the 19th century, although it is true that the name shot up in frequency in 1918. The district of Lorraine gets its name from the Latin *Lothari regnum*, a more popular version of the official name *Lotharingia*, 'territory of LOTHAIR', the name of an early medieval ruler. Lorraine became very popular in the 1950s and 60s and developed many variants.

PET FORM **Lor(r)i(e)** • VARIANTS **Laraine, Lauraine, Lorayne, Loraine, Lourene**
★ Lorraine Chase (1951–), English actress
★ Lorraine Kelly (1959–), Scottish television presenter and journalist
☆ The character of Lorraine Forrester in Angela Brazil's *The Head Girl at the Gables* (1919) is an early example of English use
☆ 'Sweet Lorraine' was a popular song by Cliff Burwell and Mitchell Parish, published in 1928 and recorded many times since

Lorrin *see* **Lauren**

Lotfi *see* **Lutfi**

Lothair *m*
The French form of the Germanic name *Hlothart* formed from *hlod*, 'glory', and *hari*, 'army'. The name is mainly found in Germany, or

elsewhere in its later form LUTHER. Use
of the form *Lothario* as a term for a
seducer comes from a character in
William Davenant's 1630 play *The
Cruel Brother*.
VARIANT **Lothar**

Lotte *see* **Elizabeth**

Lottie *f*
A pet form of CHARLOTTE, now
sometimes given as an independent
name.
VARIANTS **Lotta, Lotti** *German* **Lotte**

Lotus *f*
This is an unusual modern flower
name. The lotus is an important symbol
of purity and enlightenment in Eastern
religions because it bears beautiful
blossoms despite growing in mud,
and the name is sometimes chosen for
its religious symbolism. PADMA is the
Indian equivalent.

Lou *see* **Louis, Louise**

**Louan, Louana, Louane, Louanna,
Louanne** *see* **Luana**

Loudon *m*
Loudon is a surname, a variant of
Lowdon, which can have two sources;
it is either from a place name meaning
'low valley', or from the Scottish
regional name Lothian, of unknown
origin. It has come into use through
the fame of the singer and performer
Loudon Wainwright III.

Louella *f*
A blend of sounds such as *Lou-* of
LOUISE and the common feminine
ending *-ella*. It had a certain popularity
in the USA in the first half of the 20th
century.
VARIANT **Luella**
★ Louella Parsons (1881–1972), US
   gossip columnist

Loughlin *see* **Lachlan**

Louis *m*
This is the French form of the name
which usually appears in English
as LEWIS. It is a traditional Germanic
name, which was originally *Hlodowig*
formed from *hlod*, 'glory, fame', and
wig, 'battle'. It was a royal name in
Merovingian France where it became
Chlodowic (see CLOVIS), which was
turned into *Lodovicus* (see LUDOVIC) in
Latin, and Louis in popular speech.
The name remained dominant in the
French royal family, being borne by
18 French kings, as well as appearing
in the name of the last French king,
Louis-Philippe. Even though the
spelling Louis is more frequently used
in the USA, the pronunciation used
is often the Old French one, reflected
in the English form Lewis, rather than
the modern French 'loo-ee'. See also
ALOYSIUS.
PET FORMS **Lou, Loui(e)** • VARIANTS *Scots
Gaelic* **Luthais** *Hungarian* **Lajos** *Italian*
Luigi *Spanish* **Luis**
★ Robert Louis Stevenson (1850–94),
   Scottish writer
★ Louis Armstrong (1901–71), US jazz
   trumpeter and singer

Louise *f*
This is the feminine equivalent of
LOUIS. It was introduced to England
in the 17th century, when the court
of Charles II returned from exile in
France, most notably in the person
of Louise de Kérouaille (1649–1734),
mistress of Charles II and later Duchess
of Portsmouth. In the 18th century
Louisa became the more common
form, but Louise returned in the 19th
and has remained in steady use ever
since.
PET FORMS **Lou, Loulou, Lulu** • VARIANTS
Louisa *Irish* **Labhoise** *German* **Luise** *Greek*
Louiza *Italian* **Luigia, Luigina** *Polish* **Luiza**
Scandinavian **Lovisa, Lovise** *Spanish* **Luisa**

Loup *see* **Lope**

Lourdes *f*
A mainly Catholic name, taken from 'Our Lady of Lourdes', referring to the French village close to the place where St Bernadette had visions of the Virgin Mary in 1858, and where the healing spring has since become a major centre of pilgrimage. The name received a lot of publicity when the singer Madonna chose it for her daughter in 1996.
VARIANT **Lurdes**

Lourene *see* **Lorraine**

Lourens *see* **Laurence**

Loveday *fm*
In the Middle Ages a loveday was a day appointed to settle disputes. The term had become a first name by the 13th century. It is now particularly associated with Cornwall where it is still in use, usually as a feminine name.
PET FORM **Lowdy**

Lovis *see* **Ludovic**

Lovisa, Lovise *see* **Louise**

Lowdy *see* **Loveday**

Lowena *f*
A Cornish name, from the word for 'joy', which has spread to the rest of the UK.
VARIANT **Lowenna**

Lowri *see* **Laura**

Loy *see* **Eligius**

Lu, Lù *see* **Lucy, Luke**

Luana *f*
A name, which can be analysed as a combination of *Lou* from LOUISE plus ANNA, but which was brought to public attention by the 1932 film *Bird of Paradise* where it was used as the name of the Polynesian girl heroine. The name is currently common in France, and is well established in both the USA and Italy.
VARIANTS **Luanna, Luann(e), Loua(n)na, Louan(n)(e)**
☆ Luann Van Houten in the television cartoon *The Simpsons*

Luc, Luca, Lúcá, Lucca *see* **Luke**

Lucas *m*
A Latinate form of LUKE, also found in a number of European languages, which has been a popular choice in recent years.

Lucasta *f*
This is a name invented by the poet Richard Lovelace for one of the women to whom his poems are addressed, appearing in a volume published in 1648. The person addressed may have been a certain Lucy Sacheverel, in which case the name is both a pun on her name, and on the Latin *lux casta*, 'chaste light', *lux* also being the source of LUCY.

Lucetta, Luci *see* **Lucy**

Lucia *f*
Both a feminine of LUCIAN and the Italian form of LUCY.
☆ *Lucia di Lammermoor*, an 1835 opera by Donizetti, based on *The Bride of Lammermoor* by Sir Walter Scott

Lucian, Lucius *m*
Lucius is a Roman name derived from *lux*, 'light' (which appears as *luc-* in inflected forms), and thus is the masculine equivalent of LUCY. Lucian is a variant that developed in Roman times. Both forms were the names of several early saints.
FEMININE **Lucienne** • VARIANTS *French* **Lucien** *Italian, Spanish* **Lucio, Luciano, Luciana**
★ Lucian Freud (1922–), Berlin-born British painter
☆ Sir Lucius O'Trigger, comic Irish knight in Sheridan's 1775 play *The Rivals*. Sheridan probably chose Lucius as a

typically Irish name because it was
used to anglicize LACHTNA

Lucie *see* Lucy

Lucille *f*
A French feminine form of LUCIUS,
adapted from the Roman form *Lucilla*.
VARIANT **Lucilla**
★ Lucille Ball (1911–89), US
comedienne

Lucinda *f*
This appears to have been coined
by Cervantes for a character in his
Don Quixote (1605), based on *Lucia*
(LUCY) and the *-inda* ending found in
the names of many women in the
medieval romances he was lovingly
parodying. The name was rapidly taken
up by other writers, but did not come
into general use as a given name until
the 18th century, when it enjoyed
some popularity.
PET FORMS **Lucy, Cindy, Cindi, Sindy**
• VARIANT *French* **Lucinde**
★ Lucinda Green (1953–   ), English
three-day eventer
★ Lucinda Williams (1953–   ), US singer
☆ Lucinda Leplastrier in Peter Carey's
1988 novel *Oscar and Lucinda*

Lucius *see* Lucian

Lucretia *f*
Lucretia is a Roman family name,
possibly derived from the Latin *lucrum*,
'wealth'. In Roman legendary history
Lucretia was a virtuous wife who
was raped by the son of the ruling
TARQUIN, and who committed suicide
as a result. The populace was said to
be so outraged that they rebelled and
founded the Roman Republic. The
name was not uncommon in the 19th
century, particularly in the USA, where
it is still more likely to be found, and
has developed a number of variants
especially among African Americans.
PET FORM **Crete** • VARIANTS **Lucrece,**

Lacrisha, Lacreesha *French* **Lucrèce**
Italian **Lucrezia**
★ Lucretia Mott (1793–1880), US Quaker
minister, feminist and abolitionist
★ Lucrezia Borgia (1480–1519), Italian
aristocrat, notorious as a poisoner and
libertine
☆ *The Rape of Lucrece* is a 1594 poem
by Shakespeare telling the story of the
Roman Lucretia
☆ Lucretia Tox is a minor character in
Charles Dickens's *Dombey and Son*
(1848)

Lucy *f*
Lucy comes from the Latin *lux*,
meaning 'light', which takes the form
luc- in inflected forms. The Roman
form of the name was LUCIA, and in
antiquity it was thought of as a name
given to a child born at first light. It
was also associated with the goddess
Lucina, a name given to Juno in her
aspect as goddess of birth, the one
who leads the infant into the light
of day. St Lucy was a 4th-century
martyr, about whom little is known
for certain, although there is a lively
legend. Because of the meaning of her
name she, like St CLARE, was invoked
to protect against blindness and eye
trouble. Lucy was used in the Middle
Ages, was widespread in the 18th
century and is currently popular. See
also LUZ.
PET FORMS **Luce, Lu, Lulu** • VARIANTS
Luci(e), Lucia, Lucette, Lucetta *Scots
Gaelic* **Liùsaidh** *Welsh* **Lleucu** *French*
Lucie *Polish* **Lucja** *Portuguese* **Luzia**

Ludmila *f*
A Russian name, from the Old Slavic
elements *lud*, 'people', and *mil*,
'loved'. St Ludmilla is the patron saint
of Bohemia.
PET FORMS **Mi(l)la, Millie** • VARIANTS
Ludmilla *Russian* **Lyudmila, Lyuda**

Ludovic *m*
This is from *Ludovicus*, a Latin form
of LOUIS. It is little used by English
speakers but is associated with the
Western Isles of Scotland, where it
was historically used to anglicize the
old Gaelic name *Mael Domhnaich*,
'servant of the Lord'.
FEMININE **Ludovica** • PET FORM **Ludo**
• VARIANTS **Ludovick** *Dutch* **Lodewijk**
German **Ludwig** *Italian* **Lodovico** *Polish*
Ludwik *Scandinavian* **Ludvig**, **Lovis**
★ Sir Ludovic Kennedy (1919–),
 Scottish broadcaster and writer
☆ Ludovic 'Ludo' Bagman in the *Harry
 Potter* books by J K Rowling

Luella *see* **Louella**

Lughaidh *m* **Luiseach** *f*
These are traditional Irish names
derived from the name of the god
Lugh, which means 'brightness'.
Lughaidh, pronounced 'LOO-ee' is
traditionally anglicized as LEWIS or
LOUIS; Luiseach, pronounced 'LEE-sha',
was traditionally anglicized as LUCY, but
is now associated with LAOISE.

Luigi, **Luis** *see* **Louis**

Luigia, **Luigina**, **Luisa**, **Luise** *see*
Louise

Luiseach *see* **Lughaidh**

Luiza *see* **Louise**

Luke *m*
This currently popular name developed
in the Middle Ages as the English form
of the Latin LUCAS, which in turn came
from the New Testament Greek *Loukas*,
'man from Lucania', in southern Italy.
As Luke, reputedly a doctor and artist
who was converted by St Paul, was
author of one of the four Gospels the
name spread throughout the Christian
world.
VARIANTS **Lucas** *Irish* **Lúcá**, **Lúcás** *Scots
Gaelic* **Lùcas** *Welsh* **Luc** *Dutch, Spanish*

Lucas *French* **Luc** *German* **Lukas** *Italian*
Luca *Polish* **Lukasz** *Russian* **Luka**
☆ Luke Skywalker in the *Star Wars* films

Lukmaan *see* **Luqman**

Lulu *f*
A name that started life as a German
pet form of LOUISE, although it is now
sometimes used as a pet form of LUCY.
It can also be an Arabic name meaning
'pearls', *Lulua* in the singular.
PET FORM **Lu** • VARIANT **Lula**
★ Lulu (1948–), Scottish singer and
 actress
☆ *Lulu* is an opera by Alban Berg, first
 performed in 1937

Luna *f*
This is the word for 'moon' in Latin,
as well as in Spanish and Italian, and
thus is an alternative to SELINA. It was
in regular if quiet use, at least in the
USA, in the 19th century and early
years of the 20th, but then disappeared
until 2003, the year it was given to
the character Luna Lovegood, in the
Harry Potter books. It has, however,
remained in use by non-English
speakers, growing in frequency in
Italy, and is common among Sephardic
Jews.

Luned *see* **Eluned**, **Lynette**

Lunet *see* **Eluned**

Lupe, **Lupita** *see* **Guadalupe**

Luqman *m*
Luqman was the name of a holy
man, famous for his wisdom, who is
mentioned in the Koran. He is said
to have lived around the time of King
David.
VARIANT **Lukmaan**

Lurdes *see* **Lourdes**

Luthais *see* **Louis**

Luther *m*

This is a Germanic surname formed from *liut*, 'people', and *heri*, 'army'. It was adopted by Protestants in honour of the religious reformer Martin Luther (1483–1546), and in recent times has been chosen in honour of the assassinated civil rights activist Martin Luther King (1929–68).

★ Luther Vandross (1951–2005), US singer
★ Luther Blissett (1958–), Jamaican-born English national footballer, whose name was borrowed in 1994 as a nom de plume for a group of post-modern artists and activists

Luz *f*

A Spanish name meaning 'light' taken from the title of *Nuestra Señora de la Luz*, 'Our Lady of Light', for the Virgin Mary.

Luzia *see* Lucy

Lwyd *see* Lloyd

Lyall *see* Lyle

Lydia *f*

Lydia is an old name for a district in what is now Turkey, which came to be used as a female name in much the same way as DORIS. It is the name of a woman, 'a seller of purple', converted by St Paul in the New Testament, and was adopted by the Puritans along with the other post-Reformation New Testament names. However, its form makes it seem closer to the Latinate names that were popular among fashionable people, and as a result it has, at least in literature, had a more frivolous feel than its antecedents suggest.

VARIANT French **Lydie**

★ Lydia Pinkham (1819–83), US manufacturer of patent medicines, also known as 'Lily the Pink'
☆ Lydia Languish in Sheridan's 1775 play *The Rivals*
☆ Lydia is the name of one of the sillier Bennet sisters in Jane Austen's 1813 novel *Pride and Prejudice*
☆ 'Lydia the Tattooed Lady', a song by Harold Arlen and Yip Harburg often performed by Groucho Marx

Lyla *see* Layla

Lyle, Lyall *m*

Although in theory these are different, mainly Scottish and US names, there is considerable overlap in use. Both are surnames that have come to be used as first names. Lyle comes from the Anglo-Norman *de l'isle*, 'of the island', and Lyall may be from the Old Norse name *Liulfr*, the second part of which is *ulfr*, 'wolf', while the first part remains a mystery.

★ Lyle Lovett (1956–), US country music singer-songwriter
☆ Lyle Lanley is a smooth-talking con man who persuades the people of Springfield to buy an expensive monorail, in the television cartoon *The Simpsons*

Lyn *mf*

As a masculine name this is either from a pet form of LLYWELYN, or from a surname based on the Welsh *llyn*, 'lake'. As a feminine name it is from a pet form of names either beginning Lin- or Lyn- such as LINDA or LINDSAY, or ending in the sound, such as CAROLYN.

VARIANT **Lynn**

★ Lynn Redgrave (1943–), English actress

Lynda, Lyndi, Lyndie *see* Linda

Lyndon *m*

This is a surname, from an English place name where lime or LINDEN trees grew, used as a first name. It is most often found in the USA, where use was encouraged by the fame of President Lyndon Baines Johnson (1908–73).

VARIANT **Lindon**

★ Lyndon LaRouche (1922–), US economist and activist

Lyndsay, **Lyndsey** see **Lindsay**

Lynette f

This name has two sources. In modern use it can be an elaboration of LYN. In earlier use it is found in Tennyson's *Idylls of the King* as the heroine of his story of 'Gareth and Lynette' published in 1872, in which case it is his form of the Welsh name ELUNED.

Lynford see **Linford**

Lynsey see **Lindsay**

Lyosha see **Alexander**

Lyov see **Leo**

Lyra f

This is the Latin for 'lyre' and is used for the name of a constellation. Although it has been recorded prior to its appearance in Philip Pullman's *His*

Dark Materials trilogy (1995–2000) as the name of heroine Lyra Belacqua, the books have increased its use.

Lyric f

A name that has come into use since the mid-1990s, probably as part of the trend for names associated with music.

Lys see **Elizabeth**

Lysander m

A Greek name formed from elements *lysis*, 'release, freeing', and *andros*, 'of man'. It was the name of a famous Spartan general who defeated the Athenians in the Peloponnesian War in 405 BC.

FEMININE **Lysandra** • VARIANT *Spanish* **Isandro**

★ Lysander Spooner (1808–87), US political theorist and individualist

☆ Lysander is one of the two male leads in Shakespeare's *A Midsummer Night's Dream*

Lyssa see **Alice**

Lyuda, **Lyudmila** see **Ludmila**

M

Maaike *see* **Mary**

Maarten, Maartje *see* **Martin**

Maas *see* **Thomas**

Mabel *f*
This has been used as an alternative
to the fuller AMABEL, 'lovable', since at
least the 12th century. It was one of the
medieval names that came back into
fashion in the 19th century, revived by
its use in Charlotte M Yonge's novel
The Heir of Redclyffe (1854). At the
same time the pronunciation changed
from a short 'a' sound (as in 'mad') to
the sound as in 'may'.
PET FORMS **Mab(s), May** • VARIANTS
Maybelle, Mabelline, Mable *Welsh* **Mabli**
★ Mabel Philipson (1887–1951) was a
music hall actress who became one
of the first women to be elected to
parliament
☆ Mabel is the lead female in Gilbert and
Sullivan's *The Pirates of Penzance*

Mabon *m* **Mabyn** *f*
These Welsh names come from the
word for 'youth, son'. Mabon was
the name of a Celtic god, and came
into use after it was adopted as his
bardic name by William Abraham
(1842–1922), Welsh trade unionist and
Member of Parliament. Mabyn was
a 6th-century saint, one of the many
sanctified children of King Brychan.

Mac, Mack *m*
Originally a nickname for anyone with
a surname beginning *Mc* or *Mac*, this
is now found as a given name.

Macaria, Macario *see* **Makarios**

Mac Dara *see* **Dara**

Macaulay *mf*
A Scottish surname meaning 'son of
AULAY', which came into fashion after
the actor Macaulay Culkin became a
child star in 1990. The name seems to
have been better used in the UK than
in the USA.
VARIANTS **Macaulee, Macauley**

Mace *see* **Mason**

Machteld *see* **Matilda**

Maciej *see* **Matthew**

Mackenzie *mf*
This is a Scottish surname meaning
'son of *Cainneach* (KENNETH)'. As a first
name, it started to gain currency in
the 1980s. It is currently particularly
popular as a female name in the USA
and as a masculine one in Scotland.
See also KENZIE.
VARIANTS **Makenzie, Mckenzie**
★ Mackenzie Crook (1971–), English
actor
★ Mackenzie Phillips (1959–), US
actress credited with spreading the
feminine use of the name

Macsen *m*
This is the Welsh form of the Roman
name MAXIMUS which is beginning to
appear outside Wales.
★ Macsen Wledig ('the Emperor') is
the name given in Welsh legend to
Magnus Maximus (d.388) who was
proclaimed Roman emperor by his
troops in Britain in AD 383

Macy *fm*
This is the name of the US chain of
department stores founded by Rowland
Hussey Macy, in the 19th century, used

as a first name. The surname came from a Norman baronial name, from a place that once belonged to someone with the Gallo-Roman name *Maccius*. It was in occasional use in the USA in the 19th century, but started to be used in earnest about 1990, no doubt helped by the popularity of names with the same sounds such as STACEY and TRACY. Use is predominantly feminine.

VARIANTS **Macey, Maci(e)**

★ Macy Gray (1967–), US singer

Maddox *m*

A Welsh surname meaning 'son of MADOC', which has come into use since it was chosen by the US actress Angelina Jolie for her adopted son in 2002.

Madeleine *f*

The name of the biblical Mary Magdelene (Mary of Magdela, a settlement near the Sea of Galilee) became Madeleine in French, and in this form became a popular name in the 19th century. The medieval form had been *Magdalen*, which was usually pronounced 'maudlin'. This then became a vocabulary word for someone tearful, from the tradition that Mary Magdalene had washed Christ's feet with her tears. The name has many variants both in English and in other languages.

PET FORMS **Maddie, Maddy** • VARIANTS **Madaleine, Madeline, Madelaine, Madlyn, Madoline, Magdalen** *Irish* **Madailéin** *Welsh* **Madlen** *Czech* **Madlenka, Lenka** *German* **Magdalena, Magdalene, Magda, Marlene, Lena** *Italian* **Maddalena** *Portuguese* **Madalena** *Scandinavian* **Magdolone, Malena, Malin** *Spanish* **Malena**

Madge *f*

A pet form of MARGARET and occasionally MADELEINE.

Madhur *f*

This name comes from the Sanskrit *madhura*, 'sweet, honey'. It is a modern name, although the form *Madhu* (masculine in south India, feminine in the north), which is also the name of a spring month in the Hindu year, is old.

VARIANTS **Madhukar** (m) 'honey-maker, bee', **Madur**

★ Madhur Jaffrey (1933–), British–US cookery writer and actress

Madiha *f*

This is an Arabic name, from the word for 'praiseworthy'.

VARIANT **Madeeha**

Madison *fm*

This is an English surname, formed from a pet form of either MADELEINE or MAUD combined with 'son', used as a first name. It was introduced as a first name in the 1984 film *Splash*, when the main character chose it for herself after seeing a street sign for Madison Avenue, New York. It has since become very popular, particularly in the USA, where it has been in the top five names since the start of the 21st century. It is primarily a feminine name.

VARIANTS **Maddison, Madisyn, Madyson**

Madlyn, Madoline *see* Madeleine

Madoc *m*

A Welsh name probably meaning 'fortunate'. See also MADDOX and MARMADUKE.

VARIANT **Madog**

★ Madog ab Owain Gwynedd (fl.1150–80) is said to have sailed west and discovered America, c.1150

Madonna *f*

The Italian for 'my lady' and a title of the Virgin Mary. It has been used in the USA since at least the beginning of the 20th century. Compare the more popular DONNA.

★ Madonna (1958–), US pop singer and actress

Mads *see* **Matthew**

Mae *see* **May**

Maegan *see* **Megan**

Mael Maedoc, Mael Sechnaill *see* **Malachi**

Maelmor *see* **Miles**

Maéva *f*
This is a Tahitian name meaning 'welcome'. It was popularized in France with the publication in 1972 of a children's book called *Maéva la petite Tahitienne* ('Maéva the Little Tahitian'), by Jacques Chegaray.

Maeve *f*
This is an ancient Irish name which means 'she who intoxicates'. In the great early Irish epic, *The Tain*, Maeve, Queen of Connacht, is the driving force in the war between her country and Ulster. In later tradition she becomes one of the queens of the fairies, and appears in Shakespeare's *Romeo and Juliet* as Queen Mab.
PET FORM **Maeveen** • VARIANTS **Meave, Mave** *Irish* **Meadhbh, Medb**
★ Maeve Binchy (1940–), Irish novelist

Mafalda *see* **Matilda**

Magali *f*
The origin of this French name is in doubt, but it is thought to be a shortened form of *Malgalida* which is a Provençal form of *Margarita* (MARGARET). There was a popular saint called Magali, about whom little is known except that she may have been martyred in the 4th century, but her cult was suppressed by the Church in 1969. The name was used in the Middle Ages, and then reintroduced in the 19th century through the works

of the Provençal poet Frédéric Mistral, particularly his 'Mirèio' (1859).
VARIANT **Magalie**
★ Magali Noël (1932–), Turkish-French singer, actress and comedienne

Magda, Magdalen, Magdalena, Magdalene, Magdolone *see* **Madeleine**

Magenta *f*
The Battle of Magenta in Italy, part of the Italian War of Independence, was fought in 1859, shortly before the dye that gives the reddish-purple colour was discovered. Magenta is said to be used in Italy as a first name, but among English speakers it is mainly confined to fiction.
☆ Magenta is a character in the 1975 musical *The Rocky Horror Picture Show*

Maggie *see* **Margaret**

Magid, Magida *see* **Majid**

Magnus *m*
The great French ruler *Charlemagne*, crowned Holy Roman Emperor of the West on Christmas Day 800, was really just a simple CHARLES, but got his name by the addition of the Old French *le Magne*, 'the Great'. This became *Carolus Magnus* in Latin. After St Olaf, King of Norway converted to Christianity in the 990s, he chose the second half of Charlemagne's Latin name, Magnus, for one of his sons. The name thus entered the Norwegian royal family and spread from there. It still has strong northern associations and among English speakers is far more likely to be found in Scotland, with its Viking past, than elsewhere. It is particularly used in Orkney, where the cathedral is dedicated to St Magnus, Earl of Orkney c.1108–15.
VARIANTS *Irish* **Maghnus, Mánus** *Scots Gaelic* **Mànus**
★ Magnus Magnusson (1929–2007),

Iceland-born Scottish journalist and broadcaster

★ Magnus Pyke (1908–92), English scientist and broadcaster

Magrit see **Margaret**

Maha f
This is the Arabic word for a wild cow or oryx, chosen as a name because of the beauty of these animals' large and expressive eyes.

Mahati f
This is an Indian name from the Sanskrit meaning 'great'.
VARIANT **Mahita**

Mahdi see **Mehdi**

Mahek see **Mehek**

Mahendra m
An Indian name meaning 'great Indra' from the Sanskrit *maha*, 'great', combined with the name of the god Indra.
VARIANTS **Mahinder, Mohinder**

Mahlon see **Marlon**

Mahmoud m **Mahmouda** f
This Arabic name means 'praiseworthy, laudable' and is very close in meaning to MOHAMMED.
VARIANTS **Mahmud(a), Mahmood(a)**

Mai see **May**

Maia see **Maya**

Maidie f
This name, apparently from the vocabulary word 'maid', has been recorded in Ireland, mostly in the late 19th and early 20th centuries.

Maike see **Mary**

Maikel see **Michael**

Maiken, Màili, Mair, Máire see **Mary**

Mairead, Mairéad, Mairghead see **Margaret**

Màiri, Máiria see **Mary**

Mairin see **Maureen**

Máirtín see **Martin**

Mairwen see **Mary**

Maisie f
Originally this was a pet form of the Scottish name *Mairead*, the Gaelic form of MARGARET. While it still has a Scottish flavour, it has been widely used elsewhere, and was particularly common in the late 19th century and in the 1920s.
VARIANTS **Maisy, Mysie**
☆ *What Maisie Knew* is the title of an 1897 novel by Henry James

Maitias, Maitiú see **Matthew**

Maja see **Mary, Maya**

Majella f
A name occasionally used by Roman Catholics in honour of St Gerard Majella (1725–55), canonized in 1904. He is the patron of childbirth and small children.

Majid m **Majida** f
These are Arabic names meaning 'glorious, praiseworthy'.
VARIANTS **Majeed(a), Magid(a)**

Makaio see **Matthew**

Makarios m
This is a Greek name derived from *makar*, 'blessed, happy'. It was borne by several early saints.
VARIANTS *Italian, Spanish* **Macario** (m), **Macaria** (f) *Russian* **Makari**
★ Archbishop Makarios III (1913–77), archbishop of Cyprus who became the island's first post-independence president

Makayla f
A variant of MICHAELA (see MICHELLE) which began to be used in the USA

in the 1980s and is now very popular
there.
VARIANTS **Makaila, Makala**

Makenzie *see* **Mackenzie**

Maks, Maksim *see* **Maxim**

Maksimilian *see* **Maximilian**

Maksym *see* **Maxim**

Maksymilian *see* **Maximilian**

Malachi, Malachy *m*
Strictly speaking these are two different
names, but in practice it is unlikely
that most users distinguish between
them. Malachi is a biblical name,
borne by a minor prophet in the Old
Testament whose name comes from
the Hebrew meaning 'my messenger'.
The name was used by the Puritans
and has been experiencing something
of a revival in the USA since the
1990s. Malachy is an Irish name,
used to represent a number of old
Irish names. It was borne by two High
Kings of Ireland, both with the proper
name of *Mael Sechnaill*, 'servant of
St Secundus', and, perhaps more
importantly, by a 12th-century saint,
properly called *Mael Maedoc*. He was
archbishop of Armagh and a great
Church reformer.
VARIANT **Malakai**

Malak *fm*
The Arabic for 'angel'; use is
predominantly feminine. *Malaika* is the
same name in plural form.

Malcolm *m*
This Scottish name arose because of
the importance in Scottish history of
St COLUMBA. Gaelic has two elements
meaning 'servant of' that could go
in front of a name: *gille*, giving such
names as *Gillespie*, and *mael*, which
indicates service in the sense of being
a devotee. Rather than simply naming
a boy after an admired saint, parents

would choose a name that dedicated
the child to the saint. In the case of
Malcolm, the child would have been
called *Mael Coluim*, 'devotee of
Columba'. Malcolm became a royal
name, being borne by four kings
who reigned between 943 and 1165,
and was also well used among the
aristocracy, which helped spread the
name throughout Scotland. However,
it only came into significant use
outside Scotland in the 1920s.
FEMININES **Malcomina, Malina** • PET FORMS
Mal, Calum, Callum, Colm

Maldwyn *see* **Baldwin**

Maleek, Maleeka *see* **Malik**

Malena *see* **Madeleine**

Malgorzata *see* **Margaret**

Malia *f*
This is a Hawaiian form of MARY, 'r'
regularly becoming 'l' in Hawaiian
variants. The name became popular in
Hawaii in the 1980s, and it has been
growing in use elsewhere since the
mid-1990s.
VARIANTS **Maliyah, Maleah**

Malik *m* **Malika** *f*
These are respectively the Arabic for
'king' and 'queen'. Malik is one of
the titles of Allah, and the name is
often combined to form *Abdul Malik*,
'servant of the King'. Malik is one of
the Arabic names taken up by African
Americans.
VARIANT **Maleek(a)**

Malin *see* **Madeleine**

Malkah *f*
This is the Hebrew for 'queen', and
was traditionally given to girls born
during Purim, the feast that celebrated
the actions of Queen ESTHER to save her
people from persecution.
MASCULINE **Melek**

Mallory *f*
This name became popular in the USA in the 1980s when it was borne by a character in the television series *Family Ties*. It comes from the surname, which in turn comes from the Old French *malheure*, 'misfortune, bad luck'. It has occasionally been used as a boy's name since at least the 17th century.
VARIANTS **Malerie, Malory**

Mallt *see* **Matilda**

Malo *m*
This is a French name that appears in medieval Latin as *Maclovius*, and may represent a Celtic name *Mac-lug*, 'son of Lug', Lug being the Gaulish equivalent of *Lugh*, the Irish god of light. St Malo, after whom the port is named, is reputed to have been born in Wales in the 6th century, and to have moved to Brittany with other missionaries.

Malvina *f*
This is a name created by James Macpherson (1736–96) from the Gaelic *mala mhìn*, 'smooth brow'. Macpherson published a series of poems which were supposedly ancient Celtic and which he claimed were composed by OSSIAN. However, although certainly drawn from Gaelic tradition, the poems were mainly Macpherson's own work. This did not stop them becoming very fashionable and one admirer was Napoleon. Napoleon had made one of his generals, Bernadotte, king of Norway and Sweden, and was godfather to a number of his children. He used this opportunity to give the children fashionable new names from the Ossianic poems. As royal names they were passed on to the general public, which explains why a number of Ossianic names, Malvina included, are more common in Scandinavia than elsewhere. See further SELMA, OSCAR.

VARIANTS **Melvina, Malvena**
★ Malvina Reynolds (1900–78), US folk-singer and activist who wrote the song 'Little Boxes'

Mamadou *see* **Mohammed**

Mamie *f*
A pet form of MARGARET or MARY, sometimes used as an independent name.
★ Mamie Eisenhower (1896–1979), US First Lady

Manas *m*
An Indian name from the Sanskrit for 'mind, intelligence'.

Manda *see* **Amanda**

Mandeep *mf*
This Indian name comes from the Sanskrit for 'light of the mind or heart'.

Mandi, Mandie, Mandy *see* **Amanda, Miranda**

Manfred *m*
An Old Germanic name formed from the elements meaning 'man' and *frid*, 'peace'. Although introduced to England by the Normans, it has never been common among English speakers. It has, however, been well used by German speakers, and was a royal name in some ruling families. The name acquired romantic overtones when Byron used it for the brooding and tormented central character in his 1817 poem *Manfred*.
VARIANT *Italian* **Manfredo**
★ Manfred of Hohenstaufen (1232–66), warrior king of Sicily
★ Manfred Mann (1940–), South African musician who founded the British pop band named after him

Mani *see* **Marnie**

Manju, Manjula *f*
Manju is the Sanskrit for 'lovely, beautiful'. It forms the basis of a

number of names, such as Manjula, which has much the same meaning; for example *Manjubala* and *Manjulika*, 'charming girls', and *Manjusha*, 'girl with a lovely voice'.

☆ Manjula Nahasapeemapetilon, in the television cartoon *The Simpsons*

Manny, Manoel, Manoela, Manola, Manolo *see* Emmanuel

Manon *f*

This is a pet form of *Marie*, the French form of MARY. It is particularly associated with the southern part of France, and is common in Holland and French Canada. Manon is also a Welsh name, from the Old Welsh meaning 'queen'.

☆ *Manon Lescaut*, a novel written in 1731 by French author the Abbé Prévost, which first introduced the name to the general public. It has been adapted for opera and cinema a number of times

☆ *Manon des Sources*, 1953 film by the French writer-director Marcel Pagnol, remade in 1986 to great critical acclaim

Manpreet *mf*

An Indian name, particularly used by Sikhs, meaning 'happiness of the heart'.

Mansur *m* Mansura *f*

An Arabic name meaning 'helped, victorious', with strong religious overtones.

VARIANTS **Mansoor(a), Mansour(a)**

Manu *m*

This is the Sanskrit for 'thinking, wise', and in Hindu tradition is the name of the progenitor of the human race. In Western tradition Manu can be found as a pet form, for both sexes, of names based on EMMANUEL.

Manuel, Manuela, Manuelita *see* Emmanuel

Manus, Mánus, Mànus *see* Magnus

Manya *see* Mary

Maoileas, Maolmuire, Maolra *see* Miles

Maqsud *m* Maqsuda *f*

These names are from the Arabic for 'intended, aimed at'.

VARIANT **Maqsood(a)**

Mara *f*

This is the Hebrew for 'bitter'. In the Bible the newly-widowed NAOMI, whose name means 'pleasantness', says 'Call me not Naomi, call me Mara: for the Almighty has dealt very bitterly with me' (Ruth 1.20). Mara is also a pet form of MARIA (MARY) in some central European languages, and occasionally of TAMARA.

VARIANT **Marah**

☆ Mara Jade is the name of Luke Skywalker's wife, in the spin-off games and books from the *Star Wars* films

☆ Mara is the name of a badger in the *Redwall* series of children's books, by Brian Jacques

Maralyn *see* Marilyn

Marata, Marete *see* Margaret

Marc *see* Mark

Marcel *m* Marcella *f*

The Roman family name *Marcus* (see MARK) early on developed a variant *Marcellus*. Marcel is used in many countries, but is predominantly French, thanks to the fame of a saint who was a 3rd-century missionary to Gaul and was martyred for his faith. There is also a St Marcella who, in the 4th century, was one of the women who supported St Jerome in his work. See also MARCIA, MARCY.

VARIANTS **Marcelyn** *Scots Gaelic* **Marsaili** (also used for Margery) *Welsh* **Marchell** (f) *French* **Marcelle, Marcel(l)ine, Celine, Marcellette, Marcellin** *German* **Marcellus**

Hungarian **Marcell** Italian **Marcello,**
Marcellino Polish **Marceli, Marcelina**
Portuguese **Marcelin(h)o** Spanish **Marcela,**
Marcelo, Marcelino
- ★ Marcel Proust (1871–1922), French
  novelist
- ★ Marcel Marceau (1923–2007), French
  mime artist

Marcia, Marcy f
A name from the same root as MARCEL.
There have been a number of rather
obscure saints called Marcia. The
name has been used by English
speakers since the 18th century, and
has developed two pronunciations.
These are 'MAR-see-a', the dominant
one in the UK, and 'MAR-sha', mainly
found in the USA and reflected in the
alternative spelling Marsha. The pet
forms are currently better used in the
UK than the full forms.
PET FORM **Marci(e)** • VARIANT **Marsha**
- ★ Marcia Cross (1962–), US actress
  known for her role in Desperate
  Housewives
- ★ Marsha Hunt (1946–), US singer,
  novelist and actress

Marco, Marcus see Mark

Maredudd see Meredith

Marek see Mark

Margaret f
Margaret comes from the Latin
Margarita meaning 'pearl', a long-
standing symbol of purity and
completeness. As the French form,
Marguerite, also came to be used
as the name of the daisy, Margaret
is the source of both PEARL and DAISY.
There have been a number of saints
called Margaret. The earliest (if she
ever existed which is unlikely) was St
Margaret of Antioch, who is supposed
to have lived in the 4th century. She is
said to have been persecuted for her
faith, which she refused to renounce.
Satan appeared to her in the form of

a dragon and swallowed her, but she
was wearing a cross and the fiend
could not tolerate this inside him, so
she burst unscathed from his side.
She was an enormously popular saint,
despite attempts by the Church to
discourage her cult, and as a result
there are innumerable versions
of her name spread throughout
European languages. In the eastern
Mediterranean she is known as MARINA.
In the past, Margaret was particularly
popular in Scotland, which has its own
St Margaret, an 11th-century member
of the deposed Anglo-Saxon ruling
house of England, who was married to
Malcolm III of Scotland.
PET FORMS **Maggie, Meg, Megie, Madge,**
Mamie, Marge, Margie, May, Peg,
Peggy • VARIANTS **Marjory, Marguerita,**
Rita Irish **Mairéad** Scots Gaelic **Mairead,**
Mairghead Welsh **Mar(g)ed, Margiad,**
Mererid, Marget, Mati, Megan Czech
Markéta Dutch **Margriet** French
Marguerite, Margot, Magali German
Margaret(h)a, Margarethe, Magrit,
Margret, Meta Hebrew **Margalit**
Italian **Margherita** Polish **Malgorzata**
Russian, Spanish **Margarita** Scandinavian
Margrethe, Margit, Marit, Marete,
Merata, Mette
- ★ Margaret Thatcher (1925–), first
  female British prime minister
- ★ Margaret Mead (1901–78), US
  anthropologist

Margery see Marjory

Margot f
Margot, usually pronounced 'MAR-go',
is a pet form of MARGUERITE, which is a
French form of MARGARET. The variant
Margaux was introduced by the model
and actress Margaux Hemingway.
VARIANTS **Margo, Margaux**
- ★ Dame Margot Fonteyn (née Margaret
  Hookham) (1919–91), English ballerina

Marguerite f
A French form of MARGARET. It is also

the name for cultivated daisy flowers, so called because they share the white colour of the pearl, from which Margaret derives.

★ Marguerite de Valois (1553–1615), French princess and later queen consort and author. Affectionately known as Queen Margot

Maria, Mariah f

Maria is the Latin for MARY, and is also the standard form of the name in a number of other languages. English speakers began to use it, in addition to Mary, in the 18th century. In modern English it is usually pronounced 'ma-REE-a', but an older way is to rhyme the middle 'i' with the pronoun 'I' and the variant Mariah evolved to reflect this. The older pronunciation was brought to public attention by a song, 'They Call the Wind Maria', in the 1951 Lerner and Loewe musical *Paint Your Wagon*.

PET FORM **Ria**

★ Maria Marten (1801–27), a young English woman murdered by her lover William Corder at the Red Barn, whose fate was the subject of ballads and melodramatic plays still performed

★ Mariah Carey (1969–), US singer whose fame has done much to promote the alternative form of the name

Mariam, Mariamne see Miriam

Marian, Marianne f

In English, during the Middle Ages, *Marion* developed as a pet form of *Marie* or Mary. This was later analysed as a blend of Mary and ANNE, which affected the spelling, and although the spelling Marion is still used it is now less common than the form Marian. Meanwhile in France the name Marianne had developed as a form of *Mariamne* (see MIRIAM), although this too was later analysed as a combination of Marie and Anne.

Marion was also regularly used as a masculine name in the USA. It can be found among the top 100 boys' names in the 19th century, and remained in the top 500 into the 1970s. Although now rare, it is still in use. This has been analysed as from a Continental name Marian, a form of MARIUS, but the US masculine form is always spelt with an 'o'. Far more likely is that it represents one of the many examples of the American use of patriotic surnames as first names, in this case the name of Francis Marion (1732–95) a prominent guerrilla fighter in the American War of Independence nicknamed 'the Swamp Fox'.

VARIANT **Marianna**

★ Marianne Moore (1887–1972), US poet

★ Marion Morrison (1907–79), better known as the actor John Wayne

☆ In the course of the 19th century, the name Marianne came to symbolize the French Republic and Liberty

☆ Marianne Dashwood in Jane Austen's 1811 novel *Sense and Sensibility*

Marianela see Estelle

Maribel see Mary

Mariel, Mariella f

Mariel is usually analysed as a variant of MARY or MURIEL, but in the case of the actress Mariel Hemingway (b.1961), who brought the name to public attention, it is the name of a Cuban town used as a first name. Its spread was no doubt helped by the existence of Mariella, an Italian pet form of Mary.

VARIANT **Marielle**

★ Mariella Frostrup (1962–), Norwegian-born British journalist and television presenter

☆ Mariel is the name of a heroic mouse in the popular *Redwall* series of children's books by Brian Jacques

Marie-Reine *see* **Regina**

Marietta, Mariette *see* **Mary**

Marigold *f*
The old name for the marigold flower was simply 'gold' from its rich orange-yellow colour. However, the flower was much admired not only for its colour, but also for its excellent healing properties. It was important enough as a medicinal plant for the apothecaries to adopt it as their symbol. The plant came to be associated with the Virgin Mary, and her name was added to that of the plant in the 14th century, to give marigold. As a given name it came into use in the 19th century, but is not much used today.
PET FORM **Goldie**

Marilla *see* **Rilla**

Marilyn *f*
A name formed as a blend of MARY with either ELLEN or LYN. It has been recorded from the 18th century, but did not really take off until the 20th, initially in the USA.
VARIANTS **Marilene, Marilynn(e), Marylin(n), Maralyn, Mary Lyn(ne)**
★ Marilyn Monroe (1926–62), US film star whose fame made the name international

Marina
The origin of this name is probably from the family name *Marinus* a variant of MARIUS, but because the name Marina is the same as the Latin for 'of the sea' it has long been interpreted in this way. Marina is the name by which St Margaret of Antioch is known in the eastern Mediterranean, and as such is popular in Greece. Although the name has been recorded in England from the 14th century, it was Princess Marina of Greece who made the name more current in the UK, after she married the Duke of Kent in 1934.

VARIANTS **Maren, Maryn, Mareena** *French* **Marine** *Scandinavian* **Marna, Marnie**
★ Marina Warner (1946–   ), English literary critic and writer
★ Marina Sirtis (1955–   ), Anglo-American actress
☆ Marina is the heroine of Shakespeare's *Pericles*. She was given the name because she was born at sea

Marion *see* **Marian, Marianne**

Maris, Marisa, Marissa *see* **Mary**

Marisol *f*
This is a Spanish name, a blend of MARIA and SOL, 'sun'.
VARIANT **Maresol**

Marit *see* **Margaret**

Maritza *see* **Mary**

Marius *m*
This is a Latin family name used as a first name. The origin is uncertain although a connection with *Mars*, the Roman god of war, has been suggested, as has a link to the word *mas* (which inflects to *maris*), 'virile'. Marius was borne by an important Roman general who lived in the 1st century BC, but more significantly the name can function as a masculine equivalent of MARIA (MARY). Marius is variously pronounced with the first syllable rhyming with 'mare', 'man' or 'mar'.
VARIANTS *German, Polish* **Marian** *Greek* **Marios** *Italian, Spanish* **Mario**
★ Marius Goring (1912–98), English actor
☆ Marius is a character in Victor Hugo's 1862 novel *Les Misérables*

Marjory *f*
This is the more common modern form of the earlier *Margery*, a pet form of MARGARET. Puns on the name Margery and the herb marjoram go back at least to the poet John Skelton writing at the end of the 15th century, and

this association may have influenced the spelling with a 'j'. Certainly the French use their name for the herb, *Marjolaine*, as a feminine name.
PET FORMS **Marge, Margie** • VARIANT **Margery**

Mark, Marcus *m*

The Latin name Marcus was one of the few forenames in general use in Rome, and so is very common in Roman history. Its origins are unknown, but may be the same as MARIUS. As the name of one of the four Evangelists it spread through the western world, although it was not much used by English speakers in the Middle Ages, becoming more common after the Reformation. The French spelling, *Marc*, is currently well used as an alternative form. For feminines see under MARCEL. The Cornish King Mark, in the story of Tristan and Isolde, is probably a separate name, from Celtic *march*, 'horse', altered to conform with the Latin name.
VARIANTS *Irish and Scots Gaelic* **Marcas** *Welsh* **Marc** *Cornish* **Margh** *French* **Marc** *German* **Markus** *Italian, Polish* **Marek**, **Marco** *Spanish* **Marco, Marcos**

Marlene *f*

This name originated as a German pet form of the name Mary Magdalene. It became widely known during World War II, when the German song 'Lili Marlene' was a hit with both sides. This fame was reinforced by the popularity of the film star Marlene Dietrich (1901–92), who had left Germany before the start of the war and found fame in Hollywood. In both these cases the name is pronounced 'mar-lane-uh' in the German fashion. However, an alternative pronunciation 'mar-leen', reflecting the spelling, soon developed in English.
VARIANTS **Marleen, Marle(e)na, Marla, Marlee, Marlie**

Marley *mf*

This is a surname, originally a place name with various origins, used as a first name. It seems to have come into use to commemorate the Jamaican reggae singer Bob Marley (1945–81). Feminine forms overlap with the variants of MARLENE.

Marlon *m*

This name is something of a mystery. It was introduced to the general public, and went on to become very popular, through the fame of the actor Marlon Brando, who inherited it from his father. Since the Brando family was of French origin, it has been suggested that the name could be derived from French *Marc* combined with the pet suffix *-lon*. However, when names appear out of nowhere, it is often because they are surnames reused as first names, and it is worth considering this possibility. The Elizabethan playwright Christopher Marlowe signed his name in many different forms, including Marley and Marlin (and the first names *Marlo* and *Marlin* are usually considered variants of Marlon), so it is possible that Marlon is a form of such a surname. An even more likely explanation is that the name is a form of *Mahlon*. This is a biblical name, which has been interpreted as both 'sickly' and 'mild'. It was borne by Ruth's first husband who died young. Mahlon appears regularly in US records from at least the 18th century, and is likely to be even older. It did not drop out of US names statistics until 1952, by which time Marlon had already overtaken it.
VARIANTS **Marlo, Marlin**

Marmaduke *m*

This is a name of somewhat obscure origin, chiefly associated with Yorkshire. Some link it to the Welsh name MADOC, but the most likely source is a confused transference of the Irish name *Mael Maedoc*, 'devotee of St Maedoc' (see MALACHY). This name appears in the Domesday Book as *Melmidoc* which looks like a possible transitional form. Duke, the short form, is sometimes used in its own right, in which case it can be derived from the aristocratic title.

PET FORM **Duke**

★ Marmaduke Hussey (1923–2006), English administrator, former chairman of the BBC

☆ Marmaduke is the name of a Great Dane in a US strip cartoon of the same name

Marnie *f*

This started life as a pet form of the Scandinavian name *Marna*, a form of MARINA. The name was at its most popular in the 1960s–70s, but there are signs of a revival of interest in the UK.

VARIANTS **Marny, Mani**

★ Marni Nixon (1930–   ), US singer, known as 'the Voice of Hollywood' because she dubbed the singing voices of a number of actresses in musical films

☆ *Marnie* is the 1964 Hitchcock film based on a novel of the same name, written in 1961 by Winston Graham. Both the film and book influenced use of the name

Marquis *m*

This is the aristocratic title used as a first name. The title comes from someone who was in charge of one of the marches, an old term for border country. As a first name it is mainly found in the USA and, apart from the occasional 19th-century case, came into use in the 1970s, peaking in the early 90s. Some variants move towards blends with MARK or MARCUS.

VARIANTS **Markwis, Marquise**

Marsha *see* **Marcia**

Marshall *m*

This is the surname, originally given to someone who was in charge of horses, from the Germanic element *marah*, 'horse', used as a first name.

VARIANT **Marshal**

★ Marshall Mathers (1972–   ), US rapper also known as Eminem

Màrtainn, Mártan, Mårten *see* **Martin**

Martha *f*

This name comes from the Aramaic, a language spoken in the Holy Land at the time of Christ, for 'lady'. In the Gospels Martha of BETHANY is close to Christ, but busies herself with the housekeeping, while her sister Mary sits and listens to his teachings. This housewifely quality made the name a popular choice for Puritan women. Pet forms are shared with MATILDA.

PET FORMS **Mat(tie), Matty, Pattie, Patty, Mamie** • VARIANTS *French, German* **Marthe** *Italian, Spanish, Polish* **Marta** *Russian* **Marfa** *Scandinavian* **Marte, Merete**

★ Martha Stewart (1941–   ), US businesswoman, writer and broadcaster

☆ Martha Jones, character in *Dr Who*

Martin *m* Martina *f*

Martin comes from the Roman name *Martinus*, which probably derives from *Mars*, the Roman god of war. It was borne by St Martin of Tours who was a 4th-century Roman soldier. He famously cut his soldier's cloak in half to share it with a beggar, and afterwards became a pacifist, priest and eventually archbishop of Tours. He was a very popular saint and his name spread through Europe.

PET FORMS **Mart(y), Martie, Tina** • VARIANTS **Martinella** *Irish* **Máirtín, Mártan** *Scots Gaelic* **Màrtainn** *Welsh* **Martyn** *Dutch* **Maarten, Marten, Martijn, Tijn** (ms), **Maartje, Tineke** (fs) *French* **Martine** (f) *German* **Merten** *Italian* **Martino, Tino**

Polish **Marcin** (m), **Martyna** (f) *Portuguese* **Martinho** *Scandinavian* **Mårten, Morten** *Spanish* **Martí**

★ Martin Luther (1483–1546), German religious reformer, after whom Martin Luther King (1929–68) was named
★ Martina Navratilova (1956–), US tennis player

Marvin *m*
This is the surname used as a first name. The origin of the surname is not known for sure, but in at least some cases is from MERFYN. The name has been more used in North America than in the UK.

FEMININES **Marva, Marvalee** • PET FORM **Marv**

★ Marvin Gaye (1939–84), US soul singer
★ Marvin Hagler (1954–), US boxer
☆ Marvin the Paranoid Android in the various versions of Douglas Adams's *The Hitchhiker's Guide to the Galaxy*

Marwa *mf*
This is the Arabic for 'flint', and is the name of a hill near Mecca that is important in the hadj pilgrimage. Hajar, wife of Ibrahim, ran between the two hills Safa and Marwa searching for water for her infant son Ismail, ancestor of the Arab people. It says in the Koran 'Behold, Safa and Marwa are among the symbols of Allah' (surat al-Baqarah 2.158). Marwa is also the name of a fragrant plant. The name is used for girls more often than boys.

VARIANTS **Marwah**

Mary *f*
The Latin MARIA became *Marie* in French and Mary in English, all of which have been well used by English speakers over the centuries. The Latin name, in turn, is a variant of the Jewish name MIRIAM. Maria is the form given in the New Testament and, as the name of the mother of Christ, was important throughout Europe. As a

result, it became thoroughly detached from its original Hebrew form and was instead interpreted as deriving from the Latin *stilla maris*, 'drop of the sea', or *stella maris*, 'star of the sea'. The popularity of the name also meant that innumerable variants developed in different languages. In some languages, two forms of the name developed, one for use as a given name, the other reserved initially for the Virgin Mary, but which later came to be given to children, which increased the number of forms still further. Mary has been rather out of favour in recent years, except in combined forms such as *Mary-Jane* or *Marie-Claire*.

PET FORMS **Maisie, Mamie, Minnie, May, Mimi, Molly, Polly** • VARIANTS **Maria, Marianne, Maree, Mariel, Marylou, Marissa, Marlene** *Irish* **Máire, Moira, Maura, Máiria** *Scots Gaelic* **M(h)àiri, Màili** *Welsh* **Mair, Mari, Mairwen** *Dutch* **Marja, Maaike, Marijke, Marijse, Marike, Marloes** *French* **Marie, Manon, Marielle, Mariette, Marise** *German* **Maike, Mareike, Mariele, Maja, Marlis, Meike, Mitzi** *Hawaiian* **Malia** *Hungarian* **Mara, Marica** *Italian* **Mariella, Marietta, Marilena** *Russian* **Marya, Manya, Masha** *Scandinavian* **Maiken, Mia, My** *Spanish* **Marisol, Maribel, Marisela, Maritza**

Maryam, Maryamne, Maryana *see* Miriam

Masha *see* Mary

Mason *m*
A surname, from the occupation, which has been very popular in the USA in recent years and is growing in use in the UK.

PET FORM **Mace**

Massimiliano *see* Maximilian

Massimo *see* Maxim

Masud *m* **Masuda** *f*
Arabic names meaning 'fortunate, happy, lucky'.
VARIANTS **Masood(a)**

Masum *m* **Masuma** *f*
Arabic names meaning 'innocent, sinless, infallible, protected'. *Al-Masum*, 'the innocent', is an epithet of Muhammad. *Masun(a)* is a related name.
VARIANT **Masoom(a)**

Mat *see* **Martha**

Mathias *see* **Matthew**

Mati *see* **Margaret**

Matilda *f*
This is a Germanic name formed from the elements *maht*, 'might', and *hild*, 'battle'. It was introduced to England by William the Conqueror, whose wife bore the name, and his Norman followers. Significantly it was also the name of William's granddaughter, who after his death claimed the throne as the rightful heir. This plunged England into civil war. Matilda managed to seize power briefly in 1141, but in the end had to be content to let her cousin Stephen reign with the stipulation that her son should become Henry II. The name was the Latin or learned form of her name, the spoken form normally being modified from the French *Mahaud* or *Mahaut* to MAUD. Matilda was revived as a given name in the late 18th century, although at first uses were mainly literary. The 'unsuitable' behaviour of the 12th-century Matilda seems to have influenced use of the name, and fictional women bearing it tend to be portrayed behaving in deviant ways, as in the case of Mary Shelley's second novel *Mathilda* (1819) with its themes of incest and suicide. However, as the 19th century progressed this attitude was lost.
PET FORMS **Tilly, Tillie, Tilda, Mat(ie),**

Matty, Patty • VARIANTS **Mathilda** *Welsh* **Mallt** *Dutch* **Machteld, Mechteld** *French* **Mathilde** *German* **Mathilde, Mecht(h)ild(e)** *Italian* **Mafalda** *Polish* **Matylda** *Scandinavian* **Mathilda** *Spanish* **Matilde**
☆ Matilda Wormwood, heroine of Roald Dahl's 1988 novel *Matilda*

Matthew, Matthias *m*
These are the New Testament forms of the Hebrew name *Mattathia*, 'gift of God'. Two forms are used in the Authorized Version to distinguish Matthew, author of the first Gospel, and Matthias, the man who was elected to fill the place of the twelfth disciple after the treachery and death of Judas Iscariot. However, not all biblical translations follow this tradition, and the variants do not have this distinction in other languages. Matthew was moderately well used in the Middle Ages, but became more popular after the Reformation. Matthias has never been as common.
PET FORM **Mat(t)** • VARIANTS **Mathew, Mathias** *Irish* **Maitiú, Maitias** *Scots Gaelic* **Mat(h)a** *Dutch* **Mattijs, Thijs, Ties** *French* **Mat(t)hieu, Mathis** *German* **Mathias, Mathis, Matthäus, Mattias** *Hawaiian* **Makaio** *Italian* **Matteo** *Polish* **Mateusz, Maciej** *Portuguese* **Mateus, Matheus, Matias** *Russian* **Matvei, Matvey, Motya** *Scandinavian* **Matteus, Mathies, Mats, Mads** *Spanish* **Mateo, Matías**

Mattie, Matty *see* **Martha**

Maud *f*
This was the usual medieval spoken form of the name otherwise known as MATILDA. It was a popular name among the medieval English nobility, but then died out, before being revived in the 19th century. This revival was in part helped by Tennyson's long, melancholy poem *Maud* (1855), part of which was set to music as the popular drawing-

room song 'Come into the Garden, Maud'.

PET FORM **Maudie** • VARIANT **Maude**

★ Maud Gonne (1865–1953), Irish nationalist and actress

☆ Maudie Littlehampton, cartoon character created by Osbert Lancaster to poke fun at the upper classes

Maura *f*

This is usually the anglicized form of *Maire*, the Irish form of MARY. There is an obscure 5th-century saint called Maura, and it has been suggested that her name may be from a different source, the Gaelic *mor*, 'great'. Maura is the usual Irish form of the name, the variants being better used elsewhere. In Italy and Spain Maura can be a feminine form of MAURICE.

VARIANTS **Moira, Moyra**

★ Moira Stewart (1949–), English journalist and newsreader

★ Moira Lister (1923–2007), South African-born British actress

Maureen *f*

Maureen is the anglicized form of *Máirín*, a pet form of *Maire* (see MAURA). Technically, *Moreen* is a variant not of Maureen but of *Muireann* (*Muirinn* in Gaelic), meaning 'sea-white', or it may be the anglicized form of *Móirín*, a pet form of *Mor*, 'great'. However, there is considerable overlap in usage. Forms such as *Murron* are particularly Scottish. See also MIRIN.

PET FORM **Mo** • VARIANTS **Mairin, Maurene, Maurine, Moreen, Murron, Murrin, Murren**

★ Maureen O'Hara (1920–), Irish actress

★ Maureen Lipman (1946–), English actress and writer

Maurice *m*

The Latin *Maurus* was used of anyone who was dark-skinned, and also of North African Moors. It was a widespread name and included among its bearers a Byzantine emperor. *Maurus* became Maurice in French, and was brought to England by the Normans. It was a popular name in the Middle Ages, to the extent that it produced the surnames Morris and Morse, both of which are also used as first names. *Morris* was common from the mid-19th to early 20th century, but neither Maurice nor Morris is much used today. Maurice was also used by Jews as an English form of MOSES. In Ireland it has been given as an English form of the Irish name *Muirgheas*, formed from *muir*, 'sea', and *gus*, choice'. In the USA there is a tendency to pronounce Maurice in the French way with the accent on the second syllable, but in the UK Morris and Maurice are pronounced identically.

PET FORMS **Mo, Moss, Maurie, Maury** • VARIANTS **Morris, Morse** *Irish* **Muiris** *Welsh* **Meuric, Meurig, Merrick** *Dutch* **Maurits** *German* **Moritz** *Italian* **Maurizio** *Polish* **Maurycy** *Russian* **Mavriki** *Spanish* **Mauricio**

★ Maurice Chevalier (1888–1972), French actor and singer

Mave *see* **Maeve**

Maverick *m*

This term for an unconventional, nonconformist person comes from the career of Samuel A Maverick (1803–70), a Texas rancher who refused to brand his cattle, so that all unbranded cattle came to be called mavericks. The name appeared in the USA briefly in the late 1950s, when the television cowboy series *Maverick*, telling the adventures of one Bret Maverick, was popular. It reappeared again in 1994 (and has since grown in use) when a film was made based on the old television series. The spread of the name may have been helped by the use of Maverick as a nickname for the lead character in the 1986 film *Top*

Gun. The name does not yet seem to have made much of an impact in the UK.

Mavis *f*
This is a dialect word for a type of bird, the song thrush, which seems to have been invented by Marie Corelli for a character in her 1895 novel *The Sorrows of Satan*.

Mavriki *see* **Maurice**

Max *m*
Originally a pet form of any name beginning *Max-*, the short form is now more popular than the full forms.

Maxim, Maximus *m*
The Latin name Maximus, 'the greatest', started out as a title awarded for some achievement, but later on joined the stock of given names. Magnus Maximus (literally 'Great the Greatest') was a 4th-century Roman general who served in Britain before withdrawing troops from the province to help him win a position as one of the rulers of the crumbling Empire. He becomes MACSEN (or *Maxen*) Wledig in Welsh tradition, and was claimed as the ancestor of many of the ruling families in Wales. Maxim is also found used as a short form of MAXIMILIAN.
PET FORM **Max** • VARIANTS *French* **Maxime** *Italian* **Massimo** *Polish* **Maksym** *Russian* **Maksim, Maks** *Spanish* **Maximiano, Maximino, Maximo, Maxima**
☆ Maximus Decimus Meridius, the hero of the 2000 film *Gladiator*
☆ Maxim de Winter in the 1938 Daphne du Maurier novel and subsequent film adaptation, *Rebecca*

Maximilian *m*
There was a Latin name *Maximilianus*, a pet form of MAXIMUS. However, although this was borne by a saint, it was not current when a 15th-century Holy Roman Emperor decided to call his son Maximilian, formed from a blend of the names of two of the Roman generals he most admired, Quintus Fabius Maximus and Publius Cornelius Scipio Aemilianus. Maximilian became a standard name in the Habsburg families, and still retains some of its aristocratic associations.
FEMININE **Maximiliana** • PET FORM **Max** • VARIANTS **Maximillian, Maximillion** *Dutch* **Maximiliaan** *French* **Maximilien, Maximilienne** *Italian* **Massimiliano** *Polish* **Maksymilian** *Russian* **Maksimilian** *Spanish* **Maximiliano**

Maxine *f*
A feminine version of male names beginning with *Max-*, which was introduced in the 19th century and had its peak of popularity in the 1930s.
VARIANT **Maxene**

Maxwell *m*
A surname from a Scottish place name meaning 'Mack's well', used as a first name. It was borne by the Canadian-born newspaper magnate 'Max' Aitken (William Maxwell Aitken, Lord Beaverbrook, 1879–1964), who introduced it to the general public.

May *f*
This name can have several origins. It can be either a pet form of names beginning with *Ma-* such as MABEL, MARGARET and MARY; a month name; or a flower name. May was popular in the later 19th century and into the early years of the 20th. It has also been a popular element in two-part names.
VARIANTS **Mae, Mai**
★ Mae West (1893–1980), US vaudeville performer and film actress, after whose pneumatic form inflatable life jackets were nicknamed
★ Mai Zetterling (1925–94), Swedish actress and director

Maya¹ *f*
This popular Indian name comes

from the Sanskrit for 'illusion'. It is the traditional name of the mother of the Buddha, and an epithet of the goddess Durga.

Maya² f
This popular modern name has a multiplicity of possible roots. The most famous bearer of the name is US author Maya Angelou, and in her case it is a nickname derived from the way her brother used to say 'my sister'. Besides this a major source is the name *Maja*, a pet form of MARIA in several European languages, and pronounced with the 'j' as a 'y' sound. Other sources include the Central American people, the Mayans, a Jewish name meaning 'water' and a respelling of the name MIA. Ultimately, there may be no direct source, but merely the use of an attractive-sounding combination of letters.
VARIANTS **Miya, Mya(h), Maia**

Maybelle *see* **Mabel**

Maygan *see* **Megan**

Mayr *see* **Meir**

McCauley *see* **Macaulay**

Mckayla *see* **Michelle**

Mckenzie *see* **Mackenzie**

Mea *see* **Mia**

Meadhbh, Medb *see* **Maeve**

Meadow f
The vocabulary word that came into use at the beginning of the 21st century, probably in response to the character of Meadow Soprano in the cult television series *The Sopranos*, first shown in 1999.

Meagan, Meaghan *see* **Megan**

Meave *see* **Maeve**

Mechteld, Mechthild, Mechthilde,

Mechtild, Mechtilde *see* **Matilda**

Meena f
Meena means 'fish' in Sanskrit, and is also the name of the constellation Pisces. The name can also be a pet form of the longer *Meenakshi*, 'fish-eyes' (a compliment), one of the epithets of the goddess Lakshmi.
VARIANTS **Mena, Mina**

Meera f
This is an Indian name meaning 'sea, ocean', and thus the equivalent of MARINA. It was the name of a 16th-century princess noted for her devotion to Krishna.
VARIANT **Mira**
★ Meera Syal (1964–), English actress, writer and comedienne

Mees *see* **Bartholomew**

Meg f
A pet form of MARGARET. Initially Margaret was shortened to *Mag* or *Maggie*, and then the 'a' changed to 'e'. At one time this was a typically Scottish pet form. The name can also be found as a pet form of MEGAN and similar names.
PET FORM **Meggie**
★ Meg Ryan (1961–), US actress
☆ Meg March in Louisa M Alcott's 1868 novel *Little Women*

Megan f
This is a Welsh pet form of MARGARET, which has now become widely popular among English speakers. The original Welsh pronunciation is 'MEG-an', but an alternative pronunciation 'ME-gan' has developed since it spread beyond Wales. The peculiar looking pseudo-Irish forms that have also developed seem to have their origin in the Australian author Colleen McCullough's popular 1977 novel *The Thorn Birds* in which she names a character *Meghan*.

VARIANTS **Meghan, Meagan, Maygan, Maegan**

Megie *see* **Margaret**

Mehdi *m*
An Arabic name meaning 'the rightly-guided', and one of the titles of Muhammad. It is particularly popular among Muslims of North African descent.

Mehek *f*
This is an Indian name meaning 'fragrance'.
VARIANTS **Mahek, Mehik**

Mehitabel *f*
This is a Hebrew name meaning 'God makes happy'. Although it is only mentioned in passing in the Bible, it was nonetheless taken up by Puritans, and was well used by their descendants in the USA into at least the 18th century.
PET FORM **Hetty** • VARIANT **Mehetabel**
☆ *Archy and Mehitabel*, 1927 work by Don Marquis about the adventures of a New York cockroach and cat

Mehmet *see* **Mohammed**

Meical *see* **Michael**

Meike *see* **Mary**

Meilyr *m*
This Welsh name goes back to the Old Celtic *Maglorix* formed from *maglor*, 'chief', and *rix*, 'ruler, king'. It was the name of an early saint.
VARIANT **Meilir**

Meinir *f*
This Welsh name has been interpreted as derived either from *main*, 'slender', and *hir*, 'long', or from a word meaning 'maiden'.
VARIANT **Meinwen**

Meir *m*
This is a traditional Jewish name from the Hebrew for 'giving light'.

VARIANTS **Meier, M(e)y(e)r, Mayr**

Meirion *m*
This Welsh name goes back to the Roman name *Marianus*, a form of MARIUS. According to tradition, it was borne by a grandson of the great British war leader Cunedda, who is said to have given his name to the Welsh district of Meirionnydd (Merioneth).
FEMININES **Meriona, Merionwen**

Mel *mf*
A pet form of any name beginning *Mel-* such as MELANIE or MELVIN, but in Ireland it can be an independent masculine name, after an early saint.

Melanie *f*
This name comes from the Greek *melaina*, 'dark, black', and was used as a title for the Greek goddess Demeter (see DEMETRIUS) in her winter aspect. It came into wider use via the Latin name *Melania*, borne by a 5th-century Roman saint who gave her considerable wealth away to the poor. This became Melanie in French, and was common in the Middle Ages. The name had all but died out when it was used by Margaret Mitchell, in her 1936 novel *Gone with the Wind*, for the character of the long-suffering Melanie Wilkes. This reintroduced the name, which grew rapidly in popularity after the film adaptation of 1939.
PET FORM **Mel(ie)** • VARIANTS **Melany** *Cornish* **Melony**

Melchior *m*
In Christian tradition, this is the name of one of the three kings, or Magi, who visited Christ at the Nativity. It is thought to be Persian, from the elements *melk*, 'king', and *quart*, 'city'. The other two kings are BALTHASAR and CASPER.
VARIANT *Italian* **Melchiorre**

Melek *see* **Malik, Malkah**

Melia *see* **Amelia**

Melicent *see* **Millicent**

Melinda *f*
This name is found in the 1706 play
by George Farquhar, *The Recruiting
Officer*. As it was not uncommon
for Restoration dramatists to invent
names for their female characters, it
may have been Farquhar's creation,
probably based on MELISSA, or at least
on the Greek element *mel*, 'honey,
sweetness'.
PET FORM **Mindy**
★ Melinda Gates (1964–), co-chair of
the Bill and Melinda Gates Foundation
★ Melinda Messenger (1971–),
English glamour model and television
presenter
☆ *Mork & Mindy*, 1970s–80s television
sitcom

Melisande, Melisenda *see* **Millicent**

Melisent *see* **Millicent**

Melissa *f*
In Greek mythology Melissa, meaning
'honey-bee', was the name of the
nymph who nursed the infant Zeus. It
was introduced to English speakers in
Spenser's *The Faerie Queene* (1590),
but does not seem to have been used
as a given name until the 18th century.
Melita is an ancient variant of the
name.
PET FORMS **Lissa, Missie** • VARIANTS
Melit(t)a, Melyssa *Hawaiian* **Melika**
Spanish **Melisa**
★ Melissa was the wife of Periander
(c.625–585 BC), tyrant of Corinth
☆ Melissa is a prophetess in Ariosto's
1516 poem 'Orlando Furioso', which
helped spread the name

Melody *f*
This is the vocabulary word used as a
first name. Although it has been noted
from the 18th century, the name really
came into use in the 1920s, peaking

in the USA, where it has always been
more popular, in the 1960s.
VARIANT **Melodi(e)**

Melony *see* **Melanie**

Melville *m*
The Scottish aristocratic surname,
ultimately from a place called *Malville*,
'bad settlement', which is occasionally
used as a first name.

Melvin *m*
The origin of Melvin is not clear. It is
a Scottish surname, which may come
from a Gaelic name or be a variant of
MELVILLE. It was well established in the
later 19th century as a first name, but
is now out of fashion even in Scotland.
Melvina is both a variant of MALVINA
and a rare feminine. *Melva* has also
been recorded.
PET FORM **Mel** • VARIANT **Melvyn**
★ Melvin 'Mel' Brooks (1926–), US
film actor and director
★ Melvyn Bragg (1939–), English
broadcaster and novelist

Melvina *see* **Malvina**

Mena *see* **Meena**

Menahem *m*
This is a Jewish name meaning
'comforter, consolation'. It was
traditionally given to boys born
following the annual day of mourning
that marks the destruction of the
temple at Jerusalem, and was also used
for a child born after the death of a
sibling. In the ancient Mediterranean
the Greek name *Menelaus*,
'withstanding the people', was used as
a Gentile form of Menahem.
VARIANT *Yiddish* **Mendel**
★ Menachem Begin (1913–92), Israeli
statesman and Nobel Prize winner

Merata *see* **Margaret**

Mercedes *f*
This name comes from the Spanish

title of the Virgin Mary, *Maria de las Mercedes*, 'Mary of Mercies'. Some modern uses may be derived from the élite car name, which was in turn named after the manufacturer's daughter.

PET FORMS **Merche** (Spanish), **Mercy**, **Sadie**
• VARIANT **Mercedez**
★ Mercedes Lackey (1950–   ), US fantasy author
★ Mercedes McNab (1980–   ), Canadian actress

Mercy *f*

This is a religious virtue used as a first name. Although it was in circulation earlier, it was the Puritans who really took up the name, along with the other virtue names. It has barely been used in the USA since the 19th century, and is only quietly used in the UK. It is also found as a pet form of MERCEDES.

PET FORM **Merry** • **Mercia**
☆ Mercy and Charity, known as Merry and Cherry, are the daughters of the hypocritical Mr Pecksmith in Dickens's 1844 novel *Martin Chuzzlewit*

Meredith *mf*

This is an old Welsh masculine name, originally *Maredudd* or *Meredydd*, now predominantly used as a feminine name. It was probably formed from *mawredd*, 'greatness, magnificence', and *iudd*, 'lord, chief'. The change to a feminine name had occurred in the USA by the early years of the 20th century, and it has been a more popular female name in the USA than in the UK.

VARIANTS *Welsh* **Maredudd**, **Meredydd**, **Merêd**
★ Meredith Wilson (m) (1902–84), musical writer and composer, best known for *The Music Man*

Mererid *see* **Margaret**

Merete *see* **Martha**

Merfyn *see* **Mervyn**

Meriadoc *m*

This is the name of a Welsh saint who possibly lived in the 6th century. Little is known of him for sure, but he appears to have done missionary work in Cornwall, where he may be called *Meriasek*, and in Brittany.

☆ Meriadoc 'Merry' Brandybuck, hobbit, in J R R Tolkien's *The Lord of the Rings*

Meriel *see* **Muriel**

Meriona, Merionwen *see* **Meirion**

Merle *mf*

As a feminine name this may go back to the 1890 children's story *Wanted a King* by Maggie Brown, in which she uses it for the little girl heroine. It is possible either that she took this from the Old French *merle*, 'blackbird', that she used it as a variant of *Meriel* (see MURIEL), or that she simply made it up. As a masculine name, in use in the 19th century, peaking in popularity in the 1920s and common in the USA until the end of the 1980s, it is probably a form of *Merrill*, a surname derived from Muriel. *Merlene* may either be a variant of Merle or of MARLENE.

★ Merle Haggard (1937–   ), US country music singer and songwriter
★ Merle Oberon (1911–79), Indian-born British actress who made the feminine form of the name familiar

Merlin *m*

This is the name of the great mage who, with his wisdom, guided King Arthur. It is a form of the Welsh name *Myrddin*. According to early legend Merlin was born at Caermarthen and the town was named after him (in Welsh *Caerfyrddin* means 'Merlin's fort'). In fact, Caermarthen comes from the old Roman name *Moridunum* meaning 'sea fort', and it is more probable that Merlin was named after

the place. The variant *Merlyn* is used
for both sexes.

VARIANTS **Merlyn** *Welsh* **Myrddin**

★ Merlyn Lowther (1954–   ), first female
chief cashier of the Bank of England,
whose signature appeared on bank
notes for many years

Merne *see* **Morna**

Merrick *see* **Maurice**

Merrill *see* **Murdo**

Merry *see* **Mercy, Meredith,
Meriadoc**

Merten *see* **Martin**

Mervyn *m*
This is the anglicized form of the
Welsh name *Merfyn*, the first element
of which means either 'sea' or
'marrow', and the second 'eminent'.
It was the name of a 9th-century
king who founded a new dynasty
in Gwynedd. It was not much used
outside Wales until the 1930s, when it
grew in popularity, but it is now out of
favour again.

PET FORM **Merv** • VARIANT **Mervin**

★ Mervyn Peake (1911–68), English
writer and artist

Meryem *see* **Miriam**

Meryl *f*
A recent name, usually analysed as a
variant of *Meriel*, a form of MURIEL.

★ Meryl Streep (1949–   ), US actress

Messiah *m*
This religious term, from the Hebrew
for 'anointed', was not unusual as a
given name in Jewish communities in
the Middle Ages. It was usually found
in the form *Moshiah*, and given to
express the hope that the new baby
might be the longed-for Messiah. It
has just started to come back as a first
name in the USA. (Compare SALVADOR.)

Meta, Mette *see* **Margaret**

Meuric, Meurig *see* **Maurice**

Meyer, Meyr *see* **Meir**

Mhairi, Mhàiri *see* **Mary**

Mia *f*
This started life as a Scandinavian and
German pet form of MARIA, but is not
now generally associated with the
name. Some users may also recognize
it as the Italian and Spanish for 'my'.
The name was little used outside its
native areas until the 1960s, when it
was introduced to the English-speaking
public by the actress Mia Farrow
(b.1945). It is currently very popular in
many countries. There is some overlap
between uses of this name and of MAYA.

VARIANTS **Mea, Miah**

Miah *see* **Jeremiah**

Micah *m*
This is a biblical name, a contraction
of *Micaiah*, 'who is like Yahweh
(God)?', and thus has the same
meaning as the similar MICHAEL. It was
borne by one of the Old Testament
prophets, whose prophecies date
from the 8th century BC. The name
was quietly used by the Puritans. It
is one of the 'new' Old Testament
names that were taken up in the USA
in the late 20th century, and is now a
popular choice there, as well as being
frequently given to girls. It is beginning
to spread to the UK. Pet forms and
variants overlap considerably with
those of Michael. In the USA there
is some variation in pronunciation,
between a first syllable sounded as
'me' or the more traditional 'my'.

VARIANTS **Mica, Mika(h), Myca(h),
Myka(h)**

★ Mica Paris (1969–   ), English singer
☆ Micah Sanders in the television series
Heroes

Michael *m*
This name means 'who is like God?'.

It is the traditional name of one of the archangels, usually depicted in Christian art as a soldier, often in full armour, defeating Satan in the form of a dragon, or sometimes portrayed as the 'weigher of souls'. Michael is also the patron saint of soldiers and of several nations. The name has been consistently popular with English speakers since the Middle Ages, except for a brief decline in the 19th century. In the USA it has been either the most popular or second most popular choice for boys since 1954, and was in the top ten choices for the previous decade. The lowest rank it has had there since records began in 1880 was 59th. The Russian pet form *Misha*, sometimes altered to *Mischa*, can also be found used for girls.

PET FORMS **Mike, Mick, Mick(e)y, Mikey, Mich, Midge** • VARIANTS *Cornish* **Myghal** *Irish* **Mícheál** *Scots Gaelic* **Mìcheal** *Welsh* **Meical, Mihangel** *Dutch* **Maikel, Michiel, Michaël** *Finnish* **Mika, Mikko** *French, German* **Michel** *Italian* **Michele, Michaelangelo** *Polish* **Michal** *Russian* **Mikhail, Misha** *Scandinavian* **Mikael, Mikkel** *Spanish* **Miguel**

Michaela *see* Michelle

Michal *f*
This name, which may mean 'brook', is borne by a biblical character, a daughter of Saul who married David. In Hebrew the name is pronounced 'mee-khal'. However, it is not clear to what extent users are choosing the Hebrew name as opposed to forming a feminine of MICHAEL, especially as *Mikal* is also a Czech and Slovak form of Michael.

Michelle, Michaela *f*
Michelle was originally the French feminine form of MICHAEL and Michaela the form used in German and other languages. They are both now naturalized to the extent that they have

spawned independent names: SHELLEY and KAYLA. Michelle was taken up in the 1940s and was particularly popular in the 1970s and 80s, influenced by the 1966 Beatles song 'Michelle', but it has now been eclipsed by Michaela and its variants.

PET FORMS **Mikki, Chelle, Shell, Shelley, Kayla** • VARIANTS **Michel(a), Michayla, Makayla, Mckayla, Mikella, Mikayla** *French* **Michèle, Micheline** *Hawaiian* **Mikala** *Italian* **Micaela, Michelangela** *Polish* **Michalina** *Scandinavian* **Mikaela** *Spanish* **Micaela, Miguela**

Mick, Mike *see* Michael

Midge *see* Margaret, Marjory, Michael

Mies *see* Bartholomew

Mignon *f*
This is a French term of endearment, meaning 'little one'. It came into use as a first name with Goethe's 1795 novel *Wilhelm Meister's Apprenticeship*, and was boosted after the novel was turned into a successful opera, called *Mignon*, by Ambroise Thomas in 1866. The even rarer *Mignonette* may be a pet form of this, or the flower name.
★ Mignon Anderson (1892–1983), US silent film star
★ Mignon Dunn (1931–), US mezzo-soprano

Miguel *see* Michael

Miguela *see* Michelle

Mihangel *see* Michael

Mihir *m*
This Indian name comes from a term for the sun.
★ Mihir Bose (1947–), Indian-born BBC journalist

Mika *see* Micah, Michael

Mikael *see* Michael

Mikaela *see* **Michelle**

Mikah *see* **Micah**

Mikala, Mikayla, Mikella, Mikki
see **Michelle**

Mikey, Mikhail, Mikkel *see* **Michael**

Mikki *see* **Michelle**

Mikko *see* **Michael**

Mikolaj, Mikołaj *see* **Nicholas**

Mila *f*
A Slavic name which functions as a
short form of names such as MILOSLAVA
and LUDMILA, and is also the Slavic
word for 'dear'.

Milagros *f*
A Spanish name taken from the Marian
title *Nuestra Señora de los Milagros*,
'Our Lady of Miracles'.

Milan *m*
A Slavic name, originally a short form
of names based on *mil*, 'gracious'.
★ Milan Kundera (1929–), Czech-born
French novelist

Mildred *f*
Mildred is a reduced form of the Old
English name *Mildthryth*, formed from
mild, 'gentle', and *thyth*, 'strength'. It
was borne by a 7th-century saint and is
one of the few Old English names that
has remained in almost continuous
use, although now, after a spurt of
popularity in the 19th century, it is a
rare choice.
PET FORMS **Millie, Milly**

Milena *f*
The feminine of MILAN, which also
functions as a pet form of HELEN. In Italy
it is used as a blend of MARIA and ELENA
(see HELEN). The variant *Millenna* has
been recorded as chosen for babies
born in the millennium year.

Miles *m*
This name is something of a mystery.
It was brought to England by the
Normans, but no convincing
explanation of its origin or meaning
has ever been found. It is usually
agreed that the fact that *miles* (unlike
the name, pronounced with two
syllables rather one) is the Latin for
'soldier' is pure coincidence. It usually
appears in medieval documents
as *Milo*. All forms of the name are
associated with Ireland, where it has
been used to 'translate' *Maoileas*,
'servant of Jesus', and *Maolmuire* or
Maolra, 'servant of Mary'. Miles and its
variants have been quite fashionable in
recent years.
VARIANTS **Milo, Mylo, Myles**
★ Miles Davis (1926–91), US jazz
trumpeter and bandleader
★ Myles Standish (c.1584–1656), English
soldier and colonist, prominent among
the Pilgrim Fathers
☆ Milo Minderbender in the novel
Catch-22 (1961) by Joseph Heller

Miley *f*
A very recently coined name, which
has been introduced by the young
actress Miley Cyrus (Destiny Hope
Cyrus, b.1992). In her case it is a
shortening of her childhood nickname
Smiley. The name fits neatly with
currently fashionable sounds and has
been rapidly taken up. Although Miley
Cyrus only came to public attention in
the *Hannah Montana* television show
in 2006, the name appeared in the US
charts for 2007 ranked at 278.

Mili *see* **Millie**

Milla *see* **Camilla, Ludmila, Mila**

Milli *see* **Millie**

Millicent *f*
The Germanic name *Amalswint*,
formed from *amal*, 'work', and *swinth*,
'strength', was turned into *Melisande*

in French, and when it was brought over to England by the Normans it became Millicent. It was one of the names that fell out of use after the Middle Ages but which was revived in the 19th century.

PET FORMS **Millie, Milly** • VARIANTS **Melicent, Melisent, Melisenda**

★ Dame Millicent Fawcett (1847–1929), English suffragette and educational reformer

★ Millicent Martin (1934–), English singer, actress and comedienne

☆ *Pelléas and Mélisande*, tragic 1892 play by Maurice Maeterlinck, turned into an opera by Debussy in 1902

Millie, Milly *f*
Originally a pet form of any name containing the syllable 'mil' such as CAMILLA, EMILY, MILDRED or MILLICENT, this is now a very popular independent name. Currently Millie is the better used, but both are widespread.

PET FORM **Mills** • VARIANT **Mi(l)li**

Milo *see* Miles

Miloslav *m* Miloslava *f*
Slavic names formed from the elements *mil*, 'favour', and *slav*, 'glory'.

PET FORM **Milos(z)**

Milton *m*
An English surname formed from elements meaning 'mill' and 'settlement'. It came into use in honour of the poet John Milton (1608–74), and has been more common in North America than in the UK.

★ Milton Friedman (1912–2006), US economist

Mima *see* Jemima

Mimi *f*
An Italian pet form of MARIA, although sometimes found of other names beginning with 'M'. It was made famous by the character in Puccini's 1896 opera *La Bohème*.

Mimosa *see* Acacia

Min *see* Jasmine

Mina *f*
Originally a pet form of names ending in *-mina*, such as WILHELMINA. The name has a special role in the Scottish Highlands, where there is a custom of feminizing masculine names by adding the ending *-ina*, creating names such as *Jamesina*. There Mina can be a pet form (sometimes used independently) of names such as *Calumina* and *Normina*. For the Indian name see under MEENA.

VARIANTS **Minna, Minne**

Mindy *see* Melinda

Minerva *f*
The name of the Roman goddess of wisdom and war, which has occasionally been used as a given name since the Renaissance, but not as frequently as her Greek equivalent ATHENE.

☆ Professor Minerva McGonagall in the *Harry Potter* books by J K Rowling

Minette *f*
Minette was Charles I's nickname for his daughter HENRIETTA, Duchess of Orleans (1644–70). As she was known more familiarly as *Henriette*, the second half of the name would appear to have been taken from this form. Minette has also been recorded as a pet form of various names beginning with 'M' such as MARIA. It has been used quietly but regularly as a given name since the 17th century.

★ Minette Walters (1949–), English crime novelist

Minique *see* Dominique

Minna *see* Wilhelmina

Minnie *f*
Now an independent name, this was

originally a pet form of MARY, WILHELMINA
and other similar names.

★ Minnie Driver (1970–   ), English
  actress
☆ The cartoon character, Minnie Mouse
☆ Minnie is the heroine of Puccini's
  opera *The Girl of the Golden West* (*La
  fanciulla del West*).

Minta, Minty *see* **Araminta**

Mir *see* **Ameer**

Mira *f*
This is usually either a variant of MYRA,
or a short form of names containing
Mira-, such as MIRABEL and MIRANDA. See
also MEERA for the Indian name.

Mirabel *f*
This name is based on the Latin
mirabilis, 'wonderful', but can also
be analysed as deriving from the
mir of 'admire' and *bel(le)*, French
for 'beautiful'. The name was in use
in the Middle Ages, and was briefly
fashionable in the 19th century. It also
appears in 18th-century dramas as a
masculine name, but this use should
probably be thought of as a surname.
Mirabel is also a common place name
in French-speaking areas, as well as
being a variety of plum, and the French
regard this as the root of the name.
VARIANTS **Mirabelle, Mirabella**
★ Mirabel Topham (1891–1980),
  racecourse owner

Mirain *f*
This is a Welsh name meaning 'lovely,
splendid', which came into use around
1900.

Miranda *f*
This comes from the Latin word
meaning 'worthy to be admired,
deserving admiration', and was coined
by Shakespeare for the only female
character in *The Tempest*. It was taken
up as a first name in the 19th century,
but is not currently in favour in the UK,
although it is well used in the USA.
PET FORMS **Mandie, Mandy, Randa,
Randi(e), Mira, Randy**
★ Miranda Richardson (1958–   ), English
  actress

Mireille *f*
This is the French form of the
Provençal name *Mireio*, probably
formed from the Provençal *mirar*, 'to
admire', and thus similar to MIRANDA.
It is, however, sometimes described
as the Provençal form of MIRIAM. This
is because the name was invented by
the Provençal nationalist and poet
Frédéric Mistral. He wrote a poem
called 'Mirèio', in 1859, which was
turned into the opera *Mireille* by
Gounod in 1864. Mistral was invited
to be godfather to a girl he wanted
to call Mireille, at a time when only
names from an approved list could be
given. He therefore boldly asserted
that Mireille was the Provençal form
of Miriam, and no one dared to
contradict the great man.
VARIANTS **Mireo, Mirea** *Italian* **Mirella**
★ Mireille Mathieu (1946–   ), French
  singer

Miriam *f*
In the Old Testament Miriam is the
sister of Moses. The meaning is not
known, and it is probable that Miriam's
name, like those of her brothers AARON
and MOSES, was Egyptian in origin. The
Hebrew form of the name is *Maryam*
which shows how it could then
develop into the New Testament form
MARY. In Aramaic, the language spoken
in the Holy Land, the name would
have been *Mariam*, while yet another
form, *Mariamne*, is used by the 1st-
century AD historian Josephus for the
wife of King Herod.
PET FORM **Mitzi** • VARIANTS **Myriam** *Arabic*
Maryam *Dutch, German* **Mirjam** *Russian*
Maryana *Turkish* **Meryem** *Yiddish* **Mirele**

Mirin *f*

Both St Mirin's Cathedral and St Mirren FC in Paisley, Scotland, are named after a 7th-century Irish abbot who founded a monastery in the town. However, in Scotland the name is used for girls, not inappropriate if it is, as it appears, the same as the Irish name *Muireann* or *Muirinn*, derived from *muir*, 'sea', and *fionn*, 'fair, white'. This is always feminine nowadays, but was used for both sexes in the past. In Irish legend *Muireann* was the mother of Finn MacCool. See also MAUREEN.
VARIANTS **Mirrin, Mora(i)nn, Mir(r)yn** *Irish* **Muirinn**

Miroslav *m* Miroslava

A Slavic name formed from *meri*, 'great, famous', and *slav*, 'glory'.

Mirza *m*

This is an Islamic name which comes from the Persian word for 'prince'.

Misbah *mf*

An Arabic name from the word for 'light'. The term is an epithet of Muhammad.
VARIANT **Misba**

Mischa, Misha *see* Michael

Missie *see* Melissa

Misty *f*

This vocabulary word was in use by the early 1960s, probably encouraged by the popularity of the Errol Garner/ Johnny Burke song 'Misty', first published in 1954. Use of the name increased dramatically after the 1971 film *Play Misty for Me*, which featured the song prominently, and it spent several years in the top 50 names in the USA. It was never as popular in the UK, and is now in decline as a parental choice.

Mitchell *m*

A surname which developed from the name MICHAEL, reused as a first name.
PET FORM **Mitch** • VARIANT **Mitchel**

Mitya *see* Demetrius

Mitzi *see* Mary, Miriam

Miya *see* Maya

Mo *see* Maureen, Maurice

Moc *see* Morgan

Modestine *f*

This is a French pet form of the name *Modeste*, which is used for both sexes. This goes back to Roman times, and originally meant 'measured, regulated'. It was borne by a number of early saints. Related names, which include *Modesty*, have never really caught on among English speakers, but have been used for both sexes in other languages.
VARIANTS *Italian, Spanish* **Modesta, Modesto** *Russian* **Modest, Modya, Desya** (ms)

☆ Modestine is the name of the donkey in Robert Louis Stevenson's *Travels with a Donkey in the Cévennes* (1879)
☆ Modesty Blaise, a character who first appeared in a strip cartoon written by Peter O'Donnell in 1963, and who has subsequently featured in novels and in film

Moelwyn *m* Moelwen *f*

Moelwyn is a Welsh name, after a mountain in North Wales. It is formed from *moel*, 'bald, bare', and *gwyn*, 'white'. A related name is *Moelona*, the pen name of Elizabeth Jones. She took her name from the farm where she was born, *Moylon*, which is also formed from *moel*. The pet form *Lona* is quite well used in Wales.

Mohammed *m*

This name, the most widely used in the Islamic world and given in honour of the Prophet, means 'praised,

praiseworthy'. It appears in a range
of spellings, reflecting both the
difficulties of transcribing Arabic into
Roman script and the wide variety of
regions covered by Islam. Scholars
tend to prefer a spelling with a 'u',
but Mohammed is the most popular
form as a given name in the UK, while
Mohamed is preferred in the USA.
VARIANTS **Moham(m)ad, Mohamed,
Muham(m)ad, Muham(m)ed** *West
African* **Mamadou**

Mohinder *see* **Mahendra**

Moira *see* **Mary, Maura**

Móirín *see* **Maureen**

Moises, Moisey, Moishe *see* **Moses**

Molly *f*
Molly started out as a pet form of MARY,
but is now a popular independent
name. It appears to have developed
from the 'r' in Mary being playfully
changed to 'll', in the same way that
Sarah became Sally. *Mally* was then
changed to Molly, which in some cases
was then further changed to POLLY.
Molly is quite often used in combined
names such as *Molly-Rose*.
VARIANT **Mollie**

Mona *f*
This is the anglicized form of the
Irish name *Muadhnait*, formed from
muadh, 'noble'. It spread from Ireland
to other English-speaking areas in the
late 19th century. Some may choose
the name with reference to different
sources. In Wales it can be based on
the place name *Môn*, the Welsh for
Anglesey; alternatively it can be used
as a pet form of MONICA; some derive it
from the Greek *monos*, 'single, only,
unique', while others may take it from
Leonardo's painting of the *Mona Lisa*.
For the Arabic name see MUNA.

Monica *f*
This was the name of St Augustine's
strong-minded mother in the 4th
century. His autobiographical text
was widely read, and she features
in it as the person who introduced
him to Christianity. St Monica's name
spread far as a result, but it is not
known where it originated. As she
was North African it may have been
a Carthaginian name, or from some
other local language. It was later
linked to the Latin *monere*, 'to warn,
advise', but this was not the source.
PET FORM **Mona** • VARIANTS *French* **Monique**
German, Polish, Scandinavian **Monika**
★ Monica Seles (1973–   ), Yugoslav-born
   US tennis player

Montana *fm*
Montana is the name of the US
state used as a first name, more
often feminine than masculine. It
derives from the Latin *montanus*,
'mountainous'. It has been used as a
first name since the 1990s.

Montserrat *f*
The Latin place name *mons serratus*,
'jagged mountain', became Montserrat,
the name of a mountain near
Barcelona. A monastery founded there
in the 10th century has a remarkable
black statue of the Madonna, known
as the 'Virgin of Montserrat', in whose
honour Montserrat is used as a given
name.
★ Montserrat Caballé (1933–   ), Spanish
   soprano
★ Montserrat Figueras (1948–   ), Spanish
   soprano

Monty *m*
This is a pet form of two aristocratic
surnames used as first names. *Montague*
was a Norman baronial name taken
from the place name, *Montaigu*,
meaning 'pointed hill', which came into
general use as a first name in the 19th
century. *Montgomery*, from *mont*, 'hill',

combined with the Germanic personal name *Gomeric*, 'man' plus 'power', seems to have come into use slightly later, and is particularly associated with Field-Marshal Bernard Montgomery (1887–1976). There is an unlikely third possible source, *Montmorency*, another aristocratic surname which has always been rare as a first name. The shorter form is now commoner than the full forms. Monty may be given as a nickname to someone with one of the above surnames, or with an unusual name with similar sounds, as in the case of the cricketer Mudhsuden Singh Panesar.

VARIANT **Montagu**

★ Monty Don (1955–   ), German-born British gardening writer and broadcaster

★ Montgomery Clift (1920–66), US actor

☆ Montmorency was the name of the dog in Jerome K Jerome's *Three Men in a Boat* (1889)

Moosa *see* **Moses**

Mor *see* **Maureen**

Morag *f*
Morag is a Scots Gaelic name derived from *Mor*, 'great' (see further MAUREEN). It has been given as a pet name to the monster said to inhabit Loch Morar, in much the same was that *Nessie* has been given to the Loch Ness monster.

Morainn, Morann *see* **Mirin**

Moray *see* **Murray**

Mordecai *m*
In the Bible Mordecai is the foster-father of ESTHER. Since their story is set in Persia it is not surprising that Mordecai is a Persian name, although it is more surprising that it incorporates the name of a Persian god, for it means 'servant of Marduk'. It has mainly been confined to the Jewish community, although it was used occasionally by

Nonconformists between the 17th and 19th centuries. Jews have traditionally given the name to boys born around the time of the feast of Purim, which celebrates the escape of Mordecai and the other exiled Jews from the plottings of Haman.

PET FORMS **Mord(y), Mort(y)** • VARIANTS *Yiddish* **Motke, Motl**

★ Mordecai Richler (1931–2001), Canadian author

Moreen *see* **Maureen**

Morfudd *f*
Morfudd is an ancient Welsh name of obscure origin. It was borne by a Welsh princess, the sister of OWAIN, who probably lived in the 6th century. The name is also famous in Welsh poetry as one of the rivals to DYDDGU for the attention of the great 14th-century poet Dafydd ap Gwilym. This Morfudd was a married woman whose more ample charms are contrasted with the slim Dyddgu. She is described as 'like the sun' with golden hair.

VARIANT **Morfyd(d)**

Morgan *mf*
It seems likely that several names have fallen together to form this early name. In the earliest records it is spelt *Morcant*, and it has been suggested that this should be analysed as *mor*, 'sea', and *cant*, 'circle, edge'. However *mawr*, 'great', has also been suggested for the first element, and *can*, 'bright', or *gen*, 'born', for the second. Nor is it clear if *Morgan(a)* or *Morgain(e)* le Fay of Arthurian legend is the same name: a connection with The *Morrigain* ('Great Queen'), the Irish goddess of death and war, has been proposed as an explanation in this case. In Welsh use the name is always masculine, but since the 1980s it has been more frequently chosen for girls.

VARIANTS **Morgen, Morgyn** *Welsh* **Morcant, Moc**

★ Morgan Fairchild (1950–), US actress

Moritz *see* **Maurice**

Morna *f*
This is the anglicized form of the Irish and Scots Gaelic name *Muirne*, 'beloved'. In James Macpherson's Ossianic poems it was the name of Fingal's mother.
VARIANTS **Myrna**, **Merne** *Gaelic* **Muirne**
★ Myrna Loy (1905–93), US film actress and comedienne
☆ Morna Dunroon is the heroine of the sensational novelist Harriet Jay's 1876 book *The Dark Colleen*, which helped spread the name

Morris, **Morse** *see* **Maurice**

Morten *see* **Martin**

Mortimer *m*
This is an aristocratic surname taken up as a first name in the 19th century. It comes from a French place name, literally meaning 'dead sea', which probably referred to stagnant water or a marsh. In the past it was used by Jews to anglicize MOSES, and in Ireland it was used as a substitute for *Muirairtach* or *Murtagh*, 'seaman, mariner'.
PET FORM **Mort(y)**
★ Sir Mortimer Wheeler (1890–1976), English archaeologist
☆ Mortimer Brewster, the character played by Cary Grant in the 1944 film *Arsenic and Old Lace*
☆ Mortimer Lightwood in Charles Dickens's *Our Mutual Friend* (1865)

Morven, **Morvern** *f*
In James Macpherson's Ossianic poems, Morven is the name of a mythical kingdom in Scotland. In reality Morvern is a part of north Argyll called *a' Mhorbhairne*, 'the big gap', in Gaelic. Morven is the more common form of the name, which is mainly restricted to Scotland.
VARIANT **Morvyn**

☆ *Morvern Callar* is the title of a 1995 novel by Alan Warner, filmed in 2002, which has given the name recent exposure

Morwenna *f*
This is a Welsh and Cornish name meaning 'maiden', which is *morwyn* in Welsh. St Morwenna was a 5th-century saint who gave her name to several churches in Cornwall.
VARIANT **Morwen**
★ Morwenna Banks (1964–), English actress and comedienne

Moses *m*
The name of the man who in the Bible leads the Jews out of Egypt is probably Egyptian in origin, although we are told (Exodus 2.10) that Moses was so called because Pharaoh's daughter drew him up out of the water, implying that the name comes from the Hebrew for 'to draw'. Moses was used regularly in the UK into the 17th century, after which it became a specifically Jewish name, but continued in general use in the USA. It is also well used by Spanish speakers. The shortening *Moss* can also be a use of the surname or a pet form of MAURICE.
PET FORM **Moss** • VARIANTS *Arabic* **Musa**, **Moosa** *Dutch* **Mozes** *Hebrew* **Moshe** *Russian* **Moisey** *Spanish* **Moises** *Yiddish* **Moishe**

Moss *see* **Maurice**, **Moses**

Mostyn *m*
This is the name of a village in North Wales which became a surname and then a first name. It comes from Old English 'moss settlement'.

Motke, **Motl** *see* **Mordecai**

Motya *see* **Matthew**

Mounia *see* **Muna**

Mourad *see* **Murad**

Moustafa see **Mustafa**

Moyra see **Maura**

Mozes see **Moses**

Mstislav m
A Russian name from the Slavic elements mshcha, 'vengeance', and slav, 'glory'. It was the name of several early rulers of the area.
★ Mstislav Rostropovich (1927–2007), Russian cellist and conductor

Muadhnait see **Mona**

Mubarak m
An Arabic name, meaning 'blessed, fortunate, auspicious'.

Mubasher m
An Arabic name meaning 'bringer of good news' and one of the titles of the Prophet.
VARIANTS **Mubashar, Mubashsher**

Muhamad, Muhamed, Muhammad, Muhammed see **Mohammed**

Muirairtach see **Mortimer**

Muireadhach see **Murdo**

Muireann, Muirinn see **Maureen, Mirin**

Muirgheal, Muireall see **Muriel**

Muirgheas, Muiris see **Maurice**

Muirne see **Morna**

Muna f
An Arabic name, meaning 'wise, desire'.
VARIANTS **Mona, Mounia, Munya**

Munasir see **Naser**

Mungo m
Mungo, meaning 'my dear', is an alternative name for St Kentigern, whose nickname it was. St Mungo is the patron saint of Glasgow, which he

is credited with founding. Kentigern ('chief prince' in Old Celtic) was a British chief who was a missionary to the area around Glasgow in the late 6th century. The name is mainly confined to Scotland.
★ Mungo Park (1771–1806), Scottish explorer
☆ Mungojerrie is one of T S Eliot's cats in Old Possum's Book of Practical Cats (1939), the basis of the musical Cats

Munir m **Munira** f
This means 'bright, shining' in Arabic.

Murad m
An Arabic name meaning 'wish, intention'.
VARIANT **Mourad**

Murdo m
This is a Scottish name, the anglicized spelling of Muireadhach or Murchadh, meaning 'sea-warrior', and used to signify 'lord'. It is also the source of the surname Murdoch, which is found as a variant of the name. Outside Scotland there have been problems understanding this name, and we find the occasional 19th-century instance of it being turned into Murder.
FEMININES **Murdag, Murdina, Murdan**
• VARIANT **Murdoch**

Muriel f
The origin of this name lies with the Scots Gaelic name Muireall, Muirgheal in Irish, formed from the elements muir, 'sea', and geal, 'bright'. It came into general use alongside other Celtic names in the 19th century.
VARIANTS **Meryl, Meriel, Merrill**

Murphy mf
An Irish surname, meaning 'descendant of Murchadh ('sea warrior')'. See MURDO.
☆ Murphy Brown was a US sitcom (1988–98), which established Murphy as a feminine name in the USA

Murray *m*
A Scottish surname from Moray in north-east Scotland. The place name means 'settlement by the sea'.
VARIANTS **Murry, Moray**

Murren, Murrin, Murron *see* **Maureen**

Murtagh *see* **Mortimer**

Musa *see* **Moses**

Mustafa *m*
This is an Arabic name meaning 'chosen'. It is one of the epithets of Muhammad.
VARIANTS **Mustapha, Moustafa**

My *see* **Mary**

Mya, Myah *see* **Mia, Maya**

Myca, Mycah *see* **Micah**

Myer *see* **Meir**

Myfanwy *f*
A Welsh name which can be analysed both as *my*, 'my', and *banw*, 'woman', and as *my* combined with *manwy*, 'precious'. There is a popular Welsh song 'Myfanwy', published in 1875, with music by Joseph Parry and lyrics by Richard Davies. There is a tradition that it was written about Parry's childhood sweetheart. Another Myfanwy was celebrated by the 14th-century poet Hywel ab Einion.
PET FORM **Myfi**

Myghal *see* **Michael**

Myka, Mykah *see* **Micah**

Mylene *f*
Mylene is a French name, a pet form of the compound *Marie-Hélène*, now used as an independent name.
VARIANTS **Myleen(e)** *French* **Mylène**
★ Myleene Klass (1978–   ), English musician and television presenter

Myles, Mylo *see* **Miles**

Myr *see* **Meir**

Myra *f*
This name was invented by the poet Fulke Greville (1554–1628) for a woman addressed in his poetry. He may have been playing on the idea of 'admiration', but we cannot know for sure. Unfortunately the notoriety of the 'Moors Murderer' Myra Hindley has put this name out of circulation. In the USA it has been used as a feminine form of MYRON.
VARIANT **Mira**
☆ *Myra Breckinridge*, 1968 satirical novel by Gore Vidal

Myrddin *see* **Merlin**

Myriam *see* **Miriam**

Myrna *see* **Morna**

Myron *m*
This is a Greek name from the word for 'myrrh'. Because of the Christian story that myrrh was one of the gifts brought by the Magi at the Nativity, it was used by early Christians and there are a number of Eastern Orthodox saints with the name. However, modern use is with reference to the 5th-century BC Greek sculptor, whose most famous work is the 'Discus Thrower'. It was taken up with some enthusiasm by Americans in the 19th century, along with a number of other names from the classical past, for example VIRGIL.

Myrtle *f*
This is one of the plant names taken up in the 19th century, when it was traditional to include myrtle in wedding bouquets. It is now rare.
PET FORM **Myrtie** • VARIANTS **Myrtilla, Myrtill** *Arabic* **Myrrha**

Mysie *see* **Maisie**

N

Naamah *f* **Naam** *m*
Naamah is a biblical name from the word for 'pleasant' in Hebrew. It is borne by two characters in the Bible: the sister of Tubal-Cain and a wife of Solomon. In Jewish tradition the former was so beautiful that she caused the angels to fall from grace. The name is also traditionally that of Noah's wife. Naamah is usually pronounced with the stress on the first syllable in English, but on the last in Hebrew. Naam is the masculine equivalent.
VARIANT *Hebrew* **Na'am**

Na'ami *see* **Naomi**

Naaser, Naasir, Naasira *see* **Naser**

Nab *see* **Abel**

Nabeel *m* **Nabeela** *f*
An Arabic name meaning 'noble, honourable'.
PET FORM **Nabs** (English) • VARIANTS **Nabil, Nabila**

Nacho, Nacio *see* **Ignatius**

Nada¹ *see* **Nadia¹**

Nada² *f*
An Arabic name meaning both 'generosity, liberality' and 'dew'.
VARIANT **Nadaa**

Nadeja, Nadejda, Naděžda, Nadezhda *see* **Nadia¹**

Nadi *see* **Nadiyya**

Nadia¹ *f*
The Russian name *Nadezhda*, meaning 'hope', has the pet form *Nadya*, which is usually spelt Nadia in English. The name is popular throughout the Slavic world, and has been well established among English speakers since the early 20th century.
VARIANTS *Czech* **Naděžda, Nadeja, Nada** *French* **Nadine** *German* **Nadja** *Polish* **Nadzieja** *Russian, Bulgarian* **Nadejda**
★ Nadia Boulanger (1887–1979), French musician

Nadia² *see* **Nadiyya**

Nadim *m*
The Arabic verb *nadima*, 'to drink together', gives the name Nadim meaning 'a drinking companion', and hence a confidant. It is a pre-Islamic name.
FEMININE **Nadima** • VARIANT **Nadeem** (mainly India and Pakistan)

Nadine *f*
Nadine is a French elaboration of NADIA¹ which is occasionally used by English speakers. In France Nadine is also used as a pet form of *Bernardine*, a variant of BERNADETTE.
★ Nadine Gordimer (1923–   ), Nobel Prize-winning South African author and activist

Nadir *m* **Nadira** *f*
This is an Arabic name meaning 'rare, precious'. Nadira can also come from a different Arabic word meaning 'radiant'.
VARIANT **Nadra** (f)

Nadiya *see* **Nadiyya**

Nadiyya *f*
An Arabic name meaning 'delicate, tender, moist'.
VARIANTS **Nadi, Nadia, Nadiya**

Nadja *see* **Nadia** ¹

Nadra *see* **Nadir**

Nadya, Nadzieja *see* **Nadia**[1]

Naeem *m*
An Arabic name meaning 'happiness, contentment'. NAIM is a related name.

Naftala *see* **Naphtali**

Nagendra *f*
The Sanskrit word *naga* primarily means 'snake', but can also be used to mean 'elephant'. This has been combined with the name of the god Indra to indicate 'lord, great'. Nagendra is found in ancient texts to mean a large snake or elephant, and was used from the late Middle Ages as a personal name.

Nagib, Nagiba *see* **Najib**

Nahum *m*
A biblical name borne by a prophet whose prophecies, foretelling the downfall of Assyria, are collected in a minor book of the Old Testament. Nahum means 'comforter' and may originally have been a shortening of a longer name with a sense such as 'God is my comforter'. It is regularly used by the Jewish community, and was well represented among English speakers in the 17th century. The English pronunciation is generally 'nay-em', while Hebrew pronounces the 'u' as a long 'oo' sound.
VARIANTS *Russian* **Naum**
★ Nahum Tate (1652–1715), Irish poet and dramatist

Nai *see* **Naomi**

Naim *m* **Naima** *f*
An Arabic name meaning 'tranquil, peaceful, at ease'. NAEEM is a related name.
VARIANTS **Na'im, Naïm** (m), **Na'ima, Naïma** (f)
★ Naim Attallah (1931–   ), publisher and author

Nainsí, Nancie, Nandag, Nansi *see* **Nancy**

Nais, Naïs *see* **Anaïs**

Najib *m* **Najiba** *f*
An Arabic name meaning 'noble, high-minded', hence 'intelligent'.
VARIANTS **Nagib, Nagiba**

Naldo *m*
An Italian pet form of any masculine name with this ending, such as *Rinaldo* (see REYNOLD).

Nalini *f*
A Indian name from the Sanskrit for 'lovely'.

Nan *see* **Nancy** , **Nanda**

Nana *see* **Athene**

Nancy *f*
Nancy probably started life as a short form of both ANNE and AGNES (via ANNIS), but it has been used as an independent name since at least the 18th century. In the Middle Ages it was normal to say 'mine' rather than 'my' in front of a vowel, and there are a number of names beginning with vowels that have short forms beginning with 'N', such as NED, the 'n' becoming attached to the original form *Ed* from the affectionate 'mine Ed'.
PET FORMS **Nan, Nannie, Nanny, Nanette**
• VARIANTS **Nanci(e), Nansi** *Irish* **Nainsí**
Scottish **Nandag** (pet form) *Welsh* **Nanci**
Finnish **Nannie** *French* **Ninon**
★ Nancy Reagan (1921–   ), US First Lady
★ Nancy Sinatra (1940–   ), US singer
★ Nanette Newman (1934–   ), English actress
☆ Nancy in Charles Dickens's 1838 novel *Oliver Twist*
☆ Nancy Drew, girl detective, whose adventures have been told since 1930
☆ *No, No, Nanette*, title of a 1925 musical

Nanda¹ *f*
A pet form of Italian *Ferdinanda* or Spanish *Hernanda*, feminine forms of FERDINAND, now used as an independent name.

Nanda² *m*
An Indian name from the Sanskrit for 'joy'. The Nanda dynasty ruled eastern India in the 5th and 4th centuries BC. Nanda was the name of the Buddha's half-brother and, in Hindu mythology, of Krishna's foster-father.

Nando, **Nándor**, **Nandy** *see* **Ferdinand**

Nanette, **Nannie**, **Nanny** *see* **Nancy**

Naoise *m*
In Irish legend, Naoise (pronounced 'neesha') eloped with DEIRDRE, the betrothed of King Conchobar (see CONNOR). After many adventures Naoise was killed by Conchobar and Deirdre died of grief. Because of the feminine-sounding pronunciation, Naoise is very occasionally found used for girls.

Naomh *f*
This is a modern Irish name meaning 'holy, saint'. It is pronounced 'nav' or 'neev', so can have the same pronunciation as NIAMH with which it is often confused. Naomh is sometimes chosen for a girl born on a Sunday.

Naomhán *see* **Nevan**

Naomi *f*
In the Old Testament book of Ruth, Naomi, mother-in-law of Ruth, returns to her homeland after the deaths of her husband and sons, a tragedy that causes her to rename herself MARA, 'bitterness'. It has long been a stock name in the Jewish community, and was adopted by the Puritans in the 17th century. As a result, it has been used steadily in the USA. It has been popular in many countries since the 1970s. The traditional English pronunciation was to stress the first syllable, 'NAY-uh-me', but 'nay-OH-me' is now widely heard. NOAM is the masculine equivalent.
PET FORMS **Nai**, **Nay**, **Nomi**, **Omi** • VARIANTS **Naomia**, **Noemie**, **Niome** *French* **Noémie** *Hebrew* **Na'omi**, **Na'ami** *Italian, Czech* **Noemi** *Portuguese* **Noemí**, **Noëmia** *Spanish* **Noemí**, **Nohemi**
★ Naomi Campbell (1970–), English model

Naphtali *m*
This is a biblical name, usually interpreted as meaning 'to wrestle', but sometimes interpreted as 'to be crafty'. The origin of the name is said to lie in the rivalry between sisters RACHEL and LEAH, both wives of the patriarch JACOB. Rachel had no children, and used her maid Bilhah as a surrogate mother. When Bilhah had a son, the story goes 'Rachel said, With great wrestlings have I wrestled with my sister, and I have prevailed: and she called his name Naphtali' (Genesis 30.8).
VARIANTS **Naftali**, **Naphthali**, **Naftala** (f)

Nápla *f*
An Irish first name derived from the old form of the name ANNABEL.

Napoleon *m*
The origin of the name Napoleon probably goes back to the German name *Nibelung*, which in turn is thought to derive from *Nebel*, meaning 'mist'. This would make the mythical *Nibelungen*, creators of the magical ring celebrated in Wagner's operas, 'the sons of the mist'. The name must have been introduced to Italy by one of the early groups of medieval Germanic immigrants, such as the Lombards. There it was later influenced by the place name *Napoli* (Naples) and the word *leone*, 'lion'. Forms such as *Napoleone* are found, mainly in northern Italy, from the 13th century.

The Bonaparte family took the name with them when they emigrated to Corsica in the 16th century. The name is so strongly associated with the French Emperor Napoleon that it is now rarely used other than in direct reference to him.

VARIANTS *French* **Napoléon** *Italian* **Napoleóne**

★ Napoleon Bonaparte (1769–1821), French general and emperor
☆ Napoleon the pig in George Orwell's *Animal Farm* (1945)

Narcissus *m*

The Greek name *Nakissos* became Narcissus in Latin, which was imported directly into English. In Greek mythology Narcissus was a beautiful youth who was punished for rejecting love by being made to fall in love with his own reflection, which he saw when stooping to drink from a still pool. Eventually the gods transformed him into the flower that still bears his name today. The name appears to be pre-Greek in form, so its true meaning is lost, but the Greeks associated it with their word *narke* 'numbness, torpor', the source of words such as 'narcotic', and the plant was credited with soporific qualities. Narcissus was widely used in Roman times, particularly among freedmen. St Paul (Romans 16.11) writes to 'them that be of the household of Narcissus that are in the Lord', giving the name Christian respectability, which was further endorsed by two saints: one a Greek bishop of Jerusalem in the early 3rd century, the other a Spanish bishop martyred in the 4th century. The name was used by English speakers in the past, most prominently in the 16th century and early 19th, but the rather effeminate beauty associated with the myth and Freud's identification of the Narcissus complex, meant it fell out of favour. However, the name remains in use in other languages, while the rare feminine, *Narcissa*, is literary, used by both Alexander Pope in his *Moral Essays* (1731–5) and Smollett for the heroine of *The Adventures of Roderick Random* (1748).

VARIANTS *French* **Narcisse** *Italian, Spanish, Portuguese* **Narciso**

Narelle *f*

This is an Australian name of debated origin. It can be traced back to at least the late 19th century when the Australian soprano Molly Callaghan took the stage name Marie Narelle, reputedly taking the second part of the name from an untraced Aboriginal 'Queen of the Moruya tribe'. The name first became widespread in the 1940s and was among the most popular names in Australia in the 1970s.

Narinder *m*

This is a name from the Sanskrit *nara*, 'man', and the name of the god Indra ('mighty'). The resulting expression 'an Indra among men' has been used to refer to a ruler or a powerful person, but later also came to indicate a physician.

VARIANTS **Narendra, Narender, Narendhra**

Naseem, Naseema *see* Nasim, Nasima

Naser *m* Nasira *f*

This is an Arabic name formed from *naser*, 'help', meaning 'helper, defender, supporter'. It can be combined with other elements to form names such as *Nasir-ud-Din*, 'defender of the Faith'.

VARIANTS **Naasir, Nasser, Nasseer, Munasir, Naasira**

Nash *m*

This is a surname used as a first name. The surname usually comes from Middle English *atten ash*, the equivalent of 'at an Ash', given to someone who lived by a distinctive ash tree, which was then divided before, rather than after, the 'n'. It is mainly found in the USA, where use increased dramatically from 1997, when it was used for the eponymous hero of the long-running television cop show *Nash Bridges*.

Nasim *mf* **Nasima** *f*
This comes from the Arabic *nasim*, meaning both 'a breeze' and 'the breath of life'. Since the word is grammatically feminine it can be used for both sexes.
VARIANTS **Nassim, Nassima, Naseem, Naseema**

Nason *see* **Nathan**

Nasr *m*
Nasr comes from the Arabic word for 'victory'. It is often found combined in forms such as *Nasrullah*, 'victory of Allah', or *Nasreddin*, 'victory of the Faith'. In India Nasr is sometimes a variant spelling of NASER.
VARIANTS **Nasr-ud-Din, Nasraddin, Nasruddin**
☆ Nasreddin is a famous character in Islamic folklore, who combines wisdom and foolishness in equal measure

Nasrin *f*
Nasrin comes from the Persian for 'wild rose', and is used throughout the Islamic world.

Nass *see* **Athanasius**

Nastasia, Nastassja, Nastasya, Nastya *see* **Anastasia**

Nat *see* **Natalie, Nathan, Nathaniel**

Natacha *see* **Natasha**

Natalie *f*
The Latin expression *dies natalis*, 'birthday', developed strong Christian associations in the early centuries AD, as it was ascribed to a martyr's feast

day (commemorating the day a martyr was born into eternal life), and also to Christmas, the birthday of Christ. It was adopted early on as a first name by Christians, both in the masculine *Natalis* and the feminine *Natalia*, a form used in many languages. It became particularly popular in Russia, where it was used for girls born around Christmas (compare NOEL). It was adopted by the French from Russian, and from there passed to the English-speaking world. In the UK its popularity was at its height in the 1970s.
PET FORMS **Nat, Talia, Tallie** • VARIANTS **Natalia, Natalee** *French* **Nathalie** *Russian* **Natalya, Natasha**
★ Natalie Wood (1938–81), US film actress
★ Natalie Imbruglia (1975–), Australian singer and actress

Natasha *f*
Natasha was originally a Russian pet form of NATALIE which is now widely used in the English-speaking world. A successful 1972 BBC television adaptation of Tolstoy's *War and Peace* gave a boost to the spread of the name.
PET FORM **Tasha** • VARIANTS **Natashia** *French* **Natacha** *Dutch* **Natasja**
☆ Natasha Rostova in Tolstoy's *War and Peace* (1869)

Nathan *m*
Nathan is from the Hebrew *natan*, 'given [by God]', an element also found in names such as JONATHAN and NATHANIEL, for which Nathan is sometimes used as a short form. In the Old Testament it is borne by a minor prophet who reproaches David for engineering the death of Uriah, and is the name of one of David's sons. Nathan is also a pet form of ATHANASIUS.
FEMININE **Nathania** • PET FORMS **Nat, Nate, Natty** (archaic) • VARIANTS **Nathen** *Hebrew* **Natan, Nason** (m), **Netanya, Natanya** (f)

Nathaniel *m*
Nathaniel is the standard English form of the biblical Greek *Nathanael*. The name means 'God has given' and is formed from the same element that is found in NATHAN combined with the element -*el* found in so many biblical names, such as DANIEL and ELISABETH (see ELIZABETH). It is thought that the New Testament apostle known as Nathaniel is the same as BARTHOLOMEW. Nathaniel came into use in England in the 17th century, along with other New Testament names, and was taken by settlers to America, where it became firmly established among the stock of names.

PET FORMS **Nat, Nathan, Natty** • VARIANTS **Nathanial** *Italian* **Natanaele** *Hebrew* **Natanel** (m), **Nataniel(l)a** (f)
★ Nathaniel Hawthorne (1804–64), US writer
★ Nat 'King' Cole (1919–65), US singer and pianist
☆ Natty (Nathaniel) Bumppo, hero of the so-called 'Leatherstocking' novels of James Fenimore Cooper which include *The Last of the Mohicans* (1826)

Natividad *see* Noel

Naum *see* Nahum

Navin *m*
Navin is an Indian name, from the Sanskrit word for 'new'.
VARIANT **Naveen**

Nay *see* Naomi

Nazaire *m*
Early Latin-speaking Christians adopted, as one of their distinctive names, *Nazarius*, 'of Nazareth', in honour of the home town of Christ. There were at least two early martyrs of this name, as well as an early evangelizing French bishop. Nazaire is the French form of the name, which passed into a number of Romance languages, but has never been used much by English speakers.
VARIANTS *Italian* **Nazario** *Spanish* **Nazario** (m), **Nazaret** (f)

Nea *see* Linnea

Neacal, Neacel *see* Nicholas

Neal, Neale *see* Neil

Ned *m*
Ned is a pet form of any name beginning with *Ed-*, such as EDMUND or EDWIN and, most commonly, EDWARD. It is sometimes used as an independent name, while the *Ed-* names are now more frequently shortened to forms based on ED or TED. Ned developed in the Middle Ages when it was standard practice to say 'mine' for 'my' in front of a vowel. Thus forms such as 'mine Ed' would be heard, from which the 'n' became attached to the Ed to form Ned, a process also found in names like NANCY.

PET FORMS **Neddy, Neddie**
☆ Ned Flanders in the television cartoon series *The Simpsons*
☆ Neddy Seagoon in the 1950s radio series *The Goon Show*

Neela *see* Nila

Neelam *see* Nilam

Nehemiah *m*
The Old Testament book of Nehemiah gives an account of how Nehemiah became governor of Jerusalem in the 5th-century BC, and restored and rebuilt the city which had been left in a state of decay after the Persian conquest. The name came into restricted use in the 17th century among Puritans, but was rare thereafter until a recent revival in the USA.

Neil *m*
Neil is traditionally the commonest spelling outside Ireland of the Irish name *Niall*, the meaning of which is

not known, although 'champion' is a suggested interpretation. In Ireland Niall is generally pronounced in the same way as Neil, with a long 'ee', while elsewhere it is often 'ni-al'. Although the name was widely used by English speakers in the 20th century, and is still regularly chosen, it is currently only really popular in Ireland, where *Niallghus*, formed from Niall and *gus*, Irish Gaelic for 'strength', is also used. Neil is the source of NELSON and NIGEL.

FEMININE **Nelda** • VARIANTS **Neal(e)**, **Niel**, **Nial** *Icelandic* **Njal**

★ Neil Armstrong (1930–), US astronaut, the first person to walk on the moon
★ Niall of the Nine Hostages (d.c.405 AD), Irish king and raider, founder of the O'Neal family, and in some traditions said to have brought St Patrick to Ireland as a slave

Neirin *see* **Aneurin**

Nelda *see* **Neil**

Nele *see* **Cornelia**

Nell, **Nelly** *f*
Nell is the pet form of a number of names, such as ELEANOR, ELLEN and HELEN, the initial 'N' coming from the running on of the 'n' from the old form 'mine' in front of the vowel, as in names like NED. It was also used as an independent name from the 17th century until the 20th, when it fell out of favour. It came to be seen as a slightly comic name, perhaps influenced by expressions such as 'not on your nelly' and 'nervous nelly'. *Nellie* is also used as a pet form of CORNELIA.

VARIANT **Nellie**

★ Nell Gwyn (c.1650–87), English actress and mistress of Charles II
★ Nelly Furtado (1978–), Canadian singer

★ Dame Nellie Melba (1861–1931), Australian operatic soprano
☆ Little Nell, character in Charles Dickens's *The Old Curiosity Shop* (1840)

Nels *see* **Nicholas**

Nelson *m*
Nelson, in its basic sense of 'son of NEIL, has been recorded in Ireland from the Middle Ages, but only came into general use as an English first name in honour of Admiral Lord Horatio Nelson (1758–1805), hero of the Battle of Trafalgar. Historically, the name has been most often used in the USA.

★ Nelson Mandela (1918–), South African statesman
★ Nelson Rockefeller (1908–79), US politician
☆ Nelson Muntz, from the television cartoon series *The Simpsons*

Nena *see* **Nina**

Nerina *f*
There is some debate as to the origin of this name. It is possible it is a feminine form of *Nero*, an Italian pet form of *Raniero* (see RAYNER), but it is more likely to be from *Nerio*, the name of a 1st-century soldier baptized by St Paul. His name comes from *Nereus*, borne by the Greek 'old man of the sea', which ultimately comes from the Greek for 'water'. Alternatively, it could derive directly from Nereus, and his many daughters, the Nereids. The form *Nerine* is often described as a variant of Nerina, but may come directly from the flower name. This in turn also goes back to the Nereids, given as the flower's scientific name because bulbs of the best-known variety, also known as the Guernsey lily, were regarded as a gift from the sea. They flourished in Guernsey after the local Dean was given some bulbs by sailors shipwrecked there, in about

1655, on their way back from the plant's native South Africa.

VARIANT **Nerene**

Nerissa *f*

This is a name coined by Shakespeare for the character of PORTIA's witty and charming maid in his play *The Merchant of Venice*. He is thought to have based it on the same source as that of NERINA. It is one of the less common Shakespearean names, but is occasionally found.

VARIANT **Nerisse**

Nero *see* **Nerina, Rayner**

Nerys *f*

There is some debate as to the origins of this 20th-century Welsh name, but it is usually derived from Welsh *ner*, 'lord', and can thus be interpreted as meaning 'lady'. Another interpretation is that it is a short form of NERISSA.

★ Nerys Hughes (1941–), Welsh actress

Ness, Nessie, Nest, Nesta *see* **Agnes, Vanessa**

Nessa *see* **Vanessa**

Nestor *m*

In Greek mythology Nestor is the king of Pylos in the western Peloponnese, who took part in many famous adventures in his youth, but who is best known from Homer's *Iliad* and *Odyssey*. In these stories, he is shown as an ancient man who is, however, still vigorous and a byword for his wisdom and oratory. It is difficult to be sure of the origin of such an ancient name, but it has been linked to the Greek for 'homecoming'. The name has rarely been used in the UK, but can be found in the USA and in the naming traditions of other languages.

★ Néstor Kirchner (1950–), president of Argentina

☆ Nestor, Captain Haddock's long-suffering butler in the *Tintin* books of Hergé

Net, Netta, Nettie, Netty *see* **Agnes, Janet**

Netanya *see* **Nathan**

Netta, Nettie *see* **Annette, Janet**

Nevada *f*

This is one of the US state names that have become fashionable in the USA and spread from there to other countries. It is not as popular as choices such as DAKOTA, but is nonetheless used regularly. Since the name comes from the Spanish for 'snow-capped' it links with names such as NIEVES.

Nevaeh *f*

This is the word 'heaven' spelt backwards. Despite the fact that Nevaeh looks odd and people are not sure how to pronounce it, ever since the Christian rock singer, Sonny Sandoval, announced that he was giving the name to his daughter its popularity has grown rapidly in the USA. By 2006 it was among the top 50 names chosen for girls there. A more instinctive, but self-defeating, spelling Neveah has already appeared. Names formed by spelling words backwards are not uncommon fashions internationally. For example, when Lenin was in power, his name spelt backwards, NINEL, appeared in the USSR.

Nevan *m*

Nevan is the anglicized form of the Irish *Naomhán*, meaning 'little saint'. This was probably originally a nickname, possibly given to St Abban, which may explain why so little is known about St Nevan, and why people cannot even agree on his holy day. In the past it was common enough to be a source of the widespread

Scottish surname Niven, sometimes found as a first name, and is currently undergoing something of a revival in Ireland. The feminine equivalent is NAOMH.

VARIANTS **Nevin, Niven**

Neve see **Niamh**

Neves see **Nieves**

Neville m
There are several places in Normandy called *Neuville*, or with similar spellings, all of which simply mean 'new town'. Sir Gilbert de Nevil was one of the knights who helped William the Conqueror take England in 1066, and Neville was emerging as an important noble surname by the 13th century. The family reached the height of its power in the 15th century with Sir Richard Neville, Earl of Warwick, known as 'Warwick the Kingmaker', and his vast extended family. The name was already beginning to be used as a first name in the 16th century, but really came into its own in the 19th and earlier part of the 20th century when aristocratic names were at their most popular.

PET FORM **Nev** • VARIANTS **Nevil(l), Nevile**
★ Neville Chamberlain (1869–1940), English statesman
★ Nevil Shute (1899–1960), English novelist

Newton m
Newton is an English surname meaning 'new settlement'. It was common in the USA in the late 19th century, and continued in decreasing use into the mid-20th century. It most often commemorated the scientist Sir Isaac Newton (1642–1727).

PET FORM **Newt**
★ Newton 'Newt' Gingrich (1943–), US politician

Neža see **Agnes**

Ngaire see **Nyree**

Ni see **Aneurin**

Nia[1] f
In Wales Nia is a Welsh spelling of the Irish name NIAMH. It came to the attention of the Welsh public through the 1916 poem by T Gwynn Jones, *Nia Ben Aur* ('Nia of the Golden Head'), which retold the Irish myth of OSSIAN and Niamh, but the name really took off when the story was turned into a Welsh musical, first performed at the Eisteddfod in 1974. It has since become one of the most popular girls' names in Wales.

Nia[2] f
This is a modern African-American name based, it is said, on the Swahili for 'intention, purpose'. Nia is also the name of one of the seven days of the alternative Christmas festival, Kwanzaa, when you reflect on your purpose in life.

VARIANTS **Nya, Nyah**

Nial, Niall see **Neil**

Niamh f
Niamh is an Irish name, which means 'brightness, radiance'. In Irish mythology, Niamh of the Golden Hair was the daughter of the sea god Mannanan, and the lover of Oisin. Another Niamh was the last mistress of the great Ulster hero Cuchulainn. The name was once confined to Ireland, where it has recently been very popular. However, since the 1990s it has also been a popular name in England and Scotland. It is usually pronounced 'neev', but in some parts of Ireland may have a two-syllable pronunciation such as 'nee-av'.

VARIANTS **Neve, Nia, Niav, Nya**
★ Niamh Cusack (1959–), Irish actress
★ Neve Campbell (1973–), Canadian actress

Nic *see* **Dominic**, **Nicholas**

Nichola *see* **Nicola**

Nicholas *m*
Nicholas comes from the early
Greek name *Nikolaos*, formed from
the words *nike*, 'victory', and *laos*,
'people', and so is usually interpreted
as 'victory of the people'. Early on the
element *nike* was given a Christian
interpretation, which led to a number
of similar names being incorporated
into the stock of Western names,
although they are now rarely used
by English speakers. These include
NICODEMUS, *Nicomedes* (*nike* plus
medos, 'meditation') and *Nicephorus*
(*nike* plus *phoros*, 'one who brings'),
all of which can share short forms with
Nicholas. The reason that Nicholas
became the best known of these names
was the popularity of a 4th-century
bishop, St Nicholas of Myra, one of
the most widely venerated bishops in
the Middle Ages. He was the patron
saint of children, and among the
many legends told about him are that
he restored three murdered boys to
life, and that he gave three poor girls
bags of gold as dowries. This last story
was combined with existing northern
legends of a magician who punished
naughty children and rewarded good
ones and, using the standard Germanic
shortening of his name, gave rise to
the legend of Santa Claus. The name
was in use in England even before
the Norman Conquest, and was very
popular throughout the Middle Ages,
usually as *Nicol*, which is the source
of a number of surnames, while its pet
form COLIN become an independent
name.
PET FORMS **Nick**, **Nicky**, **Nic(o)** • VARIANTS
Nickolas *Irish* **Nioclás** *Scots Gaelic*
Neacal, **Neacel** *Scottish* **Nichol**, **Nicol**
French **Nicolas** *German* **Nikolaus**,
Niklaus, **Claus**, **Klaus** *Greek* **Nicolaos**,

Nicos *Italian* **Nicola**, **Nic(c)olò** *Polish*
Mikołaj *Russian* **Nikolai**, **Kolya** (pet form)
Scandinavian **Nils**, **Nels** *Spanish* **Nicolás**,
Nocolao

Nicodemus *m*
This is a Greek name formed from
nike, 'victory', and *demos*, 'people'. In
the New Testament it is the name of a
man who helped Joseph of Arimathea
to entomb Christ's body. It was most
used in the UK from the 17th to 19th
centuries.
VARIANTS *French* **Nicodème** *Italian*
Nicodemo, **Nico** *Polish* **Nicodem** *Russian*
Nikodim
☆ Nicodemus (Noddy) Boffin in Charles
   Dickens's 1865 novel *Our Mutual
   Friend*
☆ Nicodemus is the leader of the rats
   in Robert O'Brien's 1971 children's
   classic *Mrs Frisby and the Rats of
   NIMH*

Nicol, **Nicolas** *see* **Nicholas**

Nicola, **Nicole** *f*
These are two of a number of feminine
versions of NICHOLAS. In the Middle
Ages *Nicol* was used for both sexes,
with Nicola mainly restricted to official
Latin documents, but this distinctively
feminine form gradually came into
spoken use as well. Nicole was
originally a French variant. The French
have also used *Nicolette* since the
Middle Ages, and its short form COLETTE
became an independent name. Nicola
is also a masculine name in Italy (see
NICHOLAS).
PET FORMS **Nickie**, **Nikki**, **Nico**, **Nicky**
• VARIANTS **Nichola**, **Nichol(e)**, **Nikole**,
Nicolette, **Nicoletta** *Dutch* **Nicolet**,
Klasina, **Klazina** *French* **Nicoline** *German*
Nikola *Greek* **Nikoleta** *Spanish* **Nicolasa**
★ Nicole Kidman (1967–), US-
   Australian actress

Niel *see* **Neil**

Nieves *f*

This is a Spanish name meaning 'snows' based, as are a number of other Spanish names, on a title of the Virgin Mary *Nuestra Señora de las Nieves*, 'Our Lady of the Snows'. It is occasionally used for men.

VARIANTS **Nieve** *Portuguese* **Neves** (pet form)

Nigel *m*

The Irish name NEIL was adopted by Viking settlers in Ireland as *Njal* and entered the general stock of Norse names. Their descendants in Normandy used the name in the form *Ni(h)el*. This appeared in medieval Latin documents as *Nigellus* because the name was misinterpreted as a diminutive of *niger*, 'black'. The name probably only existed in this written form until it was used by Sir Walter Scott in his 1822 novel *The Fortunes of Nigel*, and thereafter entered the general stock of names in the UK. However, it remained rare in the USA before the 1970s. There is an early example of the feminine in a madrigal by Thomas Morley (1557–1602) called 'No No No No Nigella', but this is probably an original coinage to indicate a dark-haired beauty. In modern use *Nigella* can also be from the Latin name for the flower known as 'love-in-a-mist'.

FEMININES **Nigelia, Nigella** • PET FORM **Nige**

★ Nigel Mansell (1953–   ), English racing driver
★ Nigella Lawson (1960–   ), English television chef and author, named after her father, politician Nigel Lawson (1932–   )

Nik *see* **Nicholas, Nicola**

Nika *see* **Veronica**

Nikhil *m* Nikhila *f*

This comes from the Sanskrit word meaning 'entire, boundless' and is a popular name among Hindus.

Nikita[1] *mf*

Nikita is the Russian form of the Greek name *Aniketos*, or *Anicetos*. This name, still found in Greece and elsewhere, means 'unconquerable'. It was a title given to Alexander the Great by the Delphic oracle when he went to consult it, but was Christianized when an *Anicetus* became pope in the middle of the 2nd century. Nikita was restricted to Russia and its neighbours, where it is always masculine, until the later 20th century. It then started to be used as a girl's name in the West. The name had become famous during the Cold War with the Russian premier Nikita Khrushchev, but because it ended in an 'a', seemed feminine to Western ears. It had already started to be used in the USA for girls by the early 1970s. In 1985 the singer Elton John had an international hit with a song called 'Nikita'. Although the lyrics did not specify gender, the accompanying video depicted Nikita as female. Use of Nikita for girls peaked in the USA in 1986, the year the song was in the Top Ten there. This was followed in 1990 by a French film, released to critical acclaim in various countries, entitled either *Nikita* or *La Femme Nikita*. The success of this was followed by the cult television series *Nikita*, based on the central character. Some users may regard this feminine use as a form of NICOLA.

★ Nikita Khrushchev (1894–1971), Soviet politician

Nikita[2] *mf*

This is an Indian name, from the Sanskrit for 'the earth'.

VARIANT **Nikhita**

Nikki *see* **Nicholas, Nicola**

Niklaus *see* **Nicholas**

Nikodim *see* **Nicodemus**

Nikola *see* **Nicola**

Nikolai, Nikolaus *see* **Nicholas**

Nikole, Nikoleta *see* **Nicola**

Nila *f*
Nila is from the Sanskrit for 'dark
blue'. For Hindus the colour blue has
a religious significance, and in Hindu
iconography divinities and those who
fight evil are shown with blue skin.
In the West some uses may be as a
feminine form of NEIL.
VARIANT **Neela**

Nilam *mf*
Related to NILA, this is the Sanskrit word
for 'sapphire' derived from the same
root as the word for 'blue'. *Nilima*,
'blueness', used for girls, is another
related name.
VARIANT **Neelam**

Nilda *see* **Brunhilde**

Nils *see* **Nicholas**

Nima¹, Nimat *mf*
These are Arabic names derived from
the word for 'blessing, grace', the first
being singular, the second plural.
VARIANTS **Ni'ma, Ni'mat**

Nima² *f*
This is a Hebrew name which means
'picture, portrait'.

Nimrod *m*
In the Bible, Nimrod is the legendary
founder of the Assyrian Empire, and
is described as the first of the heroes.
The name is almost undoubtedly
Babylonian, and its meaning lost,
although it is sometimes glossed as
'man of might' or 'hunter'. Indeed,
Nimrod is described as 'a mighty
hunter before the Lord' in the book of
Genesis and, as a result, the name was
often used to indicate a keen hunter.
However, since it was also frequently

used ironically of an inept hunter, it
is occasionally found in the USA with
the general sense of 'nincompoop'.

Nina *f*
Nina is often described as a Russian
name, derived from the pet form of
such names as *Antonina* (see ANTONIA),
but this is not the full story. Although
this is indeed the primary source, in
France, where Nina has been used
as an independent name since the
17th century, it represents a pet form
of *Jeanne* (see JOAN) or ANNE, while
in Italy it comes from names such as
Giovannina (also a form of JOAN) or
ANNA.
VARIANTS **Nena, Ninetta, Ninette** *France*
Ninon (pet form)
★ Nina Simone (1933–2003), US singer,
  pianist and composer
★ Ninon (Anne) de Lenclos (1620–1705),
  French courtesan, poet and feminist
★ Dame Ninette de Valois (1898–2001),
  Irish ballerina.

Ninel *f*
In the USSR, when Lenin was in
power, this was regularly given
as a girl's name. It was formed by
spelling the name Lenin backwards.
At the time, patriotic names based
on Communist slogans, acronyms or
industry were in vogue. For example,
the boy's name KIM was common, but
it was not from the same source as in
the West, but taken from the initials
of *Kommunisticheskiy International
Molodezhi*, 'Communist Youth
International'.

Ninette *see* **Anne, Nina**

Ninian *m*
According to legend, dating back to
Bede in the 8th century, Ninian was
a 5th-century missionary who was
the evangelist of the southern Picts in
Scotland. The story places his monastic
centre at Whithorn in south-west

Scotland, and archaeologists have indeed found remains of church buildings of the right date in this location. The name is used quite regularly, but its meaning is not known.

Nino *see* **John**

Ninon *see* **Nancy**, **Nina**

Nioclás *see* **Nicholas**

Niome *see* **Naomi**

Nirvana *f*
The Sanskrit word for the state of final bliss in Buddhism which is a modern coinage as a first name.

Nisha *f*
This is a name from the Sanskrit word for 'night'. Related names are *Nishit(h)*, meaning 'midnight', and *Nishani*, 'night's end, dawn', which are used for boys.
VARIANT **Nishi**

Nita *see* **Anne**, **Jane**

Niven , **Nixen** *see* **Nevan**

Nizar *m*
This is an Arabic name, probably meaning 'little one'.

Njal *see* **Neil**

Noah *m*
The biblical story of Noah building an ark to save both human and animal life from the Flood is well known; less well known is the story of his shame after he planted the first vines and got drunk on the results. The name was hardly used until the Puritans adopted it in the 17th century. They took it to the USA, where it has usually been more common than in the UK. There has been a revival of use in all English-speaking areas in recent years, and it has once again been particularly popular in the USA. The meaning

is disputed, but is traditionally interpreted as either 'rest' or 'comfort'.
VARIANTS *French* **Noé** *Hebrew* **Noach**
★ Noah Webster (1758–1843), US lexicographer, compiler of the first US dictionary of English

Noam *m*
Noam is a modern Hebrew name from the vocabulary word meaning 'pleasantness, joy, delight'. It thus shares a root with NAOMI for which it serves as a masculine. The name is either pronounced 'no-am' after the Hebrew or, particularly in the USA, 'nome'.
★ Noam Chomsky (1928–   ), US linguist and political activist

Nocolao *see* **Nicholas**

Noé *see* **Noah**

Noel *mf* **Noelle** *f*
Noel is the French for Christmas, derived from the Latin *natalis*, in full *dies natalis Domini*, 'the birthday of the Lord'. The name thus has the same origin as NATALIE. In the past Noel, which was well established as a first name by 1200, was the standard form for both sexes, but since the 16th century various feminine forms have also been adopted. The more elaborate of these were particularly common in Australia in the 20th century, although some of them may also be feminine forms of NOLAN. The name has traditionally been used for those born around Christmas. The Spanish also have two other names connected with Christmas, *Natividad*, 'Nativity' and *Belén*, 'Bethlehem'.
VARIANTS **Nowel(l)**, **Noele**, **Noelene**, **Noeline**, **Noella** *French* **Noël**, **Noëlle**, **Noëllie** *Spanish* **Noelia**
★ Sir Noël Coward (1899–1973), English actor, playwright and composer
★ Noel Gallagher (1967–   ), English rock musician in the band Oasis

Noemi, Noemí, Noëmia, Noemie, Noémie *see* **Naomi**

Noga *f*
This is a Jewish name, meaning 'brightness, morning light'. In the Old Testament it is found as a masculine name, given to one of the sons of David, and is still occasionally used for boys.
VARIANT **Nogah**

Nohemi *see* **Naomi**

Nola *see* **Nuala**

Nolan *m*
This is an Irish surname which has been particularly well used as a first name in Australia. The surname means 'descendant of the little charioteer'. There are feminine forms, *Nolene* and *Noleen*, and *Nola*, usually a form of NUALA, is also used as a feminine.

Noll, Nollie *see* **Olga**

Nomi *see* **Naomi**

Nona, Nonie *f*
These are names that can have a number of sources. Nona is the Latin for 'ninth [girl]', and was sometimes used in the 19th century for the ninth child or ninth daughter (compare QUINTUS and other related names). Nona can also be a pet form of *Anona*, a name created for a 1903 song, and its own pet form in turn can be Nonie, which may also be a diminutive of NORA or IONE. Finally, there is a 5th- to 6th-century Welsh saint *Non*, Nona or *Nonna*, mother of the Welsh patron saint David. It is thought her name may have come from the Latin *nonna*, 'nun'.

Noor, Noora *see* **Nur**

Nora *f*
In Ireland the name HONORIA was popular in the form *Honora*. This was shortened to Nora, which became an independent name, and exported to the UK and Scandinavia, where it is still popular. Nora could also be used as a pet form of ELEANOR and LEONORA. It was at its peak of popularity in the later 19th and first half of the 20th centuries.
PET FORMS **Nonie, Noreen** • VARIANTS **Norah, Norleen, Norlene, Norita** (mainly US), **Noreena** *Irish* **Nóra**
★ Norah Jones (1979–), US singer-songwriter
☆ Nora Helmer, heroine of Ibsen's 1879 play *A Doll's House*

Norbert *m*
Norbert is a Germanic name, formed from the elements *nord*, 'north', also found in NORMAN, and the common element *berht*, 'bright, famous', found in names such as ROBERT. St Norbert was born c.1080 into one of the German royal families, and led a profligate lifestyle until, according to legend, he was struck by lightning. Thereafter he took holy orders and led a devout life. The name was revived in the UK along with other medieval names in the later 19th century, and was in regular use in the USA until the end of the 1960s. It is currently popular in Hungary, but is now rare in France, once its stronghold. It is, however, kept in the public eye by frequent sightings that road users have of the lorries of the international trucking firm Norbert Dentressangle.
PET FORMS **Norrie, Bert, Bertie**
★ Norbert Wiener (1894–1964), US mathematician and founding father of cybernetics

Norina *see* **Honoria**

Norma *f*
Although this name is sometimes used as a feminine form of NORMAN, it seems to have been invented by Felice Romani who wrote the libretto

of Bellini's 1832 opera *Norma*. It was the success of this opera that led to the name being adopted by both Italian and English speakers.

★ Norma Shearer (1902–83), Canadian actress

★ Norma Jean Baker (1926–62), true name of the actress Marilyn Monroe

☆ Norma Desmond, faded film star in Billy Wilder's 1950 film *Sunset Boulevard*

Norman *m*
'Northman' was a standard medieval term for a Viking. The term was used both of the Viking settlers in the British Isles and of those who settled in the part of France now known as Normandy (itself occasionally used as a feminine name, sometimes in the form *Normandie*). As a result Norman was in use as a first name even before 1066 and the Norman Conquest. In the Scottish Highlands it was used as the English equivalent of Gaelic TORMOD. This was adopted from another Viking name formed from the name of the Scandinavian god Thor and the element *mod*, 'mind, courage'.
PET FORMS **Norm, Norrie** • VARIANTS *Scottish* **Normanna, Normina** (rare feminines) *Canadian French* **Normand** (m), **Normande** (f)

★ Norman Mailer (1923–2007), US novelist and journalist

★ Normandie Keith (1972–   ), US model and socialite

Norrie *see* **Norbert, Norman**

Norris *m*
This is a surname which derives from NORMAN, used as a first name. It was most common in the later 19th century, and is now rare.
VARIANT **Noris**

★ Norris McWhirter (1925–2004), co-founder of *The Guinness Book of Records* and political activist

Nour *see* **Nur**

Novalee *f*
This is a name coined for the US novel *Where the Heart Is* by Billie Letts. The novel gained publicity when chosen by television presenter Oprah Winfrey for her book club in 1998, and also after it was made into a film released in 2000. As a result the name has started to be given to babies in the USA.

Nowel, Nowell *see* **Noel**

Nuala *f*
This is a pet form of the Irish name FINOLA now used as an independent name. It was particularly popular in Ireland in the middle of the 20th century.
VARIANT **Nola**

Nunia, Nuniatina, Nunzia, Nunziatina *see* **Annunziata**

Nur *mf*
This is an Arabic name, meaning 'light, illumination', which is one of the titles of Allah.
VARIANTS **Nour, Noor, Nu(o)ra** (f), **Noora** (f), **Nur-ud-Din** 'light of the faith' (m), **Nurallah** 'light of Allah' (m)

★ Nur Jahan, 'light of the world' (d.1645), wife of the Mughal emperor Jahangir, and the power behind his throne

Nya *see* **Nia, Niamh**

Nye *see* **Aneurin**

Nyree *f*
This is the usual English spelling of the Maori name correctly spelt *Ngaire*. Its meaning is not known. It came into limited use outside New Zealand after the actress Nyree Dawn Porter (1940–2001) gained fame in the highly successful 1967 television adaptation of John Galsworthy's *The Forsyte Saga*.

O

Obadiah *m*
This is a Hebrew name meaning 'servant of the Lord', and is thus the equivalent of the Arabic ABDULLAH. The name seems to have been quite common in the past, for there are an unusually large number of Obadiahs in the Bible. The best-known of these is a minor prophet whose vision of impending doom and disaster forms the shortest book of the Old Testament. The name was adopted by the Puritans, along with other Old Testament names, in the 17th century, and by the following century was being used by writers as a typical Nonconformist name. It remained in use in the UK until at least the 19th century, but has always been more common in the USA.

VARIANTS **Obediah** *Hebrew (modern)*
Ovadia

☆ Obadiah Slope, sanctimonious and scheming clergyman in Anthony Trollope's 1857 novel *Barchester Towers*

Oberon *see* Aubrey

Ocean *mf*
Names based on the word 'ocean', whether in its Latin form *oceanus* or in the local language, have a long history. *Oceanus* is recorded from Roman times, and there is a St Ocean, although he is so obscure that there seems to be no agreement on his holy day. Use by English speakers has always been rare (although it is on the increase) and often for a special reason. Thus a baby born in transit across the Atlantic on the *Mayflower*, as it took emigrants to settle in America in 1620, was christened Oceanus Hopkins. He does not seem to have flourished for he soon disappears from the records. Names from this root are more common in other languages, when they are usually feminine. It is particularly well used in France, where *Océane* was the top girl's name in 2000. The reason for its growth in popularity has been much debated, but it is worth noting that the name started being used in the 1970s at about the same time as the opening of the motorway known as the *Autoroute Océane*, which regularly takes thousands of the French on their summer holidays.

VARIANTS *French* **Océane, Océanne**
Spanish, Italian **Oceania**

Octavia *f* Octavius *m*
Octavius was a Roman family name, originally from the Latin word for 'eighth', and therefore sometimes given to an eighth child. One Octavius was nephew to Julius Caesar, who had left instructions in his will that Octavius should be adopted as his son and heir. Octavius changed his name to Caesar, adding to it *Octavian*, 'belonging to the Octavii', thus creating another variant. Octavian later became emperor of Rome and his name was changed once again to *Augustus* (see AUGUSTINE). Octavia would simply be the standard name for female members of the Octavius family. Although use of these names has been recorded from the 16th century, they have never been particularly common among English speakers, apart from a brief vogue in

the 19th century. They have, however, been well used among speakers of Romance languages, and immigrants have influenced use in the USA.

A short form of Octavian probably lies behind the independent, mainly African-American name DAVION.

PET FORMS **Tave**, **Tavie**, **Tavia** (f), **Tavius**, **Tavian** (m) • VARIANTS French **Octavie**, **Octavienne** (f), **Octave**, **Octavien** (m) *Italian* **Ottavia** (f), **Ottavio**, **Ottaviano** (m) *Spanish* **Octavio** (m)

★ Octavia Hill (1838–1912), English social campaigner, particularly for social housing

Odette *f* Odo *m*

The Germanic name element *od-*, originally meaning 'patrimony', acquired the sense 'prosperity, happiness'. It is a common name element found in the German *Ute* (f) and ULRIC (m) and in the Spanish ELODIE (f). In English it is found in many names in the form *Ed-*, for example EDWARD and EDITH. The simple masculine form of the name, Odo, is seldom used today (although the German variant OTTO is well-known in Germany), but is still familiar to historians through Odo of Bayeux, half-brother to William the Conqueror, bishop of Bayeux, warrior, and earl of Kent. *Ode* or *Oda* was the feminine form of the name, borne by a 12th-century French saint, who is said to have cut off her nose to be sure that she could escape marriage and become a nun. Odette was originally a pet form of the name, which has outlasted the original. See also UDO.

VARIANT **Odetta**

★ Odette Sansom (1912–95), French-born British agent in Nazi-occupied France during World War II, whose exploits were portrayed in the film *Odette* in 1950

☆ Odette is a character in the 1877 ballet *Swan Lake*

Odharnait, **Odhran** *see* **Orrin**

Odile *f*

Odile comes from the same root as ODETTE. The name spread from the fame of the 8th-century St Odile. She is said to have been born blind and to have been brought up in a convent after being rejected by her father. She rose to be abbess, after which she is said to have regained her sight. She is patron saint of Alsace. In France the compound name *Marie-Odile* is well used.

VARIANTS **Odilia** *French* **Odille**, **Othilie** (f), **Odilon** (m)

★ Odilon Redon (1840–1916), French symbolist painter who is regarded as a precursor to the Surrealists

☆ Odile is a character in the 1877 ballet *Swan Lake*

Odran *see* **Orrin**

Odysseus *see* **Ulysses**

Oengus *see* **Angus**

Ofelia *see* **Ophelia**

Ofra *see* **Oprah**

Ogier *see* **Edgar**

Ohran *see* **Orrin**

Oighrig *see* **Effie**

Oilbhe *see* **Ailbe**

Oilibhear *see* **Oliver**

Oisin *see* **Ossian**

Ola *see* **Alexandra**

Olaf *m*

The Old Norse form of this name, *Anleifr*, later *Óláfr*, was formed from the elements *anu*, 'ancestor', and *leifr*, 'heir', so is often interpreted as meaning 'heir of his fathers'. The name was exported to numerous countries by the Vikings. In France it became the name *Olivier*, source of OLIVER. The intermediate form *Olvir*, found, for example, in the *Orkney Saga* of about 1200, shows how this could happen. As the Orkneys, Hebrides and Ireland were for a long time under Norse rule the name entered into the stock of Gaelic names, although not in an instantly recognizable form. Olaf is most likely to be found used by English speakers in the USA where it was introduced by Scandinavian immigrants.

VARIANTS *Irish* **Auliffe, Amhlaoibh** *Scottish* **Aulay, Orley** *Danish, Norwegian* **Ole** *Norwegian, Swedish* **Ola** *Swedish* **Olof, Olov**

★ St Olaf (c.995–1030), King Olaf II and patron saint of Norway, who supported the country's conversion to Christianity

Olalla *see* Eulalia

Ole *see* Olaf

Olek *see* Alexander

Olga *f* Oleg *m*

Olga is the Russian form of HELGA. The name was taken to Russia by the 9th-century Viking settlers who founded what was to become modern Russia, and became an important Russian name thanks to St Olga of Kiev (d.969). She was the widow of Prince Igor of Kiev and converted to Christianity in 955, after which she promoted the preaching of Christianity. Despite having been used by English speakers since the 19th century the name still has distinctly Russian overtones. The masculine equivalent, Oleg, is even less naturalized.

★ Olga Korbut (1956–), Belarussian gymnast

☆ Olga da Polga is the heroine of a series of children's books by Michael Bond

Olimpia *see* Olympia

Olive, Olivia *f*

Both Olive and Olivia have been recorded in a number of countries since the Middle Ages, but the form Olivia, currently one of the dominant names among English speakers, seems to have been introduced into English by Shakespeare for the grand lady in his *Twelfth Night* (1601).

PET FORMS **Ollie, Liv, Livia, Liv(v)y**

• VARIANTS **Olyvia, Alivia** (mainly USA) *Polish* **Oliwia**

★ Olivia de Havilland (1916–), US actress

★ Olivia Newton-John (1948–), English-born Australian singer and actress

Oliver *m*

Although the name is often associated with the olive tree, it is almost undoubtedly Germanic in origin, and is generally thought to be the same as OLAF. The name appears in its French form, *Olivier*, in the Old French epic *The Song of Roland*. This deals with historical events of 778 in a highly fictionalized way. The earliest surviving manuscript of the poem dates from the 12th century, although the work itself is older. While we know that ROLAND was a genuine historical person, it is not known if his faithful friend was real. Throughout the poem Oliver's wisdom is emphasized, a useful counterbalance to Roland's rashness. These two warriors are the pre-eminent members of a group, the 'Twelve Peers', who serve King Charlemagne. All the other peers have Germanic names, which is why it is thought that Oliver's must also have a Germanic origin. Stories of the Twelve Peers were found throughout Europe during the Middle Ages, which made Oliver's name widely used. It was part of the standard stock of names well into the 17th century, but in 1661 Oliver

Cromwell (1599–1658), who had become Lord Protector of the Realm after the execution of King Charles I, was exhumed and posthumously executed following the Restoration of the monarchy, and the name became deeply unpopular. When Charles Dickens wrote his 1838 novel *Oliver Twist* the choice of name for the orphan foundling was meant to be yet another indication of the callousness of the workhouse in which he grew up. However, the novel was probably instrumental in the revival of the name in the 19th century. In recent years Oliver has been among the most popular names in the British Isles and in many other countries.

PET FORMS **Ol(l)ie**, **Olly**, **Noll(ie)** (archaic)

• VARIANTS *Scots Gaelic* **Oilibhear** *Welsh* **Havelock**

★ St Oliver Plunkett (1629–81), Irish bishop and last Catholic martyr in Britain

★ Oliver Hardy (1892–1957), US comic actor

Olof, Olov *see* Olaf

Olwen *f*
This Welsh name means 'white footprint', and it is explained in the medieval Welsh story of *Culhwch and Olwen*, where her name is first found, that she was so beautiful that four white trefoil flowers would appear wherever she had trodden.

Olympia *f*
The Greek name *Olympias*, referring to Mount Olympus, home of the gods, was used for both sexes. A female St Olympias lived c.368–409 and was a disciple of St John Chrysostom. The name has been seldom used by English speakers, but has remained in use in Greece and was common in France from the 17th century. There, the name gained notoriety in 1863 when

Manet exhibited a painting entitled *Olympia*, which portrayed a woman looking challengingly at the viewer and unashamedly nude, without any of the excusing trappings of classical antiquity.

VARIANTS **Olimpia** *French* **Olympe**

★ Olympias (d.316 BC), Macedonian queen, mother of Alexander the Great

★ Olympia Dukakis (1931–), US actress

Olyvia *see* Olive

Omar[1] *m*
This is a popular Arabic name meaning 'prosperous' based on a word meaning 'life'. Its popularity may be linked to the fact that it was the name of the second caliph, Omar the First (also known as 'Umar ibn al-Khattab, c.581–644). Although Omar[2] is mainly found in the USA, it is probably this Omar which has been steadily increasing in use there in recent years, spawning blends such as *Omarion*.

VARIANTS **Umar**, **Oumar**, **Omer**, **Umer**, **Umair**

★ Omar Khayyam (c.1048–c.1122), Persian poet, mathematician and astronomer

★ Omar Sharif (1932–), Egyptian actor

Omar[2] *m*
This is a Hebrew name probably meaning 'talkative'. It appears in the Bible as a character who is only mentioned in passing (Genesis 36.11), but it was used by the Puritans who took it with them to the USA.

★ Omar Bradley (1893–1981), US general who distinguished himself in World War II

Omi *see* Naomi

Omri *m*
This is a Hebrew name which appears to mean 'my sheaf [of grain]'. It was borne by one of the kings of Israel,

of whom it says in 1 Kings 16 that he 'wrought evil in the eyes of the Lord', which meant that the name was not used in the past. However, the Bible also shows him to have been a warrior and developer of the country, who built, among other things, the city of Samaria. This made the name attractive to settlers in Israel, and it is now well used there. Elsewhere Omri is occasionally given to girls.

☆ Omri is the name of the hero of Lynne Reid Banks's *The Indian in the Cupboard* series of children's books (published from 1980) and of the 1995 film adaptation

Ona *see* **Oona**

Onan *see* **Adamnan**

Ondine *see* **Undine**

Ondrej *see* **Andrew**

Ónora *see* **Honoria**

Onyx *f*
The is one of the rarer jewel names. The semi-precious stone takes many forms, but is best known for the banded black and white type which is often used to carve intaglios, and the pure black form. It may be that some uses of onyx as a name are deliberately used with reference to this blackness.

Oona *f*
This name probably comes from the Irish word *uan*, 'lamb', and thus is considered the Irish equivalent of AGNES. The original Irish form is *Úna*, but spellings with a double 'oo' are now more common. The name is an ancient one, which was popular in medieval Ireland. According to legend Oona and FINBAR are king and queen of the fairies, although evidence suggests that they were originally a god and goddess. Another bearer of the name is found in the song of 'Fair Oona' ('Úna

Bhán'). This is a story of unrequited love ending in death, set in the context of the 17th-century land-grab by the English.

VARIANTS **Oonagh**, **Ona** (this can also be a short form of names ending in these letters), **Una**

★ Oona O'Neill Chaplin (1926–91), actress, daughter of the playwright Eugene O'Neill and wife of Charlie Chaplin

★ Oona King (1967–), English politician and broadcaster

Opal *f*
This is one of the less common jewel names, which was first used in the 19th century, when gem names were particularly in vogue. It is sometimes chosen for those born in October because the opal is the gemstone for that month. The word comes from the Sanskrit for 'precious stone'.

VARIANT **Opaline**

Ophelia *f*
Use of this name comes from the character in Shakespeare's play *Hamlet*, first performed c.1601. In the play Ophelia runs mad with grief and dies by drowning. This fate does not seem to have put parents off using the name, particularly in England and France, where it was quite fashionable in the 19th century. The name appears to come from the Greek *ophelos*, 'help'. It is first recorded in the form *Ofelia* in the 'Arcadia' of the Italian poet Jacopo Sannazzaro which was first published in 1504, and widely reprinted thereafter. It is thought that Shakespeare picked up the name from Sannazzaro.

VARIANTS *French* **Ophélie** *Italian, Spanish* **Ofelia**

Oprah, **Ophrah** *f*
The name Oprah, made famous by Oprah Winfey, is a simplified form

of *Ophrah* which is a biblical name meaning 'fawn' (compare OSSIAN). In the Bible it is used of a man (1 Chronicles 4.14), but nowadays it is usually given to girls. It is a common name in Israel. There is a further related name *Orpah*, from the Hebrew for a female deer. In the biblical book of Ruth this is the name of another of NAOMI's daughters-in-law. Despite the respect in which Oprah Winfey is held, her name is hardly ever used by English-speaking parents.

VARIANTS **Ophra** *Modern Hebrew* **Ofra**

Oral, Oralee, Oralie *see* **Aurelia**

Oran, Oren *see* **Orrin**

Orel *see* **Aurelia**

Orflaith, Orfhlaith *see* **Orla**

Oriana *f*
Oriana is first found in the romance *Amadis of Gaul* written in Spanish by Garcia Rodrigues de Montalvo and published in 1508, but believed to be based on a medieval French original. It is the name of a British princess who is wooed and won by the exemplary knight Amadis. Both names passed into general use, although only Oriana now survives. Use appears to be on the increase. The name probably comes from French *or*, or Spanish *oro*, both words going back to Latin *aurum*, 'gold'. This certainly seems to have been in the minds of the Elizabethan poets who praised Elizabeth I as 'the incomparable Oriana'. There is some evidence that the name was popular on the Western frontier of the USA in the late 19th century.

VARIANTS **Orianna, Orianne** *French* **Oriane, Auriane**

☆ Duchesse Oriane de Guermantes in Marcel Proust's *À la Recherche du Temps Perdu* (1913–27)

Oriel, Oriole *see* **Aurelia**

Orin *see* **Orrin**

Örjan *see* **George**

Orla *f*
Orla is the modern form of an old Irish name *Orlaith* meaning 'Golden Lady'. It was borne by both a sister and niece of Brian Boru (c.941–1014), and was one of the commonest names in 12th-century Ireland. It has been strongly revived in recent years, both in Ireland and Scotland, and is beginning to be used in non-Celtic areas. As is so often the case with people struggling with the difficulties of Irish and Gaelic spellings, it has developed a number of different forms.

VARIANTS **Orlagh, Orlah, Orlaidh, Orlaigh, Orlaithe, Aurnia** *Older Irish* **Orfhlaith**

Orlando *m*
This is the Italian form of ROLAND. It became widely known throughout Renaissance Europe with two very influential Italian romantic epics *Orlando Innamorato* (1487), by Matteo Maria Boiardo, and *Orlando Furioso* (1516–33), by Ludovico Ariosto.

VARIANT **Orlanda** (f)

★ Orlando Gibbons (1583–1625), English composer
★ Orlando Bloom (1977–   ), English actor
☆ Orlando in Shakespeare's *As You Like It*
☆ Orlando, the protagonist of Virginia Woolf's 1928 novel *Orlando*
☆ Orlando the Marmalade Cat in Kathleen Hale's children's books

Orley *see* **Olaf**

Orpah *see* **Oprah**

Orrin *m*
Orrin is the commonest US form of a masculine (and occasionally feminine) name which takes many forms, and may have more than one source. The main root is probably the Irish name *Oran* or *Odhran* meaning 'brownish

grey, swarthy', borne by at least 19 Irish saints, and currently quite popular in Ireland. Orrin has been used in the USA since at least the 18th century, and was mildly popular in the later 19th century. In some cases it may be a form of *Oren*, an obscure biblical name meaning 'pine tree'.

VARIANTS **Orin, Ohran, Orran, Oryn, Odran** *Irish* **Odhran, Odharnait**

☆ Orin is used by Eugene O'Neill for the character Orin Mannon, based on the Greek *Orestes*, in his 1931 play *Mourning Becomes Electra*.

☆ Orrin P Quest, brother to Orfamay Quest, in Raymond Chandler's 1949 novel *The Little Sister*, names chosen to be typical of those used in a Midwestern small town

Orson *m*

Orson comes from the medieval French *o(u)rsin*, 'little bear, bear-cub'. In the medieval romance of *Valentine and Orson* the two heroes were twin brothers separated at birth, Valentine being raised at court while Orson, abandoned in the woods, was rescued and raised by a she-bear. The feminine equivalent is usually URSULA, although there is a rare form *Orsina*.

★ Orson Welles (1915–85), US actor and film director

★ Orson Scott Card (1951–), US novelist, best known for his science fiction

Orville *m*

Orville is a common French place name, used as an aristocratic-sounding title by Fanny Burney for the hero of her 1778 novel *Evelina*.

VARIANT **Orval**

★ Orville Wright (1871–1948), US pioneer of aeroplane design

☆ Orville the Duck, a green puppet operated by Keith Harris

Oryn *see* **Orrin**

Osama *m*

This is an Arabic name meaning 'lion'.

VARIANT **Usama**

★ Osama bin Laden (c.1957–), Saudi Arabian terrorist leader

Osanne *see* **Hosanna**

Osbert *m*

This is an Old English name formed from the elements *os*, 'god', and *beorht*, 'bright, famous'. It was revived along with other early names in the 19th century, but is now rarely used.

PET FORMS **Os, Oz, Ozzie**

★ Sir Osbert Sitwell (1892–1969), English writer and patron of the arts

★ Sir Osbert Lancaster (1908–86), English cartoonist and writer

Oscar *m*

In Irish mythology Oscar, 'deer lover', was the son of *Oisin*, 'fawn' (see OSSIAN). The name was revived by James Macpherson (1736–96) for one of the heroes of the Ossianic poems he published as remnants of ancient Scots Gaelic verse, but which were in fact largely his own work. Macpherson's poetry was immensely successful, and among his admirers was the French Emperor Napoleon. He had placed his marshal, Jean-Baptiste Bernadotte, on the throne of Sweden, and when he was asked to become godfather to the new king's first son, chose the name Oscar for him. This child later became King Oscar I of Sweden. This is how Oscar became a typically Scandinavian name, along with other Ossianic names such as SELMA and MALVINA. King Oscar, in turn, had at one time as court physician an Irish doctor called Sir William Wilde. He also chose Ossianic names for his son, calling him Oscar FINGAL O'Flahertie Wilde. Oscar had never been particularly widely used in the UK, and rapidly became identified with the flamboyant playwright. As a result, after the scandal of Oscar Wilde's trial in 1895 the name become virtually unusable and dropped out of use for many decades, until there was a revival in the 1990s. However, in the USA the influence of Scandinavian immigrants meant that the name remained in regular use there.

PET FORMS **Os, Ossie, Oz, Ozzie** • VARIANTS *Scandinavian* **Oskar**

★ Oscar Petersen (1925–2007), Canadian jazz pianist and composer

Osheen *see* **Ossian**

Osher *see* **Asher**

Osian *see* **Ossian**

Osip *see* **Joseph**

Oskar *see* **Oscar**

Osman *m*
Osman is the Turkish form of the Arabic name *Uthman*. Uthman was borne by the son-in-law of the Prophet Muhammad, who was the third caliph. He was instrumental in the writing down of the Koran. Osman I (1258–1326) was the founder of the dynasty that established the Ottoman Empire, which was centred in Turkey, but at its height covered large areas of Europe and the Middle East. The meaning of the name comes from the large bird, the bustard.

VARIANTS **Usman, Uthman, Ousman**

Ossian *m*
This is the traditional English version of the Irish name *Oisin*, currently a popular name in Ireland. The English form is often pronounced as it is spelt, but the Irish form is pronounced 'oh-sheen'. In legend Ossian is the son of FINN Mac Cool and the goddess SADHBH. She had been turned into a deer by the Dark Druid and gave birth to Ossian in this form. After seven years Finn found

them in the forest and, recognizing who they were, gave his son the name Ossian, 'little deer, fawn'. In adulthood Ossian was known as both a great warrior and poet, and was the lover of NIAMH. The name was revived alongside other Irish names by the Ossianic poems of James Macpherson (see further under OSCAR).

PET FORM **Ossie** • VARIANTS **Ossia** (f), **Osian, Osheen, Oisin**

Ossie *see* **Oscar**

Oswald *m*
This is an Old English name formed from the elements *os*, 'god', and *weald*, 'rule'. There were two Anglo-Saxon saints called Oswald, one was a bishop, the other a king of Northumbria. The latter was a convert to Christianity and, since he died in battle in 641 fighting a pagan king, he was considered a martyr.

PET FORMS **Oz, Ozzie** • VARIANTS *Scandinavian* **Osvald** *Spanish, Italian, Portuguese* **Oswaldo**

★ Sir Oswald Mosley (1896–1980), English politician and leader of the British Union of Fascists
★ Osvaldo Ardiles (1952–), Argentine football player

Oswin *m*
Oswin is an Old English name formed from the elements *os*, 'god', and *wine*, 'friend'. It was borne by a 7th-century king of Northumbria who was a cousin of St OSWALD. This may be why, when he was assassinated by his brother *Oswy*, he too was made a saint.

Otha *m*
This name is something of a mystery. It is well used as a masculine name in the USA, being recorded from the 19th century and appearing in the top 1000 names into the 1960s despite its feminine-looking ending. It is occasionally used for females.

It is most probably a variant of OTTO, via the form *Otho*, but more research needs to be done.

★ Otha Wearin (1903–90), US politician and author
★ Otha or Othar Turner (1907–2003), US blues musician
★ Otha Elias Bates (1928–2008), US rock and roll singer and guitarist better known as Bo Diddley

Othilie *see* **Odile**

Otis *m*
This is a surname used as a first name. The source of the surname is the Germanic name ODO. It is particularly used as a first name in the USA, adopted in honour of the Revolutionary hero James Otis (1725–83).

★ Otis Redding (1941–67), US soul singer

Ottavia, **Ottaviano**, **Ottavio** *see* **Octavia**

Otto *m* **Ottilie** *f*
This name derives from the Germanic element *od*, 'riches, prosperity' (see ODETTE) and was originally a short form of a number of names starting with this element. Otto is essentially a German name, and is not common among English speakers. Ottilie is both French and German, and has *Ottoline* as a pet form.

★ Prince Otto von Bismarck (1815–98), Prusso-German statesman, first chancellor of the German Empire
★ Lady Ottoline Morrell (1873–1938), English hostess and patron of the arts

Oumar *see* **Omar**[1]

Ousman *see* **Osman**

Ovadia *see* **Obadiah**

Owain, **Owen** *m*
This name can have a number of different sources, and it is often impossible to determine which is being used. The main source of the name is from Wales, found as early as the 6th century, when Owain son of Urien was king of Rheged. This historical figure became Sir *Yvain* in French Arthurian romance. The origin of the name is much debated. There are three main theories. One holds that Owain is the Welsh form of the name EUGENE. Another theory has it that the name comes from Welsh *oen*, 'lamb', while the final suggestion is that it means 'born of *Esos*', Esos being the name of an old Celtic god. Owain became Owen as a surname, and this in turn can be used as a first name. However, Owen can also be the anglicized form of the Irish names EOIN or EOGHAN.
VARIANT **Owein**

★ Owen Glendower (Owain Glyndŵr) (c.1350–c.1416), the last native Welshman to hold the title Prince of Wales

Oz, **Ozzie**, **Ozzy** *m*
This is a pet form of any name beginning *Os-*, which is sometimes used as an independent first name or nickname.
VARIANT **Ozzie**

Ozanne *see* **Hosanna**

P

Paavali, Paavo, Pablo *see* **Paul**

Paca *see* **Frances**

Paco *see* **Francis**

Pàdar *see* **Patrick**

Paddy *m*
This is a pet form of PATRICK, sometimes used as a first name. It was so common in 19th-century Ireland that it became a generic term (now considered offensive) for an Irishman, but at present Patrick is not well used by Irish parents, and even the Irish form of the name, *Padraig*, which is the source of the 'd' in Paddy, is near the bottom of the top 100 names.
FEMININE **Pádraigín**

Padma *mf*
This is the Sanskrit for 'lotus', a plant which plays an important role in Hindu mythology. Padma can be used as a name for both the god Rama and the goddess Lakshmi.
VARIANTS **Padme, Padmini** ('lotus pond'), **Padmaja** ('born of the lotus')
★ Padma Lakshmi (1970–), Indian model, actress and TV presenter

Padraic *see* **Patrick**

Pàdraid *see* **Peter**

Pàdraig, Pádraig, Pádraigín, Padrig *see* **Patrick**

Pagan *mf*
The original meaning of the Latin *paganus* was 'country dweller', just as *urbanus*, source of URBAN, meant 'town dweller'. It was only later that it came to mean, first of all, someone who was not in the military (a largely urban phenomenon, along with conversion to Christianity), then, someone who was not among the Soldiers of Christ. Pagan was a perfectly respectable name in the Middle Ages; it is recorded in England in the 11th century, and is well attested in Scotland in the 12th century. There is also a 15th-century Italian St Paganus. The name died out at the Reformation in the UK, but has recently enjoyed a revival, usually for girls.
VARIANT **Paygan**

Page *see* **Paige**

Pàidean, Páidín *see* **Patrick**

Paige *f*
This is the surname, from the occupation of page, used as a first name. It is usually given to girls, although it is occasionally used for boys. For some reason not yet ascertained, it started being chosen for girls in the USA in the 1950s, and is currently among the most popular choices throughout the English-speaking world.
VARIANT **Page**

Pàl, Pål *see* **Paul**

Pàlan *see* **Bartholomew**

Pallav *m* **Pallavi** *f*
This is from the Sanskrit word for 'budding leaf, shoot'.
VARIANT **Pallab**
★ Pallab Ghosh (1962–), BBC science correspondent

Palle *see* **Paul**

Paloma *f*
Paloma is the Spanish for 'dove'. It came into wider use as a first name after the artist Picasso chose it for one of his daughters.

Pamela *f*
This is a name invented by the Elizabethan poet and soldier Sir Philip Sydney, for his pastoral romance 'Arcadia' (1590). From the rhythm of the verse in which it is used it is clear that he put the stress on -*mel*-, rather than on *Pam*- as is usual today. He appears to have coined the name from the Greek elements *pan*, 'all', and *meli*, 'honey', to produce a name meaning something like 'all sweetness'. The name remained largely a literary curiosity until the 18th century, when Samuel Richardson published his epistolary novel *Pamela* (1740). Although little read today, the novel was a great success at the time, and the name began to be better known, although it was not in general use until the 20th century.
PET FORMS **Pam, Pammy** • VARIANTS **Pamella, Pamala, Pamelia**

Pancho *see* **Francis**

Pandora *f*
In Greek mythology Pandora, whose name is formed from *pan*, 'all', and *doron*, 'gift', is the first woman, created by the gods to punish men for accepting the gift of fire, stolen from the gods by Prometheus. Pandora was created curious, so when she was given a box and told that on no account should she open it, the gods could be sure she would disobey. The box contained all the evil gifts of the gods, the ills that afflict mankind, and when Pandora opened it they flew out and have remained in the world ever since. But Hope was also in the box, to keep humanity from despair.
PET FORM **Panda**
☆ Pandora Braithwaite, love-object of Adrian Mole in Sue Townsend's comic novels, published from 1982

Pansy *f*
This is one of the flower names introduced in the 19th century, but not much used today. It is derived from the French *pensée*, 'thought', because of the way in which the 'face' on older varieties of the flower appeared to be cast down in thought.
☆ Pansy Potter, The Strong Man's Daughter in *The Beano*
☆ Pansy Parkinson, student at Hogwarts, in J K Rowling's *Harry Potter* books (1997 onwards)

Paola, Paolo *see* **Paul**

Paquita *see* **Frances**

Paquito *see* **Francis**

Pär *see* **Peter**

Pàra, Páraic *see* **Patrick**

Paraskevi *f* Paraskevas *m*
Paraskevi literally means 'preparation' but is used to mean 'Friday', a day of holy preparation in Greek. As well as being a day, it is the name of at least four female saints venerated in the Orthodox Church. The best known of these was a 2nd-century saint who is patron of the blind. According to her legend she restored the sight of the Roman Emperor Antoninus Pius, even though he had tortured her for her faith. As Paraskevi is a feminine word, Paraskevas is unusual in being a masculine name formed from a feminine. Paraskevi is a popular name in Greece, and its variants are widespread throughout the area of influence of the Orthodox Church.
VARIANTS *Greek* **Paraskeve** *Russian* **Praskovya, Praskoviya**

Paris *mf*
Use of Paris as a masculine first name
can be either from the Trojan prince
who, in Greek mythology, caused the
Trojan war by abducting the beautiful
HELEN, or from the French city. Feminine
use is usually with reference to the
city, which is named after the tribe of
the *Parisii* who lived in the area in the
1st century BC.
★ Paris Hilton (1981–), US socialite

Parker *m*
Use of this surname, which would
originally have been given to someone
who acted as a park-keeper or
gamekeeper, has been increasing
steadily in the USA. It is now
occasionally given to girls.
VARIANT **Park**

Parmindar *f*
This is an Indian girl's name,
particularly used by Sikhs. It is
interpreted as meaning 'God of gods,
supreme god'.
VARIANT **Parminder**
★ Parminder Nagra (1975–), English
actress

Parnel *see* **Petronella**

**Parthalan, Parthlan, Partlan,
Partnan** *see* **Barclay, Bartholomew**

Parvaiz *m*
This is a Muslim name, introduced to
the Indian subcontinent by one of the
sons of the Mughal Emperor Jahangir
(1569–1627). It comes from the Persian
for 'victorious, fortunate'.
VARIANTS **Pervez, Parvez, Parwez**
★ Pervez Musharraf (1943–), Pakistani
soldier and politician

Parvati *f*
This is the Sanskrit for 'daughter of the
mountain', and is one of the names
of the god Shiva's wife, the mother of

Ganesh, who is considered a daughter
of the Himalayas.
VARIANTS **Parvathi, Parvathy**
☆ Parvati Patel in the *Harry Potter* books
by J K Rowling

Parvin *f*
This is the Persian name for the
constellation known in the West as the
Pleiades. It is mainly used by Muslims.
VARIANT **Parveen**

Parzifal *see* **Percival**

Pascal *m* **Pascale** *f*
The Hebrew term for the Jewish festival
of Passover, *pesach*, became *paskha* in
New Testament Greek, which gave the
Latin term *paschalis*. Because Passover
and the Crucifixion coincided, this
acquired a Christian sense, 'relating
to Easter'. The name was initially
masculine, and given to children born
around Easter. Pascal was a popular
name in the Middle Ages, particularly
in Cornwall, where it developed
into the typically Cornish surname
Pascoe. It died out thereafter, and was
reintroduced from France, where it was
particularly common in the 1960s.
VARIANTS **Pascaline** (f) *Italian* **Pasquale,
Pasqualino** (m), **Pasqualina** (f) *Spanish*
Pascula (m), **Pascuala** (f)

Pasha *see* **Paul**

Pat *see* **Patrick, Patricia**

Patience *f*
Patience is one of the Christian virtues
introduced as first names by the
Puritans in the 17th century. They used
the name for both sexes, but it is now
exclusively feminine. The name has
been given in conjunction with other
virtue names, for example twins have
been called Patience and Prudence,
and in the 17th century Sir Thomas
Carew, Speaker of the House of
Commons, even went so far as to call

his four daughters Patience, Prudence, Temperance and Silence (see TACEY).
PET FORM **Patty**

Patricia f

Patricia is the most frequently used of the feminine equivalents of PATRICK, having spread from English to a number of other languages. Originally Patricia would simply have been the female form of *Patricius*, a Roman family name meaning 'patrician, noble'. There was a 7th-century St Patricia of Naples, patron saint of the city, whose legend describes her as a Byzantine princess. Medieval British records of the name Patricia are, however, misleading. Patrick was used for both sexes at that time, but would appear in Latin as Patricia when referring to a female. It was not until the 18th century, probably in Scotland, that the form Patricia started to be used as a given name. It was rare for a long time, but in 1886 one of Queen Victoria's granddaughters was named Patricia. The popularity of the name increased thereafter, peaking in the 1960s.
PET FORMS **Pat, Patsy, Patti(e), Patty, Tish(a), Tricia, Trish, Trisha** • VARIANTS *Irish* **Pádraigín** *French* **Patrice** (masculine in France, but elsewhere sometimes used for girls) *Italian* **Patrizia**

Patrick m

St Patrick, the 5th-century missionary to Ireland and its patron saint, adopted the name *Patricius* (see further PATRICIA) when he was ordained, his original name having been *Sucat*. He was a Briton who had been captured by raiders and taken as a slave to Ireland. He managed to escape, then trained in France as a priest and returned to Ireland as a missionary. He was held in such reverence by the Irish that his name was not adopted as a first name until the 17th century. Patrick is still the most popular form of the name in Ireland, although there are numerous other forms of the name either in Gaelic or anglicized forms of these. (see below and at PADDY)
PET FORMS **Pat, Paddy, Patsy** • VARIANTS **Patryk** *Irish* **Pádraig, Páraic, Padraic, Porick, Páidín, Paudeen** (pet forms) *Scots Gaelic* **Pàdraig, Pàra, Pàdar** (these can, confusingly, also be used for Peter) **Pàidean** (pet form), **Padrig** *Welsh* **Padrig** (Wales also has its own St Padarn, 'fatherly') *French* **Patrice** *Italian* **Patrizio** *Spanish, Portuguese* **Patricio**

Patsy, Pattie, Patty *see* Martha, Matilda, Patricia, Patrick

Paudeen *see* Patrick

Paul m Paula f

Paulus is the Latin for 'small, insignificant', and was the name chosen by the repentant St Paul the Apostle to replace his original name of SAUL, under which he had persecuted Christians. Paulus was already a Roman family name, so it was easy for the feminine form of this, Paula, to become established as the feminine of Paul. Despite the enormous influence of St Paul on the spread of Christianity, his name was rare in England during the Middle Ages, and only came into regular use in the 17th century. The Latin pronunciation of the name changed during Roman times and this, along with the inherent instability of its sounds, has meant that there is great variety in the forms the name takes internationally.
VARIANTS *Irish* **Pól** *Scots Gaelic* **Pàl** *Czech* **Pavel, Pavla** *Dutch* **Pauwel** *Finnish* **Paavo, Paavali, Pauli** *French* **Paulette** (f) *Greek* **Pavlos** *Italian* **Paolo, Paola** *Polish* **Pawel** *Russian* **Pavel, Pasha, Pava** *Scandinavian* **Poul, Palle, Pål, Påvel** *Spanish* **Pablo, Paulino**

Pauline *f*
Although Pauline serves as a feminine
form of PAUL, strictly speaking it comes
from a slightly different root, the
Latin family name *Paulinus*, meaning
'related to the *Paulus* family'. Paulinus
was a well established Roman family
name, giving *Paulina*, which was borne
by the mother of the Emperor Hadrian,
and also by several early Christian
martyrs.
VARIANTS *Czech* **Pavlina** *Dutch* **Paulien**

Pava *see* **Paul**

Pavan *m*
This is a Hindu name, meaning 'wind,
breeze'.
VARIANT **Pawan**

Pavel, **Påvel**, **Pavla** *see* **Paul**

Pavlina *see* **Pauline**

Pavlos *see* **Paul**

Pawan *see* **Pavan**

Pawel *see* **Paul**

Paygan *see* **Pagan**

Payton *see* **Peyton**

Peaches *f*
One of the most recent trends in name
fashions has been to use plant-related
names outside the traditional range of
flowers, and in particular fruit names.
It is possible to find almost any fruit
name, from banana to raspberry, used
as a first name, but Peaches is probably
the most common. This can be
explained in part because it has had a
high media profile, and in part because
it was already well-established as a
term of endearment.
★ Peaches Honeyblossom Michelle
   Charlotte Angel Vanessa Geldof
   (1989–), English media personality,
   daughter of Bob Geldof and Paula
   Yates

Peadar *see* **Peter**

Pearce *see* **Peter**, **Piers**

Pearl
This is one of the 19th-century
jewel names, which may have been
introduced, or at least popularized,
in the USA by Nathaniel Hawthorne
(see below). Before its use as a jewel
name it could also function as a pet
form of MARGARET, as this name means
'pearl'. Yiddish speakers also used the
name, usually in the form *Perle*, as
a Gentile equivalent of the Hebrew
name *Penninnah*. This means 'coral'
in biblical Hebrew, and the name
is borne by a minor character in the
Bible, but in modern Hebrew it means
pearl. In the USA, Pearl is occasionally
found as a masculine name, as in the
case of Pearl Zane Grey, better known
as the author ZANE Grey.
VARIANTS **Perl** *French* **Perle** *Italian, Spanish*
Perla
★ Pearl S Buck (1892–1973), US novelist
   and Nobel Prize winner
☆ Pearl, daughter of the heroine Hester
   Prynne, in Nathaniel Hawthorne's
   1850 novel *The Scarlet Letter*

Peder, **Pedr**, **Pedran**, **Pedro** *see*
Peter

Pedrog *see* **Petroc**

Peer *see* **Peter**

Peg, **Peggy** *f*
These are pet forms of the name
MARGARET, now also used as
independent names. Margaret
becomes Peg, or Peggy, via the
pet form MEG. In the past changing
the initial letter of a pet form was
a common way of creating a new
diminutive. Thus *Dick* comes from
RICHARD via *Rick*, *Bob* from ROBERT via
Rob. The change of 'M' to 'P' was
particularly common, giving pairs such
as *Matty* and *Patty*, *Molly* and *Polly*.

VARIANTS *Irish* **Peig, Peigín, Pegeen** *Scots Gaelic* **Peigi**

★ Dame Peggy Ashcroft (1907–91), English actress

☆ 'Peggy Sue', 1957 song written and performed by Buddy Holly

Pehr *see* Peter

Peig, Peigi, Peigín *see* Peg

Pekka *see* Peter

Pelagia *f* Pelagius *m*
The Greek word *pelagios* means 'ocean', and was one of the titles of sea-born Aphrodite, goddess of love. This made it a suitable name for a high-class courtesan from Antioch who, according to legend, was converted to Christianity and ended her life a penitent hermit on the Mount of Olives before being canonized. Pelagius was the name of a 4th-century Briton who wrote numerous theological works. He denied the doctrine of Original Sin and was declared a heretic. He is credited with creating the first Western European heresy. In his case, it has been suggested that Pelagius may have been a translation of the British name now found as MORGAN. These names are rare among English speakers, but well used in other languages.

VARIANTS *French* **Pélagie** (f) *Russian* **Pelageya** (f) *Spanish* **Pelayo** (m)

Pelé *m*
This is the nickname of the Brazilian footballer whose given name is Edson Arantes do Nascimento (b.1940), universally known to his admirers as Pelé. He is said to have got the name from his pronunciation of *Bilé*, borne by another footballer he had admired as a child. The name has occasionally been chosen by parents in his honour.

Peleg *m*
This is a biblical name meaning 'division' in Hebrew. Although Peleg is only mentioned in passing in the Bible, it has become a common name in modern Israel.

Pelham *m*
In 1716 Thomas Pelham-Thomas was created Duke of Newcastle. Pelham is, therefore, one of the less common of the 19th-century aristocratic names. The origin of Pelham as a surname lies in a place name which refers to the settlement of someone with the Old English name of *Peola*.

★ Sir P G (Pelham George) Wodehouse (1881–1975), English novelist

Pella *see* Petronella

Pelle *see* Peter

Pelligrino, Pen *see* Peregrine

Penka *see* Petra

Penelope *f*
In Homer's *Odyssey*, Penelope is the wife of Odysseus (see ULYSSES), who becomes a byword for fidelity. While her husband is away for ten years fighting the Trojan war, and then wandering for another ten years travelling home, she never gives up the hope that he is still alive. She is besieged by suitors after her property, but puts them off by saying she has to weave a shroud for her old father-in-law before she can think of marriage. Every day she lets them see she is working hard, but each night she secretly unpicks her work, so that it is never finished. Because of this, it has been suggested that the name is derived from the Greek *pene*, a weaver's bobbin. However, the *Odyssey* includes puns on the Greek word *penelops*, the term for a type of duck, and this is often taken as its origin. It seems most likely that the source of the name is lost. It may even be pre-Greek, like a number of

Homeric names. As Penelope provides such an excellent role model for traditional feminine virtues, it is not surprising that the name was in use by the 16th century, albeit rarely. It was at its most popular in the middle of the 20th century.

PET FORMS **Pen**, **Penny**

★ Penelope Lively (1933–), English novelist and children's author
★ Penélope Cruz (1974–), Spanish actress

Penninnah see **Pearl**

Pepa see **Petronella**

Pepe, **Pepito** see **Joseph**

Pepita see **Josephine**

Peppe, **Peppi** see **Joseph**

Per see **Peter**

Perais see **Peter**, **Pierce**

Perce see **Pierce**, **Percival**, **Percy**

Percival m
Although the surname Perceval, derived from the Norman place name Pecheval, already existed, as a first name this seems to have been invented by the French author Chrétien de Troyes for his romance *Perceval or the Story of the Grail* written c.1191. This was the first of the Holy Grail stories, and was an immense success throughout Europe, being translated and adapted into many other languages. The name appears in several countries by the third quarter of the 13th century, although it is not recorded in England until the 14th. There are several views as to the origin and meaning of the name. One theory is that it is a drastic re-working of the Welsh name *Peredur*. As most names in early Arthurian literature are Celtic in origin, this would seem reasonable. However, although Peredur is indeed

the name of the hero in the Welsh version of the story, the surviving Welsh text is some hundred years later than Chrétien's version, and so cannot support this. In any case, it would be unhelpful as the source of Peredur is not known. *Perceval*, the form Chrétien uses, can easily be analysed as being formed from the medieval French *perce*, 'pierce', and *val*, 'valley'. This still leaves the problem of why he should be given such a name. Wolfram von Eschenbach, in his German version of the story *Parzival*, written by 1220, does indeed explain that he was so named by his mother because his father died shortly before his birth and the sorrow had pierced her to her inner depths (represented by the valley), but this sounds like an attempt to explain the choice of name, rather its original meaning. One recent scholar has come up with the attractive suggestion that *val* should be interpreted as 'veil' rather than 'valley', for Percival is only his childhood name, not his real name, and the story deals with his attempts to find his true self as well as to lift the veil hiding a number of other mysteries.

PET FORMS **Perce**, **Percy**, **Val** • VARIANTS *French* **Perceval** *German* **Parzifal**

Percy m
As well as being a short form of PERCIVAL, Percy is an independent name, which started out as a French surname. The surname comes from a number of places called *Perci*, which in turn come from the Late Latin *Persius* (meaning 'Persian') plus the ending -*acum*, indicating a settlement belonging to someone. A family with this surname came over with William the Conqueror, and was prominent in the medieval aristocracy. The earliest recorded use as a first name came after the heiress to the Percy family,

Lady Elizabeth Percy, married the 6th Duke of Somerset. Their third son, who died in 1721, was given his mother's maiden name, as was not uncommon at the time. The surname thereafter entered the family as a first name, and was given to a distant relative, the poet Percy Bysshe Shelley (1793–1822). His fame was probably influential in the spread of the name in the 19th century, when aristocratic surnames used as first names were particularly popular.

PET FORM **Perce**

Perdita f

This is one of the less common first names derived from Shakespeare's plays. It means 'lost [girl]', and appears in *The Winter's Tale* (1610). In the play Perdita's father, crazed with jealousy and believing her not to be his, orders her to be exposed. Her innocent mother says 'and for the babe is counted lost for ever, Perdita I prithee call't'.

PET FORMS **Perdie, Purdie**

☆ Perdita is the name of one of the dogs in Dodie Smith's 1956 book *The Hundred and One Dalmatians* and the 1961 Disney film adaptation

Peredur see Percival

Peregrine m

In the Middle Ages the classical Latin word *peregrinus*, 'stranger, foreigner', took on the meaning 'wandering' and as a noun 'pilgrim, crusader', and thus became a Christian name. It was used occasionally in the Middle Ages, no doubt helped by the fame of a 7th-century Italian saint. The name became much more common from the 16th century onwards. The first recorded use in this revival was for Peregrine Bertie, 13th Baron WILLOUGHBY, Beck and Eresby (1555–1601). His family were ardent Protestants and had gone into exile on the Continent when Mary

I tried to forcibly restore Catholicism as the state religion in 1555. Peregrine was thus born in exile and named for his family's wanderings. He later became a noted and popular general. He called one of his own children Peregrine, and the name entered the stock of those used in his family, members of which married into other noble families, including the PELHAMS and Osbornes, who in turn adopted the name. Meanwhile, it had also spread to more humble families. The idea that this earthly life was but a journey or pilgrimage to the eternal life was a popular one at the time, especially among Nonconformists (compare the use of the name *Pilgrim* in Bunyan's *Pilgrim's Progress*) and the name crops up regularly in such families. It was used steadily through to the 19th century, but became much rarer in the 20th.

PET FORMS **Perry, Pen** • VARIANTS *Italian* **Pelligrino** (Italians also use *Palmiro*, 'pilgrim', as a first name)

★ Sir Peregrine Worsthorne (1923–), English journalist

☆ Peregrine Pickle, eponymous hero of Tobias Smollett's 1751 novel

☆ Peregrine 'Pippin' Took, hobbit, in J R R Tolkien's *The Lord of the Rings*

Perl, Perla, Perle see Pearl

Pernilla, Pernille see Petronella

Perrine see Petra

Perry m

As well as being a pet form of PEREGRINE, Perry can have two other sources. One is directly from the surname, which most often comes from the Old English word for a pear tree. In the USA it can also derive from the surname, but used in honour of two brothers, Commodore Oliver Perry (1785–1819), 'the hero of Lake Erie', who defeated the British there in 1813, and Commodore Matthew Perry (1794–1858), 'Father of the Steam Navy', who was instrumental in opening up Japan to the Western world in the mid-19th century.

★ Perry Como (1912–2001), US singer

☆ Perry Mason, lawyer in Erle Stanley Gardner's novels, published from 1933 onwards, and later in the long-running television series

Perse *see* **Pierce**

Persephone *f*
In Greek mythology Persephone was goddess of both the underworld and spring. According to the myth she was abducted by Hades, god of the underworld, and taken down to his kingdom. Her mother Demeter, goddess of fertility, searched everywhere for her in tears, and the earth became barren. Only when the two were reunited did plants begin to grow again. However, Persephone has to spend some of the year with Hades, where she rules beside him. When she goes to the underworld, winter comes to the world, and spring arrives with her return. The meaning of her name has been much debated. See also ADONIS.
VARIANT *Latin* **Proserpine**

Persis *f*
This is simply the Greek for 'Persian woman'. It was used quietly from the Reformation onwards because it appears as a name in the New Testament (Romans 16.12), where St Paul writes 'Salute the beloved Persis, which laboured much in the Lord'. Unfortunately, we know nothing more about her. The name is also used by those of Persian descent.
VARIANT **Persia**

★ Persis Khambatta (1950–98), Indian actress

Pertronel *see* **Petronella**

Pervez *see* **Parvaiz**

Pesah *m*
This is the Hebrew word for the Jewish feast of Passover, which has traditionally been used for boys born at this time of year, just as PASCAL has been used for Christian boys born at Easter.
VARIANT **Pesach**

Peta *f*
This is one of the many attempts to form a girl's name from PETER. It seems to date only from the 20th century. For other feminine forms see PETRA and PETRONELLA.

★ Peta Wilson (1970–   ), Australian actress

Petal *f*
Although this vocabulary word is usually a pet name, it is occasionally given as a birth name.

Peter *m*
One of the core names in the Western tradition, Peter comes, via Latin, from the Greek *petros* meaning 'stone, rock'. The name started out as a nickname for the Apostle SIMON, for Jesus said to him 'thou art Peter, and upon this rock I will build my church' (Matthew 16.18). In the original Aramaic the name was *Cephas*, but this does not seem to have been taken up. As St Peter, Simon Peter is considered the founder of the organized Christian Church, and was the first pope. He was a very popular saint, and is depicted in art with a key, for he is said to hold the keys to heaven.
PET FORMS **Pete**, **Peterkin** (archaic)
• VARIANTS **Pearce**, **Piers** *Irish* **Peadar**, **Perais**, **Piaras**, **Ferris** *Scots Gaelic* **Pàdraid** (used for both Patrick and Peter) *Welsh* **Pedr**, **Pedran**, **Petran** *Arabic* **Bo(u)tros**, **Butros** *Czech* **Petr** *Dutch* **Piet**, **Pierter**, **Petrus** *Finnish* **Pekka**, **Petri** *French* **Pierre**,

Pierrot, Pierrick (Breton form) *German* **Petrus** *Greek* **Petros** *Italian* **Pietro, Piero** *Polish* **Piotr** *Russian* **Pyotr, Petia** *Scandinavian* **Per, Peer, Petter, Pär, Pehr, Pelle, Peder** *Spanish, Portuguese* **Pedro**

Petra *f*

This is one of the feminine forms of PETER, which is firmly established in many European countries, but only became well used among English speakers in the 20th century. For convenience other feminine forms of Peter, including those from other languages, apart from the ones listed under PETA, PETRA and PETRONELLA are given in the variant list below.

PET FORM **Pet** • VARIANTS *English* **Petrina, Petrona** *Bulgarian* **Penka, Petia** *French* **Perrine, Pierette** *Italian* **Piera, Pierina, Piertrina** *Russian* **Petia, Petya**

★ Petra Kelly (1947–92), German environmental campaigner and politician
★ Petra, pet dog on the children's television programme *Blue Peter* (1962–77)

Petroc *m*

This is the name of the most prominent Cornish saint, who lived in the 6th century. He may have been born in South Wales, but since at the time there was little distinction between the lands either side of the Bristol Channel, Cornwall can safely claim him for its own. He was buried at Padstow (a name which means 'holy place of St Petroc') but the reliquary containing his head can still be seen at Bodmin, where he lived and worked for much of his life. The name is mainly confined to Cornwall, but churches dedicated to him can also be found in Wales and Brittany. In Welsh legend he is one of the seven warriors to survive Arthur's last battle at Camlan.

VARIANT *Welsh* **Pedrog**

★ Petroc Trelawny (1971–), English music broadcaster

Petronella *f*

The Roman family name *Petronius* – kept alive because it was borne by the author of the Rabelaisian 1st-century AD satire *The Satyricon* – gave the feminine name *Petronia*. The pet form of this would have been *Petronilla*. Experts are divided as to whether or not the name came from *petrus*, 'a rock', the same source as PETER, but this was certainly the interpretation favoured in the early Middle Ages. There was an early saint Petronilla, and legend had it that she was the daughter of St Peter, who starved herself to death rather than marry. She became the patron saint of the kings of France, and so the name became popular there in the Middle Ages. It was also popular in England, as can be seen from the number of surnames with forms like Parnell which derive from it. It developed shortened forms in both English and French which led to the full form falling out of favour. In England, between the 14th and 18th centuries, *Pernel* or *Parnel* came to be used as a colloquial term for a priest's mistress, while in France a girl called *Péronelle* featured in a 15th-century army marching song, and from that became a term for a foolish, chattering girl. It is said the song was still being sung in the 19th century.

PET FORMS **Pet, Petsy, Pepa** • VARIANTS **Petronilla, Pertronel, Petronil(l), Parnel** *Dutch* **Pietronella** *French* **Pétronelle** *Scandinavian* **Pernilla, Pernille, Pella** *Spanish* **Petrona**

★ Petronella Wyatt (1969–), English journalist and writer

Peyton *mf*

This is a surname from an English place name, which is being used increasingly as a first name in the

USA. It is currently slightly more common for girls than for boys. Peyton is recorded in the USA for boys as an occasional name in the 19th century, and started to return to fashion at the end of the 1980s. As a girl's name its popularity was boosted in 1992. Surprisingly, this seems to have been as a result of the film *The Hand that Rocks the Cradle* released that year, in which a vicious, female murderer is called Peyton. This is one of many examples of the way in which parents will ignore the associations of a name if the sounds suit the zeitgeist.

VARIANT **Payton**

Phaedra *f*
In Greek mythology this is the name of Theseus's third wife, who falls in love with her step-son Hippolytos, with tragic results. In some versions of the story this is to punish him for having rejected the sensuality of the goddess Aphrodite in favour of the chastity of Artemis. The myth has been a popular subject in literature and art. The name comes from the Greek *phaidros*, 'bright', and is usually pronounced 'FAY-dra' in English, but 'FEE-dra' in modern Greek, a pronunciation which is followed in some other languages.

VARIANTS **Faedra, Faidra**

Phebe *see* **Phoebe**

Phelan *see* **Faolan**

Phelim *see* **Felim**

Phemie *see* **Euphemia**

Phia *see* **Sophia**

Philbert *m*
This name was originally *Filiberht*, being a Germanic name formed from the elements *fili*, 'very, much', and the common element *berht*, 'bright'. However, influenced by the Greek element *phil*, 'love', the spelling was

changed to a 'Ph', although the 'F' spelling remains in some languages. It was the name of a Frankish monk, born into the ruling elite of France in the early 7th century, who founded a number of monasteries including that at Jumièges. The name was popular in the Middle Ages, particularly in France, but is now rare.

VARIANTS *Dutch, German* **Filibert** *French* **Philbert, Filbert** *Italian* **Filiberto**

Philemon *m*
This is from the Greek for 'affectionate'. It is a rare name, but appears in the New Testament borne by a recipient of one of St Paul's epistles, who is said to have been martyred for his faith, while another tradition makes him bishop of Colossae. It was taken up by the Puritans in the 17th century, and is still occasionally found. The name was well established in Greece prior to St Paul. In mythology Philemon and Baucis were an old married couple rewarded for their hospitality when they entertained visiting gods who were in disguise.

VARIANTS *French* **Philémon** *Spanish* **Filemón**
☆ Philemon was the name the psychologist Carl Jung gave to a spirit guide who gave him crucial insights

Philip *m*
The Greek name *Philippos*, the source of Philip, means 'lover of horses'. It was a well-used name in ancient Greece, and was traditional in the Macedonian royal family, the father of Alexander the Great being one of the bearers. It was also the name of one of the twelve Apostles, making it a common name in the Christian world.

PET FORMS **Phil, Pip, Flip** • VARIANTS **Phillip** *Irish* **Philib** *Scots Gaelic* **Filib** *Czech, Dutch, Polish, Scandinavian* **Filip** *Finnish* **Vilppu** *French* **Philippe** *German* **Philipp** *Italian*

Filippo *Russian* **Filipp** *Spanish, Portuguese* **Felipe, Filipe**

★ Philip II of Macedonia (382–336 BC), king of Macedonia, military general, and father of Alexander the Great

Philippa *f*

This is the most common feminine form of PHILIP. In the Middle Ages it was usual in a number of languages for both men and women to be called the equivalent of Philip, with Philippa only being used in official Latin documents, a habit which persisted until at least the 17th century in England and the 18th century in France. Feminine forms of the name Philip came into general use in the 19th century.

PET FORMS **Pippa, Philly** • VARIANTS **Phillip(p)a, Philippina** *French* **Philippine** *Polish* **Filipa, Philipina** *Spanish* **Felipa** *Russian* **Filippa**

☆ Pippa in Robert Browning's 1841 poem 'Pippa Passes'

Phillice, Phillida, Phillis, Philly *see* Phyllis

Philomena *f*

Philomena, along with the masculine form *Philomenos*, comes from the Greek for 'strength' and 'love', so is interpreted as 'strongly beloved'. The name was used by early Christians, and was given to both sexes in the Middle Ages. The name became popular in the 19th century following the discovery in 1802 of a Latin inscription *Filomena pax tecum*, 'Peace be with you Philomena', in the Roman catacombs, along with some bones. These were thought to be the bones of a saint, and many miraculous healings were recorded at her tomb. However, later interpretation has suggested that the inscription merely means 'Peace be with you, greatly beloved one', and the name has rather fallen out of fashion,

particularly after the saint was dropped from the liturgical calendar in 1961.

VARIANTS **Filomena** *French* **Philomène**

Phineas *m*

Although the traditional interpretation of this biblical name is 'serpent's mouth', indicating an oracle, it is probably originally an Egyptian name *Panhsj* meaning 'dark-skinned, Nubian'. There are two characters in the Old Testament with this name. It was adopted by the Puritans in the 17th century and taken by them to the USA. It was regularly used there until falling out of favour in the 19th century.

PET FORM **Fin(n)** • VARIANTS **Phinehas, Phin(n)eaus** (the form used in the Authorized Version of the Bible) *Hebrew* **Pinchas**

★ Phineas T Barnum (1810–91), US showman

★ Pinchas Zukerman (1948–), Israeli violinist

Phoebe *f* Phoebus *m*

The Greek word *phoibe* means 'bright, shining'. Phoebus was one of the commonest epithets for Apollo, the god of the sun. It is rare as a masculine name, except in Yiddish, where it becomes FAIVISH and its variants. Phoebe was used as a title for Apollo's sister, Artemis, in her moon aspect. It was well used in the 17th century and has been a very popular name in recent years. In the past Phoebe has also been used as a pet form of EUPHEMIA.

VARIANT **Phebe**

Phoenix *mf*

A recent introduction, this name is more used for boys than girls, perhaps because it serves as a masculine substitute for the popular PHOEBE. In mythology the phoenix is a unique bird that regenerates itself in old age through fire. The spread of the name may have been helped by the prominent role the phoenix plays in J K Rowling's *Harry Potter* books.

Phylicia *see* **Felicity**

Phyllis *f*
This name comes from the Greek world *phyllis* meaning 'foliage', which in inflected forms takes a 'd' giving the less common name *Phyllida*. In mythology Phyllis is a maiden seduced by Demophon when he stops at the house of her father, the King of Thrace, on his way home from the Trojan war. He continues his journey home, but promises to return when he has assured his father he is safe. However, he is delayed by adverse winds and Phyllis, thinking she has been abandoned, hangs herself in despair. In pity, the gods turn her into an almond tree. This story is movingly told by the Latin poet Ovid, and from him passed into Western culture. Chaucer repeats the story in three different works in the 14th century, and a couple of centuries later the name is used regularly in pastoral and lyric poetry. As a given name it was well used in the earlier 20th century, but is currently out of favour. There is some overlap between variants of this name and of FELICITY.
PET FORMS **Phyl, Philly** • VARIANTS **Phillis, Phillice, Felic, Phillida, Phyllida, Phy(l)licia**
★ Phyllis Diller (1917–), US actress
★ Phyllida Law (1932–), Scottish actress

Pia *f* **Pius** *m*
The Latin *pius* (*pia* in the feminine) originally had the sense of 'dutiful', but rapidly acquired the meaning of 'pious'. Pius was the name chosen by twelve popes, but is little used as a first name by English Speakers, although is sometimes chosen by African parents.

In the past, Pia was mainly used by Italians or Scandinavians, but has enjoyed a certain popularity with English speakers in the last 30 years.
VARIANTS *French* **Pie** (m) *Italian* **Pio** (m)
★ Pia Zadora (1954–), US actress
★ St Pio of Pietrelcina (1887–1968), known as Padre Pio, Catholic priest, canonized in 2002

Piaras *see* **Peter, Pierce**

Pie *see* **Pia**

Piera *see* **Petra**

Pierce, Piers *m*
Piers was the standard medieval English form of the name now more commonly found as PETER, formed from the Norman French variant of the French *Pierre*. It was very popular in the Middle Ages, as can be seen by the number of surnames, such as Pierce, it produced. In Ireland the form *Pearce* is used with particular significance as the surname of Patrick Pearce, leader of the 1916 Easter Rising.
VARIANTS **Perse, Perce** *Irish* **Piaras, Perais**
★ Piers Morgan (1965–), English journalist
★ Pierce Brosnan (1953–), Irish-born US actor
☆ Piers Plowman, eponymous hero of a long 14th-century religious poem by William Langland

Pierette, Pierina *see* **Petra**

Piero, Pierre, Pierrick, Pierrot, Pierter *see* **Peter**

Piertrina *see* **Petra**

Piet, Pietro *see* **Peter**

Pietronella *see* **Petronella**

Pilar *f*
This is one of the many Spanish names derived from a title of the Virgin Mary, in this case *Nuestra Señora del Pilar*,

'Our Lady of the Pillar'. The title comes from the story that St James the Greater had a vision of Mary on a pillar at Saragossa. The name is pronounce with the stress on the second syllable.
PET FORM **Pili**
☆ Pilar is the gypsy wife of guerrilla leader Pablo, in Ernest Hemingway's 1940 novel of the Spanish Civil War *For Whom the Bell Tolls*

Pim *see* **William**

Pinchas *see* **Phineas**

Pio *see* **Pia**

Piotr *see* **Peter**

Pip *see* **Philip**

Piper *f*
This occupational surname was introduced to the general public in the 1950s by the actress Piper Laurie (née Rosetta Jacobs), but only became fashionable after it was given to one of the main characters in the television series *Charmed*. This was first shown in 1998, and Piper made its first appearance in the USA top 1000 first names, at 700, the following year. It has climbed steadily ever since, and a number of celebrities have chosen it for their children. It is occasionally used for boys.
VARIANT **Pyper**

Pippa *see* **Philippa**

Pista, **Pisti** *see* **Stephen**

Pius *see* **Pia**

Pixie *f*
Although this is usually a pet name, it is sometimes given as personal name. The origin of the vocabulary word is not known.
★ Pixie Geldof (1990–), daughter of Bob Geldof and Paula Yates
☆ Pixie Frou Frou is the name of the

daughter in satirical strip cartoon *Celeb*, by Charles Peattie, Russell Taylor and Mark Warren, featured in *Private Eye*

Placido *m*
This comes from Latin *placidus* meaning 'calm, untroubled'. It was a popular name among early Christians, and this form is still well used in Italy, Spain and Portugal.
FEMININES **Placida**, **Placidia** • VARIANTS
French **Placide** (m and f), **Placidie** (f)
★ Placido Domingo (1941–), Spanish tenor

Pól *see* **Paul**

Pollonia, **Pollonie** *see* **Apollo**

Polly *f*
This was originally a pet form of MOLLY, itself a pet form of MARY, whiwhich is now used as an independent name. The change from 'm' to 'p' was a common one in the past (see PEG). Polly has been used as an independent name since at least the 18th century, while blends such as *Pollyanna* tend to date from either the 19th or 20th century.
PET FORM **Poll**
☆ Pollyanna Whittier, optimistic orphan in Eleanor H Porter's series of children's novels, starting with *Pollyanna* in 1913

Pooja *see* **Puja**

Poonam *f*
Poonam is from the Sanskrit for 'full moon'.
VARIANTS **Poornima**, **Purnima** ('night of the full moon')

Poppy *f*
This is one of the flower names introduced in the late 19th century. It was well used in the first two decades of the 20th century, then declined until a recent revival in the UK, where it is

currently among the top 30 names for girls.

VARIANT **Poppie**

Porick see Patrick

Porter m

This is an occupational surname, either from the job of porter or of doorkeeper (from French *portier*), which is increasingly being used as a first name.

Portia f

The Roman family name *Porcius* (feminine *Porcia*), which probably came from the word for 'pig', was turned into a less porcine Portia in two of Shakespeare's plays, although the pronunciation 'POR-sha' remained unchanged. In *Julius Caesar*, Portia is the wife of Brutus, but modern use of the name probably comes from the heroine of *The Merchant of Venice*. This Portia is charming, witty and affectionate, as well as being able to take on a man's role and win her case as a lawyer. In the USA the name appears as *Porsha* or *Porsche*. There has been some debate about the source of these variants. Some regard them as the use of an élite brand name as a first name, a recognized but comparatively rare phenomenon. However, as the names are all pronounced identically, Portia must surely have had at least some influence on them.

Posy f

Posy started out as a nursery form of JOSEPHINE, but this has been lost to the more obvious sense of the term for a bunch of flowers. It is an uncommon given name.

VARIANT **Posey**

★ Posy Simmonds (1945–   ), English cartoonist and graphic novelist

Poul see Paul

Prabhakar m

This is a Hindu name, from the Sanskrit meaning 'maker of light'. It is one of the titles of the sun, and also a byname of the god Shiva.

VARIANTS **Prabhaukar, Prabhakara**

Prabhhjot mf

This is an Indian name from the Sanskrit meaning 'light of God', which is particularly favoured by Sikhs.

VARIANT **Prabhjo(i)t**

Pradeep, Prakash m

These comes from the Sanskrit for 'light', Pradeep having the secondary meaning of 'lantern' and Prakash the secondary meaning of 'glory'.

VARIANTS **Pradip, Preedeep**

Pranav m

At the beginning of Hindu texts there is usually a sacred syllable, transcribed in the West as *Om*. In Sanskrit it is called Pranav, which means 'shout of praise', and serves much the same function as 'amen' in Christian texts.

Praskoviya, Praskovya see Paraskevi

Pravin m

This is an Indian name, from the Sanskrit for 'skilful'.

VARIANT **Praveen**

Precious fm

Although this is often simply a term of affection used by parents for small children, it has been recorded as a given name since at least the 18th century. It is most common in the USA, particularly for girls, but use is growing in other English-speaking areas.

☆ Precious Ramotswe, Botswanan heroine of Alexander McCall Smith's *The No. 1 Ladies' Detective Agency* books, published from 1998

Preedeep see Pradeep

Prem *m* **Prema** *f*
These come from the Sanskrit word for
'love'. There are many names based
on this word, such as *Premal* (m) and
Premala (f), 'full of love'.

Prescilla, Prescillia *see* **Priscilla**

Presley *mf*
As a surname, Presley means 'priest's
meadow'. It is inextricably linked
with ELVIS Presley, and even if parents
are not using it as a first name with
specific reference to the singer, the
link must give it status. It is, perhaps
surprisingly, used more for girls than
boys. Use has been climbing steadily
in the USA since the late 1990s, and is
increasing elsewhere.

Preston *m*
As a place name Preston means
'village with a priest'. As a first name
Preston, presumably transferred
from the place-derived surname, has
been quite a popular choice for boys
in the USA for some years, and is
increasingly used in the UK.
★ Preston Sturges (1898–1959), US
  screenwriter, film director and inventor
★ (Samuel) Preston (1982–), lead
  singer of The Ordinary Boys

Prianka *see* **Priya**

Primo *m*
Primo is from the Latin *primus*
meaning 'first'. It was well used by
early Christians, and there are four
saints with the name. On occasion it
has been chosen for a first-born child.
It is used by Italians, Spanish and
Portuguese, but is rare among English
speakers.
★ Primo Levi (1919–87), Italian writer
  and chemist

Primrose *f*
This is one of the flower names
introduced in the later 19th century
which, like so many of them, peaked

in popularity in the 1920s, although
it is still used occasionally today. The
name of the flower, with its strong
associations with early spring, comes
from the Latin *prima rosa*, 'first rose [ie
flower]'. The Latin name of the family
to which the plant belongs, *Primula*, is
also sometimes used.

Prince *m* **Princess** *f*
These are pet names for children,
which are now being used as given
names. They both derive from the
Latin *princeps*, 'first, chief', which in
turn comes from *primus*, the source
of PRIMO. Spread has no doubt been
helped by the prominence of the singer
Prince.
★ Prince (1958–), US musician

Priscilla *f*
Priscilla is a pet form of the Roman
family name *Priscus* (*Prisca* in the
feminine) which in turn started out as
a nickname meaning 'ancient'. Both
a Prisca and a Priscilla are mentioned
in the New Testament, the first at 2
Timothy 4.19 and the latter at Acts
18.2, and they are thought to be the
same character. Both names were
adopted by the Puritans in the 16th
century, although Prisca is now very
rare. The name is now more common
in its short form CILLA.
PET FORMS **Cilla, Prissy** • VARIANTS **Pricillia,
Prescill(i)a**
★ Priscilla Beaulieu Presley (1945–),
  US actress and former wife of Elvis
  Presley

Priya *f*
This is a name based on the Sanskrit
word for 'beloved'.
VARIANTS **Prianka, Prisha, Priyasha**

Proinsias *see* **Frances**

Proserpine *see* **Persephone**

Prosper *m*
This comes from the same Latin

root meaning 'fortunate, happy' that supplies the English word 'prosperous'. It was popular in the ancient world, particularly in the 5th century, when several saints bearing the name appear to have lived. It was one of the names introduced to England by the Puritans, but is now rare. It was more popular in France, where one of the saints had been bishop of Orleans, but even there has been little used since the end of the 19th century.

★ Prosper Mérimée (1803–70), French novelist

☆ Prospero in Shakespeare's *The Tempest*

Prudence *f*

This name was famous in the past as a masculine name, through the Latin hymns of the 3rd-century theologian *Prudentius*, full name *Aurelius Prudentius Clemens*. As the word *prudens* had a meaning in Latin that was closer to 'wisdom' than the 'caution' associated with prudence in English, it has been suggested that the masculine name was originally used as a male equivalent of SOPHIA. The feminine *Prudentia* was also used in the past. Prudence was one of the virtue names enthusiastically taken up by the Puritans in the 17th and 18th centuries, and was used as the name of a character in John Bunyan's Christian allegory *The Pilgrim's Progress* (1674).

PET FORMS **Pru(e)**, **Purdy** • VARIANTS *Italian* **Prudenzio** *Spanish* **Prudencio**

★ Prue Leith (1940–), South African-born cookery expert

Prunella *f*

The immediate source of this name is something of a mystery. While it seems evident that it must derive ultimately from the Latin *prunis*, 'plum', root of the English word 'prune', it is not clear why it should come to be a name. Prunella also exists as a

vocabulary word; it is the name for a type of silk fabric, rarely encountered today. In addition, it is the Latin name for a wild flower, known in English as 'self-heal', and for the common bird otherwise known as the hedge sparrow or dunnock. But this does not really provide a reason for the name. One possible source is the French name *Prune*. This too means 'plum' and was introduced in France with the Revolutionary calendar of 1793. This replaced the names of months and saints' days, which traditionally influenced the choice of a child's name, with the names of agricultural animals and plants. Prune was the name day of 18 August.

PET FORM **Pru(e)**

★ Prunella Scales (1932–), English actress

Psyche *f*

The Greek word *psykhe* means both 'soul, spirit' and 'butterfly'. In the delightful myth of Cupid and Psyche, most notably told by Apuleius in his *Golden Ass* in the 2nd century AD, Psyche is a girl so beautiful that Cupid himself falls in love with her. His mother does her best to come between them, but after many trials they are happily reunited.

Puja *f*

This is a popular Indian female name, which comes from the Sanskrit word for 'worship, an act of devotion'. It is the term used for making an offering to a deity to ask for blessing.

VARIANT **Pooja**

Purdie, Purdy *see* **Perdita, Prudence**

Purnima *see* **Poonam**

Pyotr *see* **Peter**

Pyper *see* **Piper**

Q

Qasim *m* **Qasima** *f*
These are from the Arabic for 'divider, distributor' and refer to charitable acts.

Queenie *f*
This is a name with a number of sources. It can simply be a pet form either of Queen or of REGINA. In the 19th century, during the reign of Queen Victoria, it was a pet form of the name VICTORIA.

Quentin *m*
This comes from the Latin name *Quintinus*, originally used for a fifth child or son. It was popular in France in the Middle Ages, used in honour of St Quentin who was a 3rd-century missionary in northern France. Quentin had a revival in 19th-century Britain, and it is once again popular in France. The name is occasionally found for females.
VARIANTS **Quintin, Quinton, Quintus, Quintana** (f)
★ Quentin Bryce (1942–), first female Governor-General of Australia
★ Quentin Tarantino (1963–), US film director and screenwriter
★ Quintin Hogg, Viscount Hailsham (1907–2001), English jurist and politician

Quincy *m*
This was originally an aristocratic surname, derived from the lands held in the area of *Cuinchy* in Normandy. However, as a first name it is mainly used in the USA, most probably thanks to the fame of John Quincy Adams, 6th

US president. He was born in Quincy, Massachusetts, which was named after his maternal great grandfather, so his middle name may well have been chosen because it was his grandmother's maiden name, as was customary at the time.
VARIANT **Quincey**

Quinlan *m*
This is an Irish surname with more than one origin, which is coming into fashion as a first name.
★ Quinlan Terry (1937–), English architect

Quinn *mf*
This is a transferred use of the Irish surname, which means 'descendant of CONN'. It has been in regular use as a boy's name in the USA for a number of years. Since the mid-1990s it has been increasingly chosen for girls, perhaps under the influence of the successful television series *Dr Quinn, Medicine Woman*. Quinn is occasionally used as a short form of TARQUIN.
VARIANT **Quin**
☆ 'The Mighty Quinn', a 1967 song by Bob Dylan, also known as 'Quinn the Eskimo'

Quintana, Quintin, Quinton, Quintus *see* **Quentin**

Qusay *m*
This is an Arabic name, perhaps meaning 'distant', which was borne by an ancestor of the Prophet Muhammad.

R

Rab, Rabbie *see* **Robert**

Rabi *m* **Rabia** *f*
Arabic names meaning 'spring, springtime'.
VARIANT **Rabee(a)**

Rabih *m* **Rabiha** *f*
Arabic names meaning 'winner, gainer'.

Rabindra, Rabindranath *see* **Ravi**

Rachel *f*
This is the Hebrew word for 'ewe'. In the biblical book of Genesis Rachel is the second and favourite wife of Jacob; she does not get on with her sister and co-wife LEAH, who tricked Jacob into marrying her first. Rachel is the mother of JOSEPH and BENJAMIN. The name was mainly Jewish until it was taken up as part of the trend to use Old Testament names in the 17th century. At one time it was thought of as a typical Quaker name. It is currently a popular choice, and appears frequently in the spelling *Rachael*, based on the pronunciation. See also ROCHELLE.
PET FORMS **Rach, Rae, Ray, Shel, Shelley**
• VARIANTS **Rachael, Racheal, Raeshel, Rachelle, Rachyl** *Irish* **Ráichéal** *Arabic* **Rahil** *Italian* **Rachele** *Scandinavian* **Rakel** *Spanish* **Raquel** *Yiddish* **Ruchel**

Rachid, Rachida *see* **Rashid**

Radha *f*
This is the name of the favourite wife of the god Krishna. It means 'success' in Sanskrit.

Radwan *m*
An Arabic name meaning 'pleasure, contentment'.

Rae, Raelene *f*
Rae was originally a pet form of RACHEL, but is now often regarded as a feminine of RAYMOND or RAY. It is primarily an Australian name, although it has spread to other countries. Rae is often used in combination with other names and has developed elaborations such as Raelene.
VARIANTS **Rai(e), Raeleen, Raelyn**

Raegan *see* **Reagan**

Raeshel *see* **Rachel**

Raeven *see* **Raven**

Raf, Rafa, Rafael, Rafaello, Rafaël *see* **Raphael**

Rafe *see* **Ralph**

Raffaele *see* **Raphael**

Rafferty *mf*
Originally an Irish surname, which came from *O Robhartaigh*, 'descendant of *Robhartach*', Robhartach being an old Irish first name meaning 'wielder of prosperity'.

Rafi *m* **Rafia** *f*
An Arabic name meaning 'high ranking, exalted, noble', it is one of the titles of Allah. Rafi can also be a pet form of RAPHAEL.

Rafiq *m* **Rafiqa** *f*
These are from the Arabic for 'close friend' but can also be interpreted as meaning 'kind, gentle'.

Raga *see* **Raja**

Raganvald *see* **Ronald**

Raghid *m* **Raghida** *f*
Arabic names meaning 'carefree, enjoyable'.
VARIANT **Raghda**

Raghnall *see* **Randall, Reginald, Ronald**

Raghu *m*
This is an Indian name, from the Sanskrit for 'swift'.
VARIANT **Ragu**

Ragnar *see* **Rayner**

Rahil *see* **Rachel**

Rahim *m* **Rahima** *f*
Rahim means 'kind, compassionate' in Arabic and is one of the 99 names of Allah. See also ABDUL.
VARIANT **Raheem(a)**

Rahman *m* **Rahmat** *mf*
Rahman is an Arabic name meaning 'most compassionate', and is one of the titles of Allah. Rahmat is closely related and means 'mercy, compassion, kindness'. In Islamic tradition Rahmat was the name of a granddaughter of Yusuf [Joseph] and wife of Ayyub [Job].

Rai *see* **Rae**

Raibeart *see* **Robert**

Ráichéal *see* **Rachel**

Raiden *m*
Raiden is one of the major characters in the *Mortal Kombat* video games. It has started to be used in the USA as a given name, probably because it fits in with the craze there for any name that rhymes with AIDAN. As the character in the game is a thunder god, the name would appear to be modelled on that of the Japanese thunder god, *Raijin*.
VARIANT **Rayden**

Raie *see* **Rae**

Raimonda, Raimondo, Raimund, Raimunde, Raimundo *see* **Raymond**

Raina *see* **Regina**

Rainard *see* **Reynard**

Raine *see* **Regina**

Rainer, Rainier *see* **Rayner**

Rianna *see* **Adrianna**

Raj *m*
A popular Indian name meaning 'prince, king' in Sanskrit. It can also be found as the short form of a number of other names including *Rajesh*, 'ruler of kings', *Rajinder* or *Rajendra*, 'lord of kings', *Rajneesh* or *Rajnish*, 'lord of the night'. *Rajni* or *Rani*, 'queen', and *Rajkamari*, 'princess', are female counterparts.
VARIANTS **Raja, Ranee**

Raja *f*
An Arabic name meaning 'hope, anticipation'.
VARIANT **Raga**

Rajiv *m*
This is an Indian name, literally meaning 'striped', but used for the sacred blue lotus.
VARIANTS **Rajeev, Rajib**
★ Rajiv Gandhi (1944–91), assassinated Indian prime minister

Rajmund *see* **Raymond**

Rakel *see* **Rachel**

Rakesh *m*
An Indian name meaning 'lord of the full moon' formed from the Sanskrit *raka*, 'day of the full moon', and *isha*, 'lord, ruler'.

Ralph *m*
This is the contracted form of the Old Norse name *Rathulfr* formed from the elements *rath*, 'counsel', and *ulfr*, 'wolf'. It was introduced to Britain by

Viking invaders before the Norman Conquest, but use was later reinforced by *Radulf*, the Norman form of the same name, and became *Ralf* in the Middle Ages. By the 17th century it was often spelt *Rafe*, to reflect the preferred pronunciation at the time, which is still sometimes found. The spelling Ralph was introduced in the 18th century to make the name look more classical. The current preferred pronunciation sounding the 'l' is a spelling pronunciation which appears to date from the beginning of the 20th century.

PET FORM **Ralphie** • VARIANTS **Rafe**, **Ralf** *French* **Raoul** *Italian, Spanish* **Raul**
- ★ Ralph Waldo Emerson (1803–82), US poet and essayist
- ★ Ralph Vaughn Williams (1872–1958), English composer
- ☆ Ralph Wiggum in the television cartoon series *The Simpsons*

Rama *m*
Rama is the Sanskrit for 'pleasing' and another name for the god Vishnu. It is also a shortening of the name *Ramachandra* (*chandra* means 'moon'), the hero of the *Ramayana* who is regarded as an avatar of Vishnu.
VARIANT **Ram**

Ramadan *f*
This is the Arabic name for the ninth month of the lunar calendar, during which Muslims fast.

Ramadeep *mf*
This is an Indian name, particularly associated with Sikhs, formed from RAMA and *deep*, 'light, lamp'.

Ramon *see* Raymond

Ramona *f*
This is the feminine of *Ramon*, the Spanish form of RAYMOND. It spread to the English-speaking world by way of Helen Hunt Jackson's 1884 novel *Ramona* and its later film adaptations,

and also by a 1959 song called 'Ramona'.
- ☆ Ramona Povey, battle-axe wife in the long-running (1959–76) BBC radio series *The Navy Lark*

Ramsay *m*
This is a Scottish surname used as a first name. Its origin is in a place name in Huntingdonshire derived from Old English *hramsa*, 'ramsons, wild garlic'. The surname was introduced to Scotland when David of Scotland, exiled to England in 1093, returned to the Scottish court with a number of close followers from the East Anglian area. They took with them surnames such as Ramsay, GRAHAM and LINDSAY, all of which are now regarded as typically Scottish. The name is mainly confined to Scotland, and strongly associated with Prime Minister (James) Ramsay MacDonald (1866–1937).
VARIANT **Ramsey**

Ran *see* Randall, Randolf

Rana *f*
Rana is an Arabic name meaning 'an eye-catching object' based on the Arabic *rana*, 'to gaze'. See also RANIA.

Ranait *see* Ronit

Ranald *see* Ronald

Randa[1] *f*
This is the Arabic word for a type of sweetly-scented tree that grows in deserts.

Randa[2] *see* Miranda

Randall *m*
This is a surname used as a first name. It comes from a medieval pet form of RANDOLF and similar names. In Ireland Randall is used to anglicize *Raghnall*, the Irish form of REGINALD.
PET FORMS **Ran**, **Randy** • VARIANTS **Randle**, **Randal**

★ Randy Newman (1943–), US singer-songwriter

☆ Randle Patrick McMurphy is the lead character in Ken Kesey's 1962 novel *One Flew Over the Cuckoo's Nest*

Randi, Randie *see* Miranda

Randolf *m*
After the Norman Conquest, the Old Norse name *Randulfr* was replaced by the Norman equivalent Randolf, formed from *rand*, 'shield rim', and *wulf*, 'wolf'. The name became rare after the Middle Ages, but was revived in the 18th century when it was often spelt *Randolph*, influenced by classical Greek spelling.
PET FORMS **Ran, Randy, Dolph, Dolf**
★ Randolph Scott (1898–1987), US actor
★ Randolph Churchill (1911–68), English journalist and politician, son of Sir Winston Churchill and named after his grandfather Lord Randolph Churchill (1849–95)

Randy *see* Miranda, Randall, Randolf

Ranee, Rani *see* Raj

Ranerio *see* Rayner

Rania *f*
This name comes from the Arabic for 'gazing' and is used with reference to gazing at a loved one. See also RANA.
VARIANTS **Raniyah, Ranya**

Raniero *see* Rayner

Ranjit *m*
This comes from a Sanskrit word that covers the meanings 'coloured, pleased, delighted'.
★ Ranjit Singh (1780–1839), founder of the Sikh kingdom which covered most of the Punjab and Kashmir

Ranulf *m*
This is a Scottish name, introduced by Norse settlers in the early Middle Ages.

It is a form of the old Norse *Raginulfr*, from *regin*, 'advice, decision', and *ulfr*, 'wolf'. Some regard it as a form of RANDOLF. As with related names, the 'f' appears as 'ph' in later spellings.
PET FORM **Ran** • VARIANT **Ranolph**
★ Sir Ranulph Fiennes (1944–), English explorer and adventurer

Ranya *see* Rania

Raoul *see* Ralph

Raphael *m*
This is borne by one of the great archangels in Jewish tradition. He is particularly associated with healing, and his name comes from the Hebrew for 'God has healed'. Raphael has been particularly popular in France recently, and is growing in use in the UK, where it has never been common.
PET FORMS **Raph(i), Rafa, Rafi** • VARIANTS *Dutch* **Rafaël, Raf** *French* **Raphaël** *German* **Rafael** *Italian* **Raffaele, Rafaello** *Spanish* **Rafael, Rafa**
★ Raffaello Santi or Sanzio (1483–1520), Italian painter usually simply known as Raphael
★ Rafael 'Rafa' Nadal (1986–), Spanish tennis player

Raphaella *f*
This is the feminine form of RAPHAEL which has recently been taken up as a fashionable name in the UK.
VARIANT **Raphaela**

Raquel *f*
This is the Spanish form of RACHEL, which has come into use among English speakers thanks to the fame of US actress Raquel Welch (Raquel Tejada, b.1940).
VARIANT **Raquelle**

Rasha *f*
An Arabic name meaning 'young gazelle'.

Rashad, Rashid *m*

These are related Arabic names, Rashad being from the Arabic for 'right guidance, integrity of conduct', and Rashid being from 'wise, rightly guided'. There is a further name, *Rashed*, 'right-minded, rightly guided'. Rashad is one of the Arabic names taken up by African Americans, resulting in a number of new coinages based on *Rash-* as a combining form.
FEMININES **Rasheda, Rashida** • VARIANT **Rachid**

Rasmus *see* Erasmus

Rastus *see* Erastus

Rasul *m*

An Arabic name meaning 'prophet, messenger'.

Rathnait *see* Ronit

Raul *see* Ralph

Raven *mf*

The large black bird called the raven was revered by followers of the Old Norse god Odin (who used the name *Hrafn* 'raven', both by itself and in compound names), as well as by a number of West Coast Native American tribes. Ravens also play a significant part in Celtic mythology. Raven is one of the standard comparisons for blackness, and it was probably usually with reference to black hair or skin that this name first came into use in the USA in the 1970s. However, it must have become detached from such specific associations by the time it peaked in popularity there in the late 1990s. It is most often used for girls. It is tempting to see the occasional use of *Ravin* as a first name as a respelling of this name.
VARIANTS **Ravyn, Raeven**

★ Raven-Symoné (1985–), US actress and singer who has made the name better known in the USA

Ravi *m*

This is the Sanskrit for 'sun', and is one of the names of the Hindu sun god. It is a popular Indian name, and often crops up in fiction as being typically Indian. The variant *Ravindra* combines Ravi with the name of INDRA, mightiest of gods, giving a sense 'lord of the sun'.
VARIANTS **Rabindra, Rabindranath**

★ Ravi Shankar (1920–), Indian musician and composer

★ Rabindranath Tagore (1861–1941), Indian philosopher and poet whose works had a major influence on Western understanding of Indian thought

Rawiya *f*

This is an Arabic name from a term used for a reciter or transmitter of classical Arabic poetry.
VARIANT **Rawia**

Ray *mf*

Usually a pet form of RAYMOND or RACHEL, but also used for other names and as an independent name.
VARIANT **Rae**

Raya *see* Regina

Rayden *see* Raiden

Raymond *m*

The Germanic name *Reginmund*, formed from *ragin*, 'advice', and *mund*, 'protector', became *Reimund* or *Raimund* in the mouths of the Normans who brought it to England. There are rare English names that can act as feminine variants listed under RAE, but other languages have regular feminines.
PET FORM **Ray** • VARIANTS **Raymund** *Ireland* **Redmond** *French* **Raymonde** (f) *German* **Raimunde, Raimund, Reimund** *Italian* **Raimonda** (f), **Raimondo** *Polish* **Rajmund** *Spanish* **Raimundo, Ramon, Raymundo, Ramona** (f)

★ Raymond Blanc (1949–   ), UK-based French chef and restaurateur

☆ *Everybody Loves Raymond*, US sitcom starring Ray Romano

Raynard *see* Reynard

Rayner *m*
The Germanic name *Reginhar*, from *ragin*, 'advice', and *heri*, 'army', was one of those brought over by the Normans, and was common in the Middle Ages in the form Rayner. Thereafter it was rare, but was back in use by the end of the 18th century, in at least some cases reintroduced from the surname which had survived. Other uses may have come from Continental forms which had never died out.

PET FORM **Ray** • VARIANTS Dutch **Reinier** *French* **Rainier** *German* **Rainer** *Italian* **Raniero, Nero** *Scandinavian* **Ragnar, Regner** *Spanish* **Ranerio**

★ Prince Rainier III of Monaco (1923–2005)

★ Rainer Maria Rilke (1875–1926), Austrian lyric poet

☆ Rainier Wolfcastle, Austrian-American action film star in the television cartoon *The Simpsons*

Raza *m* Razia *f*
These come from an Arabic word meaning 'contentment, satisfaction', used with reference to winning approval from Allah.

VARIANTS **Raziyah, Riza, Rida**

Razin *m* Razina *f*
Arabic names meaning 'calm, composed, self-possessed'.

Reagan, Regan *mf*
There is considerable confusion over the origin and history of these names. The problem is augmented by the number of variant spellings which can make it unclear whether the user means the name to be pronounced with the first syllable to rhyme with

'me' or 'may'. Reagan can at least be clearly identified as often being a transference of the Irish surname Re(a)gan from *O Riagain*, 'descendant of *Riagan*', a name which may mean 'impatient'. Reagan is often associated with the US presidency of Ronald Reagan, but the name was already in use, even for girls, before he became a prominent politician. The form Regan can obviously be linked to the wicked daughter of that name in Shakespeare's *King Lear*, but this does not seem a likely source of its popularity. More significant is the use of Regan for the name of the possessed girl in the 1971 novel by William Peter Blatty, *The Exorcist*, and the very successful film adaptation made in 1973. This coincides with the fact that both Reagan and Regan start being used as girls' names in the USA around 1974. Although it may seem unlikely that parents would want to choose the name of this character, there are plenty of examples of this sort of transference, if the sound of the name is in vogue at the time. See a further example at GAGE. Blatty presumably got the name from Shakespeare. It has been suggested that Shakespeare's name is a form of the Irish *riogan*, 'queen', which is pronounced 'ree-gan'. An alternative interpretation is that Regan represents a direct shortening of the name REGINA, also meaning 'queen'.

VARIANTS **Reegan, Reigan, Re(e)gin, Raegan**

Réaltán *f*
This is a modern Irish name meaning 'little star'. It is pronounced 'RAYL-tawn' or 'RAYL-teen'.

VARIANT **Réaltín**

Reanna *see* Rhiannon

Rebecca *f*
In the Old Testament (Genesis 24–27) Rebecca is the wife of Isaac

and the mother of Jacob and Esau. The meaning of the name is not known and, as she was not Hebrew herself, may not have come from that language. It was one of the names taken up by the Puritans, and has been well used since the early 20th century.

PET FORMS **Becca, Beck(y), Beckie, Reba** • VARIANTS **Rebeka, Rebe(c)kah** *Hebrew* **Rivka, Riva** *Spanish* **Rebeca**

☆ Rebecca is the name of the learned and spirited Jewish woman in Sir Walter Scott's 1820 novel *Ivanhoe*
☆ Rebecca de Winter, deceased rival of the narrator in the 1938 novel *Rebecca*, by Daphne du Maurier, which was adapted for film in 1940
☆ *Rebecca of Sunnybrook Farm*, 1903 children's novel by Kate Douglas Wiggin

Red *mf*
This is usually a nickname for someone with red hair, and is normally given to males. There are many standard first names, such as RORY, inspired by hair colour.

★ Red Skelton (1913–97), US actor
★ Red Buttons (1919–2006), US actor

Redmond *m*
This is the anglicized form of *Réamann*, the Irish form of RAYMOND.
VARIANT **Redmund**

★ Redmond O'Hanlon (1640–81), Irish outlaw
★ Redmond O'Hanlon (1947–), English travel writer

Redvers *m*
A name which had a brief vogue in the early 20th century. It was used in honour of Sir Redvers Buller (1836–1908), who was prominent as a general in the Boer War. While his actions were often criticized back home, his care for the soldiers under his command made him popular with the troops. Buller was a Devon man, and his unusual first name seems to

have been that of a local noble family in the 11th century.

Reece *see* **Rhys**

Reegan, Reegin *see* **Reagan**

Reenie *see* **René**

Rees, Reese *see* **Rhys**

Regan, Regin *see* **Reagan**

Regina *f*
This is the Latin word for 'queen'. There was a 3rd-century saint of the name, and it can also be used in honour of the Virgin Mary, Queen of the Heavens (*Regina Coeli* in Latin).

PET FORMS **Gena, Gina, Queenie** • VARIANTS **Regena, Raine** *Bulgarian* **Raina, Raya** *French* **Reine, Marie-Reine, Régine**

Reginald, Reynold *m*
In the Middle Ages the French name *Reinald* or *Reynaud* was written in Latin *Reginaldus*, showing an awareness of the name's Germanic origins in the elements *ragin*, 'advice', and *wald*, 'rule'. The spoken form became Reynold, a popular name in the Middle Ages. Variants based on the Latin spelling began to appear in the 15th century, but then died out. The name was revived in the 19th century, probably thanks to its appearance in Walter Scott's 1820 novel *Ivanhoe*. Its success in the 19th and early 20th centuries means that it is now out of favour, although the pet forms are occasionally given as independent names. RAYNER is a related name. See also RONALD.

PET FORMS **Reg(gie), Rex** • VARIANTS *Welsh* **Rheinallt** *Dutch* **Reinout** *French* **Renaud, Reynaud** *German* **Reinhold** *Italian* **Rinaldo** *Spanish* **Reinaldo, Reynaldo**

★ Reginald Bosanquet (1932–84), English newsreader
☆ Reginald 'Reggie' Perrin in David

Nobbs's novels and the television series

Regine, Régine, Reine *see* **Regina**

Régis *see* **Rex**

Regner *see* **Rayner**

Reigan *see* **Reagan**

Reimund *see* **Raymond**

Reinaldo, Reinhold *see* **Reginald**

Reinier *see* **Rayner**

Reinout *see* **Reginald**

Reis, Reise, Reisel *see* **Rose**

Remi, Remigio *see* **Rémy**

Remus *m*
Remus was the name of one of the two legendary founders of the city of Rome. He and his twin brother Romulus were abandoned as babies and raised by a she-wolf. When they began to build Rome they quarrelled over which of them would give his name to the city and Romulus killed his brother.
VARIANT *Italian, Spanish* **Remo**
☆ Remus Lupin, wizard and werewolf in the *Harry Potter* books by J K Rowling

Rémy *m*
This name has a special place in French culture, for it was St Rémy who converted the Frankish king Clovis in the 5th century and made what was to become France a Christian country. Rémy comes from the Roman name *Remigius*, from the Latin *remigis*, 'oarsman'.
VARIANTS **Remi** *Italian, Spanish* **Remigio**

Renan *see* **Ronan**

Renard *see* **Reynard**

Renaud *see* **Reginald**

René *m* **Renée** *f*
This name comes from the Latin *Renatus* meaning 'reborn'. In early Christian times it was not uncommon to adopt a new name at baptism, to indicate a new start in life, and Renatus was a popular choice for this. Nowadays, this significance has largely been lost. English speakers often drop the accent, and Rene, which is also a diminutive of IRENE, can be found as a feminine form.
VARIANTS **Re(e)nie, Rena(e), Rena** *Italian, German, Spanish* **Renata** *German* **Renate** (f) *Italian, Spanish* **Renato**

Renie *see* **Irene, René**

Renzo *see* **Laurence**

Reuben *m*
The biblical book of Genesis 29.32 explains this name as meaning 'behold a son'. It was borne by one of Jacob's sons who later founded one of the twelve tribes of Israel. Reuben was mainly confined to the Jewish community until the Protestant Reformation. By the 19th century the name was considered old-fashioned and only used by bumpkins, which led to the development of the US slang word 'rube'. The spelling *Ruben* is found in Spanish and several other languages, and is currently vastly more usual in the USA, although Reuben still dominates in the UK. The name is currently enjoying a considerable revival.
VARIANTS **Ruben** *Hebrew* **Reuven**

Rex *m*
This is the Latin word for 'king', which appears to have only come into use as a first name in the 19th century. Initially it seems to have been primarily given as a pet form of REGINALD. The French name *Régis*, bestowed in honour of the French saint

Jean-François Régis, comes from the same Latin root as Rex.

VARIANT *French* **Régis**

★ Rex Whistler (1905–44), English artist
★ Sir Rex Harrison (1908–90), English actor
☆ Rex Gascoigne in George Eliot's 1875 novel *Daniel Deronda*

Reynald *see* **Ronald**

Reynaldo *see* **Reginald**

Reynard *m*

This is the French form of the Germanic name formed from *regin*, 'advice', and *wald*, 'brave'. The meaning of the name made it suitable for the devious fox found in the medieval beast stories that often go under the collective title of *Reynard the Fox*.

VARIANTS **Rainard, Raynard, Renard**

Reynaud, Reynold *see* **Reginald**

Rhamantus *f*

A modern Welsh name meaning 'romantic'.

Rhea *f*

This name is identified with Rhea Silvia, mother of ROMULUS and REMUS in Roman legend, but this is quite likely to be a coincidence. Rhea was probably originally a respelling of *Ria*, pet form of MARIA. Certainly the large, flightless bird bearing the name is unlikely to be a source.

★ Rhea Perlman (1948–   ), US actress

Rheanna *see* **Rhiannon**

Rheinallt *see* **Reginald**

Rhett *m*

This name was introduced to the general public by Margaret Mitchell in her 1936 novel *Gone with the Wind*. This book has had a major influence on modern naming habits, although Rhett has been less successful than other names popularized by the work such as ASHLEY and MELANIE. The story is set in the American Civil War and Mitchell drew extensively on real people involved in the conflict for her choice of names. Consequently her use of this name for the charming Rhett Butler can be linked to Robert Bramwell Rhett (1800–76) a prominent politician of the time. The rare *Rhetta* has been described as a feminine form of Rhett, but may be derived from *Margaretta* (MARGARET).

Rhiain *f*

This is the Welsh word for 'maiden'. It is sometimes found combined with *wen*, 'fair, blessed', to form *Rhianwen*. It is also used as a pet form of RHIANNON.

VARIANTS **Rhian, Rhianedd, Rhianydd, Rhianu, Rian**

Rhiannon *f*

In the outstanding collection of medieval Welsh stories known as *The Mabinogion*, Rhiannon is a queen unjustly accused of killing her own son. She is a mysterious figure with strange powers, and is probably the faint echo of a Celtic goddess, for the name appears to be a form of *Rigantona*, meaning 'great queen', recorded from Roman times. Rhiannon was not used as a given name until the 20th century, but has now reached far beyond Wales. In the course of this spread it has developed a number of variants which make it conform more to English name forms. The current craze for introducing extra 'h's in names may owe much to this name.

VARIANTS **Rhianon, Rhianna, Rhiann, Rheanna, Rianna** (also a pet form of **Adrianna**) **Reanna**

★ Rhianna (1983–   ), English R&B singer
★ Rihanna (1988–   ), Barbadian singer

Rhidian *m*

This is a Welsh name of uncertain

meaning, although it may be connected with the Welsh word *rhyd*, 'ford'. It comes from the place name of Llanrhidian, which should mean 'the church of St Rhidian', but may in fact be a corruption of something else.

VARIANT **Rhydian**

★ Rhidian Brook (1964–), Welsh writer and broadcaster
★ Rhidian Roberts (1983–), Welsh singer

Rhisiart *see* Richard

Rhoda *f*

This is from the Greek *rhoda*, 'rose', which, since the island of Rhodes got its name from the same source, can also be interpreted as 'woman from Rhodes'. It appears in the Bible (Acts 12), as belonging to a servant of Mary, the mother of John. In the Scottish Highlands it has been found as a feminine of RODERICK. The name was popular c.1900, but is seldom used now.

☆ *Rhoda* was a popular US sitcom in the 1970s

Rhodri *m*

This is an old Welsh name found in early legend and genealogies. It is formed from the elements *rhod*, 'wheel, disc, orb', and *rhi*, 'ruler'. It is sometimes regarded as the Welsh equivalent of the Germanic name RODERICK, but is unconnected.

VARIANT **Rhodrhi**

★ Rhodri Morgan (1939–), Welsh politician

Rhona *f*

This name seems to have appeared in Scotland c.1870, and has been analysed either as a Highland feminine of RONALD, or as a use of the name of the Hebridean island Rona (Gaelic for 'rough island'), with the spelling in both cases influenced by RHODA. It was spread further afield in the 1930s with

the creation of the long-lasting fashion label Rhona Roy, but the name is once again mainly confined to Scotland. In Wales it is used as a short form of RHONWEN.

VARIANT **Rona**

Rhonda *f*

This is probably a modern blend of RHODA and RHONA, although it can be interpreted as Welsh *rhon*, 'spear', combined with *da*, 'good', or as a form of Rhondda, a Welsh valley called after its river, the name of which means 'noisy'.

★ Rhonda Fleming (1923–), US actress who gave the name prominence and for whom it may have been coined
☆ 'Help Me, Rhonda', a 1965 song by The Beach Boys

Rhonwen *f*

Welsh name formed from the elements *rhon*, 'lance', and *wen*, 'fair', indicating a slim beauty. In Welsh texts it is used for the daughter of Hengist known as ROWENA in English texts.

PET FORMS **Rhona** • VARIANT **Ronwen**

Rhun *m*

Pronounced *rin*, this is an old Welsh name of unknown meaning. Rhun ap Maelgwn or Rhun Hir ('the Tall') was a (probably mythological) king of the 6th century in Gwynedd.

FEMININE **Rhunedd**

☆ Prince Rhun is a character in Lloyd Alexander's *Chronicles of Prydain* children's books, which draw heavily on Welsh mythology

Rhydderch *m*

This is an old Welsh name meaning 'reddish-brown' and is likely to be one of the names that come from hair colour. It is frequently found in early Welsh history and legend, with its most famous bearer being Rhydderch Hael ('the Generous') of the 6th century, commemorated as one of

'the Three Generous Men of the Isle of Britain' in Welsh lore. It is often anglicized as RODERICK.
VARIANT **Riderch**

Rhydian see Rhidian

Rhys, Reece mf
This is an old Welsh name usually interpreted as meaning 'ardour', although some would prefer 'hero'. The spellings Reece and *Rees* evolved as surnames derived from the first name. In Wales it is always masculine, but since becoming popular elsewhere it has also come to be used as a feminine.
VARIANT **Rees(e)**

★ Rhys Ifans (1968–), Welsh actor
★ Reese Witherspoon (1976–), US actress
☆ Rhys Williams is a character in the television series *Torchwood*

Ria see Maria, Rhea

Rian see Rhiain, Ryan

Rianna see Rhiannon

Ribbon f
An unusual first name, based on the vocabulary word.
VARIANT **Ribon**

Ric, Rick see Cedric, Derek, Eric, Richard

Rica see Frederica

Richard m
Long one of the core Germanic names in English use, this name is currently being used surprisingly little by British parents, although it is still popular in the USA. It is formed from the elements *ric*, 'power, rule', and *hard*, 'brave'. It became a royal name in the 12th century with the accession of King Richard I, 'the Lionheart', with whom the name is still strongly associated. Its steady popularity from

then on is attested by the numerous pet forms it developed.
FEMININES **Ric(c)arda, Richelle, Richardine, Richenda** • PET FORMS **Dick, Dickon, Dicky, Rick, Ricky, Rich(ie), Ritchie** • VARIANTS *Irish* **Risteárd** *Scots Gaelic* **Ruiseart** *Welsh* **Rhisiart** *Dutch* **Rikhart** *German* **Ri(c)kert** *Italian* **Riccardo** *Polish* **Ryszard** *Spanish* **Ricardo, Rico**

Richelle f
This is used as a feminine form of RICHARD but in Ireland, particularly as *Richella* or *Richael*, it is also the name of a virgin saint whose feast day is 19 May.

Rickert see Richard

Ricky mf
A pet form of any name containing the element *ric*, most commonly RICHARD, ERIC and FREDERICK. For girls it is usually a pet form of ERICA. Like all such forms it is also used as an independent name.
VARIANTS **Rikki, Ricki(e)**

★ Ricki Lake (1968–), US actress and chat-show host

Rico see Henry, Richard

Rida see Raza

Riderch see Rhydderch

Ridley m
A surname, from one of a number of place names with various origins, used as a first name.
★ Sir Ridley Scott (1937–), English film director

Ridwan m Ridwana f
An Arabic name meaning 'contentment, satisfaction'.
VARIANT **Rizwa(a)n(a)**

Rika see Frederica

Rike see Frederick

Rikert, Rikhart see Richard

Rikke see Frederick

Rikki see **Ricky**

Riley mf
This is a surname used as a first name. The surname can either be English, derived from a place name, or a variant of the Irish Reilly, 'descendant of *Raghallach*', a name of unknown meaning. It has become a popular choice with parents in recent years. The expression 'living the life of Riley' may have helped its spread.
VARIANTS **Rilee, Rylie, Ryleigh**

Rilla f
A name which came into use with Lucy Maud Montgomery's *Anne of Green Gables* books, in which Rilla is the name of Anne's youngest child. It is a shortening of *Marilla*, which is in turn a pet form of Amarilla, a variant of AMARYLLIS, in use in North America in the 18th and 19th centuries.

Rima f
A name created by Henry Hudson in his 1904 novel *Green Mansions* for a strange, wild girl who lives in the South American jungle. This romantic story was enormously successful and the name came into quiet use for a while, but is now very rare. *Rim* or *Rima* is also an Arabic name meaning 'white antelope'.

Rinaldo see **Reginald**

Rio see **River**

Riona see **Catherine, Catriona**

Risteárd see **Richard**

Rita f
This short form of *Margarita* (see MARGARET) was a popular choice of name in the 1940s and 50s, but is now rarely chosen.
★ Rita Hayworth (1918–87), US film actress and dancer
★ Rita Tushingham (1942–), English actress

☆ 'Lovely Rita Meter Maid', a Beatles song from 1967
☆ Rita Skeeter, sensationalist reporter in the *Harry Potter* books by J K Rowling
☆ *Educating Rita*, a 1979 play by Willy Russell

Ritchie see **Richard**

Riva see **Rebecca**

Rivan, Riven see **Ruthven**

River, Rio mf
River is a word that has come into use as first name largely under the influence of the actor River Phoenix (1970–93). The Spanish equivalent, Rio, is also used, for both sexes; for boys it has been popularized by the English footballer Rio Ferdinand (b.1978), while its use for girls has been encouraged by the Duran Duran song.
☆ River Tam is a character in the cult television sci-fi series *Firefly*

Rivka see **Rebecca**

Riza see **Raza**

Rizwaan, Rizwaana, Rizwan, Rizwana see **Ridwan**

Roald m
A Norwegian name formed from the Old Norse elements *hrothr*, 'fame', and *valdr*, 'rule', introduced to the English-speaking world by the children's author Roald Dahl (1916–90).

Roanaid see **Ronit**

Roar see **Roger**

Robert m
A Germanic name formed from the elements *hrod*, 'fame', and *berht*, 'bright, famous'. Like many such names it was introduced by the Normans, replacing the Old English equivalent *Hreobeorht*. It was a common name in the Middle Ages and

has remained consistently popular ever since. There are two obsolete short forms, *Hob* (source of hobgoblin) and *Dob*. RUPERT is the same name arrived at by a different route.

PET FORMS **Bob, Bobby, Bert, Rob(bie), Robin** • VARIANTS *Irish* **Roibéard** *Scots Gaelic* **Raibeart** *Scottish* **Rab(bie)** *Welsh* **Robat, Hopcyn** *Dutch* **Robrecht, Robbe(rt)** *Italian, Spanish* **Roberto**

Roberta *f*

This is the most common of the feminine forms of ROBERT. It came into fashion in the 1870s and remained well used into the 20th century. In the USA it appeared in the top 100 names for girls into the 1950s. There is a long tradition in Scotland of forming feminines from masculine names that are not regularly feminized elsewhere. Since historic characters such as Robert the Bruce and Robert Burns have made Robert an esteemed name in Scotland, it is not surprising that Roberta has been well used there, and that it has developed other feminine forms which include *Robena* or *Robina* (see ROBIN).

PET FORMS **Bobbi, Bobbie, Berta** • VARIANT *Italian, Spanish* **Robertina**

★ Roberta Flack (1937–), US singer
☆ *Roberta* was a Jerome Kern musical of 1933, filmed with Fred Astaire and Ginger Rogers in 1935

Robhartach *see* **Rafferty**

Robin *mf*

This was originally a pet form of ROBERT, but has long been used as an independent name. The spelling *Robyn* is an old one, but is now considered a modern variant of Robin. Although both spellings are used for both sexes, there is a tendency for Robin to be used as a masculine name and Robyn as a feminine. Robin, or Robyn, has only been used as a feminine since the middle of the 20th century; prior

to that, the standard form was *Robina*. This was widespread in the 17th and 18th centuries; by the 19th century, it had become more common in Scotland than in England, and now it has almost died out. Robin has seldom been chosen in the USA, except for quiet use in recent years.

FEMININE **Robina** • VARIANTS **Robyn, Robynne**

★ Robin Hood (c.1250–c.1350), semi-legendary English outlaw

Robson *m*

This is a surname, meaning 'son of ROB(ERT)', used as a first name.

★ Robson Green (1964–), English actor. In his case he was given his grandmother's maiden name
★ Robson 'Robinho' de Souza (1984–), Brazilian footballer

Robyn *see* **Robin**

Rocco *m*

This is the Italian form of a Germanic name from the element *hrok*, 'rest', or perhaps a similar word meaning 'rook'. It came into use because of a French man, known in France as St Roch, who stopped while on pilgrimage to Rome to nurse plague victims until he died of the disease himself. He subsequently became the patron saint of the sick. The pet form is sometimes used as an independent name or nickname.

PET FORM **Rocky**

★ Sir Rocco Forte (1945–), English hotelier
★ Rocky Marciano (1923–69), US heavyweight boxing champion

Rochelle *f*

Although this appears to be a French first name, and indeed there is a French word *rochelle*, meaning 'little rock', found in the name of the port of La Rochelle, it is not actually used in France. It is probably best to regard Rochelle either as an invented name or as a variant of RACHEL. As it first appeared in US statistics in 1921, it is conceivable that the name was popularized by soldiers returning from World War I, as LORRAINE was, but this is a tenuous link. What made the name generally known was the popularity of the US film actress Rochelle Hudson (1916–72) who was prominent in the 1930s.

VARIANT **Roshelle**

Rocky *see* **Rocco**

Rod, **Roddy** *see* **Roderick**, **Rodney**

Roderick *m*
A Germanic name formed from the elements *hrod*, 'fame', and *ric*, 'rule, power'. Introduced by the Normans, it became rare thereafter except in Celtic-speaking areas such as Wales, where it was used to anglicize both RHODRI and RHYDDERCH, and Scotland where it has been used for *Ruairidh* (see RORY). It was revived among English speakers at the beginning of the 19th century. This revival took a slightly different form from the general fashion for the medieval. The name had already been used by Smollett (see below) when Sir Walter Scott, who played an important role in such revivals, published a poem in 1811 called 'The Vision of Don Roderick'. This work caught the public's attention because it was written to raise money for those wounded in the Peninsular War. It told of the last Visigothic king of Spain's dabbling in magic, which revealed to him Spain's future, first as a Moorish state, followed by the restoration of Christianity. This king is usually known to history by the Spanish variant, *Rodrigo*. There is a rare Scottish feminine form, *Rodina*.

PET FORM **Rod(dy)** • VARIANTS **Broderick** *French* **Rodrigue** *Italian, Portuguese, Spanish* **Rodrigo** *Portuguese* **Rui** *Spanish* **Ruy** *Russian* **Rurik**

★ Roddy Doyle (1958–   ), Irish novelist
★ Rod Stewart (1945–   ), British singer, born in London of Scottish and English parents
☆ *Roderick Random* is a 1748 novel by Tobias Smollett

Rodge, **Rodger** *see* **Roger**

Rodney *m*
This surname, of uncertain origin, has been recorded as a first name from the 17th century, but came into general use in honour of Admiral Sir George Rodney (1718–91), whose exploits included bringing most of the West Indies under British rule. Despite this patriotic origin the name was a popular choice in the USA in the 1960s and 70s. Rodney is now little used in the UK.

PET FORM **Rod(dy)**
★ Rod Steiger (1925–2002), US actor

Rodolpho *see* **Rudolf**

Roel, **Roeland** *see* **Roland**

Roger *m*
There was an Old English name *Hrothgar*, famous from the Old English epic poem *Beowulf*, which was formed from the elements *hroth*, 'fame', and *gar*, 'spear'. After the Norman Conquest this name was replaced by the French variant *Rogier*, which then became Roger. It was a popular name among the Norman aristocracy, and although it declined in popularity after the Middle Ages it remained in regular use. There is an old pet form *Hodge*, or *Hodgekin*, which is the source of the surnames Hodges and Hodgekins. This died out after it became used as a name for a typical rustic or country bumpkin.

PET FORM **Ro(d)ge** • VARIANTS **Rodger** *Dutch* **Rogier**, **Rutger** *German* **Rüdiger** *Italian* **Ruggierro** *Portuguese* **Rogério** *Scandinavian* **Roar**

★ Sir Roger Moore (1927–), English actor

★ Rutger Hauer (1944–), Dutch actor

Rohan[1] *m*
This is a popular Indian name from *rohana*, the Sanskrit for 'ascending', which is the name of a holy mountain in Sri Lanka.

Rohan[2] *m*
In Scotland this has been recorded as a variant of the Gaelic *Ruadhan* (see ROWAN). Rohan is also an aristocratic surname and a French place name, and uses may occasionally be with reference to these.

Rohan[3] *f*
In recent years there have been cases where the name Rohan has been given to girls, after the land described in J R R Tolkien's *The Lord of the Rings*. He created the name from an old Germanic root for 'horse', and gave its meaning as 'horse country'.
VARIANT **Rohanne**

Roibéard *see* Robert

Roisin *f*
This was originally a pet form (*Róisín*) of the Irish name *Róis*, 'rose', but is now much more common than the full form. It has been popular in Ireland for a number of years and has now spread beyond the country. Depending on where in Ireland it is used, it can be pronounced 'rosh-een' or 'ro-sheen'.
VARIANT **Rosheen**

Roksana *see* Roxana

Roland *m*
This is a Germanic name formed from *hrod*, 'fame', and *land*, 'land'. It was famous throughout Europe in the Middle Ages as the name of the great warrior nephew of Charlemagne, who was killed with his great friend OLIVER at the Battle of Roncevalles. When the Normans charged the Anglo-Saxons

at the Battle of Hastings in 1066, they were led into battle by a minstrel singing of Roland's deeds. The name was common enough in the Middle Ages to develop into the surname *Rowland*, now used as an alternative spelling of the first name.
PET FORMS **Rol(e)y**, **Rowl(e)y** • VARIANTS **Rowland** *Welsh* **Rolant** *Dutch* **Roeland**, **Roel** *French* **Rolande** (f) *Italian* **Orlando** *Russian* **Rolan** *Spanish* **Rolando**, **Roldán**

★ Sir Rowland Hill (1795–1879), English founder of the penny post

☆ 'Childe Roland to the Dark Tower Came', 1845 poem by Robert Browning that inspired Stephen King to write the *Dark Tower* series of books

Rolf *m*
This is the English form of the Old Norse name *Hrolfr*, a pet form of *Hrofwulf*, RUDOLF. It died out after the Middle Ages, then reappeared in the early 19th century, perhaps as an import from Germany where the name had remained in use. In Latin texts the Old French form of the name, *Roul*, appears as *Rollo*, most famously as the name of the Viking lord who took over Normandy and made himself the first duke of Normandy. Rollo started to reappear in literature in the 17th century, but does not seem to have been used as a given name until the 19th century. Since Rollo was also an aristocratic surname, the revival may have been, at least in part, from this source.
VARIANTS **Rollo**, **Rolph**

Roma, Romaine *f*
Roma is simply the Latin word for 'Rome' while Romaine is the French for 'Roman woman', the feminine of ROMAN. Roma is also found as a pet form of ROSEMARY. These names have never been common among English speakers, but there is currently some

interest being shown by parents, particularly in Roma.

VARIANTS **Romane, Romayne, Romana** *Spanish* **Romina**

★ Roma Downey (1960–), Northern Irish actress

Roman, Romeo *m*

Roman simply means 'citizen of Rome'. It was borne by a 6th-century Syrian saint who is remembered for the hymns he wrote, and by a 10th-century saint involved in the conversion of Russia. The name is not part of the core stock in English, but is well used in other countries. Romeo is a related, Italian name, originally meaning 'pilgrim to Rome'. Its strongest association is with Shakespeare's tragic hero. Use of this name has been climbing steadily in the USA since the end of the 20th century, and it came to public attention in the UK when it was chosen by the Beckhams for one of their sons.

★ Roman Polanski (1933–), French-Polish film director, scriptwriter and actor

★ Roman Abramovich (1966–), Russian plutocrat

Romey *see* **Rosemary**

Romilly *fm*

This is a French place name, probably derived ultimately from the name ROMULUS, which became a surname and then a first name. The most famous bearers of the surname were Sir Samuel Romilly (1757–1818) and his son John, both of whom were prominent reforming lawyers and politicians. The first name may have come into use in their honour, or influenced by the use of 'young Romilly', a surname that could be mistaken for a first name, in Wordsworth's 1807 poem 'The Force of Prayer'. The name does not seem to have been used as a given name before the 20th century. An early example was the case of the poet and detective story writer Romilly John (b.1906). He was the son of the painter Augustus John who liked to choose unique or very unusual names for his numerous children. The name is quietly but regularly used, now mostly as a feminine name.

VARIANT **Romily**

☆ Romilly MacAran, heroine of *Hawkmistress*, a 1982 novel in the 'Darkover' fantasy series by Marion Zimmer Bradley. This may have led to an increased use of the name for girls in the 1980s

Romola *f* Romulus *m*

Romulus is the name of one of the twins who founded Rome (see further at REMUS), and simply means 'of Rome'. Romola is the feminine form, introduced to English speakers by George Eliot's 1863 novel of the name, set in Renaissance Florence. The name has been used quietly but regularly ever since.

VARIANT *Italian* **Romolo**

Romy *see* **Rosemary**

Ron *mf*

A modern Hebrew name meaning 'joy, song'. There is a female-only variant RONIT, and Ron is also a pet form of names found under RONNIE.

Rona *see* **Rhona, Ronald**

Ronald *m*

This is the Scottish and northern English form of the Old Norse *Ragnvaldr*, which became REGINALD or REYNALD elsewhere. It has since spread to the rest of the English-speaking world. *Ranald* is particularly Scottish variant. There is a rare feminine *Ronalda*, and *Ronnette*. *Rona* or RHONA may also be used as a feminine variants.

PET FORMS **Ron, Ronnie** • VARIANTS *Scottish* **Raghnall, Raganvald**

★ Ronald Reagan (1911–2004), US president and former film actor

☆ Ron Weasley in J K Rowling's *Harry Potter* books

Ronan *m*

Ronan comes from the Gaelic *rón*, 'seal', and means 'little seal' It is an old Irish and Scots Gaelic name, which was borne by a number of saints, one of whom was a missionary to Brittany. The name was introduced to the general English-speaking word by Sir Walter Scott's 1823 novel *St Ronan's Well*.

VARIANTS *Irish* **Rónán** *Breton* **Renan**

Roni, Ronni, Ronnie *mf*

These are pet forms of various names containing the sound 'ron'. For males it is usually RONALD, but also AARON; for females VERONICA.

PET FORM **Ron** • VARIANT **Ronee**

★ Ronnie Spector (1943–   ), lead singer of the Ronettes

Ronit *f*

This is the anglicized form of the Scottish and Irish name *Rathnait*, formed from *rath*, 'prosperity, grace' and interpreted as 'little graceful one'. It is the name of an Irish saint. See also RON.

VARIANTS **Ranait, Roanaid**

Ronja *see* Veronica

Ronwen *see* Rhonwen

Roo *mf*

Short form of names such as RUPERT and RUTH.

Roosje *see* Rose

Rory *m*

This is a Gaelic name based on *ruadh*, 'red', meaning 'red-haired' or 'fiery', although the Irish form of the name, *Ruaidhrí*, has been interpreted as

deriving from *ruadh* combined with *rí*, 'king'. It is an old name going back to at least the 12th century, and is still popular in Scotland and Ireland. In the past Rory has been anglicized as RODERICK.

VARIANTS **Rorie, Ruairi** *Irish* **Ruaidhrí** *Scots Gaelic* **Ruairidh, Ruaraidh**

Ros *see* Rosalind, Rosamund

Rosa *see* Rose

Rosaleen *f*

This variant of ROSE was used to translate the Irish name ROISIN in James Mangan's 1846 poem 'Dark Rosaleen' ('Róisín Dubh' in Gaelic). This poem purports to be a love song, but the love is really that for Ireland, at a time when Irish nationalism was persecuted. Thus Dark Rosaleen came to be a symbol of Irish nationalism.

☆ Rosaleen was the name of the Little Red Riding Hood figure in the 1984 film *The Company of Wolves*

Rosalie *f*

This is the French form of the name of a saint, otherwise known as *Rosalia*. She is said to have been a Sicilian noblewoman who was born in 1130, and who died alone in the cave she had turned into a hermitage. When Sicily was attacked by a plague in 1624 she appeared to a woman in a vision, after which her bones were found and taken to Palermo, and the plague was halted. She subsequently became the patron saint of Palermo.

Rosalind *f*

There has been much debate over the exact origins of this name. It is generally agreed that it was not a 'rose' name originally, although the modern form has been affected by the Latin *rosa linda*, 'lovely rose'. The name was Germanic, and currently the most prevalent interpretation is that its elements are *hros*, 'horse', and *linde*, 'soft, supple'. Identifying its history is not made any easier by the fact that numerous variants have been in use since the Middle Ages, obscuring the original form.

PET FORMS **Ros, Roz** • VARIANTS **Rosalin, Rosaline, Rosalyn(n)(e), Ros(e)lyn** *Spanish, Italian* **Rosalinda**

★ Rosalind Russell (1907–76), US actress
★ Rosalynn Carter (1927–), US humanitarian and First Lady
☆ Rosalind is the heroine of Shakespeare's *As You Like It*, but even here she is also called *Rosaline*

Rosamund *f*

This was originally a Germanic name from the elements *hros*, 'horse', and *mund*, 'protection', but like ROSALIND its history has been influenced by the possible Latin interpretations of the name, in this case either *rose mundi*, 'rose of the world', or *rosa munda*, 'pure rose', both titles of the Virgin Mary. The name was introduced by the Normans and has been in use ever since, although it is not currently a popular choice. The form *Rosamond* is the norm in the USA, where the name has always been much rarer.

PET FORMS **Ros, Roz** • VARIANTS **Rosamond, Rosamunde**

★ Rosamond Lehmann (1901–90), English novelist
★ Rosamunde Pilcher (1924–), English author

Rosasharn *see* Sharon

Roscoe *m*

A surname from a place name used as a first name. The place name comes from the north of England and is formed from the Old Norse elements *ra*, 'roe deer', and *skogr*, 'wood'. It was well used in the USA in the 19th and early 20th centuries.

★ Roscoe 'Fatty' Arbuckle (1887–1933), US silent-film star

★ Roscoe Tanner (1951–), US tennis player

Rose *f*

Originally, this was probably not used with reference to the flower, but was a short form of names related to ROSAMUND and ROSALIND formed from the element *hros*, 'horse', or from *hrod*, 'fame' 'kind', both of them common Germanic elements. We know this because in the early Middle Ages we find the name spelt *Roese*, *Rohese*, or *Rohesia* in Latin rather than *Rosa*. However, Rose soon became identified with the flower, which had strong symbolic associations, particularly with the Virgin Mary (see Rosamund). The name was particularly popular in the 19th century, and is also currently fashionable. It often blends with other names to form compounds, some of which are listed below, and is also used as a pet form of ROSEMARY.

PET FORM **Rosie** • VARIANTS **Rosa, Rosabel(le)** *Dutch* **Roosje** *French* **Roselle, Rosette, Rosine** *Italian* **Roseangela, Rosella, Rosetta, Rosina** *Spanish* **Rosita** *Yiddish* **Reis(el)**

☆ Briar Rose is the traditional name for the princess in the fairytale *Sleeping Beauty*. Both Briar Rose and Briar are occasionally found as given names

Roseanna, Roseanne *f*

A blend of ROSE and ANNE or ANNA that has been in use since at least the 18th century.

VARIANTS **Rosannah, Roseann, Rozanne**

★ Rosanna Arquette (1959–), US actress
★ Roseanne Barr (1952–), US comedienne

Rosemary *f*

Although this looks like a blend of ROSE and MARY, it is from the herb's Latin name *ros marinus*, 'sea dew', given because the plant thrives near the sea, and because of the misty colour of its leaves. As a first name it came into use in the 19th century. *Rom(e)y* is a short form which originated in Germany.

PET FORMS **Rose, Rosie** • VARIANT **Rosemarie**

- ★ Rosemary Clooney (1928–2002), US singer and actress
- ★ Romy Schneider (1938–82), Austrian actress
- ☆ Rosemary is the name of the woman who gives birth to the son of Satan in the horror film *Rosemary's Baby* (1968)

Rosetta, Rosette *see* **Rose**

Roshan *mf*
A Muslim name which comes from the Persian for 'shining, splendid, renowned'. Closely related are the feminine names *Roshni*, meaning 'brilliance, lustre', and *Roshanara*, which is 'light of the assembly'. ROXANA is probably also related.

Rosheen *see* **Roisin**

Roshelle *see* **Rochelle**

Roshni *see* **Roshan**

Rosina, Rosita *see* **Rose**

Roslyn, Roslynne *see* **Rosalind**

Ross *m*
This is a Scottish surname, from the Gaelic word for 'headland', now a popular first name, particularly in Scotland. It is occasionally given to girls. It has been used as a first name since at least the 16th century.

- ★ Ross Perot (1930–   ), US businessman and politician
- ★ Ross Noble (1976–   ), English comedian
- ☆ Ross Geller in the television series *Friends*

Rowan¹ *m*
This is the anglicized form of the Irish *Ruadhán*, 'little red one'. It was the name of a 6th-century Irish saint who

founded a monastery at Lothra in County Tipperary. His bell still survives and is in the British Museum.

VARIANT **Rowen**

Rowan² *f*
Although there is considerable overlap between the two forms of Rowan, feminine uses are usually linked to the small tree called the rowan, otherwise known as mountain ash. This name comes from the Old Norse for the tree, *rogn*. Variants shade into forms of ROWENA.

VARIANTS **Rowen, Rowann(e), Rowanna**

Rowena *f*
This is the name given in Geoffrey of Monmouth's 12th-century *History of the Kings of Britain* to the daughter of the Saxon leader Hengist. Her beauty so overwhelmed Vortigern that he was willing to sacrifice large tracts of Britain to the Saxons in return for her hand. In the Welsh version of events her name is given as RHONWEN. The origin of Rowena is not clear. The name came into general use after Sir Walter Scott used it for the Saxon woman loved by the hero of his 1820 novel *Ivanhoe*.

VARIANT **Rowenna**

Rowland, Rowley, Rowly *see* **Roland**

Roxana *f*
This is the Latin form of a Persian or Bactrian name, perhaps *Roschana* or *Roshanak*, thought to mean 'dawn', 'light', 'luminous beauty' or perhaps 'little star'. It has always had strong romantic associations, as early historians claimed that the marriage between the Princess Roxana and Alexander the Great in the 4th century BC was not to form an alliance between Alexander and her father, but because Alexander had fallen in love with her

beauty. The pet forms are also found as independent names. See also ROSHAN.

PET FORMS **Roxie, Roxy** • VARIANTS **Roxanne, Roxanna** *Arabic* **Ruk(h)s(h)ana** *Polish, Russian* **Roksana**

☆ Roxane is the love interest in Edmond Rostand's 1897 play *Cyrano de Bergerac*

☆ Roxie Hart is the acquitted murderer in the musical *Chicago*

Roy *m*
This comes from the Scots Gaelic name *Ruadh*, 'red', originally a nickname given to someone with red hair. Outside Scotland it can be a shortening of ELROY or LEROY and thus appear as a form of the Old French *roy*, 'king'.

VARIANT *Scots Gaelic* **Ruadh**

★ Roy Rogers (1911–98), US cowboy singer and actor
★ Roy Scheider (1932–2008), US actor

Royston *m*
Royston is a surname from a place name in Hertfordshire meaning 'Rose's settlement'.

★ Royston Vasey (better-known as Roy 'Chubby' Brown) (1945–), English comedian whose real name has been used as a place name in the television comedy series *The League of Gentlemen*
★ Royston Drenthe (1987–), Dutch footballer

Roz *see* **Rosalind, Rosamund**

Rozanne *see* **Roseanna**

Ruadh *see* **Roy**

Ruadhan *see* **Rowan**

Ruairi, Ruaidhrí, Ruairidh, Ruaraidh *see* **Rory**

Ruben *see* **Reuben**

Ruby *f*
This is a jewel name that originally came into use in the 19th century and was common into the 20th. It then fell from favour, but has recently had a strong revival to become one of the most popular names in the UK.

VARIANT **Rubi(e)**

★ Ruby Wax (1953–), UK-based US actress and comedienne.

☆ 'Ruby Tuesday', a 1967 Rolling Stones song

Ruchel *see* **Rachel**

Rüdiger *see* **Roger**

Rudolf, Rudy *m*
This is the German form of the name ROLF, introduced to English speakers in the 19th century.

VARIANTS **Rudolph** *Italian, Spanish* **Rodolpho**

★ Rudy Vallee (1901–86), US musician
★ Rudolph Valentino (1895–1926), Italian-born US silent-film star
☆ 'Rudolph the Red-Nosed Reindeer', a popular Christmas song

Rue, Ruf *see* **Ruth**

Rufus *m*
This was a Latin name which meant 'red-haired'. There were a number of saints called Rufus, but this did not prevent it coming into use in the 17th century when saints names were generally rejected.

VARIANTS *Italian, Spanish* **Rufino** *Russian* **Rufina** (f)

Ruggierro *see* **Roger**

Rui *see* **Roderick**

Ruiseart *see* **Richard**

Rukhsana, Rukhshana, Ruksana, Rukshana *see* **Roxana**

Rupert *m*
This is a German form of the name ROBERT. It was introduced into England in the 17th century by the dashing Cavalier Prince Rupert of the Rhine,

who came to support his uncle King Charles I in the English Civil War. The name is hardly used in the USA where it is regarded as typically English.

★ Rupert Brooke (1887–1915), English poet
★ Rupert Murdoch (1931–), US newspaper publisher
☆ Rupert Bear, long-running children's strip cartoon

Rupinder f
An Indian name, particularly used by Sikhs, meaning 'greatest beauty'. It is formed from the Sanskrit *rupa*, 'beauty', and the name of the god INDRA, used to indicate greatness.

Ruqayah f
This Arabic name probably means 'charm, charming' and was borne by one of Muhammad's daughters.
VARIANTS **Ruqay(y)a, Ruqaiya**

Rurik see Roderick

Rushdi m
An Arabic name, meaning 'sensible conduct, emotional maturity'.

Russell f
The French nickname *rousel*, 'little red one', became an English surname. It was among the aristocratic surnames taken up as first names in the 19th century. The pet forms are sometimes found used independently.
PET FORMS **Russ, Rusty** • VARIANT **Rusel**

Rut, Ruta see Ruth

Rutger see Roger

Ruth f
Ruth is an Old Testament name of uncertain meaning. It has been linked to the Hebrew for 'friend', but since Ruth was a Moabite her name may not have any Hebrew meaning. The biblical Book of Ruth describes Ruth's devotion to her mother-in-law Naomi, and also tells the story of how Boaz, whom Ruth later married, saw her gleaning in his field and ordered his men to drop grain on purpose, so that she could have more to collect. It was one of the names taken up by the Puritans in the 16th century.
PET FORMS **Ruthi(e), Rue, Roo** • VARIANTS *German, Italian, Scandinavian, Spanish* **Rut** *Polish* **Ruta** *Russian* **Ruf**

★ Ruth Rendell (1930–), English detective-story writer
★ Ruth Kelly (1968–), British politician, born in Northern Ireland

Ruthven f
Ruthven is a Scottish clan name and aristocratic title used as a first name. It can be interpreted either as from Old Norse *rauthr*, 'red', with 'fen', or from Gaelic *ruadh*, 'red', and *abhuinn*, 'river'. The traditional pronunciation is 'ree-vn' and the forms *Riven* or *Rivan* are occasionally found as first names in Scotland.

★ Ruthven Todd (1914–78), Scottish poet
☆ Sir Ruthven Murgatroyd in Gilbert and Sullivan's 1887 operetta *Ruddigore*

Ruy see Roderick

Ryan m
This is an Irish surname from the old personal name *Rian*. The meaning of this is uncertain, but it may be a pet form of *rí*, 'king'. The name increased in popularity in the 1970s when US actor Ryan O'Neal made it well known, and it is now widely popular.
FEMININE **Ryanne** • VARIANT **Rian**

★ Ryan Giggs (1973–), Welsh footballer

Ryleigh, Rylie see Riley

Ryszard see Richard

S

Saabiha *see* **Sabah**

Saabir, Saabira *see* **Sabir**

Saad *m*
An Arabic name meaning 'good luck, fortune'.
VARIANT **Sa'd**

Saalim, Saalima *see* **Salim**

Saami *see* **Sami**

Saamia *see* **Sami, Somaya**

Sabah *fm*
An Arabic name meaning 'morning'. It is one of a number of related names where morning is transferred by association to ideas of light and beauty in the traditional interpretation of the names. Thus for boys we find *Saabih*, 'coming in the morning', *Sabuh*, 'shining, brilliant'; for girls *Saabiha*, 'coming in the morning', *Sabaha*, 'beauty', *Sabia*, 'charming', *Sabih*, 'pretty', *Sabiha*, 'morning', *Sabuh*, 'shining, brilliant'. Sabah is often described as a feminine name, but in the Gulf States it is also a popular masculine name. Saba is also the Arabic name of the kingdom of SHEBA.
PET FORM **Sabbouha** • VARIANT **Saba**
★ Sabah (1927–), Lebanese singer famous throughout the Arab world

Sabia¹ *f*
An Arabic name meaning 'captivating, charming'.

Sabia² *see* **Sadhbh**

Sabina¹ *f*
This name means 'Sabine woman'. According to classical tradition, the Sabines were a tribe who neighboured the Romans in the early days of Rome. After ROMULUS had built the city he managed to attract settlers, but they were mainly men. In order to find wives the Romans invited the Sabines to a festival and then carried off the women. This event, known as 'The Rape [literally 'carrying off'] of the Sabine Women' became a popular subject in art. The Sabine men only managed to arrange an attack on Rome after some of the women had borne children by the Roman men. As the two forces were drawn up for battle the women placed themselves between the armies, pointing out that whatever the outcome they would lose, either brothers and fathers, or the fathers of their children, and insisted on peace being made. They were honoured as conciliators. Sabina was borne by a number of early saints, and is well used in other languages, but did not enter the stock of English names until the 19th century, except in Ireland, where it was used to anglicize SADHBH, and sometimes *Sile* (SHEILA).
PET FORM **Bina** • VARIANT *French, German* **Sabine**

Sabina² *f*
A Muslim name meaning 'flower'.

Sabir *m* **Sabira** *f*
An Arabic name meaning 'patient, enduring'. *Sabri* (m) and *Sabriya(h)* and *Sabra* (fs) are related names.
VARIANTS **Saabir(a), Sabeer(a), Sabuh, Sabur(a), Sabriyya(h)**

Sable *f*
This name combines both a sense of

'blackness and of 'richness' derived from the precious black fur called sable. The name is mainly found in the USA when it has been in use since at least the first part of the 20th century.

Sabra, Sabri, Sabriya, Sabriyah, Sabuh, Sabur, Sabura see **Sabir**

Sabrina f
British legend has it that the River Severn gets its name from Sabrina, the daughter of Locrine, second king of Britain, who was thrown into the river on the orders of her wicked stepmother. This was picked up by Milton in his masque *Comus*, containing lines addressed to 'Sabrina fair' which were once a standard school text. *Sabrina Fair* was then taken for the title of a 1953 play by Samuel A Taylor, filmed the following year as *Sabrina* starring Audrey Hepburn. This did much to transform the name from one of legend to a fashionable first name.
VARIANTS **Sabryna, Sabrine, Zabrina**
★ Sabrina (Norma Anne Sykes) (1936–), voluptuous English starlet
☆ Sabrina Spellman in the television series *Sabrina the Teenage Witch*

Sacha see **Sasha**

Sachairi see **Zach**

Sa'd see **Saad**

Sade f
This is the name of a Nigerian-born singer-songwriter and her group, which was taken up particularly by those of African descent, mainly in the 1980s. The singer's full name is Helen Folasade Adu, and *Folosade* is said to mean 'honour bestows a crown' in Yoruba. The name is pronounced 'SHAR-day' and is sometimes found in spellings that reflect this.
VARIANTS **Sharday, Shardae**

Sadhbh f
This means 'sweet, goodness' in Irish and is pronounce *sive* rhyming with 'alive'. In Irish legend Sadhbh was the poet Ossian's mother, who had been magically enchanted to take the form of a deer until released by Finn Mac Cool. The name was well used in the Middle Ages and is popular today in Ireland. In the past it was anglicized as *Sabia* or SALLY, with the pet form turned into SABINA.
PET FORM **Saidhbhín** • VARIANTS **Sive, Sabia**

Sadie f
This is a pet form of SARAH which began to be used as an independent name in the 19th century. It is more often found in the USA than in the UK. It can also be used as a pet form of MERCEDES.
☆ Sadie Hawkins Day (the Saturday after 9 November) was invented by Al Capp for his cartoon *Li'l Abner*. In the cartoon it is the day that women can chase men and force them into marriage. In North America some schools hold dances on that day, during which the conventional male–female dating roles are reversed

Saeed see **Said**

Safa mf
This is an Arabic name meaning 'purity, sincerity'. The masculine can also appear as *Saafi*. Safa should strictly be spelt *Safaa*, to distinguish it from Safa, the name of the hill outside Mecca that is the counterpart of MARWA, but English spelling does not happily make distinctions that are apparent in Arabic script. The names *Safi* (m) and *Safiya* (f) are related to Safa,, for they mean 'pure (ie close) friend'. Safiya was borne by one of the wives of Muhammad.
VARIANTS **Saffi, Safiy(y)a(h)**

Saffron f
This is the name of a type of crocus

and of the valuable, bright yellow spice that comes from its stamens. It came into use as a first name in the 1960s.

PET FORMS **Safi, Saffie, Saffy**

★ Saffron Burrows (1972–), English actress

☆ Saffron 'Saffy' Monsoon, the responsible daughter in the television comedy series *Absolutely Fabulous*

Safi, Safiya *see* **Safa**

Safrawa, Safura *see* **Zipporah**

Safyre *see* **Sapphire**

Sage *mf*
The plant sage got its name from the reputation tea made from its leaves had for making you sage or wise. The name can therefore be seen as either a plant name or a virtue name. It was popular in Wales from the late Middle Ages until the 17th century, but then seems largely to have disappeared until the 20th century. It has been used regularly for both sexes in the USA since the 1990s.

Sahar *f*
An Arabic name meaning 'dawn, early morning'.

Sahara *f*
A recently-introduced name; the place name simply means 'desert' in Arabic.

Said *m*
An Arabic name meaning 'happy, lucky'.

VARIANTS **Saeed, Sa'id, Sayeed**

★ Saeed Jaffrey (1929–), Indian actor

Saidhbhín *see* **Sadhbh**

Saif *m*
An Arabic name, meaning 'sword'.

VARIANTS **Sayf, Seif**

Saira *f*
This is an Arabic name, perhaps meaning 'traveller'.

VARIANT **Sairah**

Sajid *m* **Sajida** *f*
An Arabic name, meaning 'bowing in adoration'. The related *Sajjad(a)* means 'worshipper [of Allah]'.

VARIANTS **Sajed(a), Sajjid(a)**

Sal *see* **Sally, Salvador**

Salah *m*
Salah is the Arabic for 'goodness, righteousness'. The expanded name *Salah-ud-din* 'righteousness of religion' is usually found as *Saladdin* in Western history.

VARIANTS **Saleh, Salahudin**

Salih *m* **Saliha** *f*
This name means 'virtuous ' in Arabic.

VARIANTS **Salihah, Salha**

Salim *m* **Salma** *f*
This Arabic name comes from the word for 'safe'.

VARIANTS **Saleem(a), Saalim(a), Selim(a)**

★ Salma Hayek (1966–), Mexican-born US actress of partly Lebanese descent

Sally *f*
This was originally a pet form of SARAH, the 'r' having changed to 'l' as in so many names (compare MARY and MOLLY). It was in use by the end of the 17th century, and was a popular given name in the 20th century.

PET FORM **Sal** • VARIANTS **Sallie, Sali**

Salma *see* **Salim**

Salman *m*
An Arabic name meaning 'safe'. Salman the Persian was one of the Prophet Muhammad's companions.

★ Salman Rushdie (1947–), Indian-born British novelist

★ Salman Khan (1965–), Indian actor

Salome *f*

This name comes from the Aramaic for 'peace', a word related to the Hebrew *shalom* which is also a first name but used for both sexes. Salome is notorious as the woman who danced the dance of the seven veils to persuade her uncle to give her the head of John the Baptist (much of the story is based on non-biblical tradition). There was, however, another biblical Salome. She was one of the women who stood at the foot of the cross and who discovered Christ's empty tomb. For some, this has been enough to supersede the reputation of the other Salome. The stress in English is usually on the second syllable, but some prefer to emphasize the first. SOLOMON is the masculine equivalent.

Salomon *see* Solomon

Salvador *m*

This is from the Late Latin *Salvator* meaning 'saviour'. It is rare in the UK, but both this form and the Italian *Salvatore* have been used by immigrant families in the USA.

PET FORM **Sal** • VARIANTS *Italian* **Salvatore, Tore**

★ Salvador Dalí (1904–89), Spanish artist

Sam *mf*

A pet form of any name containing the 'sam' sound, particularly SAMUEL and SAMANTHA.

PET FORMS **Sammy, Sammie**

Samantha *f*

This name appeared in the USA in the 18th century, but no one has yet managed to discover how and why. It is usually suggested that it serves as a female equivalent of SAMUEL. The name was regularly used in the USA in the 19th century and for the first few years of the 20th. It then declined, but was brought back to public attention with the character of Tracy Samantha Lord, the spoilt upper-class heiress in *The Philadelphia Story*, first shown as a play in 1939, and released as a very successful film the following year. The author presumably used it as an old-fashioned name suitable for the pompously old-fashioned family she came from. The film was turned into a musical, *High Society*, in 1956, and a song from it 'I Love You, Samantha' was a great hit. The name did not then seem old-fashioned, but fresh and new, and it began to be used again. However, what really popularized the name and introduced it to the UK was the use of it for the central character in the television comedy *Bewitched* in 1964.

PET FORMS **Sam(my), Sammie**

Samar *mf* Samir *m*

Samar comes from the Arabic meaning 'pleasant conversation' particularly that held in the evening, when the day's work is over. Samir is the term for the man with whom this conversation is shared, with *Samara* as a feminine. Samira has entered the stock of Western names by way of a horror film *The Ring* (2002). This, like REGAN, is a case where an unpleasant character nevertheless has a name which appeals to parents and becomes fashionable.

VARIANT **Sameer(a)**

Sami *m* Samiya *f*

An Arabic name meaning 'exalted, eminent'.

PET FORM **Soumaya** • VARIANTS **Saami(a), Samia, Samya**

Samih *m* Samiha *f*

An Arabic name meaning 'tolerant, magnanimous'.

Samir *see* Samar

Samiya, Samya *see* Sami

Sammy *see* Sam

Samson *m*

In the Bible Samson is the strong man who loses his strength after his Philistine mistress DELILAH cuts off his hair, which he has dedicated to God. The Hebrew form of the name is *Shimson*, which probably comes from *shemesh*, 'sun', or means 'son of [the sun god] *Samash*'. Since Samson shares many adventures with heroes from other mythologies it is thought that the stories told of him may be reworked remnants from pre-Hebrew religions. Samson was a popular name in the Middle Ages, particularly in Cornwall, where it was used in honour of St Samson, a 6th-century Celtic saint.

PET FORM **Sam(my)** • VARIANTS **Sampson** *Italian* **Sansone**

Samuel *m*

In the Old Testament Samuel was the last of the ruling judges, who anointed first SAUL and then DAVID as king. The name is *Shemu'el* in Hebrew, which can be interpreted variously as 'name of God', 'God has heard', or 'asked of God'. The latter would be relevant to the story that Hannah, his mother, had prayed fervently to God for a son, and promised to dedicate the child to the temple if her prayers were answered, a promise that she kept. The name was rare among English speakers until it was taken up in a big way by the Puritans, and remained well used into the 19th century. After a period of being out of fashion it became popular again in the 1990s both in its full form and the shortened *Sam*.

PET FORMS **Sam, Sammy** • VARIANTS *Welsh* **Sawyl** *Italian* **Samuele, Samuela** *Russian* **Samuil** *Yiddish* **Shmuel**

Sana, Saniyya *f*

These are Arabic names, Sana meaning 'brilliance, radiance', while Saniyya means 'brilliant, radiant'.

Sanchia *f* Sancho *m*

The Latin *sanctus*, 'holy', developed a Late Latin form *Sanctius*, 'saintly, holy', which evolved into first names in Spain and Italy. It is sometimes chosen for a child born on All Saints' Day (1 November). The feminine forms in particular are recorded in British history from at least the 13th century, and have begun to reappear on occasion.

VARIANTS **Sancha** *Italian* **Santa, Santuzza, Santino**

☆ Sancho Panza, the peasant squire in Cervantes' *Don Quixote* (1605–15)

☆ Santino 'Sonny' Corleone, heir apparent to the Mafia family in the 1972 film *The Godfather*

Sandaidh, Sander *see* Alexander

Sandi, Sandie *see* Alexandra

Sandor *see* Alexander

Sandra *f*

This was originally a pet form of *Alessandra*, the Italian equivalent of ALEXANDRA. It was brought to the attention of English speakers by George Meredith's 1864 novel *Emilia in England*, whose heroine was called Emilia Sandra Belloni, particularly when the novel was reissued in 1886 as *Sandra Belloni*. The Scottish equivalent pet form was *Saundra*, which was turned into *Sondra* by Theodore Dreiser in his 1925 novel *An American Tragedy*, filmed in 1931, thus introducing the general public to a further variant. Sandra is occasionally found as a pet form of other names ending in the sound, such as CASSANDRA.

VARIANTS **Sondra, Sandrine, Zandra, Xandra, Xandrine** *Italian* **Sandro** (m)

★ Zandra Rhodes (1940–), English fashion designer

★ Sondra Locke (1947–), US actress and film director

Sandrine *see* **Alexandra**

Sandy *mf*
This was originally a Scottish pet form of ALEXANDER or ALEXANDRA. It is also used as a nickname for someone with appropriately-coloured hair.
VARIANTS **Sandi(e)** *Scots* **Sawney** *Scots Gaelic* **Sandaidh**
★ Sandy Lyle (1958–), Scottish golfer
★ Sandy Denny (1947–78), English folk singer
☆ Sandy is the lead female character in the musical *Grease*

Sangeeta *f*
An Indian name meaning 'musical'.
VARIANT **Sanjita**
★ Sangeeta Bijlani (1965–), Bollywood actress and former 'Miss India'

Sania, Saniyya *see* **Sana**

Sanjay, Sanjit *m*
Sanjay is a popular Indian name, from the Sanskrit for 'triumphant'. In the great Indian epic of the *Mahabharata*, Sanjay is the charioteer of a blind king and has to tell his master everything that is happening, thus acting as narrator of the work. The related Sanjit means 'complete victory'.
VARIANTS **Sanjaya, Sanjeet**
★ Sanjay Gandhi (1946–80), Indian politician
☆ Sanjay is the brother of Apu and helps him at the Kwik-E-Mart in the television cartoon *The Simpsons*

Sanjiv *m*
An Indian name meaning 'living, reviving' from the Sanskrit *sanjiva*.
VARIANT **Sanjeev**
★ Sanjeev Bhaskar (1964–), English comedian and actor

Sanna *see* **Susan**

Sansone *see* **Samson**

Santa, Santuzza *see* **Sanchia**

Sante *see* **Ashanti**

Santiago *m*
Meaning 'St James', formed from the word for 'saint' combined with IAGO (the old form of JAMES), this is a popular Spanish name, well used in the USA. It is chosen with specific reference to the great pilgrimage site of the Cathedral of St James at Compostella in Spain.
PET FORMS **Diego, Santi**

Santino *see* **Sanchia**

Saoirse *f*
This is the Irish for 'freedom' coined with reference to Irish independence. It has been used since the 1920s and is currently a popular choice in Ireland. It is usually pronounced 'SEER-sha', but is sometimes found as 'SAYR-sha'. It is occasionally used for males.

Sapphire *f*
This is one of the rarer jewel names, although it is increasing in use. It was introduced in the 19th century, but probably did not catch on in the way of PEARL or RUBY because of its biblical associations. In the Acts of the Apostles Sapphira and her husband Ananias are early Christians who sell some land for charity, but falsely claim they have handed over all the money when they have in fact kept some for themselves. They are struck dead for their deceit.
PET FORM **Sapphy** • VARIANT **Safyre**

Sara, Sarah *f*
This is the Hebrew for 'noble lady, princess' and was borne by the wife of Abraham, making her the mother of the Jewish race. Sara is the form of the name found in the New Testament. This is sometimes pronounced with the vowel long, as in 'far', but is often nowadays simply an alternative spelling for Sarah. Sara is also the form used in many other languages, from Arabic to Scandinavian. The name

came into use after the Reformation, when Old Testament name were popular, and sometimes appears in spellings which reflect contemporary pronunciations such as 'Sarey' or 'Sarra'. Its popularity is attested by the independent use of the pet forms.
PET FORMS **Sadie, Sally, Sassa, Sassie**
• VARIANTS **Sera** *Spanish* **Sarita, Zarita** *Yiddish* **Sarit, Suri, Tzeitel**

Sarafina *see* **Seraphina**

Saraid *f*
A traditional Irish name meaning 'excellent, best'. It is pronounced 'SAR-ad' or 'SOR-it'. It was traditionally anglicized as SARAH.
VARIANT **Sárait**

Sarina *see* **Serena**

Sasha *mf*
This was originally a Russian pet form of ALEXANDER. It was first taken up outside Russia by the French, in the form *Sacha*, in the early years of the 20th century when Diaghilev's *Ballets Russes* created a craze for all things Russian.
PET FORMS *Russian* **Sashura, Shura**
• VARIANTS **Sacha, Sascha**
★ Sacha Distel (1933–2004), French singer
☆ Sasha is a major character in Virginia Woolf's 1928 novel *Orlando*

Saskia *f*
This is a Dutch name of uncertain origin, perhaps from *sachs*, 'Saxon'. It was borne by the wife of the artist Rembrandt. The name is currently fashionable.
★ Saskia Reeves (1962–   ), English actress
☆ Princess Saskia is the heroine of the 1922 John Buchan novel *Huntingtower*, filmed in 1927, which may have helped to introduce the name to a wider audience

Sassa *see* **Astrid**, **Sarah**

Sassie *see* **Sara**

Saud *m*
An Arabic name meaning 'very happy, very fortunate'.

Saul *m*
This is a Hebrew name meaning 'asked for or prayed for'. In the Old Testament it was borne by the king who made a favourite, and then an enemy, of David; in the New Testament it was the name of St PAUL before he changed it on conversion to Christianity. It was one of the biblical names taken up at the Reformation, but became rare in the 19th century. There has been a recent revival in the name as part of the new interest in the rarer biblical names.
VARIANT *Hebrew* **Shaul**
★ Saul Bellow (1915–2005), US author

Saundra *see* **Sandra**

Sausan *see* **Susan**

Savannah *f*
This name, probably taken from the US city in Georgia rather than directly from the vocabulary word, was well used in the 19th century and into the 20th, but then died out. It was reintroduced by the 1982 film *Savannah Smiles*, in which it was the name of a cute little girl in search of love. It re-entered the name charts the following year, in 465th place, and has climbed steadily ever since, reaching 30th place by 2007. It is only quietly used in the UK.
VARIANT **Savan(n)a**

Saverio *see* **Xavier**

Sawney *see* **Sandy**

Sawyl *see* **Samuel**

Saxon *m*
The name of one of the major tribes to form the Anglo-Saxons comes ultimately from *sahs*, the Germanic term for the distinctive knife they used for fighting. It was taken up as a first name in the 19th century when there was a great revival of Anglo-Saxon names.
☆ Saxon Ashe, 1940s fictional detective

Sayeed *see* **Said**

Sayf *see* **Saif**

Sayyid *m* **Sayyida** *f*
This is the Arabic for 'lord, master' and the female equivalent. It was originally given to any descendant of the Prophet, but by the 19th century it had come to mean little more than 'sir' or 'madam', and from there came to be used as a first name. The form *Syed* is a common variant on the Indian subcontinent.
VARIANTS **Say(y)ed(a)**, **Sayeed(a)**, **Sayad**

Scarlett *f*
This is the most obvious of the many names that have come into circulation from Margaret Mitchell's 1936 novel *Gone with the Wind*, and particularly the 1939 film adaptation (compare MELANIE, ASHLEY). Scarlett is actually the character's middle name, and was her grandmother's maiden name. Despite the fame of the character the name was used only sporadically until the 1980s but is increasing in use.
VARIANT **Scarlet**
★ Scarlett Johansson (1984–), American actress of Danish and Polish descent

Schlomo *see* **Solomon**

Schuyler *see* **Skyler**

Scott *m*
Originally a surname indicating someone from Scotland. It was particularly popular as a first name in the 1960s–90s, but is still regularly used, particularly in Scotland. Outside that country, use may have been influenced by the fame of Captain Scott ('Scott of the Antarctic', 1868–1912) and of the author F Scott Fitzgerald (1896–1940). The pet form is sometimes given to someone with Scottish ancestry or with the surname Scott – as in Montgomery 'Scotty' Scott, the engineer in the television series *Star Trek*.
PET FORMS **Scottie**, **Scotty**
★ Scott Walker (1943–), US singer

Scout *f*
This name comes from HARPER Lee's 1960 novel *To Kill a Mockingbird*. The child narrator of the novel is called Jean Louise Finch, but is always known by her nickname, Scout. The name has grown in use since US actors Bruce Willis and Demi Moore chose it for their daughter in 1991.

Se, Sé, Seaghdh, Seaghdha *see* **Shay**

Seamus *m*
This is the nearest the Irish language, which lacks a 'j' sound, comes to the name JAMES. Because it was a popular name it developed variant spellings both in Irish and in other languages, when it spread to the rest of the world. In Scotland the name came to be spelt HAMISH.
VARIANTS **Shamus, She(a)mus** *Irish* **Séamus, Séamas, Seumus**
★ Seamus Heaney (1939–), Northern Irish Nobel Prize-winning poet

Sean *m*
This is the Irish form of JOHN which has spread widely beyond its native land since the 1920s. In the process it has developed many variant forms, based on the way the 'S' is pronounced as 'Sh'. Sean evolved as the nearest the

Irish language, which does not have a 'j' sound, could come to the French form of John, *Jean*. *Seanna* is a rare feminine, while the standard Irish female equivalent is SIOBHAN. See also EOIN, SHAWN. Sean and SHANE have been popular in Ireland in recent years and have also started to be used as feminine names.

VARIANTS **Shane, Shayne, Shaun, Shawn** *Irish* **Séan**

★ Sir Sean Connery (1930–), Scottish film actor
★ Sean Bean (1959–), English actor
★ Shane Warne (1969–), Australian cricketer
☆ The Northern Irish variant *Shane* gained publicity and came into wider use after Jack Shaefer published a Western novel called *Shane* in 1949, which was very successfully filmed in 1953 and turned into a television series in the 1960s

Seanán *see* **Senan**

Searlait *see* **Charlotte**

Searlas, Séarlas *see* **Charles**

Seathan *see* **John**

Seathrun, Seathrún *see* **Geoffrey**

Sebastian *m*
This name means 'man from *Sebaste*' in Latin. Sebaste was a town in Asia Minor whose name came from the Greek for 'venerable' and which was a direct translation of the Roman imperial title *Augustus*. St Sebastian introduced the name to the common stock of European names. His martyrdom, which included being used as target practice by his fellow Roman soldiers, was a popular subject in art.

PET FORM **Seb** • VARIANTS *Dutch* **Sebastiaan, Bastiaan** *French* **Sebastien, Bastien, Sebastienne** *German* **Bastian** *Italian*

Sebastiono, Sebastiana *Portuguese* **Sebastião** *Russian* **Sevastian, Sevastyan**

★ Sebastian Coe (1956–), English athlete and politician
★ Johann Sebastian Bach (1685–1750), German composer
☆ Sebastian Flyte in Evelyn Waugh's 1945 novel *Brideshead Revisited*

Sˌebnem *see* **Shabnam**

Sedric, Sedrick *see* **Cedric**

Seeta, Seetha *see* **Sita**

Ségolène *f*
This is the French version of a Germanic name formed from *sigu*, 'victory', and *linde*, 'gentle, soft'. In German mythology *Sieglinde*, the German form, was mother of the great hero Siegfried.

PET FORMS **Ségo, Sigi**

★ Ségolène Royal (1953–), French politician

Seif *see* **Saif**

Seissylt *see* **Cecil, Sextus**

Selig *m*
A Yiddish name, meaning 'blessed, happy, fortunate', from the German *selig* of the same meaning. For feminines see under ZELDA.

VARIANT **Zelig**

Selim, Selima *see* **Salim**

Selina *f*
This name, introduced in the 17th century, is probably a Latinate form of *Selene*, goddess of the moon, and thus companion to the names DIANA and CYNTHIA that were also coming into use at the same time. Others would like to link it to the same root as CELIA.

VARIANTS **Selena, Celina**

★ Selina Scott (1951–), English newsreader and television presenter
☆ Selina Kyle is the real name of Catwoman in the *Batman* stories

Selma *f*

This is one of the many names introduced with James Macpherson's Ossianic poems (see further under OSCAR). In this case, it was not the name of a person but of the castle of the hero FINGAL. However, when the poems, which were popular in Scandinavia, were translated into Swedish, Fingal's longing to see Selma again was interpreted in such a way that the name could be regarded as a personal one, and it entered the stock of Swedish names. Use was reinforced first by a series of poems featuring the name Selma, by Frans Mikael Franzén (1772–1849), and later by the enormous popularity of the Swedish writer Selma Lagerlöf (1858–1940). Selma was taken to the USA by Swedish immigrants, and so entered the stock of names there, but has never been common in the UK. Some 20th-century uses in the USA may be with reference to Selma, Alabama, from where Martin Luther King began a 50-mile civil rights march in 1965. Selma can also be found as a feminine of SALIM.

VARIANT **Zelma**

☆ Selma Bouvier in the television cartoon *The Simpsons*

Selwyn *m*

A surname used as a first name. The surname can come from a number of sources, including an Old English name formed from the elements *sele*, 'hall', and *wine*, 'friend', and a form of SILVESTER. Use of the name in the 19th century may have come directly from the surname, at least in New Zealand, in honour of Bishop George Augustus Selwyn.

VARIANT **Selwin**

★ Selwyn Lloyd (1904–78), English politician

★ John Selwyn Gummer (1939–   ), English politician

Semaj *m*

This is the name JAMES spelt backwards. There has been a vogue for this name in the USA over the last decade. Compare NEVAEH.

Semyon *see* **Simon**

Senan *m*

Pronounced 'SHAN-awn', this is a traditional Irish name meaning 'old, ancient', which has been a regular parental choice in Ireland in recent years. There was a 6th-century saint of the name who is particularly associated with County Clare, and whose story contains so many wonders that it passes into the realm of mythology. There is a much rarer feminine equivalent *Seanach*, sometimes found as *Shannagh*.

VARIANT *Irish* **Seanán**

Sender *see* **Alexander**

Senga *f*

This rare Scottish name has been around for some years, and is usually analysed as AGNES spelt backwards (compare SEMAJ). However, it may well be a development of Gaelic *seang*, 'slender'.

Seocan *see* **John**

Seoirse *see* **George**

Seona *see* **Shona**

Seonade, Sèonade *see* **Sinead**

Seònaid, Seonag *see* **Shona**

Seòras *see* **George**

Seòsaidh, Seosamh *see* **Joseph**

Seosaimhn *see* **Josephine**

Sepp, Seppel *see* **Joseph**

Septimus *m*
The Latin for 'seventh', this was mainly used in the 19th century, when large families were common, for a seventh child. The feminine *Septima* was rarer.
☆ Rev Septimus Harding in Anthony Trollope's 1855 novel *The Warden* and the subsequent Barchester novels
☆ Septimus Weasley, grandfather of the Weasley children in the *Harry Potter* books by J K Rowling

Sera *see* **Sarah**, **Seraphina**

Seraphina *f*
This comes from the Hebrew *seraphim*, 'fiery ones', an order of angels particularly known from the biblical book of Isaiah 6.2. There was an obscure 5th-century saint of the name. The masculine *Seraphino* is much rarer.
PET FORM **Sera** • VARIANTS **Sarafina** *French* **Sérafin**, **Sérafine** *Greek* **Serafeim** *Italian* **Serafina**, **Serafino**, **Fina** *Russian* **Serafima**
☆ Serafina Pekkala, witch in Philip Pullman's *His Dark Materials* trilogy

Seren *f*
This is a Welsh name, meaning 'star', which is beginning to spread outside Wales.

Serena *f*
This is a Late Latin name from *serenus*, 'serene, tranquil'. It was borne by a minor early saint, but until the 20th century was mainly a literary name, having been used by Edmund Spenser in *The Faerie Queene* (1590). The variant *Serina* was used by Thomas Otway in his 1680 play, *The Orphan*. In the UK there is some overlap between variants of this name and SEREN, while in the USA the abstract noun *Serenity* is a popular choice – more so than Serena.
VARIANTS **Sarina**, **Sereen**
★ Serena Williams (1981–), US tennis player

Serge *m*
The Latin name *Sergius*, of unknown origin, was borne by an early Christian martyr who has the unusual distinction of being the patron saint of desert nomads, and by four early popes. More importantly it was borne by a 14th-century Russian saint who was a major reformer in the Church and who made the name typically Russian. The name came into use in France in the 20th century and has occasionally crossed from France to the UK.
VARIANTS *Greek* **Sergios** *Italian*, *Spanish* **Sergio** *Polish* **Sergiusz** *Russian* **Sergei**, **Sergey**

Serif, **Serifa** *see* **Sharif**

Sesto *see* **Sextus**

Seth *m*
In chapter four of the biblical book of Genesis we are told 'And Adam knew his wife again; and she bare a son, and called his name Seth: For God, said she, hath appointed me another seed instead of Abel, whom Cain slew'. This has led to the name traditionally being interpreted as 'appointed', but it actually means 'a setting, a cutting', the pun being on the word translated as 'seed'. Found occasionally in the Middle Ages, it was one of the Old Testament names adopted by the Puritans. By the end of the 19th century it was rare, and could be used as a comically rustic name, as in Stella Gibbons's 1932 novel *Cold Comfort Farm*. In recent years there has been a strong revival of the name.
★ Seth Green (1974–), US actor

Seumas *see* **Seamus**

Sevastian, **Sevastyan** *see* **Sebastian**

Severus *m*
Severus was a Latin family name which meant 'stern, severe', and was borne by a dynasty of Roman emperors,

including Septimus Severus. It was also the name of a number of early saints. However, although well established and used for both sexes in other languages, Severus has not been much used by English speakers.

PET FORM **Seve** • VARIANTS *French* **Sévère**, **Séverin**, **Séverine** *German* **Severin**, **Sören** *Italian, Spanish* **Severo**, **Severino**, **Severiano** *Polish* **Seweryn**, **Seweryna** *Scandinavian* **Søren**

★ Seve Ballesteros (1957–), Spanish golfer
★ Søren Kierkegaard (1813–55), Danish philosopher
☆ Severus Snape in the *Harry Potter* books by J K Rowling

Sextus *m*
Meaning 'sixth' in Latin, this was a name traditionally given to a sixth child and, like SEPTIMUS, was common in the Victorian period. It was also the name of five popes, but is now rare.

VARIANTS **Sixtus** *Italian* **Sesto**, **Sisto**
★ Ed (Edmund Sixtus) Muskie (1914–96), US politician whose parents had seven children

Seymour *m*
Seymour is a surname turned first name. As with so many surnames taken up in the 19th century, it is an aristocratic name, the most famous bearer of which was Jane Seymour, the third of Henry VIII's six wives. The surname can have several sources, most notably the French village (now a Parisian suburb) of St-Maur-des-Fosses, the saint's name being a local variant of MAURICE.

PET FORM **Sy**
☆ Seymour Skinner, school principal in *The Simpsons*

Shabnam *f*
This is a Muslim name from the Persian for 'dew' and, by analogy, 'a string of pearls'.

VARIANTS **Shabnum** *Turkish* **S̜ebnem**

Shadi *m* Shadiya *f*
These are Arabic names meaning 'singer' from *shada*, 'to sing'.

Shae *see* Shay

Shaela *see* Shayla

Shafi *m* Shafiqa *f*
An Arabic name meaning 'kind-hearted, compassionate, affectionate'.

Shahnaz *m*
A Persian name formed from the elements *shah*, 'king', and *naz*, 'pride, glory'.

VARIANT **Shenaz**

Shahrazad *see* Sheherazade

Shai *see* Shay

Shaina *see* Shayna

Shakil *m* Shakila *f*
Arabic names from the word for 'handsome, beautiful'. This was one of the Arabic names taken up by African Americans in the 1980s.

Shakir *m* Shakira *f*
From the Arabic for 'thankful, grateful'.
★ Shakira Caine (née Baksh) (1947–), Guyanese model and actress
★ Shakira (1977–), Colombian singer of partly Lebanese descent

Shalimar *f*
This is a 20th-century name, probably introduced in response to Laurence Hope's *Kashmiri Song* (1901) which opens with 'Pale hands I loved beside the Shalimar'. This refers to the Shalimar Gardens, a famous Mughal garden in Kashmir; there is also another well-known garden of the same name in Lahore. The poem was turned into a popular song, featured in the scandalous 1921 film *The Sheik*, sung by Rudolph Valentino, and recorded by many others. The name

was in general use by the 1940s and is probably earlier. Recently, the exotic connotations of the name have been reinforced by its use for a perfume.
VARIANT **Shalamar**

Shalom see **Salome**

Shamus see **Seamus**

Shan, Shana, Shanae f
These names seem to be modern inventions, simply based on a fashionable sound. The picture is somewhat obscured by the fact that Shana and *Shani* are also found as pet forms of *Siân* (see JANE), and indeed Shan can be a respelling of Siân. See also SHAYNA and SHANIA with which variants overlap. These names are also used as pet forms and variants of other *Shan-* names.
VARIANTS **Shanea, Shani, Shanna(h)**

Shanade see **Sinead**

Shane see **Sean**

Shanel, Shanelle see **Chanel**

Shania f
A name popularized by the Canadian singer Shania Twain (b. Eilleen Edwards, 1965). It is said to be from the Ojibwa for 'I'm on my way'. It is pronounced 'she-NYE-a'.
VARIANT **Shanea**

Shanice, Shanika f
These belong to a group of names which were well used, particularly by African Americans, mainly between the 1970s and 90s. They were formed from the fashionable element *Shan-* combined with other fashionable elements, and have no particular significance.
VARIANT **Shaniqua**
★ Shanice (1973–   ), US singer

Shanna see **Shan, Shannon, Susan**

Shannagh see **Senan**

Shannon fm
The name of the River Shannon, in Ireland, comes from the Gaelic *sean*, 'old' (see SENAN, which may have had an influence) and *abhann*, 'river'. Shannon is also a surname. As a first name it became popular in the USA in the 1940s, and was used for both sexes, before spreading to other countries. As with many other new names associated with Ireland, it seems to have first come into use among those of Irish descent outside the country, and was slow to be adopted in Ireland itself. However, Shannon is now a popular choice for girls in Ireland, but is increasingly rare for boys everywhere.
PET FORMS **Shan(na), Shannie** • VARIANTS **Shan(n)en, Shan(n)yn, Shanon**

Shanta, Shanti f
The Sanskrit *santa* means 'pacified, calm', while *santi* is the abstract noun 'tranquillity'. These names are sometimes found in the West, from their use in some disciplines of yoga. Shanti can also be a pet form of the name ASHANTI.

Shantal, Shantel, Shantelle see **Chantal**

Shanti see **Shanta**

Shardae, Sharday see **Sade**

Shareen f
This name has two different sources: it can be an elaboration of SHARON, or it can be a Muslim name, meaning 'dear', a variant of SHIRIN.

Sharel, Sharelle see **Cheryl**

Shari see **Sharon**

Sharif m **Sharifa** f
This is an Arabic name meaning 'venerable, respected', and is a

term used of the descendants of
Muhammad.

VARIANTS **Sharifah, Shareef(a), S(h)erif(a)**

Sharleen, Sharlene see **Charlene**

Sharlotte see **Charlotte**

Sharmaine, Sharmane see
Charmaine

Sharon f
Sharon is the name of a coastal plain
in Palestine, esteemed in the Bible
for its fertility and beauty. In the
biblical Song of Solomon (2.1) the
author rejoices in his vigour and love,
saying 'I am the rose of Sharon, and
the lily of the valleys'. By the 18th
century, Sharon had been adopted as
a masculine first name, most notably
in the person of historian Sharon
Turner (1768–1847), but then fell out
of use. It was reintroduced in the USA,
in the 1920s, as a feminine name.
Although it was already in circulation,
it is thought that the serial novel *The
Skyrocket* (1925), by Adela Rogers St
Johns, may have encouraged its use.
John Steinbeck obviously regarded
Sharon as a suitable name for a young
Midwestern woman in the 1930s,
as he uses 'Rose of Sharon' (usually
appearing as *Rosasharn*) for a character
in his 1939 novel *The Grapes of
Wrath*. The early pronunciation of the
name, at least in the UK, was to rhyme
the first syllable with 'share', but by the
time of its peak popularity in the 1960s
and 70s the 'a' was usually short as in
'shall'. The excessive prevalence of the
name in this period, alongside that of
TRACY, resulted in its becoming a term
of disparagement which led to a rapid
decline in use. There are a number
of elaborations of the name which
are also found, such as *Sharonda* and
Sharona.

PET FORMS **Shari, Shaz(za)** • VARIANTS
Sharron, Sharyn

★ Sharon Osbourne (1952–), English
music promoter and television
personality

★ Sharon Stone (1958–), US actress

☆ Sharon Falconer in the 1927 novel
Elmer Gantry, by Sinclair Lewis, filmed
in 1960

Sharrel, Sharrelle see **Cheryl**

Shaul see **Saul**

Shaun see **Sean, Shawn**

Shavon, Shavawn see **Siobhan**

Shawn mf
This is a respelling of SEAN, the Irish
equivalent of JOHN, based on its
pronunciation. Although SIOBHAN is
the standard Irish feminine of Sean,
Shawn has recently come to be used as
an alternative. There are a number of
other feminines: *Shawna*; *Shawnelle*;
Shawndelle; and *Shawnda*; and,
based on other forms of Sean, *Seanna*,
Shauna and *Seaneen*. The names
Shaunee, *Shauni* and *Shawnie* can
either be further variants or else forms
of the name of the Native American
Shawnee nation, which is also found
as a first name.

Shay mf
This is the most common form of the
first name from the Irish surname
[O']Shea, which comes from the old
name *Séaghdha* meaning 'hawklike'.
The name takes a number of forms
and has been growing in use since the
1970s. The Scottish variant has been
anglicized as *Shaw*.

VARIANTS **Shae, Shea, Shaye, Shai, Shi,
Sheigh** Irish **Sé** Scots Gaelic **Seaghdh**

Shayla f
This can be analysed either as a variant
of SHEILA, or as a blend of names
such as Sheila and KAYLA. There are a
number of recent similar names such
as *Shaylee* and *Shaylyn*.

VARIANTS **Shaela, Shaylah, Shailie, Shayleigh, Shalynn, Shealynn**

Shayna *f*
This is a Yiddish name meaning 'beautiful' which has spread beyond the Jewish community.
VARIANTS **Shaina, Sheine**

Shayne *see* **Sean**

Shaz, **Shazza** *see* **Sharon**

Shea *see* **Shay**

Shealynn *see* **Shayla**

Sheamus *see* **Seamus**

Sheary *see* **Geoffrey**

Sheba *f*
Historically, Sheba was usually a pet form of BATHSHEBA. However, the name, which has never been common, has become separated from its source, and is now more likely to be associated with the glamour of the Queen of Sheba – traditionally called *Bilqis* in Arabic tradition, but unnamed in either the Old Testament or the Koran. See also SABAH.

Sheena *f*
This is the anglicized form of *Sine* the Irish and Scots Gaelic equivalent of JANE, and the form that it is most often found outside Scotland.
VARIANTS **Sheenagh, Shena**
★ Sheena Easton (1959–), Scottish singer
☆ Sheena, Queen of the Jungle, the eponymous heroine of the 1930s comic book series which has since been made into a film and two television series
☆ 'Sheena is a Punk Rocker', a 1977 song by the Ramones

Sheigh *see* Shay

Sheila *f*
This is the anglicized spelling of the name *Síle*, an Irish form of CICILY. It started to be used outside Ireland in the 19th century, and was at its most popular in the 1930s, by which time it had lost a sense of being Irish and its connection with Cicily. It has also developed numerous spellings. The name is not often chosen at the moment. The Australian slang use of 'sheila' as a generic term for 'woman' was coined in the 19th century. See also SHAYLA. In the past Síle could be anglicized as SABINA.
VARIANTS **She(e)lagh, Sheelah, Shelegh, Shelia, Shyla, Shiela, Shela**

Sheine *see* **Shayna**

Shel *see* **Rachel**

Shelby *fm*
This is a surname of uncertain origin used as a first name. Although it has been used as a masculine name since the 19th century and as a feminine name from the 1930s, its popularity as a feminine name started in 1989 when it was used for a character in the film *Steel Magnolias*.
PET FORM **Sheb** • VARIANT **Shelbie**

Sheldon *m*
This is a surname, from a number of sources, which has been used as a first name since the 19th century, most frequently in the USA.
PET FORM **Shelly**
★ Sheldon Glashow (1932–), US Nobel Prize-winning physicist

Shelley *f*
This now independent name can come from a number of sources. It can be a use of the surname, sometimes with specific reference to the poet Percy Bysshe Shelley. This was usually the context in which it was given as a masculine name in the past. It can also be a variant of SHIRLEY. Most often it is

a pet form of names such as MICHELLE or RACHEL that contain the 'shel' sound.

PET FORM **Shell** • VARIANTS **Shelly, Shellie**

★ Shelley Winters (1920–2006), US actress who did much to publicize the name

Shemus see **Seamus**

Shenaz see **Shahnaz**

Sher m
This is the Persian for 'lion', which has become an Indian name, partly influenced by the fame of the 16th-century Mughal ruler Sher Shah.

Shereen see **Shirin**

Sheridan mf
A surname, from an old Irish name of unknown meaning. Once exclusively masculine, it is now more likely to be given to girls.

PET FORM **Sherry**

★ Sheridan Le Fanu (1814–73), Irish novelist and journalist
★ Sheridan Morley (1941–2007), English critic and writer

Sherif, Sherifa see **Sharif**

Sherill see **Cheryl**

Sherilyn see **Cherilyn**

Sherman m
This is mainly a US name, from a surname originally given to someone who sheared the nap on cloth. Its use as a first name is linked to the fame of General William Tecumseh Sherman (1820–91).

☆ Sherman McCoy, protagonist of Tom Wolfe's 1987 novel *The Bonfire of the Vanities*

Sherry f
A variant of CHERIE or pet form of SHERIDAN, which may occasionally be used with reference to the wine (compare BRANDY).

VARIANT **Sherri(e)**

Sheryl see **Cheryl**

Shevaun see **Siobhan**

Shi see **Shay**

Shiane see **Cheyenne**

Shiela see **Sheila**

Shiloh fm
A name which has recently been in the news as a celebrity choice, this has actually been used as a masculine name among Jews since the early Middle Ages. Interpreted to mean 'he who has been appointed', it appears in a prophetic passage in the biblical book of Genesis (49.10) which was thought to refer to the coming of the Messiah.

Shilpa f
This is an Indian name, from the Sanskrit for 'work of art, decoration'.
VARIANT **Silpa**
★ Shilpa Shetty (1975–   ), Indian actress

Shimme, Shimmel, Shimon see **Simon**

Shinade see **Sinead**

Shirin f
This is borne by a heroine of the great Persian epic the *Shahnama* and later stories, which tell of the love between her and Farhad. The name has spread to Western use. It means 'sweet, charming, agreeable'. See also SHAREEN.
VARIANTS **Shireen, Shereen**

Shirley f
This was originally a surname which could come from a number of place names with different meanings. It was in use in the 18th century as a masculine name, and is still very occasionally found as such – for example, the wrestler known as 'Big Daddy' was born Shirley Crabtree

(1937–97). It became established as a feminine name after Charlotte Brontë published her 1849 novel *Shirley*. The name was particularly popular in the 1930s when child star Shirley Temple (b.1928) was charming filmgoers with her singing and dancing.

PET FORMS **Shirl**, **Sherry** • VARIANTS **Shirlee**, **Shirly**, **Shirlene**

★ Shirley MacLaine (1934–   ), US actress
★ Dame Shirley Bassey (1937–   ), Welsh singer

Shivani *f*
This is one of the names of the Hindu goddess Parvati, in her role as consort to Shiva.

★ Shivani (1923–2003), popular Indian writer

Shivaun *see* **Siobhan**

Shlomit *see* **Shula**

Shmuel *see* **Samuel**

Sholto *m*
This is the anglicized form of the Gaelic *Sioltach* meaning 'sower' and, by implication, 'fruitful'. It is traditionally associated with the Douglas family, which is said to have been founded by a bearer of the name, and is most likely to be found coupled with that surname.

Shona *f*
This is the anglicized form of the Scots Gaelic form of SINEAD, *Seonag* or *Seònaid*, all forms of JOAN. Shona is still predominantly a Scottish name, but has spread elsewhere. SHEENA is related.

VARIANTS **Shonagh**, **Seona** *Scots Gaelic* **Seonag**, **Seònaid**, **Deònaid**

Shontelle *see* **Chantal**

Shoshana, Shoshanah, Shoshanna, Shoshannah *see* **Susan**

Shree *see* **Shri**

Shreya *f*
This means 'auspicious, lucky' in Sanskrit.

Shri *f*
This name, meaning 'radiance, beauty' in Sanskrit, is one of the names of the goddess Lakshmi.

VARIANTS **Sri**, **Siri**, **S(h)ree**

Shug, Shuggie *see* **Hugh**

Shula, Shulamit *f*
This is the Hebrew for 'peacefulness' from *shalom*, 'peace'. A popular name in Israel, it comes from a passage in the biblical Song of Solomon (6.13) in which peace is personified in the words 'Return, return, O *Shulamite*; return, return, that we may look upon thee'. The short form Shula has become familiar in the UK through the character of that name in the long-running radio soap *The Archers*, although in her case it was purportedly formed from a random selection of letters.

VARIANTS **Shulam(m)ite**, **Shulamith** *Hebrew* **Shlomit**

Shura *see* **Alexander, Alexandra, Sasha**

Shyann, Shyanne *see* **Cheyenne**

Shyla *see* **Sheila**

Si *see* **Simon**

Siân *see* **Jane**

Sianade *see* **Sinead**

Siarl *see* **Charles**

Sib, Sibb *see* **Sybil**

Sibéal *see* **Isabel**

Sibilla, Sibyl *see* **Sybil**

Sidney *mf*
This is an aristocratic surname which can be derived either from the French

place name St Denis or from an English place name meaning 'wide meadow'. It came into use as a first name for both sexes in the 16th century, and was spelt indiscriminately Sidney or *Sydney*, the two forms often being used for the same person. Nowadays the 'y' spelling tends to be reserved for females. Sidney continued in steady use for both sexes into the 19th century when aristocratic surnames became popular and the male use became predominant. However, the name is now out of favour as a masculine, and is far more likely to be found as a feminine, particularly in the USA where it has been among the most popular feminine names of the 21st century. Although *Cyd*, as in the actress and dancer Cyd Charisse (1922–2008), looks like a variant and is treated as such, it was in fact a childhood nickname, based on the word 'sister'.

PET FORMS **Sid, Syd** • VARIANTS **Sydney, Sidnee, Sydne(e)**

★ Sydney Owenson, Lady Morgan (1783–1859), Irish novelist and nationalist
☆ Sydney Carton, romantic hero of Dickens's *A Tale of Two Cities* (1859)

Sidonia *f*

This simply means 'woman of Sidon'. It is found in medieval England as *Sidony*, but was most used in France in the 19th century as *Sidonie*, a form that sometimes made its way into English. It has been suggested that Sidony was the source of the feminine form of SIDNEY, but there is little evidence to support this view.

PET FORM **Siddy** • VARIANTS **Sidony, Sidonea**

★ Sidonie-Gabrielle Colette (1873–1954), French author, usually just called Colette
☆ Sidonie Verdurin, character in Marcel Proust's *À la recherche du temps perdu*

Sidra *f*

This is a Muslim name. It comes from the term for a tree that is said to grow in Paradise.

Sieffre *see* Geoffrey

Siegfried *m*

An old Germanic name formed from *sige*, 'victory', and *frid*, 'peace'. It was borne by a doomed hero in ancient Germanic legend, the best-known version of which is found in the *Nibelungenlied*. The name was revived in the 19th century after Wagner retold the story in his *Ring* cycle of operas. In Norse legend the hero is called *Sigurd* (see SIGMUND).

PET FORM **Sigi**

★ Siegfried Sassoon (1886–1967), English poet and novelist
☆ Siegfried Farnon is the senior vet in the semi-autobiographical novels of James Herriot

Sieglinde *see* Ségolène

Sieman *see* Simon

Sienna *f*

This name sometimes appears as *Siena*, the spelling of the Italian city, but more often as Sienna, familiar as the spelling of the brown pigment. The pigment is called after the city which got its name from the Etruscan tribe who founded it, the *Saina*.

VARIANT **Siena**

★ Sienna Miller (1981–), English actress, born in New York
★ Sienna Guillory (1975–), English actress and model

Sierra *f*

This is the Spanish word for a mountain range that has been popular in the USA since the 1980s. There is some overlap with CIARA.

Sigi *see* Ségolène, Siegfried, Sigrid

Sigmund *m*

This is an Old Germanic name, particularly associated with Scandinavia, formed from *sigr*, 'victory', and *mund*, 'protector'. In Norse mythology Sigmund is the father of *Signy* ('victory' plus 'new') and her brother *Sigurd* ('victory' plus 'guardian'). Sigurd is the dragon-slayer who fulfils the same role as SIEGFRIED in German mythology. Similarly from Norse mythology is the name of the Valkyrie *Sigrun*, from 'victory' and *run*, 'secret lore, rune'. See also SÉGOLÈNE.

VARIANTS **Signi**, **Signe**

★ Sigmund Freud (1856–1939), Austrian neurologist, the founder of psychoanalysis

Sigourney *f*

This is a surname of uncertain origin, most notably that of the popular 19th-century US author Lydia Sigourney (1791–1865). F Scott Fitzgerald took her name for the character of Sigourney Howard in his 1925 novel *The Great Gatsby*. The actress Sigourney Weaver, who has made the name widely known, chose to change her given name of Susan to Sigourney when a child because, it is said, she liked the Fitzgerald character.

Sigrid *f*

This is an Old Norse name from *sigr*, 'victory', and *frithr*, 'fair', which is occasionally found among English speakers, particularly those of Scandinavian descent in the USA. The name has been out of fashion in Scandinavia for some time, but is just beginning to show increased use.

PET FORM **Sigi**

Silas *m*

This is a New Testament name, a shortening of the Greek *Silouanus*, a form of SILVESTER. Both forms of the name are used in the biblical Acts of the Apostles to describe a companion of St Paul in his ministry. There is a certain fashion for the name at the moment.

☆ Silas Marner, eponymous hero of George Eliot's 1861 novel

☆ Silas is the name of the fanatical albino monk in *The Da Vinci Code*

Sile *see* **Sheila**

Silence *see* **Patience**, **Tacey**

Silke *see* **Celia**

Silpa *see* **Shilpa**

Silvester *m* Silvestra *f*

Silvester comes from the Latin *silvestris*, 'of the woods'. It was borne by three early popes including one who was made a saint. It has never been a particularly common name in English, but is well used in other languages. Silvestra has been even rarer.

PET FORM **Sly** • VARIANTS **Silas**, **Sylvestra**, **Sylvester** *French* **Sylvestre** *German* **Vester**, **Fester** *Italian* **Silvestro** *Polish* **Sylwester**

★ Sylvester Stallone (1946–   ), US film actor and director

☆ Sylvester the Cat in the *Looney Toons* cartoons

Silvia *f*

Like SILVESTER, Silvia comes from the Latin *silva*, 'wood'. In Roman legend Rhea Silvia was the mother of ROMULUS and REMUS, the founders of Rome. Silvia entered the stock of Christian names as that of the 6th-century St Silvia, mother of St Gregory the Great. From there it entered the stock of Italian names, and seems to have come to England via Shakespeare's *Two Gentlemen of Verona*, in which it is used as a typically Italian name.

VARIANTS **Sylvia** *French* **Sylvie**, **Silvie** *Italian*, *Spanish* **Silvio** (m) *Polish* **Sylwia**

★ Sylvia Plath (1932–63), US poet

★ Sylvia Syms (1934–), English actress

Sim *see* Simon

Simchas *mf*
A Hebrew name meaning 'joy'. It can also be used to mean 'a festive occasion', and has a religious overtone.

Simeon *m*
This variant form of the name SIMON is particularly associated with the old man who blessed the infant Jesus at the Temple, recognizing him as the Messiah (Bible, Luke 2.25). In the Old Testament it is found as the name of one of the twelve sons of Jacob who founded the tribes of Israel. It was also borne by several distinguished medieval rabbis and saints.
VARIANT **Symeon**

Simon *m* Simone *f*
This is the standard form of the name also found as SIMEON. It comes from the Hebrew word *sham'a*, 'to listen'. There are a number of Simons in both the Old and New Testament, with probably the most significant one for the stock of European names being the Apostle Simon Peter. The name was very popular in the Middle Ages, when it often appeared as *Sim* or *Simkin*, declined after the Reformation and became very fashionable again in the 1960s and 70s. Simon is not now well used, but the French-derived feminine Simone is much more common.
PET FORMS **Si, Sim** • VARIANTS **Simonette, Symon** *Dutch* **Sieman** *Hebrew* **Shimon** *Italian* **Simona, Simonetta** *Polish* **Szymon** *Portuguese* **Simão** *Russian* **Semyon** *Scandinavian* **Simen** *Spanish* **Simón** *Yiddish* **Shimme(l)**
★ Simon Cowell (1959–), English music producer and television personality
★ Simone Signoret (1921–85), French actress

Sinclair *m*
This is a Scottish aristocratic and clan name, originally a Norman French form of a place in France called Saint-Claire. It became established as a first name alongside other such surnames in the 19th century.
★ Sinclair Lewis (1885–1951), US novelist

Sindy *see* Cindy

Sine *see* Sheena

Sìne, Síne *see* Jane

Sinead *f*
Pronounced 'shi-NAYD', this is the Irish form of JANET, arrived at via the French form *Jeanette*. The 's' is the nearest Irish gets to a French 'j' sound. The name has become widespread outside Ireland, and because Irish spellings are difficult to reconcile with the sounds, has developed numerous phonetic variants.
VARIANTS **Shinade, Shanade, Seonade, Sianade** *Scots Gaelic* **Sèonade**
★ Sinead Cusack (1948–), Irish actress

Sinjin *see* St John

Sinty *see* Hyacinth

Siobhan *f*
This is the Irish form of JOAN, developed via the Norman French *Jeanne* (compare SINEAD). It has become widely popular outside Ireland, but because of the disparity of the pronunciation, 'shi-VAWN', with non-Irish spelling systems, is often found in respelt forms.
VARIANTS **Shavon, Shavawn, Shevaun, Shivaun, Chevonne** *Scots Gaelic* **Siubhan**
★ Siobhan McKenna (1923–86), Irish actress

Siôn, Sioni, Sionyn *see* John

Siôr, Siors, Siorus *see* George

Siothrun, Siothrún *see* Geoffrey

Siri *see* **Shri, Sigrid**

Siriol *f*
This is a Welsh name, from the vocabulary word meaning 'happy, contented, cheerful'. It is a modern name which is currently popular with Welsh parents.

Sis, Sisley, Sissie, Sissy *see* **Cicily**

Sisto *see* **Sextus**

Sita *f*
This is the Sanskrit for 'furrow' and is the name of the Hindu goddess of harvest. She appears in the *Ramayana* as the wife of Rama.
VARIANT **Seet(h)a**

Siubhan *see* **Siobhan**

Siùsaidh, Siùsan *see* **Susan**

Sive *see* **Sadhbh**

Siwan *see* **Joan**

Sjef *see* **Joseph**

Skye *mf*
This is the name of the Hebridean island renowned for its beauty and back-to-nature lifestyle. It also carries with it the associations of the vocabulary word 'sky', and may sometimes be used in this sense. It is given to both sexes, but most often to girls. Use may also have some overlap with SKYLER, below. It is a modern name, but in the 21st century has been popular in the USA, the British Isles and Australia.
VARIANT **Sky**
★ Ione Skye (Leitch) (1971–   ), British-born US actress, who drew attention to the name
★ Skye Sweetnam (1988–   ), Canadian singer

Skyler *mf*
This is a modern respelling of *Schuyler*, which is a Dutch surname meaning 'scholar'. There were Schuylers prominent in the early history of New York. The name is thought to have been adopted in honour of the US general and senator Philip Schuyler (1733–1804). It was well established in the 19th century; an early bearer of the name was Schuyler Colfax (1823–85), 17th vice-president of the USA. The 'Sky' spelling of the name began to appear in the USA in the 1980s, perhaps influenced by TYLER.
VARIANTS **Schuyler, Skyla(r)**

Slaney *f*
This is a traditional Irish name meaning 'health' which was once borne by a goddess. It is pronounced 'SLAW-nyeh' or 'SLAWN-ya'. In the Middle Ages the name was particularly associated with the O'Briens and MacNamaras.
VARIANTS **Slany, Slania, Slanie** *Irish* **Sláine**

Sly *see* **Silvester**

Sofia, Sofie, Sofiya *see* **Sophia**

Sofronia *see* **Sophronia**

Sol *fm*
Sol is a Spanish and Portuguese name meaning 'the sun'. It can also be a short form of names such as SOLDEDAD and MARISOL, and as a masculine, SOLOMON.

Solange *f*
The Latin *sollemnis*, 'solemn, religous', became the Late Latin name *Sollemnia*, 'religious festival', which in turn became Solange in French popular speech, with *Solène* being a more learned form. Solange was the name of a 9th-century French saint, whose legend describes her as a young shepherdess pledged to virginity, who died rather than be ravished by a local lord. George Sand chose the name for her daughter in 1828, but otherwise it was not used in modern times until the 1920s in France.

★ Solange (1986–), US singer and actress

☆ Solange is one of the main characters in Salvador Dali's only novel *Hidden Faces* (1944)

Soledad *f*
A Spanish religious name, taken from a title of the Virgin Mary, *Nuestra Señora de la Soledad*, 'Our Lady of Solitude'.

Solomon *m*
This name comes from the Hebrew *shalom*, 'peace'. In the Old Testament Solomon is the wise and magnificent king of Israel, who is credited with writing several books of the Bible and who embellished the Temple. There has been increased interest in the name in recent years.
PET FORMS **Sol, Solly** • VARIANTS *Arabic* **Sulaiman, Sulayman** *French, Polish, Scandinavian* **Salomon** *Turkish* **Süleiman, Süleyman** *Yiddish* **Schlomo, Zalman**
☆ Solomon Grundy in the traditional rhyme about him

Somaya *f*
This started out as a pet form of the name *Saamia*, 'high', but is now used independently. See also SAMI.
VARIANTS **Sommia, Sumay(y)a**
★ Sumayyah bint Khayyat (6th century), the first person to be martyred for being a Muslim

Somerled, Somhairle *see* Sorley

Sondra *see* Sandra

Sonia *f*
Originally a Russian pet form of SOPHIA, this has been used as an independent name by English speakers since the beginning of the 20th century. While in the UK the standard pronunciation is 'SON-ya', in the USA the first syllable can also be 'sawn'.
VARIANTS **Sonya** *German* **Sonja, Sonje**
★ Sonia Delaunay (1885–1979), Ukrainian-French artist

☆ Red Sonja, the She-Devil with a Sword, a comic-book character from 1973, adapted for film in 1985

Sonny *m*
In the past this was mainly a nickname from 'son' or else a pet form of names such as *Sandro* (see SANDRA) or *Santino* (see SANCHIA). It is now increasingly being used as an independent name.
VARIANT **Sonni**

Soo *see* Susan

Sophia, Sophie *f*
This name comes from the Greek word for 'wisdom', originally with specific reference to the *Hagia Sophia*, the 'holy wisdom'. As well as meaning 'holy', *Hagia* is also used as the word for 'saint' (which comes from the Latin equivalent), so it is not surprising that legends grew up about a St Sophia. The name was well used in Europe in the Middle Ages, but only caught on in England in the 17th century and really took off in the 18th, under the influence of the Hanoverians, as Sophia was a German royal name. Sophie is the French form of the name, which is currently the more usual choice for parents, although both are popular.
PET FORMS **Sonia, Phia** • VARIANTS **Sofia, Sofie, Sophy** *Polish* **Zofia, Zosia** *Russian* **Sofiya** *Slovak* **Zofia** *Yiddish* **Tzofiya**

Sophronia *f*
This comes from the Greek name *Sophronios*, from *sophron* meaning 'self-controlled, sensible', related to the source of SOPHIA. The name has been recorded in the UK from the 14th century, but has never been common. It was most used in the 19th century.
PET FORM **Frona** • VARIANTS **Sophronie** *Italian* **Sofronia**
☆ Sophronia Lammle in Charles Dickens's 1865 novel *Our Mutual Friend*

☆ Sofronia is a heroine in Torquato Tasso's 1581 epic *Jerusalem Delivered*, and the best-known use of the name

Soraya *f*
This is a Muslim name which has spread to the West. It comes from the Persian name for the constellation known as the Pleiades.
VARIANTS **Suray(y)a**, **Thurayya**
★ Soraya (1969–2006), US singer of Lebanese-Colombian descent
★ Soraya Tarzi (1899–1968), wife of the last king of Afghanistan, promoter of women's rights

Sorcha *f*
This is an old Irish name meaning 'radiant, bright'. It is pronounced variously 'SUR-a-ka', 'SOR-ha', 'SURK-ha' and 'SORR-kha' and is currently popular in Ireland. In the past it was anglicized as SARAH or SALLY, or sometimes *Clara* (see CLARE) because of the similarity of meaning.
VARIANT **Sorche**
★ Sorcha Cusack (1949–   ), Irish actress
☆ The main character in Juliet Marillier's popular 1999 novel *Daughter of the Forest* is called Sorcha

Sören, **Søren** *see* **Severus**

Sorley *m*
Sorley is the anglicized form of *Somerled*, a Scottish Highland name from the Old Norse *Somarlithr*, 'summer traveller'. This would originally have been a nickname, and has been linked to Viking raiding. It was the name of the founder of the Clan Macdonald and was in regular use among their rulers in the Middle Ages.
VARIANTS **Summerlad** *Irish* **Somhairle**
★ Sorley MacLean (Somhairle MacGill-Eain) (1911–96), Scottish poet who wrote in both English and Gaelic

Sorrel *f*
This can be regarded as being taken from the plant name, or it can refer to the rich red-brown colour found in animals, such as red setters and some breeds of horse, as well as in human hair.
VARIANT **Sor(r)el(l)**
☆ Sorel Bliss in Noël Coward's 1925 play *Hay Fever*. This use may have been inspired by Agnes Sorel, the 15th-century mistress of the French King Charles VII, who was famous for her beauty

Soumaya *see* **Sami**

Spencer *m*
Originally a term for a steward of a manor (who was a *dispenser* of things), this was one of the aristocratic surnames taken up in the 19th century. It is occasionally given to females.
VARIANT **Spenser**
★ Spencer Perceval (1762–1812), English statesman, the only British prime minister so far to have been assassinated
★ Spencer Tracy (1900–67), US film actor who did much to popularize the name in the 20th century

Speranza *f*
This is an Italian name meaning 'hope' used as a personification by Dante in his *Divine Comedy*. Speranza was the pen name under which Lady Jane Wilde (1821–96), mother of the more famous Oscar, wrote Irish nationalist journalism.
VARIANTS *French* **Espérance** *Spanish* **Esperanza**

Spike *m*
This is usually a nickname, often given with reference to someone with spiky, or a tuft of, hair.
★ Spike Jones (1911–65), US bandleader
★ Spike Milligan (1918–2002), Irish humorist

★ Spike Lee (1957–), US film director

Spiro *see* **Spyridon**

Spring *f*
This is the name of the season used as a first name. Although it has been recorded since the 19th century it is rare, unlike SUMMER. This is perhaps because of the alternative, mechanical sense of the word.

★ Spring Byington (1886–1971), US actress

Spyridon *m*
This is a Greek name, derived ultimately from the Latin *spiritus*. The name is popular in Greece and is particularly associated with Corfu, which is home to the body of the 4th-century St Spyridon. The saint's relics are said to have protected the island from a plague.

PET FORMS **Spyro(s)**, **Spiro** • VARIANT **Spyridion**

★ Spyridon Marinatos (1901–74), Greek archaeologist, who discovered the Minoan city buried in volcanic ash at Thera

★ Spiro Agnew (1918–96), disgraced US vice-president under Nixon

Sree, Sri *see* **Shri**

St John *m*
This religious name was introduced in the 19th century, and is now rare. It was given in honour of St John the Baptist and as a first name, although not always as a surname, is pronounced 'sinj(e)n'.

VARIANT **Sinjin**

☆ St John Rivers, evangelical clergyman in Charlotte Brontë's *Jane Eyre* (1847)

Stacey *mf*
This comes from a surname, which in turn came from a medieval first name derived from a pet form of EUSTACE. As a girl's name it can also be a pet form of ANASTASIA. It was in occasional use as a masculine name in the USA from the 19th century, then became rare until the 1930s when it began to be revived. It appeared as a female name in the USA in the 1950s and had become very popular by the 1970s. The spelling *Stacy* tends to be preferred in the USA, but Stacey is more usual in the UK.

VARIANTS **Stacy, Staci(e)**

★ Stacy Keach (m) (1941–), US actor

☆ Malibu Stacy is the brand name of the doll that parodies the Barbie® in the television cartoon *The Simpsons*

Staffan *see* **Stephen**

Stanislas *m*
This is the Latinate form of the Slavic name *Stanislav*, formed from the elements *stan*, 'stand', and *slav*, 'glory'. St Stanislav of Cracow (1030–79) was a bishop who was murdered, probably by King Boleslaw the Cruel of Poland, whose immoral way of life he had attacked. The name is used in Ireland to anglicize the Irish *Anéislis*, 'careful, thoughtful'.

VARIANTS *German* **Stanislaus** *Italian* **Stanislao**

★ Stanislaus Joyce (1884–1955), Irish author and assistant to his more famous brother James

Stanley *m*
An aristocratic surname from a place name formed from Old English *stan*, 'stone', and *leah*, 'field'. It was in use as a first name by the 18th century, but became popular in the 19th thanks to the fame of Henry Morton Stanley (1841–1904), who uttered the immortal line 'Dr Livingston, I presume'.

PET FORM **Stan**

★ Stanley Baldwin (1867–1947), English politician and prime minister

★ Sir Stanley Matthews (1915–2000), English footballer

Star *f*

This is the vocabulary word which has occasionally been used as a first name since at least the beginning of the 20th century. Compare STELLA.

VARIANTS **Starr, Starla**

Stasia *see* **Anastasia**

Stavros *m* **Stavroula** *f*

Stavros is the Greek word for the Cross used as a first name. These are popular names in Greece.

★ Stavros Spyros Niarchos (1909–96), Greek shipping magnate

☆ Stavros, the Greek takeaway owner, was a character created by the comedian Harry Enfield in the 1980s

Steeny, Stefan *see* **Stephen**

Stefanie, Steff, Steffie *see* **Stephanie**

Stelios *m*

This Greek name is a shortening of the name *Stylianos*, from *stylos* meaning 'pillar'. St Stylianos of Paphlagonia was a 9th-century hermit who is the patron saint of children. *Styliani*, shortened to STELLA is the feminine form.

★ Sir Stelios Haji-Ioannou (1941–), Greek-born businessman who founded the economy airline easyJet

Stella *f*

This is the Latin for 'star'. It was used in the Middle Ages in titles for the Virgin Mary, where she was addressed in poetry as *Stella Maris*, 'star of the sea', and *Stella Coeli*, 'star of the sky'. In the 16th century, after the Reformation, it was introduced as a literary name by Sir Philip Sidney in his sonnets *Astrophel* ['star-lover' in Greek] *and Stella*; a series of poems addressed to Lady Penelope Devereux. Stella remained in regular literary use through to the 19th century, most notably in Swift's *Journal to Stella* (1710–13). It started to be used as a

given name in the 19th century, by which time it had appeared in several novels, which may have helped the transition. The name was popular in the later 19th century and into the early 20th, and is undergoing something of a revival at the moment. See also ESTELLE.

★ Stella Tennant (1970–), Scottish model

★ Stella McCartney (1972–), English fashion designer

Stéphane *see* **Stephen**

Stephanie *f*

This name began as a French feminine of STEPHEN, derived from Latin *Stephania*, originally *Stephana*, the feminine of *Stephanus*. St Stephanie was a 2nd-century martyr from Damascus. Stephanie was introduced to English speakers in the late 19th century, and was very popular in the 1990s.

PET FORMS **Steph, Steff, Steffie, Steffy, Stevie •** VARIANTS **Stephany, Stephani** *Dutch* **Stefana** *French* **Fanny, Stéphanie** *German* **Stefanie, Steffi(e)** *Hawaiian* **Kekepania** *Italian* **Stefania** *Polish* **Stefania, Stefcia** *Spanish* **Estefanía**

★ Stephanie Beacham (1947–), English actress

★ Steffi Graf (1969–), German tennis player

Stephen, Steven *m*

Of the two spellings of this name, Stephen is marginally the preferred one in the UK, while Steven has the edge in the USA. The name comes from the Greek *Stephanos* meaning 'crown', and was borne by the first man to achieve the crown of martyrdom for Christianity. The Feast of Stephen is celebrated on 26 December. There is a later, 10th-century, St Stephen who was the first Christian king of Hungary, and is the patron saint of the country.

England also had a King Stephen (c.1097–1154), although his reputation is far from saintly. The name, however, has remained in regular use since his time.

PET FORMS **Ste(ve)**, **Stevie** • VARIANTS *Irish* **Stiofáa** *Scots Gaelic* **Steafan**, **Steaphan** *Scottish* **Steenie** *Welsh* **Steffan** *Dutch* **Stef**, **Stefanus** *French* **Étienne**, **Stéphane** *German* **Stefan**, **Steffen**, **Stephan** *Greek* **Stefanos**, **Stephanos** *Hungarian* **Istvan**, **Pista**, **Pisti** *Italian* **Stefano** *Polish* **Szczepan** *Portuguese* **Estevão** *Scandinavian* **Staffan** *Spanish* **Estavan**, **Esteban**

★ Stephen Hawking (1942–), English theoretical physicist
★ Steven Spielberg (1946–), US film producer and director

Sterling *see* Stirling

Stevie *mf*
Developed from the short form *Steve*, this is a pet form of both STEPHEN and STEPHANIE, now given as an independent name. It is also found as a form of similar names.
VARIANTS **Stevi**, **Stevey**

★ Stevie Smith (f) (1902–71), English poet and novelist
★ Stevie Wonder (m) (1950–), US soul, pop and rock singer and instrumentalist

Stewart *see* Stuart

Stian *see* Christian, Stig

Stig *m*
Stig is a Scandinavian name, originally a short form of the Old Norse *Stígandr*, 'wanderer'. However, it is better known to English speakers as the name given to the Stone Age boy in Clive King's children's classic *Stig of the Dump* (1963).
VARIANT **Stian**

Stijn *see* Augustine

Stiofáa *see* Stephen

Stirling *m*
This is the name of a Scottish town which became a surname and then a first name. The origin of the place name is not known, although Celtic *ystre Velyn*, 'house of Melyn', has been suggested. *Sterling* is the more usual form in the USA. The name is occasionally used for females.
VARIANT **Sterling**

★ Sir Stirling Moss (1929–), English racing driver

Storm *mf* Stormy *f*
These meteorological names began to appear in the 1960s, but did not make their mark until the 1990s. Storm is mainly masculine in the USA, but more often feminine in the UK.
VARIANT **Stormee**

☆ Storm Logan (m) was a character in the television soap *The Bold and the Beautiful*
☆ Storm (f) is a character in the Marvel comics *X-Men*, and the films made of them

Strachan *m*
This is a Scottish surname, turned into a first name, meaning 'little valley'.
VARIANT **Strahan**

Struan *m*
This is a Scottish aristocratic title and surname, from a place name derived from Gaelic *sruthan*, 'streams'. It has been used since at least the 19th century and is currently in regular use.

Stuart *m*
This Scottish name became a surname after King David I of Scotland bestowed the title of Hereditary Steward of Scotland on Walter Stewart (a respelling of the word) in the 12th century. The family was prominent in Scottish politics and marriage into the royal family led to the first Stuart king Robert II (1316–90). Stuart is the French respelling of Stewart, and was

the form used by Mary Queen of Scots who was half French and spent much of her childhood in France. The name became widely popular in Britain in the 1950s and 60s, and is still well used in Scotland.

PET FORM **Stu** • VARIANT **Stewart**

★ Stuart Sutcliffe (1940–62), English musician, 'the fifth Beatle'

Su see **Susan**

Suad f
An Arabic name of uncertain origin, perhaps meaning 'happiness'.

Sudha f
This is an Indian name, from the Sanskrit for 'nectar'.

Sue, **Sukie** see **Susan**

Suelo see **Consuelo**

Sulaiman, **Sulayman**, **Süleiman** see **Solomon**

Sultan m **Sultana** f
These names come from the Arabic for 'ruler'.

Sumaya, **Sumayya** see **Somaya**

Summer f
A season name that came into use in the 1970s and is now becoming increasingly popular.

★ Summer Glau (1981–   ), US actress
☆ Summer Swann, character in the television soap *EastEnders*

Summerlad see **Sorley**

Sunil m
This is an Indian word from the Sanskrit for 'very dark blue'. Blue has religious associations for Hindus, and is the colour of the god Vishnu's skin. The word is also used to describe the pomegranate tree and the flax plant.

Sunita f
An Indian name formed from Sanskrit

su, 'good, well', and *nita*, 'conducted'. In the past it was a masculine name, but is now feminine. It was borne by a male follower of the Buddha. The variant *Suniti* is the legendary mother of the pole star. Compare SUSHIL.

VARIANT **Suniti**

★ Sunita Williams (1965–   ), US astronaut
☆ Sunita Alahan, character in the television soap *Coronation Street*

Sunniva f
This Scandinavian name is a form of the Old English name *Sunngifu*, 'sun gift'. A saint bearing the name is said to have fled a forced marriage and taken refuge in Scandinavia. The locals suspected she and her followers had been stealing sheep and killed them.

VARIANTS **Synnöva**, **Synnøve**

Sunny mf
The vocabulary word, often a nickname for someone cheerful, but also sometimes found as a given name, perhaps influenced by SONNY.

Suraj m
The Sanskrit for 'born of the gods'. The related *Surya* is the name of the sun god.

Suraya, **Surayya** see **Soraya**

Suri f
This name received a lot of publicity recently when it was chosen by actors Tom Cruise and Katie Holmes for their daughter. They said they had chosen it as a name with two meanings, one is a Yiddish pet form of SARAH, and the other is the Persian word for 'red', borne by the red damascus rose.

Surinder m
An Indian name from Sanskrit *sura*, 'god', and the name of the god INDRA used in the sense 'mighty'.

VARIANT **Surendra**

Susan, Susanna, Susannah *f*
The Hebrew name *Shoshana* comes
from *shoshan*, which means 'rose'
in modern Hebrew, but in biblical
Hebrew meant 'lily, lily of the valley'.
This becomes Susannah is the Old
Testament and Susanna in the New.
These forms were used from the
Middle Ages. Susan is the standard
English form of the name dating from
the 17th century; it was popular in
the middle of the 20th century, but is
seldom chosen today.
PET FORMS **Su(e), Soo, Suzie, Susie,
Sukie, Shan(n)a, Zanna** • VARIANTS
Suzan, Suzanna(h) *Scots Gaelic* **Siùsan,
Siùsaidh** *Arabic* **Sausan** *French* **Suzanne,
Suzette** *German* **Susann(e)** *Hebrew*
Shoshan(n)a(h) *Hungarian* **Zsuzsanna,
Zsazsa, Zsuzsa** *Polish* **Zuzanna** *Russian*
Syuzanna *Scandinavian* **Sanna** *Spanish*
Susanita
★ Susan B Anthony (1820–1906), US
   social reformer and women's suffrage
   leader
★ Susan Sarandon (1946–   ), US film
   actress
☆ *Lady Susan*, short novel by Jane
   Austen, unpublished in her lifetime

Sushil *m* **Sushila** *f*
An Indian name from the Sanskrit *su*,
'good', and *shila*, 'conduct', usually
interpreted as meaning 'good-
tempered, well-disposed'. Sushila is
the wife of the god Krishna. Compare
SUNITA.
VARIANT **Susheela**

**Susie, Suzan, Suzanna, Suzannah,
Suzanne, Suzette, Suzie, Suzy** *see*
Susan

Sven, Sweyn *m*
Sven is a Scandinavian name from the
Old Norse *Sveinn*, 'boy'. Sweyn is an
old spelling which is sometimes used.
VARIANTS **Svein, Svend, Swein**

★ Sven-Göran Eriksson (1948–   ),
   Swedish football manager
★ Svein I Haraldsson, 'Fork-Beard'
   (d.1014), Danish king who also ruled
   Norway and England, father of Canute

Svetlana *f*
Svetlana is a Russian name from the
Slavic element *svet*, 'holy, light'. It
came into use as a translation of the
Greek name *Photine*, an Orthodox
saint of the 1st century, and was
popularized by the poem *Svetlana*
(1813) by the Russian poet Vasily
Zhukovsky. The masculine equivalent
is *Svyatoslav* formed from *svyanto*,
'bright', and *slav*, 'glory'.
PET FORMS **Sveta, Lana**
★ Svetlana Alliluyeva (1926–   ),
   daughter of Joseph Stalin who defected
   to the USA in 1967
★ Svetlana Khorkina (1979–   ), Russian
   gymnast

Swein, Sweyn *see* **Sven**

Swithin *m*
This comes from the Old English
emphatic word *swith*, usually
translated in this context as 'strong'.
It was the name of a 9th-century saint
who was bishop of Winchester. The
name became rare after the Norman
Conquest, but was occasionally
revived in the 19th century.
VARIANT **Swithun**
★ St Swithun Wells (c.1536–91), English
   Catholic martyr
☆ Swithin St Cleeve in Anthony Trollope's
   1882 novel *Two on a Tower*

Sy *see* **Seymour**

Sybil *f*
This is the more usual modern form
of the name also spelt *Sibyl*, the
confusion of the vowels going back
to ancient times. The name comes
from the Greek *Sibylla* or *Sybilla*, the
term for a female prophet or oracle.

From the early Christian period it was believed that a sibyl had prophesied the coming of Christ – even St Augustine was prepared to accept the validity of the sibyls – and so the name could be used by Christians. Sybil was introduced into England by the Normans, but the history of the name in the Middle Ages can be blurred by confusion with shortened forms of ISABEL, particularly in Gaelic regions where *Sibéal* is actually a form of Isabel, but may be anglicized as Sybil. The name became rarer after the Middle Ages, until revived in the 19th century, influenced by Benjamin Disraeli's 1845 novel *Sybil*.

PET FORM **Sib(b)** • VARIANTS **Cybill, Sibilla, Sibyl, Sybilla** *French, German* **Sybille**

★ Dame Sybil Thorndike (1882–1976), English actress

★ Cybill Shepherd (1950–   ), US actress

☆ Sybil Fawlty in the television comedy *Fawlty Towers*

Syd, Sydne, Sydnee, Sydney *see* **Sidney**

Syed *see* **Sayyid**

Sylvester, Sylvestra, Sylvestre, Sylwester *see* **Silvester**

Sylvia, Sylvie, Sylwia *see* **Silvia**

Symeon *see* **Simeon**

Symon *see* **Simon**

Symphony *f*
One of the more recent musical names, simply taken from the vocabulary word.

Synnöva, Synnøve *see* **Sunniva**

Syril *see* **Cyril**

Syuzanna *see* **Susan**

Szczepan *see* **Stephen**

Szymon *see* **Simon**

T

Tabitha f
This is the word for 'gazelle' in Aramaic, the everyday language of the Holy Land at the time of Christ. In the New Testament (Acts 9.36) Tabitha, whose name is DORCAS in Greek, is a Christian woman restored to life by St Peter. Tabitha was one of the biblical names taken up by the Puritans, and it was brought back to public attention in the 1960s when it was used for the daughter in the popular television series *Bewitched*, and in a spin-off series named after her.
PET FORMS **Tabbie, Tabby** • VARIANTS
Tabatha, Tabetha *German* **Tabea**
☆ Tabitha Twitchit in Beatrix Potter's *Tale of Samuel Whiskers* (1908). Tabitha is a traditional name for a tabby cat

Tacey f
St Paul (1 Corinthians 14.34) says that women should keep silence in church. *Tace* is the Latin for 'be silent' and was adopted in this form, or as Tacey, by the Puritans as a suitable name for their daughters. *Silence* itself has also been recorded as a first name from this time. The form *Tacita* is both a Latinate form of Tacey and the feminine form of the Roman family name *Tacitus* (ultimately from the same source). Tacey is chosen surprisingly often in this more liberated world. The variant *Tacy* can also be a pet form of
ANASTASIA.
VARIANT **Tacy**
☆ Tacy (Anastasia) Kelly is the name of a child in the 'Betsy-Tacy' series of children's novels, written by US author Maud Hart Lovelace in the 1940s.

They are mentioned in the 1998 film *You've Got Mail*

Tad m
This is usually a pet form of THADDEUS or TADHG, but is also found as an independent name, and was particularly common between the 1950s and 80s. It is also given as a nickname, often to someone small.
PET FORM **Taddy**
★ Tad Lincoln (1853–71), youngest child of President Abraham Lincoln
★ Tad Williams (1957–), US author

Taddeo, Tadeo, Tadeusz *see* **Thaddeus**

Tadhg m
This is an old Irish name meaning 'poet', usually pronounced as in the first syllable of 'tiger'. Despite, or perhaps because of, the Northern Irish use of the variant *Teague* as a term of opprobrium, the name has been a popular choice in Ireland in recent years, particularly in the southern part of the country. It is also found in Scotland. In the past it was anglicized as TAD, THADDEUS, *Thady* or *Tim*. See also TEAGAN.
VARIANT **Teige**

Taegan, Taegen *see* **Teagan**

Taffy *see* **David**

Taghrid f
An Arabic name meaning 'song, singing' particularly of birds.

Taha m
This Arabic name is formed from the first two letters of the 20th sura

[chapter] of the Koran, and is also the title of the sura. Taha is an epithet of the Prophet.

Tahir *m* Tahira *f*
This is an Arabic name meaning 'virtuous, pure'. The name Tahira is given to both the Prophet's wife KHADIJA and his daughter FATIMA.

Tahl, Tahlia *see* Talia

Tahnee *see* Tawny

Takla *see* Thecla

Tala *see* Talia

Talbot *m*
An old aristocratic surname of disputed origin, used as a first name.

Talfryn *m*
This is a modern Welsh name which comes from a place name made up of the elements *tal*, 'high' or 'end of, furthest point', and *bryn*, 'hill'.
★ Talfryn Thomas (1922–82), Welsh actor

Talia[1] *f*
This was originally a pet form of *Natalia* (NATALIE), which is now used as an independent name. It is also an occasional variant of THALIA.
VARIANTS **Talya, Tallie, Tala**
★ Talia Shire (1946–   ), US actress

Talia[2] *f*
A Hebrew name derived from *tal*, 'dew'. Talia means 'dew from God'. *Tal*, 'dew', and *Tali*, 'my dew', are also used.
VARIANTS **Talya, Tahlia, Tahl**

Taliesin *m*
This is an ancient Welsh name formed from *tal*, 'brow', and *iesin*, 'shining'. It is pronounced 'tahl-YES-in' by the Welsh, but tends to be 'ta-li-ES-in' otherwise. It was the name of one of the great early bards who may or may not have existed. There is certainly

surviving poetry attributed to him, but there are also legends that give him magical powers. The name has appeared frequently in recent fantasy fiction, and is spreading outside Wales. It is occasionally given to girls.

Talitha *f*
This is the Aramaic word for 'little girl', adopted as a first name from the Bible passage (Mark 5.41) in which Jesus raises a little girl from the dead, saying, Mark tells us, 'Talitha cumi; which is, being interpreted, Damsel, I say unto thee, arise'.

Tallie *see* Natalie, Talia

Tallulah *f*
The actress Tallulah Bankhead (1902– 68), who brought this name to public attention, was named after her grandmother. She, in turn, is thought to have been named after the Tallulah waterfalls in Georgia, Tallulah meaning 'leaping waters' in Choctaw. However there is also an Irish name *Tuilelaith*, usually anglicized as Talulla(h), which could have been the source of the name. Tuilelaith is traditionally pronounced 'TIL-a-la' or 'TIL-yeh-la'; it means 'abundant lady' and was the name of two medieval Irish saints. Tallulah has become rather fashionable in recent years.
☆ Tallulah is the name of a lead character, memorably played by Jodie Foster, in the 1976 musical film *Bugsy Malone*. It is likely that this encouraged the spread of the name, since Tallulah Bankhead had a rather notorious reputation and the name did not come into more general use until after the film

Tam *see* Thomas

Tamara *f*
This was originally a Russian name, probably formed from the biblical

name *Tamar*, the Hebrew for 'date-palm'. It was borne by a saint, Tamara of Georgia (1184–1213), who was queen of Georgia during the period regarded as its Golden Age.

PET FORMS **Tam(my)**, **Mara**, **Tara** • VARIANT **Thamar**

★ Tamara de Lempicka (1898–1980), Polish-born painter based in Paris
★ Tamara Mellon (1969–), founder of the Jimmy Choo shoe company

Tàmhas *see* **Thomas**

Tamika *f*
This is the US form of the Japanese name *Tamiko*, altered to conform with Western expectations that names ending in '-o' are masculine, and those ending in '-a' are feminine. Tamiko is made up of elements *ta*, 'many', *mi*, 'beautiful', and *ko*, 'child', but can also be interpreted as 'beautiful flower'. Both forms entered the stock of US names after the television film *A Girl Called Tamiko* was shown in 1962, with Tamika eventually winning out as the standard form. The anti-racist theme of the film particularly appealed to African-American parents.

★ Tamiko Jones (1945–), US singer

Tamir *m*
An Arabic name meaning 'rich in dates'.

Tammy *f*
A pet form of names such as TAMARA and TAMSIN, now used as an independent name. Use increased in the USA after a song called 'Tammy' spent several weeks in the hit parade in 1957. The name is currently out of favour in the USA, but regularly used in the UK. As a masculine name it can be a pet form of Tam (see THOMAS).

VARIANT **Tam(m)i(e)**

★ Tammy Wynette (1942–98), US country singer

Tamsin *f*
This is an old form of THOMASINA. It was in general use in the Middle Ages, but subsequently was restricted to Cornwall. It was revived in the 1950s and has been used steadily since then.

PET FORMS **Tam**, **Tammy** • VARIANT **Tamzin**

★ Tamsin Greig (1967–), British actress

Tancred *m*
This is a Germanic name formed from the elements *thank*, 'thought', and *rad*, 'counsel'. Its best-known bearer was a Norman Sicilian who was one of the leaders of the First Crusade. Although common in the Middle Ages, the name is now rare, and modern uses may be from the surname or the 1847 novel of the name by Benjamin Disraeli.

Tania *see* **Tanya**

Tanika[1] *f*
This is an Indian name, from the Sanskrit word for 'rope'.

★ Tanika Gupta, OBE (1963–), English playwright

Tanika[2] *f*
A mainly African-American name, coined in the 1970s from fashionable elements of names such as TAMIKA and TANYA.

Tanish *m* **Tanisha**[1] *f*
A Hindu name, meaning 'ambition'.

Tanisha[2] *f*
A mainly African-American name coined from fashionable sounds and used from the 1970s to the end of the 90s. It has also been linked to the name *Tani*, used by the Hausa of Nigeria, meaning 'girl born on Monday'.

Tanith *f*
This is the name of the ancient Phoenician goddess of love and fertility. It probably means 'serpent

lady'. In Carthage she was known as *Tanit*, and was the patron of the city.
★ Tanith Lee (1947–), English writer

Tanner *m*
This is a surname, from the occupation, which has been a popular choice in the USA since the 1990s, and is beginning to appear in the UK.

Tansy *f*
This is a plant name, which comes from a corruption of its old Greek name *athanasia*, 'immortality'. Tansy can also be a pet form of ANASTASIA or ANASTASIUS.
VARIANT **Tansi**

Tanvir *m*
This is a popular name in the Indian subcontinent, meaning 'strong body'.
VARIANT **Tanveer**
★ Tanvir (1923–), pen name of the noted Indian playwright Habib Ahmen Khan, also known as Habib Tanvir

Tanya *f*
This was originally a pet form of the Russian name TATIANA now used as an independent name. It came into fashion in the 1940s and remained well used into the 1990s. The variant forms *Tawnia* and *Tonya* reflect phonetic spellings from dialectic variations in US pronunciation, the name having been very popular in the USA in the 1970s. Tonya overlaps with pet forms of ANTONIA (see ANTHONY).
VARIANTS **Tania, Tonya, Tawnia, Taniya(h)** *German* **Tanja**
★ Tanya Tucker (1958–), US country singer
★ Tonya Harding (1970–), US figure-skating champion whose career ended in scandal
☆ Tawnia Baker was the female sidekick in some episodes of the 1980s television adventure series *The A-Team*

Taoufiq *see* Tawfiq

Taqi *m* Taqiya *f*
This is an Arabic name meaning 'God-fearing, devout, pious'.
VARIANT **Taqiyya**

Taqwa *f*
An Arabic name taken from the Islamic concept of 'God-consciousness', an elevated awareness of God in life.
VARIANT **Taqwah**

Tara[1] *fm*
This is the name of the Irish 'hill of the high kings' used as a first name. Tara comes from the Gaelic *teamhair*, 'hill', and was the ancient place where the high kings of Ireland were crowned. In many cases the name was probably an indirect use, taken from the plantation in *Gone with the Wind* that is called Tara after the hill. The name was popular in the USA in the 1970s but, as was so often the case, was slow to take off in Ireland itself, although it is now a popular choice. It is usually feminine, but early uses – the name was not given until the late 19th century – were sometimes masculine. Tara Guinness, for example, whose death inspired the Beatles song 'A Day in the Life', was male.
★ Tara Palmer-Tomkinson (1971–), English socialite
★ Tara Lipinski (1982–), US champion figure skater
☆ Tara King, character in the 1960s television series *The Avengers*, who helped spread the name

Tara[2] *m*
An Indian name which can have two sources, either as an epithet of the gods Rudra and Vishnu, meaning 'saviour', or from a word meaning 'shining'.

Tara[3] *f*
An Indian name from the Sanskrit meaning 'star'. The name is associated with several divine females in a

number of Eastern religions including Hinduism, Jainism and Buddhism.

Tariq *m*

This means 'he who pounds at the door' and is the Arabic name for the morning star. This is one of the Islamic names that have been taken up by African Americans who have developed it into variants such as *Tyreek*, *Tyrik* or *Tyriq*.

VARIANTS **Tarik**, **Tareq**, **Tarek**

★ Tariq Ali (1943–), British-Pakistani author and activist

★ Tariq ibn Ziyad (d.720), Berber general who conquered Spain

Tarlach, Tárlach *see* Turlough

Tarquin *m*

This was borne by the last two kings of Rome; the monarchy was deposed and replaced with a Republic when the royal family's behaviour outraged the Roman citizens (see LUCRETIA). The name is probably Etruscan and the meaning is not known.

PET FORM **Quinn**

★ Tarquin Olivier (1936–), son and biographer of the actor Sir Laurence Olivier

☆ Tarquin (Quinn) Blackwood, vampire in Anne Rice's *Vampire Chronicles*

Tarub *f*

An Arabic name meaning 'lively, merry'.

☆ *Tarub, Baghdad's Famous Female Cook*, an 1897 novel by the German author Paul Scheerbart

Tarun *m*

An Indian name from a Sanskrit word with a sense of 'young, tender', which can imply both tender feelings of affection and youth, or newness, such as the rising sun or growing plants.

Taryn *f*

This name was coined by the US actors Tyrone Power and Linda Christian as a blend of their own names for their daughter Taryn Power (b.1953), who later followed her parents into film thus publicizing the name.

★ Taryn Manning (1978–), US actress and singer

Tasgall *m*

Tasgall is a Scots Gaelic name which comes from the Old Norse name *Ásketill*, 'cauldron of the gods', formed from *áss*, 'god', and *ketill*, 'cauldron'. It was anglicized as *Taskall*.

VARIANTS **Taskall**, **Taskill**

Tasha *f*

A short form of NATASHA sometimes used as an independent name. It is also used as a combining element to form names such as LATASHA.

☆ Tasha (Natasha) Yar, character in the television series *Star Trek: The Next Generation*

Tasia *see* Anastasia

Taslim *m* Taslima *f*

An Arabic name meaning 'greeting, salutation'.

★ Taslima Nasreen (1962–), Bangladeshi medical doctor and feminist novelist, whose works have caused outrage in parts of her country

Tasnim *f*

Tasnim is the name of a spring found in Paradise, transferred to a first name.

VARIANT **Tasneem**

Tasoula *see* Anastasia

Tate *m*

A surname, from the Old English personal name *Tata*, which is currently a fashionable first name.

★ Tate Donovan (1963–), US actor

Tatiana *f*

This Russian name belonged to a 3rd-century saint, patron of students, who was especially venerated in the

Orthodox Church. Tatiana derives from the Roman family name *Tatius*. The origin of this is much debated, but one attractive theory is that it comes from Latin *Tata*, the equivalent of 'Daddy'. Tatiana did not spread beyond the Eastern bloc to be taken up by English speakers until the 1980s. The name is well used in South America.

PET FORM **Tanya** • VARIANTS **Tatian(n)a, Tatyana** *French* **Tatienne** *Slavic* **Tatjana**

★ Grand Duchess Tatiana Nikolaevna of Russia (1897–1918), second daughter of Tsar Nicholas II, last tsar of Russia

☆ Tatiana Larina in Alexander Pushkin's *Eugene Onegin* (1833)

Tatum *f*

This is a surname from the same source as TATE, used as a first name. It was introduced in 1963, when US actor Ryan O'Neal named his daughter after the jazz musician Art Tatum. It is more rarely found as a masculine name, and is mainly confined to the USA.

Taufik, Taufiq *see* Tawfiq

Tave, Tavia, Tavian, Tavie, Tavion, Tavius *see* Octavia

Tawfiq *m*

An Arabic name formed from *wafiqua*, 'to be successful', and meaning 'good fortune, prosperity, success'. It is based on a quote from the Koran, 'My success is granted only by Allah'.

VARIANTS **Taoufiq, Taufiq, Taufik, Tewfik**

★ Tawfiq of Egypt (1852–92), khedive of Egypt

Tawnia *see* Tanya

Tawny *f*

A modern name from the vocabulary word, which comes from the Old French *tané* meaning 'light brown, tanned'. It is usually linked to hair colour. It had a brief vogue as a parental choice in the 1980s.

VARIANTS **Tawnee, Tawney, Tawnie, Tahnee**

★ Tawny Kitaen (1961–   ), US actress

★ Tawny Cypress (1976–   ), US actress

Tawnya *see* Tanya

Taylor *mf*

This is a surname, from the occupation, used as a first name. It has recently been very popular for girls in the USA, overtaking the use for boys which peaked in the early 1990s. In the UK it is still more popular for boys, but the girls are catching up.

VARIANTS **Taylar, Tayler, Tayla**

★ Taylor Caldwell (1900–85), Anglo-American popular novelist, credited with influencing use of the name as a feminine

Tayyab *m* Tayyiba *f*

An Arabic name from the word meaning 'good-natured, generous, good'.

VARIANT **Tayyib**

Tazim *m* Tazima

An Arabic name meaning 'glorification, honour, exaltation'.

Tea *see* Dorothy

Teagan *mf*

This name presents real problems for the analyst, and it is inextricably confused with TEGAN. Teagan can be interpreted as an Irish surname, from *O Tadhgáin*, 'descendant of little TADHG'. Tegan, on the other hand, is a female Cornish and Welsh name based on *teg*, 'pretty, fair, precious'. Both, however, share the same variants, making the distinction rather artificial. What is unusual is that Tegan came into circulation first, but that Teagan then became both a masculine and feminine name. The usual trend is for masculine names to become feminine.

VARIANTS **Tegan, Teigan, Taegan, Teagen**

★ Teagan Clive (1959–), US bodybuilder, writer and actress

Tearlach, Teàrlach see **Charles**

Tearra see **Tiara**

Tecla see **Thecla**

Ted, Teddy m
Usually pet forms of any one of the many names beginning Ed-, particularly EDWARD, but also names such as EDMUND and EDWIN. Ted and Teddy are also found as independent names, although this pet form is somewhat out of fashion. Teddy bears, however, are named after the US President Theodore 'Teddy' Roosevelt (1858–1919).
★ Teddy Sheringham (1966–), English footballer
★ Ted Bundy (1946–89), US lawyer and serial killer
☆ Ted (Theodore) Logan is a character in the *Bill and Ted* films

Teddie see **Theodora**

Teena see **Tina**

Teesha see **Letitia**

Tegan f
This is a name formed from the Welsh or Cornish teg, 'fair, precious, pretty'. It was first brought to public attention in the 1980s by the *Dr Who* character Tegan Jovanka, who was Australian. Consequently the name took off in Australia, and it is here that the variant *Teagan* seems to have become established, reflecting the same variation in analysing the syllable break and vowel lengthening found earlier with MEGAN. This has led to total confusion between this name and the originally masculine TEAGAN.
VARIANTS **Teagan, Te(a)gen, Teigan, Teighan, Tiegan**
★ Tegan Rain Quin (1980–), one-half

of the Canadian singer-songwriter duo Tegan and Sara
☆ Tiegan Brook was a character in the Australian soap *Home and Away*

Tegwen f **Tegwyn** m
A Welsh name formed from teg, 'pretty, precious, fair', and (g)wen or (g)wyn, 'fair'. The name is particularly used for blond(e)s. Tegedd, 'lovely form', is a feminine variant.

Teigan see **Teagan, Tegan**

Teige see **Tadhg**

Teighan see **Tegan**

Tekla see **Thecla**

Tel see **Terence, Terry**

Teleri f
This is a variant of the Welsh name ELERI, with the initial 'T' coming from the respectful element ty, literally 'your'. In Welsh tradition it was borne by one of the maidens at King Arthur's court. J R R Tolkien also used Teleri in his works, as the name of an elf clan. The name is widespread in Wales.

Telma see **Thelma**

Temperance f
Temperance was one of the virtue names, such as HOPE and PATIENCE, created by the Puritans in the 17th century. It was used quietly but regularly into the 19th century, but is now rare. There are signs, however, that it may be coming back into use after fictional uses.
☆ Temperance 'Tempe' Brennan is a character created by Kathy Reichs for her forensic anthropology novels, which have been made into the television series *Bones*

Tempest mf
This name has a rather complex history. It is evidently the vocabulary

word, but early uses in the north of England from the 16th century are actually a surname reused as a first name. As a modern, mainly feminine name, it goes back to at least the early part of the 20th century. Compare STORM and STORMY.

★ Tempestt Bledsoe (1973–), US actress. There is a report of a parent mistakenly naming a child *Temptress* after this actress

Tenniel *m*
A surname, of uncertain meaning but perhaps a form of DANIEL, sometimes found as a first name.
VARIANT **Teniel**

★ Tenniel Evans (1926–), Kenyan-born British actor

Teo, Teodor *see* **Theodore**

Teobaldo *see* **Theobald**

Teodora *see* **Theodora**

Teodoro *see* **Theodore**

Teofil, Teofilo *see* **Theophilus**

Terence *m*
Terence is the English name for the Roman playwright known in Latin as *Publius Terentius Afer*. However, the name came into use, not so much in honour of the playwright Terence, but largely because it was thought that TERRY must be a pet form of a longer name and there was felt to be a need for a 'respectable' version. Terence was particularly well used in Ireland in the 19th century to anglicize TURLOUGH. In the UK its popularity peaked in the 1950s and it is seldom chosen now. The spellings with a double 'rr' are the more common in the USA. The pet form *Tel* is a recent coinage.
PET FORMS **Tel, Terry** • VARIANTS **Terrance, Terrence**

★ Sir Terence Conran (1931–), English designer and businessman

★ Terence Stamp (1939–), English film actor and author

Teresa, Teresia, Teresinha, Teresita, Tereza, Terezinha *see* **Theresa**

Tero *see* **Andrew**

Terra *f*
While this may occasionally represent the Latin for 'earth', most uses of the name are probably as a dialect variant of TARA, particularly in the USA where Tara is often pronounced with a short 'a' sound and may be almost indistinguishable from the sound of Terra. Alternatively, some uses may simply be a variant of TIERRA.

Terrell *m*
This is from a surname, also found as a place name in the USA, that comes ultimately from French *tirer*, 'to pull', and is thus a variant of TYRELL. It can also be seen as a variant of TERENCE. Terrell has been in use since at least the early part of the 20th century, but was particularly taken up by African Americans in the 1970s and 80s. This may have been in honour of Mary Church Terrell (1863–1954), a campaigner for both women's and civil rights, whose remarkable career made her both the first woman and the first African American in many fields.
VARIANTS **Terel, Terryl**

Terry *mf*
While this is the regular pet form of TERENCE, it is actually older as a name in English. The Germanic name *Theodoric* became the English name DEREK (where its history is explained) via Germanic languages. However, in French it had become THIERRY, a name brought to Britain by the Norman French. This was simplified in English to Terry, probably via its use as a surname. Terry also serves as a pet form of other names such as THEODORE;

for women it can be a pet form of
THERESA and is sometimes given as an
independent name.

PET FORM **Tel** • VARIANT **Ter(r)i(e)**

★ Sir Terry Wogan (1938–　), Irish
broadcaster and writer

★ Sir Terry Pratchett (1948–　), English
author

Tessa f
This is a pet form of THERESA now used
as an independent name. There is
some mystery in its origin. It appears
in 19th-century novels, such as George
Eliot's *Romola* (1863), where it is
treated as an Italian form, but there is
no record of its use at this time in Italy.
It has now lost all sense of the exotic.

PET FORMS **Tess, Tessie**

★ Tessa Jowell (1947–　), English
politician

★ Tessie O'Shea (1913–95), Welsh
comedienne

☆ *Tess of the D'Urbervilles*, an 1891
novel by Thomas Hardy

Tessan *see* **Theresa**

Tettie, Tetty *see* **Elizabeth**

Teun, Teunis *see* **Anthony**

Tevin m
A modern name modelled on the
sound of names such as KEVIN. It was
introduced by the US R&B singer Tevin
Campbell (b.1976), and entered the US
name charts in 1990, the year he had
his first hit, staying there for a decade.

Tevye *see* **Tobias**

Tewfik *see* **Tawfiq**

Tex m
This is rarely a given name, but is
usually a nickname for a Texan. Texas
got its name from a local Native
American tribe whose name means
'friendly'. A female given name,
Texanna, based on the state name, has
been recorded.

★ Tex Avery (1908–80), US animated
cartoon director

★ Tex Ritter (1905–74), Texan country
singer

Teyrnon *see* **Tiernan**

Thaddeus m
This biblical name presents us
with some problems. Thaddeus is
listed among the twelve Apostles
in St Matthew's Gospel, but not in
the others. As St Jude appears in
Thaddeus's place elsewhere, it may
well have been an alternative name for
him. We are not even sure what the
name means, or even which language
it comes from. Suggestions put forward
are that it is from the Aramaic word for
'praise', that it is the Aramaic version
of the Greek name THEODORE, or that
it is from the Hebrew for 'valiant' or
'wise' or 'heart'. It has never been
a particularly well-used name by
English speakers, except in Ireland,
where it was used to anglicize TADHG,
particularly in the distinctively Irish
pet form *Thady*. It is also common in
Eastern Europe.

PET FORM **Tad** • VARIANTS **Thaddaeus** *Italian*
Taddeo *Polish* **Tadeusz** *Russian* **Faddei,
Faddey** *Spanish* **Tadeo**

★ Thad (Thaddeus) Jones (1923–86), US
jazz musician

Thais f
Thais was a courtesan who was the
mistress of Alexander the Great and
travelled with him on his campaigns.
The fame of this Thais meant that it
almost became a generic term for
a courtesan and was often adopted
as a working name. St Thais, in the
4th century, is said to have been a
reformed prostitute. Both women
were the subjects of literary works in
19th-century France, and it was in that

country in the 1980s that the name began to become fashionable.
VARIANT **Thaïs**

Thalia *f*
In ancient Greek tradition, Thalia was the name of the Muse of comedy and pastoral poetry, and was also borne by one of the three Graces. The name comes from *thallo*, 'to blossom, flourish'. Thalia is common in South America and is increasingly used by English speakers. Compare AGLAIA.
VARIANT **Talia**
★ Thalía (1971–   ), Mexican actress and singer whose success coincided with the revival of this name in the USA

Thamar *see* Tamara

Thana *f*
An Arabic name meaning 'praise, commendation'.

Thanasis *see* Athanasius

Thandie *f*
This name, introduced to the public by Anglo-Zambian actress Thandie Newton (1972–   ), is a contracted form of *Thandiwe*, meaning 'beloved' in Ndebele.

Thane *m*
An old aristocratic rank and a surname that is sometimes used as a first name.

Thanos *see* Athanasius

Thea *f*
Pet form of names containing the element *theos*, 'god', particularly *Dorothea* (DOROTHY) and THEODORA, that is currently more popular as a given name than the full forms.
★ Thea Musgrave (1928–   ), Scottish composer

Thecla *f*
St Thecla was the first female Christian martyr, and thus the counterpart of St STEPHEN. However, while the account of

Stephen's death is recorded in the New Testament and accepted as authentic, the lurid tales of Thecla's martyrdom are related in the apocryphal *Acts of Paul and Thecla* and are not considered reliable. Nevertheless, although now obscure, she was once a very popular saint and in the 4th century St Thecla's church in Milan was one of the largest buildings in the world. Thecla had entered the stock of English names by the 8th century, as a religious name at least, for it is recorded as belonging to an Anglo-Saxon nun. The name is a shortened form of *Theokleia* formed from the Greek *theos*, 'God', and *kleia*, 'glory'.
VARIANTS **Tecla, T(h)ekla, Takla**

Theda *f*
A pet form of THEODORA and related names, made famous by the notorious silent-film actress Theda Bara (1890–1955), whose given name was THEODOSIA Goodman.

Thekla *see* Thecla

Thelma *f*
This name seems to have been invented by the popular author Marie Corelli for her 1887 novel *Thelma*. In this story the heroine is Norwegian, but there is no record of the name in use there at the time. Nevertheless, the name in the form *Telma* is currently well used in Iceland. Thelma was popular among English speakers in the 1920s and 30s, but is a rare parental choice today.
★ Thelma Todd (1905–35), US actress
★ Thelma Barlow (1929–   ), English actress who played Mavis Wilton in *Coronation Street* for many years
☆ *Thelma and Louise*, 1991 film

Thelonius *m*
This may look Greek, but it is actually the Latin form of the name of a 7th-century Saxon St *Tillo* or *Tielo*, who

was kidnapped by raiders and then became a missionary in France. Tillo is a pet form of names beginning *Diet-* such as *Dietrich* (see DEREK). It is also the source of the name *Till*, famous from the folk-tale trickster Till Eulenspiegel.

VARIANT **Thelonious**

★ Thelonious Monk (1917–82), US jazz pianist and composer

Theo *m*

A pet form of THEODORE and other names beginning *Theo-*, that is currently more popular as a given name than the full forms.

VARIANTS *French* **Théo** *Italian, Spanish* **Teo**

★ Theo Walcott (1989–   ), English footballer

Theobald *m*

Theobald is a Germanic name made up of the elements *theud*, 'people', and *bald*, 'bold', which is now rare in English, but still used in other languages. It was introduced by the Normans and in everyday speech became *Tibald* or *Tybalt*, the name of Romeo's friend in Shakespeare's *Romeo and Juliet*. This was also a traditional name for cats, from the same beast epics that called the fox Reynard, and the pet forms *Tibs*, *Tibby* and *Tiddles* still survive as cat names.

VARIANTS *Irish* **Tiobóld** *French* **Thibau(l)t** *Italian, Spanish* **Teobaldo**

★ Theobald Wolfe Tone (1763–98), Irish patriot better known simply as Wolfe Tone

Theodora *f*

This name is formed from *theos*, 'god', and *doron*, 'gift', combining the same elements as DOROTHY but in reverse. A form of the name is found in the Mycenaean Linear B clay tablets dating from the late Bronze Age, which must make it one of the oldest names in continuous use. It was a common

name among the ruling classes in the Byzantine Empire and is still in regular use in Eastern Europe. It came to the UK in the 17th century, but has never been popular.

PET FORMS **Thea, Dora, Theo, Teddie, Theda** • VARIANTS *Italian, Spanish* **Teodora** *Russian* **Feodora, Fedora**

Theodore *m*

Like THEODORA this is an ancient name, originally pagan, formed from the elements *theos*, 'god', and *doron*, 'gift'. It was widespread among early Christians and was borne by a number of saints. However, it was rare among English speakers until the 19th century. At present it is probably more popular than it has ever been, particularly in the short form THEO.

PET FORMS **Theo, Teddy** • VARIANTS *Dutch* **Theodoor** *French* **Théodore** *German, Scandinavian* **Theodor** *Greek* **Theodoros** *Italian, Spanish* **Teodoro** *Jewish* **Todros** *Polish, Scandinavian* **Teodor** *Russian* **Fe(o)dor, Fyodor, Fedya**

★ Theodore Roosevelt (1858–1919), 26th US president

★ Theodor Seuss Geisel (1904–91), US children's author better known as Dr Seuss

☆ Theodore 'Laurie' Laurence in Louisa May Alcott's *Little Women* (1868)

Theodoric *see* Derek, Terry

Theodosia *f* Theodosius *m*

Closely related to THEODORE, these names are formed from *theos*, 'god', and *dosis*, 'giving'. There were early saints of both names, as well as Byzantine rulers. However, it has not been as popular in Western Europe as its related names, with which it shares pet forms.

★ Theodosia Burr Alston (1783–1813?), daughter of controversial US vice-president Aaron Burr who disappeared under mysterious circumstances, and

was the subject of Anya Seton's novel
My Theodosia
★ Theodosia Burr Goodman (1885–
1955), real name of US actress Theda
Bara

Theophania *see* **Tiffany**

Theophilus *m*
A Greek name meaning 'friend of
God', formed from the elements
theos, 'god', and *philos*, 'friend'. It is
important in early Christianity as the
name of the person to whom both the
Gospel of St Luke and the Acts of the
Apostles are addressed. There were
also several early saints of the name.
Both AMADEUS and the German GOTTLIEB
are translations of this name.
PET FORM **Theo** • VARIANTS *French*
Théophile *Polish* **Teofil** *Italian, Spanish*
Teofilo *Russian* **Feofil**
★ Théophile Gautier (1811–72), French
poet and novelist
☆ Theophilus P Wildebeeste, comic
character created by Lenny Henry

Theresa *f*
The meaning of this name is
not known, although all sorts of
suggestions have been made regarding
its origin. It first appears in the 4th
century in the form *Therasia*, as the
name of the Spanish wife of St Paulinus
of Nole. It was regularly used in the
Iberian peninsula, and only spread
to other countries in the 16th century
with the fame of the reforming nun St
Teresa of Avila, one of the first women
to be declared a Doctor of the Church,
although this did not happen until
1970.
PET FORMS **Terry, Tessa** • VARIANTS **Teresa**
Irish **Toiréasa, Treasa** *Dutch, German,*
Scandinavian **Theresia, Thera** *French*
Thérèse *Portuguese* **Tereza, Teresinha,**
Terezinha *Scandinavian* **Teresia, Tessan**
Spanish **Teresita**

★ St Thérèse of Lisieux (1873–97), French
nun and virgin saint
★ Mother Teresa of Calcutta (1910–97),
Albanian nun, missionary and Nobel
Prize winner

Thetis *see* **Achilles**

Thibault, Thibaut *see* **Theobald**

Thierry *m*
This is the French form of DEREK. It
was popular in the Middle Ages, then
used only quietly until a 20th-century
revival.
VARIANT **Thieri**

Thijs *see* **Matthew**

Thirza *f*
This is a Hebrew name, meaning
'favourable, pleasantness', found both
as an obscure personal name and as
a place name in the Old Testament. It
was taken up quietly by the Puritans. It
was in regular use in the 19th century
and modern use may owe something
to the choice of the name, in the form
Tirzah, for the sister of Ben Hur in Lew
Wallace's 1880 novel and subsequent
films.
VARIANTS **Tirza(h), T(h)irsa(h)**

Thomas *m*
As the name of one of the more
prominent of the twelve Apostles,
Thomas has been a popular choice
in the UK for over 1,000 years, and
is currently particularly popular.
The name comes from the Aramaic
for 'twin', and so was presumably
a nickname. There is a non-biblical
tradition that Thomas's name was
originally Judas, and that it was
changed to distinguish him from
the other two Apostles called Judas.
During the Middle Ages, use of the
name in England was more likely to
be in honour, not of the Apostle, but
of St Thomas à Becket, an immensely
popular English saint.

PET FORMS **Tom(my), Tommie, Thom**
• VARIANTS *Irish* **Tomás** *Scottish* **Tam** *Scots Gaelic* **Tòmas, Tàmhas** *Welsh* **Tomos, Twm** *Dutch* **Maas** *Italian* **Tommaso** *Polish* **Tomasz, Tomek** *Portuguese* **Tomé** *Russian* **Foma** *Scandinavian* **Tomas** *Spanish* **Tomás**

Thomasina *f*

Nowadays TAMSIN or TAMMY are the most common feminine forms of THOMAS, but Thomasina has been used since the Middle Ages as an alternative. At present, it is most often encountered as the name of a cat.

VARIANTS **Thomsine, Tomasina** *Spanish* **Tomasa**

☆ Thomasina Tittlemouse, a cat in Beatrix Potter's *Tale of the Flopsy Bunnies* (1909)

Thor *m*

Although his name means 'thunder', the Norse god Thor was very much more than a weather god. He was also a fertility god, a god of war, and in many Norse societies functioned as the patron god of communities. He played a more intimate role in people's lives than his more distant superior Odin. His hammer symbol was sometimes worn much as a cross is by Christians. There were a large number of Norse names that began with *Thor-*, and which were shortened to his name. The name was revived in Scandinavia in the 18th century.

VARIANT **Tor**

★ Thor Heyerdahl (1914–2002), Norwegian anthropologist and explorer

Thora *f*

This is a feminine form of THOR, the name of a Norse god. It probably started out as a pet form of several longer names beginning *Thor-*. Thora crops up regularly in early Scandinavian records and features among the Norse settlers in Scotland.

One notable bearer was the mother of St Magnus of Orkney. Elsewhere the name was at its most popular in the later 19th century.

VARIANTS **Thyra**

★ Dame Thora Hird (1911–2003), English actress
★ Thora Birch (1982–), US actress

Thorfinn *m*

This Norse name, formed from THOR and the ethnic name Finn, was common among Vikings. It was used regularly in the Orkney ruling house, which included Thorfinn Skullsplitter in the 10th century and Thorfinn the Mighty in the 11th. Another Thorfinn was a settler in Vinland in North America. The name is still regularly used in Scandinavia. See also TORIN.

Thorkel *see* **Torquil**

Thornton *m*

A surname from a place which was a settlement with thorn bushes, used as a first name.

★ Thornton Wilder (1897–1975), US writer and playwright

Thorsten, Thorstein *see* **Torsten**

Thorwald *see* **Torvald**

Thurayya *see* **Soraya**

Thurstan *m*

This is the modern form of *Thórsteinn* formed from THOR and the Old Norse *steinn*, 'stone' (see TORSTEN). It was a popular Old Norse name, but modern use may come from the surname, which can also come from a place name based on Thor and *ton*, 'settlement'. Passing through French, the name became DUSTIN.

VARIANTS **Thurston** *German, Scandinavian* **Torsten**

★ (Robert) Thurston Dart (1921–71), English musicologist, keyboard player and conductor

★ Thurston Moore (1958–   ), US rock musician

Thyra *see* **Thora, Tyra**

Tia *f*
This name is something of a mystery. It has been described as a pet form of names ending in *-tia*, such as LETITIA or LUCRETIA, but as these endings are usually pronounced 'sha' rather than 'tee-a' it seems unlikely that this is the main source. An alternative suggestion is that the name is linked to the liqueur called Tia Maria, which was invented in the 1940s at around the same time that Tia first appeared, although the name has become popular far more recently. The brand name is actually a use of the Spanish term *tia* which means something like 'auntie', but it could easily have been interpreted as a personal name. Whatever its origin, there is no doubt that use of the name increased after it appeared in Alexander Key's 1968 science fiction novel *Escape to Witch Mountain*, particularly after the novel was turned into a film in 1975. In this case Key claimed to have made the name up as a suitable one for an alien.
★ Tia Carrere (1967–   ), US model and actress

Tiago *m*
This is a shortened form of SANTIAGO, particularly common in Portugal. It may be the source of DIEGO.

Tiana *f*
This name, which came into use in the USA in the 1970s, can be analysed as a shortening of names such as *Christiana* and *Gratiana*, but its origin probably lies as much in its combination of fashionable sounds. The popularity of the name TINA may have influenced use.
VARIANT **Tianna**

Tiara *f*
The vocabulary word used as a first name, probably under the influence of TIANA and TIERRA. Variants overlap to some extent with the latter. It is mainly confined to the USA and has only been in use since the 1980s.
VARIANTS **Tearra, Tiarra**

Tiarnan *see* **Tiernan**

Tib, Tibby *see* **Isabel**

Tibald *see* **Theobald**

Tibor *m*
This is the Hungarian form of the Roman name *Tibertius*, meaning 'of the River Tiber' after the river running through Rome, which also gave its name to the resort of Tibur, now called Tivoli. Tibertius was borne by a 4th-century martyr.

Ticia *see* **Letitia**

Tiegan *see* **Tegan**

Tiego *see* **Diego**

Tiernan *mf*
This is the anglicized form of the old Irish name *Tighearnán*, 'little lord', also found as a surname. Originally exclusively male this is now occasionally used for females.
VARIANTS **Tiarnan, Tigernán, Tyrnan** *Welsh* **Teyrnon**

Tierney *mf*
This is an Irish surname from the old Irish name *Tighearnach*, which comes from *tigherearna*, 'lord', ultimately the same root as TIERNAN. St Tierney of Clones is said to have had St Brigid herself as his godmother. The name is now predominantly feminine.

Tierra *f*
Tierra forms a trio of names, with TIANA and TIARA, which depend as much on sound as meaning. They all came into

use in the 1970s or early 80s. Use of Tierra, which is the Spanish for 'earth', may have been influenced by the much more popular SIERRA.

Ties *see* **Matthew**

Tiesha *see* **Letitia**

Tiffany *f*
The early Greek Christians had a name *Theophania*, meaning 'Epiphany', formed from *theos*, 'God', and *phainein*, 'to appear'. This passed into Old French as *Tiphaine* and appears in medieval English as *Tiffania*, *Tiphany* or *Tiffany*. The name was given to children born on or around the Feast of the Epiphany marking the arrival of the Magi on 6 January. The name died out after the Middle Ages except as a surname. One bearer of the surname was the famous French jeweller who set up shop in New York. The name was revived after Truman Capote's 1958 novella *Breakfast at Tiffany's* was turned into a very successful film in 1961.
VARIANT *French* **Tiphaine**
☆ Tiffany Aching is the heroine of some of Terry Pratchett's children's *Discworld* novels

Tigernán *see* **Tiernan**

Tighearnach *see* **Tierney**

Tighearnán *see* **Tiernan**

Tijn *see* **Augustine, Martin**

Tilda, Tilly *f*
These are pet forms of MATILDA, now used as independent names. Tilly is currently in fashion.
VARIANT **Tillie**
★ Tilda Swinton (1960–), Scottish actress

Till *see* **Thelonius**

Tillie *see* **Matilda**

Timothy *m*
The Greek name *Timotheus* from *time*, 'honour', and *theos*, 'god', was the name of a man who appears in the biblical Acts of the Apostles as an assistant to St Paul. His name, along with those of his grandmother Lois and mother Eunice, was taken up at the Reformation and was steadily used from the 18th century. It is currently only used quietly after enjoying a peak of popularity in the 1980s. There are rare feminines *Timotha* and *Timothea*.
PET FORMS **Tim(my)**, **Timmie** ● VARIANTS *French* **Timothée** *Italian, Spanish* **Timoteo** *Polish* **Tymoteusz** *Russian* **Timofei, Timofey**

Tina *f*
Originally a pet form of names such as CHRISTINA and MARTINA, this has been used as an independent name since the 19th century. In Holland it is also a pet form of *Catharina*.
VARIANTS **Teena, Tyna**
★ Tina Turner (1938–), US pop singer and film actress

Tineke *see* **Martin**

Tino *see* **Martin, Valentine**

Tióbóld *see* **Theobald**

Tiphaine *see* **Tiffany**

Tira *see* **Tyra**

Tiree *mf*
This is the name of a Scottish island in the Hebrides which, like IONA and SKYE, is now being used as a first name, particularly in Scotland. The variant *Tyree*, the usual form in the USA, probably comes from the surname derived from the place.
PET FORM **Ty** ● VARIANTS **Tyree, Tyrese**
★ Tyree Washington (1976–), US athlete

Tirion *f*
A modern Welsh name from the vocabulary word meaning 'kind, gentle'. Tirion is also the name of a city in Tolkien's fiction.

Tirsa, Tirsah, Tirza, Tirzah *see* **Thirza**

Tish, Tisha *see* **Letitia, Patricia**

Titus *m*
This is a Roman family name of unknown meaning. As well as being borne by a Roman emperor, it was also the name of a companion of TIMOTHY, and so was available to join the stock of biblical names used after the Reformation. However, after Titus Oates was imprisoned for devising the so-called Popish Plot in 1678, the name fell out of general use. It was revived in the later 20th century, perhaps influenced by the character of Titus Groan in Mervyn Peake's *Gormenghast* trilogy (1949–59).
VARIANTS *Italian, Spanish* **Tito** *Polish* **Tytus** *Russian* **Tit**
★ Sir Titus Salt (1803–76), English manufacturer and philanthropist, who founded the village of Saltaire

Toal *see* **Tuathal**

Tobias, Toby *m*
The Greek name Tobias is a form of the Hebrew *Tobiah* meaning 'God is good'. The biblical book of Tobit in the Apocrypha tells a story of spirits and magic in which the young Tobias, with the help of the angel Raphael, cures his father's blindness and wins himself a suitable wife. Tobias travels on his adventures with his dog. This is why the traditional English form of Tobias, Toby, was later used for the dog in the Punch and Judy show. *Tobin*, occasionally found as a first name, comes from a surname developed from

Tobias. Both forms of the name are currently moderately popular.
VARIANTS **Tobi, Tobey** *Polish* **Tobiasz** *Yiddish* **Tevye, Tovia, Tuvya**
★ Tobias Smollett (1721–71), Scottish author
★ Tobey Maguire (1975–), US actor

Todd *m*
A surname, from an old name for 'fox', used as a first name.
VARIANT **Tod**
★ Todd Rundgren (1948–), US singer-songwriter
★ Tod Sloan (1874–1933), US jockey, source of the rhyming slang expression 'on your tod'
☆ Todd Flanders in television cartoon *The Simpsons*

Todros *see* **Theodore**

Toinette *see* **Anthony**

Toirdhealbhach *see* **Turlough**

Toiréasa *see* **Theresa**

Tolly, Tolomey, Tolomy *see* **Bartholomew**

Tom, Tomas, Tòmas, Tomás *see* **Thomas**

Tomasa, Tomasina *see* **Thomasina**

Tomasz, Tomé, Tomek, Tommaso, Tommie, Tommy, Tomos *see* **Thomas**

Ton *see* **Anthony**

Tone *m*
This is used in Ireland in honour of the Irish patriot Wolfe Tone (1763–98). Tone is also found as a pet form of TONY.

Toni *f* **Tony** *m*
These are pet forms of ANTONIA and ANTHONY and their variants, now found as independent names.
PET FORM **Tone**

★ Toni Morrison (1931–   ), Nobel Prize-winning US novelist
★ Tony Curtis (1925–   ), US actor and painter

Toni, Tonia, Tonya see Antonia, Tanya

Tonio see Anthony

Topaz f
This unusual jewel name has been used occasionally since the 19th century. There are medieval records of it as a masculine name, but that was simply a variant of TOBIAS.
☆ Topaz Mortmain in Dodie Smith's 1948 novel *I Capture the Castle*

Topher see Christopher

Topsy f
This name, usually a nickname, was introduced in Harriet Beecher Stowe's *Uncle Tom's Cabin* (1852), for the little slave girl left in such ignorance as to her origins that all she can say is 'I s'pect I growed'.
☆ *Topsy and Tim*, children's books first published in the 1960s

Tor see Thor

Torcall see Torquil

Tore see Salvador

Tori, Toria, Torie see Victoria

Torin m
This name, used mainly in Scotland, is of debated origin. It has also been suggested that it is a variant of the surname Torrence, which is from a Scottish place name meaning 'hillock'. It is often said to be from an Irish Gaelic word meaning 'chief', but this word is not cited, and it is difficult to find one that would fit. The name is growing in popularity. However, the most likely explanation is that it is a Scottish development of THORFINN, a name prominent in northern Scottish history.
VARIANTS **Torrin, Torran**
★ Torin Thatcher (1905–81), Indian-born British actor
★ Torin Douglas (1950–   ), English journalist and broadcaster

Tormod m
Traditional Scots Gaelic name which originally came from the Old Norse name *Thormothr*, from the god THOR combined with *mothr*, 'mind, mood'. It was anglicized as NORMAN.

Torquil m
This is the anglicized form of the Scots Gaelic name *Torcall*, which in turn comes from the Old Norse name *Thorketill*, formed from the name of the god THOR and *ketill*, 'cauldron'. The name is particularly used in the Macleod family.
VARIANTS *Scots Gaelic* **Torcall** *Scandinavian* **Torkel, Thorkel**

Torri, Torrie see Victoria

Torsten m
A Scandinavian and German name from the Old Norse name *Thorsteinn*, 'Thor's stone', perhaps referring to an altar. The name became THURSTAN in English.
VARIANTS **Thorste(i)n, Torstein**
★ Thorstein Veblen (1857–1929), Norwegian-born US economist and social critic who invented the concept of conspicuous consumption

Torvald m
From the Old Norse name *Thorvaldr* which combines THOR with the word for 'ruler'.
VARIANT **Thorwald**
☆ Torvald Helmer in Ibsen's 1879 play *A Doll's House*

Tory see Victoria

Tottie see Charlotte

Toussaint *m*

An old French name, dating from the 12th century, meaning 'All Saints'. Traditionally it is given to babies born on 1 November, All Saints' Day. It is the French equivalent of names such as SANTOS. Well used into the 19th century in France, it is now mainly confined to Corsica and the Antilles. Elsewhere, it is usually found associated with Toussaint-Louverture (1743–1803) slave leader of the Haitian Revolution.

FEMININE **Toussainte**

Tovia *see* Tobias

Toya *f*

A Hispanic pet form of VICTORIA that has now become established as an independent name, sometimes in the form LATOYA,

VARIANT **Toyah**

★ Toyah Wilcox (1958–), English singer and actress

Tracy *fm*

Tracy started out as an aristocratic surname, taken from a French place name. This in turn derived from a Roman personal name *Thracius*, 'man from Thrace'. Tracy was used as a masculine first name from the 19th century, and became quite popular in the USA, getting into the top 100 names there in the 1960s. This was probably helped by the popularity of the film star Spencer Tracy (1900–67). However, by the 1960s the feminine use of the name, introduced in *The Philadelphia Story* (see further at SAMANTHA), had overtaken the masculine, which led to a rapid decline in masculine use. The name was so popular for girls in the 1960s and 70s that its status was lowered. In the USA the more masculine-sounding short form *Trace* is still in regular use as a masculine name. As a feminine,

Tracy is also found as a pet form of THERESA.

PET FORM **Trace** • VARIANT **Tracey**

★ Tracey Ullman (1959–), English-born comedienne and author
★ Trace Adkins (1962–), US country singer-songwriter

Trahaearn *m*

A Welsh name formed from *haearn*, 'iron', with the intensifying element *tra* in front. In legend it was the name of the father of MACSEN. Some uses of the variant *Traherne* may be from the surname.

VARIANTS **Traherne, Treharne**

★ Trahaearn ap Caradog (d.1081), king of Gwynedd

Travis *m*

This is a surname, from the Old French *traverse*, 'a crossing', now used as a first name. The surname would have related to someone either living at a crossroads, or working at a crossing place such as a toll bridge. It came into use as a first name in the USA in honour of William Travis (1809–36), commander of the Texan forces at the Battle of the Alamo. It was a very popular name in the USA in the 1990s.

VARIANT **Travers**

☆ Travis Bickle in the 1976 film *Taxi Driver*
☆ Travis McGee, detective in the popular novels of John D MacDonald (1964 onwards). There are records of the popularity of this character inspiring parental choice

Treasa *see* Theresa

Trefor *see* Trevor

Treharne *see* Trahaearn

Trent *m*

A surname from the English river, used as a first name. It is mainly found in the USA and is sometimes a shortening of TRENTON.

★ Trent Lott (1941–), US politician
★ Trent Reznor (1965–), US musician also known as 'Nine Inch Nails'

Trenton *m*
This is the name of the New Jersey city, founded by William Trent, used as a first name. In the American War of Independence it was the site of a decisive defeat of the British by General George Washington (1776). However, it did not come into use as a first name until the 1960s, and use may have been inspired by the slightly earlier TRENT, which also serves as a pet form.
PET FORM **Trent**

Trevelyan *m*
A Cornish surname sometimes found as a first name. The surname is composed of *tref*, 'farmstead', and the old personal name *Elian*.

Trevor *m*
This is the English form of the Welsh name *Trefor*, from a place name derived from *tref*, 'farmstead', and *mawr*, 'large'. It is an old Welsh name, found from at least the 10th century. The name spread from Wales in the 1860s and was very popular in the middle years of the 20th century.
PET FORM **Trev**

★ Trevor Howard (1916–88), English actor
★ Trevor Phillips (1953–), English broadcaster and civil rights advocate

Trey *m*
Originally a nickname developed in the USA for a son who is the third generation in his family to bear the same name, the second being JUNIOR. Trey is an old term for the three in a suit of playing cards. It has been used as an independent name in the USA since the 1960s and has spread to other countries.
VARIANT **Tre**

★ Trey Parker (1969–), US creator of television cartoon *South Park*

Tricia *see* **Patricia**

Trina *f*
Originally a short form of *Catrina* or *Caterina*, variants of CATHERINE, and of other similar names. It is now used as an independent name.
★ Trina (1978–), US rapper

Trinity *f*
This is the religious term for the Christian concept of the Godhead, comprising the Father, Son and Holy Ghost. Although recorded as a first name at the time of the Reformation, it was very rare and has only been regularly used since the 20th century. It is currently popular in the USA. The Spanish *Trinidad* is older, and may have influenced the name. Although *Trini* is used as a pet form, the fashionista Trinny Woodall is not a Trinity but a Sarah-Jane, who was nicknamed Trinny after a childish prank compared to that of the girls of St Trinian's.
PET FORM **Trin(i)** • VARIANT *Spanish* **Trinidad**
☆ Trinity is a character in the 1999 film *The Matrix*. Use of the name increased enormously in the USA the following year

Triona *see* **Catriona**

Tris *see* **Beatrice**

Trish, **Trisha** *see* **Patricia**

Triss *see* **Beatrice**

Tristan *m*
In early Celtic legend Tristan, the nephew of King Mark of Cornwall, was sent to fetch the beautiful ISOLDE from Ireland to be Mark's bride. On the voyage home they mistakenly drank the love potion intended for Mark and Isolde's wedding night, and were doomed to tragic love. A story was told

that Tristan's mother chose his name just before she died in childbirth. The original form of Tristan may have been something like *Drustans* or *Drystan*, but the name was taken up by French romance writers who identified it with the word *trist*, 'sad'. Forms of the name have always been very variable. The popularity of the name has increased enormously in the last 20 years. In the USA it is also used for females, sometimes as *Trista* or *Tristana*.

PET FORM **Tris** • VARIANTS **Tristain, Tristen, Tristin, Tristram, Tristran, Trystan**

★ Tristan Tzara (1896–1963), Romanian poet, father of Dada

☆ Tristan Farnon, character in James Herriot's novels

☆ Tristram Shandy, eponymous protagonist of Lawrence Sterne's novel (1759–67)

Trixie *f*
A pet form of BEATRICE, now used as an independent name.
PET FORM **Trix** • VARIANT **Trixi**

Troalach *see* **Turlough**

Troilus *see* **Cressida**

Troy *m*
Although Troy looks as if it is taken from the ancient city besieged by the Greeks, it was originally a surname, transferred to a first name, that came from the city of Troyes in France. However, modern use may be associated with the ancient city. The name was given a boost in the 1960s by the teen idol film star Troy Donahue (1936–2001, birth name Merle Johnson), and is now enjoying a revival.

☆ Troy McClure, faded actor in television cartoon *The Simpsons*

Trudy *f*
A pet form of GERTRUDE or names

containing similar sounds, now used as an independent name.
PET FORM **Tru** • VARIANTS **Trudi(e)**, *Dutch* **Truus**

★ Trudie Styler (1954–), English actress and producer

Trystan *see* **Tristan**

Tsetsiliya *see* **Cecilia**

Tuathal *m*
An old Irish name, pronounced 'TOO-uh-hul', meaning 'ruler of the people'. It was a popular name in the Middle Ages, but has been rare since the 19th century.
VARIANTS **Toal, Tully**

Tucker *m*
A surname reused as a first name. In the past a tucker was someone who worked as a cloth-fuller. The name has been increasingly used in the USA since the 1980s.

Tudor *m*
This is the anglicized form of the Welsh name *Tudur*, which is derived from the Old Celtic *Teutorix*, formed from elements meaning 'people, tribe' and 'ruler, king'. This makes it the Welsh equivalent of TERRY, although it has also been used as the Welsh form of THEODORE. St Tudor was an early saint who figures largely in Welsh genealogies. Tudor is also the Romanian form of Theodore.
VARIANTS *Welsh* **Tudur, Tudyr**

Tudwal *m*
A Welsh name formed from *tud*, 'people, tribe', which is also found in TUDOR, and *gwal*, 'wall, defender'. It was the name of a 7th-century bishop and saint.

Tuilelaith *see* **Tallulah**

Tully *see* **Tuathal**

Turlough *m*

Pronounced *TUR(-a)-lakh*, this is the anglicized form of the Irish *Tárlach*, itself a shortening of the magnificently long *Toirdhealbhach*. This comes from *toirdhealbh*, 'prompting', and means 'instigator'. There were several early rulers of the name. TERENCE was used as the English equivalent.

VARIANTS *Irish* **Tárlach, Toirdhealbhach, Troalach**

★ Turlough Carolan (1670–1738), composer, known as the last of the great Irish harpists.

Tuvya *see* Tobias

Twila *see* Twyla

Twm *see* Thomas

Twyla *f*

This name has been used in the USA since the 19th century. Various suggestions have been put forward regarding its origins, including the idea that it is based on the word *twilight*, or that it is a Cajun pronunciation of French *étoile*, 'star'. Another possibility is that it represents a shortened pronunciation of the Irish name *Tuilelaith* (see TALLULAH) which has been anglicized in the past as *Twilleliah*.

VARIANT **Twila**

★ Twyla Tharp (1941–), US dancer and choreographer

☆ Twyla and Gawain, children in Terry Pratchett's *Hogfather*

Ty *m*

A pet form of names with this sound, particularly TYRONE and TYLER, increasingly used as an independent name.

VARIANT **Tye**

Tybalt *see* Theobald

Tycho *m*

This is the Latin form of the name of St *Tychon*, a Cypriot bishop who died c.450 and who was active in suppressing the last vestiges of paganism on the island. Nowadays it is primarily used in memory of the Danish astronomer Tycho Brahe (1546–1601).

Tyler *mf*

This is an occupational surname which has risen in popularity alongside TAYLOR and TUCKER, but has been more successful than these on both sides of the Atlantic. It is still predominantly masculine, although it is also used as a feminine.

PET FORM **Ty** • VARIANTS **Tylar, Tylor**

★ Tyler Brûlé (1968–), UK-based Canadian journalist and founding publisher of the magazine *Wallpaper*

Tymoteusz *see* Timothy

Tyna *see* Tina

Tyra *f*

Tyra is usually analysed as a Scandinavian name, a feminine version of the Old Norse god *Tyr*. However, its function as a modern name is to fill the gap for an exclusively feminine name among fashionable-sounding names such as TYLER and TYRONE. The name was introduced to the general public in the form *Tira* by Mae West in her 1933 film *I'm No Angel*, but did not catch on in the USA until the 1960s when male names beginning *Ty-* were becoming popular. It arrived in the UK somewhat later.

VARIANT **Tira**

★ Tyra Banks (1973–), US model and television presenter

Tyree *see* Tiree

Tyreek *see* Tariq

Tyrell *m*

A surname from the Old French *tirel*, a term for an animal that pulled on the reins, from *tirer*, 'to pull'. It is a variant of TERRELL, and although it has been used occasionally for many years, is probably currently chosen because it fits so well into the group of names starting *Ty-* which have become so fashionable.

★ Tyrell Biggs (1960–   ), US heavyweight boxer

Tyrese *see* **Tiree**

Tyrik, Tyriq *see* **Tariq**

Tyrnan *see* **Tiernan**

Tyrone *m*
Tyrone is a Northern Irish county, which in Irish is *Tir Eoghain*, 'land of EOGHAN'. As a first name, it was introduced to the general public by the US actor Tyrone Power (1914–58), who in turn was named after his great-grandfather, an Irish actor.

PET FORM **Ty**
★ Sir Tyrone Guthrie (1900–71), English theatrical producer
☆ Tyrone Slothrop, character in Thomas Pynchon's 1973 novel *Gravity's Rainbow*

Tyson *m*
A surname, of mixed origins, used as a first name. Although it is now strongly associated with the boxer Mike Tyson, the surname started to be used as a first name in the 1930s, so he could only have influenced its popularity.

Tytus *see* **Titus**

Tzafrir *see* **Zephyr**

Tzeitel *see* **Sara**

Tzion *see* **Zion**

Tzofiya *see* **Sophia**

U

Uailan, Uailean, Ualain, Ualan, Ualean *see* **Valentine**

Ubayd *m* **Ubayda** *f*
This is the diminutive of the Arabic *abd*, 'servant' (see ABDUL), and means 'lowly servant'. As a given name the word has religious connotations and can also be found as *Ubaydullah*, 'lowly servant of Allah'. This was the name of a cousin of Muhammad.
VARIANT **Ubaid(a)**

Udo *m*
This German name comes from the same root as ODO, meaning 'riches'. It is probably a surviving short form of earlier two-part names. It is in regular use in German-speaking areas, but has never really been part of the English stock of names.

Uffe *see* **Ulf**

Ughtred *m*
This was an Old English name spelt *Uhtraed*, made up of the elements *uht*, 'sawn', and *raed*, 'council', which survived the Norman Conquest and became an aristocratic surname. This is probably what led to its quiet revival in the 19th century.
VARIANT **U(t)hred**

Ugo, Ugolin *see* **Hugo**

Uhred *see* **Ughtred**

Uilleac, Uilleag *see* **Ulick**

Uilleam, Uilliam *see* **William**

Uinseann *see* **Vincent**

Uisdean *m*
A traditional Scots Gaelic name,
adopted from the Old Norse *Eysteinn*, formed from *ei*, 'ever, always', and *steinn*, 'stone'. It was usually anglicized as HUGH.
VARIANTS **Ùisdean, Hùisdean**
★ Uisdean Cam (d.1780), also known as 'One-eyed Hugh'. He was the stepfather of Flora Macdonald (1722–90), the Jacobite heroine who helped the escape of Bonnie Prince Charlie

Ulf *m*
This comes from the Old Norse *ulfr*, meaning 'wolf'. Before the Norman Conquest, it was a common name in England among those of Danish descent, but is now confined to Scandinavia.
VARIANTS **Ulffe, Uffe, Ulv**

Ulick *m*
This Irish name is probably from the Old Norse name *Hugleikr*, formed from *hugr*, 'heart, mind, spirit', and *leikr*, 'play'. In the past it was anglicized as WILLIAM (of which it is sometimes described as a form), HUGH or ULYSSES. It was a traditional name in the Burke family.
FEMININE **Ulicia** • VARIANTS *Irish* **Uilleac, Uilleag**
★ Ulick O'Connor (1928–), Irish author

Ulises, Ulisse *see* **Ulysses**

Ulla *see* **Ulric**

Ulric *m* **Ulrica** *f*
Ulric represents a falling together of two different names. The first is an Old English name originally found as *Wulfric*, formed from the word for wolf combined with *ric*, 'power,

rule'. The second is an anglicized or Scandinavian form of the German name *Ulrich*, formed from the same second element, but in which the first element comes from *oudal*, 'prosperity'. Ulrica is the Scandinavian feminine of this name.

PET FORM **Ulla** • VARIANTS **Ulrick, Ulrika, Ulrice**

★ Ulrika Jonsson (1967–), Swedish-born British television presenter.

☆ Ulrica in Verdi's 1859 opera *Un ballo in maschera*

☆ Ulrica is a character in Sir Walter Scott's 1820 novel *Ivanhoe*

Ultan *m*

This Irish name means 'Ulsterman'. St Ultan was a 7th-century monk who was a missionary in East Anglia and later in Merovingian Gaul.

VARIANT *Irish* **Ultach**

Ulv *see* **Ulf**

Ulysses *m*

This is the Latin form of the name of the Greek hero *Odysseus*. It has been recorded intermittently from the 16th century, but was only at all usual in the USA. There it came into fashion in the 19th century, alongside other classical names such as VIRGIL, and is still quietly but regularly used. In Ireland the name has been used to anglicize ULICK.

VARIANTS *Italian* **Ulisse** *Spanish* **Ulises**

★ Ulysses S Grant (1822–85), US general and president. It is probably his fame that keeps the name alive in the USA

Uma *f*

This is an Indian name from the Sanskrit for 'flax, turmeric'. It is a name for the goddess Parvati.

★ Uma Thurman (1970–), US actress

☆ Uma is a beautiful girl in R L Stevenson's 1892 novella *The Beach of Falesá*

Umar, Umair *see* **Omar**

Umayma *f*

An Arabic name meaning 'little mother'.

VARIANT **Umaima**

Umberto *see* **Humbert**

Umer *see* **Omar**[1]

Umm *see* **Abu**

Una *f*

Úna is the Irish Gaelic spelling of the name now usually found as OONA. It can also be interpreted as deriving from the Latin for 'one', and was used in this sense by the poet Spenser for the heroine of book I of *The Faerie Queene* (1590–96). In this work Una personifies truth, for there is only one truth while falsehoods are many. However, it should be remembered that Spenser spent much of his working life in Ireland, and may have been influenced by the Irish name.

★ Una Stubbs (1937–), English actress

Unaiza *f*

An Arabic name meaning 'friendly, affable'.

VARIANT **Unaysah**

Undine *f*

From the Latin *unda*, meaning 'wave', this name was created by the medieval author Paracelsus as a term for water spirits. In German folk tradition Undines are water spirits who can acquire a soul by marrying a human and bearing a child. This idea was used by the German author Baron de la Motte Fouqué, who turned it into a tragic novella called *Undine* (1811). This in turn was made into several operas and ballets, making the name well known. Undine is rarely used in real life, but frequently encountered in fictional settings.

VARIANT *French* **Ondine**

Unice *see* **Eunice**

Unity *f*

This is the vocabulary word used as a first name. It was adopted by the Puritans, but since then has been most used in Ireland as a variant of UNA.

★ Unity Mitford (1914–48), English socialite, the Mitford sister who supported Hitler

Urban *m*

Urban, from Latin *urbanus*, means 'city-dweller' and was the name of several early saints and popes. It was adopted as a Christian name because country-dwellers, who tended to have less exposure to the new religions, were called *paganus* in Latin, a name that came to mean PAGAN.

Uri *m*

This is a Hebrew name meaning 'light'. It is borne by a minor character in the Old Testament.

★ Uri Geller (1946–), Israeli paranormalist

Uriah *m*

This is a Hebrew name meaning 'God is light'. In the Bible Uriah is Bathsheba's husband, and his death is arranged by King David so that he can marry Bathsheba himself (2 Samuel 11). It was used after the Reformation, but was never popular, and became all but unusable after Dickens created the unpleasant character of Uriah Heep in his 1850 novel *David Copperfield*.

Uriel *m*

A Hebrew name meaning 'God is my light'. It is borne by two minor characters in the Old Testament, and is the name of an archangel in Hebrew tradition.

Urien *m*

The traditional interpretation of this Welsh name is that it derives from Latin *urbigenus*, 'city-born', a variant of URBAN. However, it is now thought that it could be formed from the Old Celtic elements *orbo*, 'privileged', and *gen*, 'birth'. Urien of Rheged appears in Welsh legend, and may be the same figure as the real-life 6th-century king and war leader who was father of OWAIN.

Ursula *f*

This name, meaning 'little she-bear' and thus the feminine form of ORSON, was borne by a 4th-century martyr whose highly romanticized legend was a popular subject for medieval art. The name is used quietly but regularly.

★ Ursula K Le Guin (1929–), US science-fiction writer
★ Ursula Andress (1936–), Swiss actress
★ Ursula Vernon (1977–), US artist and writer

Usama *see* Osama

Usha *f*

From the Sanskrit for 'dawn' this is the name of the Hindu goddess of the dawn, the daughter of heaven.
VARIANT **Ushas**

Usman *see* Osman

Ustinya *see* Justin

Ute *see* Odette

Uthman *see* Osman

Uthred *see* Ughtred

Uzair *m*

This well-used name is the Arabic equivalent of EZRA.
VARIANT **Uzayr**

Uzi *m*

This is a Jewish name, from the Hebrew for 'power, might'. It is also used as a short form for the biblical names *Uz(z)iah*, 'power of Yahweh', and *Uz(z)iel*, 'power of God'.

Vaclav *see* **Wenceslas**

Vadim *m*
A medieval Russian and Slavic name, perhaps from the Slavic element *volod*, 'rule', or possibly a variant of VLADIMIR. PET FORM **Vadik**

Vaila *f*
This is the name of one of the Shetland islands that has come into use as a first name in Scotland (compare IONA, SKYE). The island gets its name from the Old Norse for 'valley'.

Val *mf*
Pet form of any name beginning *Val-*, or of names such as PERCIVAL, sometimes found as an independent name.
★ Val (Michael Valentine) Doonican (m) (1927–), Irish singer
★ Val Kilmer (m) (1959–), US actor

Valda *f*
In use since at least the beginning of the 20th century, this is probably an elaboration of VAL, or a blend of Val with a name such as LINDA.
★ Valda Trevlyn Grieve (1906–89), Cornish nationalist, publisher and wife of the poet Hugh MacDiarmid
★ Valda Aveling (1920–2007), Australian pianist
☆ Valda Sheergold is a character in the Australian soap *Neighbours*

Valdemar *see* **Vladimir**

Valentine *mf*
The Roman family name *Valentinus* came from *valens* (also used as a name) meaning 'strong, health'. It was borne by a 3rd-century martyr, about whom very little is known for sure. The reason St Valentine's Day is celebrated as it is, is because his feast day fell in the middle of the ancient Roman fertility festival of the *Lupercalia*, and the traditions were transferred to his day. While Valentine is usually masculine, it is sometimes found as a female name, although *Valentina* is also used.
PET FORM **Val** • VARIANTS *Scots Gaelic* **Uala(i)n** *Welsh* **Folant** *Dutch* **Valentijn** *French* **Valentin** (m) *Italian* **Valentino**, **Valentina** *Polish* **Walenty**, **Walentyna** *Spanish* **Valentín**
★ Valentine Dyall (1908–85), deep-voiced English actor, primarily in radio
★ Valentina Tereshkova (1937–), Russian cosmonaut, and first woman in space

Valerie *f* **Valery** *m*
This is the English form of the Latin name *Valeria*, the feminine of *Valerius*, from the Latin *valere*, 'to be strong, healthy', and thus related to VALENTINE. There are both male and female saints of this name. One, St Valerie, is said to have been decapitated and then carried her head to the church where the bishop who had baptized her was saying Mass. A 7th-century St Valery founded a monastery in France at a place still called Saint-Valery-sur-Somme. The masculine form is much rarer than the feminine among English speakers, but is well used in other languages.
PET FORM **Val** • VARIANTS **Valary** *French* **Valère**, **Valéry** (ms), **Valérie** *German* **Valeska** (f) *Italian, Spanish* **Valeria**, **Valerio** *Polish* **Walerian**, **Walery** (ms), **Waleria** *Russian* **Valeri(y)** (m), **Valeriya**

★ Valerie Singleton (1937–), English television and radio presenter
★ Valéry Giscard d'Estaing (1926–), French politician

Valter *see* **Walter**

Van *see* **Ivan**

Vance *m*
This is a English surname, from a respelling of the word 'fens', used as a first name.
★ Vance Packard (1914–96), US author and social commentator

Vanda *see* **Wanda**

Vanessa *f*
This name was invented in 1726, for use in a poem, by the Anglo-Irish writer Jonathan Swift. It was formed from elements of the name of a woman called Esther Vanhomrigh, to whom the poem was addressed.
PET FORMS **Ness(ie)**, **Nessa**
★ Vanessa Redgrave (1937–), English actress
★ Vanessa Paradis (1972–), French singer and actress

Vanni *see* **John**

Vanya *see* **Ivan**

Varfolomei, **Varfolomey** *see* **Bartholomew**

Varvara, **Varya** *see* **Barbara**

Vashti *f*
In the biblical book of Esther, Vashti is the wife of the Persian king Ahasuerus. During a feast, the king summons Vashti before his guests and orders her to display her beauty. She refuses and, rather than being praised for her modesty, she is deposed for fear that other women will follow her example and disobey their husbands. Esther then takes her place. Despite being held up as an example of womanly disobedience, the name was used by

the Puritans for their daughters, and even appeared among the most high-minded New England families. It is still quietly but regularly used, and is now felt by some to be a feminist choice.
★ Vashti Bunyan (1945–), English singer-songwriter
☆ Vashti is the mother in E M Forster's influential 1909 story *The Machine Stops*

Vasili, **Vasiliki**, **Vasilis**, **Vasilios**, **Vasilisa**, **Vasiliy**, **Vaska** *see* **Basil**

Vaughan *m*
This Welsh surname comes from the nickname *bychan*, 'small', which mutates under certain grammatical conditions to *fychan*, the first letter of which is pronounced in Welsh with a 'v' sound.
VARIANT **Vaughn**

Vedant *m*
This is an Indian name which refers to the *Vedas*, the oldest sacred texts in Hinduism. Vedant is often combined with other elements to form more complex names of religious significance.

Velda *f*
The US author Mickey Spillane claimed to have coined the name Velda for Mike Hammer's secretary, in his series of books about the hard-boiled private detective, the first of which was published in 1947. Unfortunately for Spillane this cannot be the case, as Velda had been recorded in use in the USA by the 1890s, although there is no doubt that he gave the name publicity. However, the meaning and origin of the name remain unknown.
☆ Velda is the name given by the archaeo-geneticist Bryan Sykes to the theoretical ancestress who has passed her genes down to the Basque people

Velma f

A name of rather obscure origins which has been in use in the USA since the 19th century. The most likely explanation is that it represents a form of the German pronunciation of *Wilma*, a pet form of WILHELMINA.

★ Velma Middleton (1917–61), US jazz singer
☆ Velma Dace Dinkley, the bright one in the television cartoon *Scooby Doo*
☆ Velma Kelly, murderess in the musical *Chicago*

Velvel *see* William

Velvela *see* Wilhelmina

Velvet f

This is an unusual female name from the vocabulary word. It was made famous by Enid Bagnold's 1935 novel *National Velvet*, and particularly by the 1944 film adaptation starring the young Elizabeth Taylor as the heroine, Velvet Brown.

Venceslao, Venceslas *see* Wenceslas

Vendela *see* Wendell

Venedikt *see* Benedict

Venetia f

This name is of somewhat obscure origin. It is the Latin name for Venice, and modern users probably link it with the city. However, the name has been in use since the Middle Ages, and early users seem to have associated it with the goddess VENUS.

★ Venetia Stanley (1600–33), famous for her beauty, independence and learning. When she died she was mourned by some of the foremost poets of the time, and her husband Sir Kenelm Digby, once one of the most prominent men of his day, remained in seclusion for two years
★ Venetia Stanley (1887–1948), descendant of the above and also famed for her beauty, who attracted so much interest from Prime Minister H H Asquith, that he even wrote letters to her while he was in Cabinet meetings
☆ *Venetia*, an 1837 novel by Benjamin Disraeli which re-ignited interest in the name

Veniamin *see* Benjamin

Venus f

This is the name of the Roman goddess, usually described as the goddess of love and beauty but actually much more than that, who was considered mother of the Roman race.

★ Venus Williams (1980–), US tennis player

Venyamnin *see* Benjamin

Vera f

This was originally a Russian name, being the Russian for 'faith'. However, it also looks like a feminine form of the Latin *verus*, 'truth', and some people use it in that way. The name had spread to English speakers by the 19th century. Vera is also a pet form of VERONICA or VERENA, while in Greece it is a pet form of *Varvara* (BARBARA).
VARIANTS Slavic **Viera** Russian pet forms **Verochka, Verusia**

★ Dame Vera Lynn (1917–), English singer
★ Vera Brittain (1893–1970), English writer, feminist and pacifist

Verena f

The source of the name Verena is unknown, perhaps because it is not of European origin. It may be Egyptian (transformed through Latin) if we can believe the legend of St Verena, said to have been an Egyptian nurse who in the 3rd century travelled with the Theban legion to Switzerland. When the legion was martyred she settled near Zurich. The name is still most used in Switzerland.

PET FORM **Vera** • VARIANTS French **Vérène** German **Vreni**

☆ Verena Tarrant in Henry James's *The Bostonian* (1886)

Vergil *see* **Virgil**

Verity *f*

This is the old-fashioned word for 'truth' which was one of the virtue names adopted in the 17th century. It is currently attracting some interest from parents.

VARIANTS **Verily**, **Verita**

★ Verity Lambert (1935–2007), English television producer

☆ Verity is the character played by Madonna in the 2002 James Bond film *Die Another Day*

Verna *f*

This is a 19th-century coinage which can be linked with the Latin *vernus*, 'spring', or else be regarded as a feminine form of VERNON.

★ Verna Felton (1890–1966), US actress who voiced many characters in Disney cartoons

★ Verna Bloom (1939–), US actress

Vernon *m*

Vernon is a French place name which comes from a Gaulish word meaning 'where alders grow'. A Richard de Vernon was one of the Norman conquerors of England, and he founded a noble family. Vernon became a popular first name in the 19th century when aristocratic surnames were in fashion.

PET FORM **Vern(e)**

★ Vernon Scannell (1922–2007), English poet

★ Vernon Kay (1974–), English radio and television presenter

☆ Vernon Dursley, Harry Potter's uncle in the *Harry Potter* books by J K Rowling

Veronica *f*

Veronica is a good illustration of how a name can change because of what people think it should mean. Historically the name is a Latin form of BERENICE, but looks as if it could be from the Latin expression *vera icon*, 'true image'. A story evolved to suit this meaning, telling of a woman who used her veil to wipe the sweat from Christ's face as he was carrying the cross to Golgotha, and found that a true image of his features was left imprinted on the cloth. The name was occasionally used from the Middle Ages, but did not become common until the 19th century.

PET FORMS **Vera**, **Roni** • VARIANTS French **Veronique** German, Scandinavian **Veronika** Polish **Weronika**, **Wera** Russian **Veronika**, **Nika**, **Ronja**

★ Veronica Lake (1922–73), US film actress

★ Veronica Giuliani (1660–1727), Italian saint and mystic

☆ *Veronica Mars*, US television series

Vesta *f*

This is the name of the Roman goddess of hearth and home, who was served by the Vestal Virgins. Although the name was taken up in the 19th century, it never really became established in the stock of English names, despite being given prominence on the stage. It is possible this was because of the association of the word with a brand of matches.

★ Vesta Tilley (1864–1952), English comedienne

★ Vesta Victoria (1873–1951), English music hall performer

Vester *see* **Silvester**

Vevina *see* **Beibhinn**

Vi *see* **Violet**, **Vivian**

Vicente *see* **Vincent**

Victor *m*

Victor comes from the Late Latin *victorius*, 'conqueror'. It was adopted as a name by early Christians, to signify Christ's victory over death. It was borne by a number of early saints, but did not come into general use in the UK until the 19th century, during Queen Victoria's reign.

PET FORM **Vic** • VARIANTS *Welsh* **Gwythyr, Gwydyr** *German, Scandinavian, Russian* **Viktor** *Italian* **Vittore, Vittorino, Vittorio, Vico** *Polish* **Wiktor** *Portuguese* **Vítor** *Russian* **Vitya** *Spanish* **Victorino**

★ Victor Hugo (1802–85), French poet and writer
★ Victor Spinetti (1933–   ), Welsh actor
☆ Viktor Krum in the *Harry Potter* books by J K Rowling
☆ Victor Frankenstein in Mary Shelley's 1818 novel *Frankenstein*

Victoria *f*
This name was little known in the UK before Queen Victoria (1819–1901), who was named after her German mother Mary Louise Victoria of Saxe-Coburg. It came into general use after Victoria's accession in 1837, but was at its most popular in the 1960s and 70s, being the most prominent name in the first wave of 19th-century revivals, and is still well used. As a result of this popularity, a number of pet forms have hived off into independent names. Those in the *Tori* group are particularly common.

PET FORMS **Vic, Vickie, Vicky, Vi(k)ki, Queenie, To(r)ri(e), Tory, Toria, Toya, Vita** • VARIANTS *Scots Gaelic* **Bhictoria** *French* **Victoire, Victorine** *German, Scandinavian* **Viktoria** *Hawaiian* **Wikolia** *Italian* **Vittoria** *Polish* **Wiktoria** *Russian* **Viktoriya**

★ Victoria Principal (1950–   ), US actress
★ Victoria Beckham (1974–   ), English singer, Spice Girl and fashionista
☆ Victoria (Vic) Iphigenia Warshawski, heroine of Sara Paretsky's *V I Warshawski* novels

Vida *f*
This is usually either a short form of the Scottish name *Davida* (see DAVINA) or a variant of VITA.

Vidal *see* **Vita, Vitus**

Viera *see* **Vera**

Viggo *m*
This is a form of the old Scandinavian name *Vigge*, originally a short form of names beginning with the element *vig*, 'war'. Viggo is a popular name in Sweden.

★ Viggo Vrun (1885–1978), Norwegian mathematician
★ Viggo Mortensen (1958–   ), Danish-American actor

Vijay *m* Vijaya *mf*
This popular Indian name means 'victory' in Sanskrit. It is common in Hindu mythology, particularly as an epithet for the hero ARJUN, and was the name of a semi-legendary king of Sri Lanka in the 6th century. The initial 'V' mutates to a 'B' in Bengali forms of the name. Vijay can also be used in compound names such as the feminines *Vijaylakshmi* and *Vijayshree*, both epithets of the goddess Lakshmi.

VARIANTS **Bijay, Bijoy, V-J**

★ Vijay Singh (1963–   ), Fijian golfer

Viki, Vikki *see* **Victoria**

Vikram *m*
This is one of the names of the Indian god Vishnu which can be interpreted as 'stride' (indicating purposeful action), 'heroism' and 'strength'.

★ Vikram Seth (1952–   ), Indian poet, novelist and travel writer
★ Vikramaditya (375–414), meaning 'Vikram son of Aditi (the sun)', an Indian king. Vikram is often a short form of this name

Viktor *see* **Victor**

Viktoria, Viktoriya *see* **Victoria**

Vilhelm *see* **William**

Vilhelmina, Vilma *see* **Wilhelmina**

Vilmar *see* **Wilmer**

Vilmos *see* **William**

Vilppu *see* **Philip**

Vimal *m* **Vimala** *f*
From the Sanskrit meaning 'pure,
stainless' these names are particularly
found in Buddhist texts.

Vina *see* **Davina, Lavinia**

Vinay *m*
This Indian name is from the Sanskrit
for 'modesty, humility, leading,
guidance'.

Vincent *f*
The Roman name *Vincentius* was
formed from the verb *vincere*, 'to
conquer'. It was borne by a number
of early saints for the same reason that
the related VICTOR was a popular choice
for early Christians, but nowadays
the saint most closely associated with
the name is the French St Vincent de
Paul (1581–1660). Although Vincent
was used occasionally by English
speakers from the Middle Ages, it did
not become widespread until the 19th
century.
PET FORMS **Vince, Vinnie, Vinny** • VARIANTS
Irish **Uinseann** *German* **Vinzent, Vincenz**
Italian **Vincente, Vincenzo, Enzo** *Polish*
Wincenty *Russian* **Vinkenti** *Spanish*
Vicente
★ Vincent Van Gogh (1853–90), Dutch
   Post-Impressionist painter
★ Vinnie Jones (1965–   ), English
   footballer and actor

Vinia *see* **Lavinia**

Viola, Violet *f*
Although Viola has been less common
in English than Violet, it is the elder of
these two flower names, having been
in use in Italy since the Middle Ages,
when it was taken directly from the
Latin word for 'violet'. The choice of

Viola by English speakers is mostly
directly inspired by Shakespeare's
use of the name in *Twelfth Night*.
The English equivalent, Violet, had
appeared in Scotland by the 15th
century, but does not seem to have
become established in England until
the 18th century. This is despite the
fact that an Italian form, *Violante*, had
been borne by Violante Visconti, who
married Lionel, second son of Edward
III, in 1368. Violet was a popular name
in the 19th century and, after some
years in the wilderness, is showing
some signs of returning to favour.
PET FORM **Vi** • VARIANTS *French* **Violette**
Italian **Violetta** *Spanish* **Violeta**
★ Lady Violet Bonham-Carter (1887–
   1969), English politician and publicist
☆ Violetta Valéry in Verdi's 1853 opera
   La Traviata, adapted from Alexandre
   Dumas's 1848 novel *La Dame aux
   Camélias*

Virgil *m*
This name, famous as that of the 1st-
century BC Latin poet, is mainly used
in the USA. The older spelling of the
name is *Vergil* and both forms are
found. Virgil sometimes appears as a
Latin form of the Gaelic name FERGAL.
VARIANTS **Vergil** *Italian, Spanish* **Virgilio**
★ Virgil Thomson (1896–1989), US
   composer and critic
☆ Virgil Tibbs in John Ball's 1965 novel,
   and in the 1967 film adaptation, *In the
   Heat of the Night*
☆ Virgil Tracy in the 1960s television
   puppet series *Thunderbirds*

Virginia *f*
The Romans told a story of a Roman
girl called Virginia whose father
chose to kill her rather than see her
dishonoured. However, the name did
not enter the stock of Western names,
although its sense, the Latin for 'virgin',
was revived when Queen Elizabeth I,
the 'Virgin Queen', was on the throne.
It was in her honour that early English

settlers in North America named the province of Virginia, and the first baby girl born to them there, in 1587, was given the name of the place, thus reintroducing the personal name.

PET FORMS **Ginger, Gina, Gigi, Ginnie, Ginny, Jinny** • VARIANTS *French* **Virginie, Ginette**

★ Virginia Woolf (1882–1941), English novelist, critic and essayist

★ Virginia McKenna (1931–   ), English actress

Vishal *m*
An Indian name from the Sanskrit for 'wide, spacious'.

Vishnu *m*
The name of one of the great gods of Hinduism, derived from the Sanskrit for 'all-pervasive'. He is god of the sun and protector of the universe.

Vita *f* **Vitus** *m*
The Latin word *vita* means 'life' and was adopted early on as a specifically Christian name. St Vitus was a 4th-century child martyred in Sicily. Vita is the feminine form of this name in some countries. For English speakers it can also be used as a pet form of names such as VICTORIA. Related to Vitus was the Late Latin *Vitalis*, 'of life, vital', which was also borne by several early saints, and gave rise to names in a number of languages. The history of Vitus and Vitalis can be somewhat confused by the fact that, early on, both names were muddled up with the Germanic *Wido*, source of GUY.

VARIANTS *Italian* **Vitale, Vitalia** *Russian* **Vitali(y), Vitya** *Spanish* **Vidal**

★ Vita (Victoria) Sackville-West (1892–1962), English poet, novelist and garden designer

★ Vidal Sassoon (1928–   ), English hairdresser

Vítor, Vittore *see* **Victor**

Vittoria *see* **Victoria**

Vittorino, Vittorio, Vitya *see* **Victor**

Vivian *fm*
The Roman name *Vivianus* came from *vivus*, 'alive, lively'. It was originally a masculine name, used in honour of a 5th-century French bishop who protected his people from the invading Visigoths. It can still be found as a masculine name, but is now more often feminine, as are its variants.

PET FORMS **Vi, Viv(i)** • VARIANTS **Vivien, Vyvian** *French* **Vivianne,** *Italian, Spanish* **Viviana**

V-J *see* **Vijay**

Vladimir *m*
A Russian name formed from the Slavonic elements *volod*, 'rule', and *mer*, 'great, famous'. Its popularity in Slavic countries comes from St Vladimir of Kiev (c.958–1015) whose conversion to Christianity started the conversion of Russia.

PET FORM **Vlad** • VARIANTS *German* **Waldemar** *Polish* **Włodzimierz, Waldek, Waldus', Włodek** *Russian* **Volodya, Vova** *Scandinavian* **Valdemar**

★ Vladimir Ilyich Lenin (1870–1924), Russian revolutionary and founder of Leninism

★ Vladimir Nabokov (1899–1977), Russian-born US novelist

Vladislav *see* **Ladislas**

Vlas, Vlasi, Vlasis, Vlassis *see* **Blaise**

Volodya *see* **Vladimir**

Vonda *see* **Wanda**

Vova *see* **Vladimir**

Vreni *see* **Verena**

Vyacheslav *see* **Wenceslas**

Vyvian, Vyvyan *see* **Vivian**

W

Waclaw *see* **Wenceslas**

Wade *m*
This is a surname, from the Old English word for a ford, used as a first name. There was a prior use of Wade, as the name of a shadowy legendary figure in Old English stories, but this is unlikely to be a source. Wade has been used steadily in the USA since the 19th century.
VARIANT **Wayde**
★ Wade Hampton III (1818–1902), US Confederate general and politician, and the reason Margaret Mitchell calls Scarlett O'Hara's first child Wade Hampton Hamilton, in *Gone With the Wind*. Hampton's grandfather, Wade Hampton I (c.1751–1835), was also a prominent general and politician

Wafa *f* **Wafi** *m*
Wafa comes from the Arabic word for 'faithfulness, fidelity, faith'. *Wafiya* is a related name meaning 'trustworthy, reliable'. This becomes Wafi in the masculine, with *Wafai* having a closely related meaning.
VARIANT **Wafiyya**

Wafiq *m* **Wafiqa** *f*
These names, from the same root as WAFI, mean 'friend, companion'.

Waldek, **Waldemar** *see* **Vladimir**

Waldo *m*
The Germanic element *wald*, 'power', was used in a number of compound names, of which Waldo survives as a shortened form. It may have passed into the stock of Western names from the Waldensians, a sect who played a

prominent part in the Reformation, and who were in turn named after a 12th-century reformer, Peter Waldo.
★ Ralph Waldo Emerson (1803–82), US poet and essayist. His fame is the immediate source of the name in the USA
☆ *Waldo*, a 1942 novella by Robert A Heinlein, about a disabled man who invents remote manipulators to overcome his problems. This led to the use of 'waldos' as a term for such devices

Waldus´ *see* **Vladimir**

Walenty, **Walentyna** *see* **Valentine**

Waleria, **Walerian**, **Walery** *see* **Valerie**

Walid *m*
Walif is the Arabic for 'newborn child', hence 'son'.
★ Walid Jumblatt (1949–), Lebanese politician

Wallace *m*
The Norman French word *waleis* originally meant 'foreign', and then became a generic term for the Celtic races. This became a Scottish surname, and was used as a first name in honour of the Scottish warrior and patriot Sir William Wallace (c.1270–1305).
PET FORMS **Wal**, **Wally** • VARIANT **Wallis**
★ Wallace Beery (1885–1949), US actor
★ Wallace Stevens (1879–1955), US poet
☆ Wallace in the claymation *Wallace and Gromit* films

Walter *m*
There was an Old English name *Wealdhere*, formed from elements

meaning 'rule' and 'army', the same elements as HAROLD in reverse order. At the Norman Conquest the Normans introduced their own version of this Germanic name, which appears in records as the forms Walter and *Gualter*. This became a popular name, and records also show that it was pronounced 'water' in the Middle Ages and beyond, which explains old pet forms such as *Wat* and *Wattie* and the surname from the name, Watkin.
PET FORMS **Walt, Wal(ly)** • VARIANTS *Scots Gaelic* **Bhaltair, Bhàtair** *Welsh* **Gwalter, Gwatcyn** *Dutch* **Wouter** *French* **Gautier** *German* **Walther** *Portuguese* **Gualter** *Scandinavian* **Valter** *Spanish* **Gualtiero**
★ Walt Whitman (1819–92), US poet
★ Walt Disney (1901–66), US artist and film producer, founder of the animation company
★ Walter Matthau (1920–2000), US actor
☆ Watkin Wombat in the Australian children's classic *The Magic Pudding* (1918), by Norman Lindsay

Wanda *f*
The earliest recorded use of the name Wanda is for an 8th-century Polish queen, but there is no indication of where it came from. The origin of the name may have been lost, although a Germanic tribal name, 'the Wends', has been suggested as a source. The name was introduced to English speakers by the novelist Ouida, who published a work called *Wanda* in 1883. Forms beginning with an initial 'V' reflect the Polish pronunciation.
VARIANTS **Vonda** *Italian* **Vanda**
★ Vonda McIntyre (1948–   ), US author
☆ The 1988 film, *A Fish Called Wanda*

Ward *see* **Howard**

Warren *m*
This is a surname used as a first name since at least the 17th century. The surname can have different sources,

either from the vocabulary word 'warren', from the French place name La Verenne near Nantes, or from a Germanic name *Varin*, 'guard'.
★ Warren G Harding (1865–1923), 29th US president
★ Warren Beatty (1937–   ), US film actor, director and producer

Warwick *m*
This is a surname from the name of the English city, which means 'settlement by a weir'. As a first name, Warwick has been particularly well used in Australia.
PET FORM **Warrie** • VARIANT **Warrick**
★ Warwick Deeping (1877–1950), English novelist

Washington *m*
The surname of George Washington (1732–99), the first president of the USA, which comes from a town in the north of England, used as a first name.
★ Washington Irving (1783–1859), US writer

Wasim *m* **Wasima** *f*
The Arabic for 'handsome, beautiful' used as a first name. *Wasma*, 'pretty face', is also used for females.
VARIANT **Wassim**

Wat, Watkin *see* **Walter**

Wawrzyniec *see* **Laurence**

Wayde *see* **Wade**

Wayland *m*
This is an old Germanic name from the elements *wig*, 'war', and 'land'. It was the name of a legendary smith in Germanic tradition.
VARIANTS **Waylon** *German* **Wieland**
★ Waylon Jennings (1937–2002), US country music singer and songwriter
☆ Waylon Smithers in the television cartoon *The Simpsons*

Wayne *m*

This is an occupational surname for a wagon maker, used as first name. Its popularity is due to the fame of US actor John Wayne (Marion Michael Morrison, 1907–79). He is said to have taken his screen name from US general and politician Anthony Wayne (1745–96).

★ Wayne Rooney (1985–   ), English footballer

☆ Wayne Campbell in the 1992 film *Wayne's World*

Webster *m*

This is an occupational surname, from an old word for 'weaver', used as a first name. It came into use in the USA in the 19th century, perhaps in honour of the statesman Daniel Webster (1782–1852).

★ Webster Booth (1902–84), English actor and singer who formed a famous singing duo with Anne Ziegler

Wenceslas *m*

This is a Slavic name from the elements *ventie*, 'more, greater', and *slav*, 'glory'. Good King Wenceslas was actually a 10th-century duke of Bohemia, and is the patron saint of the region.

VARIANTS *Czech* **Vaclav** *German* **Wenzel** *Italian* **Venceslao** *Polish* **Wacław** *Spanish* **Venceslas** *Russian* **Vyacheslav**

★ Václav Havel (1936–   ), Czech dramatist and statesman

Wendell *m*

This comes from the German name *Wendel*, derived from an old ethnic grouping among the early medieval northern tribes, 'the Wends'. Thus it may be a masculine equivalent of WANDA. Its use as a first name in the USA is in honour of the US author Oliver Wendell Holmes (1809–94), and his equally respected son of the same name.

VARIANTS **Wendel** *German* **Wendelin** *Swedish* **Vendela** (f)

★ Wendell Willkie (1892–1944), US politician

Wendy *f*

This name was introduced to the general public by J M Barrie in 1904, when he used it for the girl in his play *Peter Pan*. He claimed to have coined it from a nickname *Fwendy-Wendy* which was given to him by a little girl who regarded him as her friend. However, there is some evidence that the name was already in use as a pet form of GWENDOLEN. Wendy became popular after *Peter Pan* and peaked in use in the 1960s.

PET FORM **Wen(d)** • VARIANTS **Wendi, Wenda**

★ Wendy Craig (1934–   ), English actress

★ Wendy Cope (1945–   ), English poet

Wenona *see* **Winona**

Wera *see* **Veronica**

Werner *m*

A German name from the elements *war*, 'guard', and *heri*, 'army'.

VARIANTS **Wernher, Wetzel, Wernicke**

★ Werner Herzog (1942–   ), German actor and film director

★ Wernher von Braun (1912–77), German-born US rocket pioneer

☆ 'Werner' was an 1823 work by Lord Byron

Weronika *see* **Veronica**

Werther *m*

This German name comes from the elements *wert*, 'worthy', and *heri*, 'army'. It is strongly associated with the highly romantic 1787 novel *The Sorrows of Young Werther* by Goethe.

VARIANT **Werter**

Wesley *m*

This is a surname, from a place

meaning 'west meadow', used as a first name. It came into use in honour of John Wesley (1703–91) founder of the Methodist Church.

PET FORM **Wes**

★ Wesley Snipes (1962–   ), US actor
★ John Wesley Hardin (1853–95), US outlaw
☆ Wesley Wyndham-Price in the television series *Buffy the Vampire Slayer* and *Angel*

Weston *m*
This is a surname, from a place meaning 'west settlement', used as a first name, mainly in the USA.

Wetzel *see* Werner

Whitley *f*
A surname, meaning 'white wood', used as a first name. It came into use in the 1980s, particularly among African Americans, as a result of its appearance in the television sitcom *A Different World*, a programme which also introduced *Jaleesa*.

Whitney *fm*
This is a surname, from a place meaning 'white island', used as a first name. As a masculine name it probably comes from the fame of the US geologist Josiah Dwight Whitney (1819–96), after whom the highest peak in the Rockies was named. As a feminine name its popularity comes from the two performers listed below.

VARIANT **Witney**

★ Whitney Blake (1926–2002), US actress
★ Whitney Houston (1963–   ), US pop and soul singer named after Whitney Blake

Wieland *see* Wayland

Wikolia, Wiktor, Wiktoria *see* Victoria

Wilbert *m*
Originally a Dutch name from the Germanic elements *wil*, 'desire', and *berht*, 'bright'. It was one of the old names revived in the 19th century, and was well used in the USA in the early years of the 20th century.

★ Rev Wilbert Awdry (1911–97), English author and clergyman, creator of Thomas the Tank Engine

Wilbur *m*
This was originally an Old English female name *Wilburg*, from the elements *wil*, 'will, desire', and *burh*, 'fortress', which became a surname and then a first name. It was well used in the USA from the late 19th century into the early part of the 20th.

★ Wilbur Wright (1867–1912), US aviation pioneer
★ Wilbur Smith (1933–   ), US-based novelist
☆ Wilbur the pig in E B White's 1952 children's book *Charlotte's Web*

Wilfrid *m*
St Wilfrid, whose name was formed from elements *wil*, 'will, desire', and *frith*, 'peace' was an outstanding Northumbrian bishop in the 7th century. His name became rare after the Norman Conquest until it was revived in the 19th century, when it was often changed to *Wilfred* to conform with other *-fred* names.

PET FORMS **Wilf, Fred** • VARIANT **Wilfred**

★ Wilfred Owen (1893–1918), English World War I poet
★ Wilfred Pickles (1904–78), English comic and radio host

Wilhelmina *f*
This is a German and Dutch feminine form of WILLIAM. It was common in the 19th century, as the wide variety of pet forms shows, but is now rare among English speakers, although the pet forms are still found. It was most

often used in the USA, where it was introduced by immigrants.

PET FORMS **Mina, Willa, Wilma, Minnie, Velma, Ilma** • VARIANTS *German* **Wilhelmine, Elma, Helma, Helmine, Minna** *Scandinavian* **Vilhelmina, Vilma, Helmi** *Yiddish* **Velvela**

★ Wilhelmina Krafft (1778–1828), Swedish artist
★ Wilhelmina of the Netherlands (1880–1962), highly respected queen of the Netherlands
☆ Mina (Wilhelmina) Harker in Bram Stoker's 1897 novel *Dracula*
☆ Wilhelmina Slater in the television show *Ugly Betty*

Wilkie *m*

A surname, from an old pet form of WILLIAM, occasionally used as a first name. In the case of the most famous bearer, author Wilkie Collins (1824–89), it was a pet form of his given name of William.

Willa *f*

This is generally interpreted as an independently formed feminine of WILLIAM, although it also serves as a pet form of WILHELMINA.

★ Willa Cather (1873–1947), US fiction writer, poet and journalist
★ Willa Baum (1926–2006), US pioneer of oral history

William *m*

A Germanic name composed of the elements *wil*, 'will, desire', and *helm*, 'protection'. It was already widespread on the Continent, in various forms, before being brought to England by William the Conqueror, and has remained one of the most-used names among English speakers ever since.

PET FORMS **Will(y), Willie, Bill, Billy** • VARIANTS *Irish* **Liam, Uilliam** *Scots Gaelic* **Uilleam** *Welsh* **Gwil(l)ym, Gwilim, Gwil** *Manx* **Illiam** *Dutch* **Willem, Wim, Pim, Jelle** *French* **Guillaume** *German*

Wilhelm, Willi, Wim *Hungarian* **Vilmos** *Italian* **Guglielmo** *Portuguese* **Guilherme** *Scandinavian* **Vilhelm** *Spanish* **Guillermo** *Yiddish* **Velvel**

★ William Shakespeare (1564–1616), English playwright, poet and actor
★ William Butler Yeats (1865–1939), Irish poet

Willis *m*

An English surname, derived from WILLIAM, occasionally used as a first name.

★ Willis Hall (1929–2005), English dramatist
★ Willis E Lamb (1913–   ), US Nobel Prize-winning physicist

Willoughby *m*

This aristocratic surname, from a place meaning 'willow settlement', was among those which became fashionable as first names in the 19th century. It has, however, been recorded in East Anglia as a female name from at least 1700. It is seldom used today.

★ Willoughby Smith (1828–91), English electrical engineer
☆ Willoughby the Dog, a *Looney Tunes* character

Willow *f*

This is the tree name used as a first name. It has been in circulation for some years, often appearing in fictional contexts, but has only recently become popular. This can be directly linked to the character of Willow Rosenberg in the cult television series *Buffy the Vampire Slayer*. The hit series was first shown in 1997 and Willow entered the US name charts in 1998. The name sometimes fills the role of a feminine form of WILLIAM.

PET FORM **Will**

☆ Willow is a male character in the 1988 fantasy film *Willow*

Wilma *f*
A pet form of WILHELMINA mainly found in the USA, where it was introduced by German settlers in the 19th century.
☆ Wilma Flintstone in the television cartoon *The Flintstones*

Wilmer *m*
A Old English name formed from *wil*, 'will, desire', and *maer*, 'famous', which later died out, but not before it had become a surname. This was then reused as a first name, particularly in the USA. Although it is out of favour among English speakers, it is not uncommon in Latin America and the Scandinavian form is currently well used in Sweden.
VARIANTS **Wilmar** *Scandinavian* **Vilmar**
☆ Wilmer Cook is the name of the manic gunman working for Gutman in *The Maltese Falcon*

Wilson *m*
Wilson is another of the surnames derived from WILLIAM, now occasionally chosen as a first name. Use in the USA is influenced by the fame of President WOODROW Wilson.
★ Wilson Pickett (1941–2006), US soul singer

Wim *see* **William**

Win *see* **Gwen**

Wincenty *see* **Vincent**

Winifred *f*
This is the anglicized form of the Welsh name GWENFREWI, which has become hopelessly muddled up with similar names, such as the masculine Old English name *Winfred* (from *wynn*, 'joy', and *frith*, 'peace'). It came into use among English speakers in the 16th century, and was popular in the 19th and early 20th centuries.
PET FORMS **Win(nie)**, **Winn**, **Fred**, **Freda**
• VARIANTS **Gwinifred**, **Winnifred**

★ Winifred 'Winnie' Ewing (1929–), Scottish politician
★ Winnie Mandela (1936–), South African civil rights activist

Winn *see* **Gwen**

Winona *f*
This is a Sioux term meaning 'first-born daughter'. The name appears in Longfellow's *Hiawatha* (1855) as *Wenona*. As well as being recorded as a genuine Native American name, it is a common place name in North America.
VARIANT **Wynon(n)a**
★ Winona Ryder (1971–), US actress named after the town near where she was born
★ Wynonna Judd (1964–), US country singer

Winsome *mf*
The vocabulary word sometimes used as a first name, especially in Australia.

Winston *m*
This is a surname, transferred from a place name, now used as a first name. Winston was a traditional name in the Churchill family. The first Sir Winston Churchill (1629–88) was given his mother's maiden name, and his son became the first duke of Malborough. The name was passed down to his most famous namesake, whose father was a younger son of a later duke. The name became a popular 20th-century name in honour of the great World War II leader.
★ Winston Graham (1908–2003), English novelist
☆ Winston Smith in George Orwell's 1949 novel *Nineteen Eighty-Four*

Wistan *see* **Wystan**

Witney *see* **Whitney**

Wladislaw, **Władysław**, **Władysława** *see* **Ladislas**

Włodek *see* **Vladimir**

Włodysław *see* **Ladislas**

Włodzimierz *see* **Vladimir**

Wmffre *see* **Humphrey**

Wolf *m*
This can either be from the vocabulary word, found in both English and German, or from a shortening of various German names containing the word for example, *Wolfgang* (wolf plus *gang*, 'going'), *Wolfger* (wolf plus *ger*, 'spear') and *Wolfram* (wolf plus *hramm*, 'raven'). The spelling *Wolfe* is sometimes found in Ireland, transferred from the surname of Irish nationalist Theobald Wolfe TONE.
VARIANT *Scandinavian* **Ulf**
★ Wolfram von Eschenbach (c.1170–c.1220), German poet
★ Wolf Mankowitz (1924–98), English author, playwright and antique dealer
★ Wolfgang Amadeus Mozart (1756–91), Austrian composer

Woodrow, Woody *m*
This is a surname, originally given to someone living in a row of houses near a wood, which entered the stock of US names in honour of President (Thomas) Woodrow WILSON (1856–1924). It is regularly shortened to Woody, which can also be a given name or a nickname.

★ Woody Guthrie (1912–67), US folk singer, songwriter and activist
★ Woody Herman (1913–87), US bandleader, alto saxophonist and clarinettist
★ Woody Harrelson (1961–), US actor
☆ Animated cartoon character Woody Woodpecker

Wouter *see* **Walter**

Wulfric *see* **Ulric**

Wyatt *m*
A surname which is a contracted form of the Old English name *Wigheard*, formed from elements *wig*, 'battle', and *heard*, 'brave'. The modern use of Wyatt as a first name is probably linked to the fame of the US lawman and gunfighter Wyatt Earp (1848–1929).

Wyn, Wynne *see* **Gwen**

Wynfor, Wynford *see* **Gwynfor**

Wynona, Wynonna *see* **Winona**

Wystan *m*
This name, which comes from Old English *wig*, 'battle', and *stan*, 'stone', was borne by a 9th-century saint who was murdered soon after becoming king of Mercia.
VARIANT **Wistan**
★ Wystan Hugh Auden (1907–73), English-born US poet and essayist

X

Xabier *see* **Xavier**

Xander *m*
This was originally a pet form of
ALEXANDER, but is now increasingly used
as an independent name. Use of this
name has shot up since it was borne
by a major character in the television
series *Buffy the Vampire Slayer*.
PET FORMS **Xan, Zan** • VARIANT **Zander**
★ Xander Berkley (1955–), US actor

Xandra, Xandrine *see* **Alexandra,
Sandra**

Xanthe *f*
A Greek name meaning 'yellow,
golden, blonde', and thus an
equivalent of FLAVIA. It is the name of a
sea nymph and of an Amazon in Greek
mythology. The name is pronounced
'zan-thee'.
VARIANT **Xanthia**
★ Xanthe Elbrick (1978–), English
actress

Xara *see* **Zara**

Xavier *m*
This is the surname of St Francis Xavier
(1506–52), one of the founders of
the Jesuits, used as a first name. His
surname is Basque in origin, being a
standard Spanish spelling of the name
Etcheberria or *Etxaberria*, a common
Basque surname meaning 'new house'.
It is often found preceded by Francis.
FEMININES **Xavia, Zavia, Xaviera, Xaverine,
Xavière** • VARIANTS **Xabier, Javier, Zavier**
German **Xaver** *Italian* **Saverio**
★ Xavier Cugat (1900–90), Spanish-born
Cuban bandleader
★ Xabi (Xabier) Alonso (1981–),
Spanish footballer who plays for
Liverpool FC

Xena *f*
This name gained publicity through the
television series *Xena, Warrior Princess*.
It can be interpreted either as a variant
of XENIA, or as deriving directly from
Greek *xena*, 'stranger, foreigner',
or alternatively as a variant of ZENA.
The name Xena has been given to a
recently discovered minor planet.

Xenia *f*
Xenia means 'hospitality' in Greek and
is derived from *xenos*, 'stranger'. It is
the name of several saints venerated
in the Eastern Church, including St
Xenia of St Petersburg, an 18th-century
widow who gave away her possessions
and who was only canonized in 1988,
and 5th-century St Xenia of Rome,
who is said to have fled to Greece to
avoid marriage and became a nun
famous for her powers of healing.
VARIANTS *Polish* **Ksenia** *Russian* **Aksinya**

Ximena *f*
This is borne by El Cid's wife in the
great Spanish epic named after him.
The meaning of Ximena is not known,
although it has been suggested that
it may be an old Spanish feminine
of SIMON. It is quite a popular name
among Spanish speakers in the USA, in
both the 'X' and 'J' variant spellings.
VARIANTS **Jimena** *French* **Chimène**

Xiomara *f*
A Spanish name of obscure origin.
It may be a variant of *Guiomar*, a
Spanish name of Germanic derivation
meaning 'famous in battle'.

Xitlalli *see* **Citlali**

Y

Yadav *m*
An Indian name from the Sanskrit meaning 'descendant of *Yadu*', Yadu being one of the names of Krishna.

Yadira *f*
This is a popular name in Latin America, in use since at least the 1940s, although its origins are obscure. It has been suggested that it is a respelling of Spanish *Jadira*, 'jade', or that it is a form of an Arabic name. However, as there is a liking in the region for invented names beginning with 'Y', it may simply have been made up.
VARIANT **Yadhira**
★ Yadhira Carrillo (1974–), Mexican soap star

Yael *see* **Jael**

Yahya *see* **John**

Yair *mf*
A Hebrew name meaning 'he shines'. It is found in the Old Testament as the name of a judge and as the son of Manasseh.
VARIANTS **Yaire**, **Jair** *Spanish* **Jairo**

Yakim *see* **Joachim**

Yakov *see* **Jacob**

Yan, Yanni, Yannic, Yannick, Yannis *see* **John**

Yaqub *see* **Jacob**

Yarden, Yardena *see* **Jordan**

Yaroslav *see* **Jaroslaw**

Yasar *m*
An Arabic name meaning 'prosperity, ease'.
★ Yasar Kemal (1923–), Turkish author

Yashpal *m*
An Indian name meaning 'protector of splendour' in Sanskrit.

Yasim *see* **Jasmine**

Yasin *m*
An Arabic name formed from the first two letters of the 36th sura of the Koran.
VARIANTS **Yaseen, Yassin(e)**

Yasir *m*
An Arabic name meaning 'easy, prosperous', related to YASAR.
FEMININES **Yusriyya, Y(o)usra** • VARIANTS **Yusri, Yasser**
★ Yasser Arafat (1929–2004), Palestinian resistance leader

Yasmeen, Yasmin *see* **Jasmine**

Yechezkel *see* **Ezekiel**

Yefim *see* **Euphemia**

Yefrem *see* **Ephraim**

Yegor *see* **George**

Yehoshua *see* **Joshua**

Yehudi *see* **Jude**

Yehudit *see* **Judith**

Yekaterina *see* **Catherine**

Yelena *see* **Helen, Jelena, Lena**

Yelisei *see* **Elisha**

Yelizaveta *see* **Elizabeth**

Yemelyan *see* **Emil**

Yentl *f*
A Yiddish name, which seems to have come from the French nickname *Gentille*, 'kind, nice, noble'.
VARIANT **Yente**
☆ *Yentl* is a 1983 film based on a story by Isaac Bashevis Singer

Yesenia *f*
This is a Latin American name, taken from a type of tree found throughout the area, which has the Latin name *Jessenia*. It was introduced in a 1970 film, set in the 19th century, which was later developed into a popular television soap opera.
VARIANTS **Yessenia**, **Jes(s)enia**

Yesfir *see* **Esther**

Yeshua *see* **Joshua**

Yetta *f*
A Jewish name of unknown origin, although it may be no more than a variant of *Etta*, a pet form of any name ending in the sound, such as HENRIETTA or *Marietta*.

Yevgeni *see* **Eugene**

Ygor *see* **Igor**

Yiaanni, **Yiaannis** *see* **John**

Yidel *see* **Judith**

Yiorgos *see* **George**

Yitzak *see* **Isaac**

Ynyr *m*
A Welsh name which is probably an early development of the Roman name *Honorius* (HONORIA). It is well attested in the surviving records from the 6th to 13th century, and has come back into use in modern times.

Yolanda *f*
This is an old name of obscure origin. It is possible to argue for a Germanic

derivation, but if this is the case it has become hopelessly confused with other names. It was well used by the medieval French aristocracy, and appears in records as *Yolande*, *Iolande* and *Iolante*, among other forms. These could also be from the Italian *Violante* (VIOLET) or from its Greek equivalent IOLANTHE.
VARIANTS **Yolande** *Dutch, Italian, Polish* **Jolanda** *Italian* **Iolanda**

Yonah *see* **Jonah**

Yonatan, **Yoni** *see* **Jonathan**

Yorath *see* **Iorworth**

Yorgos *see* **George**

Yos, **Yosel**, **Yosi**, **Yoske**, **Yousef** *see* **Joseph**

Yousra, **Yusra** *see* **Yasir**

Youssef *see* **Joseph**

Ysabel, **Ysobel** *see* **Isabel**

Ysanne, **Yselle** *f*
Modern coinages, which combine the sound of *Yseult* (ISOLDE) with familiar name endings.
★ Ysanne Churchman (1925–), English actress, best known for playing Grace Archer in long-running radio soap *The Archers*

Yseult, **Yseut** *see* **Isolde**

Yudel *see* **Judah**

Yuli *see* **Julian**

Yulia *see* **Julia**

Yuliy *see* **Julian**

Yuliya *see* **Julia**

Yunus *see* **Jonah**

Yuri, **Yuriy** *see* **George**

Yusef, **Yusuf** *see* **Joseph**

Yushua *see* **Joshua**

Yusra, **Yusri**, **Yusriyya** *see* **Yasir**

Yussel *see* **Joseph**

Yustina *see* **Justin**

Yutke *see* **Judith**

Yves *m*
This French name, particularly common among Bretons, comes from a shortening of Germanic names containing the element *iv*, 'yew'. Its popularity with Bretons comes from St Yves, or *Ivo*, of Kermatin, the patron saint of the area. In the Middle Ages *Yvon* developed as a pet form, and it is thought that the Arthurian knight *Yvain* (see also OWAIN) may have derived his name from this.
PET FORM **Yvon** • VARIANTS **Ivo**, **Ives**
★ Yves Montand (1921–91), Italian-born French singer and actor
★ Yves Klein (1928–62), French artist

Yvette *f*
A feminine form of YVES, more frequently used by English speakers than by the French.
★ Yvette Fielding (1968–), English broadcaster and actress
★ Yvette Cooper (1969–), Scottish economist and politician

Yvon *see* **Yves**

Yvonne *f*
This is a feminine form of YVES, formed from the pet form *Yvon*. It is currently rarely used by the French, being much more common among English speakers, with whom it was very popular in the first part of the 20th century.
VARIANTS **Yvone**, **Evonne**, **Ivonne**
★ Yvonne de Carlo (1922–2007), Canadian actress
★ Yvonne Ridley (1968–), English journalist

Z

Zaahir *m*
This Arabic name means 'manifest, plain, clear'. *Al Zaahir*, 'The Evident', is one of the titles of Allah. See also ZAHIR.

Zaaki, Zaakia *see* **Zaki**

Zaakira *see* **Zakir**

Zabrina *see* **Sabrina**

Zach, Zachary *m*
The Hebrew name *Zechariah*, 'God has remembered', appears in the Greek of the New Testament as *Zacharias*, father of John the Baptist, and became Zachary in English. The name was taken up by the Puritans and used regularly thereafter, but is currently more popular, particularly in its short forms, than it has ever been. Consequently it has developed many variants. The form *Zac* or *Zack* can also be used as a pet form of ISAAC.
PET FORMS **Zac, Zack, Zak** • VARIANTS
Zacharias, Zechariah, Zachery, Zackery *Scots Gaelic* **Sachairi** *Arabic* **Zakari(y)a** *French* **Zacharie** *Polish* **Zachariasz** *Russian* **Zakhar**
★ Zachary Scott (1914–65), US actor
★ Zac Goldsmith (1975–), English environmentalist and politician

Zadok *m*
This is a Hebrew name meaning 'just, righteous'. In the Old Testament it is borne by several characters, including the priest who anoints Solomon. It is very rare as a given name outside the Jewish community.
VARIANT **Zadoc**
☆ Zadok Allen is a key character in H

P Lovecraft's 1936 story *The Shadow over Innsmouth*

Zahid *m* **Zahida** *f*
An Arabic name, meaning 'pious, devout'.
VARIANT **Zahidaa**

Zahir *m* **Zahira** *f*
Arabic names from the Arabic word for 'helper, supporter, protector', a term used in the Koran to describe angels. The name is also found in compounds such as *Zahir-ud-Din*, 'protector of religion'.
VARIANT **Zaheerah**
★ Zahir-ud-Din Babur (d.1530), founder of the Mughal Empire

Zahra, Zahrah *f*
Strictly speaking these are two different Arabic names, Zahra or *Zahraa* coming from the word for 'brilliant bright', and Zahrah meaning 'blossom, flower'. However, the differences between the Arabic and Roman alphabets mean that, in practice, the two are not readily distinguished in their variant spellings. Zahra is a name used of the Prophet's daughter Fatima. See also ZARA.

Zaid *see* **Zayd**

Zain, Zaina *see* **Zayn**

Zainab, Zaineddin, Zainub *see* **Zaynab**

Zak, Zakaria, Zakariya, Zakhar *see* **Zach**

Zaki *m* **Zakiya** *f*
An Arabic name meaning 'pure, chaste, sinless'.

VARIANTS **Zaaki, Za(a)kia**

Zakir *m* **Zakira** *f*
An Arabic name using a term for one who eulogizes Allah.
VARIANT **Zaakira**

Zalman *see* **Solomon**

Zan, Zander *see* **Xander**

Zandra *see* **Alexandra, Sandra**

Zane *m*
This is a surname of unknown meaning, used as a first name. It was introduced to the general public by the author Zane Grey (1872–1939), whose given name was Pearl Zane Grey. Zane was his mother's maiden name and she was a descendant of Ebenezer Zane, who founded Grey's hometown of Zanevill in Ohio. Not surprisingly, Grey dropped his first name when publishing his novels of the Wild West. See also ZAYN.

Zanna *see* **Susan**

Zara *f*
This name came to public attention in 1981 when it was chosen by Princess Anne for her second child, Zara Phillips. However, the name has featured in English literature for some time. William Congreve used it for an African queen in his 1693 play *The Mourning Bride*. In 1732 Voltaire gave it to the heroine of his tragedy *Zaire* (itself sometimes used as a first name in the USA), and when Aaron Hill translated the play in 1735 he called it *Zara*. It is not clear if the name should be thought of as a form of SARAH or of ZAHRA. Although Princess Anne's choice of the name initially had only a small effect on its use, as Zara Phillips has become more famous its popularity has increased.
VARIANT **Xara**

Zarina *f*
A Muslim name, from the Persian for 'golden'.
VARIANTS **Zareen, Zarin(e)**

Zarita *see* **Sarah**

Zavia, Zavier *see* **Xavier**

Zayd *m*
An Arabic name meaning 'increase, growth'. It was borne by an adopted son of Muhammad.
VARIANT **Zaid**

Zayn *m* **Zayna** *f*
These come from an Arabic word meaning 'beautiful, handsome'. *Zayn-ud-Din* means 'beauty of religion'.
VARIANTS **Zain(a), Zaynah, Zaineddin, Zinedine**
★ Zinedine Zidane (1972–), French footballer nicknamed *Zizou*

Zaynab *f*
This is the Arabic name for a type of sweetly scented flower, used as a first name. It was popular in the Prophet's family, being the name of two of his wives, a daughter and a granddaughter. It is one of the most frequently used names in the Islamic world, reflected in the wide variety of forms it takes.
VARIANTS **Ze(y)nab, Zainab, Zainub, Zeynep, Zaynah**

Zbigniew *m*
A Polish name formed from Slavic elements *zbit*, 'to dispel', and *gniew*, 'anger'.
★ Zbigniew Brzezinski (1928–), Polish-born US academic and politician

Zebedee *m*
Zebedee is the New Testament Greek form of the Hebrew name *Zebadiah*, 'God has bestowed'. In the New Testament it is the name of a prosperous fisherman on the Sea of Galilee, who is father of the Apostles John and James the Great.

PET FORM **Zeb** • VARIANT **Zebadiah**

☆ On the children's television show *The Magic Roundabout* Zebedee was the character, half-man, half-spring, who said 'Time for bed'

Zebulun *m*

In the Old Testament Zebulun, whose name probably means 'exaltation', was one of the sons of Jacob. Although taken up by the Puritans, the name has never been common, although it was occasionally used in the USA during the 19th century and has been very quietly revived there in recent years.

★ Zebulon Montgomery Pike (1779–1813), US soldier and explorer after whom Pikes Peak in Colorado is named

Zechariah *see* Zach

Zedekiah *m*

A Hebrew name meaning 'justice of God', which was borne by three Old Testament characters, including the last king of Judah. It is very rare, but the short form was occasionally used in the USA, mainly in the 19th century, or in fictional contexts.

PET FORM **Zed**

Zeenat *see* Zinat

Zeev *m*

This is a Jewish name, from the Hebrew for 'wolf'. It has been used to translate the many other names with this meaning. It is particularly associated with the tribe of Benjamin, who, Jacob said on his deathbed, would 'ravin as a wolf'. It is pronounced with two syllables, 'ze-ev'.

VARIANT **Zev**

Zef *see* Joseph

Zeferino *see* Zephyr

Zeke *see* Ezekiel

Zelda, Zelde *f*

This name may be either a pet form of GRISELDA or a Yiddish form of SELIG. However, these may not be the immediate source of the name as used today. The woman who brought fame to the name, Zelda Fitzgerald (1900–48), was named after two 19th-century literary works: Jane Howard's *Zelda: A Tale of the Massachusetts Colony* (1866) and Robert Edward Francillon's *Zelda's Fortune* (1874). In both these stories Zelda is regarded as a gypsy name.

☆ Zelda is the heroine of a very successful series of computer games

Zelig *see* Selig

Zelma *see* Selma

Zelpha *see* Zilpah

Zena *f*

This name can have a variety of sources. It is used a Scottish pet form of *Alexina* (ALEXANDRA), can also be a variant of XENA, XENIA or ZINA, or may be a shortening of names such as ZENOBIA or ZINNIA. In addition, it can be taken from the Persian word for 'woman'. Alternatively, Zena may simply be chosen because parents like the sound. The name has been in use since the 19th century.

Zenab *see* Zaynab

Zenaida *see* Zinaida

Zenap *see* Zaynab

Zenith *mf*

The vocabulary word which has occasionally been used as a first name in modern times.

Zeno *m*

This is the English form of the Greek *Zenon*, derived from *Zeus*, king of the gods. Zeno was borne by two ancient Greek philosophers: Zeno of Elea (c.490–430 BC) is remembered from the conundrum of Zeno's arrow; Zeno of Citium (c.334–262 BC) was the founder of the Stoic school of philosophy. The form Zenon is particularly used in Poland.

VARIANT **Zen(n)on**

Zenobia f

This was the name of a queen of Palmyra in the 3rd century AD who was famous for her beauty and wisdom. It appears to be a feminine form of the Greek name *Senobios*, derived from ZENO, a form of the name of the god *Zeus* combined with *bios*, 'life, life force'. However, on inscriptions in Palmyra her name appears as *Septimia Bathzabbai*, the second half possibly meaning something like 'dowry of God', and it may be that Zenobia was an attempt to create something recognizable from this name. Others have tried to link the name with the Arabic ZAYNAB, but this is less convincing. For some unknown reason the name was well used in Cornwall in the 16th century.

VARIANTS *Cornish* **Zenoby** *Greek* **Zenovia**
☆ Zenobia is a feminist character in Nathaniel Hawthorne's 1852 novel *The Blithedale Romance*

Zephaniah m

This name is usually interpreted as meaning 'hidden by God' or 'protected by God'. It is borne by one of the minor prophets in the Old Testament.

PET FORM **Zeph** • VARIANT **Zephania**

Zephyr fm Zephirine f

The vocabulary word 'zephyr', from Greek *Zephyros* the name of the west wind and the god that ruled it, has occasionally been used as a first name in English. It is also found in Catholic countries, given in honour of the 3rd-century pope St *Zephyrinus*, whose name was taken from the Greek.

Of the feminine forms Zephirine is probably the best known, from the thornless, pink, climbing rose named after Zephirine Drouhin.

VARIANTS **Zephyra** *French* **Zéphirin**, **Zéphyrine** *Hebrew* **Tzafrir** *Portuguese* **Zeferino** *Spanish* **Ceferino**

Zeta *see* Zita

Zev *see* Zeev

Zeynab, Zeynep *see* Zaynab

Zhubin *see* Zubin

Zia m

An Arabic name which means 'light, illumination, splendour'.

VARIANTS **Ziya**, **Ziaur**
★ Muhammad Zia-ul-Haq (1924–88), Pakistani soldier and politician
★ Ziaur Rahman (1935–81), Bangladeshi soldier and politician

Zillah f

Zillah is the second wife of Lamech in the biblical book of Genesis. The name was used in the years after the Reformation, and was revived in the 19th century, but is now rare. It is said to be a traditional name among the Romany.

VARIANT **Zilla**
☆ Zillah is the innocent maiden in Robert Southey's 1799 poem 'The Rose'
☆ Zillah is the name of the housekeeper in Emily Brontë's 1847 novel *Wuthering Heights*

Zilpah f

In the Bible Zilpah was the name of a slave girl belonging to Leah who has two sons, Asher and Gad, by Leah's husband Jacob. Probably because of this slightly uncomfortable background the name has only ever been quietly used.

VARIANTS **Zilpha**, **Zelpha**
★ Zilpha Snyder (1927–), US children's author

Zina, Zinaida *f*
Zina is a Russian pet form of Zinaida. This in turn comes from the Greek *Zenais* which derives from *Zeus*, king of the gods. Zinaida is a common Russian name, but is not much used by English speakers. Those who do choose it may have been influenced by Turgenev's 1869 novella *First Love*. Zina can also be a respelling of the names referred to at ZENA, and is an Arabic name meaning 'ornament', a term used of a lovely woman.
VARIANT *Spanish* **Zenaida**
★ Zina Garrison (1963–   ), US tennis player

Zinat *f*
An Arabic name meaning 'adornment, decoration'.
VARIANT **Zeenat**

Zinedine *see* **Zayn**

Zinnia *f*
One of the rarer 19th-century flower names. The plant was named after the German botanist Johan Zinn (1727–59).
☆ Zinnia Wormwood is Matilda's neglectful mother, in Roald Dahl's 1988 children's book *Matilda*

Zion *m*
Zion is used in the Bible as an alternative term for Jerusalem, although strictly speaking it is the name of the central citadel of the city. It is also the term used by Rastafarians for a land of freedom. It has a long history as a Jewish name, but seems to have been introduced to the common stock of names in 1997, when US singer Lauryn Hill and Rohan Marley, son of the Rastafarian singer Bob Marley, bestowed it on their son. The name entered the US name charts the following year and has been climbing steadily ever since. It is also starting to be used in the UK.
VARIANT *Yiddish* **Tzion**

Zipporah *f*
Now rarely found outside the Jewish community, this is the name of the wife of Moses. It means 'bird' in Hebrew. It was occasionally used by English speakers in the 18th and 19th centuries.
VARIANTS *Arabic* **Safura, Safrawa**

Zita *f*
This name comes from an Italian dialect word meaning 'child'. It was borne by a 13th-century saint who is the patron of domestic servants.
★ Zita of Bourbon-Parma (1892–1989), last empress of the Austro-Hungarian Empire

Ziya *see* **Zia**

Zoe *f*
This is the Greek word for 'life'. It was popular with early Christians because it linked with ideas of eternal life. It is also the Greek equivalent of the Hebrew EVE. It has been steadily popular in the UK since the 1970s.
VARIANTS **Zowie, Zoie, Zoey** *Polish* **Zoja** *Russian* **Zoya**

Zofia *see* **Sophia**

Zoha *fm*
As a feminine name this is the Arabic for 'morning light', and is mainly used by those of Indian descent. As a masculine name it can be a variant of *Zuha*, the title of the 93rd sura of the Koran.

Zohra *f*
An Arabic name derived from that of the planet Venus.
VARIANTS **Zurha, Zorah**

Zoie, Zoja *see* **Zoe**

Zola *f*
A 20th-century first name, apparently from the surname of French author

Emile Zola (1840–1902). His father was Italian, and the surname comes from an Italian dialect word for a 'bank' or 'mound of earth'. The name is also used in South Africa from the Zulu for 'quiet, tranquil'.
★ Zola Taylor (1938–2007), US lead singer of The Platters
★ Zola Budd (1966–   ), South African athlete

Zoltan *m*
This Hungarian name may be from the Turkish title, Sultan. It became established in Hungary after it was borne by a 10th-century ruler.
VARIANT **Zsolt**

Zorah *see* **Zohra**

Zosia *see* **Sophia**

Zowie, **Zoya** *see* **Zoe**

Zsazsa *see* **Susan**

Zsolt *see* **Zoltan**

Zsuzsa, **Zsuzsanna** *see* **Susan**

Zubaida *f*
An Arabic name, meaning 'marigold'. It can also be a pet form of *Zubda*, meaning 'the cream of something, the élite'.

Zubin *m*
A name from the Sanskrit for 'spear'.
VARIANT **Zhubin**
★ Zubin Mehta (1936–   ), Indian-born US conductor

Zuleika *f*
In both Jewish and Arabic tradition, this is the name of Potiphar's wife who tried to seduce Joseph, although the name is not given in either the Old Testament or the Koran.
VARIANTS *Arabic* **Zulaikha**, **Zulaykha**
☆ Zuleika was the name of the heroine in Lord Byron's narrative poem *The Bride of Abydos* (1813)
☆ *Zuleika Dobson, or an Oxford Love Story* was a satirical novel by Max Beerbohm published in 1911. The name is now strongly associated with its heroine

Zulfiquar *m*
This was the name of the Prophet Muhammad's sword. It means 'cleaver of vertebrae'.
VARIANT **Zulfaqaar**, **Zulfikar**
★ Zulfikar Ali Bhutto (1928–79), Pakistani statesman

Zurha *see* **Zohra**

Zuriel *m*
This is the name of a minor figure in the Old Testament, and also of the angel that presides over the sign of Libra in some mystic beliefs. The name means 'my rock is God', and shows slight signs of revival.

Zuzanna *see* **Susan**

Zyta *see* **Felicity**

How important is your name?

Popular names

One of the 'facts' regularly quoted about first names is that experiments have shown that unusual names have negative effects on people, and so should not be given to children. And yet all the evidence shows that modern parents have not followed this advice. From the 12th century through to the beginning of the 19th century, some 20 per cent of children born in any year were likely to be given the most popular name for either sex, 50 per cent of them would have one of the three most popular names and 80 per cent would have one of the top ten. But from 1800 onwards these percentages declined rapidly.

Percentage of children given popular names in the UK

		Boys	Girls
1900	top name	9%	7%
	top three names	23%	16%
	top ten names	51%	39%
1950s	top name	6%	6%
	top three names	17%	13%
	top ten names	38%	32%
1990s	top name	4%	3%
	top three names	11%	9%
	top ten names	28%	24%

In the USA – and most figures for name statistics are quoted for the USA, as the government there makes full information available which is not accessible in the UK – the figures show a similar pattern, although the mixed cultural heritage means that names have always been more diverse in the USA, and the statistics do reflect the conservatism of the USA in the 1950s.

Percentage of children given popular names in the USA

		Boys	Girls
1900	top name	6%	5%
	top three names	15%	9%
	top ten names	31%	18%
1950	top name	5%	5%
	top three names	14%	11%
	top ten names	33%	23%
2007	top name	1%	0.9%
	top three names	3%	2.5%
	top ten names	9%	8%

These statistics raise two main questions. What has been going on socially to change people's naming habits so radically in the last 200 years? And why do parents ignore the perceived wisdom about avoiding unusual names?

Social changes

The first question cannot be answered by science, as parents from previous centuries cannot be asked, but there are some obvious factors in society that can explain the changes. The first of these is the Industrial Revolution and the resulting urbanization of society. This meant that, as people left their small communities to gather in large cities, the old naming traditions could be disrupted. In addition, simply because they were exposed to so many more people, they were also likely to encounter a greater pool of names to choose from. City living would also mean that there was a need for a greater store of names. In a village it would not matter if there were ten Johns, as you would know them all and would be able to distinguish them by some handy term, much as is still done in parts of Wales, where the milkman might be referred to as 'Dai the Milk' and the local shopkeeper as 'Dai the Shop'. In cities you need to be able to distinguish between people you do not know intimately, and different names serve this function. The introduction of mass education was another influence. The Romantic movement had introduced a taste for exotic names in literature. The cult of the medieval that it brought with it lies behind the revival of Anglo-Saxon names, and these and other exotic names worked their way into popular literature. From the mid-19th century we see an increasing use of names from popular novelists and similar sources.

The rapid increase in the pool of names that occurred during the 20th century, and particularly since the 1950s, can be explained by another major social shift, this time in how people address each other. If you read Victorian novels you will be familiar with the fact that, once you became an adult, only your nearest and dearest used your first name. Sometimes even husband and wife addressed each other as Mr and Mrs rather than by their first names. Anthony Trollope, in an admittedly extreme case, shows us in The Warden (1855) Mrs Grantly going no further than to call her husband 'Archdeacon' even when in bed with him.

A child in the 1950s might be given the right to address close friends of their parents as 'Auntie This' or 'Uncle That', but otherwise would never think to address an adult by their first name. Yet nowadays it is quite normal for complete strangers to write letters addressing you by your first name. This means that a first name has moved from being a way of distinguishing between, say, Mr John Smith and Mr George Smith. By dropping the use of a surname we have halved the distinguishing names for people, so it is no surprise if in response we have had to vastly increase the pool of first names.

Naming against the grain

This brings us back to the problem of why everyone 'knows' we should not do exactly what people are actually doing – choosing unusual names. I regularly speak on the subject of first names, and when some celebrity chooses an outlandish name for their child I am called by radio stations and asked whether this is bad for the child, with the implication: surely they will be bullied at school? I usually answer that, alas, if a child is going to attract the attention of bullies, then the bullies will always find something to pick on – if it is not their name, then it will be something else. As for the outlandish names of celebrity children, it has been suggested that it might be good for them rather than bad, as it at least gives them something to be famous for in their own right, rather than being totally overshadowed by their parent's fame.

The psychology of names

Where then does the idea that unusual names are bad for you come from? Sadly, it has its source in some rather poor science. The concept entered the public domain from some experiments done in the USA in the 1950s. College students were asked to rate a list of names for various qualities, and the results showed that the students assessed people with names from a core group much more positively than names they felt to be more unusual. These results rapidly passed into the public domain. It was only later that people re-examined these experiments and spotted some of the faults in them. First of all, this was the buttoned-down 1950s, and attitudes have changed since then. More importantly, there were inherent flaws in the experiments. The group of students used for the testing were all from the same narrow socio-economic group – their positive responses were to names that they identified as fitting in with their group. As important was that some of the names used were ethnically marked, and the names which were identifiably associated with African-Americans were responded to particularly negatively. What in fact the students were doing was showing their class and race biases, and in this they were at least showing themselves more socially aware than their professors.

This lack of ability to take into account the complexity of first names by psychologists is very striking. Indeed, as an outsider interested in the history and origin of first names, it always surprises me how cloth-eared psychologists seem to be when it comes to what are unusual names, and how people might respond to them. Take, for example a US study published in 1977 (Richard L

Zweingenhaft's 'The Other Side of Unusual First Names' in *The Journal of Social Psychology*). Most of what he has to say makes excellent sense. His experiments led him to conclude that an unusual name is not necessarily a disadvantage. He shows that 'unusually-named members of the upper class were more, not less, likely to be found in *Who's Who*', and he stressed 'the importance of considering the socioeconomic class, race, and sex of the individual before generalizing about the impact of an unusual first name.' He made allowances for differences of race and gender in his experiments, giving his students a set of variable names and variable descriptions of the family background of parents choosing a name for a child, and concluded 'The socioeconomic status of the parent was an important variable in their evaluations. In addition, the various unusual first names were given widely different evaluation from one another, one unusual name was given very positive ratings.'

And yet… He explains very carefully how he chose what was a common and what was an uncommon name by looking at a pool of over 11,000 school students. However, he was so wrapped up in his procedure that he failed to consider the wider social implications of the names he chose as unusual. One of the masculine names he chose as unusual was McKinley. He had already discussed the use of surnames as first names among the upper classes, but failed to mention this when he discusses its high ranking among students, and totally ignored the fact that as the surname of a president of the USA it was likely to have positive associations. Moreover, it was really not that unusual a name. Although it had dropped out of the USA's top 1,000 names for boys after 1966, it had been in regular use from the late 19th century until then. The other unusual boy's name he used was Talmadge, which was poorly ranked. Hardly surprising when you take into account that not only are the sounds in it associated with female names (Madge in particular), but it was well known as a feminine name in the form of the film star Norma Talmadge. Courtney was the unusual female name that was well received by the students. This is hardly surprising as it was actually the 76th most popular name for girls in 1977, had been rising steadily in popularity since the early 60s and was to reach 17th in rank in 1990. These sorts of objections can be found to many such studies.

From Sharon to Chloe

There is still conflicting evidence from these studies on the effects of unusual names. I very much doubt that it will ever be possible to prove anything conclusively, as assessment of even what is an unusual name is so subjective. It is often said that no one can speak in the UK without being condemned by someone else on class grounds. Much the same applies to names – so much so that it sometimes seems that a parent can't win. There is enormous variation in attitudes to and fashions for names even within the UK, let alone among English speakers in other countries. Separate statistics for England and Wales, Scotland and Northern Ireland are published in the UK, in which you can easily see the variation between these countries. You can focus even more closely and find variation within regions and even within cities and streets. The divisions are even greater across the socioeconomic and cultural divides. For every person who thinks it is cute or clever to name a child Princess Tiáamii, there will be another group who will tut-tut about poor taste. This is not all in one direction – you have only to listen to comedians (often a good source of social observation) mocking supposedly 'posh' names like Tarquin to realize how much we judge people by their choice of names. These judgements are often based on ignorance. The British, for example, may feel that President Obama's daughter Malia has a strange name, although an American probably would not. The name is popular in Hawaii where he grew up, being the local form of Maria, and is rising in popularity in the rest of the USA.

However, the judgemental are influenced not just by class but also by time. Take the two most mocked names of recent years, Sharon and Tracy. Much scorned in the 1990s as 'chav' names, there was a time when they seemed as exotic and upper class as Tarquin. It is their very success that has brought them into disrepute. Sad to say a lovely name like Chloe, once rare but enormously popular throughout the world in the late 20th and early 21st centuries, may one day seem as déclassé and dated as Sharon. A study of the way in which names can pass from the rare and elite to the over-popular can readily be found in Levitt and Dubner's popular book *Freakonomics* (2005). There they discuss research into the socioeconomic factors linked to first names. Not only do they show the way in which names change class, they also look at the links between the years a mother has spent in school (often an indicator of socioeconomic status) and the spelling of a name. They list ten different spellings of the popular name Jasmine, showing that mothers whose children are given the more conventional spellings had, on average, noticeably more education that those who chose spellings such as Jazmyne – something prospective parents might like to keep in mind.

African-American names

They also tackle the vexed question of distinctively African-American names. Studies have shown that if identical job applications are submitted but with either a typically white middle class name or a typically African-American name, the person with a 'white' name will get more job interviews – evidence that in this case names can matter. They discuss how much this is due to overt racism, and how much to judgements we make about the type of background a person with any given name is likely to have. They conclude that trends such as the use of typically African-American names emerge out of class solidarity and are the *result* of socioeconomic conditions rather than a *cause*:

> *The data show that, on average, a person with a distinctively black name…*
> *does have a worse life outcome than a woman named Molly or a man named*
> *Jake. But this isn't the fault of their names. If two black boys, Jake Williams*
> *and DeShawn Williams, are born in the same neighborhood and into the*
> *same familial and economic circumstances, they would likely have similar life*
> *outcomes. But the kind of parents who name their son Jake don't tend to live*
> *in the same neighborhoods or share economic circumstances with the kind*
> *of parents who name their son DeShawn. And that's why, on average, a boy*

named Jake will tend to earn more money and get more education than a boy named DeShawn. A DeShawn is more likely to have been handicapped by a low-income, low-education, single-parent background. His name is an indicator – not a cause – of his outcome.'

The most important overall conclusion that Levitt and Dubner make from the point of view of someone trying to choose names is that the Californian data shows us 'how parents see themselves – and more significantly, what kind of expectations they have for their children.'

Naming your child

So what should a parent today do? My personal advice is to do your research and think hard about the long-term effects of a name on a child:

- Research what other people are calling their children, and learn from that. There is plenty of material around for this. Governments publish statistics and there are good (as well as bad) websites on first names. These can tell you about names in steady use and those that are going out of fashion, as well as the popular ones.

- Take note of what people in your circle are calling their children, particularly the very young ones.

- Think carefully about the combination of first name and surname, considering rhythm, combinations of initials and overall effect.

- Don't try to be too clever – take a warning from examples such as the US couple who wanted to call their child Destiny and misspelt it Density, or the poor child in Scotland whose parents followed the fashion there for names which combine variants of the name Anna and Lisa, but came up with the form Analyse.

- Remember that your little baby will one day be an adult. Names that are cute on a baby may be a hindrance when the child is grown. Names that are too fashionable may date them.

- Try to give them choice. The current fashion is to give children a pet form of a name, but why restrict their choice? Call a child Ellie and she is stuck with it. Give the child the full form Eleanor and you can still call her Ellie, but if she wants she can choose all sorts of other pet forms or go by the full, formal form when it suits her in adult life.

Above all, be resigned to the fact that your child will probably reproach you for your choice at some point in his or her life!

First Name Popularity Tables

The latest available data from official sources is given. Where names have equal ranking in popularity the tied names are indicated by "=" or "*=".

Top 30 first names in England and Wales 2007

	Boys	Girls		Boys	Girls
1	Jack	Grace	16	Lewis	Hannah
2	Thomas	Ruby	17	Mohammed	Megan
3	Oliver	Olivia	18	Jake	Katie
4	Joshua	Emily	19	Dylan	Isabella
5	Harry	Jessica	20	Jacob	Isabelle
6	Charlie	Sophie	21	Luke	Millie
7	Daniel	Chloe	22	Callum	Abigail
8	William	Lily	23	Alexander	Amy
9	James	Ella	24	Matthew	Daisy
10	Alfie	Amelia	25	Ryan	Freya
11	Samuel	Lucy	26	Adam	Emma
12	George	Charlotte	27	Tyler	Erin
13	Joseph	Ellie	28	Liam	Poppy
14	Benjamin	Mia	29	Harvey	Molly
15	Ethan	Evie	30	Max	Holly

Source: Office of National Statistics, UK

Top 20 first names in Scotland 2008

	Boys	Girls		Boys	Girls
1	Jack	Sophie	11	Alexander	Ellie
2	Lewis	Emily	12	Aiden =	Jessica
3	Daniel	Olivia	13	Dylan =	Amy
4	Liam	Chloe	14	Aaron	Isla
5	James =	Emma	15	Ben	Grace
6	Ryan =	Lucy	16	Kyle	Eva
7	Callum	Ava	17	Jamie	Rebecca
8	Logan	Katie	18	Finlay	Leah
9	Matthew	Erin	19	Adam	Freya
10	Cameron	Hannah	20	Andrew	Holly

Source: 'Popular Forenames – Babies' First Names 2008'
General Register Office for Scotland, Crown copyright © 2008

Top 20 first names in Northern Ireland 2008

	Boys	Girls		Boys	Girls
1	Jack	Katie	11	Ethan =	Elie
2	Matthew	Sophie	12	Jamie =	Sarah
3	Daniel	Grace	13	Adam	Erin
4	James	Jessica	14	Aaron	Anna
5	Ryan	Emma	15	Ben	Aoife
6	Joshua	Lucy	16	Luke	Caitlin =
7	Conor	Emily	17	Callum =	Leah =
8	Thomas	Chloe	18	Harry =	Niamh =
9	Dylan	Hannah	19	Lewis	Ella
10	Charlie	Eva	20	Sean	Olivia

Copyright: © NISRA

Top 20 first names in the Republic of Ireland 2007

	Boys	Girls		Boys	Girls
1	Jack	Sarah	11	Dylan	Amy
2	Sean	Emma	12	Aaron	Ciara
3	Conor	Ella	13	Darragh	Hannah
4	Daniel	Katie	14	Thomas	Lucy
5	James	Sophie	15	Matthew	Chloe
6	Adam	Ava	16	David	Leah
7	Ryan	Aoife	17	Jamie	Caoimhe
8	Luke	Emily	18	Oisin	Niamh
9	Cian	Grace	19	Patrick	Rachel
10	Michael	Kate	20	Alex	Anna

Copyright: © Central Statistics Office, Republic of Ireland

Top 20 first names in the USA 2007

	Boys	Girls		Boys	Girls
1	Jacob	Emily	11	Alexander	Addison
2	Michael	Isabella	12	David	Samantha
3	Ethan	Emma	13	Joseph	Ashley
4	Joshua	Ava	14	Noah	Alyssa
5	Daniel	Madison	15	James	Mia
6	Christopher	Sophia	16	Ryan	Chloe
7	Anthony	Olivia	17	Logan	Natalie
8	William	Abigail	18	Jayden	Sarah
9	Matthew	Hannah	19	John	Alexis
10	Andrew	Elizabeth	20	Nicholas	Grace

Source: US Office of Policy, Social Security Administration

Top 20 first names in Alberta, Canada 2008

	Boys	Girls		Boys	Girls
1	Ethan	Ava	11	Benjamin	Grace
2	Jacob	Olivia	12	Evan	Taylor
3	Alexander	Emma	13	Lucas	Ella
4	Joshua	Emily	14	Daniel	Abigail
5	Liam	Sarah	15	Jack	Brooklyn
6	Logan	Isabella	16	William	Brooke
7	Nathan	Sophia	17	Jayden	Sophie
8	Matthew	Madison	18	Carter	Hailey
9	Noah	Hannah	19	Ryan	Addison
10	Owen	Chloe	20	Aiden	Elizabeth

Source: 'Top 25 Baby Names of 2008' © 2009 Government of Alberta

Top 20 first names in British Columbia, Canada 2008

	Boys	Girls		Boys	Girls
1	Ethan	Ava	11	Lucas =	Madison =
2	Jacob =	Chloe	12	Daniel *=	Sarah
3	James =	Emma	13	Ryan *=	Lily
4	Logan *=	Emily =	14	Owen	Sophia
5	Nathan *=	Hannah =	15	Alexander	Elizabeth =
6	Noah	Olivia	16	Jack	Maya =
7	Joshua	Ella	17	Aiden =	Taylor =
8	Matthew	Sophie	18	Evan =	Brooklyn *=
9	Benjamin =	Abigail	19	Samuel	Julia *=
10	Liam =	Isabella =	20	Nicholas	Hailey

Copyright: © 2008, Province of British Columbia

Top 20 first names in Ontario, Canada 2006

	Boys	Girls		Boys	Girls
1	Ethan	Emma	11	Nicholas	Julia
2	Matthew	Olivia	12	William	Sophia
3	Joshua	Emily	13	Lucas	Grace
4	Jacob	Ava	14	Michael	Samantha
5	Ryan	Sarah	15	Benjamin	Chloe
6	Noah	Isabella	16	Andrew	Victoria
7	Nathan	Hannah	17	Liam	Lauren
8	Daniel	Abigail	18	Logan	Maya
9	Alexander	Madison	19	Evan	Jessica
10	Owen	Ella	20	Jack	Hailey

Copyright: © Queen's Printer for Ontario, 2006

Top 20 first names in New South Wales, Australia 2008

	Boys	Girls		Boys	Girls
1	Jack	Mia	11	Ethan	Amelia
2	William	Chloe	12	Daniel	Grace
3	Lachlan	Isabella	13	Noah	Lily
4	Joshua	Emily	14	Samuel	Matilda
5	Cooper	Olivia	15	Liam	Ruby
6	Riley	Ella	16	Ryan	Jessica
7	Thomas	Charlotte	17	Alexander	Zoe
8	Oliver	Sienna	18	Max	Hannah
9	James	Sophie	19	Jacob	Sarah
10	Benjamin	Ava	20	Jayden	Emma

Reproduced with the permission of the NSW Registry of Births Deaths & Marriages for and on behalf of the Crown in and for the State of New South Wales. It is subject to Crown copyright.

Top 20 first names in Victoria, Australia 2008

	Boys	Girls		Boys	Girls
1	William	Mia	11	Ethan	Ruby
2	Jack	Olivia	12	Benjamin	Lily
3	Thomas	Chloe	13	Lucas	Matilda
4	Joshua	Isabella	14	Samuel	Grace
5	James	Charlotte	15	Daniel	Amelia
6	Lachlan	Ava	16	Max	Hannah
7	Oliver	Sienna	17	Charlie	Zoe
8	Riley	Emily	18	Alexander	Jessica
9	Cooper	Ella	19	Liam	Emma
10	Noah	Sophie	20	Ryan	Lucy

Source: Victorian Registry of Births, Deaths and Marriages © State of Victoria 2009

Top 20 first names in New Zealand 2008

	Boys	Girls		Boys	Girls
1	Jack	Sophie	11	Thomas	Hannah
2	James	Olivia	12	Jacob	Chloe
3	William	Ella	13	Ethan	Ruby
4	Samuel	Isabella	14	Jayden	Lucy
5	Joshua	Charlotte	15	Noah	Ava
6	Riley	Lily	16	Ryan	Amelia
7	Liam	Emma	17	Lucas	Madison
8	Oliver	Emily	18	Luke	Maia
9	Benjamin	Jessica	19	Max	Mia
10	Daniel	Grace	20	Hunter	Holly

Source: The New Zealand Office of Births, Deaths and Marriages, Department of Internal Affairs.